MW01231055

Baseballs and Battlefields

Matthew A. Neville

Preface

I should probably explain how I got to this point in my life. I was born in Santa Rosa, California, the county seat for the Sonoma Valley wine country. I was born to very young parents in 1969, raised by my paternal grandparents until 3rd grade, then with my father and his new wife until my sophomore year. Typical split family issues sent me to my mother's house in St. Helena for a semester, finally ending up back with my grandparents for my junior and senior year.

Bouncing around three different high schools didn't leave me with very many life long friends; I had no feeling of roots or hometown. I attended the local junior college for about a year before I inevitably began to get into trouble. I was already contemplating joining the service when I found myself at the mercy of a judge in South Lake Tahoe who made no qualms about my military career choice. When the words, "MY Marine Corps..." came out of his mouth, my destiny was set in stone. "Bring me your enlistment papers, pay 50 bucks, and get out of my court." Oohrah.

I served in the United States Marine Corps from 1989 to 1995; participating in Operations Desert Shield/Desert Storm; and Operation Restore Hope in lovely downtown Mogadishu, Somalia; more affectionately known as "Black Hawk Down." It's still hard for me to watch that movie. I was discharged after six years and a couple months with a small service related disability percentage, from injuries incurred during deployment. No Purple Heart, because we weren't in a combat zone. No Combat Action Ribbon, because we were on a "humanitarian" mission. No Humanitarian Medal, because we used too much force. Instead, we received a star on the Sea Service Deployment Ribbon, a Marine Expeditionary Medal, and a lifetime of not so great memories. Try to explain that one at the local VFW. Anyway, I digress.

While I was enlisted, I married my soon to be ex-wife, and had two beautiful daughters. After my discharge, we moved to Arizona where I worked as an HVAC technician, bouncing from job to job. It didn't take long for my wife to decide she had had enough; marriage was easier when I was half way across the world. So I soon found myself a single dad, fighting for visitation, and barely getting by due to paying child support.

i

The Arizona housing boom took off around 2002. I finally found myself in a position to buy a home. Of course at this time nobody thought this was a bubble that was soon to burst. I took a position with KB Home as a construction superintendent, which I was surprisingly good at. I had found my dream job. I quickly rose through the ranks, thanks only to my boss and mentor who was also a veteran. He took me under his wing, understood my background and how to effectively train me. My income rose from 36K a year to just under 100k with bonuses, in just 3 short years. I was on cloud nine. Then the economy failed, the housing bubble burst, layoffs were eminent. The stress of meeting deadlines for quarterly and year end totals was brutal. It was a cut throat time where you couldn't trust even your closest co-workers not to undermine you in an attempt to save their own careers. That's when everything changed.

I remember waking up one morning about 30 minutes before the alarm went off, shaken from a horrible dream that I knew was about to become reality. We had been late on delivering a home to a family who had their entire life in a Uhaul truck, living at a motel for the past week, and I was about to tell them it was gonna be at least another week. Suddenly my chest felt tight, real tight. Then the pain hit. I thought I was having a heart attack. After an ER visit, it was diagnosed as an anxiety attack, and I was given a referral to a mental health provider for anxiety and depression. After two visits with the shrink, his exact statement was, "I can't believe you're functioning at this level. Have you ever been diagnosed with PTSD?" This got the ball rolling with a claim to the VA.

By 2007 I was unemployed, had two foreclosures and a short sale on my rental properties, and I was facing a foreclosure on my last property. I was literally just a few weeks from being homeless when, by the grace of God, the VA concluded that I had been suffering with PTSD for quite sometime and gave me a 70% disability rating with back pay because of it. They also made this a total and permanent finding, and awarded me "Unemployability." This meant I was unemployable, therefore paying me at 100% instead of just 70%, with full base privileges, and complete healthcare. The timing was truly miraculous. I was literally given what veterans call the "golden egg." This egg saved my life, but it also almost ended it.

I decided to relocate to a small town in NE Arizona for a completely fresh start; a small town called Pinetop, about a 3 hour drive from Phoenix up to "Rim Country." Pine trees, fresh air, cool temperatures. It was like heaven from the 120f degree concrete jungle known as Phoenix. I moved into a one bedroom trailer, joined the local gym, and started having breakfast with some old friends I used to know from Phoenix. At 38 years old, the "old man" retired lifestyle was a totally new fit, but not a very good one.

My breakfast friends actually owned the restaurant that we would meet at. The restaurant had a nightclub attached where I soon found myself working as the doorman. Remember the unemployability part? It didn't allow me to have anything taxable hit my income. With the housing market crash and a very unstable economy, I wasn't about to do anything that would jeopardize my only steady source of income. But, I couldn't just sit there spinning my wheels. So I worked as a doorman on and off at the local bars. It gave me something to do, something to look forward to, and some breathing room when it came time to pay the bills. But it wasn't enough.

One day I decided to start working toward a bucket list item of mine. At least then, even if it was just saving every penny I could for 5 years to finance this goal, I'd be moving forward. Baby steps. The bucket list item was to touch all 50 states. I needed a vehicle, a camper/RV, a trailer for my Harley, and I'd be outta here. That was the 5 year plan.

Working the bar scene in a small town will take its toll on you. Whether it was the time I spent working and saving toward the trip, or maybe the cumulation of the Creator's grander plan, I found myself at a place where I was done. Mentally, emotionally, financially, just done. I was able to purchase a new truck at a ridiculously high payment and interest rate, an old cab-over camper that was in decent shape, and a small covered trailer from a close friend who needed Christmas cash. Suddenly I realized that the 5 year plan was complete. Launch code initiated.

Another sign that it was time to go was when my old male dog passed just a month before we had planned to leave. This was actually a blessing, being 12 years old and in failing health, he would have been a handful to take care of on the road. Deuce hung around long enough to train Kimber, my new female puppy. In the few months Deuce had with her, he taught her the glory of chasing a ball, the joy of cookies after peeing outside, and the love of traveling in the truck. Everything she needed to soon be one of the most well traveled pups in modern history.

Kimber's breed is important and rather unique. She is a full-bred English Staffordshire Bull Terrier, commonly called an English Staffy; not a very common breed. Super athletic and full of energy, Staffys are truly a big dog in a little dog frame. Her appearance is that of a calf high, 30lb "pit bull" puppy. This is important when it comes to places we travel that have pit bull bans. The fact that she looks like a puppy is good because people aren't afraid of her. Then once I point out she is an adult dog they look at her differently. Not as a scary pit bull but as an oddity, albeit a damn cute one. Everyone wants a Kimber once they meet mine.

After several months of prepping and planning to begin my life of living on the road, I was finally set. But wandering around the country aimlessly seemed a little too much like homelessness. As a Marine I needed a plan, I needed a mission. One of the great loves of my life is the sport of baseball. My whole family are huge baseball fans. I remember coming home from school to see my grandfather in his chair watching the San Francisco Giants on television, while my grandmother sat in the kitchen working crosswords while listening to the same game on the radio. Best part was when a great play was made, she would run into the living room to see the instant replay. Ahh the good old days. One of the things my grandfather, my dad, and myself wanted to do, was see all 30 of the MLB parks. Another bucket list item for myself, and something to honor my grandfather by doing. Perfect.

Now what to do about the states that have no Major League Baseball teams. My grandfather also served in the United States Navy shortly after Pearl Harbor. He was very proud of his service, telling me stories and jokes from that era, which may have given me my interest in military history. A history that America is ripe in. So I decided to visit all of our nation's National Battlefields, and any other place that bullets flew in the name of freedom, transforming a young country into the greatest nation on earth.

So the mission was taking shape. The goal was to touch all 50 states, seeing a game in every MLB park, and setting foot on all the major battlefields along the way. Basically exploring America's two favorite pastimes, baseball and war. I decided to make it interesting by adding in a time factor. I wanted to be in Hawaii for my 50th State, on my 50th birthday. When I mentioned to my youngest daughter, now married with her own children, that I wanted to touch all 50 states by age 50, her cheeky response was, "Ya better hurry up." That was it, gauntlet thrown. There was no way I was gonna let that fly. Touch 50 in five years it is.

The first leg of the journey would be yet another bucket list item of mine from a very young age. I wanted to drive the west coast from San Diego to Seattle, along the Pacific Coast Highway. I still had some loose ties requiring me back in Arizona by summer's end, so this would be it for year one. Plus, I didn't want to take off across the country without a trial run. Year two would be what I call the Mountain States Run, year three would be the Southern States, Northeastern/Lakes/Plains States for year four, and finally Alaska and Hawaii for year five. This was of course a broad itinerary, and an ambitious mark to hit. I would have to coordinate the six months of the baseball season schedule, along with trying to hit some non-baseball states during fall and winter months.

Ok, so the plan was set, the Rig was loaded and tested on some short weekend camping trips. All systems go. First, let me explain what I mean by "The Rig." The truck I purchased was a 2013 Ram 1500 4x4. It had an extended crew cab, 4 doors, with the 5.7 Hemi gasoline motor. With my credit being non-existent due to the housing crash, I began my enslavement to a 20.2% interest payment on a new truck. I looked at it as a rent payment since I'd be living in it. Gotta look at the glass half full, right? It was also my ticket to my dream. I was told that after 18 months I'd be able to refinance; which was bullshit. But at least I now owned a very reliable mode of transportation for my trip, like buying a horse to pull my covered wagon.

Modifications had to be made as the truck was only a 1500 and not rated for that much weight. I installed 5K pound airbags for the rear suspension and an onboard compressor to remedy this, along with a 2.5 inch leveling kit in the front to increase the clearance, both of which I installed myself at a friends 4x4 shop, saving every dime I could.

Next part of the Rig was my actual home. I bought an 1983 Cabover, slide-in, truck camper from a friend for $900. It was still in good shape, no leaks, fridge worked on propane and electric, 3 burner gas stove, queen size bed, dinette table, ample storage, small sink with water tank, and a propane gas heater. All it was missing was a bathroom and air conditioning.

The last piece of the Rig was my 6x8 covered trailer that became my garage. I carried my 1979 Harley Davidson, a beach cruiser bicycle, tools and BBQ toward the center and rear of the trailer, while the front had cabinets for food, clothes and a spot for the port-a-potty.

This was my world on wheels, minus a small storage shed in Arizona with some household junk in it. I sold most everything I own, so this was literally my entire world, a scary yet incredibly liberating feeling. Going from a six figure income and 4 homes, to living in a camper on $2900 a month, took some serious lifestyle adjustment. But it was the absolute best, most life changing decision I ever made. So, grab a beer, have seat, and let me tell you about the next 5 years of my life. I think you will be surprised, hopefully entertained, and most importantly.... inspired.

Slainte!

WEST COAST RUN

2015

May 25th, 2015. And so it began. Memorial Day. A completely unplanned departure date, although a very fitting one. Kimber and I said our goodbyes the night before and headed out of the small town of Buckeye, AZ just before dawn. I stopped at the end of the driveway just before entering the road. My body tingled with excitement, or maybe it was a mild anxiety attack; either way we were headed west. West until we hit water, then North until we hit Canada. As I pulled the Rig out onto the empty city street, I couldn't help but think, "I'm officially homeless. Sweet, let's do this." Pacific Coast Highway, here we come.

The weeks before the trip, I had realized while combing over maps, campsites, mileage, costs, budget, etc., that I was completely stressing myself out. Stress was something that had no place with me while on this trip. So I decided to do as the age old bumper sticker proclaims, and let Jesus be my co-pilot. I quickly learned that you may pick the actual destination, but the road decides your path; hopefully with a little divine intervention along the way. So our first stop would be the famous Dog Beach, where Kimber could experience the ocean for the very first time. From there... I guess we would see.

Even with the five years of preparation and thought put into this trip, what I experienced next caught me by surprise. I felt alive. For the first time, in what has been many faded years, I felt truly alive. Not just alive, but alive and FREE. In a way I can only describe as both exhilarating and equally terrifying.

Complete and utter freedom was something that I suddenly realized I had never experienced on this level. We have all grown up hearing how freedom is something precious, something worth fighting for, even dying for. As a Marine, I thought I knew what freedom was. I was mistaken. For the first time in my entire existence, I was truly free. I mean short of a post apocalyptic world, this was about as free as I was gonna get on a VA pension.

California

We hit the California border around 1000 hours, crossing over through the small town of Yuma. Being a California Native, I had a pretty good idea what to expect of my home state, even though it had been a solid twenty years since I'd set foot on Cali soil. A lot had changed since then. I'd be lying if I said I wasn't somewhat concerned for our safety on this trip. I had a concealed weapon permit from the state of Arizona, but it wasn't valid in any of the three western coast states. The thought of being stopped in California for whatever reason and being found with a firearm was terrifying. I would go to jail, Kimber would go to jail, my house would go to jail. It was just not worth it. So effectively, I'd been disarmed due to the fact that I'm a law abiding citizen. Oh well, I got a softball bat and a Pygmy Pit. I was good.

I remembered it was about an eight hour drive from San Diego to Phoenix. What I didn't remember was the state law that said vehicles pulling trailers had to stay under 55 mph. This didn't concern me as much as it concerned the drivers behind me. Many a one-fingered salute were rendered as we ventured into my former home state. Somethings never change. Look, it made zero sense for me to get a speeding ticket, time was one thing I had plenty of. Suddenly elderly drivers made perfect sense.

About 12 hours later, we pulled into Robb Park, a sports complex with softball and soccer fields, where I noticed several other RVs and campers parked. Kimber and I both definitely needed to stretch our legs. When I got out of the truck I noticed the rear end sagging quite a bit. Apparently we lost the air in the airbag suspension I had installed. This was why I did the bag upgrade myself, so I knew how to fix it. Thankfully, I had packed enough tools on the trailer to open a small auto repair shop. Within a few minutes, I replaced a portion of air line that had melted, re-routed the line, and were back to full suspension. Lesson learned.

We were just outside the Ocean Beach area so I locked down the Rig, put Kimber on a leash, and set out to explore. I was looking for a bicycle shop to tune up my old beach cruiser, as we explored the once familiar beach town. I can repair air lines on my truck but can't tune up a bicycle, go figure. Kimber hadn't spent much time on leash as we usually just played ball at the park with my old dog, Deuce. So she was in learning mode, slightly hesitant of the traffic and big city noises, obviously overwhelmed, but stayed the course as best she could.

During our walk we came across a couple of surfer kids passing by. I say kids but they were probably in their early 20's. I asked if they knew where a bike shop was and described what I needed done. One of the boys said, with a very heavy Irish accent, that he worked at a shop in Mission Beach and he'd hook me up for 30 bucks. I got the name of the place and said thanks. What a coincidence that the first person I met on this trip was an Irish bicycle mechanic. I asked him what his name was. He smiled while offering his hand to shake and said, "I'm Mick." I had to laugh at my own Irish heritage. Mick the Mick. I replied, "Well of course you are."

It was starting to get dark so we headed back to the Rig. I stopped to ask some folks in an RV nearby if it was ok to sleep here. They said no, the police run folks out of here at dark. With that heads up, we chose to play it safe our first night out and stayed at a 24hr Walmart Supercenter. The first of what would be many to come. So just to clarify, certain Walmarts allow overnight parking, mostly ones in subdivisions or rural areas. Not so much in the big cities. This one happened to have several 18 wheelers and a few campers scattered in the rear parking lot, which I learned to be a welcoming sign. I quietly parked between a 5th wheel and a big rig, broke out some leftovers on the stove, and settled in for the night. Day one complete.

The next day, bright and early, we drove down to Dog Beach for Kimber to see her first wave. The leash laws on the beach are ridiculously strict in California. Dog Beach was the only public beach that allowed dogs, let alone off leash. It was about 0600, so we easily found a parking space for the Rig, grabbed the ball, and headed to the water. With only a few dogs and their humans out, Kimber and I pretty much had the run of the beach. First thing she did was get a serious case of the "zoomies." Rear end slung low, head up, ears back, she ran through the sand throwing rooster tails up behind her like a dune buggy. Then she saw the wave. She completely froze, watching as the wave came towards her. It got to within a few feet of her, before retreating back into the ocean. This is when Kimber became brave and gave chase, only to flee in terror as the retreating wave returned with reinforcements, overtaking her as she fled. When she realized it was only water, a newfound sense of courage took over. She turned and gave chase after the wave again, barking and growling along the way, only to dig her paws into the wet sand upon reversing direction before the next incoming set. This went on for several minutes while I was bent over in hysterical laughter.

With Kimber sufficiently worn out and resting comfortably in the camper, I decided to break out my Harley and go find where Mick's bike shop was. It had been years since I'd been to the Mission Beach area, with its old rollercoaster and the normal plethora of tourist traps still in place. It was early still, most shops were still closed or just opening up. I found Mick's shop about halfway between Pacific Beach and Mission Beach, a little place called RADD sports. It too was closed for another couple hours, so I decided to scout the area for a parking place big enough for the Rig.

Just a couple miles north of Radd Sports was a fast food restaurant where I stopped for coffee and a bite to eat. While I sat by the window eating, I noticed a small apartment complex across the street. Everybody was emerging from their apartments and heading to work or school. Cars were pulling out and the streets were basically empty, with a perfect spot for the truck and trailer just up the street. I rushed back to the Rig, knowing that the beach crowd would be there soon enough and I'd have no chance to find a double space for the trailer. Luckily, the spots were still there and a perfect fit for the Rig. We were set for at least a day or maybe two.

Once situated, I put Kimber on leash and went to explore the boardwalk. I learned very quickly that I hit the jackpot for a "boondock" spot. The fast food restaurant was open late for bathroom use; and just across the main drag, right before the beach, was a public restroom with free surfer showers. Awesome! And being right across the street from an apartment complex with only street parking, there were always different cars coming and going. With no undue attention and by keeping the lights low, nobody even gave us a second glance.

After a walk down the boardwalk which was absolutely torture for Kimber who didn't understand why she couldn't spin rooster tails in the sand or chase the target rich pigeon environment. We headed down to the bike shop to see Mick. Radd Sports was a cool little beach cruiser and surfboard rental shop, with a fleet of bicycles out front and racks of surfboards inside. I was excited to get my own beach cruiser road worthy and on the boardwalk, but unfortunately Mick didn't work until tomorrow and they had no other mechanics coming in. No biggie, we could wait. With that we headed back to the rig for some lunch and a much needed nap. Earlier during our walk, Kimber and I happened upon a small, just off the boardwalk bar, called the 701 Surf Club. Advertising a $1 Taco Tuesday special with a Trivia night. Sounded like my kinda place. So after getting cleaned up, I left Kimber to hold down the fort while I headed out for tacos and beer. The 701 Surf Club did not disappoint. Great fish and carnitas tacos, cold draft beer, and team trivia just starting up. Good times.

After I saddled up to the bar and put in my order, two guys walked in and sat down on the stools next to me. I noticed one of them had an Arizona State University cap on. Of course, I immediately told him I was a fan and even came close to graduating from ASU West, once upon a time. What happened next was unreal. Turned out the guy with the cap was an Army Ranger veteran named Mike who served in Iraq, and was now living in Surprise, AZ. Wait, what? Surprise!? This was the town where I had worked as a homebuilder prior to receiving my VA disability. Then I learned that his ex-wife lives in Show Low, a town near Pinetop where I started my 5 year plan to travel. What an incredibly small world. Then came the kicker. Turned out Mike goes to the same church as my friends in Buckeye and was walking into the 1100 sermon while we were walking out of the 0930 sermon last Sunday! Now that's crazy. I gave my new friend the Facebook info where I'd be posting my trip, hopefully he will keep in touch.

One quick note about Ranger veterans and those of us lucky enough to have served in Somalia. (Sarcasm) There's a special brotherhood between branches when it comes to Operation Restore Hope. I served with a Marine Expeditionary Unit (MEU) that were some of the first Marines on the ground, securing the airport, golf course, and Lido Pier area. I was an electronic technician assigned as a Corporal of the Guard at Lido Pier. The Rangers showed up later, which unfortunately led to the story for the movie "Black Hawk Down." I was literally home, being processed for discharge, watching the pilots being dragged through the streets on tv, tears in my eyes. I was pissed. Anyway, this was an emotional battle for the Rangers and is a bit of a legend now that it was over 25 years ago. So young Rangers and this old Marine have something in common. I'd never realized how important this was until later.

The next morning, I was eager to get the bike in and worked on so I could continue up the coast. When I got to Radd Sports, once again Mick wasn't working. Thankfully, the guy who was working said he could handle it. Bummer, I missed my Irish friend, but I was happy to get the bike back on the road. Another goal of mine was to take surf lessons. I wasn't a surfer growing up, preferring the road rash of skateboarding instead. Surf lessons and learning to surf was another bucket list item that I intended to check the box for. Turned out my new bike mechanic, Manny, was also an old surf instructor who had been surfing his entire life, a true local, still shredding at age 49. He offered to take me out for a few hours on his next day off.

5

This was perfect. One on one instruction, with a guy my age, for a smoking price. I was stoked. We made plans for the following Saturday, and then Kimber and I headed out to our very first battlefield.

Since California has very few actual battlefields, I had to do some serious research to locate one, so of course I asked Google. Up popped the Battle of San Pasqual, just outside the town of Escondido where my ex-wife had worked when we were married. I was familiar with the area, but after 20 years it might as well have been a first time visit. I found a route that went by an Anytime Fitness, where I bought a membership for nationwide showers, gym access, and boondocking if necessary. Nobody would know if I'm in there working out at 3am, or crashed out in my camper. Either way, it was one of the best preps I could have made for the trip. So a pit stop for a good hot shower was definitely in order.

I was just east of Escondido on a small, two lane country road when the navigation on my phone announced that "You have arrived." I looked around to see just a small turnout with a roadside assistance phone box in front of what looked like an old rock fence. Across the street, and apparently upwind of us, was a large and very active dairy farm. When I got out to look around and let Kimber stretch her legs, I noticed the rock wall had an opening with an unkept, dirt trail leading to a large stone. The stone looked to have had a plaque that was removed or vandalized. Well that sucked. Then I noticed a branch of the trail went to another rock behind a tree. This one had a plaque that read, "Battle of San Pasqual, Dec. 6, 1846. Brigadier General S. W. Kearney Commanded. United States Forces. Originally marked by Daughters of the American Revolution of California in 1924. New plaque dedicated 1993." American Revolution of California? In 1846? None of this made any sense, at least not to my standard level of government education. I took plenty of pictures and retired to the Rig for some lunch. I'd have to look into this deeper.

Turns out that the Battle of San Pasqual was a military skirmish that took place during the Mexican-American War. This was the largest and bloodiest battle in California history, ending with both sides claiming victory. Although 17 American soldiers were killed, and the Mexican Californios only sustained some injuries, the Americans were able to turn the Mexican forces and reach San Diego. Some interesting facts about the Battle of San Pasqual are worth mentioning. The 2,000 mile march from Fort Leavenworth to San Pasqual Valley is the longest forced march in U.S. Army history, with a portion of the march led by the famous American scout, Kit Carson. Now that's pretty cool.

I was really disturbed to find out that the stone with the missing plaque had indeed been vandalized, and had the names of all those who lost their lives engraved. What is it in people that makes them have so little respect for our nation's history and for those who died, that they see this as acceptable or even noble? Full disclosure; it wasn't until a couple days after our visit to the battlefield that I learned there was another entrance, complete with visitor center, trails and more monuments. This is what I get for searching for battlefields on Google Maps. Lesson number two learned.

After lunch it was time to find a secure campsite for a few days, where I could safely drop the trailer before venturing into downtown San Diego for a Padres game. No safer place to be than on a United States Marine Corps Base, especially one I was previously stationed on and familiar with. With a smile a mile wide and butterflies in my stomach, I pulled up to the Camp Pendleton main gate like I had hundreds of times before.

I hadn't been on a Marine base since I got out of the service, so I wasn't sure what the security would be like. Here we live in a post 9/11 world, where lone wolf terrorism is a reality, and I pull up to a Marine installation with a beard, camper, and covered trailer in tow. Ya, I was pretty sure they were gonna go to DEFCON 4 on my ass.

All the traffic was funneled down to two lanes, with a 100% ID check in full swing. This wasn't new, they would do this back in my day on Friday and Saturday nights, looking for drunk drivers. By the looks of the Marine in full battle dress holding a shotgun, while the Military Police scanned ID cards into some sort of a palm pilot card scanner, I was pretty sure they weren't looking for drunks. Surprisingly, with just a swipe of my military ID and a "have a good one bro" from the MP, I was back home. Once a Marine, Always a Marine, OOHRAH.

I went for a drive around the base, or at least tried to. Everything was so different, I was amazed at the growth. The old barracks where I had lived looked like brand new condos, all shiny and modern. I gotta admit I was kinda jealous, this place was nice! It wasn't long before I was lost and had to ask a young Marine for directions to Delmar Beach Club and the RV Park. The place had definitely grown, and I'd definitely gotten older.

Back in my days, Delmar Beach was the recreational beach for Camp Pendleton. It had an enlisted club called Sharky's, another cabana bar/cantina by the water, and some water toy rentals. I was shocked at what Del Mar had become. A full-on resort style beach like you would see on a Sandals commercial. There was a brand new bar/cantina, rows of white beach chairs lined up facing the water, covered cabanas with couches, and a full stage for concerts. The RV park had full hookups, shower hut, and parking right on the beach for $40 a night. A little pricey for my budget but this place was amazing, and perfect for dropping the trailer. I was concerned whether they had an open spot as busy as it was, and the fact that folks reserved these spots months in advance. Luckily they had a spot, one row back from the water, for two nights. It was meant to be!

Walking out of the camp office I met a couple guys handing out flyers for an upcoming concert. They had seen Kimber hanging out of the window and wanted to say hello. The effect she has on people is uncanny. Turned out they were civilian concert promoters, putting on a free concert for the Marines. They handed me a flyer, pointed to where they were camping, and invited me over for a beer while they set up for the show. Hell ya, I'm in!

We soon found our spot, situated between two massive class 3 RVs. These are the ones that look like buses and are as expensive as a regular house. As I thought to myself, one day I'll ascend to the level of these RV grand masters, about then the owner of the coach popped out of the front door and came over to say hello. Enter my buddy Alex.

Alex was an older guy I pegged to be a little older than my dad, maybe late 60s early 70s. A former Army infantry officer who served in Vietnam, now a retired Massachusetts state trooper, was there taking sailing lessons with his wife Dawn. These people were awesome! I could sit and listen to Alex's war stories, both foreign and domestic, for hours. With his heavy New Englander accent he reminded me of one of my favorite movies, *The Departed*, with Jack Nicholson and Matt Damon. To this day, when I talk to Alex I call him "Troopah." Here's the insane part, they now live in Sun City, AZ; the senior community next door to Surprise, where I had lived while working for the homebuilders. What!?!

We sat at the picnic bench between our rigs, drinking beers and talking about our glory days in the service. Kimber of course was running around with her ball, trying to entice us into a game of fetch. After explaining to Alex what my trip was about, he and his wife asked if I would like them to watch Kimber while I went to the Padres game the following evening. Wow! See what I mean, everybody falls head over heels for this dog! It would allow me to go to the game and enjoy myself without worrying about Kimber in the camper alone. I absolutely took them up on their offer and set a time to drop Kimber off the next day.

After some beers with the concert guys that night, I retired to the camper with the sound of Marine Cobra attack helicopters patrolling the coast. A comforting change from the "Ghetto Birds" or police helicopters that you hear flying around the night sky of Phoenix. My peace was disturbed early the following morning by the sound of something mechanical and big, shaking the ground as it seemed to get closer. I opened the door to the camper, blurry eyed and confused, just in time to see three Amtracks (AAV) roll through the campgrounds. This is basically a tank without the turret, armored personnel carriers that can float on water and drive on land. I had to laugh. Yup, definitely the best campground security that I'd ever seen! A few other campers emerged from their rigs to investigate, some not so happy. You're on a Marine base for God's sake, what did you expect? It used to really bother me when folks who lived outside of Luke AFB back in Phoenix would complain about the jet noise. First of all, you moved there knowing the base is there. Second, that's the sound of freedom, people! When I was building houses and jets would fly over head, I'd stop and snap a quick salute and yell "Go get 'em boys!" I just don't understand folks sometimes, but I digress.

Kimber and I were wide awake after that, so we headed to the beach for some ball time before it got crowded. I could spend hours watching Kimber do her thing when it comes to playing ball. From an early age, Kimber realized that she could get to the ball before old Deuce could, if she launched about three feet before the ball and literally dove at it. She would then do a tuck and roll, pop up facing the opposite way, and be on the way back before Deuce could even slow down enough to turn around. It was impressive, but we were in sand this time. She quickly learned that she couldn't dive at the ball the same way she did on the grass back home. After the first throw and subsequent dive, she came back looking like she had run face first into a giant sugar cookie. Her face was completely covered in sand, with just her little dark brown eyes peeking out. I about fell over laughing. She apparently wasn't a fan of having a mouthful of sand on every dive, so she learned to stop and gently pick up the ball, giving it a good shake before returning it. Smart dog!

After breakfast we heard the band starting to warm up and headed over toward the stage area. Gerry, one of the concert promoters, also played the ukulele and sang in a reggae band. I'm not a huge reggae fan, but these guys were really good; pulling off some Bob Marley covers along with some original work. I was impressed. While they were warming up on stage, I saw his buddy Mike and friends at the cabana, waving us over to join them. We had a blast hanging with Mike and some other band guys, kicking it under the cabana on the beach while listening to Gerry rock the reggae. Life doesn't get much better than that!

As usual, Kimber was working her magic on our new friend Mike. He was infatuated with her. He invited us to come to Dana Point when we were done to stay at his place for a couple days. See, Mike's girlfriend Katie wanted a dog, a big dog, like a Lab. So Mike was hoping by Katie seeing Kimber that she would opt for a smaller dog. Specifically a smaller dog with smaller poop, being as he assumed he would be the one cleaning the yard. I was happy to oblige the brother. Unfortunately, the AC/DC cover band who was the headliner didn't go on stage until later that night when I would be at the Padres game. So Mike and I exchanged numbers and made plans to see him at his place in Dana Point on Sunday. See what I mean about the road just taking you?

I headed back to the Rig to get cleaned up for the game and drop Kimber at the neighbors. Friday night, 6pm game time, traffic would be brutal; definitely wanted to get an early start. Just as I stepped outside to knock on Alex's door, they pulled up in their little car they tow behind their RV. He and Dawn had just got back from sailing lessons and needed to go to the store. Before Dawn could even ask, Kimber jumped in the car and was ready to go. Guess that answered that. It made me feel good that my baby girl would be spoiled rotten for a few hours while I was gone. She won't want to come home!

I was so grateful that I decided to leave the trailer at the campsite instead of trying to weave it through I5, rush-hour traffic. Pulling a trailer sucks, big time. Either way, I made it to Petco Park about an hour before first pitch. Luckily, they had uncovered parking for the camper, and a few people setting up their tailgate activities. I found a spot, relaxed for a few minutes, and then made my way to the Park. Here we go, game one!

Petco Park, San Diego, CA

May 29th, 2015. Petco Park is the fairly new home of the San Diego Padres. Last time I saw a Padres game was at the old Jack Murphy Stadium that the Padres shared with the Chargers. I remember watching some of the greats there: Tony Gwynn, Dave Winfield, and Rollie Fingers to name a few. It was located on the outskirts of San Diego, right off of Interstate 8. Later named

Qualcomm Stadium, it was these massive stadium sized venues that I remember from my childhood: Candlestick Park, Oakland Coliseum, Jack Murphy Stadium, etc. Typically built from the late 1960s to the early 1980s, they usually had easy freeway access, acres of parking, and plenty of seats. The new Petco Park was NOT one of these stadiums.

A lot of the major cities seem to be doing this downtown renovation project, where they build a ballpark in a warehouse or other dilapidated industrial area, in order to draw the hotels, restaurants, condos, and other associated businesses revolving around tourism. It's a great idea, but has its serious drawbacks, parking being the big one. You're usually stuck trying to find a parking garage, street parking, or even nearby houses offering their front lawn for 20 bucks. Traffic control being the second issue. City surface streets obviously just aren't capable of accommodating this level of congestion. Although picturesque, these ballparks were a logistical nightmare for the Rig.

Getting to Petco Park wasn't too bad. Just a few blocks off the freeway. There seemed to be plenty of parking lots, thankfully one being non-covered for the camper height. There seemed to be a lot of construction going on even though the park was built in 2003. Twenty bucks to park was pretty much what I had assumed, the uphill hike to the park, I didn't see coming.   All   in all, the park was very modern looking from the outside, and blended in nicely with the neighboring architecture.

When I reached the ticket booth, I asked if they had any veteran specials or discounts. Most parks do have a military/veterans discount, but they're usually only available at the box office on the day of the game. Some season ticket holders donate unused tickets, some teams give free tickets on weekday games, some give free upgraded seats or a significant discount. It never hurts to ask, you earned it! The Padres were no exception. I asked for the cheapest veteran seat behind home plate, 12 bucks later I was on my way to game number 1.

My Dad used to call that a "get in" ticket. The cheapest one that got you in the door. I'm usually gonna be at the game solo, walking around taking photos and seeing the sights, so paying for an expensive seat up close doesn't make sense. I like the view from the upper deck without a net in front of me, looking down at the entire field in full view. That and day games during the week are pretty much empty, with ushers being much more laxed on checking tickets.

Ok, so back to Petco Park. Another super cool aspect of downtown ballparks is the backdrop or the cityscape that you see usually above the outfield seats. Petco sits so that the city skyline is

11

lit up behind the outfield seats, showcasing the most recognizable aspect of any city. Beautiful. The most interesting feature of this stadium is the "Park in the Park." For ten bucks you can get into what seems like a city park, with slight rolling hills of grass, complete with couches and ottomans, behind right and center fields! You could see over the low right field fence to watch the game live, or watch the huge video screen that was on the centerfield fence. There was a micro whiffle ball park for the kids, with employees pitching and running the games. There was a stage with a band playing, all the regular concession stands, and kids running everywhere. All with full access to the rest of the park. A very cool, first come first serve, standing room only sort of venue that I highly recommend. Only bummer was Petco Park didn't allow pets; only service and support animals. A bit of irony there for ya.

I just happened to attend the Military/Veteran and First Responder Appreciation Night. I gotta say, San Diego has always been a military town and has deep regards for her military and veterans. They had some military folks and first responders take the field first, being introduced one by one like baseball players, taking a position on the field with a ball in hand. Then the Padres players ran out to their positions and signed their ball for them. It was super cool with all the military and first responders being asked to rise for a huge standing ovation. It really made me feel proud.

Inside the actual park were numerous displays about the military and the local Naval port. The most impressive was a huge scale model of the USS Midway, surrounded by walls enshrined with the MLB players' names who had served their country. I snapped some pictures of the walls to possibly use as the inside cover lining for this book. It was a powerful and moving display.

I usually roll out during the seventh inning stretch unless the game was close. Padres were down by a handful of runs so I opted to make the best of traffic with an early departure. Besides it had been a good 5 hours, I missed my pup and I was sure she was worried sick about me. Petco Park, MLB park #1... COMPLETE!

When I knocked on Alex and Dawn's door, I assumed Kimber would have heard the truck and would be waiting eagerly to greet me. Ya, not so much. Hell she wasn't even on the way! She was sprawled out on the couch next to Alex, apparently on her own little blanket, barely raising her head enough to acknowledge my presence, while wagging her tail... twice, before fading back into a treat induced, food coma. Yup, I told ya she'd be worried about me. After exchanging numbers we said goodbye to Alex and Dawn, I scooped up Kimber and headed for the Rig. I needed to rest up for my attempt at surfing lessons in the morning.

I got to the Mission Beach public parking lot at about 8am, and had my run of the place. After wearing Kimber out with a good ball session in the near-by grass, I grabbed the beach cruiser out of the trailer and rode down to meet Manny at the bike shop. It wasn't long before I had a wetsuit on and was given the "big boy" board. This thing was twice as tall as me and just as wide; I wondered if a sail was supposed to come with it. We stacked the boards in the back of Manny's truck and off we went.

I won't bore you with the play by play, because there wasn't any. After ground drills and about 2 hours in and out of the water, I think I actually stood up and surfed once for about 3 seconds. I was completely exhausted. No wonder you don't see any fat surfers. It was a serious workout but I was determined. Manny helped me out the best he could, and also enjoyed getting in the water after a long hiatus. After about 4 hours, we opted for some coffee and called it quits. When we got back to the shop, low and behold, my Irish buddy Mick was working! After some visiting and a few pictures with the RADD Sports crew, I turned the beach cruiser in the direction of the Rig and headed back to Kimber, who once again was sleeping belly up on the camper bed, in full reveal to the warm sun. California dreaming for sure.

The next day, we were back on the road, heading North to Dana Point and my new buddy Mike's place. Turned out that not only was Mike a super awesome guy, but also a professional boogie boarder. To prove both these points, Mike had a stack of boogie boards that had scratches or blemishes, basically seconds of $250 boards that he sold to kids on the beach for 5 bucks. He said he wanted the kids to respect the board by having to pay something for it, but really just wanted to see more kids in the water enjoying his passion for the sport. How freakin' awesome is that!? He even gave me his personal "leash" off of his own board, to put on a board that he gave to me. Thanks man! Afterward, I got a tour of the house and met his girlfriend Katie, then headed out for some lunch.

It was the end of hockey season with the playoffs coming up. Katie was a huge Ducks fan and wanted to watch the game, so we headed to what I thought was gonna be a sports bar. Instead we ended up turning into the Dana Point Yacht Club, one of Mike's favorite hangouts. When we walked in, we were obviously the youngest folks in the restaurant, with most of Mike's buddies being my Dad's age. When I asked him about it, he said he came here because there was never any drama and old guys are freakin' hilarious. Which I found out in short order.

Mike introduced me to a Korean War veteran named Sammy, who was also a fellow Marine. He told me a story about his time as a Marine Officer aboard ship, when his bunk was literally on a torpedo, with another one suspended from a chain about 6 inches above his head. He told me, "That was the most well oiled chain in the whole damn Navy." Gotta love it.

After some great jokes and even better steaks we stopped by Mike's best friend, Tommy's house, a super awesome guy with an amazing home in the Dana Point Hills. He tossed me a T-shirt that read "Joe Jost's" and told me I had to check this place out if I was going through Long Beach. A famous bar where a couple of different movies were filmed, famous for their draft beer and sandwiches. Sounded like my kinda place! I put it on the itinerary, thanks Tommy!

The next day, Kimber and I set out on foot for some local exploring. Dana Point is the home to the old school long boards and paddle boards. I watched guys my age, paddling like hell while standing on their board to get past the breakers, then turn around and catch a wave to ride in. Old guy surfing, without the need to jump up onto the board. I'm gonna have to remember that. From there we met up with Gerry's band at a local bar and grill for some cocktails and reggae. Finally returning to Mike and Katie's for a home cooked meal and a good night's rest. What a great week with absolutely amazing new friends. I could get used to this traveling thing.

Angel Stadium, Anaheim, CA

June 1st, 2015. The two days spent in Dana Point set us up perfectly for a Monday night game in Anaheim. Ok so, full disclosure, I'm not a fan of the Los Angeles metro area, which Anaheim is a part of. There's a big difference between Northern California and Southern California. Not just the terrain, traffic, congestion, but it's the over all attitude of locals in general. Add to that the rivalry between sports teams, Californians can be pretty territorial when it comes to north and south, and that's putting it mildly. Just ask any San Francisco Giants' fan what they think of the Los Angeles Dodgers, or vice versa.

From Dana Point I chose to roll up Interstate 5 to Anaheim. I was really apprehensive about parking the Rig and leaving Kimber in some of the neighborhoods around the ball park, so we got there early to scout out a spot big enough to fit the truck and trailer. Unbelievably, as we drove past one of the main entrances to the park, I spotted several RVs parked across the street. It was an industrial park with mainly mechanics, auto-body shops, and supply houses. I found a spot between two other RVs that were parked in the shade of some trees. Wow, this was perfect! No lot attendants, no meters, no signs saying what times to park, and most of all, no fee.

After a quick lunch, I put Kimber on a leash to go walk around the ballpark and buy our ticket. That's when I realized there was actually an armada of RVs that went around most of the surrounding side streets. Some with out of state plates, most with a favorite MLB team sticker. I was glad to see that we were in good company. The Rig tends to stick out when it's by itself. When urban boondocking, attention is not your friend. That and I'd feel safer with Kimber in the camper tonight.

Angel Stadium, unlike Petco Park, sits in the center of an ocean of concrete, just off of Interstate 5 and Hwy 57. This is one of the "stadium" style parks I was talking about earlier. Now that I look back at my second game, I could have just as easily parked at the stadium, but not for free.

Kimber was not amused with being left in the camper. With pre-game traffic and commotion outside, she wasn't having it. I walked her around the neighborhood once the concrete had cooled down, in an effort to tire her out. All to no avail. I hated leaving her there, but she was gonna have to learn to get used to it, and so would I.

I crossed the street at the direction of the motorcycle cop who was directing traffic. On the other side of the intersection I saw two more motors officers standing next to their police bikes. These things looked like something out of *Judge Dredd*. Super futuristic looking BMW motorcycles with all kinds of cool features to hold the tools of their trade. The best was a saddle bag mount for a M4 carbine. Pretty crazy to see a mini M-16 mounted to a motorcycle saddle bag lid. I stopped and pointed at the set up and said, "I'd love to get one of those for my Harley." The look on the cop's face was one that compelled me to assure him that I was a former Marine who now lived in Arizona. Mutual expressions of relief and laughter followed. I really needed to remember where I am before I open my mouth.

The inside of the park was pretty standard for these giant concrete stadiums. Walking along the main concourse, there are several exhibits from their 2002 World Series Championship team. The most impressive was a intricately carved, Waterford Crystal, baseball bat and ball. They also had the World Series trophy and ring on display. Some of the greatest players of all time played for the California Angels: Nolan Ryan, Rod Carew, and Bobby Grich just to name a few. Bet ya didn't know the original owner and founder of the Anaheim Angels was none other than Gene Autry, American country music legend. Ya, neither did I. Angel Stadium, MLB park #2… COMPLETE!

Dodger Stadium, Los Angeles, CA

June 4th, 2015. The next day I was eager to get back to the coast. We set out just after rush hour, hoping to find a break in the traffic. Ya right, good luck with that. Los Angeles traffic knows no such boundaries. It pretty much sucks 24/7.

So we were stuck in traffic on the 55, somewhere between Anaheim and Newport Beach, when it hit me like a shovel to the face. I thought the smell was coming from a broken sewer line, or maybe a waste disposal truck, affectionately known as a shitter sucker in Marinese, ahead of me and had to be leaking. It was bad, and getting progressively worse. Then I saw Kimber trying to get as far away from the driver's side of the back seat as possible. Pretty sure she would've jumped out if the window was open. When I adjusted my rear view mirror, I realized that my little princess had dropped a grenade in the seat behind me. If anyone reading this knows me very well, you know that my sense of smell is directly connected to an insane gag reflex. Ever see the dad diaper change videos? Yup that's me. It was like a can of mace was shot in my face right in the middle of rush hour traffic. I did mention I was in L.A., right? Merging lanes with a truck and trailer like a drunken cruise ship captain, trying not to breathe through my nose, eyes watering, and stomach working to relieve me of last night's Angel Dog… somehow we made it to the shoulder. Barely. After cleaning up, reassuring Kimber that I wasn't gonna die and neither was she, we bee-lined for the beach. Wow, that sucked.

We drove back to the Pacific Coast Highway (PCH) and headed north. Passing all the famous beaches, we stopped at Newport Beach for a much needed leg stretch and to recover from our L.A. commute. I didn't want to spend much time in L.A. as you could imagine, but I did want to check out Joe Jost's; so we headed to Long Beach for lunch.

Joe Jost's used to be a barbershop that sold sandwiches way back in the day. I'm talking turn of the century, 1900s. The bartender who served me was not only a sandwich making expert, but a Joe Jost's historian. He told me that the health department stepped in and made them choose

16

either haircuts or sandwiches way back in the day. Glad they made the right choice! Then when prohibition raised its ugly head, the bar installed a giant root beer sign, showing they were complying and one of the good guys not selling alcohol. The sign is still there today. Now the bar has been the setting for a couple of modern movies. Angelina Jolie served the beers here in *Gone in 60 seconds*, and the late Whitney Houston shared a booth with her co-star Kevin Costner in *The Bodyguard*.

The house special is called the 1+1+1. This is a sandwich consisting of a hotdog slit lengthwise with a pickle wedge inserted, between two slices of rye bread, accompanied by a pickled, hard boiled egg that has been soaking in pepperoncini juice, served on a bed of pretzels with black pepper, and a Pabst Blue Ribbon draft poured in the old chalice style cold glass. Awesome! Like stepping back in time. Apparently, they have shipped out these 1+1+1s all over the country to folks requesting them from their death beds. Ya, it's that good. Thanks for the shirt and the recommendation Tommy!

After checking the schedule and seeing the Dodgers' next game wasn't until tomorrow, the challenge now would be finding a place to park the Rig for the night and lay low until the game. I wanted out of this town ASAP. After checking the map, I decided to take the PCH north toward Santa Monica, where I saw some state beaches. Driving past iconic beach names like Redondo, Hermosa, and Manhattan was surreal. Finally, we happened upon Venice Beach and the Boardwalk, home to the famous Muscle Beach Gold's gym. This was like a pilgrimage for me.

I got into bodybuilding when I wasn't allowed to play high school team sports my last two years, due to the one year attendance rule and all my moving around. So lifting weights became my calling, dreaming of making the Mr. Olympia competition, in the footsteps of the greats like Schwarzenegger, Zane, Columbo, and Ferrigno, all of whom trained and were "seen" at this outdoor weight pile, known as Muscle Beach.

I wasn't staying long, so I set Kimber up with a soup bone in the camper, and headed for the boardwalk. I can't even describe how disappointed I was in what happened next. Let's just say the L.A. boardwalks are a totally different world compared to San Diego and other beaches. The first thing you notice is the smell. I would compare it to a combination of the drippings leaking from the trash bag from behind a busy bar at closing... and dead fish. Second thing was being damn near accosted by guys with Jamaican accents, handing me their music CD to sample, then ripping it out of my hands when you say no to the 10 bucks they're expecting in payment.

Finally, after the multiple t-shirt and tourist trap shops with shopkeepers cat calling like carnies at a ring toss game, I saw the famous steel and iron weight sets, standing like rusted steam-punk statues abandoned to the salt air. Nobody was working out, just a sad empty relic of passed greatness. I pictured Arnold doing bench presses with young aspiring bodybuilders, and mystified bikini clad females watching every twitching muscle. Sadly I headed back to Kimber and the Rig. I really hated L.A. now, even more than usual.

Not wanting to get too far away from Dodger Stadium, we really had a hard time finding a place to park for the night. We ended up parked along the side of the PCH, near some restaurants that had cars lined up and down both sides of the road for miles. The sign said no parking between 2am and 6am, but I noticed construction vehicles also parked there after daylight, so decided to take the chance. It was a strange sound to fall asleep to, as the waves pushed massive rocks around in the surf; a very deep muffled collision sound, that I wasn't sure was comforting or frightening.

The next day I decided to roll into downtown L.A., trying to find an early spot like we did in Anaheim. The game wasn't until 6pm, but the gates were already open. When I pulled the truck and trailer up to the gate to see how much parking was, the gate guard looked at me in disbelief. He said they would have to search my camper and trailer, AND I would have to pay for two spots. So 40 bucks to park, for a damn Dodger game, in the stadium parking lot that wasn't open yet anyway. This was not a great start to seeing my most hated rival team. I'm pretty sure they knew I was Giants' fan. So off to hunt for a spot elsewhere big enough for the Rig.

The first thing that was news to me about the area around Dodger Stadium was that it's built on top of a hill. Not quite a San Francisco hill, but damn close. I turned down a side street searching for a spot, when I noticed a semi-truck and trailer about 500 feet ahead of me, blocking most of the street while making a delivery. I realized that I would have to back down the hill with the trailer, in order to turn around and take a different street. Just then the driver of the truck popped out from the cab and motioned me to come on. I really didn't think I had the room between the front of the semi and another vehicle parked across the street, but the driver seemed confident I'd make it. Big mistake. As I crept forward, trying to squeeze between the truck and parked car, I had to stop because I was inches from both. There was no way I was gonna fit.

As I came to a stop, wedged between the semi and the other car, a pedestrian walked by, looked at the situation and said "Ya, good luck with that." I was stuck, it wasn't gonna happen.

That's when one of the Hispanic workers who spoke English told me I was gonna brake an axle from the torque, which apparently is what the semi did! Whoa what? The semi wasn't moving either. Jesus, no wonder the driver was flipping out. I told the guy I'd put the truck in low 4WD, if I had the clearance, I'd make it. That's when he shouted something in Spanish, and about a dozen guys jumped up from watching amusingly and sprung into action. The driver put the truck in neutral and all those men, literally pushed the semi back about 3 inches, and I was able to squeeze by. That's it, I was livid. Not at the construction crew or the truck driver, but at L.A. in general.

When I set out to write this memoir, I thought I should try to be politically correct and not too abrasive when discussing my not so favorite teams and the cities who support them. Well that lasted about a week. Oh well, noble thought, stand by for rant and rave. L.A. SUCKS! The traffic sucks, the beaches suck, the politics suck, and their freaking baseball team sucks. God, I hate L.A. Remember when I said stress would have no place with me on this trip? Well the bitch just hitched a ride. The fact that I was stressing out over a Dodger game, made it that much worse. I had 6 hours to figure this out before game time. Ok, rant complete, I feel better.

I remembered seeing a campground sign north of Malibu Lagoon State Beach where we boondocked last night. I needed to get out of town ASAP, my anxiety was at full tilt. Hopefully they had a spot, I'd be able to drop the trailer and drive back to the stadium. If not, I was thinking I may have to fly back for a game or stop back on the way home to AZ. There was no way I was gonna let this city change my plans.

A couple hours later we pulled up to the gate of the Malibu Creek State Park Campground. It was warm and all the windows to the truck were down, giving Kimber the opportunity to say hello to the Park Rangers in the booth. The two young female Ranger interns were instantly infatuated with Kimber, go figure. They had plenty of spots, but the cheapest was $65 a night! I slowly felt anxiety start to creep in. I explained what we were doing and asked if they had a DAV or military discount, and there was no way I'd be able to afford 65 a night. That's when one of the girls petting Kimber, said her brother was in Afghanistan and if I was a vet, I stayed for free, never once taking her eyes or hands off Kimber. My mouth hit the floor, "Seriously?!" Yup, I was all set up in a quiet campground about an hour or so from Dodger Stadium for the night. Looking back at this, I wish I would've just paid the 40 bucks and let them search the truck. Live and learn.

There was only one problem, they chained the entrance at night, so you could only walk in after dark. This was comforting to know the trailer would be safe, but I'd have no way to get back to the campsite after the ballgame. The only answer was to leave Kimber and the Rig there while I took the Harley into L.A. Anxiety crept in again, while more excerpts of how I hate the F'ing Dodgers flew out. Not much I could do, and we were at this campsite for a reason. So I wore Kimber out the best I could with a solid session of ball, set her up in the camper with food, water, a light, and the radio on, and took off for the game. I just wanted to get this over with.

It had been 20 years since I rode a bike on the California freeways, not much had changed except maybe my fearlessness. I decided to take Hwy 101 into the city this time, taking me straight to the stadium. After a nerve racking hour and a half ride, I rolled into the parking lot unscathed, except for the $20 gut punch to park my motorcycle. I parked as close as I could to the entrance, expecting only to stay long enough to take some pictures and watch a few innings.

Dodger Stadium is rather unique for being a Stadium style park because of its downtown location and expansive onsite parking. The twenty dollar fee regardless of vehicle is high, but worth the convenience. The park was built in 1962, making it the oldest active MLB park west of the Mississippi River, and third oldest overall behind Fenway and Wrigley. Dodger Stadium also boasts the largest capacity by seat count of any major league park.

I purchased my "get in" ticket and headed for the security check turnstiles. Turned out it was bobble head day for some Dodger player I didn't even know, or cared to, at this point. That's why my get in ticket was $25, gut punch number two. After taking a few pictures and a video, I sat for a couple innings and took in the experience of Dodger Stadium. When I had my fill (about 3 innings), I handed my bobble head to the usher with instructions to give it to some kid who didn't get one and bailed back to the bike. I couldn't stand Kimber being this far away and alone, especially near L.A. Dodger Stadium, MLB park #3… COMPLETE!

The next morning we pulled out onto the PCH once again, heading north. I stopped at one of the few predetermined spots I had mapped out for an early lunch, the famous Neptune's Net. This was the roadside seafood joint in one of my favorite movies, *Point Break*. While I sat with an amazing Shrimp Po' Boy in my hand, taking in the fresh sea air, I broke out the road atlas to see what was next. This was the part of the trip I was looking forward to the most, uncharted territories. In all my years of growing up in California, I had never been on the coast between L.A. and San Francisco. I was excited to finally see this part of my old "home" state.

After driving a few hours, I stopped at a rest stop on the side of the highway for a much needed bathroom break and leg stretch. I put Kimber on a leash and walked to the back of the property along the fence to let Kimber do her thing. Apparently I had taken the back route and didn't see the signs warning me of what happened next. Kimber suddenly jumped back from the fence at the same time I heard the menacing but familiar sound. A solid 3 ft rattlesnake was making a hasty get away, much like Kimber and myself, but in the opposite direction. Thank God Kimber had a leash on; I pulled so hard, poor Kimber launched in the air and flew about 3 feet, but was at least out of strike range. After my blood pressure normalized, we got back on the road. Note to self. Kimber stays on leash!

One thing I didn't expect or plan for was how crowded the campgrounds would be. I should've realized that schools would be out for summer, and California beaches have summer visitors from all over the world. I decided to put in for the night near Pismo Beach. Campsite after campsite, both public and private were filled to capacity. Without a reservation you were pretty much screwed. One camp host said I should try Grover's Beach after looking at my Rig and saying, "It looks like you can handle the sand."

Grover's Beach State Beach allows you to park anywhere on the beach that you wish for only 10 bucks a night. I was stoked to finally find a spot to park, super cheap, and right on the beach too! Not being familiar with driving on the sand, I followed the tracks that went through the dryer portion, thinking this was safer than the wet sand. Mistake numero uno. Within a few hundred feet I was stuck. Great, now what?

Parked just a few yards away was a couple sitting on the trunk of their car taking in the scenery. The gentleman noticed I was having trouble and came over to see if he could help. This is when I met my friend Mark and his wife. Mark was about my age, a former military brat, born and raised in Germany and still residing there. Now visiting the states, he was showing his wife the sights of the iconic California Coast.

Unable to free the Rig ourselves, we decided to flag down a 4x4 truck passing by to see if he could pull my truck and trailer to more solid land. Thankfully, it was easy work for this guy's diesel truck to set us free. I sat and relaxed with Mark and his wife while sipping on a couple of much needed cocktails. We traded information, set Mark up on my book page, and promised to meet again but on his side of the world. Looking forward to it, brother.

I moved the Rig further down the 5 mile beach, to a more secluded spot with no other campers, being it was only Thursday afternoon. The first night on Grover's Beach was incredibly peaceful and awe inspiring. A passing Park Ranger suggested that I back into the spot where I want to camp, giving me a downhill run for when I want to leave. Also to deflate my tires to about 20 psi for better traction. Solid advice to be remembered for sure. Once situated, Kimber and I were treated to an amazing sunset over the Pacific Ocean, something I haven't seen in over 20 years. Tranquil and serene... and then morning came.

The next day I realized that I had made mistake number two. Not noticing on the map that Grover Beach was a designated off road vehicle state park, I awoke to the sound of ATVs. My serene campsite just turned into the equivalent of the pits at a NASCAR race. I suddenly found myself in the center of an oval track, with Quads, Sandrails, and any other ATV you could think of, circling my camp. I also noticed a small armada of toy haulers and campers making their way up the beach to the camping zone. The beach was filling up like crazy. Flatbeds of quads for rent to people who obviously shouldn't be on motorized equipment. That night, the Park Ranger Law Enforcement went up and down the beach at least 5 times, with full lights and sirens. Needless to say, we were out the next day.

Not in the mood for driving much after a very restless night's sleep, we only ventured as far as San Simeon State Park, just north of the small town of Cambria, CA. This being a little more of a remote campsite, there were plenty of spots to choose from. This time when I pulled up and asked about veteran discounts, the ranger told me to go to the California State Park Headquarters just up the road and apply for a disabled discount pass. Apparently, you had to be a California resident to get the free camping pass, but I did receive a half price card! Which was awesome. I was quickly learning that every penny counts.

When I returned to the campsite, half price card in hand, I explained to the Ranger that I had to be a California Veteran to get the free camping access he had told me about. His reply was, "Bullshit! Not on my watch. How long do you want to stay?" and with a swipe of his pen I was staying for 5 nights... for free. My jaw hit the floor. We found a perfect spot, completely set up camp, and settled in for a much needed break.

The campsite sat on the east side of the PCH, but was close enough to the water to enjoy the sounds and smells of the ocean. Kimber and I explored the area with huge patches of wild blackberry and fields of wild dill and mustard, the smells were amazing. I was getting hungry now, so we headed into Cambria for supplies, a cool little hippy town with a good selection of places to eat, but no real grocery store to mention. Walmart was about 20 miles inland and I needed to eat now, opting for some pizza in town. Kimber was getting restless, not being able to be off leash in a few days, so after asking around we found a dog park to let her unwind.

This was a special little park where the love for our canine companions was abundant. There were a few canine patrons enjoying the day, running after balls and frolicking with other pups while their humans watched on. At the entrance to the park was a wine barrel cut in half, both sides full of tennis balls. They also had "chuckers" and some paddle ball rackets for humans to hit the balls farther than they could throw. The local racquet club donated all the balls and the gear. How cool is that! Balls were flying everywhere, and Kimber was in absolute heaven.

After a couple hours of ball time with her new friends, Kimber was sufficiently worn out enough that I could do some laundry. I was in desperate need of some clean clothes, but the laundromat vending machines were out of soap. I did manage to find some at a nearby gas station for an ungodly price, but it was an emergency. Now armed with a duffel bag full of laundry, a roll of quarters, and the most expensive soap by the ounce I'd ever purchased, I settled in on a hard plastic chair and read a local newspaper while my clothes were in the wash.

Another laundromat patron, a very pretty blonde woman in her late 20s or early 30s, also needed some soap. Of course being the gentleman I am, I leaped into action, offering her the last of my precious detergent. Soon into our conversation she told me that her husband was also a former Marine, and went out to their truck to get him. Husband? I quickly ran our conversation through my mind's "husband" filter, making sure I shouldn't be looking for the rear exit. That's when I met Steve, a mountain of a man, about the same age as his wife, dressed like George Strait, complete with starched wrangler jeans and a white cowboy hat. He was a traveling rodeo announcer from Montana, working the rodeo circuit in California. We talked quite a bit about our beloved Marine Corps and about politics in general, while our clothes dried. He invited us to his ranch in Billings, Montana, when I'm out that way. Some super cool folks I hope to see again real soon.

With the laundry clean and folded, I decided to head inland to the Paso Robles Walmart for supplies. The drive inland was beautiful, but hot. After being on the coast this whole way, and coming from the much drier AZ air, the inland temperature of 92f felt more like 112f. This was an issue for Kimber in the camper while I shopped. This would have to be a very quick supply run.

When we arrived at Wally World, the parking lot temperature was well above 100f. With no cooling in the camper, I was lucky enough to find a spot with shade. I opened up all the windows, put down a bowl of cold water, turned on the fans, and literally sprinted through Walmart, getting supplies in record time. When I returned to the camper, the wind had kicked up and Kimber was sound asleep on the cool floor. This gave me some time to run into Big 5 sporting goods in search of a camp chair.

As usual, once in Big 5 I found myself drawn into a conversation with the gun counter clerk and another local patron regarding firearm laws. Always a risky move in the Soviet State of California, but what the hell, I'm your huckleberry. I explained how I was traveling the country alone with only a small dog and a baseball bat due to California's gun laws, and how being a vet with a concealed weapons permit back home, this was rather disheartening. Then I noticed they sold bear spray, which I was gonna need in Oregon and Washington anyway. So I asked the clerk for a can and said, "Well this will have to do I guess." That's when the local said, "We don't have many bears around here," apparently confused by what I was insinuating. "No, I mean for the 2 legged variety," I replied. When the local finally caught on, his face wrinkled up like he swallowed a bug, grunted and walked off. The clerk and I had a good laugh; he wasn't from California either.

The next couple of days Kimber and I just kicked it around the camp, enjoying the scenery and the cool weather. Soon enough we had a small car pull into the spot next to us, for our first neighbors in a couple days. Out popped a middle-aged couple with their teen-aged daughter. They were struggling to set up a small tent, and sent their daughter over to ask for a mallet. Apparently her English was best of the three. She was about 13 years old, speaking in broken English with a heavy French accent. I was happy to help. When she returned the tool, she brought her mother with her, thanking me in the same broken English. I introduced myself and Kimber, who was all over the young girl like a long lost friend she hadn't seen in years. Kimber truly is an ambassador for her breed. They explained they were obviously from France and were spending the summer traveling the coast. What an amazing vacation for that young girl! She would have some serious bragging rights when she goes back to school. The next day when they were packing up, the little girl came over and asked for a picture with me and Kimber, and exchanged Facebook info. It was the cutest thing ever, providing me with a warm fuzzy feeling the rest of the day.

Also at that campsite I met another couple who were traveling in a Cabover camper, but pulling a small fishing boat. We started talking about our campers and where we were from. Turned out they were newly married high school teachers from the Bay Area, if I remember right. They were my age with no kids, that did a lot of traveling and fishing during their summer months off. They recommended I stop at a Patrick's Point State Park near the Oregon border, a place they said I just gotta see. I put it on the itinerary, thanks guys! Happy Trails.

After five days at San Simeon, I was itching to get back on the road. I wanted to put in some miles, anxious to get to the next ballpark, since there were no real battlefields along the California Coast. The few stops we made were at places I had heard of, but never experienced in my time there. We stopped to watch a massive herd of sea lions enjoying the summer sun. We took a walk through the southern most Redwood grove in Los Padres National Forest. Had a quick lunch and short hike at Big Sur State Park, and finally stopped in Monterrey to explore the famous Cannery Row that afternoon.

After the usual chore of finding parking for the Rig, Kimber and I set out to see the sights of Cannery Row. It was happy hour and all the restaurants were vying for your attention with amazing food specials. Most of the original cannery was gone, with high end retail and restaurants filling in the formally industrial pier space. Monterrey had amazing clear blue water, great food, and just big enough of a town to not get bored. I will definitely be back to visit again.

Evening was setting in and we needed to find a boondock spot for the Rig. It was going to get harder now that we were starting to enter the congested Bay Area. One thing that I've learned during my short time of urban boondocking, is to look for the big rigs. These guys are the pros and know the quiet spots to bed down for the night. You'll see them on frontage roads where there are commercial motels like Motel 6 or Embassy Suites, which was exactly the case just an exit away from the Cannery. Even better was the Kona Lounge inside one of the hotels where I watched an NBA playoff game and joked with some Army Vets from the nearby base. I was actually supposed to go to the Defense Language Institute in Monterrey to be a Russian linguist, but the Corps had other plans for me. When I told my new Army buddy this, he replied, "Oh that's too bad, you'd be a local by now. Everybody who comes here, stays here." I would have to agree. Put Monterrey on your bucket list for sure!

Up early and on the road, we stopped in Santa Cruz for coffee and to watch some absolutely insane people surfing the Santa Cruz cliff line. Next to a lighthouse was a memorial to the people who I could only assume died surfing there. The surfers were lined up and ready, waiting on the next set of waves to break. They'd catch a wave, surf past this cliff and lighthouse, then with nothing but giant jagged rocks to land on, they would paddle hard to make it to the rock shore and climb out before the next wave slammed them on the jetty. It was insane, but impressive for sure.

As we moved further north the PCH became a regular four lane highway, with more traffic and skinnier lanes. With the width of the camper pretty much taking up the whole lane, I was definitely not looking forward to the bridges and tunnels I knew were coming up. It would be like guiding a bull through the proverbial china shop. My only saving grace being that if the semi-truck in front of me fit, then so would I.

Then came the ticket booths on the south end of the Golden Gate Bridge. Memories of our school bus mirrors scraping the sides as we came home from an away basketball game, came flooding back to life. I lined it up and literally closed my eyes. No scraping, no sparks. But we weren't out of trouble yet. Now we had to navigate the bridge itself with its never ending lane changes, neon orange cones trying to guide your way. Finally we hit one last tunnel, the smallest yet, where I took up the outside two lanes just to make sure I wasn't gonna lose my camper roof, until I made the Stinson Beach exit and headed back to the PCH.

Note to reader. If you have an RV or a rig pulling a trailer... DO NOT TAKE THE STINSON BEACH EXIT! Definitely the wrong exit for this rig. After finally getting through the traffic congestion, we began to ascend Mt. Tamalpias, the last obstacle separating us from the coast. The higher we climbed, the narrower and more curvy the road became. Making it that much more agonizing was the multitude of bicyclists on both sides of the road, that had little to no shoulder. The curves were so tight that I had to take the middle of the road to clear the trailer, making on-coming bikes and cars wait. Rock on one side, cliff on the other, bicyclists like fleas, and here comes the bull. It was brutal, with multiple single finger salutes from all parties involved.

After finally reaching Hwy 1 again, I was now in familiar territory. It was starting to get dark and a much needed shower was in order. The nearest Anytime Fitness was in the town of

Petaluma, that happened to be next to a Walmart. Perfect. We were now in Sonoma County, short of a couple quick visits, it had been 20 years since I had been "home."

After my shower at the gym and some dinner in the camper, we pulled into the Petaluma Walmart for the evening. Unfortunately, this was not a 24hr store and had signs prohibiting overnight parking. There were no big rigs or campers in the parking lot, and I just had a creepy feeling about the place. That weird "spidey sense" took over, veterans know what I mean, so I pushed further north.

I decided to take the road toward the small town of Sebastopol, CA, where I was raised by my paternal grandparents. I started to get an unsettled feeling about something I knew was coming. My Dad and I hadn't spoke in about 12 years, pretty much since my grandfather had passed, for reasons that are better left for another book. Surprisingly, he contacted me just before I left, letting me know he had some old "military" papers from my enlistment that he thought I might want. I told him to hang on to them and he could give them to me himself, then explained my upcoming adventure. Later, I found out from an old Babe Ruth baseball teammate, John, that he had seen my Dad in Starbucks and told him about my upcoming journey. So after years of John and my Dad not seeing each other, and only after John and I had reconnected on FB, the door to me re-connecting with my father was open again. The Lord works in mysterious ways indeed.

The next day would be the day I'd drive to Sonoma and see my Dad. So let me explain really quick, the towns and time frames. My parents were in high school when I was born, and lived in Sebastopol, CA where I spent my childhood with my paternal grandparents. After remarrying, my Dad and his new wife moved me to Sonoma. It was a typical split family, with typical turmoil and drama. We'll just leave it at that. From there it was decided that I would move to St. Helena with my mother, which lasted a single semester; then finally ending up back in Sebastopol for my final year and a half of high school... at the same school my parents graduated from. Talk about full circle. Hopefully that clears it up a little.

The anxiety level for the next day's meeting wasn't going to allow me to get much sleep, so I drove on to Sebastopol, just as dusk set in. I drove by my grandparents' house, almost not recognizing the street. It was as if the trees had suddenly become massive and grew over the streets, or the concrete itself had shrunk. Everything seemed so small. It was a good feeling, a welcome one. The closest one I have of "home." I had to find a place to park soon, so I pointed the Rig toward the city park where my grandmother and I used to walk down to feed the ducks. She would save the heels of her bread just for this occasion.

There was a lot of curb parking along the park side of the street, with houses on the other. There was a Little League baseball game in full swing that filled the streets with plenty of non local vehicles, so blending in was easy. We parked next to the pool where I used to take swimming lessons, put Kimber on a leash and went to watch the kids play ball. Amazing memories came flooding back. Memories that were hard to assimilate as an adult. Playing on the swing set, feeding ducks, little league games, all from a new "adult" perspective. It was almost surreal. Not growing up around these things day to day where they stay familiar, and now experiencing them as they were back then, was truly a mind blowing moment. After the game we retired to the camper for a surprisingly good night's sleep.

That day I called my Dad to let him know I was in Sebastopol. We decided on meeting at his place later that afternoon for dinner, which gave Kimber and I the day to explore Sonoma, a place that I hadn't seen or spent much time in since middle school. Remember my time there wasn't the highlight of my childhood, so a lot of apprehension and not so great memories showed up this time. It was a strange combination of facing my fears and healing, I guess you could say. Like something that had to be done, strings that were once severed, needed tying. Once again not living in, or even seeing this town since I was a child, unfortunately only triggered childhood memories. Like seeing through a ten year old's eyes, feeling a boy's emotions, but accepting it on a new adult level, was something I wasn't quite sure how to handle.

As Kimber and I walked around the square in downtown Sonoma, a one square block city park with your typical iconic town hall building in the center, I realized how much things had changed. It used to be a typical Saturday when you'd come to the "plaza" for a picnic with your dogs, frisbees flying, kids in swings, maybe an art festival going on. Either way, dogs were welcome. Now as we headed for the park, we were met with signs reading, "No Dogs." Period. Not even on a leash. For as liberal as California is in general, you'd sure think they'd have a different view of dogs. Add the fact that Kimber looking like a small pit-bull puppy didn't exactly help the issue. Ya, don't get me started on that.

I found an off leash dog park just up the road by where I used to play Babe Ruth baseball. Arnold Field was the place of my fondest memories of Sonoma. This was the last place that I actually played baseball, short of a junior college try-out. Pretty much anytime I spent on a baseball field were the best times of my life. There was a game going on, and I had to use the bathroom and get Kimber some water, so we walked into the park. Wow, the memories were amazing. Everything was essentially the same, except for maybe some new paint and different advertisers on the left field wall.

I hoisted Kimber up to get a drink out of the water faucet. While holding her I looked around, taking in the scene, when I noticed people were looking at me like I had committed a crime. What, because the dog drank out of the faucet? Give me a break. I walked her around the grandstand to where the bathrooms were, unfortunately having to take her in with me. Another patron in the bathroom was washing his hands, muttering something to himself. When he turned, looked at Kimber and said, "You can't have that dog in here." I told him I was sorry but I was here alone. "I just gotta pee." Then he said, "No, in the park. No dogs in the park." Jesus, again? No wonder people were tripping on me and Kimber at the faucet. This made me chuckle. Then I noticed he had a Sonoma Dragons ball cap on. This was where I attended school my first two years of high school, and where my Dad retired as a teacher from. I apologized and said we would leave, and that we didn't know about the rule. To change the mood, I pointed at his cap and said he might know my Dad, and mentioned his name. Immediately, the gentleman named Mario replied, "You're Matt, you pitched for the Lions. I remember you." WHAT!? Mario used to announce the Babe Ruth games and had been a part of the Sonoma sports scene ever since. I couldn't believe that he remembered me after 30 plus years. That felt good.

Across the street next to the police department was the dog park. Kimber was ecstatic to be able to act like a dog again, chasing the ball and saying hello to the other pups. Two ladies came into the park with their little Shitzu, a lady in her 50s with her elderly mother. Then it happened. Just as I threw the ball for Kimber, the lady in her eighties took a small step backward, right into Kimber's path. Anyone who's seen Kimber play ball knows that it's a 100% full contact sport for whatever's between her and her beloved ball. Kimber barely clipped the poor woman's leg as she barreled by, and down she went. Oh Jesus, no!

I could see the headlines, "Pitbull put down after dog park attack." Remember what I said about people's perceptions of breeds; this has happened to me before. Kimber's predecessor was put down for biting a woman during a dog fight, only because she looked like a Pitbull. If ya try to stop a dog fight, good chance you'll get bit. But because of her appearance, the prosecutor was determined. It was one of the worst times of my life, and no way in hell I could do that again. So right about then my fight or flight syndrome was pinging!

I jumped up to help the lady, apologizing profusely, only to be told by her daughter to leave her alone. This wasn't good. I could tell she was seeing this as Kimber's fault. It was time for me to get out of there. I grabbed the ball and told Kimber, "No more of that for you." That's when the elderly woman, now sitting at the picnic bench, said, "Let the dog play, wasn't her fault." That was reassuring, but the look on her daughter's face was not. After a few more minutes, I leashed Kimber and headed off down a bike path before going back to the camper. It's sad that in this age of endless litigation from a sue happy culture, I was relieved my license plate was miles away.

We got to my Dad's about 4pm for dinner, extremely nervous yet thrilled to reconnect with him after all these years. When he opened the door, I just said "Hi Dad" and hugged my father for the first time in ages. We sat outside at his pool house, watching the Warriors game, drinking some of his home made beer, while we caught up. It was good to sit with my Dad like a man, an equal, no reason to hide feelings, and for the first time, content just to be me. It was liberating to sit with my Dad, drinking a beer with him for the first time, not hiding my full sleeve tattoos, not hiding differing opinions on politics; finally (hopefully) he could accept me just for me and the man I'd become. Maybe healing is a better word than liberating. Either way, I'm glad it happened. Whatever happened next was up to him. I made the peace I needed to make, even though I think it was pretty overwhelming for my Dad and his latest wife. For then at least, I had my Dad back.

The only thing I asked from my Dad was that we could catch a San Francisco Giants game together, like the old days. Unfortunately, Dad's neighborhood wasn't exactly a great fit for the Rig. I mean the thing is a pretty big eye sore unless you're at a campground, and this being "wine country," Dad didn't want to upset the neighbors by my rig sitting there for a few days. He suggested I take a spot at the Sugar Loaf State Park campground, where he happened to be a volunteer on the weekends. Perfect! We stayed that night with Dad, heading out in the morning to Sugar Loaf.

I remember my Dad taking me to Sugar Loaf when I was a kid, located outside of Sonoma on Hwy 12, near the famous wine country town of Kenwood, CA. An absolutely beautiful park that used to be run by the state, now it was run by volunteers to keep it open to the public. How cool is that? This is a pretty special place that I hope finds a way to survive. The campsite volunteer was already gone for the day, and I didn't have exact change to drop the fee into the pay tube. So I put my VA ID card and my Drivers License on my dash board, expecting to settle with the camp host in the morning. The next day the camp host came by; I jumped out of the camper to explain I didn't have change last night, and tried to hand him my cash. He held up his hand, refusing to take my money. "I saw your IDs. Boss says veterans stay for free." To this day I'm not sure if my Dad had a hand in that or not; either way, I stayed in Sonoma Valley for 5 days... free. Do you have any idea how much a room costs in that town!? All I can say is wow!

AT&T Park, San Francisco, CA

June 15th, 2015. It was amazing to think I was going to catch a Giants game with my Dad after all these years. The last game I remember seeing with him was back in the early 80s, I think. Back when freezing your ass off in the upper decks of Candlestick Park, eating a frozen chocolate malt with a wooden spoon, trying to catch glimpses of Atlee Hammacher on the mound between fog banks rolling in, was the norm. This was baseball, the good old days.

AT&T Park was the perfect example of a monster stadium being scrapped for a smaller downtown location. Where Candlestick was located more on the outskirts of San Francisco, moving the park to the wharf area would obviously bring in more revenue to the city, including the parking. So here's a pro tip for seeing the Giants at home. Park at Larkspur Ferry Landing which is north of the San Francisco Bay, across the street from the infamous San Quentin Prison. For 6 bucks a ticket, park and take the Ferry across the Bay, dropping you off directly in front of the park. The ride is about an hour long, cruising the San Francisco Bay, with amazing views of the city and Port of San Francisco. The Ferry even has a full bar! Here's the great part. The ferry is waiting for you after the seventh inning stretch, and leaves as soon as game is over. An absolutely awesome way to visit AT&T Park.

The park itself was built in 2000, and has gone through several name changes, including the most recent change in 2019 to Oracle Park. The real issue that I have about these new fancy parks, is the history lost. This isn't the same dirt that Mays and McCovey played on, it's as if sacred soil was disregarded for a shiny new model. Although the modern new parks are absolutely awesome and will bring fans to the sport of baseball for generations to come, the nostalgia is still sadly lost. The positive aspect of the move is that this park is one of the most picturesque parks on the West Coast. With just a single, massive Jumbotron in centerfield, lower deck bleachers in left, a brick promenade/walkway in right, it gives a wide open view of the Bay in the distance. Short of just finding our seats, touring the park wasn't my main priority this time, sitting and enjoying the game with my Dad took precedent. And with that… AT&T Park (Oracle Park), MLB park #4… COMPLETE!

One thing I forgot to mention, that's important for later. While my Dad and I walked around the ballpark, we passed a guy standing off to the side with a good sized Pitbull terrier. (I personally hate that term). The guy was a few years younger than me, wearing an army sweatshirt, beard and tattoos. His dog was adorned in his own Giants jersey, with a pair of those weird sunglasses that have eyes for lenses. Obviously not a "service" dog, I stopped and asked the guy how he got his dog in. He mentioned a company online, and said to just Google a support dog kit. I'd have to keep that in mind. Would be a lot less stressful for me to have her with me, than to always be worrying about her alone in the Rig, let alone safer for Kimber to be in warmer temperatures.

Back at the camper, Kimber was sleeping peacefully, barely raising her head as I opened the camper door. She was tired; this had been one crazy trip for this little girl. So for the next day we just relaxed around camp, chased the ball, and met up with Dad for another Giants game, but this time at the local bar. For the very first time, I felt like I could actually miss this place.

O.Co Coliseum, Oakland, CA

June 18th, 2015. Our last day at camp was planned so that I could leave the trailer here, and catch a weekday, day game at the Oakland Coliseum. Now it's apparently called the O.Co Coliseum (Overstock.com), so we will just go with the Coliseum, formerly known as the Oakland Coliseum. Either way, Kimber and I were going to an A's game, that's all that mattered.

The weekday, day games, also referred to as "Businessman's Special" are my favorite games to catch. School is in, most people are working, the place is generally empty except for an occasional school bus of kids and a lot of seniors. Tickets are cheap and plentiful, and so is the parking in Oakland. Some parks even give a free veteran/military ticket for the Monday through Thursday afternoon games. This would come in handy later on.

Kimber and I easily found parking as the Oakland Coliseum is another one of the monster stadium style parks. Built in 1966, it's easily accessed from local freeways, and sports an ocean of parking spaces for $20. This long time home of the Oakland A's, also plays home to the Oakland Raiders NFL franchise, actually being the last stadium to still house both sports. The field is built almost 32 feet below sea level, along with the grassy hills added to the exterior of the building, giving the intended appearance of only one level from the street. It truly is an archaic, concrete beast.

After fixing some lunch in the camper and letting Kimber chase the ball with a few of the guys tailgating nearby, I set her up with food, water, and a chewy stick before I went inside. She wasn't pleased that she was staying in the camper, but quickly drowned her worries in the rawhide pacifier. She'd be fine, but I'd still be leaving early.

When I got to the gate of the park, I passed an Oakland Police motorcycle, Harley Davidson this time, parked near the entrance. Being an old "biker" myself, I'm always stoked to see the boys in blue riding American Harley's. Something about the history and nostalgia of it. I asked one of the motors officers if I could take a picture of his bike, just in case that was frowned upon. The officer actually stopped mid sentence in his conversation with his partner, held out his hand and said, "Gimme your phone." I paused for a second, reluctantly handing over my cell. Then he motioned me back over to where his bike was and snapped several pictures with me and his bike. How freaking awesome is that. Dead stopped talking to a fellow officer to address a member of the public like that was commendable. I shook their hands and told them about the M16 mounts the Anaheim cops had. One of the officers said they wished they could have those here in Oakland. I said, "Ya me too! I'm gonna mount one on my Harley when I get home." I really gotta remember where I am before I blurt out gun ideas, especially in conversation with the local law enforcement. I quickly added that I'm a retired Marine from Arizona. One of the officers was also a Marine from a different state. A good laugh ensued, followed by more handshakes. Thanks for your service, fellas, Semper Fi.

Inside the park, I think the temperature actually rose 20 degrees. One thing about the O.Co Coliseum is that there is very little in the way of shade, especially in the upper level cheap seats. The sun was brutal and I think the ushers knew it, allowing people to pretty much sit where they wanted. I found a spot behind home plate, shaded by the upper deck. There was nobody in the entire row, so I settled in to watch the game in the shade. About that time, a family of four started walking down my row. I grabbed my stuff, assuming I'd have to move, not believing that I picked the one seat that was somebody else's. Turned out they were sitting just a chair away from me, season ticket holders, with their young son and baby daughter. The seat I had taken belonged to their friend who wouldn't be there, so we were good.

About halfway through the 5th inning, I happened to be looking at stats on my phone, when a foul ball hit the roof just in front of our seats, then hit the ground under the seat between me and the father of the young boy. It was like time froze for an instant. He was holding his son, and looking at the ball, as I turned to see where it went. Instinct took over I guess, as I picked up the ball and instantly handed it to his son. I was an interloper in his world, that wasn't my ball, that was his boy's. Just as soon as I handed the boy the ball, the entire stadium erupted with applause. I had no idea I was on the center field screen. That was my very first MLB foul ball, and I couldn't think of a better way to celebrate than to see that little boy's eyes when I gave him his ball. The funny part is, he thought I wanted it back when I asked for a picture with him. He was having none of it. Got a picture with him and his death grip on that ball. Great memory right there.

One funny story about that game. You realize how old a park is by what type of urinals they have in the men's room. I know it sounds weird but those of you my age can remember the "bathtub" urinals. Like a long, slender, porcelain trough with chrome tubes on top, leaking out a continuous stream of water. I hadn't seen those since I was a kid. I actually wanted to take a picture of the ancient plumbing, but thought that would be a little weird with a room full of men. Fast forward to me walking out of the game. I stopped in the same bathroom, standing there alone doing my business, when the whole room lit up like a bolt of lightning. I looked around just in time to see the iconic Asian tourist with a camera around his neck, taking a picture of the urinals. See, I'm not the only one. Oakland Colosseum, or whatever they call it now, MLB park #5… COMPLETE.

The next day we said goodbye to Sonoma and turned the Rig west, back to the coast. I took Hwy 12 back to Sebastopol and out to Bodega Bay. More incredible memories came flooding back. I stopped in for a bowl of the best clam chowder I know, poured into a sourdough bread bowl of course. This was real NorCal eating. Just north of Bodega was my favorite beach, Salmon Head, and then the small town of Jenner, where my grandparents first settled and where my Dad was born. My grandmother used to work in the small cafe that doubled as the Post Office, while my grandfather drove a street sweeper for the state after his Navy time.

After driving most of the day up the winding PCH, I decided to call it quits just outside of a cool little town called Gualala. There was a trailhead with parking that led down to what looked like a popular surfing beach called Moat Creek. One guy walking past, after stopping to check out the waves, said it wasn't looking good today, but this place would be packed first thing in the morning. Tomorrow is the last week of Abalone season. I didn't know Abalone had a season, good to know.

Abalone is a super tough, very large, muscle that lives in shells we call mother of pearl, at least that's what the rainbow color looked like. I remember my uncle diving for them, coming home with a bag of these huge shells, cutting the meat out, and beating the crap out of it with a metal mallet. I think they slice them first and then tenderize; either way, they hit an egg wash with breading and a pan full of hot grease. Pour some marinara over it... amazing! But if this place was gonna be full of divers, I had better be ready to go early.

The next day our first stop was for some breakfast. Fort Bragg was the next town that looked promising for some food. Not realizing it was Father's Day until I saw a sign offering a Father's Day Pancake Breakfast at the town's VFW Hall. There was also a good sized car show happening that morning, lining the streets with some pretty amazing vintage rides. The VFW Lodge itself was very old, housing a virtual museum of WW1, WW2, Korean and Vietnam War memorabilia, all donated from hometown veterans who served their country in one battle or another. Everything from uniforms to letters home to their sweethearts, it was a pretty remarkable display of American patriotism. I enjoyed some of the best green runny eggs and dollar pancakes ever. Had nothing to do with the food, everything to do with the warriors I was dining with.

We continued on the PCH until it cut inland and became Hwy 101, also known as The Redwood Hwy. Another absolutely incredible bucket list drive. That afternoon, I stopped for the night at an amazing campsite known as Richardson Grove State Park, nestled in the middle of a Giant Sequoia grove, on the shores of the Eel River. For those who have never seen a Redwood tree, a visit to the Giant Sequoias is a bucket list experience. You don't just "see" these ancient trees, you experience them. With trunks big enough to drive through, and the tops of the trees burnt from lightning strikes, it's something that words struggle to describe. You just have to see these things.

As I pulled up to the gate house, praying they had an open spot, I noticed the three young female Forestry Interns working the kiosk. Quickly, the back, driver's-side window rolled down and immediately Kimber went to work, showing her smiling face as all three girls became puppy mush. I couldn't even get the girls' attention to see about an available camping space. There was nothing but small loving hands all over Kimber and a symphony of coo's and ahh's emanating from the Ranger booth. That's my girl! Do what you do, my friend. That's when the older training Ranger said they were full and only had a "Disabled" spot left. I showed her the half price card from San Simeon and asked if this would work. With a big smile she said, "Yup, that'll do it! How many nights?" Once again I was shocked. The place was packed, mid summer, and somehow, someway, I got a spot. Not to mention it was half off! Everything truly happens for a reason, my friends. We set up camp and settled in for the evening.

The next day we hiked around the park taking in the absolutely amazing scenery. It was pretty humid compared to Arizona, definitely warm enough to take a swim in the river. There were pockets of people on the micro beaches along the river shore, mainly kids with floaties and many mindful parents nearby. We walked downstream a ways so I could unleash Kimber and watch her first experience with rushing river water. The river depth went from 6 inches to a couple of feet in some spots. I threw the ball upstream, positioning myself to catch the ball if Kimber couldn't. No worries there; with a splash, Kimber was in the deeper water. For the first time I saw her free swim; it wasn't exactly graceful but it did the job. I was completely amazed how this little dog had taken to water.

Sitting in that ice cold, crystal clear water, watching the kids play in the slower more shallow current, brought back more childhood memories of playing in the Trinity River with my cousins. Every summer I would get on a Greyhound bus heading to Redding, CA to spend the summer with my Mom and the other side of the family, always spending the day either at the Trinity River or Whiskeytown Lake. My maternal grandmother warned us about the current around the large rocks; get too close and the river will drag you under. The things adolescent nightmares are made of. Funny the things that come to mind after years of forgotten memories are stirred up by something as simple as kids in a river. I thought I must be getting old.

After two days in the Giant Sequoias, I was eager to move on, although I could've stayed there forever. From this point forward it was brand new territory again. I'd never really been north of Eureka, CA and had only been to Medford, OR when I was a kid. So the next part of the journey would be pure exploring. I was excited to drive the Oregon Coast to see what all the excitement was about; I'd heard it was beyond amazing.

We headed out fairly early, easing over the speed bumps in the campground, when I heard a loud pop. It sounded like a muffled gunshot, but it didn't seem to bother the kids playing near by. Shrugging it off, we continued out onto the highway. About 100 yards down the road my tire air pressure sensor went off. I had a flat. Well, I guess I knew where that pop noise came from; it was the plug I had repaired that tire with months ago. I didn't quite ease over that speed bump slow enough and blew out the plug. With 5 days until payday this was not great news.

I decided to give my aunt in Redding, CA a call. It had been years since I'd seen anybody on that side of the family, and I wasn't planning on heading that far inland due to the heat. Redding was on Interstate 5, the route I had planned to take back to AZ, and planned to stop in then. Now out of cash, rolling on a spare tire, with the trailer tires on their last leg too, I had to find somewhere to lay low until payday. Redding would be the biggest city to find the tires I needed anyway, so it wasn't like I had much of a choice at that point. It would be good to see my aunts, cousins, and maybe even try to re-connect with my mother. Like my Dad, we had been out of touch for years. Also like my Dad, that's an issue for a completely different novel. With just a call and an address, I had family waiting for me in Redding. I have to admit, that felt pretty good. Tire changed, spare installed, we were back on the road heading east.

The weather in Redding was exactly what I had remembered, except now since I'd been in the desert for 20 years, add humidity to the 100f heat. It was like a concrete tropical jungle. It was too hot to take Kimber outside anywhere, so we stayed with my aunt in the air conditioning for most of the 5 days. I did touch base with my mother, the meeting unfortunately didn't go as well there as it had in Sonoma. Oh well, maybe next time. Life is too short to let drama bring you down, regardless of blood. Harsh but true. I tried, and that was enough for me. Now back to exploring.

July 1st payday gave the Rig a brand new tire, and four more on the trailer. This was gonna set me back a bit, but had to be done. I was more than eager to get out of the Redding heat and back to the cool coastal breezes. We left the same way we came in, taking the hot winding Hwy

299 back to the coast. The truck temperature reading outside was 101f when I noticed the truck handling differently. A glance at the airbag gauge revealed we were sitting at zero. I lost the damn airbags again. After stopping at a rest area and trying to lay on hot concrete, it was just physically impossible to work under the truck. Besides, I would be in cooler climate in two hours; I'd drive slow and push on. Big mistake.

I took the "fishing teacher's" advice and found Patrick's Point State Park about an hour or so north of Eureka. Great advice, the place was amazing! Like a tropical rain forest in the dense coastal fog, vines crawling up the huge redwood trees, ground ferns fanning out, covering the ground that was soft as a pillow from the wet moss and fallen redwood needles. It looked like I was in the *Land of the Lost* TV show, with those creepy green lizard people and that family living in the trees. Totally just dated myself, but this was the best description. I expected to see a Raptor or T-Rex come crashing through the trees any minute.

Sadly, the beauty surrounding me was foreshadowed with worry about my Rig and fixing those airbags. The manual said to keep the bags inflated to a minimum of 5 lbs psi or they would deflate, expand out, and rub on my truck suspension springs, wearing a hole in the side of the bag. Yup, that's exactly what happened. Not just one bag, but both bags. I could hear the air escaping from the side of both airbags, as my heart began to sink. That's it, we were done. Well, there goes $800 bucks and now possibly the end to my travels. There was no way I could afford a new kit, let alone order it, find a place to have it delivered, and do the install. I was royally screwed. The thought of packing it in and limping back to Arizona on stock suspension was starting to look like my only option. Then the Jarhead in me stood up and smacked me in the back of the head. I was halfway from completing a childhood dream, let alone writing a damn book. There was no way I was turning back now. There was no way I wasn't going to finish what I told my father I had started. Absolutely not gonna happen. Realizing this completely changed my outlook and attitude about the situation. I gave a quick smile and pointed at the cloud filled sky and said aloud, "I know you got this." With that, Kimber and I enjoyed all the sights, sounds, and smells that Patrick Point had to offer for the next two days.

When we left Patrick's Point, I pulled the Rig out onto a flat concrete part of the road and checked the its rear wheel clearance. I still had a good 6 inches of travel space between tire and wheel well, with no signs of rubbing. This was welcome news, we were good to go. Looking a bit like Jed Clampett driving the Beverly Hillbillies family car, we inched our way up the last

few miles of the California Coast. There you have it, California, state number #1…
COMPLETE.

Oregon

July 1st, 2015. The Oregon Coast has been touted as the eighth wonder of the world, or whichever number they're on now. The famous lighthouse seen in pictures and the Tillamook Cheese factory were the only two places I had written down as must stops, the rest would be pretty much pure exploring. Uncharted territory, I was stoked. Once again the plan was to just hug the coast as closely as possible as we ventured north. Easy enough, I thought, let's do this.

We reached the Oregon border around 1100 and stopped to take a picture of the state's Welcome sign. One thing I learned from California is to check the various states for military or veteran discounts that I may be eligible for. The next town up was Gold Beach where I saw a large Ranger Station. Actually, this turned out to be a National Forest Service office, not the Oregon State one I had hoped for, but since I was there, might as well check with the Feds too. I was sure glad I did! Thanks to a very kind Ranger lady, who was enjoying a summer visit with her grandkids when I walked in the office door. She looked somewhat perturbed when I asked about veteran or disabled discounts, immediately explaining I needed to go online and apply, and then that they would mail the pass to me. I explained that I was traveling with no access to mail. By now it was almost lunchtime, with a fussing toddler in her arms, she quickly handed me an application and a plastic card. The card was called an "Access Pass" for half priced camping in all the national forests throughout the country, and free admission to National Parks. I'm pretty sure she was just anxious to get me to leave so she could focus on her grandbabies. With card in hand, I was happy to oblige. There were only a few National Parks in California, and a couple in Oregon, but I was glad to have that card anyway. I'd be keeping an eye out for national forests from then on. Little did I know, that card she gave me would save me thousands of dollars in the years to come.

As we drove up the Oregon Coast, I was absolutely dumbfounded by the beauty laid out before me. Every turn was like driving into a living, breathing postcard. Unlike most of the California beaches, the mountains touch the sea in Oregon. I'm not talking about just cliffs or rocks; there's plenty of those too. It was astonishing to see the actual mountain ranges ending in the Pacific Ocean. To see pine trees lining the beaches, water so clear you would think the ocean was a rushing river, and Elk Crossing signs in the parking lot. I was led to believe I had just found heaven.

Venturing inland from the beaches was a chore in itself, if not afforded the luxury of a trail. The vegetation was even more lush than California, moss hanging from the branches of coastal pines blocking out the sun. Dense vines and huge ferns made it practically impossible to navigate, but amazing to behold.

I had a buddy in the Marine Corps who was from Coos Bay, Oregon. He used to show me pictures of his hometown and its beaches, which were absolutely amazing. I always wanted to visit the place, which happened to be the next town on the map, and the largest town we had encountered so far. I was glad to see the town was large enough for a Walmart, and an apparent popular one at that. The back parking lot was taken over by an armada of RVs and big rigs. This was always a good sign. My biggest fear was to be jolted awake by someone pounding on my camper, telling me to move. Add a barking Kimber and a good old dose of PTSD, and you guessed it, not great. It was somehow comforting to be parked for the night among my traveling brethren.

In the morning, we drove the Rig downtown where we set out on foot to explore the city. We walked along the Bayshore boardwalk, passing some incredible sailboats and hardcore fishing vessels. They must've been commercial fisherman, with their long net masts and huge floodlights pointing to the water. Mostly covered in rust, I could only imagine how old some of those massive boats were. They looked ancient but apparently still serviceable.

The downtown district of Coos Bay had your standard tourist trinket shops, but also a good number of nice restaurants and bars, along with other family businesses such as barbershops, specialty stores, boutiques, etc. A very cool place I will definitely be visiting again in the future.

During our walk we happened upon a tire shop that was advertising truck lifts and suspension installs in their window. Luckily, I was able to speak with the lead mechanic about my airbags and whether my half ton truck could make it the rest of my trip. He took a look at my springs and looked for any rub marks, confirming that I still had 6 inches of travel and should be fine. "Just take it slow around the curves and plenty of room breaking," he recommended. No worries there, since I already drove like my grandfather anyway, and as long as I was rolling forward, I was good! What a relief to hear that the truck was good to go.

After about a 6 mile walk, Kimber I were exhausted and hungry. Time to look for a campsite and settle in for a day or two. On the way back to the coast we passed by a casino offering a huge 4th of July fireworks show and RV parking for 10 bucks a night. Not realizing it was gonna be the Fourth in a couple days, I made a mental note. This might be worth checking out.

I found a campsite online and headed toward the beaches. After all that walking I was ready to set up camp, fire up the grill, and relax. Wishful thinking. As soon as Kimber saw all that sand, she started freaking out, bouncing back and forth between the open windows in the backseat, with an occasional stop on the center counsel to let me know I wasn't driving fast enough. This dog was way too smart.

We found a campsite in the Sunset Bay State Park just south of the town of Charleston. An absolutely beautiful place to camp, if you're ever in the area, I highly recommend it. A secluded little bay, with a nice clean beach to play on, not much for waves, so no surfers, just a few fishing kayaks here and there. When the tide rolled out, it revealed probably the largest group of tide-pools I'd ever seen. There had to be literally a 100 yards of tide-pools, teeming with all the regular sea creature tenants. The park service offered Ranger led nature classes and hikes for adults, and the same for children. Add showers for less than 20 bucks a night, it looked like we had found home for a couple days.

One of the hikes offered was a tour of some old World War II radar sites nearby. I wanted to take Kimber, of course, so we set out to find the sites ourselves. There were no road signs or trail markers pointing to the trailhead, so I asked for directions from a local who was hiking by. We were close. Just up the paved road was an old dirt fire road that led back into the rain forest, or maybe jungle is a better description.

After a pretty good hike we found the radar site; seemed to me to be more like a type of lookout tower more than anything. All that remained was the shell of a three room block structure, covered in multi-colored graffiti, with strange chimney-like risers that had an opening on top. After further research, turned out the place was the Cape Arago Radar Station, built by the Army in 1942 as part of a chain of radar sites up and down the west coast. Used as early detection against Japanese planes and ships, these were secret sites buried in the Oregon coastal vegetation, and off limits to the locals from 1942 to 1944. The chimney stacks were actually generator flus. What a cool find!

On the 4th of July morning, Kimber and I were up bright and early after a relaxing two days at camp. I wanted to get down to the casino early in case the RV spots filled up fast. We broke camp and stopped at Walmart for some supplies and gas. I pulled up to the gas pump, bounced out of the Rig and was reaching for my wallet, when suddenly this guy popped up from behind the pump and just stood there, uncomfortably close, staring at me as I slid my credit card into the card reader. He was probably in his early 50s, wearing a dirty dark blue jacket that matched his trousers, a light blue collared shirt with some type of company patch on the chest, and a fluorescent orange safety vest. On his belt he had what looked like a two-way radio and a large set of keys, with safety boots and an old ball cap; other than that, he looked like he rolled out of a garbage dumpster.

My first inclination was that this guy was some sort of security. First thought was, "Great. What the hell did I do?" Funny how that was my first guess. After swiping my card, I glanced at him with a puzzled look and said, "Good morning." He just stood there. The hair on the back of my neck started to tingle, spidey sense kicking in. I slowly started to reach down for my keys, the only weapon I had close. I didn't know if this guy was gonna carjack me or what, he wasn't exactly dressed for a crime spree. So who was this guy? Safety conscience homeless guy, or tomorrow's headlines: "Arizona man next on the Coos Bay Killer's list." The card didn't read so I swiped it again, never letting the guy out of my peripheral vision. Then he spoke. "What do you want?" he asked. I looked at him again with the same look puzzled look. "Umm…gas?" I replied. The pump gratefully broke the awkward silence with a loud beep, telling me to go inside to see the attendant. Thank God! A reason to step away from this guy without drama. As I started to walk away he said, "Well, give it here, I'm the attendant." I stopped dead in my tracks, "Really bro?" I replied. With a big grin he said, "I saw your plates, was just messing with ya. It's actually illegal for you to pump your own gas in Oregon." I had to chuckle. "That shit will get you shot in Phoenix," I told him. We both laughed, him a little more so than me.

We got to the Mill Casino around noon. The RV park had a few spaces but were a lot more expensive than the $10 dollar advertisement; it was actually the overflow lot with no hook-ups. With laundry facility, showers, and of course the casino, it was still a steal.

It never dawned on me that Kimber may not appreciate the 4th of July as much as I do. We lived in a small town that didn't have a fireworks show, you had to go to the next town over for that. So Kimber had zero experience with what was to come. When it started getting dark, I locked up the Rig and put Kimber on the leash. I wanted to hear the music that was part of the firework display. I sat down in the last row of seats on the end, not seeing the speaker stack directly behind me. Yeah, I know. It was dark, give me a break. When they lowered the lights, I picked Kimber up onto my lap just in case it didn't go so well.

When the first shell exploded above us and the music roared to life, it was at that exact moment I realized Kimber was incredibly stronger than I had given her credit for. She sprung up from my lap like a cat, somehow managed to turn around in mid-flight, and was determined to make a break for it over my newly realized sunburned shoulder. I was able to react in time, to catch her by the waist, somewhere near my left ear, as she attempted her decent down my back. Kimber literally pulled me from the seat, clawing at the pavement for at least 500 yards, practically dragging me back to the Rig. The rest of the night was spent holding and comforting my shaking little princess. Looked like we'd be sticking to barbecues and sparklers on the 4th from then on.

Back at it, bright and early the next day, we said goodbye to Coos Bay, pointing the Rig north once again. With absolutely no traffic at 0600, the drive north was serene and at times even surreal. Lakes as smooth as glass, minus even the slightest ripple, their shores lined by pine trees, and a rainbow of wildflowers. I stopped several times, right in middle of the highway, trying to capture the scenes on my camera to no considerable avail. The Oregon Coast is an experience, incomprehensible to those only able to see it through a picture frame, or computer screen.

Reedsport, OR was the next town to catch my attention. I was taken aback by the beauty of the small coastal town. A combination of personal boats and small commercial fishing ships, all shared the antiquated docks. The streets were lined with the standard tourist gift shops, coffee houses, and a good selection of restaurants and bars. At the end of the pier, folks were setting up a Farmer's Market and art show.

After taking in the sights, having a coffee and stretching our legs, we headed back to the truck. I noticed a street sign that was facing the opposite way when we pulled up. It warned of a $6,250 fine for littering. Whoa what? Did I read that right? No wonder Oregon is so beautiful, and the locals are apparently determined to keep it that way. After scanning my immediate area for anything that may have fallen out of the truck, I picked up some trash from the gutter that wasn't even mine, not taking a chance of mistaken blame. Just then I realized how well that little sign worked.

As we continued to work our way up the coast, I spotted a road sign for the Oregon Coast Aquarium. Due to low funds, I had to skip the Monterrey Aquarium, so I decided to check the price here. As I made my way down the winding road away from the highway, I was suddenly faced with an unexpected pleasure and a hard decision. The Rogue Brewery just happened to be on the same road as the Aquarium. This was one of my all time favorite craft beers that I had no idea was in Oregon, let alone 100 yards in front of me. Then came the decision of spending cash to see some cool coastal sea life, or drinking a beer while eating some heated up coastal sea life. Decisions, decisions.

We pulled into the Rogue Brewery parking lot just before they opened for lunch at 11am. The Brewery was built near Yaquina Bay, almost directly under the 600 foot bridge that towered above us. The tide was apparently out, as there were folks digging for clams in the wet sand. I noticed an older couple around my Dad's age, shucking and cleaning their catch on a concrete table that had a hose for running water. I walked Kimber over to have a look. Wow, those were some clams alright! They were baseball size, with a 2ft "neck" and were considered small. They were Pacific Geoducks, pronounced "goo-e-ducks," and were the biggest clams I had ever seen, almost like a small abalone.

The older couple were Oregon natives who explained that while the tide was out, you walked the wet sand looking for bubbles; this marked the monster clams' air hole. When you see a hole, you're supposed to stick your finger in it to feel for the end of the clam's long neck. When you feel the clam retract from your touch, that's when you dig about 2 feet down with a pitchfork to uncover your prize. The meat from one of them is about the size of two golf balls, and the snorkel neck thing is usually cut up for chowders and other recipes. Super friendly and talkative people, but it was lunchtime.

When the brewery opened, I set Kimber up with food and water in the camper and headed in for some lunch and a draft. As you walked through the front door you almost wanted to back up to make sure you went through the correct entrance. The walkway meandered through part of the brewery with huge beer vats towering above and the smell of roasting grain, hops or barley, I assumed. Following the signs to the tasting room and the restaurant, you got a self-guided tour of the working part of the brewery. After a few samples of some new beers, I opted for an amazing barbecue pulled pork sandwich with beer cheese soup. No sea creatures were consumed… this time.

We passed through Newport, stopping at a surf shop that was having a wet suit sale. I was gonna need some thicker skin if I was ever going to get in the water this far north. Ozzie's Surf shop set me up with the ever elusive size of Large/Short. Shut up, it's a hard size to find! The shop manager, a fellow "big boy," even threw a trucker cap in with the deal. When I told him about my lessons in San Diego, the "big boy" board, and how I now understood why you didn't see any fat surfers, he laughed. "Ya need insulation up here. Gotta represent!" he proclaimed while patting his belly. We all had a laugh, as we watched Kimber steal the show outside with the girls hanging clothes. God, I love that dog. We took pictures with the shop crew, exchanged information, and headed north.

More amazing scenery, like a continuous rolling postcard that you're actually driving in. I came to a stoplight in the town of Lincoln City, where I smelled the amazing scent of smoked salmon. Barnacle Bill's Seafood Market was on the corner, with a walk up type meat counter right on the sidewalk. Reminded me of Fisherman's Wharf back in the day, walking down the sidewalk with restaurants on one side and crab carts on the other. You could order three different types of smoked salmon; dry, medium, and wet, mainly referring to the red glaze on the fish. The medium was amazing. I absolutely love smoked fish, and this was the best I'd ever had. I even opted for some smoked ling cod on a stick, to go.

The next stop was definitely planned. The Tillamook Cheese Factory, which I had no idea was in the town of Tillamook, in Tillamook County, let alone in Oregon. When I saw it on the map, it became a destination. The Sonoma Cheese Factory was my favorite lunch spot growing up, I wasn't gonna pass up a tasting bar with my favorite cheese as an adult. The factory was massive with a huge variety to sample, and to my surprise, there was also an ice cream fountain. The ice cream wasn't free, but the size of the cone you got for two bucks was insane. The place was super cool and a definite must see.

It was later in the afternoon and we were gonna need to start scouting out a place to park. We stopped for groceries in a really cool beach town called Seaside, that I definitely wanted to check out. Then by crazy luck, just up the street was a small Army post called Ft. Rilea. I was curious if they had a camping area or RV park, so I pulled up to the front gate to ask the guard, who then directed me to the housing office. Within 20 minutes I had an RV spot next to the shower house, with full hook-ups, for $20 a night. I loved staying on base, which was like a little city at my disposal. Complete with bar, bowling alley, small restaurant, gym, laundry facility, and sometimes a commissary if not a "quick mart" of some type. And of course, there was no safer place for my trailer than on a military base. I'd pay extra for that.

The next morning we unhooked the trailer and drove back to Seaside. It didn't take but a few blocks to fall in love with the place. It was exactly like a little Pacific Beach, complete with boardwalk, beach cruisers and hotels on the waterfront. Also nice restaurants, cool looking bars, even bumper cars for the kids. It was definitely a family friendly place, and a popular tourist attraction.

I decided to grab my gear, attempt to put on my new wet suit, and see if I could remember how to boogie board. After getting to the water, I realized that the only people on boards were about 200 yards out into the ocean because there were little to no waves on the shore. The break was way out there. With the life guard about a quarter mile down the beach, there was no way I was going out that far. At my age and experience... not gonna happen. So after laying in the water on my board for a minute, contemplating my new surfing career's demise, I turned to do the walk of shame in my fat boy wet suit back to Kimber and the Rig. Much to the dismay of the tourists who stopped to watch me "shred."

Back at base, the MSgt who had checked us in told me about a nearby battlefield that I needed to check out. Fort Stevens State Park was just up the road near the town of Astoria, on the mouth of the Columbia River. Sweet! I had wanted to drive into Astoria to look around anyway, so off we went, in hunt of some lunch and a coffee. After seeing how cool Seaside was, I had already started contemplating moving here. Then when I saw Astoria, I was completely hooked. The place was like a mini San Francisco, complete with commercial fishing wharfs, restaurants on the docks, breweries and bars, a small downtown area, and a very cool assortment of Victorian style houses. It was even built on a hill with two major bridges feeding the city! Imagine being in Pacific Beach, but only twenty minutes from San Francisco, with a military base in between. Ya, I could live there. It officially became my number one spot to relocate to, when my book is done. Kinda funny since I had 48 more states to go.

That afternoon Kimber and I explored Fort Stevens. I was shocked to hear that it was originally a Civil War base, built to stop the Confederates from entering the Columbia River. It was armed with a battery of what were called "Parrot Guns," basically a cannon that would pop up to fire and then return below the firing platform, concealing the gun location and giving cover to the troops.

46

Inside the museum were displays of uniforms and weapons from both the Civil War and WW2. Lots of maps and pictures from that era decorated the walls. Pictures of bomb carrying balloons that were set to drop their payload as far inland as St. Louis and Chicago via the jet streams. This was such a prevalent threat that local residents took turns on a citizen's watch, looking for Japanese balloons or aircraft appearing on the horizon.

The most interesting exhibit was the 30 minute video at the end. Unbelievably, the Japanese actually bombed the Oregon Coast nine times! Wait what? Bombs hit our mainland? I never heard this in school? Turns out that one renegade Japanese submarine commander got close enough to our shore to hit the Oregon beaches with some type of mortar. Knowing our antiquated parrot guns would not reach the sub, and rather than giving up their positions, they chose not to fire back, infuriating the troops and sparking a huge controversy.

They had interviewed American civilians and GIs that were there. One woman said she heard the bombs hit the beach, even shaking the glass in her windows. They couldn't believe they were under attack. She made the comment, "It really brought home the fact that there was an enemy out there who wanted to hurt us." Interesting. Oregon, state #2… COMPLETE!

Washington

July 8th, 2015. The next day we broke camp and headed back to Astoria. Just over one of the longest expansion bridges I had ever seen was our third state, the State of Washington. This was the first state that I had never been in, short of a layover in Spokane airport years ago. When one usually thinks of visiting Washington for the first time, the images of dark, dreary, overcast days, with a near continual form of moisture lingering about, seems to be on the forefront of the mind's images. Washington State did not disappoint. With heavy overcast, a decent layer of fog over the water, and a heavy mist that felt like I was inhaling straight from a cold air vaporizer, we entered the "Cascade State" via the Astoria Bridge.

The plan for the state was to continue up the coast on Highway 101, around the Olympic Mountains, to a small town outside of Olympia called Lacey. This was the home of a dear friend and former roommate of mine from Arizona. When he left Arizona to go back home, I promised him I'd stop in and visit when I was on my travels. I don't think he believed me back then, judging by the sound of his voice when I told him I was in Washington. He was pretty surprised.

He told me I was the only friend of his from Arizona that had made it up to see him. I was happy to keep my promise and was looking forward to seeing him again.

Not seeing any battlefields on the Washington coastline, we continued up Hwy 101 which jagged inland a little too far for my pleasing. Only near the town of Queets did I get a glimpse of the Pacific Ocean. As we began to wind around to the east, Kimber was getting anxious to stop, as was I. It was a long drive, but the scenery made the trip incredibly enjoyable, as time and miles seem to fly by.

We decided to stop at the next National Forest Campground called Sol Duc, in the heart of the Olympic National Park. The campground was about 12 miles inland, which made the temperature and the humidity rise drastically. We found a nice campsite, unpacked the Rig, and decided to explore. The first thing I noticed was the amount of insects flying around, inquisitively landing on every portion of my exposed skin. After an insect repellent shower, we headed out to find some water to possibly cool off in. Unfortunately we were out of luck. Nearby was a small stream, but with signs posted that swimming and/or fishing was not allowed, due to that section of water being a "salmon ladder." The water was amazingly clear with an incredible shade of blue and green. So much so, that a fellow onlooker stated, "There's no way that's real, they must dye it." Ignorance must be bliss.

We headed east the following morning, passing some of the most amazing lakes I'd ever seen. Mountains covered with lush pines, dropping drastically to water level, allowed for a very small beach covered in multicolor gravel. The water also was as clear and blue/green as the streams feeding them. The fog rolling down the mountain was like driving through a picture, until you actually had to drive through the fog itself. It poured over the roadway so thick that I dared not go over 35 mph or leave sight of the vehicle's tail lights in front of me.

That afternoon we pulled up to my friend's house in Lacey, WA. It's always nice to have someone local show you the sites that you would normally have missed. One of which was an impromptu fishing and crabbing trip just up the highway, back the way I had come in. Crabbing for the first time, and on one of the Puget Sound tributaries, in a small boat with 5 ft swells, was truly an experience. Little did I know the crabs' favorite bait was turkey drumsticks. After dropping a few crab pots with the turkey into the water, marking the location with an empty bleach bottle for a buoy, we headed out to open water for a little salmon fishing. It wasn't long before I realized what seasickness was all about. This was new to me, but what I did know was that if my eyes left the horizon for more than a glance, I was going to revisit what I had for lunch. My so-called friend found great pleasure in this.

After a few passes we went back to the buoys to retrieve the crab pots. To my amazement, we pulled up a pot with around 10 to 12 crabs. Unfortunately, they were mostly female, just under the required size of 6.5 inches across, both of which were a no go, and had to be released. It truly was an interesting experience, and a pretty funny one according to my buddy.

As we were attempting to fish for salmon, I told my friend's parents how much I loved smoked salmon, and they graciously invited me on a fishing trip with them to Seiku, WA, which of course I excepted. Seiku is a small fishing town just east of Neah Bay, which is the furthest northern point of the lower 48 states on the Pacific coast. The place was amazing! With Canada in sight across the Strait of Juan de Fuca, there were docks full of fishing boats of all shapes and sizes, along with RVs and campers full of fishermen ready to claim the prize of an open water King salmon. Overhead you could hear the unmistakable screeches of baby bald eagles playing in flight, wrestling with each other in the sky. Under the docks were literally thousands of small crab feeding on the heads and entrails of cleaned fish. There was nothing wasted, nature consumes all.

The grand prize and main reason to fish at this time of year, is the running of the King salmon, with the pinks and silvers also in play. Being mainly from Arizona at this point in my life, I thought I was battling a great white shark when I fought to reel in a 12 pound King, much to the amusement of my fellow fishermen who landed a 25 lb fish earlier. Unfortunately, my "trophy" catch was a native fish, meaning both its dorsal fins were intact, and could only be kept by Native Americans. Only hatchery fish, with its rear dorsal clipped, was harvestable by non-natives. I was shocked and fully prepared to break out a pocket knife and start cutting up sushi for lunch, if I didn't get to bring this thing back. The worst part was to see the fish end up floating away, because it didn't make it through the de-hooking and release. So just because I was the wrong skin color, that fish was wasted. My anger was short lived when I was told either an eagle, seal, or some other sea creature would eat that salmon. Nothing wasted indeed.

I had about five days to kill before the next Mariners game in Seattle, and with everyone needing to get back on work schedules, I decided to get back to mine. Tyler's folks were kind enough to let me stow my trailer with them while I did some exploring before the game. Kimber and I meandered our way along the coastline, slowly working our way up to Seattle, when I decided to get a bite at one of my favorite chain restaurants, Buffalo Wild Wings. While I was sitting at the bar enjoying a cold beer and watching a ballgame, I noticed the gentleman sitting to my left. He was clean cut, apparently Hispanic, 30 something, I assumed. He was enthralled with a soccer game that was on while having a phone conversation in Spanish. He didn't seem too talkative, at least not in English, or with me. So I finished my beer and meal and decided to call it a night. Luckily, the restaurant was located in a large mall parking lot with plenty of cars around. Without the trailer, we just hopped in the camper and stayed there for the night. Looking back, it wasn't the best place to park, mall security will usually run you off. Seeing that the bar would have cars there until 0200, it was an educated gamble. We luckily slept uninterrupted.

In the morning we continued to follow the coastline, leading us to the Alki beach area. I was stoked to find free roadside parking on the beach, surfer showers/bathrooms, and a Starbuck's across the street with strong WiFi. Perfect! Much like Pacific beach, I was once again surrounded by huge hotels and condos, but this time I had the amazing view of the Seattle skyline in the sleeper window every night. Kimber was pleased too, chasing her ball, this time into the frigid waters of the Puget Sound, without hesitation, and of course to the merriment of whoever could see her.

With funds tight, we stayed in the Alki Beach Area for three nights. Moving the camper to different spots each time to avoid detection. Urban camping is an adventure all in itself, but also tiring. Always on the lookout for what would be a safe place to park later that night, and then trying to sleep easy when you do. It gets very tiresome and taxing at times. I had reserved a spot at the local military base for two days while I went to the game, knowing that a relaxing evening with a hot shower was in order before heading into Seattle.

After checking into our RV spot at the Lewis McChord Joint Air Base, which was both an Air Force Base and home to the Army's 2nd Ranger Battalion, I decided to find a cold beer and watch some baseball. It was nice to have a campsite and nothing to do until the Mariners game the next night. We were close to the same Buffalo Wild Wings we ate at earlier in the week, so I headed that way. To my complete surprise, the same Hispanic dude was there, watching soccer of course. I asked him who was winning, and with a surprised look on his face he replied, "You're back!" I guess he remembered me after all, but this time he was much more talkative, and in perfect English. He noticed my eagle, globe, and anchor (Marine emblem) tattoo on my neck and asked if I was a Marine. "God, I hope so!" I replied. We laughed and shook hands as he introduced himself as Leo. I explained who I was and about the travels I was on. When I told him I was staying at Fort Lewis, he replied, "Yeah, that's where I was stationed. I was a Ranger." I had no idea he was a veteran, let alone a former Ranger. So of course when I told him I served in Mogadishu during Operation Restore Hope, he was shocked. "You were there?" he asked. Like I said before, Somalia veterans are legends of lore to younger Rangers, even if I was just an old Marine.

We chatted about the military and where we served, while we watched our respective games and had beers. I told him I was originally from California, but ended up in Arizona. He asked what part of Arizona, and when I replied with the different places, he spoke up when I mentioned working in Surprise. "I've got a battle buddy from Iraq that moved to Surprise." Not thinking much about it, I replied something about it being a small world. A couple minutes later, he showed me his phone with a picture of a Ranger in combat gear and said, "That's him." I about fell off my barstool. It was Mike, the Ranger I had met in Pacific Beach! Needless to say, after a FaceTime session, a bunch of belly laughing and disbelief, way too many beers and a regrettable hot wing challenge, I had myself a couple of new Ranger brothers.

One of my most cherished memories of the trip was when Leo reached in his pocket, slammed his open palm down on the bar, and looked at me. Under his hand was a 2nd Ranger BN challenge coin. When a military member slams a challenge coin on the bar, you're supposed to respond in kind with your own coin, or buy the next round. I said, "Ya got me there. I don't have any of my coins." He then slid the coin to me, "No, that's for you, brother." I have to admit, I choked back a couple tears. I hoped to see Leo again, maybe on my way to Alaska, so I could slam MY palm down on the bar next time. Right on, bro, stay well.

The next day, nursing a bit of a hangover, I picked up my buddy Tyler and headed north to Seattle for the game. We ended up parking downtown, a few blocks away from the ballpark. One of the places I'd always wanted to see was the fish market at Pike's Place. Every kind of fish and seafood you can imagine is prominently displayed on ice for the world to see. This is the place where they throw the fish from the ice to the wrapping station, then over to the registers for customers to pick up. Without delay, a dozen huge crabs flew through the air in rapid succession. These guys were good, and the loud applause from the crowd proved it.

Safeco Field, Seattle, WA

July 24th, 2015. Safeco Field was just a few blocks down the street from where we parked the Rig. With Kimber secured in the camper and an uneasy feeling about leaving her alone, Tyler and I headed toward the park. Safeco Field was built in 1999, strictly a baseball venue, with Century Link Field housing the NFL's Seattle Seahawks (my 49ers arch nemesis) next door. This was the first time I'd seen this type of setup, with neighboring stadiums in a downtown setting. Definitely made for quite the pre-game and post-game celebrations in the several completely packed bars and restaurants nearby.

As always, we opted for "get-in" tickets and would float around from there. As we made our way up to the third deck nose bleed seats, I saw an opportunity to represent for my 49er brethren back home. I flipped my San Francisco Giants cap around so the S.F. would be in the photo, and asked Tyler to take a quick picture. After handing him my phone, I spun around and gave a double fisted, one finger salute toward the neighboring football stadium, with the "Century Link" logo prominently displayed as my target. My buddy, a Seahawk Loyalist, caught on to my shenanigans and replied with an "Oh hell no…" After pleading with him, and reminding him he owed me for making me feed the fish on an earlier fishing expedition, he finally snapped the picture. He started yelling something about how I had better not post that on Facebook, when he noticed the people in the snack bar line watching us, shaking their heads and laughing. I'd never seen him move so quickly, head down, around the corner, and out of sight; which of course gave me the perfect amount of time to post my prize on social media, tagging my friend as being present. Good times! What else are old roommates for, anyway?

When we got to our seats, I was happy with where we were sitting. Practically the last row, on the top deck, down the left-field line. They were nosebleeds, but the view of the Seattle coastline, looking into the sunset, was breathtaking. The goldish pink reflection of the sunset bouncing off the water lit up the mirrored reflection of the skyscraper's glass like something out of a child's book about a golden city. Then as the sun crept below the horizon, the Seattle skyline came to life with a rainbow of lights, from the ballparks to the Sky Needle. Definitely one of the most picturesque cities on the trip thus far.

About the third inning, my phone began to blow up with incoming notifications. I couldn't contain my laughter. My buddy looked at me through squinted eyes and asked, "You posted that, didn't you?" By this time tears were rolling down my face, trying to hold back, as I showed him the last comment… from his mother. "Real good you two, and I bet Tyler was the one who took the picture!" she had typed. The look on his face was beyond what words could describe. Something like a cross between complete horror and extreme constipation. "Delete that shit before I get my ass kicked!" he shouted, and then pretty much wouldn't speak to me for a few innings. Probably because that's how long it took me to quit laughing. With that alone, Safeco Field, MLB park #6… COMPLETE.

The next day Kimber and I said our goodbyes to Tyler and his family as we pointed the Rig south for the first time this trip. What I didn't realize, and wouldn't until the following year, was that this would be the last time I saw my friend Tyler. Sadly, he passed away the following Christmas Eve. It broke my heart when I learned this, he was doing so well. Life is short, never ever take your time here for granted. RIP little buddy, you deserve it. On a sad note, Washington, state #3… COMPLETE!

With our inaugural run complete, and the Rig needing some much needed attention, it was time to roll back to Arizona. We made it back around the first of August, pretty much the hottest month of the year. Prescott AZ was where I had rented a storage unit, where my VA doctors were, and was substantially cooler than Phoenix. I was gonna have to sell off a lot of things from my storage unit to buy new airbags for the truck. I found a campsite near town, and started to do what I could to raise money for the repairs on the Rig – everything from setting my trailer up as a handyman outfit and doing yard work, to selling off my household goods at a local swap meet. I was determined to get back to the heaven that I had found on the open road… ASAP.

Back in California, when I lost the airbags, my sob story must have struck home with some folks on Facebook. A buddy of mine from grade school got in touch with me shortly after I made my post, saying he lives in Phoenix now and owns a tire and rim shop. "Give me a shout when you get back," he said. "We'll get those airbags fixed up." I was shocked. I hadn't heard or seen Jimmy since our sophomore year in high school. I'm not gonna lie, we weren't the nicest kids to Jimmy at times, with his platinum white hair and huge round eyeglasses. Boy was I shocked when I pulled up to his shop and a mountain of a man walked out. Apparently I'm the only one who quit growing their sophomore year. Jimmy had grown about a foot since then and become quite the high school wrestler, served a stint in the Air Force, and was now a happily married business man doing well in Phoenix. He told me when I got there that he had phoned the makers of my airbags, telling them that he's got a Marine broke down on the road and needs replacement bags ASAP. I couldn't believe that a long lost friend would go to that trouble for me. He said, "I got a soft spot for hometown boys." I wasn't sure how to respond to that. I didn't realize the kids I grew up with in Sonoma thought of me as a one of them. Pretty sure I went around the corner and let my eyes leak a little.

With not only new airbags on the rig, but also a fresh set of tires and a solar panel with two huge 12v batteries, Jimmy and the boys had the Rig better than ever. What an incredible debt I owed my friend; I couldn't possibly have thanked him enough.

After a month, I was burning up in the Arizona heat without AC in the camper. Even in Prescott, the days were pushing into the 90s, making me irritable and anxious. I decided not to end the baseball season with an Arizona game, instead I found a late season make up game in Denver. Colorado would be much cooler and I could try my hand at some trout fishing; either way, the wanderlust bug had burrowed deep into my psyche. I had to keep moving; anything to keep moving.

Colorado

September 1st, 2015. When payday finally arrived, I packed up the campsite, dropped the trailer and Harley off at my buddy's property, and headed for Colorado. The plan was to catch a Colorado Rockies game in Denver, then work my way back across the Rocky Mountains to Arizona, camping and fishing along the way. The kicker this time... we had $500 bucks and one month to do this. I didn't mind eating hotdogs and ramen for a month if it meant getting out of that heat. Colorado it was.

We took Interstate 40 into New Mexico and then north on Interstate 25 to Colorado. The drive through the painted rocks of New Mexico made the nine hour drive fly by. Passing through the urban sprawl of Albuquerque, into the gorgeous rolling hills of Santa Fe, peaked my interest for our New Mexico visit. First things first: Baseball.

We made the Colorado state line by nightfall, pulling into a rest stop just outside of Trinidad for the night. I had two days to get to Denver to catch the re-scheduled day game, so I was pleased making it this far on the first leg. We would be in Denver tomorrow morning fairly early, with plenty of time to scout out a parking spot and buy my ticket.

When you cross the Colorado border you're welcomed by a huge sign saying "Welcome to Colorful Colorado." Let me tell you, they weren't lying. The drive up to Denver was picturesque;

Rocky Mountains on my left, green farmlands to the right, a few cotton balls of pure white clouds dotted the blue sky that went on for eternity. Then suddenly your immersed in traffic. I was shocked at how big Denver was. This being my first visit to Colorado, I had no idea of the sprawling metropolis that I was about to enter. I was so grateful that I had left the trailer behind.

The ballpark was easy to get to, and parking for a weekday day game was fairly abundant. I found a parking lot directly across the street from the ticket office that hadn't put out its day of game parking signs yet. I pulled into one of the rear spots, and waited for the box office to open. I wondered if they would run us out of the lot or have us pay when they opened. It wasn't like the truck and camper was blending in well with the small "city" cars around it.

About 11am, I put Kimber on a leash and headed out for the box office. While the clerk was looking for the best "get in" ticket for me, I mentioned how I loved weekday day games. "You know that the game is this evening, right?" the clerk asked. What? No! So apparently, I read the times wrong online, leaving Kimber and I stranded in 90f weather, and getting warmer.

I had about 6 hours to kill during the hottest part of the day, it was time to scout out some shade and post up until sundown. I thought to drive around and find a park with some water, but money was tight and we had priorities. I found a spot with some temporary shade from the tall buildings across the street, just down from Coors Field. It happened to be near some condos, with a 2 hour parking meter that I fed, while Kimber and I took sponge baths under the camper fan and dined on cold cuts for lunch.

This is where I should explain Kimber and her "support" dog status. So I took the advice from the veteran back at the Giants game, and did some research into emotional support animals. I learned that the VA does not give a true service animal nor a support animal for PTSD. I also learned the guidelines for an emotional support animal, stating that the only requirement is that it must be well behaved and respond to commands. Now I'm not one to try and exploit a loop hole that isn't exactly clear, like the folks bringing support donkeys and peacocks on airplanes. I just couldn't leave Kimber in a hot camper. So I paid the 60 bucks, sent in Kimber's picture, and got a ESA ID card, red vest, and leash. If the lady with the support chihuahua in her purse can go in a bar, then Kimber sure as hell can. I also learned that not too many people want to be the guy that turns away a disabled veteran and his companion dog, after seeing my Military/VA ID right next to Kimber's ID.

Some folks don't understand why a big burly veteran, with no visible disabilities, has to have a dog in the restaurant. Regardless of temperature outside, a lot of veterans won't go out if they have to leave their dog behind. This is their life companion a lot of times, like a wife or a child. Thus causing the veteran to shutter in, avoiding the much needed contact with other humans. So folks in the airport with a support gerbil because they saw a car wreck, are really doing veterans with PTSD from combat a serious disservice. Ok, off my soapbox.

The temperature cooled down enough to make the evening comfortable, but the camper was still pretty warm inside. Looked like this would be Kimber's very first Major League Baseball game. She had been inside a few restaurants back home, walking in with her vest on like a boss that owned the place. I was amazed how she instinctively walked right next to me to our seat. I'd lead her under the table or she would back in next to my barstool on the floor, and lay down like she'd been doing it all her life. I think she also learned that she could go inside if she behaved, instead of sitting in the truck or camper. She always received a ton of attention everywhere we went and ate it up like the little diva she is. God, I love my dog.

Coors Field, Denver, CO

September 2nd, 2015. As we walked up to the turnstiles, I was a little concerned they wouldn't let Kimber in. This worry was quickly dispelled as the guy taking tickets forgot to swipe mine, being way too enthralled by the "little bitty pitty." Kimber danced around charming her new friends, at the same time staying very close to my side. One guy asked if she was a puppy in service dog training. I just smiled and said, "Actually she just turned two, she's an English Staffy, not a pit. She's doing great though," politely side-stepping the question. The security being too enamored with Kimber to follow up, they all agreed.

I'm always amazed at how people will react to Kimber. As we walked further into the ballpark, there was a Coors Field 2015 banner on a fence that I wanted to take a picture of Kimber next to. I sat her in front of it, but couldn't backup to take the shot without Kimber following me. That's when another security lady walked by and asked if I wanted her to take the picture of both of us. Of course I accepted, handing her my phone. "But only if I can get a picture with her too!" she added. See what I mean? I wish I had a copy of that picture, a black female security guard, all smiles in her uniform, as Kimber lavished her with kisses. That's what I'm talking about!

Something about the big open venue of the park spooked Kimber. So many people not looking down, kicking and stepping on her. Add the loud music, I'm sure she was probably having 4th of July flashbacks. Taking pictures and walking around the park definitely wasn't happening, so I settled into a upper level seat and calmed her down. Next thing I knew, Kimber was laying under my seat, developing a substantial peanut habit, until she faded off to sleep with her head on my foot. The little pup had had a very long day.

Coors Field, built in 1992 was the first ball park built for a National league team since Dodger Stadium in 1962. It was the architecture of the stadium that caught my attention first. Like a combination of old and modern, Art Deco steel and brick from the 1920s, with modern purple and white lighting. If Gotham City had a MLB park, this would be it. The design was actually intended to replicate Baltimore's Camden Yards, being a brick building retrofitted into a ballpark. This theme continued into the inside of the park – huge grandstand style seats behind right field, an ocean of bleacher seats from left field to center, with a waterfall display between the them. Small triangular shaped flags, flying above the bleachers gave the park that "old-timey" feel. Super cool park and just a great experience over all. Coors Field, MLB park #7… COMPLETE.

After parking at a Pilot Truck stop just a few exits away from the ballpark for the night, I was eager to get into the mountains and cooler elevations. We found our way to Interstate 70 west, luckily avoiding most rush hour traffic with a bright and early start. Out of all the major interstates in this country, I-70 through the Rockies has got to be my favorite so far. I'm not talking about the PCH or any state highways, I'm talking about the main arteries that tie this country together. Usually a boring, straight, never ending strip of concrete with very little to see along the way. That's definitely not the case in Colorado. At street level you're looking at a river that winds parallel to the road through the valleys. Just above the river you begin to see aspen groves just starting to turn yellow, nestled away in a sea of dark green spruce and pine. The forest climbs up to the tree line, before giving way to a grass and rock covered mountain cap. The colors of the rocks were amazing, differing shades of brown and orange, practically impossible to describe with words, absolutely breathtaking.

While I was scouting out camping spots for this leg of the trip, I came across a website called FreeCampsites.net (FCN) This was like a Wikipedia for campgrounds under 12 dollars, and a grip of free boondocking sites. I would learn later just how much cash this website would save me along the way. Our first stop, Breckinridge, CO at the Dillon Reservoir.

After checking in with a Ranger station about fishing information, I decided this would be my first spot to put in for a few days. There was a nice NPS campground, right on the shores of Dillon Reservoir for $22 bucks a night, which would be $11 a night with my pass. Unfortunately, it was the weekend and all spots were full. I decided to scout out a boondock site nearby until Monday when most of the campers would be gone. This turned out to be my first valuable lesson as a full time RVer. Travel on the weekend when the campgrounds are full, have your pick of the place come Monday. Lesson learned.

FCN pointed out some places to park just a few miles from town. Heading down toward Breckinridge, following the Blue River, we came to what looked like an abandoned campground, with several cars, campers, and tents spread out under the pines. There was nothing but a few rock fire rings here and there, no bathrooms or running water except the river... but it was free.

I backed the truck into a spot that had a trail leading to the river. Kimber was absolutely ecstatic to not be on a leash, exploring the immediate area but never getting too far away. I spent the rest of the day setting up camp, and firing up the bbq for a much deserved steak I found on sale at the local grocery. Time rich and money poor was something I could get used to, especially with this kind of scenery as my backyard.

The next day we spent exploring the area. There were some great trailheads for hiking just down the road, leading back into the dense forest. Kimber had a blast running the trails. Never getting too far ahead, stopping as the trail turned until I came back into her sight. It was like she had been hiking trails all her life... until she disappeared.

Lost in my own thoughts, walking back from a decent couple miles of hiking, I suddenly didn't hear Kimber running along the trail or the sound of leaves and branches crunching under her feet. I stopped and called her... nothing. Louder I yelled, walking back up the trail the way I had come; still silence. At this point I'm screaming her name, and starting to shake. She was gone. My only hope was that she knew we were going back to the truck, picked up the scent, and headed back the way we came. Then the thoughts of the busy road with cars flying by started flooding my mind. At this point I broke into a run toward camp, still yelling her name. Still nothing. Thoughts of not finding her, coyotes and bears in the area, and sitting through the night with her gone, was way more than something I would be able to handle. Then I was afraid that somebody would stop and pick her up, another scenario of her being gone. I was in tears and about to break down when I turned back once again toward the trail. Then I saw her. Sitting next to an abandoned backpacker camp that had some discarded food near by. She was scared and shaking. Probably thinking she was in trouble hearing me yelling frantically, she just sat down to wait. I fell to my knees and scooped up my puppy into my arms and just hugged her while tears ran down my face. The feeling of helplessness slowly fading from my body. Wow, that's something I never want to experience again, ever.

When we got back to camp, a new car had pulled next to the fire ring a few yards away from us. A young couple were setting up a grill, preparing their evening meal. Kimber of course, ran up to introduce herself to a guy named Tim. Tim and his girlfriend were traveling from the Bay Area of Cali, to a concert in Denver. Another complete stranger that happened to be from my neck of the woods years ago. I was telling him about our travels when he burst out, "Like Travels with Charlie!" a Steinbeck book about his travels around America with his dog. "I don't know it," I replied. "But will definitely check it out!" We hung out and grilled some dinner together, tipping back a couple craft beers and telling road trip stories. Once again another super cool stranger I met on the road, that I now call friend.

Monday, we went back to the busy campground hoping that the weekend traffic cleared out. We were in luck, the beach front sites were practically empty. God, I love the weekdays! Now we had a spot for Kimber to chase the ball into the lake, and I could try to catch a fish. At $11 dollars a night we opted for a couple of days.

Our second day there, a huge motorhome decided to take the spot right next to my rig. There were plenty of spots on each side that weren't 10 feet from me, I wasn't pleased at all. Like when there's a whole bar to sit at, and somebody has to sit on the stool right next to you. Oh well, it's just for a night. Still not great campsite etiquette, something that I was learning. Anyway, that afternoon I met the gentlemen and his wife, traveling home to Oklahoma I think it was. Super nice folks that were a blast to talk with.

Later that evening, the Oklahoma couple and I were sitting around the camp fire with some folks camping a few spots down. A French couple, traveling the US in a van were eager to hear about traveling around this country. We sat and told our travels stories for hours. At the end of the night, the gentleman from Oklahoma said something that I found profound, and was taken aback by his comment. He was talking mainly to the French couple about folks you meet on the road when he said, "Take Matt here, for instance, who's never met a stranger." Basically saying I was friendly and approachable. Wow! He had no clue to my background, military experience, or PTSD. He just saw me as a friendly, talkative guy, out traveling with his dog. It was the second time someone had made me consider the healing that was taking place while traveling. My good friend in Phoenix said I don't have those scrunched up lines between my eyes anymore, after my return from the west coast. Meaning I didn't have perma-scowl anymore. Maybe travel and PTSD do have some sort of correlation? More on this later.

One place I did want to checkout was a small town called Rifle, AZ. I mean come on, the name alone will get the attention of any Jarhead. There was a restaurant that boasted about its staff all carrying side arms. The sign on the front door read, "You should be packing, because we are." Unfortunately it was closed, but it gave us some amazing sightseeing along the way. We passed the iconic ski resort towns of Vail and Eagle, all way too ritzy for this trip, but on the list for a future visit. We continued on to the nearest Anytime Fitness in Grand Junction; a hot shower was definitely in order. With a Walmart and Buffalo Wild Wings all in the same parking lot, we found our home for the evening.

At this point we turned the Rig south, not wanting to leave the state of Colorado yet. We took Highway 50 toward Montrose, that turned into the 550 south. We noted a Walmart and Anytime Fitness in Montrose, the last until Durango, near the Arizona border. We passed through the town of Ridgeway, stopping at the most amazing little mountain town yet... Ouray, CO.

When you leave the town of Ridgeway, you travel through some of the most picturesque ranch scenes I've ever seen. Tall, painted, red rock cliffs surrounded the green pastures, spotted with massive oaks. Horses and cattle grazing peacefully side by side, while birds darted about, from tree to tree. It was truly beautiful.

There were black and white jay looking birds, with long tails and tufts of bright blue on their wings, that quickly became one of my favorite birds. They were everywhere, chasing bugs and each other, in the bright blue cloudless sky. Turned out it was a Magpie, related to the Crow. Close enough. Super cool bird.

The valley then narrowed to a river passing between the towering cliffs. The river led back into a small valley, like a giant granite bowl, where the town of Ouray sat, affectionately known as the American Alps. Like stepping back into the 1800s, Ouray hasn't changed much since the

Gold Rush days. The highway runs through the middle of town doubling as a "Main Street" lined with shops, restaurants, and other tourist businesses like Jeep tours. Unlike most tourist type towns, this one also had an ACE hardware, grocery store, post office and other signs that real working people actually lived there. It was an interesting mix of tourists and locals to say the least.

There were three national forestry campgrounds nearby. One very close to town, and two a few miles outside of town, up an old mining road called Camp Bird Road. Well, I was definitely in on the cheaper idea, so off to Thistledown Campground we went. Little did I know that the road to this campground was heavily used by off road vehicles. Lovely. But it was late in the season, starting to cool down, kids back in school, so not many whining ATV motors to deal with.

The campground was a chain of dry camp sites leading from the main road back to a decent sized stream. Cost was like 7 bucks a night with my discount card, if I remember right. I had the run of the place, it was completely empty, including an awesome spot all by itself, right on the bank of a small stream. It had a fenced in garden looking area and what looked like an old power pole. It also had running water at a spigot nearby and a vault toilet up by the road. The scenery was like something from a survivalist show with dense pine and cedar forests and huge jagged rock mountain tops. Plenty of hiking trails near camp, let alone all of the ones around town... were like hiker heaven. Exactly what I needed to bed down for a couple weeks, save money and explore the area, while I waited for Arizona to cool off.

Since I was going to be here for two weeks with no cell phone reception at camp and very little in town, I looked around for a Redbox or video store to no avail. The lady at the local coffee shop said that everybody uses the local library for videos. Interesting. Just a few blocks away, I walked into the Ouray County Library, home to one of the most impressive video collections I've ever seen. A complete wall full of hundreds of DVDs. After filling out a quick application, I was on my way home with not only the complete *Vikings* series up to that point, but also a copy of Steinbeck's *Travels with Charlie*, thanks to Tim's suggestion.

During my explorations I also found a cool little Irish pub whose staff was swooned by Kimber of course. This was my spot for cheap drafts and daytime baseball games; I was even offered a bouncer job the next summer, complete with RV site, if I was interested. Wow was that a tempting offer.

One day, as we were heading back into Montrose for supplies at Walmart and a hot shower at the gym, we stopped in for coffee at the local java shop. We had become friends with the owner that had a son in the Corps. We chatted about duty stations as she poured my coffee and asked if I was gonna have breakfast. "Not this time, I gotta run to Walmart to get supplies for the rest of the week. The first of the month better hurry up!" She chuckled. "I hear ya," she replied. About that time the guy behind me said, "Get him what he wants, I got this." Enter Fireman Mike from Hawaii.

I turned around to face a guy about my height, a few years older, holding out his hand saying thank you for my service. Mike was a retired firefighter, here enjoying some vacation time. I'm always struck when this happens, sometimes feeling guilty, but always so grateful as pride swells in my heart. "Hey, thanks man, I appreciate that. And thank you for yours," I said while shaking his hand. I ordered some breakfast and asked if he would join me. He had prior commitments but asked what I was doing the following night and invited me for a steak at "The Outlaw," a popular restaurant down the street. "Absolutely! Looking forward to it, thanks man!" I replied. The next day we met for a great steak and a couple beers. I was learning that first responders and veterans also have a bond, not only because a lot of police and fire have prior military service, but mainly as we share the love of country and devotion to fellow Americans. Super cool dude and another new "road buddy" I'm proud to call my friend.

After the maximum two weeks allowed for camping in our spot, I was sad to have to leave our little hidden paradise. I definitely could make Ouray my home if I could afford the property. I broke camp early that morning, heading south on highway 550 toward Silverton. There was a completely free campsite somewhere near Molas Pass called Little Molas Lake that caught my attention. It was right on a lake and free; I was hoping to finally catch a fish, so off we went.

I had overheard people talking about the "Million Dollar Highway" before I left for Colorado. Bikers coming into the bar where I worked, after returning from Sturgis, talked about how ya have to drive the Million Dollar Highway. I thought it was due to the price of property along Hwy 550 which could also have been an inspiration for the name. Actually, the name comes from the cedars turning the brightest gold color I've ever seen on a tree. More like a neon yellow, the leaves were bright enough to need sunglasses. What amazing timing that I just happened to be traveling the Million Dollar Highway in the fall, totally un-planned. This is one for the bucket list my friends, you must see Hwy 550 in the fall.

Another old mining town, Silverton, was even more of a tourist destination than Ouray. They had train rides and wild west type attractions. Main Street had some pretty neat stores with a few nice restaurants and bars and a very small, extremely high priced grocery store. I stocked up on hotdogs, some canned goods, and the cheapest beer I could find; we were gonna do a week here, regardless of the campsite. Hopefully, it was as nice as the website described.

Just up the hill was Molas Lake, a paid private campground with a well known fishing lake that I definitely wanted to check out after we set up camp. Thankfully, the website was spot on with its recommendation for the Little Molas Lake free campground. It was jaw droppingly beautiful and actually fairly busy; I could definitely see why. Luckily, we found a decent spot near the one set of vault toilets in the middle of camp. I was surprised to see that they were maintained, stocked with paper, and fairly clean. There was running water at a spigot, plenty of hiking trails, and a smaller version of Mulas Lake just down the trail from the campsite. I was shocked that this place was free. An absolutely great find!

While setting up camp, Kimber saw an opportunity to make new friends with the neighbors – a couple about my age from New Zealand, out mountain biking and exploring the Rockies. They both worked for the Forestry in New Zealand, vacationing in the U.S. every couple of summers. They were in a van that was situated as their bedroom, while cooking outside. The cool part was that they had bought their van, bikes, camping gear, etc. here in the states, and would pack it up and leave it in storage when they flew home. What a great way to vacation! And of course, Kimber added to her international fan club.

The next day I was up bright and early. That day, with God as my witness, I was gonna catch a damn fish! We went back to Little Molas Lake to ask about a license but they weren't open yet. I went ahead down to the water where there were a couple of other guys fishing. I asked them about bait and how much a license cost. I'm not gonna lie, I was shocked at how much an out of state 2 day license was; I could buy trout cheaper at Safeway back home. One of the guys had a spare pole, and asked if I wanted to use his. He had a two pole stamp in case anybody asked. So I happily obliged and threw some of the power bait they were using. One thing I was doing wrong, not enough bait. They would literally cover the entire hook with the bright, stinky, fish scented, play doh. As soon as the bright green ball hit the water, a nice 10" rainbow decided it was breakfast time. I finally caught a fish. I didn't care if it was somebody else's gear, all I knew was I wasn't eating ramen tonight! The guys I was fishing with were actually from Arizona and must've felt sorry for me, they gave me a couple more good sized trout for supper that night. Ok, so without paying for a license, I caught a Colorado trout and will dine on it this evening. Works for me, mission complete, check the box!

The next few days Kimber and I spent hiking and relaxing around camp. I decided to follow the creek that fed the small lake up the mountainside to see where it came from. Kimber, off leash, but this time with my eyes glued to her, stayed just a few feet ahead of me as we followed a small trail that hugged the creekside. The trail came to a stop but the creek continued up the mountainside, disappearing into the brush. Only a quarter mile in or so, I decided to go off trail and just follow the stream.

We followed the creek all the way up to above the tree line, where the pines gave way to dense thickets of shrubs. From my vantage point it looked impassable, a sea of thick brush. Then I noticed Kimber had walked easily into the brush and came back out looking at me like, "What's the hold up?" I bent down to see where she had gone and saw there was a very defined game trail just under the thick canopy of sharp branches. So very gingerly we pushed through the thickets until we came to a part of the mountainside that had nothing but fallen petrified trees in a tall grassy field. It was amazing how drastically the terrain would change as we climbed. The creek had dwindled down to just a trickle coming from a rocky area covered with green moss. The moss was as thick as a sponge, water running through your hands as you pressed on it. This was where the spring began. Just as I was admiring how dense and soft the moss was, Kimber literally plopped her entire body down on the cold, water filled plant. She appreciated them too, apparently.

We were only a few hundred yards from the rocky peak of the mountain. The air was thin, and the terrain was so steep I could only take a few steps at a time without stopping for a breath. Kimber too was wearing out, waiting for me to move before she would. Finally, we made the summit, turned my back against the giant rock that capped the mountain and just took in the sight before me.

The sign just up the road from the campgrounds entrance read Molas Pass, 10,900 ft. My GPS had us sitting at just above 12,000 ft, giving us a view across the top of the Rockies like we were in an airplane. I just sat down and leaned against the rock to take it all in. I think even Kimber knew that what we were seeing was something spiritual. She literally just climbed into my lap, facing away from me, and stared into the distance, obviously tired, but strangely still. It really was something spiritual to behold. This was the highest mountaintop I had ever climbed. Something came over me and I shouted, "Jesus is Lord!" and listened to the echo fade away in the distance. Because that's what you do from the mountain tops… right? Spiritual indeed.

After a week at Little Mulas Lake, I was way due for a shower. It was close enough to October that northern Arizona would be cool enough to camp, and payday was on the horizon. We stopped at the Durango Anytime Fitness that evening for a shower, listened to a cool little jazz band in the neighboring park and decided to stay right there for the night. Perfect ending to my first trip to the colorful state of Colorado, and we still had time to catch a game back home. Colorado, state #4… COMPLETE!

Arizona

September 28th, 2015. I decided to come back from Colorado just a few days early to hopefully catch the last Diamondbacks home series of the year, wrapping up all the west coast teams in 2015. Then I planned to check out the one battlefield I knew of in the state, down towards Tucson, called Picacho Pass. But first, I had some business to do.

I returned to Prescott, determined to sell off the old junk I had in my storage unit and get out of the $80 a month fe80e. I also decided to put the Harley up for sale, as much as it pained me to do it. This was my very first build, that two very close friends oversaw me wrestle with for over a year. They opened their bike shop to me, taught me everything from motor-building to fabricating brackets, and even let me use their tools and shop supplies. It hurt to let it go, but I finally did, to a young former Marine who wanted something to wrench on with his son. How could I say no? Gratefully now I was able to pay Jimmy back, and maybe make a financial move that would help me in the future. More on that later.

Chase Field, Phoenix, AZ

October 4th, 2015. Jimmy and I were able to catch the very last Arizona Diamondback game of the 2015 season. As I was waiting in line to buy some get in tickets, Jimmy walked up, flashed a pair of tickets, and said, "I got this." Jimmy, always making a deal, had found a scalper with some killer 2nd row seats behind the Diamondback dugout. I was stoked to be able to just kick it with my friend as a bit of a celebration for this year's travels.

I remember when they broke ground on Bank One Ballpark, now known as Chase Field, in the late 90s. I had an opportunity to work as an HVAC installer when they built the park, but opted for a civil service position at Luke AFB. My buddy who did work on the stadium used to tell me about driving golf carts inside the giant ductwork to get around. It really is amazing to be chilly in such a massive air conditioned space while it's 112f outside. Add a massive retractable dome and it becomes truly a mechanic marvel. With almost a 50k seat capacity, this park is so big that the Diamondbacks have complained they can never sell it out, thus causing blackouts on televising home games.

Chase Field has grown up a lot since the 2001 Inaugural season. What was a somewhat sparse selection of vendors, mainly due to the size of the park, has now filled in every possible space with something from Arizona. You enter through a brick courtyard that's adjacent to several bars and restaurants full of street vendors and scalpers, feeling more like a street fair than a baseball game. Inside, the welcome cold air is a bit of a surprise for most, some fans donning hoodies and sweaters. The backdrop for the park is impressive, with a massive Jumbotron dominating centerfield. There's a small pool and spa that fans can rent, right on the outfield fence, just right of center, and some very small bleacher areas just below the Jumbotron. The rest is an ocean of regular style seats, covering both right and left fields. Behind the plate and on both sides are seats three levels high with a suite level mixed in. Ya, the place is massive, no wonder they can't sell it out.

My fondest memory of Chase Field is watching one of my all time favorite players, Mark McGuire, taking batting practice before a game. He hit a ball so far into the upper left field deck that he broke the "row" on the Front Row Sports Bar sign. To this day, they've left the "row" part of the neon sign broken. (The broken sign is now inside the restaurant, replaced by a new sign) To make it even better, I had my two young daughters with me when it happened. They probably won't remember, but I sure will. Chase Field, MLB park #8… COMPLETE!

Toward the end of October, I decided it was cool enough for Kimber and me to venture into the Arizona Desert. The one battlefield that I was aware of in Arizona was the Battle of Picacho Pass, pretty much halfway between Tucson and Phoenix. After 20 years of living in Arizona, I had no idea that this was a Civil War site. This was actually the westernmost battle of the American Civil War. In 1862, Tucson was a Confederate outpost, highly treasured for its silver mines. The South had ambitions of making a port on the west coast near San Diego, while the

North sent troops from San Francisco to stop it. After a small skirmish, the Confederates retreated back to Texas.

The park had several hiking trails with some great panoramic views overlooking where the battle took place. I was surprised to hear that the park service put on a re-enactment every year, commemorating the fight. I snapped a picture of Kimber laying in front of a small cannon. Little did I know that this would be the first of many cannons to come.

The holidays have always been a rough time of year for me. Being divorced since 1996, I've usually had to take the role of the third wheel when invited by friends to attend their family celebrations. Even while being so completely grateful for being included, it just wasn't mine. It wasn't MY house, with MY kids and MY family. I don't know, maybe it's a middle-aged man thing, either way this year I was determined to change things. I had found a new desire, a new mission, or maybe just a new distraction. Either way I was gonna fill my head with new sights, rather than old memories. Since there were no baseball parks in New Mexico, yet southern enough that weather should be decent, it seemed like a perfect fit for November. So just about a week before Thanksgiving, I decided to check New Mexico off the been there, done that list.

I found a free campsite near the New Mexico state line that looked interesting. It was in the Coronado National Forest, called Cochise Stronghold. It was quite a ways off the freeway, but I was ready for a little solitude. The road wound back into what's called the Dragoon Mountains, like huge piles of giant sandstone boulders stacked up to make a mountain. Think dry grass scattered with mesquite trees and scrub oak. Pretty much looked like what you would see on some African safari show. I was literally waiting for an elephant or rhino to walk by.

The sign at the campground said that Cochise had used this area as a natural fortress for him and his fellow Apache warriors. "He battled the U.S. Calvary because of the handling of an incident that happened at Apache Pass about 30 miles east of here" the sign read. It also said that Cochise was possibly buried here, somewhere in the rocks. Interesting. After some exploring, rock climbing, and Kimber experiencing her first tarantula, we packed it in for the night. Looked like we were headed 30 miles east in the morning.

A totally unexpected battlefield, Apache Pass has some unbelievable history. It turns out that the U.S. Calvary called for a meeting with Cochise to recover a kidnapped boy and stolen livestock. Known as the Bascom Affair, 2nd Lt Bascom took Cochise into custody until the boy and cattle were returned. Cochise denying the accusations, bolted from the tent, escaping while the other Apaches in the meeting were captured. All hell broke loose for 16 days with both sides taking hostages and executing them, causing incredible strife between the two nations for 11 years. It took President Grant's intervention in 1872 to finally make peace. They say there is no known photo of Cochise or knowledge of his demise.

The Battle of Apache Pass, where a column of U.S. troops were ambushed while stopping at an underground spring for water, prompted the building of Fort Bowie. Some of the original Fort is preserved, with a small guest center. There's a path that winds through the Fort ruins, with signs describing different scenes. One picture shows a group of Apaches standing in the Fort's courtyard, with an arrow pointing to an elderly man near the edge of the crowd with his hands on his hips. Turns out that Cochise wasn't the only famous Apache from this tribe. The man in the photo was Geronimo, transferred to Ft. Bowie after his final surrender in 1886.

Just before the Fort entrance you pass a small graveyard where the original union soldiers were buried, before Fort Bowie was built. I was shocked to find a Congressional Medal of Honor recipient O. O. Spence, Pvt Co. G, killed during the Indian Wars buried there. With the grave of Geronimo's two year old son, "Littlerobe," just a few spaces over. What an amazing historical find, just happened upon out of the blue. I actually stood in the exact place that Geronimo was standing in the photo. So freaking cool!

At this point, we would actually leave the state of Arizona, but to return shortly, so was not gonna call it complete quite yet. I'm thinking next year we'd kick off with some Spring Training. AZ… to be continued.

New Mexico

November 21st, 2015. The first night in New Mexico we stopped in Las Cruces where they had an Anytime Fitness and of course a Buffalo Wild Wings. I should really be getting a sponsorship from this place. Full disclosure: when I came back from Cali, I became friends with the bar manager at the local BWW in Phoenix who showed me their points program that gives free food for purchases. After meeting Kimber and eventually becoming a close family friend, she keeps my points card nicely stocked while I'm traveling. So a free meal and a 4 dollar beer is always on my heads up display. Veteran note: in all my travels, stopping at a BWW in almost every state, they have always welcomed Kimber and loved their veterans.

The people I meet while just sitting at the bar watching a ball game never ceases to amaze me. One time, a big burley biker with a club patch on his leather vest that read "Combat Vets" sat down a couple stools away. He also had Navy patches on the front of his vest, denoting that we served about the same time. I introduced myself and asked when and where he served. Turned out that he was a fellow Restore Hope veteran (Somalia) and was also a nuclear tech, the job I almost took with the Navy until their recruiter mentioned I was the right size for a sub. Best Marine recruiting tactic ever! It's always good to meet another Mogadishu Vet, another bond with complete strangers that seems sometimes even stronger than blood.

The next morning, after a quick workout and a shower, we were back on the road. The scenery near the Carlsbad Caverns was pretty bleak – like a combination of desert and grassland, flat as can be with only very small mounds to break up the monotonous terrain. The road sign saying that the Caverns were coming up, literally pointed to nothing. Then you suddenly drove into a small hidden valley with a visitor center and amphitheater. The parking lot was full of RVs and campers of every description. One off-road beast was from France, a family of four traveling from Argentina!

It always amazes me to meet these folks that travel the world, carefree of any problems or crime along the way. It seems like us Americans are programmed to believe that everybody is out to get us, and traveling abroad is taking your life into your own hands. I would love to drive to South America, but I'm terrified to do it. Then I see these folks with two small children traveling all this way through what we would consider very dangerous countries. I just don't get it, but I'm pretty sure this giant Marine tattoo on my neck might not be appreciated in certain circles. I'll work on Canada first.

The sign out front of the entrance to the amphitheater read "Elevator broken," with caution tape blocking the elevator doors. This should have been my first clue. For some reason my brain didn't register how deep a 750 ft hole in the ground was, as I followed the rest of the herd to slaughter. Down a winding concrete path that incorporated an occasional staircase, steep enough to warrant a hand rail, a herd of people went. I looked around at my fellow unsuspecting tourists, thinking that this will truly be a thinning of the herd.

The hole in the ground we were about to enter was just a black, gaping hole in the ground with stairs leading down into it. The first thing that overwhelmed our senses was the smell. Fresh bat guano smells something like a cattle dairy after a rain shower – pure ammonia; add the unbelievable humidity, it was like you could taste it. Thankfully, it was only at the opening; after that it was just a very damp smell of water and rocks. The temperature thankfully cooled down quite a bit the farther down we went.

The best way to describe the Carlsbad Cavern is like walking into the Dante's Inferno paintings. There were lights situated behind rocks that lit up what looked like different rooms or tunnels filled with eerie shadows from the salt stalagmites, looking like demons peeking out. It really was like walking deeper and deeper into the abyss. Once you got to the bottom you saw the elevator doors, also blocked off with a sign. There were bathrooms, vending machines, and dining tables. By this point, I was starting to feel claustrophobic; I needed fresh air.

About half way up I was just about done. Thankfully, there were seats every couple hundred feet, handrails to pull on the steep parts. I started to think about the original herd up at the guano pit; hate to think how long an ambulance would take to get out here.

Just as I finally gasped my first breath of fresh guano air, I saw a young family with a mom pushing a stroller with an infant, and a toddler riding on dad's shoulders. He looked at me trying to catch my breath. "Rough?" he asked. "What goes down, must go up," I replied while glancing at his passenger and smiling. With a concerned look on his face he mumbled "Great," glancing back at his wife with a "this is your fault" look. Behind them was an entire family of Asian folks, Chinese I was assuming. Two of which were obviously the elderly grandparents. I wished there was some way to warn them. I would be shocked if those folks made it to the bottom and back with the park closing in a couple hours. Instead, I just smiled and said, "Good luck." They were gonna need it.

That night we stayed at the Carlsbad City Water District levee, a spot I found on the free camping site. Basically, a place where boats park to go fishing, a boondock spot with a few garbage cans and a public bathroom. It was the perfect place to lay low and check out the town of Carlsbad, I had to do some laundry anyway.

Thanksgiving day, I decided I wanted to brave the Black Friday crowds at Walmart to get a much needed new laptop. Closest Walmart was in Roswell, which was definitely a place I wanted to check out. It was just about dinner time when we pulled into Walmart, and I was starving. I went inside to buy a turkey kielbasa, that I promptly walked back outside and threw on the grill, while I waited for the Black Friday chaos to commence. The looks on people's faces driving by, while I was sitting in my lawn chair, Kimber laying by my feet, with the grill smoking, was priceless. "What did you do for Thanksgiving, Bro?" "Grilled turkey sausage outside of Walmart in Roswell, New Mexico. You?" Definitely one for the record books.

The next day, we drove through the very small town of Roswell. Just about every business in the one block downtown area had some sort of alien theme. The actual crash site was way outside of town that you needed a GPS to find. I thought they would've had a huge tourist bus stop sort of setup, maybe from the 50s, sadly no. It's just a piece of desert on somebody's ranch now, at least that's what the locals say.

With a quick google search of New Mexico Battlefields, the Battle of Valverde popped up. Located somewhere in the middle of the state, near Fort Craig, outside of Socorro, NM. So from Roswell, we took Hwy 380 west through the towns of Hondo, Ruidoso, and Lincoln. It was like watching my grandfather's old westerns come to life as we drove through the mountainous ranch terrain.

Weather was beginning to set in, with the sky turning an ominous dark grey and temperature dropping quickly. We pulled into a campground near the Valley of Fire National Recreation Area, complete with hot showers, flush bathrooms, and full hookups. It was pricey even at half off, but we were in the middle of nowhere with some pretty bad weather heading our way. I was actually pretty blessed to have this place just pop up out of nowhere; a phenomenon that was becoming the norm.

That night the rain and wind kept Kimber and I up most of the night. The camper was rocking from side to side like my buddy's boat in Washington. Ok, not quite that bad, but Kimber sure thought so. She was shaking under the blanket, curled up in my arm pit the entire night. It was so cold and the wind blowing so hard, that there were icicles shaped like an "L" hanging from the bottom of the camper jacks. That was new.

We stayed there two days, waiting for the storm to pass. When it was finally gone, we had a chance to explore the area. From the campsite there was a walking trail that led down a fairly steep hill into what looked like a flowing black river of lava rock that was at least a quarter mile wide and went as far downstream as you could see. Valley of Fire made sense now. It was an interesting combination of lava rock and desert botanical garden; ok back to battlefields. With blue sky overhead, we drove onto the Battle of Val Verde, pretty much out in the middle of nowhere.

71

The Battle of Val Verde was much considered a toss-up. The Confederates were making a push from Texas to New Mexico, where they would take the capital of Santa Fe before pushing on to make California part of the Confederacy. Whoa what!? The Confederates made a push for California? Never heard that in my California educated upbringing. The Civil War was so far removed from California that I didn't even have much interest for it while I was in school. That was about to change.

Then I realized, could this be the Confederates that the San Francisco Union column fought at Picacho Peak in Arizona? Val Verde was considered a draw, even though the Confederacy won the battle but failed to take Fort Craig and its much needed supplies. A tactical win, but logistical failure. These guys were basically fighting for water at this point. Taking advantage of a brief truce to remove bodies from the battlefield, the Confederacy made their move toward Santa Fe. With over 500 total casualties, this was actually the largest battle of the west.

After exploring the neighboring Ft. Craig, we turned north toward Albuquerque. Stopping for gas in the town of Peralta, on the outskirts of the city, where I just happened to notice a road marker across the street. The sign read "Peralta. One of the last skirmishes of the Civil War in New Mexico took place here on April 15, 1862. The Sibley brigade, retreating to Texas, camped at the Hacienda of governor Henry Connelly, a few miles from Peralta. Here the Confederates were routed by Union forces under Col. Edward R.S. Cansby."

So now we apparently were seeing the Confederacy retreat back to Texas. An interesting point is that the date of this skirmish is the exact same day as the Battle of Picacho Pass in Arizona. So apparently not the same troops, maybe an outpost expecting to be reinforced? Either way, the San Francisco column appears to have been sent in response to this Confederate push west. At least that's what the battlefield placards are telling us. Did I mention I love history?

Albuquerque was another sprawling city that seemed to go on forever. As you emerge north of the city on I25, you wind through some picturesque foothills with really nice homes, as you enter the state capital of Santa Fe. The Battle of Glorietta Pass took place between Santa Fe and Pecos, and is now part of the Pecos National Historical Park.

Known as the "Gettysburg of the West," the Battle of Glorietta Pass was pivotal in terms of Confederate expansion into the west. So now we find the same confederate troops (pre-Peralta) who now have actually taken the capital of Santa Fe, but are facing reinforcements from Colorado. Just by sheer luck, a small scout force from Colorado happened upon the meager

Confederate Supply camp and torched it, effectively driving Sibley back through Peralta toward Texas, ending any hopes of the Confederacy moving west. Boom! The battles of New Mexico in full circle. Super cool.

After spending the morning hiking the Glorietta Battlefield trails, I wanted to drive north to Taos. I always heard it was a place you had to experience. From Santa Fe we took Hwy 68 into Taos, an interesting artisan town dominated by southwestern art studios and a pretty cool farmers market. The weather was a lot colder than I had expected, with overcast skies and a possible storm coming in, so it was more of a driving tour day than a walking around day.

I decided to drive what was called the "Enchanted Circle" for the afternoon, and stay in Taos at the local Walmart when we came back. The Enchanted Circle is a series of small ski resort towns that make a ring around Wheeler Peak, the tallest mountain in NM. The scenery was amazing, much like last month's Colorado trip, minus the fall colors. Passing through the towns of Angel Fire, Eagle's Nest, and my favorite, Red River, I was making mental notes in my head for the next time I pass through this way, hopefully when it's not so cold.

I had no idea New Mexico had such unbelievably beautiful mountains. At over 10k feet in elevation, the Enchanted Circle is where the Texans go to ski. I passed by some absolutely amazing roadside campgrounds, closed due to the season, that I will definitely be back to check out. Stay tuned for that.

Back at Taos, the temperature was dropping drastically, so much so that the little gas propane heater in the camper just wasn't cutting it. This is when I learned to use Walmart like an equipment rental store. I bought a $65 dollar little buddy propane heater, that I really didn't have the spare cash for, but what was I gonna do, freeze? I would just save the receipt and take it back to a Walmart in Arizona. I felt kind of bad about cheating the system like that... until I woke up with ice on the INSIDE of the camper window. That was it, I was done with New Mexico. I drove the entire way to Lake Roosevelt in Arizona that day. No joke. Drastic situations call for drastic measures. New Mexico, state #5... COMPLETE.

Arizona, Part 2

December 4th, 2015. We spent the next few months at a campsite by Lake Roosevelt, just over the mountain from the Phoenix Metro Area. Since I was able to sell the Harley and pay Jimmy back, it enabled me to start prepping the Rig and trailer for next summer's journey into the

Mountain States. I also managed to sprain my knee playing softball, prompting a VA appointment in the upcoming weeks. Coupled with the fact that this next leg of the trip would have no baseball parks, I decided to do all of the Cactus League Spring Training parks while I waited to see the doc.

Having lived in Arizona since 1996, I've seen what was once known as the best secret in baseball, transform into the money making spectacle known as Cactus League Spring Training… the "destination." Long gone are the days of $5 dollar lawn seats, $6 beers, and free parking. Now it's a winter vacation spot for the snowbound Midwestern states. I mean, who wouldn't want to take a break from Chicago weather to see the Cubs play in 76f degree weather? Unfortunately, they're willing to pay the "destination" prices, which leaves the locals scrambling to afford even a spring training ticket. Like the $50 lawn seat at the new Sloan Park, also known as Wrigley West. If you're on vacation it's no biggie, if you work at circle K on the corner, that's a lot! Regular season Diamondback tickets are cheaper nowadays.

The upside to Spring Training in Arizona, besides the weather of course, is the proximity of the parks. There's usually a game going at all 9 parks in the valley that are just minutes apart from each other. There are games everyday from the last week of February to opening day of regular season. Given mostly day games with night games on the weekends, you had plenty to choose from. Except now, you better buy them online as soon as they go on sale, as sell outs are prevalent later in the season.

In between Spring Training games, Kimber and I stopped in at a local sports bar for dinner. It was a crowded Friday afternoon, with pretty much every barstool taken except the one next to me. Suddenly this guy flags down the bartender for a beer, turns the seat sideways towards me, slides into it now facing me, spread eagle, and uncomfortably close. He then takes a huge drink of his beer, looks at me and says, "So how's your day?" Slightly taken aback, and somewhat irritated, I replied, "Better now," holding up my beer before taking a sip, trying not to make eye contact. I really wasn't in the mood. Then he asked, "What do you do?" After thinking about it, I said, "I guess I'm trying to be a writer." This peaked his interest, as I told him about my travels. He then finished off his beer, wiped the corner of his mouth with a napkin and stood up while reaching for his wallet. "It's all about the relationships man, people want to hear about relationships," he said as he patted me on the back and walked out. That was it, he was gone, just like that. Those words stuck in my mind as I went forward with this journey, realizing along the

way, that he was 100% correct. Who was that guy? Either way, Arizona, state #6…
COMPLETE! Mountain States, here we come…

The Mountain States

2016

After a month and a half in Phoenix, I was anxious to start my next adventure. The plan for this summer was to continue on with the "Mountain States" since we already visited Colorado. First up would be Utah, then north to Wyoming, on to Montana, over to Idaho, and finally down to Nevada, putting us back on the border of Arizona. All of which was under somewhat of a time constraint, as I filed for bankruptcy and would need to appear in court around August. Might as well try to fix my credit while I'm voluntarily homeless.

Since I was still waiting for my VA appointment to X-ray my knee, the Arizona heat was becoming unbearable, and I was anxious to get on the road. I decided to chart out what I called the "Monument Loop" and started to prep for the road. Since I had sold my Harley, I wanted to outfit the trailer as a mobile mountain bike shop/walk-in closet of sorts. I built a work bench that separated my bicycle and full size charcoal grill/smoker (priorities!), from the carpet I had installed in the front half of the trailer. I added a plastic set of cabinets, a plastic dresser, even a spot for a plastic porta-potty; trying to stay light as possible, making the dressing room area accessible from the side door of the trailer. I was also hoping that my gas mileage would be considerably better not dragging the Harley behind me. Fingers crossed.

Utah

April 6th, 2016. I decided to take Hwy 89 out of Arizona. The map showed that it ran right through Prescott and Flagstaff, then north all the way to Montana. Staying off the freeways was a continuous goal of mine, setting the GPS to "no interstates" and following the map wherever it may lead. This would prove to be both amazing at times, yet also could be utterly frightening. I would learn this lesson well in Utah.

The plan was to head over the southeast border of Utah toward Moab. There were several national monuments that I definitely wanted to check out, plus Moab is known for its world class mountain biking at Slick Rock. From there we would see all the different monuments in the area, from Natural Bridges National Monument to Bryce Canyon. Hopefully by then I'd be back on the AZ border to see about my knee. After the VA gives me the green light, we would go back to exactly where we left off and continue north toward Salt Lake. The only must do thing on the agenda was reconnecting with my little sister, and getting out of the Arizona heat.

We crossed the Utah border on April 6th around dawn. It's an amazing sight to see the "painted desert" light up like an oil painting under a direct light. The view of the rock formations changed as the sun rose, shining light at different angles, continuously changing colors as we drove by. We continued on Hwy 163 to the small town called Mexican Hat, named after the nearby rock formation that resembles the bust of a man wearing a sombrero. As with most small border towns, the gas was extremely expensive, so I decided to wait until we got to a cheaper station further inland.

This would've been fine if I had stayed on Hwy 163 to Blanding. Instead I chose a more direct route to the Natural Bridges Monument and turned left on Hwy 261 as my GPS recommended. I had found a campsite online that was supposed to be across from a mountain bike park, somewhere in the Manti-Sal National Forest. It seemed to be just up a forest road from the monument. So it all made sense to head that way, until the road turned to gravel and I started seeing road signs saying, 10% grade ahead, not recommended for vehicles pulling trailers. Lovely. For a split second, maybe two, I contemplated turning around. Then I remembered we survived the Dodger Stadium Hill incident AND the Mt. Tamalpias nightmare; we would survive this too. With a quick prayer and a few white knuckles from maneuvering around oncoming traffic, we were up and over the steep grade with rig intact. But now we had a gas issue. Going up that steep grade used up a lot of fuel, definitely more than I had expected. Now I was kicking myself for not fueling up in Mexican Hat. Assuming we were going to be on fumes trying to reach Blanding, I popped the transmission into neutral and coasted down the backside of the grade that thankfully wasn't nearly as steep and covered about 30 miles! This little trick got us to the pump on the fumes of fumes. Man, we got lucky that time.

After filling up, I turned back around, determined to find the campsite next to the mountain bike park. The GPS had us turn off the main road onto a dirt Forest Service road, winding up a large mountain. Perfect, we must be close. As we drove deeper into the forest, the road began to narrow, patches of snow started appearing, becoming more frequent as we moved to the shaded side of the mountain. I decided to check the GPS again to see how much farther we had to go… no signal. You gotta be kidding me. It couldn't be that much farther, so we pushed on. With mud on one side of the road and what turned out to be a knee deep trench covered with snow on the other, the truck suddenly dropped off to one side, and stopped. Yup, you guessed it, we were stuck. I mean spinning in 4-low stuck... with a truck camper... and a trailer. This was not good. Thankfully, I had stocked the camper for at least 3 days of food and water; looked like I wasn't going anywhere until I dug myself out. By hand... literally. Apparently, I didn't think enough to pack a shovel. Also lovely.

About that time I heard a car motor coming up the road behind me. It was two, all-wheel drive Subaru's, out four-wheeling in the snow. I walked back to them to let them know I was stuck, and if they needed to go around to feel free. One of the guys said he couldn't believe I made it this far in. I guess I was a little overconfident of the Rig's 4WD capability, but with a lot of praying and even a little begging, I miraculously was able to inch the Rig and trailer straight back, enough to find a spot to turn around. Looking back at what normally would have been one serious meltdown, I was surprisingly calm as could be. With a nod and a wink to the big man upstairs, I gave thanks and drove back to the highway. Another extremely close call, somebody's got to be looking out for us.

It was coming up on 3pm, so I headed for the Natural Bridges Monument campsite, which of course was full. Turned out it was the last weekend of Spring Break in Utah. Wonderful. Thankfully, I remembered seeing a boondock site when we were coasting into Blanding. So we pulled in and fired up the grill, worrying about if we would find a camping spot in Moab the next day. Time would tell.

In the morning we started out to Moab, heading east on Hwy 95 and then north on Hwy 191. We stopped and checked out the Canyonlands National Park, and the Newspaper Rock Petroglyphs. Some pretty cool campsites surrounded by rocks, nice paved roads, and 2 separate campsite loops, both of which were full unfortunately. Great place for road cycling but no mountain bikes allowed off pavement. Newspaper Rock was incredible, and a must see, like prehistoric graffiti with animal drawings, but with images of what one could only say look like what we would call aliens or some sort of space beings, complete with helmets and antennae... or horns. I report, you decide. As the sign said, without a known translation what the petroglyphs mean, they are up to one's own interpretation. Crazy stuff.

Continuing north on Hwy 191 to Moab, we got into town around 1300, I was excited to find a spot and settle in for a few days of mountain biking, or as long as my knee would allow me. I'm so bad about pushing an injury and not letting it completely heal. Another one of those battles where the brain hasn't figured out how old the body has recently become. I was trying to convince myself that mountain biking is more of a "low-impact" exercise than weights or hiking, and therefore would all be ok. Again, we shall see! Anyway, we scouted out where the world renown hot spot for mountain bikes, Slick Rock Trail, was located, and decided to look for a free boondocking spot just outside of town. Wow! It was jam-packed too, full of RVs with quad trailers. There was room for a quick overnight stay but I was looking for a place to set up camp.

It was now pushing 4pm and I was getting desperate to find a spot. Finally, almost in a fit of rage, I threw up my hands and said, "Ok Lord, I give up! Where do you want us?" I pulled off to the side of the road to use the bathroom and grab some water out of the camper. When I calmed down and gathered myself together, I picked up my phone and immediately noticed an app that I had downloaded, but never used. It was a Military camping app, basically showing all military installations and military fam camps (family camping), around the country. What I didn't realize was it also had privately owned campsites that offered a free, three night stay for active duty military and retirees. It didn't say if disabled veterans qualified, so I never thought to check this app. Incredibly enough, I punched the locate button and voila, there was a private campground literally a mile down the road from Slick Rock Trail! I called them to ask if the offer was good for disabled vets, the gentleman on the other side of the phone said, "Nobody's ever asked that before, so I guess it does now. Come on over!" I put down the phone, shook my head, and smiled. Another nod, wink, and a tremendous thank you to the man upstairs. With it being the last weekend of Spring Break, the town was booked solid, and now we were staying three days for free, with electric and showers. Amazing! Kimber and I spent the rest of the day wiping down the camper and straightening up the trailer. After a much needed shower and a nice steak, we called it a night.

The following morning, I decided to let the knee rest up another day before we got on the bike. We started with a light walk around downtown Moab in search of breakfast. We found breakfast gold at the Peace Tree Café; the Moab Breakfast burrito is truly something to behold. Afterwards, we stopped at a local bike shop for a Moab sticker and headed out toward the Arches National Monument.

What a truly magical place! Absolutely awe inspiring as you gaze upon amazingly colorful rock formations. It reminded me a lot of Sedona, but on an even grander scale. It was almost painful to see these world famous hiking trails covered with hikers, backpackers, and rock climbers, but not be able to partake in the fun. We shall be back! Hiking the Arches is definitely a bucket list item I'll be looking forward to checking off. Later that evening, I shoved a frozen pack of hotdogs down into my knee brace and cinched it down for a couple hours. It did the trick, knee felt good, and Kimber was happy to dispose of the field expedient ice pack.

In the morning I was up, bright eyed and bushy-tailed, ready to attack the trail like a champ. My knee had quite a different perspective of the morning. Not great. Nonetheless, I was convinced that my medical opinion far outweighed the pain, and hit the trail anyway. Surprisingly, the pedaling of the bike just around the parking lot did indeed make my knee feel better, and was now gleefully looking forward to the ride. That's when I realized that I had left my helmet and water back in the trailer at the campsite. Rookie maneuver for sure, but I was undaunted. Well it couldn't be that dangerous, it's just the warmup loop.

As I approached the trailhead, with my buddy Jim's monster downhill bike that I borrowed for the trip, I swear I was getting the craziest looks. Then I noticed EVERYBODY had helmets on; I had a SF Giants cap on backwards. I couldn't help but feel the barbs shooting from the mother's eyes when I heard her child asking why HE doesn't have to wear a helmet. Once I made the corner, I suddenly realized that the term "practice" loop, did not mean "beginner" loop, and was anything but a warmup. It should've been called the "Go get your helmet, idiot!" loop.

Right about then an 8 year old girl just about face-planted right in front of me. Somehow contorting her body in such a way to perfectly stick the dismount, straightened her helmet, mounted the saddle, and rode off laughing. I was terrified. So not only did I not have the proper protective equipment, but I had a pretty good chance of NEEDING proper protective equipment here shortly.

After a couple of runs I was thoroughly enjoying the downhill, the uphill not so much. I was definitely out of shape. The view was enough to make you forget the pain and enjoy the scenery. Riding a bike on petrified sand dunes was like riding bikes on Mars. It was amazing! After the practice loop, I went back to camp to get my helmet and returned for a few more runs. Slick Rock Trail is definitely a mountain biker's bucket list item!

After sadly saying goodbye to Moab, we made our way up to Interstate 70, turned west to Hwy 24, then south toward the Capital Reef National Park. More amazing rock formations, but now with small pastures and crop fields nestled among the red and tan sandstone. We passed through Fruit and several other old Mormon settlement towns, where I could definitely relate to living in such beautiful country, while living off the land. A longing for a simpler time always seems to be more enticing as one gets older.

Turning south on Hwy 12, I discovered that the Granite Reef National Park was part of the Dixie National Forest, with plenty of boondock sites to choose from. We found an awesome spot near a small lake. There was only one other camper, so we pretty much had the place to ourselves. Seemed to good to be true, and then suddenly, it was exactly that. A storm rolled in and temps dropped into the 20's almost instantaneously. When it's too cold to bring the smoker to temp, then it's too cold for me!

After a walk down to the lake, Kimber and I came back to camp. It was brisk out, but Kimber was being her typical energetic self, so I grabbed her ball and gave it a toss toward the back of the campsite. The ball ran down a trail to a downed fence line and got stuck. Kimber was not pleased and came back to tell me about it. When I got to the ball I realized there was a fairly clear area just past the downed fence that was mainly rock and sand. I gave the ball a toss and then saw the "crack." With every fiber of my being I screamed for Kimber to stop as she was full throttle after the ball. Thank God she froze at the sound of my scream, as the ball seemed to disappear into the rock. The closer I got, the faster my heart was racing. That crack was a five foot wide chasm that went down at least 70 to 80 feet to a rock strewn creek. I grabbed Kimber into my arms and just hugged as hard as I could as we walked back to camp. That's it, we're out, I almost lost her that time. Thank you Jesus, thank you! Wow, I still shake just writing this.

We toughed it out another night and broke camp at sunup. We stayed on Hwy 12, passing through Boulder Town and Escalante, then stopping for a brief drive through Bryce Canyon. Bryce Canyon is a lot like Arches but with much more forest. The park is an extremely popular tourist spot, with ample but fairly pricey camping. Looked like a great place to explore and definitely planned on being back. One word of caution, beware of the parking police.

I jumped out at one of the more popular exhibits to take a couple of quick pictures. In the 10 minutes I was gone, I returned to a giant, fluorescent orange sticker on my driver side window that needed a razor blade and a blow torch to get off. Apparently even trucks with trailers are not allowed in the bus parking. Driving out of the park with this sticker on my window was like driving with the equivalent of a scarlet letter on my forehead. I could feel the smirks of passersby as I tried to peel off my criminal designator at the local gas station. Lesson learned, back on the road.

With my VA appointment slowly approaching, I decided to head back toward AZ. We headed back up to Hwy 12 and caught the 89 south to Kanab where we stopped for supplies, propane, and gas. Kanab was a cool little town, about 45 minutes from Lake Powell, on the Utah side. Thanks to freecampites.net, which has proven to be an invaluable asset, we found an awesome campsite, right on the shore of Lake Powell called Lone Rock. The half priced fee of $7 bucks a night was exactly what the doctor ordered. We spent the next 3 days grilling on the beach and throwing the ball for Kimber. This dog loves water! Afterwards we headed back into AZ through Page, down Hwy 89, wanting to take in the Grand Canyon for the first time. After living in this state on and off for 20 plus years, I think it was overdue. As we pulled into the park I was shocked to see the $30 dollar entrance fee, but relieved that it was waived with my National Forest Passport Pass. Thank you, Oregon National Forest Service lady, more than you could ever know!

I was excited to see the first exhibit, and then I saw the parking lot. WOW! I had to find a spot among the buses to fit the Rig. With orange fluorescent non-parking stickers on my mind, I decided to take the risk. I had to, the place was packed. After getting Kimber situated in the camper, I blended in with the mob and headed for the exhibit. This is when things went downhill quick.

Blending in didn't work out so well, as English was apparently a second language amongst the Chinese and some other folks who I assumed were Russian or at least Slavic. I skirted most of the crowd to get near the rail of the canyon for a quick video. Ya, that wasn't happening. Every time I held up my camera, either somebody moved in front of me or bumped me from all angles, without even a nod. At this point, I was pretty much done and felt this unbelievable need to scream, "I'm an American Veteran... MOVE!" like I had some sort of title to that in a National Park. In a way I do... don't I? More than them at least, and they call us the ugly Americans. I was pissed. Needless to say, I left the park and headed back to Prescott, eager to get my knee cleared by the doc and get back on the road.

After another agonizing week in the Phoenix Metro heat; yes, May is hot in Southern AZ, I was ecstatic to be back on the road. Doc said the knee was a possible meniscus tear but left it up to me if I wanted to see ortho, which would mean surgery, I'm sure. Silly question doc, see ya in a few months. I'll wear my brace, take it easy hiking, and build my knee back up on the bike. Or at least that was my plan; it always feels amazing when I'm done riding. One thing that's becoming blatantly obvious. Getting old sucks. To compound that notion, I was issued a brand spanking new pair of VA bi-focals, or at least the progressive alternative, and a brand new dental crown in my face... to "cap" it all off.

Finally free as a bird with only one tether left, the bankruptcy was all that was standing between me and complete freedom. We backtracked to exactly where we left off, pulling into Zion National Park around mid-afternoon. This was an absolutely awe inspiring park that should be on every outdoor enthusiast's bucket list. Not nearly as crowded as the Grand Canyon, but still a pricey entrance fee that was gratefully waived with my access pass. I did get hit for a $15 fee that I did not expect. It's called a "tunnel permit" that equates to a "stop all traffic and let this idiot through" tax. Apparently, there is a 30 mile tunnel that is only wide enough for Priuses to drive side by side in. Ok, maybe it was only 1.1 mile long, but ya could've fooled me. I pulled up to the ranger guard shack at the mouth of the tunnel, rolled down my window and the guard says, "Oh we gotta measure ya," and proceeds to whip out a tape measure and starts measuring my camper width. "Yup, two inches too wide" he reports. "That'll be 15 bucks." After I paid him, he spoke with someone on his radio, then turned back to me. "Ok, drive down the center lane, turn your lights on, don't go over 30mph and whatever you do, DON'T STOP!" He then took three steps back and waved me through while talking on the radio again. Whoa what? Don't stop!? Ok, so now I was a little worried. That same feeling when the scary-ass carnie guy at the fair clicks you into the ride, stands back, smiles, and hits the "you're going to hell" button on the puke ride. Umm...could you repeat that? Oh well, here we go. So my full-sized truck, with oversized cab-over camper, and 6x8 covered trailer in tow, start for the mouth of the tunnel. As luck would have it, the automatic headlight sensors took about three seconds to register, my heart skipping a beat as I plunged into complete darkness with the words "DON'T STOP!" screaming in my inner ear. That was the longest 1.1 miles of my life.

Unfortunately with the trailer, I wasn't able to find parking at any of the trailheads in Zion. It was pushing up on supper time and I was exhausted already. I decided to call it a day and head for the closest Walmart, my second home away from home. With the Rig pointed west at the moment, we found our way into the small town of Cedar City, Utah. From there we would be north bound until Montana.

Cedar City was incredibly windy and cold. I parked the Rig along a side road next to a Walmart, where some other tractor trailers had parked. By now it was well into dinner time, and I was famished. After setting Kimber up in the camper with food and the heater on, I decided to splurge on some Applebee's. I walked in and grabbed a seat at the bar, which was unusually empty for "happy hour." The bartender appeared and asked what I was drinking. "I'll take a Stella draft please, big one...." I replied. "Will you be eating with us tonight?" she asked. I nodded in the affirmative, then she asked, "You are of age, right?" "God I hope so!" I said with a smile. Completely unamused, she walked off, said something to her manager who glanced my way, nodded, and then she brought me my beer. She still hadn't given me a menu. I asked if I would've been turned away if I didn't order food; she nodded in the affirmative. Apparently, in Utah you have to be eating to have an alcoholic beverage. She went on to say that they do have bars here, but it's a different license classification for restaurants. Working in the bar business, I understand the weird liquor laws in different states, so that made sense. What didn't make sense was that I was paying the same price for 3.2% ABV Stella, which is brewed specific for Utah, as compared to the standard 5%. Note to self... buy beer in Wyoming.

Not wanting to take the interstate, I decided to get back to Hwy 89 for the scenic route. A friend had told me to check out the Cedar Breaks National Monument, unfortunately the road was still closed due to snow. We did happen upon a cool campsite near Duck Creek Village that I wanted to stay at. As we drove through the campgrounds we saw deer, geese, and something I had only heard about and read in the news. Polygamists. One family, with a large SUV, had an older male and 2 teenage boys dressed like Quakers, complete with suspenders, white shirts and brimmed hats setting up camp. There were three adult females with four younger girls, all with full length denim dresses and some sort of white headgear, walking to the bathroom. I didn't want to be weird about it, but I really wanted a picture of this foreign lifestyle, so I just barely raised my phone above the dash, snapping a quick picture. I had to pull over and wipe my eyes from the laughter that ensued, after glancing at my phone. The picture of the three LDS girls looked like a combination of the iconic blurry big foot picture in full stride, and the cover of The Beatles Abby Road album. Blurry, with one arm in front, opposite arm to the rear, as they walked in sequential order down the trail. Classic.

Unfortunately, all the campsites were reserved for the upcoming Memorial Day weekend. Kimber and I continued on until we came to a boondock site just off of I70 and Hwy 89. Although looking sparse, the spot turned out to be a trailhead with a horse corral. There were several camping spots with picnic tables and fire rings, tall oaks and grass, with a small creek running behind. Perfect place to set up the bbq, throw Kimber's NEW ball, and get some rest.

Nervously, I called my sister to let her know I was in the area and was hoping to drop in. As always, Jenny put me at ease and said "C'mon up!" My little sis has always been an ear for me to talk to, and it had been way too long since I had seen or spoken to her last.

The scenery along Hwy 89 was beautiful. Amazingly huge churches standing prominently among the lush green grass of what seemed to be fertile farm land. I was surprised at how massive these churches were, with such incredible architecture and workmanship, yet found within what seemed to be such a small quaint community. This seemed to be the norm through the next several small towns.

As we got closer to Herriman, which is basically a distant subdivision of Salt Lake City (SLC), and with my sister's house being up on the valley slope, it started to look like any other metropolis, except for one very obvious feature. LDS church spires everywhere, like saguaro cacti springing up from the low brush in the desert, they were literally everywhere.

It was great to see my sister after all that time. Soon as she answered the door, she said, "Wow! With glasses you look like Dad!" I'd learn this to be a recurring phenomenon. We spent the rest of the evening reminiscing about our childhood, getting to know my niece and nephews, and just reconnecting with "blood" family after way too long of an absence. Something I'd been longing for and had sorely missed in my adult life.

The next morning, I was telling my sister about Applebee's and the polygamist sighting as we watched the local news on television, over coffee. She told me about the struggles of living in SLC and not being Mormon, such as her children being told by other grade school children that their Mom and Dad weren't really married because it didn't happen in the Temple. I was astonished. Mormons are Christians too, right? Well, that would be answered soon enough. Apparently a storm had moved in the night before and lightning had struck one of the local "temples." The golden statue of the angel Moroni on top of the Bountiful Temple literally had the back of its head and most of the statue's back blown out! Wow! My sister and I just kinda looked at each other like "whaaaat?!" I was thinking that if your church was struck by lightning... the Lord might be trying to tell you something. Just saying.

Later that morning we went to check out Salt Lake City, do a little shopping, and grab some pizza with my sis and the kiddos. We stopped at Dick's Sporting Goods because I wanted to buy a watch with altimeter, thermometer, and barometer for the upcoming mountains. Not having any luck, I asked a manager where I could find them. Dressed in a short sleeve, white collared dress shirt with a tie, the manager looked up at me, then looked at my full sleeve tattooed arms, and then looked down at the shirt he was folding, and muttered, "I think they're downstairs." I was starting to get the impression that my tattoos weren't exactly the rage in Utah; at least not in SLC. My sister was even surprised by the lack of service and undeniable attitude I received.

When we rolled into downtown Salt Lake City, which is called "New Jerusalem," the first thing I noticed was that all the cars were big black SUVs, and the buildings were made out of what looked like white marble. There was a concrete or metal decorative arch that spanned across the main road leading into the "Temple Mount" with an eagle perched on what can only be described as an upside down star or pentagram. Ok, so that was weird. After parking, we set out to explore the temple grounds area. I was taken back by the absolutely beautiful architecture of the temple, but surprised by all the Masonic and pagan symbolism portrayed in the concrete walls. Various moons, suns, hands clutching each other as in a handshake, and more stars, both right side up and upside down. Not normally what you would be used to seeing on a Christian Church, at least in my experience.

I spotted an elderly gentleman handing out maps and decided to ask where the temple entrance was so I could check out the inside. "So where's the doors to get in? I'm a Christian, I'd love to see the inside," I asked. Very politely, he explained that only LDS members can enter. "Hmm... so if Jesus showed up, would they let HIM in? Pretty sure He wasn't Mormon." The look on his face showed that he had no idea what to say. "It's ok," I said. "God bless you, sir" and I walked away. This was getting old quick.

We walked around the area, taking in the colorful flowering landscaping, and other sites on the map. The Mormon Tabernacle Choir building was impressive, the woodwork and the pipe organ was incredible. Up the street, we came upon this huge building with a massive concrete wall that had a giant globe carved in it. This was the world LDS headquarters. It literally looked like something you'd see in Gotham City with Batman parked out front. Reminded me of Orwell's 1984 book for some reason. It was just ominous.

On the way back to the house we stopped for pizza at a local hotspot. I walked to the counter to order while the kids and my sis found a table upstairs. I ordered a couple pizzas, sodas for the kids, and a pitcher of beer for me and my sister. The girl taking my order was fine until I asked for the beer. She looked at me with a blank stare, turned to what I assumed was her manager and said, "he wants beer." Here we go again. I specifically ordered the pizza first to show we were eating. Granted, she may have been too young to pour the beer, but I literally stood there for 15 minutes before a guy with a ponytail and a tattoo on his arm saw me, shook his head and said, "I got you bro," and poured our pitcher. Walking back to the table, I noticed we were in fact the only ones drinking beer in the restaurant. This was almost surreal, wow!

After saying goodbye to my sister and family we headed out for a battlefield that was south of SLC, across the valley from my sister's place, near the town of Pleasant Grove. Battle Creek Falls Trailhead was the site of the first battle, or slaughter of the Native Americans in this region, specifically the Timpanogos in this instance. It's hard to call most of these Indian Wars an actual battle, sadly enough, slaughter is more correct. The trailhead was near a Kiwanis club picnic area and had one small monument that read, "Battle Creek, Mar. 15th, 1849. This monument is in memory of the first armed engagement between the Mormon pioneers and the Native Americans that inhabited the Utah Valley and serves as a reminder of the extreme sacrifice given by both people. This skirmish at the mouth of Battle Creek Canyon gave it its name." The history books, eyewitness accounts on both sides, and historians have a very different story, but with this being the only information placard on site, we will leave it at that.

From Pleasant Grove I turned NE toward the mountains. I was wanting to visit Park City, UT after reading an article in a mountain biking magazine. One of the four big national races were held here; it wasn't until the next month, but at least I could do some bike-lift assisted, downhill runs for the first time. The Hwy 189 mountain route to Park City was breathtakingly beautiful. Unfortunately, the attitude of the people there was not. I probably shouldn't lump all

LDS together, as I have amazing Mormon friends who I love dearly, who also, by the way, warned me about the Salt Lake Area. So with it still being "mud season," no bike lifts running yet, and my fill of what I call "Mormon Exceptionalism," we headed straight for the Wyoming border. I could use a real beer at this point. Utah, state #7… COMPLETE.

Wyoming

April 25th, 2016. Rarely do I ever take the interstate, wanting to see as much of the countryside and small towns as possible. Not this time. I jumped on the I80 and made a beeline for the Wyoming border, crossing the state line around 1500. We gassed up in Evanston and continued north on Hwy 89, weaving in and out of the Utah/Wyoming border until we reached the town of Cokeville. There was a campsite just before you started climbing drastically in elevation, which I knew would mean much colder temps. It was getting close to dark, so decided the Allred Flat Campground was going to be home for the night. When we pulled into this amazing campground, once again we were the only campers there, which is always a good thing for Kimber; she can stay off leash and chase the ball as much as she wants, without a camp host bothering her.

The campground was nestled along a creek in the Bridger Teton National Forest, which was more like a river in Arizona. Our site was surrounded by Aspen trees, with the babbling creek just yards away. The following morning, Kimber and I decided to take a hike and explore the path that ran along the creek, back into the woods. As we walked, I began noticing Aspen trees that were broken off and laying near the edge of the creek. Then I looked closer and realized they weren't broken off, they were chewed off! I'm talking about 4 to 6 inch diameter trees, with tooth marks that looked more like a hatchet felled the tree. That's when I saw that the creek was backed up by a beaver dam, with a large mound in the middle of the small reservoir it had created. Whoa, beavers? Suddenly I realized the hatchet that downed the tree was actually teeth marks! How big are these things!? Looking at my small dog, a good 20 yards in front of me, I started racking my brain as to whether these things were carnivores. Unsure, I called her close and decided to turn around. I was excited to get on the road anyway. Next stop, Jackson Hole, Wyoming.

I have a friend who used to go to Jackson, Wyoming who told me all the time how great it is; it was also a big mountain bike spot, so that was our next stop. I found a campsite on what turned out to be an Elk Refuge just outside the town of Jackson. This time there were plenty of campers around, but the actual campground itself was fairly empty. Most were boondocking along the cliffside, that gave a breathtaking view of the Grand Teton mountain range. Truly the most majestic mountain range I've ever seen.

After picking out our spot, I decided to set up camp right away so we could commence with exploring the area. The campsite was on the slope of a hill, so the first step coming out of the side door of the trailer was a doozy. I took a block of wood from the trailer to use as a step. Bad move. While carrying one of those heavy, "zero gravity" lawn chairs a friend gave me, I stepped out of the trailer, placed my foot on the block, and suddenly hit the ground... HARD! I must've caught the edge of the block with my heel, because it decided to roll down the hill sending me straight back with my hands full. It happened so fast I didn't even have time to drop the chair. Just barely missing the metal edged door jam of the trailer, I slammed my head on the ground, driving my right elbow into a sharp piece of granite.

I hit hard. Enough to see stars, as I slowly reached toward the back of my head, expecting to feel warm, wet blood. Luckily, I didn't bust my head open, but did have a tremendous headache for the rest of the evening. My right elbow, however, did not fair as well. I spent the next 30 minutes scrubbing small pieces of rock out of my bleeding arm. I patched it up with some gauze and duct tape, until the next morning when I could find a better first aid kit. Little did I know how this seemingly simple fall would affect the rest of my trip.

In the morning we headed to town for breakfast and to find that first aid kit. After patching myself up the best I could, Kimber and I scouted the area for mountain bike shops and trails. Unfortunately, just like Utah, it was still "mud season" with not much going on. We ventured up to the ski resort where I took the tram to the top of the mountain range for some pictures. If you've never seen the Grand Tetons, it's definitely a must for any bucket list. They truly are majestic.

Afterwards, we headed back to town for some lunch at a local brewery. Snake River Brewery was the local favorite. Fantastic food and the beer was even better. While I was enjoying my lunch, a young lady came in and sat on the stool next to mine. We started up a conversation and I learned that she too was a fellow adventurer from Maine, who was here for the white water rafting. I was impressed. Here I was, looking for a bike trail while she was barreling down the Snake river in a rubber raft at break-neck speeds. We had a great talk and afterwards I gave her my Baseballs and Battlefields book page address to keep in touch. Made me wonder just how many other people I would meet on this journey doing amazing things. Always cool to actually see people chasing their dreams and not just wishing they would just happen. That first step is always the scariest, but will be the greatest first step of your life.

I almost forgot a cool story from Jackson Hole. After my tram ride to the top of the mountains, I stopped in a bar and grill for some lunch. Looking at the menu prices told me I was in the wrong place for a quick lunch. The bartender must've read my mind as he mentioned that there was also a snack bar on the property. "But there's no beer at the snack bar," I mentioned. He laughed and noticed the Marine tattoo on my neck. "You a vet?" I smiled and nodded in the affirmative. Jokingly, I asked if he had veterans discounts available. He asked what beer I drink, then proceeded to pour a tall Stella. "No discounts, but we sure as hell will buy you a beer. Thanks man," he said as he sat the cold beer in front of me. I told him there was no better discount than that. A cold beer and a thank you is all this veteran would ever want. Thanks man!

We ended up staying in Jackson for about 4 days before I decided we had better get going. Loved me some Jackson Hole. From there we continued north on Hwy 89 to Yellowstone National Park. I wanted to see Old Faithful, maybe do some hiking. The camping area we pulled into was jam pack crowded. The camping spots were very tight and very expensive. We only signed up for a couple days and went to check out the park. Old Faithful Lodge was amazing and a super cool place to stay if you can afford it. As with all the National Parks I encountered on this trip, it was completely overrun with tourists, mainly Chinese. After waiting for almost 30 minutes to see Old Faithful do its thing, just as it started to spit water, a group of Chinese tourists all ran to the front for pictures, blocking all our views. In the best Marine Drill Instructor voice I could muster, I yelled, "SIT THE HELL DOWN!" To my surprise they did! A guy next to me with his two small children looked at me and mouthed the words "thank you." All I could wonder was why he didn't do it himself.

As we drove around the park I was kinda surprised that I hadn't seen a buffalo yet. There was plenty of signage on the roads warning you of the beasts, yet not one sighting. The next morning we packed up early and headed out. That's when I realized I wasn't being careful what I wished for. On the way out of the park, I got stuck behind one lonely bison, walking down the dead center of the road. Even with me behind him, he didn't speed up or get out of the way. After about a mile I decided to try to squeeze around him, hoping not to piss him off and have him ram the truck. He didn't even look my way. I had to chuckle, rush hour in Jellystone. Gotta love it.

I took Hwy 14 east out of the park, heading toward Sheridan, Wyoming, then north to Montana and Custer's Last Stand. Absolutely beautiful country, with some super cool camping spots down along a decent size river. The first town I came to was Cody, Wyoming. A quaint little country town known for its Buffalo Bill Center of the West exhibit. What I didn't know was that inside the Buffalo Bill Center is the largest firearms collection in the world. The actual Smithsonian Institute's firearm exhibit. Well, that pretty much decided the next two days of my life. We set up house at a small RV park just down the street for two days. Absolutely amazing history and the most incredible collection of guns that I've ever seen. What a great find!

The next day we walked downtown to see the sights of Cody. We came across a small bar with a dog friendly outdoor patio. As we walked by, one of the patrons of the bar commented on Kimber's uncanny cuteness. Turned out it was the owner of the bar who invited us in for a beer. While we were enjoying our beverage and telling her about my travels, a group of people approached the table. It was the bar owner's daughter and some friends. After introductions we all sat and enjoyed the sun and conversation. Several beers later the daughter invited me over for a bbq and campfire, which I gladly accepted. While we were sitting around the campfire some guys showed up, one carrying a guitar case. This guy was Luke Bell, an up and coming country music singer/song writer who was all over YouTube with his music videos! Like the old wild west days, we sat around the campfire singing songs and passing the bottle. The only way to spend an evening in Wyoming!

From Cody we continued east into Sheridan, Wyoming, a much bigger town but still not quite a major city. I decided to stop for the night. We parked at a local Walmart, scouted out a local brewery, and headed in for dinner and a couple of drinks. That's when it happened. I sat down at the bar and was looking at a menu when the young and extremely hot, female bartender came to take my order. I put down the menu, put my elbows down on the bar and proceeded to give her my order. About that time I felt something wet on my right elbow. That's when the bartender's face turned to pure terror as she looked down at my elbow on the bar. There was a small puddle of amber colored liquid starting to ooze from my elbow bandage and seep its way across the bar. It literally looked like a quarter cup of motor oil was seeping from my elbow. Even though I had been changing the dressing and keeping my elbow wound clean, it apparently wasn't healing and had festered. Talk about complete and utter embarrassment. I quickly apologized, grabbed Kimber and we bolted for the door.

Now I was worried. I had a bout with a staph infection years ago in my left elbow. I had cut my finger on a dirty air filter at work, didn't have time to wash it out, wrapped some duct tape around it and called it good. Ya, bad move. My elbow swelled up due to a nasty Staph infection, spiking a fever that sent me to the hospital. They had to cut out my bursa, and pack the wound for 8 weeks while the flesh healed from the inside out. It almost killed me... literally. So here I was with the opposite elbow now leaking fluid and not healing. It was ripe for infection. Thankfully, on the way out of town I saw a VA Hospital sign and decided to have it looked at. After 3 hours at the VA, they had looked at the wound, cleaned it out and bandaged it. Then the nurse handed me some antibiotics and said, "If that thing's still not healed by the time you run out of these; you better stop somewhere." Not exactly the most encouraging statement ever.

Montana

June 3rd, 2016. Montana, the Big Sky State; specific images come to mind when you think of Montana. Visions of majestic mountains, carved by rushing rivers from a millennia of glacier water. Big horn sheep, elk the size of dinosaurs, and trout fishing to die for. This was the Montana in my mind; needless to say, I was shocked when I crossed the Montana state line, heading north on Interstate 90.

The first thing I noticed was there weren't any mountains, just rolling plains that went as far as you could see. No farming going on, just empty land. That's when I realized we were on the Crow Indian Reservation, which apparently is a poor tribe judging by the condition of the housing. Sadly enough, I never understood why the majority of reservations that I saw were in such poverty. I lived right next to a reservation in Arizona that made millions from casino money, yet the homes were dilapidated and garbage strewn everywhere. This reservation was no different. Definitely not what I expected Montana to be.

Our first National Battlefield was the Little Big Horn National Battlefield and Cemetery. The Battle of Little Big Horn, more famously known as Custer's Last Stand, is also known as the Battle of Greasy Grass to the Lakota and other Plains Indians. After some research as to why one battlefield has the "National" designation and another will not, the conclusion is... there really isn't any rhyme or reason. The one glaring fact about this battle as compared to other Indian Wars battles is... the U.S. lost. Interesting.

The park itself was pristine. It also housed a National Cemetery with fallen veterans from all the major wars who were from this area. There was a large visitor center for both the cemetery and the battlefield, with the battle monuments perched on the rolling hills behind. Another interesting aspect to this park is that it's the only battlefield where they marked the ground where the soldiers actually fell, making the view of the hillside, speckled with white markers, an eerie sight.

I also noticed that there had been recent editions, information monuments on shiny new brown granite, depicting the Indians' take on the battle. Also some newer brown markers for the fallen Indian warriors that were visible when you took the walking trail. Interestingly, there were no American survivors, so everything we know of this battle is from the Indian perspective. As with some of the other battlefields, research tells a bit of a different tale than the one most taught.

June 25th, 1876, General Custer was sent to subdue an entire village made up of several different tribes to include the Sioux and Cheyenne. A traveling village was an almost impossible target to track and control, but one of this size would surely lead to a U.S. loss. Custer made a mistake of dividing his troops into three columns, trying to surround the village. With no idea of how many natives there actually were, Custer sent for reinforcements and ammunition. It was during this time that the natives attacked, completely slaughtering all the U.S. troops as they encircled their commander, chasing down and murdering U.S. troops as they fled. This would be the Plains Indians' greatest victory, as Sitting Bull fled to Canada and Crazy Horse to Nebraska.

What I found interesting was all the obviously newer additions to the antiquated park. Brand new shiny brown granite markers, carved with depictions of the Natives' viewpoint of the battle, discussing the raping of their lands and destruction of their people. Chieftains quoted as saying how the U.S. soldiers fought with gallantry, and Custer himself as a great warrior. Completely different than what I researched prior to the visit and an obvious appeasement to the politically correct historian club. Political Correctness has no place in history... period. It is what it is, and as soon as we doctor it to appease one's feelings, history is truly lost.

Authors notation: After seeing my first National Battlefield, I realized I was going to have to make a decision on the book content. It was obvious that I could literally spend years just chasing all the Indian War Battlefields, then add the Civil and Revolutionary Wars. I think I bit off more than I could chew. So I will concentrate on the National Battlefields, and then cover the notable or interesting battle sites along the way. You'll see what I mean as we go on. Also, I've decided that all the information I put forward will only be from what I learn at that specific battlefield. Only information from the parks video, museum, information placards, and Park Rangers, like a kid on a field trip, looking at each encounter with a blank slate. This also eliminates any argument over sources, adding pages of footnotes, and generally is just my interpretation of what's before me.

After walking around the battlefield until early afternoon, it was starting to get hot and I decided I had better get back to Kimber. Unfortunately, most of the National Monuments and Battlefields don't allow dogs outside of the car. Understandable since they are preserving actual history, rather than just a lone trail in the forest. So off to the next Walmart in Billings, MT that I noticed had a Buffalo Wild Wings just a few doors down. Perfect. Just in time for a cold beer and a baseball game.

Interstate 90 through Billings reminded me a lot of Redding, CA. Flat and what seemed very industrial, with a lot of businesses catering to truckers, which made obvious sense since this was the largest city we'd seen so far and on a major interstate. After dinner and waiting for it to cool down a bit, we found a quiet spot in the back of Walmart's lot to bed down for the night. Next stop was Big Hole National Battlefield, clear on the other side of the state.

I-90 seemed to roll on forever, and at this point I was in severe need of a real shower. The nearest Anytime Fitness was in Bozeman, a college town that I learned had a propensity for breweries and mountain biking. After a quick shower, we went out to find a bike shop with a trail guide for the area and hopefully some downhill lifts.

Bozeman was beautiful, and I was so done with Walmart camping at this point that I wanted to find a cool place to camp and relax for a couple days. The free camping website pointed to a grip of what looked like riverside, federal campgrounds, south of Bozeman, near Big Sky, MT. The ski resort in Big Sky also just happened to have mountain bike lifts. Sweet! The bike shop owner in Bozeman said that they probably weren't running the lifts yet; apparently we were still chasing the "mud" season north. Undaunted, I took the chance and headed toward Big Sky.

Just as promised, the place was incredible. The Gallatin National Forest Campground ended up being just $6 a night, right along the huge Gallatin River. Now this was what I expected Montana be. Mountains on each side of a green valley with a huge river running through the center. Hiking and biking trails galore, water to cool off in, and still fairly empty... this was exactly what I needed. I set up the camper, broke out the grill, and settled into the incredible beauty surrounding us.

The next day we set out on a morning hike while we waited for the mountain bike lifts to open up. We were less than a mile into our hike when we ran across the remains of an elk leg that still had plenty of meat left on the bones. That's when Kimber went back on a leash. Colorado scared me, and now I have proof why. Kimber was going to be on a short leash when we got deeper into the woods from then on. At that point it was time to head into the town of Big Sky and check out the downhill, a perfect reason to turn back toward camp, with a cautious and continuous eye behind us. I'm not sure what took down that elk, but I wasn't taking the chance that it would be back to finish its breakfast.

Big Sky was a small community nestled away in the center of the Gallatin National Forest, surrounded by the Madison Mountain Range, truly a picturesque place. With its golf course, high-end shopping center with a fantastic little brewery, and Big Sky ski resort, it was a paradise for the rich and shameless.

A couple of the ski lifts ran customized chairs that doubled as bike racks. Riders could bring their own ride, or rent a bike from the bike shop that was also part of the ski resort. Just like skiing, I purchased a lift ticket and headed for the line, this time remembering my proper protective attire... thank God. I had a helmet and gloves, that's it, while other guys looked like they just walked off the *Mad Max* movie set. Some had full BMX gear on from head to toe, one kid had what looked like football pads and pants on. After a couple near death experiences, I checked the downhill mountain bike box on the bucket list. I'm addicted, what a blast. Ya, I know, typical Jarhead adrenaline junkie. My elbow was still leaking a bit, but seemed to be getting better. After a half-day on the slopes, I was exhausted. Time to catch a six pack from the Big Sky Brewing Co, and settle in for a steak and a good night's sleep... oh and ball, lots of throwing Kimber's ball.

From Big Sky we drove west into the northern portion of the Rocky Mountains. Well, north of Colorado at least. The terrain was still grasslands, as the foothills began to grow in size. This was a very desolate place with very few gas stations, and little human life in general. One of the last valleys nestled in the foothills is where the Battle of Big Hole occurred.

The Battle of Big Hole was fought on August 9th of 1877, between the Nez Perce and the U.S. Army. The Nez Perce was a migratory tribe following the good weather and fertile hunting from Southern Idaho to Montana each year. When the treaty was signed between the tribe and the U.S. Government to move the tribe to a reservation, 1/4 of the tribe's hunters and warriors refused to comply. The group was trying to make it to the Canadian border when they were viciously attacked at night by the pursuing troops. Over 750 Nez Perce were killed, only 200 were men.

I had never heard of this place, this battle, or even of the Nez Perce story. As with the last National Battlefield, this one too had a visitor center with an introductory film made by the park service. So the information you got there was pretty much what we learned from our standard high school curriculum, so basically textbook information. That's important to remember for later. The visitor center also had its typical displays of native jewelry and clothing from the period. There were two main hiking trails to the battlefield. Unfortunately, it was starting to get pretty warm, and I couldn't take Kimber on the trails; so I took as many pictures as I could and got back to the camper. At this point I was tired of Indian Wars battlefields which never really held my interest. Then add what seemed to be nothing less than butchery by the U.S. in most circumstances, makes it very difficult to stay patriotic. Remember when I said "textbook" information? I'm starting to see the correlation between the title "national" and the author being our government. You'll understand this more very soon.

From Big Hole we continued west on Hwy 43, then north on Hwy 93 to Missoula. I was in desperate need of a hot shower and some chicken wings. Just like Billings, we found a Walmart with the gym and a BDubs all in close proximity. Perfect, a good meal and a ballgame, then a good night's rest before I'd go up to Glacier National Park. At least that was my plan. One of my favorite sayings is, "Ya wanna make God laugh... tell Him what YOUR plans are."

So with Missoula being a college town, I assumed it would have its fair share of shenanigans going on, but not at a Walmart on a Tuesday night. Who was I kidding, it's Walmart. As we pulled into the Missoula Wally World parking lot, after enjoying a nice relaxing meal, the first thing I saw was an armada of not exactly the road brethren I was used to seeing. The back of the parking lot was against a retaining wall and grass area, which apparently had become a miniature Woodstock in full swing. They had music, grills going, people dancing, all dressed like they got dunked in a tie dye tub, which was probably the only tub they'd seen in a while. One of the more ingenious "RVs" was a full-size yellow school bus with the rear third of its roof cut away, leaving a two foot wall around a sun deck of sorts. Complete with built-in bbq grill, a fake palm tree, and Christmas lights powered by the noisiest generator this side of the Rockies. Needless to say, I parked on the other end of the lot with the big rigs and travel trailers not affiliated with the love fest.

Even in middle of the semi-trucks, you could still hear the generator from the Partridge family bus. Add the fact that the sun didn't go down until around 22:30 and you got one not so restful night. I think it was about the 5th boom box or the 3rd police car rolling through that prompted my 0400 wake up call and immediate departure. I was exhausted but I was done with this Walmart.

With a huge mug of coffee in hand, and a blurry-eyed, not so chipper driver, the Rig turned north toward Glacier... I thought. About an hour into my drive through some amazing mountains and cool little towns, I saw the "Welcome to Idaho" sign. Whoa what? Idaho? Where the hell is Glacier? With a blurry-eyed turn onto Interstate 90, I completely missed the Hwy 93 exit north. After checking the map, I was going to have to backtrack halfway to Missoula to head north. Well I guess Glacier will have to wait until next time. Remember what I said about MY plans... ya, good times. Well alrighty then, welcome to Idaho. Montana, state #9... COMPLETE!

Idaho

June 8th, 2016. Rolling into Northern Idaho on Interstate 90 west, was exactly what I pictured this state to look like. Super lush, grass lined highways, giving way to steep mountains that were equally lush with evergreen trees. This was truly the definition of the American Northwest.

Apparently with not enough coffee, I had suddenly crossed the Idaho state line with road signs saying the town of Cour d'Alene was just a few miles ahead. Needing a place to rest and regain some direction, I headed toward the nearest Walmart. As usual, we slid into the multitude of RVs and fifth wheels without a problem. This was a smaller town with lots of water nearby, so lots of families camping and retired folks out to enjoy the first days of summer. No buses with porches, thankfully.

After a great power nap, I searched the area for local camping but found the state parks around there all had full hook-ups and were quite expensive. Typical of most state parks, only veterans of that state could get the discounts. I get that, I guess. So back to Walmart for the night, and to map out our next stop. The humidity was something I wasn't expecting this far north, complicating where we were going to stay for the night. With it getting late, I just prayed it would cool down enough for another night at Walmart.

Thankfully, the temperatures dropped to a very comfortable level for sleeping, so after a great night's rest we were up and rolling early again. When I stopped for gas on the outskirts of a small town, there happened to be an Anytime Fitness across the street; a shower was definitely in order. When I was getting dressed, I noticed my elbow was still pretty swollen and still leaking fluid... not to mention, last night I ran out of pills.

After the Sheridan VA not even knowing who I was, and having to enroll me in their system, let alone the care I received, I skipped searching for another VA and pulled into the first civilian hospital I could find. The Grittman Medical center emergency room was completely empty when I walked in, giving me plenty of time to explain my elbow woes to the nurse. When they heard me say "staph infection," they brought me back right away, jumping into action. After x-rays and a test on my elbow fluid for infections, they re-dressed my wound and had me wait for the test results. This was awesome, I'd be on the road in a minute, with proper care and meds. You can imagine my surprise when the ER doc came back and recommended surgery, or it would NEVER stop leaking. Incredibly enough, they just happened to have an orthopedic surgeon in house that day and said he would come back that evening to work on me! Whoa what? I would've been somewhere in Glacier National Park, with no meds, and a leaking elbow. Now I was getting surgery the same day I walked into the hospital. Did ya hear me when I said, everything happens for a reason!?

So now the challenge was to find a place for the trailer and someone to watch Kimber during this whole ordeal. Amazingly enough, the hospital staff jumped into action once again. I was quickly given the number to the local fairgrounds that also had an RV park, just a few miles from the hospital. They also gave me two different contacts for pet boarding facilities around town. So the rest of the afternoon was spent getting everything set up so I could have surgery with minimal worries for Kimber, or my gear. Gotta love a small town, and these people were amazing!

So there I was in Moscow, Idaho, looking for somewhere to take Kimber. I think I was having the worst case of separation anxiety ever, and she wasn't even gone yet. Then I remembered that my sister went to college in Idaho, so I sent her a text hoping that she knew somebody in the area. Amazingly she text me back with, "that's the town where I went to school, Moscow!" What are the chances of me deciding to stop in a small town, suddenly needing surgery, and it being a town where my sister spent four years of her life? That's insane! Unfortunately, that was over 10 years ago and she didn't know anybody still here. Still, what an amazingly small world.

About then, I got a callback from one of the numbers the nurses had given me. She sounded like a nice elderly lady, with an accent I couldn't recognize, even though it sounded strangely comforting. We made an appointment for a few hours later, in the meantime I went to look for the fairgrounds and an RV spot. Seventeen dollars a night was a little out of my price range, but what was I gonna do? It had electric, a bathroom/shower house, Safeway across the street, and several fast food places near by. No telling how long I'd be here, so might as well be comfortable. Oh and did I mention a huge grass field, begging for Kimber to play ball. Ya, we were home, I just wondered how long I could afford it.

The boarding kennel was about twenty minutes outside of town, secluded in the rolling farmland. On the way to drop Kimber off, I almost broke into tears. Pathetic, I know, but this little girl hadn't spent a night away from me since we started this trip. I could already hear her whining, running to the door, thinking I abandoned her; and damn it, there was nothing I could do about it. I hated leaving her in a strange place, but the nice Swedish lady (she sounded like my grandmother) comforted me with a walk through of the house. It was set up with several couches and chairs, all for the dogs. They had toys everywhere, tv on the animal channel, and all were playing happily or comfortably sleeping on a piece of furniture. She would be fine here. I was the one who was gonna be the mess.

Dr. Jacobson and the entire hospital staff were amazing. He explained that they would have to remove the torn bursa, make the arm immobile until the skin would heal, then my body would grow another bursa, complete with fresh motor oil, as soon as I started moving it again. With skin healed first, it eliminated the chance for that very susceptible place to become infected. Whatever you say Doc, let's do this. I got a dog missing me.

After the procedure, I woke up in my own hospital room with a real bed and cable TV. First thing I did was ask for my phone; I had to check on my girl. Soon as the phone powered up, the notification sound chirped. Pictures of Kimber playing with the other dogs, sleeping peacefully with a blanket, and eating her food, made my eyes leak with gratitude. After a quick call to the

Swedish lady, I sat back and enjoyed the creature comforts of home that I hadn't had in months. Funny that a hospital room was like Club Med to the lonely traveler. Turning down pain meds, I left the hospital as soon as they would let me. I'm coming baby.

Shortly after lunch, I was on my way to get Kimber. Driving was already an issue with the partial cast from wrist to bicep wrapped tightly in a sling. Did I mention that I'm right handed? It was very frustrating for the first few days, to say the least. I had two weeks before my follow up appointment, and I was determined to do exactly as the surgeon said; I wanted to enjoy the rest of my trip pain and worry free. Ok, well maybe worry free at least, my elbow was pretty tender.

I could see Kimber looking out the window, paws on the sill, barking wildly as I pulled up. When the Swedish lady opened the door, Kimber literally flew into my arms, trembling and whining to the point of a low howl. The lady laughed, Kimber howled, and I hid my tears of joy the best I could. Shut up, that was the longest 22 hours of my life! I thanked the lady a million times, and headed back to the fairgrounds.

During the next two weeks, I met some absolutely amazing people, all of whom welcomed Kimber and me like a long lost family. If it wasn't for missing that exit outside of Missoula, who knows what would've happened. The Lord put me right where he wanted me. What seemed like a missed opportunity, turned out to be the exact path that I needed. He led me to an amazing small town that I could easily find myself calling home someday. Idaho, state #10... COMPLETE!

To top it all off, I had told my bankruptcy lawyer that I had an accident and needed surgery. About a week into my recovery, I got an email saying that I no longer needed to appear, they would cover it! Another incredible blessing, bringing a whole new direction to the trip. With no reason to run back to Arizona, and still being fairly close to Glacier National Park, I decided to turn the Rig north again, and head back to Montana. Now, with all the time in the world, I might as well see as many states this summer as I can. So back to Montana, then on to North Dakota, South Dakota, Nebraska, Kansas, and Oklahoma, before turning west back to AZ. That was the new and improved plan, or should I say that was MY plan. With a nod and a wink to the blue sky above, Montana here we come... again.

Montana, Part 2

It was coming up on the Fourth of July when we left Idaho. We had settled into an amazingly remote and quiet campground at Lake Pend Oreille, before crossing into Montana again. It literally took over an hour, at 15mph because of the rough dirt road, to get out there. I assumed Kimber would be safe from fireworks out here, but once again I was wrong. As the campground filled up with people boating their gear over to a small dock near by, I learned that there would be fireworks shot off over the lake. From that little dock! So you're telling me, I'm camping where the town shoots its fireworks off from? Isn't that awesome. And it's only the third.

I broke camp and loaded up the Rig as fast as I could to make it out of there by nightfall. I wasn't going through another night like the last 4th of July. I set the GPS for Glacier National Park and started driving, hoping I'd find a Walmart or someplace to park away from civilization for my poor little dog's sake. That and I promised the old guy living back in there that I would leave this little bit of heaven out of the book. Vague enough I hope, thanks for the water and wood, sir!

It wasn't too far up the road, just on the Montana side of the state line, I found a Forest Service campground. It was completely black, tall dense pine trees blocking out any moon or starlight. With only a few other campers and all very quiet, we slipped into a spot and crawled into bed for the night; this time with Kimber sleeping soundly under the covers. Yes, I love my dog that much.

The Yaak River Campground, just west of Troy, Montana was amazing. Where the Kootenai and Yaak Rivers meet, just a few yards from our campsite, was the biggest, crystal clear river I'd ever seen. Like the salmon ladder in Washington, it was almost an emerald green color, and at least 50 yards wide. When I saw the sign that 26 inches was the legal size to keep a trout here, I about fell down. Anything under 26" has to go back. That's a shark in Arizona! I was amazed.

Kimber survived the Fourth with me playing music in the camper loud enough to drown out the faint sound of fireworks from the town nearby. We spent a couple days hiking the area and checking out the town of Troy. From there we headed into Kalispell for a shower and some wings, passing some amazing campgrounds along the riverside. We found the local Walmart within walking distance from a Buffalo Wild Wings and called it a night. I thought I may stay right here at Walmart for a couple days; there was a farmers market coming up that I had heard a lot about from folks in Troy.

The next day, I took Kimber for a walk and was heading back to the camper when I noticed a guy with a clip board writing down license plate numbers. Apparently the Walmart here would get so many RVs that they limited you to only one night. Which, quite honestly, is how it should be. They need to pass that word down to the Missoula love fest.

The Whitefish Farmers Market came highly recommended by the locals in Troy, so the next day we turned north toward the super cool little town of Whitefish, Montana. Much like Big Sky but larger, this was another ski resort town in the middle of the Flathead National Forest. There was also a small lake, a cool little downtown area, mountain bike parks, and of course plenty of hiking.

We stopped at a restaurant called the Bulldog Saloon. A huge sign on the front of the building sporting an English bulldog standing upright wearing boxing shorts, and a American flag painted on the wall with the word "EATS" and an arrow pointing to the door... well duh, of course I was going in that place.

I sat at the bar and was waited on by a female bartender a few years younger than me, named Michelle. I told her about my travels and asked about camping in the area. She offered to show me around when she got off work, which I gladly accepted. Always good to have a local show you the sights and who knows where the good, free, camping spots are near town! She took me to a spot just off the main road leading up to the ski resort. It was just a small parking area, but overlooking the entire valley, with an incredible view. Enough room for the truck and the camper, plus it was just an area out in the National Forest, so it was free. This was perfect as I needed a spot to bed down for a week or so, to save some money. The first of the month was a ways off, and the stay in Moscow with full hookups was a little pricey, pretty much depleting my savings.

So the next week or so we spent checking out the sights of Whitefish. It started getting busy at my little boondock site when the weekend rolled around. Apparently, I had parked in a popular area for picking huckleberries. "Hucks" are tiny berries that grow wild and are sold at a premium for syrups and wine making. I was getting some pretty sketchy looks from some folks, thinking I was moving in on their huck patch. I started thinking of that show about the ginseng pickers back east, flattening tires, shooting at other "pickers." I decided it was time to move on. Payday was on Sunday, so direct deposit hit early, just in time.

With it being a Friday, and not having reservations for camping at Glacier, I knew I didn't have much of a chance to find a spot. When we left Whitefish that morning, the sky was getting pretty dark, and as luck would have it, it was pouring rain by the time we got to the park. I mean a torrential downpour, barely able to see the taillights of the car in front of me. We pulled into the visitor center to wait out the downpour and check on camping. As expected, they were full, even in the rain. I was going to top off the gas tank while I was there, but the gas prices were ridiculous. I had 3/4 of a tank, I'd be fine.

As we emerged from Glacier National Park, traveling east on Hwy 2, I was shocked at how fast the scenery changed. Pretty much as soon as I exited the east side of Glacier Park, it almost instantly turned into rolling plains that stretch as far as the eye could see. For hours, there was nothing more than farms and the occasional small community; and of course, the seemingly continuous running trains...but no gas.

I was having Utah flashbacks, but instead of a huge uphill climb draining my tank, it was a 30 mph headwind I was battling, leaving me with a gas mileage of about 6 mpg! Now with the gas gauge well into the red, I needed to see a small town with a gas station in the next 30 miles. Thankfully Chester, MT was on the horizon. I pulled up to the first pump I saw and filled up. While pumping the gas, I checked the website for camping in the area; it was around 7pm and I wanted to get some rest. Amazingly enough, there was a small city park that allowed RVs and camping for a donation. Crazy thing is, I had been scouring the free camping page and never saw this campsite until exactly then!

Just around the corner from the gas station we found the campsite. A well maintained, pet friendly park with bathrooms and electricity as advertised. The sign said the showers were down the street at a motel. That was weird, but I was ready for a hot shower, so off we went. The hotel office was inside the local quickie mart, with about a dozen rooms behind it. One of the rooms in the hotel was the Chester Chamber of Commerce. When I said small town, I wasn't kidding. I went in to inquire about the showers. Sure enough, for 8 bucks, you got one hour in a regular motel room, complete with soap and towels. Add to that, baseball on the TV, while I soaked in a hot bathtub; that was the best 8 dollars I've ever spent.

My joy was short-lived. After dropping the key off at the office, I hopped in the truck and headed back to the park. At least that was the plan. When I started the truck, I noticed it started a little rough, and seemed to lurch a bit when I stepped on the gas. The idle was rough, even back firing as I gave it more gas to pull out into the road. There were no idiot lights on the dash, which was really strange as this truck has a ton of sensors alerting you to everything from low tire pressure to windshield wiper fluid low. I was lucky enough to have barely gotten the truck into my parking spot when it died and wouldn't start again.

This was not good. My mind began racing with possible problems that would cause these symptoms; it seemed like it was starving for fuel. I could work on an old Harley with my eyes closed, but with this new fuel injected pick-up, I had no clue. I assumed the loss in gas mileage was from the headwind, but could it be something mechanical? Maybe a fuel pump, preferably a fuel filter; any more than that would break me financially. All I knew was my PTSD was not taking this well at all. To make things worse, there was a pretty good size storm rolling in. Lovely.

I decided to walk back down to the quickie mart to ask about any mechanics in the area. Seated just to the left of me was a couple enjoying some ice cream. When I told the clerk my situation, she looked over to them inquisitively as if they might know someone to help. Turned out, the gentleman was an airplane mechanic and a Vietnam vet. The couple were kind enough to give me a lift back to the park and take a listen to my truck. He also believed it to be a fuel issue, and told me there was a Napa auto parts here in town and two mechanics shops nearby. I was going to meet with him for coffee in the morning and try to figure this out. Gotta love small town and fellow veterans.

The next morning, I met up with Steve and chatted over some coffee. He was an Air Force veteran who was actually stationed at Luke AFB in Arizona, the same base where I worked as a civilian HVAC tech. Another incredible coincidence! Who'd have thought I'd meet somebody in Chester, MT that had walked on the same dirt as me?

After coffee, Steve drove me over to the mechanic shop he had mentioned. Funny enough, it was the gas station that I had filled up at the night before. As we walked up to talk to the mechanic, I noticed something about the gas pump that I had used that I did not notice in the dark. The pump was green! I looked at Steve and just said, "Are you freaking kidding me!?" He looked at me like I had lost my mind. "I used that pump!" I said in complete disgust. I had filled my gas motor pickup truck with a full tank of diesel. Well, that shed a light, didn't it. In my own defense, we have Shamrock gas stations in AZ that have green pumps, the handle here was black and fit into my truck. Nonetheless, I was pretty damn embarrassed.

The mechanic said he really didn't want to drop a full tank of diesel on a Saturday without the owner around. I can't blame him there, it was a beautiful day. When I asked when the owner would be here, he said he was on a hunting trip and was due home Monday at the earliest. With that being said, it looked like I was spending the weekend in Chester.

Steve said that we should probably drive over to the Sheriff station to let them know my rig would be in the park for a couple more days. Steve explained the situation to the Sheriff dispatch. After a quick chuckle, she put out a radio call to the patrolling deputy, who also had a good chuckle. "No worries, good luck," she said as we turned and walked out of the station. Pretty sure the whole town knows I'm the idiot with the camper full of diesel.

The following morning I joined my new friends for church. It was a small town Methodist church that reminded me a lot of the Lutheran Church my grandmother took me to as a child. I received a very warm welcome as Yvonne, Steve's wife, introduced me to the other church members. I love how everybody knows everybody here. With a population around 600, it wasn't hard to do.

After church Steve helped me tow the rig over to the mechanic shop where I was going to spend our last night. He had to work out of town in the morning so we said our goodbyes, and I headed across the street to the small bar and grill to spend the rest of the day watching baseball. While I was enjoying a cool draft, a gentleman came in and sat next to me. We struck up a conversation; I believe he told me he too was a vet. I can't remember for sure, because I was still trying to wrap my head around that this guy was Steve's brother, who just happened to pull up a stool next to me. Yup, it's that small of a town.

The next day I was up bright and early when the owner pulled up. I explained what the situation was to which he replied, "Oh, you're the dumb ass." Ok, the small town thing was starting to get old now. I just hung my head and raised my hand. "Guilty," I muttered. He just laughed and said it was no sweat, they could pump the gas tank out from the fuel rail. He said it would run like crap, smoke a lot at first, but would be fine. When I asked how much it would be, he said he would drain the tank and fill me up with premium for a 100 bucks; a smoking deal for sure. He then shook my hand and said, "Don't feel bad, I've done it too."

Back on Hwy 2, also known as the "Highline" to the locals, Kimber and I pressed on through countless miles of wheat pastures. Truly, the amber waves of grain sung about in *America the Beautiful*. The waves being caused by the wind that seemed to always be coming at you, regardless of your direction. We camped at a county park just south of Havre, MT for the night, then ventured on in the morning until we ran across a pretty significant battlefield.

I noticed the road sign for the Nez Perce National Historic Park and made the turn south into what looked like nothing but more grain pastures. I had no clue this was here, nor planned to visit this site. Now I realized that some historic parks are actually battlefields, which added an interesting dimension to completing this mission. This was a battlefield called Bear Paw, the final battle to corral the last of the Nez Perce tribe onto a reservation. The tribe was just 40 miles from the Canadian border, where they sought to be free when captured. What sticks in my mind the most about this was the smaller sign under the large welcome sign showing a cartoon-like brown hand holding out a rifle to an open and waiting gloved hand, obviously depicting disarmament and surrender, neither of which sat well with me. Isn't that a political firestorm wrapped into one little sign? Just another not so great tale of our American Military past. An interesting and unsuspected find, which made me think that I needed a map with all the National Parks and designators. This would prove important later.

From there, we camped twice more. One night at Nelson Reservoir, where we were overcome by an unbelievable amount of mosquitos. and then on the lake near Fort Peck. It seemed like I'd never get out of the state of Montana, when finally, we hit the North Dakota border; the state where my paternal grandmother was born. Montana, part two...COMPLETE.

North Dakota

July 24th, 2016. I remember flying on the plane to North Dakota with my grandma to go see great gramma. I barely remember pheasant hunting with my great grandfather, but I do remember distinctly, two kids that were older than me, feeding stink bugs to their pet monkey. I mean come on, what kid wouldn't, right? Funny the things you remember as a small child. No recollection of the terrain or what to expect otherwise; just monkeys. So far, there wasn't much difference from the Montana plains except for the oil rigs beginning to pop up here and there. Farmland slowly morphed into oil fields, but it was still flat as far as I could see. The first town had a BDubs where we stopped for lunch. I needed to check the map for Stanley, ND, the town where my great grandparents settled from Norway, and where I had visited as a small child.

We pulled into Stanley at dusk. Pretty much a single Main Street kind of town, that apparently rolled up everything at night. I actually found a small campground across the street from the town hall where you paid for your site. The campground was completely empty so finding a spot was easy. I let Kimber out to do her thing before I ventured into the only business that was open and had food; a small sports bar about a block away had a sign screaming pizza. Perfect, I was starving.

The bar was dark with only a few people inside. I found a spot in front of a TV with baseball on and ordered my food. I asked the bartender if he had heard of my grandparents or any of the Ericksons, which he did not. About that time two older gentlemen walked in. The bartender asked them if they knew of my family. One of them said, "Wally Erickson used to own the Standard station across the street years ago. I think he lives in Bismarck with his kids." I was shocked to learn that my Grandma's little brother and wife were still alive! He also said that if I went to the insurance office down the street, that they might know more. Awesome! The same guys, who were probably my Dad's age, also told me that my great grandfather was the county magistrate and had a couple of "come to Jesus" meetings with him in a jail cell. How cool is that! I was so glad I stopped in here for pizza!

The next day I was up early, throwing the ball for Kimber at a local dog park. After sufficiently wearing Kimber out, I did some research and actually found my grandparents headstone in the local cemetery. So many memories of my great grandma coming to California to visit. I sat down in front of the marker, wiping the dust and straightening the flowers. It was an emotional moment. When my grandparents passed I felt like this part of my family was gone. That's why when I heard Wally was still alive, I was elated. Next stop, the insurance company.

When I walked into the insurance office, I have to say I got some pretty strange looks. Full sleeve tattoos aren't really a thing in Stanley. After explaining who I was and inquiring about my great uncle, a lady emerged from the back room. "I knew your great grandparents. I did Gramma Erickson's hair when she passed. My sister owns their house on the corner, across from the Catholic Church," she said. Whoa, what?! They were also close friends with my Great Aunt Rainey. I asked if they could pass my number and information on to her, which they gladly did. I didn't even get back to the truck when my phone rang with a Bismarck, ND phone number. It was my Great Aunt Rainey. Before I knew it, I was on my way to see my long lost family.

When I pulled up to the address my Aunt gave me, I was a little concerned I had the wrong place. I mean come on, Aunt Rainey had to be pushing 90 right? There was a very nice golf club on the right side of street, and what looked like the Governor's mansion on the left. She said, "yup, that's it, turn left and we're the house on the right." There were three houses on the property, and wow were they amazing. Apparently my cousins had done very well in the insulation business, and owned a nation-wide company. A far cry from the tiny little house across from the church their grandparents lived in. Super cool! I spent the next two days meeting cousins and family I had no clue even existed.

We made plans to meet up for a pitchfork fondue at the Medora Music Festival, apparently the thing to do in North Dakota. I was excited to do anything with family, so I was definitely in. In the meantime, we had about a week to kill before the show. I decided not to waste any time, turning the Rig toward South Dakota to see the "heads," or what the North Dakota locals called Mt. Rushmore. But first there was a nearby battlefield I wanted to see.

I took I-94 west to Dickinson, then north on Hwy 22 to the town of Killdeer, just south of the Killdeer Mountain Battlefield State Historic Park. It seemed like a pretty self explanatory trip according to Google, then we hit dirt roads just outside of town. The first spot Google said was the battlefield turned out to be somebody's back yard. The second spot led us to a small parking lot that had one historical marker explaining the battle, and a couple of headstones of fallen soldiers.

Interestingly enough, this Indian battle took place in 1864, at the height of the American Civil War. Another Indian slaughter of several Sioux tribes as punishment from the Minnesota's Dakota Conflict several years earlier. Encamped here were major Sioux leaders, including Medicine Bear and Sitting Bull. Instead of ending a conflict, this slaughter started one. This was a prelude to the Sioux Wars of the 1870s. Not a National Battlefield, but still some heavy hitters worth noting were here.

On the way out of the parking lot I realized that my phone had died. No biggie, I just needed to reach down and grab this... and out from my hand flew the phone, that miraculously found the only hard piece of metal capable of shattering its screen. No freaking way. To top things off, I was way the hell out here and all twisted around, thanks to Google's impeccable navigation skills. Thank God my inner boy scout/Marine picked up on some land navigation points that I remembered on the way in. Gratefully, I found concrete a few miles up, turning south to Dickinson to see about a new phone. Thanks Murphy, good times.

That evening was spent in the town of Dickinson, drowning my sorrows in a cold beer and basket of chicken wings. Tomorrow we would roll to Mt. Rushmore, find a camping spot, and see whatever else the Black Hills of South Dakota decided to throw at us. Since we were coming back to North Dakota in a week, it's to be continued…

South Dakota

July 30th, 2016. I quickly learned that driving Hwy 85 south into South Dakota is taking your life into your own hands. The same flat rolling farmland, now with a two lane highway, and a wind that magically blows into your face from every direction, is now populated with crazy truckers, bikers going to Sturgis, and RVs being blown all over the road. It was a white knuckle drive until I saw a road sign pointing at a battlefield with a camping symbol underneath. I was done driving and needed a break, so off we went into the Custer National Forest in search of a campsite.

We ended up pulling into a deserted National Forest Campground. One of the spots by the road had electric with a small, metal donation container for the use. Pretty sure this used to be the camp host's spot. The other sites were free from what I could tell. They had some pretty old vault toilets but were stocked with paper; a lot like the free spot at Little Molas Lake in Colorado. It was a good place to stop for a couple nights and check out the battlefield just up the road. We opted for a spot away from the road with a lot more shade. After setting up camp and rolling out the smoker, Kimber and I settled in for a grilled steak and some well deserved relaxation. Hwy 85 was no joke.

The Battle of Slim Buttes is what the old metal designator sign read, posted next to a mound with a flag pole planted on top. A small, metal fence enclosed the mound with a few plastic flowers laid near by, faded by the sun. According to the sign, this was one of the final Sioux War battles after the disastrous Battle of Little Big Horn. The mention of Crazy Horse was here also, but very vague as to his role, other than he made a last stand of his own shortly after this battle, but the U.S. Army had gained reinforcements by that point and Crazy Horse stood down. Didn't say if he was captured. Another crazy find, man I love that, unsuspected history right under our feet.

The only thing I really knew about South Dakota was the Sturgis Motorcycle Rally held in the Black Hills, which included Mount Rushmore of course. What I didn't realize was that bike week was kicking off next week. This posed a problem for trying to find a campsite anywhere remotely near Sturgis, or near anything that even represented a hill with cooler temperatures. All of which I learned from the restaurant owner while having breakfast at a small diner in the town of Belle Fourche.

"I know the guy down the road here that has an RV park. Tell him I sent you, and that you're a vet." I thanked him for the breakfast and the advice, and sought out the RV park a few blocks away. Thankfully, he had plenty of spots which were fairly cheap with the vet discount. I decided it would be easiest to drop the trailer here while I went to check out Mount Rushmore. It was going to be pretty warm here, but the nights seemed to cool off enough to be comfortable. So I paid the man for four nights, set up camp, and spent the rest of the day throwing the ball for Kimber and battling the flies.

Belle Fourche, SD is the geographical center of the United States, and is where all the railroads converge to buy and sell cattle from all over the country. At least that's the town lore proudly displayed at a small museum downtown. Needless to say, I began to wonder if this town had a fly problem or the flies had a town problem. This was confirmed when the bartender at the local watering hole handed me a fly swatter with my beer. What made it even more incredible was the swap out of "troops" at dusk. The flies tag-teamed with the mosquitos, slapping wings as the sun went down, for their turn at the tourists.

First thing in the morning we headed out to see the "Heads." The terrain didn't start to change until we got into the town of Spearfish, where the Black Hills began. Beautiful rolling hills with actual trees and green grass was a welcome change. Eager to get off of Hwy 85, we took the fastest route to Mt. Rushmore on I-90, then planned to take the "Hill Country" route on the way back. Maybe just maybe, we would be able to find a camping site for the return trip from North Dakota next week.

Mt. Rushmore was a lot more than just giant heads cut into the mountainside. I was surprised to see very cool exhibits about the history and construction of this iconic American landmark. They also had a minor league baseball team here in the early 1900s that played in the nearby town of Deadwood! What I found really cool was the small tourist town just outside of the exhibit that was like walking back in time. A very cool experience that needs to be a bucket list for all Americans.

The weather in the Black Hills was remarkably cooler than back at the campsite. Gorgeous mountains with streams and lakes spotted throughout. This place was amazing! We turned south to see the Crazy Horse Monument, but the price was ridiculous and I was eager to explore the area. We stopped for lunch at a brewery in Hill City, took a dip in the cool water of the Pactola Reservoir, drove through the famous towns of Lead and Deadwood, before finally heading back to camp in the cooler evening air. Pretty sure we will be doing this "run to the cool water trip" tomorrow too. Awesome!

After a couple more days swimming in the Pactola Reservoir, it was time to head north again. I wasn't looking forward to driving that road again, but I wasn't passing up an experience with my new found family for anything. Once again, headlong winds tossed the Rig and destroyed my gas mileage. I was exhausted when I finally got to the Theodore Roosevelt National Park campsite, just outside of Medora, ND.

Luckily we found a spot and settled in for the night. The next morning, we had a visit from the biggest bison I had ever seen, who decided my campsite looked like the perfect place to roll in the dirt. This thing was the size of my covered trailer. Thankfully, the rangers came through and ran the campers out, due to a calf amongst these monsters. Apparently, bison are extremely protective of their young. These things made the bison in Yellowstone look like goats. HUGE!

Medora was a resort town of sorts, with the National Park and the Medora Music festival being the main attractions. An old west theme town with restaurants and small amusement park rides, pretty much what you would expect to see in a 1950s vacation movie. The show itself was something like a country vaudeville production with music, dancers, and gymnasts, all on one stage with a country western music genre. The best part was the "pitchfork fondue." They literally took several huge steaks, speared them on a regular pitchfork, and cooked them in giant pots of oil. It was quite the experience, and I was blessed to see it with my grandmother's side of the family; a side of me that I thought was gone. North Dakota, state #11. . .COMPLETE!

That night we said our goodbyes, stayed one more night at the campsite, and ventured south again on the dreaded Hwy 85. This time, Bike Week was in full swing, with motorcycles everywhere, most of which were piloted by people who shouldn't be on a motorcycle. I'd never experienced Bike Week and now that I was scooterless, I definitely wasn't going to partake in any of the festivities this time. So on we pushed to the Badlands National Park where I wanted to visit the Wounded Knee Battlefield.

Just south of the town of Wall was the entrance to the Badlands National Park, where the free camping site was a spectacular boondock spot that shouldn't be missed. There was a small service road that led back to a huge antenna farm, perched on the highest point above the Badlands, giving an amazing view of the valley below. We parked about 20 feet from the edge of a cliff, lined up with other RVs scattered along the rim. We were just staying the evening so didn't bother taking anything out of the camper. This was a good call, as a serious storm was heading our way. The skies began turning colors, the clouds started looking like giant cotton balls, and the wind was picking up enough to rock the truck and trailer. I decided to move the Rig, pointing the front toward the storm and the direction of the wind that was pushing 70mph easy. The radio station in Grand Rapids recommended folks get in their basements where there is concrete and metal pipes to protect you. I grabbed Kimber, bailed out of the camper, and got into the back seat of the truck. This was getting bad, the wind was picking up, and that cliff seemed to be closer than I had remembered. Kimber instinctively knew something was wrong and crawled down to the floor. I held on to her collar, with one foot pushing hard to prop open my door just slightly, thinking I may have to bail if the truck started to roll. All I could think was my little 20 lb dog would be a kite if I had to jump. Twenty minutes of this felt like 2 hours, but finally the wind began to let up. We made it. Unfortunately wind sound, to this day, scares Kimber pretty bad. After the storm cell had passed, we were treated to the most amazing double rainbow, sprouting from the multiple colors of the Badlands, surrounded by blue and purple skies. It was amazing, but I was glad to leave the next morning. That was the closest to a tornado I've ever been.

The Badlands National Park was surprising. It was back to a flat and arid terrain, but the colors of the sand and stone were amazing, like giant snow cones with multiple flavors of different colored ice; the rock layer colors were incredible. We spent most of the day enjoying the scenery, hoping to end it at the site of the Wounded Knee Massacre. Unfortunately, the whole thing was set up weird. The map said something about a visitor center all the way back in Wall, and the site being on the Lakota Reservation. Either way, I wasn't going all the way back to Wall, so we pressed on to Nebraska. South Dakota, state #12. . .COMPLETE!

Nebraska

August 9th, 2016. After driving to the southern point of the Badlands and realizing there was no way out other than the entrance I came in, we ended up back tracking through Wall after all. Not pleased with the added couple hours of driving, I just wanted to get into Nebraska and find some water to camp next to. So back to the I-90 west, then south on Hwy 385. It was a nice drive, but gradually becoming warmer as we neared the Nebraska state line. Much much warmer.

Not really knowing much about Nebraska other than corn and football, I wasn't sure what to expect, but assumed more very flat farmland. What I did not expect was the heat and humidity, but then again, being in AZ the last 20 years, everywhere is humid to me.

First town we hit was Chadron, where I stopped for some gas and noticed my trailer tire was almost flat. Really!? Of course Mr. Murphy would drop in when it was over 100f and nowhere near a town of size. Luckily, there was a local mechanic shop open that patched the tire and had us back on the road, free of charge. I think it could've had something to do with the manager being a Marine veteran. . .just maybe. Thanks, man! OOHRAH.

After ducking into a Walmart for ice and food as fast as I could, Kimber and I were in hot pursuit of the first sign of water we could find. Box Butte Reservoir State Rec Area fit that bill and was 45 minutes down the road. Thank God! A very long bumpy ride into the park, paid off with plenty of spots, clean facilities, and crystal clear water. We found a great site completely covered by tree shade, right on the bank. It was like a deserted island oasis, and I was in need of some down time. We ended up sitting there on the lake for a solid three days, recharging our batteries and staying cool. Kimber was ecstatic with ball throws into the water from dawn until dusk. She wasn't ready to leave when we packed up camp and headed off to see our first Nebraska Battlefield.

The Blue Water Battlefield proved to be more elusive than I cared to give effort to find. Especially as the temps kept creeping higher. I was done with the heat. I decided to try to catch Nebraska again on a future trip, made a hard right turn onto I-80 West, and headed for the cooler altitudes of Colorado. One of the greatest joys of living on the road is driving to an altitude and temperature that is best for you; now that's true freedom. Short but sweet, then again, all you really need to see in west Nebraska is "Carhenge" right? Nebraska, state #13… COMPLETE!

The next several weeks we spent camping and sight-seeing our way back toward Arizona. We dropped in on Great Uncle Wally's son, my cousin, in Loveland; drove through Estes Park and the Rocky Mountain National Park, where we drove the highest road in the continental U.S. Pretty cool!

We wandered our way south through Silverthorne, stopping in Leadville for a few days camping at the base of Mount Elbert, the highest peak in Colorado. From there we found a great boondocking sight near the town of Salida, a place that I fell in love with. Super cool little mountain town! From Salida we found the town of Gunnison that had a huge mountain bike park and tons of free camping. It was the perfect spot to wait out the rest of the month until payday. Funds were getting low and Arizona wasn't even close to being bearable yet, weather wise.

So back in Idaho when I was resting after surgery, I did a lot of posting my book page to several other pages on Facebook, trying to drum up some followers and "likes." Someone told me the more followers your page has, the better it looks to a future publisher. Why not? I had nothing better to do at that point. A few of the pages were veteran based and I received a pretty good amount of vets interested in my travels.

So fast forward to the present. I was cooking some dinner in the camper when this car pulled up to my campsite. Understand that I'm the only one parked up on this hill, near some boulders, with my nearest neighbor a quarter mile away and out of direct sight. To make it worse, I had a bit of an altercation with a kid on a dirt bike who flew past me and Kimber on the trail. So when this twenty something kid gets out of the car and walks towards my camper, I came out with my War face on. Instantly the kid says, "I know you! Baseballs and Battlefields, my friend in the Army follows your page." I was floored. Turned out this dude was going to college here in Gunnison, saw my post on FB about the area, and knew where I was. He came to say hello. How freaking cool is that!?

I guess this Facebook thing was paying off. Little did I know what I had begun when I shared my page on those other veteran FB pages. I had no clue how it would transform my travels and set me on a mission, something I suddenly and abruptly realized was what I was missing in my life. Stick with me, this is where it starts to get good!

After Gunnison we found our way to Telluride and a National Forestry Campsite just a couple miles outside of town. Hard to beat a week in Telluride at 12 bucks a night! Finally, the weather was cool enough to start our drive back to Arizona, putting my 2016 Mountain Run in the record books. With seven more states under our belt, bringing the total to 13, I was already looking forward to next year and what the road had in store for us.

The Southern States Run

2017

When we finally made it back to Arizona, I was exhausted but motivated. The next leg of the trip was the one I was looking forward to the most, but first there was work to be done. I had lived in Texas for a few years after my stint in the Corps, so I was well aware of the southern heat, humidity, and bugs. At least I thought I was.

So modifications to the Rig were a must; first and foremost was air conditioning. A small 120v window unit replaced the rear glass in the camper, powered by a 2,000 watt generator, if I couldn't find any electric to plug into. I also decided I was done towing a trailer, so I installed a bike rack on the front receiver hitch of the truck, and a cargo basket for the rear. The generator, grill, propane tank, and 6 gallon water container fit in the basket like it was made to be. I left the tail gate down this time, which fashioned as a sort of porch. The perfect sun deck for Queen Kimber. Jimmy hooked me up with brand new tires all the way around, the Rig was set.

I also made some adjustments to the inside. Removing the center table and actually using the top to mount the AC in the window, I installed a long plywood counter running from front to back, with a regular desk chair facing the window. A perfect writing desk and miniature mobile office. It was time to get serious about writing a book. This trip was gonna be too good not to.

I found it interesting that as most people are looking to move up into more spacious homes or RVs, I was looking to downsize. Looking back at all the homes I've owned, one being progressively larger and more expensive than the next, I also watched them go away in that exact, but reverse order. I was so done dragging that trailer with very little use of everything inside it. Plus my gas mileage, mobility, ability to boondock, all increased dramatically with this setup. I think I was learning that the fewer possessions you have, the more free you actually become. I had the homes, Harleys, high-end SUVs, and also the headaches that came with all of it. This was real freedom.

Kimber also needed some special attention for this trip. With all the bugs, specifically ticks, she got the full gamut of shots. Also some sort of oral chewy that makes her bulletproof from mosquitos for 6 months. Add a natural spray repellent to her coat on hikes, she was good to go. Trying to keep her out of gator filled water would be the real trick.

With the Rig and Kimber ready to hit the road, all that was left was to chart out a rough route. I've learned very well the last two years that the road and the Lord take you where they want you. So all I knew was that I wanted to follow the coastline the best I could, and since we did AZ spring training, might as well do Florida's too, which meant I had to be there by March. There was also going to be a grip of battlefields as we began to enter the Civil War states. I decided to do the Civil War from a southern prospective this trip, covering all 16 of the predominantly Confederate states, then next year, a view from the Union prospective. It just made sense that way since the NE would be freezing right now. So that was the plan; a very ambitious one, but the only constraints we had this time was the length of the baseball season, and funds of course.

Texas

January 11th, 2017. Kimber and I crossed the Texas border just before dawn. I've traveled this leg of I-10 many times while I lived in Texarkana, TX for about three years after leaving the Marines. It was a long desolate stretch of freeway that went on for an eternity. I decided that I would revisit the Alamo in San Antonio for my first Texas battlefield, then turn south to Brownsville where I would follow the coast from the Mexican border to Virginia.

It was a two day drive to San Antonio, and I was in need of a shower. The closest Anytime Fitness before San Antonio was in the small town of Kerrville, which also had a Walmart with a Chili's across the street. Perfect. After a workout and a shower, I found a spot at the local Walmart with other traveling motorists, set Kimber up with fresh water and food, and headed over to Chili's for a much needed meal and a cold beer.

t   As I was waiting for my food, a couple came in and sat at the stools next to me. They looked like they were my age, maybe a couple years older. About that time, the bartender brought my food. "Wow, that looks good. What is that?" asked the tall dark haired lady. I told her what menu item it was and started a conversation with her and her husband. Turned out she had two sons who were active duty Marines, and she was a very proud Texas Momma. Texans understand this more than most, as the military and its veterans are highly respected in this state. It also turned out they owned a radio station in town, 94.3 RevFM, The Rock of Texas. After a meal, a few beers and some great conversation, next thing I knew, I had an interview with Harley and the morning crew, live on air the following morning! Now that's the way to kick off this leg of the trip! What a great experience, thanks to my new found friends in Kerrville.

After the interview, I was on cloud nine driving into San Antonio. An even greater sense of direction and motivation seemed to take over. I was pumped, and I now had a mission to complete. I finally felt like "somebody" again. It's amazing what having a purpose in life does for the soul. Just as startling is how life seems meaningless without one. This time though was different. I had veterans from all over the country following my Facebook page. Invites for ballgames, visits to hometown battlefields, and hearing other vets preparing to travel due to my inspiration was humbling and transformational.

The Alamo is another must see site for all Americans, especially Texans. The Battle of the Alamo was a turning point in the Texas Revolution, known for the brutality of the Mexican General, Santa Ana, who slaughtered all the Texan defenders. "Remember the Alamo!" was the battle cry that united American adventurers and Texan settlers in the war against Mexico.

After walking around downtown San Antonio, taking in the sights of the Alamo and the surrounding iconic buildings, we headed south toward the border. First overnight stop was in the small town of Alice, TX; moving on the next day to Brownsville, TX; ending at Boca Chica Beach. This was the first public beach north of the Mexican border.

Our next stop was at the Palo Alto Battlefield National Historic Park. Say that three times fast. I found the place last winter, while trying to research all the different types of National Sites which were actual battlefields. Unlike the Indian War sites, this National designator was for an obvious reason; this was the very first battle of the Mexican American War. The museum held some interesting artifacts, the first being something called a grapeshot or canister shot. Imagine an artillery shell filled with steel baseballs, like a giant shotgun shell. Absolutely brutal. The second was the ornately carved sword, that looked similar to the Marine NCO sword, given to a Lt. Pemberton for gallantry. Remember this name, he shows up again later. The grounds were basically marshlands with cannons facing each other, representing the artillery battle that this fight became. After the battlefield walk, I decided to move on, weather was inbound, and I was tired of driving.

With it being January, the beach was completely empty, except for a couple in a van from Quebec who didn't speak much English. Kimber was excited to be out of concrete parking lots, chasing the ball on the beach and continuing her battle with small gulf coast waves. I didn't see any "no overnight parking" signs, so we settled in for the night, excited to continue along the TX coastline.

The excitement slightly diminished as I realized there wasn't a main coastal highway or even a road that came close to the water. From Boca Chica Beach to Corpus Christi seemed to be marshland, with Hwy 77 being the only road heading north, a few miles inland from the gulf. So north we went for what seemed an eternity, until we came across Kingsville Naval Air Station.

It was starting to get dark on a Friday night when I pulled into the front gate of the base. I had seen online that there was an RV park here and asked the gate guard for directions. He told me where it was but added that the office was closed and to check in with the campground host. After finding a spot, the campsite host, who turned out to be the base provost Marshall (military police commander), came over to say hello. A super nice guy who was an active duty naval officer living with his wife and teenage daughter in a fifth wheel while their house was being built in town.

It seemed to be a pretty tight knit group of mainly retired military folks "snow-birding" in the mild Texas winter. The host invited me over for beers later and introduced me to the crew. There were only dry campsites left, and with the humidity, I was going to need some AC. I asked if I could run the generator, but received a resounding "hell no!" "Just run a cord from my plug. Ya'll need a cord?" I was asked. Gotta love Texas, some of the most friendly folks I've ever known.

The humidity during the winter months was something I wasn't prepared for. I knew about the summer, but needing to turn on the AC to keep dry, while I froze to death, was new for sure. My maps, books, and papers were starting to curl from the moisture, so I grabbed a hoodie and sweat pants, bundled up Kimber and myself, and turned on the AC with it being only in the 50s at night.

That Sunday I went to church with Kingsville NAS's top cop and his family. Feeling completely out of place in my T-shirt and tattoos, the congregation made me feel right at home. I can't count how many folks shook my hand and thanked me for my service. Afterwards we went back to the camp, fired up the grills, and settled in for some football that evening. One of the guys picked up Kimber's tennis ball and gave it a toss, activating "ball mode." Little did he know that he just opened the floodgates. Almost 3 hours later, and continuous pestering from my little dog, he looked at Kimber and asked if she ever got tired. Nope... no she does not.

Monday morning we decided to move on, trying to keep the time frame of making it to Florida by March. I learned that Kingsville NAS allowed you to stay as long as you wish for $350 a month rent. This was awesome! Full access to a huge gym, beautiful sports field with rubber track, huge enlisted club, and basically empty all the time as it's a reservist base. I will definitely remember this for the future, and will be looking for other bases that offer the same.

From Kingsville we drove just 45 minutes to Corpus Christi, hoping to find a campsite near the beach. Padre Island National Seashore fit this bill perfectly. Malachite Beach Campground was half price and completely full, except for the disabled parking. Not excited about using my half price card as a handicap placard, but just like California, we were lucky to get a spot, so I took it. I almost wanted to fake a limp so I wouldn't have folks pissed I took the campsite.

After a shower, I let Kimber out of the camper to do her thing. Of course she instantly saw people across the street and went to say hello. This seems like no big deal, but not everybody likes dogs, especially ones off leash and jumping into their car. Thankfully, the young couple across the road didn't seem to mind. Enter my new friends Nate and Laurel, a young couple in their early 30s from Minnesota, traveling the country in a minivan. We struck up a conversation and quickly became friends. Kimber turned out to be an amazing judge of character as we also met a couple and their kids from Oakland, CA, and a solo RVer from Canada named Rusty, thanks to her loving nature and overwhelming puppy cuteness. All of us pitched in that evening for a great taco night, telling road stories and making plans to meet up again in the future. Once again, road friends are lifelong friends. Freaking awesome!

From Padre Island we followed the coast as close as possible, stopping at a free campsite called Magnolia Beach in Port Lavaca for the night. Then on to Bay City for a famous oyster po' boy sandwich. If it wasn't so crowded on the coasts, I could definitely get used to fresh seafood all the time. Add Texas BBQ and Cajun food; I'd be 300lbs in no time.

We drove all the way to Galveston that day, once again hoping to find a coastal seashore beach. Unfortunately we were unsuccessful. I had no idea what a tourist area Galveston was, being mainly a resort like town with a lot of restaurants and hotels, and not allowing beach camping or overnight parking. Even when we pulled into the only Walmart on the island, we were immediately followed by a security car, letting me know there was no overnight parking. Great. The only campground I found nearby was a state-run park, which required reservations. This wasn't good. We had been driving all day and were in serious need of a parking spot. We ended up driving all the way to Stowell, TX where we thankfully found a free site at the local fairgrounds.

The next day we drove through Port Arthur and all the oil refineries, toward another Texan battlefield. It was bizarre to drive under the numerous pipes that ran across the road, just above the traffic lights. We passed huge oil tankers moving slowly up the waterways into Lake Sabine, finally arriving at Sabine Pass Battlefield State Historical Site.

Surprisingly this was a Civil War Battlefield, not a Texas Revolution or Mexican War site. It was here in 1863 that only 50 Confederate soldiers defeated a Union force of more than 5000 men, preserving Texas as a Confederate stronghold. But wait, we're not done yet. Fast forward to WW2. A total of 24 German submarines attacked ships in the Gulf of Mexico sinking 56 and damaging 14 more. Whoa what!?! Nazi subs off the coast of Texas? Ya, me neither. Ironically, one of the ships the Germans sank was the freighter SS Robert E. Lee.

After exploring the battlefield and taking plenty of pictures, we hit the road heading east across the Louisiana state border, wrapping up this portion of our Texas visit. I would be back later in the baseball season to catch the two Texas ballparks, unfortunately not in such nice cool weather. Texas, state #14… almost complete.

Louisiana

January 27th, 2017. We were up at the crack of dawn to visit Sabine Pass, which put us at around 7am when we crossed into Louisiana. Wanting to hug the coast as closely as possible, I took Hwy 82 west toward Holly Beach, a place recommended by a local. The first thing that caught me off guard was to stand on the coast and watch the sunrise, and eventually set, all from the same location. Being on the west coast all my life, seeing the sunset over the ocean, the change was substantial and somewhat bizarre. Either way, the view was spectacular as the morning light reflected off the surprisingly calm gulf water.

The beauty slowly escaped as you traveled further into the Louisiana marshlands. The devastation from Hurricane Katrina was still apparent and abundant. There was still wreckage and debris in some areas, where others had rebuilt, with every single structure being on stilts. From mobile homes to gas stations, the local high school and town library, all were built on stilts or concrete footings that were around ten feet in the air. I had to chuckle at the boats on the ground, tied to the deck of a mobile home on stilts, with its rope swinging in the air. Not to mention the fishing poles at the ready. Comical, yet sad.

Holly Beach was a small tourist like town that used to flourish prior to Katrina. Now it seemed to be a memory of past glory. Brand new beach houses stood with others in varied levels of construction, while other lots were covered with debris or completely bare. I was hoping to find a spot for a couple days of beach camping here, but decided to move on.

The beach started to give way to swamp, and camping spots were few and far between. It was early in the afternoon when we happened upon Palmetto Island State Park; the only campground I could find for miles. When we pulled up to the front gate, there was a line of RVs checking in, which didn't bode well for me finding a spot. Apparently this was a popular snow-bird park during the winter months, and reservations were recommended. The lady in the booth said I was welcome to look around, so we pulled in, hoping for the best.

Just as she said, the park was full of reserved spots. Pretty much empty on a Thursday evening, but nowhere to park. That was frustrating. People reserve a spot and then don't show up or come in the following day. This park didn't have a first come first serve area, and it being a state park, my federal access pass offered no help with a disabled spot.

We stopped by a fishing lake to walk Kimber and stretch our legs before we sought out the closest Walmart for the evening. We took what was called the "nature loop" trail that wandered through the woods and marsh between the different camping areas. I was of course on high alert for snakes, gators, and anything else that might consider my little dog, or me, a snack.

As we walked along the trail, it turned from dirt to fairly deep mud. That's when I noticed Kimber stop to investigate a small brown mound. Thinking it was some sort of animal poop, I yelled at Kimber to get away. But as I got closer, I realized it was a bunch of marble sized mud balls stacked up about 6 inches high with a 1-inch hole in the center. Instantly I grabbed Kimber and started walking fast. If that thing was some sort of a wasp mound, those things had to be monsters! Then I began to see them everywhere, there were literally dozens of little cannon ball mounds. Nope... we're out. I turned toward the way we came in, walking fast yet avoiding the mud ball piles like IEDs. Later that night, while throwing the ball for Kimber on a grassy patch near Walmart, I saw more of those mounds. I mentioned them to a Walmart clerk rounding up baskets. "Wasps? What wasps?" the clerk asked. I pointed at the mounds. "Man, those ain't wasps. Those are crawfish mounds." We both had a good laugh.

Full disclosure. When I lived in Texas for those few years, we used to go to Shreveport, LA quite a bit, where I developed a taste for "mudbugs," also known as crawfish. I loved to eat those little "crawdads," what we called them in the creeks of NorCal, but had no idea what their houses looked like. Mudbugs. It all made sense now. Driving through the countryside, you would see these muddy fields with some sort of grass growing in rows. Along the rows were square metal boxes every so many yards. These were the tops to the crawfish cages that were submerged under water. These were crawfish fields! I was amazed. Here I was thinking these things were in the ocean. Either way, boiled with the right amount of spice, these things are to die for! If you ain't sweatin', you ain't eatin', when it comes to mudbugs.

Later that evening I got a call from Nate and Laurel, the Minnesota couple from Texas. They said they'd be rolling through Lafayette in a couple of days and wanted to see if I was close to meet up. Perfect, I was just down the road in Abbeville, which would give me time to scout out a Walmart for us to meet and stay the night. The Breaux Bridge Walmart was the perfect spot, right off of I-10, and across the street from a great crawfish place that I tried out before my friends showed up. Perfect, this was gonna be fun.

The next day, with time to kill before Nate and Laurel arrived, Kimber and I found an awesome sports park nearby, complete with mountain bike paths and soccer fields. We were pretty much the only ones there at 9am, so I called Nate and Laurel to have them meet me here for a BBQ before heading back to Walmart for the evening.

After plans were set, Kimber and I found a picnic bench and started setting up the BBQ. That's when I noticed the parking lot starting to fill up. It was a Saturday morning and the soccer teams were showing up for games. It didn't seem out of the ordinary until I noticed that they were all grown men, not kids; and they were looking at me inquisitively. One young Hispanic girl came up and asked what kind of food I was selling, then ran back to the food truck her dad was setting up. That's when I realized I was the only white person in the park, at least that I could see. The entire parked filled up with Hispanic folks, but not Mexicans. Being from Arizona adult soccer leagues wasn't unusual, but the flags they had weren't Mexican, they were Honduran. Hundreds of Hondurans in central Louisiana? Seemed like a huge change from the Louisiana I knew many years ago.

Later that afternoon, Nate and Laurel showed up. By this time the parking lot was completely full, and I had to save a parking spot with a folding chair, which didn't help my standing with the locals. We smoked up some ribs and had a few beers while we chatted about the last few weeks' travels. That's when I started to notice the sound of a deep base and gangster looking cars start to roll through the parking lot as the day progressed. More guys in their 20s, but this time with gold teeth, gold chains, and baggy clothes. These Hondurans weren't here for soccer; and they had taken up an interest in us being there. I decided it was best if we moved on, which Nate agreed. This was definitely a shock to see in central Louisiana.

Later that evening, after finding a spot for the night at Walmart, we ventured across the street to introduce my northern friends to the heaven-sent mudbugs. If I remember right, Nate and I opted for the medium heat on a 5lb serving of crawfish between the two of us, while Laurel sensibly ordered the gumbo. She wasn't falling for it. After a pound or two in, Nate's face was bright red with beads of sweat forming quickly. They were pretty spicy for mediums, as I was sweating pretty good too. Match that with some ice cold Abita beers; good food, great friends, amazing Louisiana memories.

The next morning was a little rough, but survivable. Nate and Laurel were heading to a reserved campsite across Lake Pontchartrain from New Orleans, a state park again of some sort, and invited us to share their spot. Since the Battle of New Orleans and a visit to the French Quarter was already on my itinerary, I gladly accepted. I was hoping to see a battlefield near Baton Rouge, which was on the way, so we packed up our rigs and jumped on I-10 east. I was heading to Port Hudson, while Nate and Laurel went into Baton Rouge, making plans to meet at the Fontainebleau State Park in a day or two.

Port Hudson was the battle site that I was hoping to visit but was unfortunately closed on Mondays and didn't open until Wednesday. Since it was a state park and not a National Battlefield or monument, I decided to move on. I grabbed a quick workout and shower at the local Anytime Fitness and went to meet up with Nate and Laurel.

Setting the maps app to "avoid highways" is the best part about having GPS navigation. It's going to take you on the most direct route, on any and every old back road it can find. Places that you would never even know were there, let alone how to get to them. If you take anything away from this book, heed this advice. America is found on the backroads, not on the freeways. It's the small-town shops, and seeing the homes that folks live in. It's seeing real people in day to day lives that interest me, not a tourist trap or big city where you are people's income. They have to be nice to you, regular people, doing regular things... don't. That's where the "real" part comes in. I hate driving the freeways anyway, so I got off of I10 as soon as I could, taking a small two lane highway through the back country to the campground.

Part of the drive followed a river where once again you saw the devastation of Hurricane Katrina. The same varying levels of rebuilding going on. All the houses were on stilts like at the coast, with boats tied off to a very slow-moving river. Other lots were still just rubble, where it was obvious folks chose to leave or abandon their property rather than rebuild. Who knows, but I'm sure the stories are heart wrenching. This wasn't a very affluent area whatsoever.

Mandeville was a different story. This was a very expensive, high-end area, directly over the Pontchartrain Causeway, which is probably the longest bridge I've ever seen in my life, connecting Mandeville to New Orleans. About 20 minutes outside of town is the Fontainebleau State Park, an absolutely massive area with camping, day use picnic areas, a really nice beach area, and a whole lot of "Beware of Gator" signs. Beauty has its price, I guess. Either way, we met up with Nate and Laurel, and settled in for the night before we ventured into New Orleans. It was quite a relief to have a safe spot to drop off the bike and cargo basket before venturing into our first major city of this trip. I was pretty sure this was going to be a tight and crowded expedition when it came to parking in the French Quarter.

First step to New Orleans was the causeway, that literally felt like we were driving to Hawaii. Two lanes in each direction seemed to go on forever into the horizon. It wasn't until about mile 19 of the 24 mile bridge, that you actually saw the skyscrapers of New Orleans. Ya, it was that long. Then add the fog or low clouds, it was an interesting drive for sure.

First stop was to visit one of the many famous cemeteries, known as the "City of the Dead." Incredible to see all the massive stone tombs, closely lined together like small houses on an ancient cobblestone street, hence the description of it being a "city." From there Nate and Laurel headed downtown, while Kimber and I headed to the site of the Battle of New Orleans, on the outskirts of the city. We made plans to meet up later in the French Quarter before heading back across the lake.

The Chalmette Battlefield located just east of New Orleans, also known as the Battle of New Orleans, was the final conflict between England and America, ending the War of 1812. This is the war that saved New Orleans, began the peace with England we know today, and propelled Andrew Jackson's popularity and career to the White House. An incredible piece of land indeed.

Today it has a small visitor center with a huge obelisk marking the battle location. There are a few cannons, a very old farm house, and a path that is about a mile long around the property. It's interesting to get such a solemn feeling for what occurred here, while at the same time seeing locals use the path as a lunchtime jogging trail. I'll expand more on this thought later in the story.

Kimber and I walked the trail in the excruciating humidity. Ya I know, it was only February, but coming from AZ... it was brutal. Even Kimber was wrecked after only a mile. One of the spots on the trail was the original farm house, with a nice cool marble floor. Kimber laid spread eagle, with her belly smashed against the cold stone, while I gazed out what would have been the front door. I could only imagine being a sugar plantation owner and seeing two countries commencing ground battle with cannons and muskets... in my front yard! I tried to imagine what I would be feeling, watching this with my family. Terrified and helpless, I'm assuming, would be the two main emotions surging at that point. Kimber stood up and broke my thought; I noticed I had goosebumps, while I was sweating. History will move you, if you let it.

After lunch and a cool-down in the truck's AC, we headed to the French Quarter to meet Nate and Laurel. The looks of the locals as I drove this full-size truck and oversized camper down the one-way single lane roads, lined with parked cars on either side, were priceless. Hey, if a fire truck can do it, I can do it. I wish I had a picture of the Rig crossing Bourbon Street with a street band playing at the intersection. The whole crowd looked over at the Rig, with the driver and dog grinning out the window. Priceless.

We found a 24 hour parking lot where I backed into a spot with the camper door so close to a block wall that you couldn't get in. The French Quarter has a bit of a reputation for crime. Here's the thing, it was 8 bucks for 24 hours. Nothing like having a hotel room, walking distance from Bourbon Street, for 8 bucks a night. You tracking me!? Something to consider for the next time coming through, and something to look for in other cities.

Directly across from the parking lot was a cigar shop where I met up with Nate and Laurel. We picked out a couple sticks for later that night and walked down to Bourbon St. Now granted, this was in the early afternoon, on a weekday, so there were mainly vendors making deliveries and trash trucks taking out last night's party. Either way, it smelled exactly like the trash can behind the bar, after the bag rips, when you take it to the dumpster. Bartenders and bouncers can smell these words. Ya, the stench was bad. We walked a few blocks and headed back on Royal St., a much cleaner and family friendly experience. After we had our fill of the French Quarter, we headed back to camp for a BBQ and cigars.

When I got back to camp, Nate and Laurel had already stopped to get beer at the local liquor store. They had these small styrofoam cups filled with daiquiris, free with the twelve pack of beer. What?! Apparently the owner was trying to get the word out about the new slushee machines with free samples. I wanted one and Nate was ready for another, so we headed over to sample the wares. When the guy handed them to us... through the drive-thru window... they had the regular plastic top with a straw on the side, not stuck in the lid. As an old bar scene worker, I instantly asked about open container laws. The owner said, "As long as you don't put the straw in it, it's not open. Just crack the lid and sip it." Welcome to NOLA!! The daiquiris were really good. So good that the 32oz cup drained fast enough to make for a pretty rough ride out of Louisiana the next morning. Nate and Laurel were heading to the NE, while I continued along the coast toward Florida. Saying goodbye to my friends, we made plans for when I made it up to Minnesota. Louisiana, state #15... COMPLETE!

Mississippi

February 3rd, 2017. We crossed the Mississippi state line with a full bank account and no idea what to expect. This was the furthest into the "deep" South that I had ever been. So the plan was to venture north into Mississippi, over to Alabama and back down to the coast, panhandle to panhandle, setting us up to enter Florida March 1st, just in time for Spring Training to kick off. There were several National Battlefields to explore, especially now moving from the Indian and Mexican Wars headfirst into the heart of the American Civil War. A war that I had no real opinion of and quite honestly didn't have that much excitement for learning about. I was more of a Revolutionary War, American Patriot, 'Murica!, sort of guy. Little did I know how much my eyes would be opened to this part of American history; the history that I thought I knew.

So when it came to the Civil War, I really didn't have a dog in the race. My family was all pretty much west coast born and bred, and the ones that did come over from Norway and Sweden, came well after the war. The only hint at having any type of ties to the Civil War would be my maternal, great grandfather's last name... Jackson. There were some possible Scotch/Irish ties to both Andrew Jackson and Stonewall Jackson, most of which I considered to just be some tall family tales. So with that being said, we had two weeks to check out Mississippi; this should be interesting.

The first thing you notice about driving the coastal road into Gulfport is the absolutely incredible white sand beaches. Later I would find out that this stretch of beach was the largest man-made beach in the world. What? Man-made? An old local gentlemen told me that they brought all the sand in from the Mississippi River after Hurricane Katrina. "Think about it, no waves in the gulf. Can't make sand," he said. He had a point. Now those white sand beaches are resorts with massive casinos, a hidden spot that would rival any tropical destination. I'd remember this for sure.

I had to stop and let Kimber play on the beach, her next favorite venue to a baseball field. The sand was perfectly white and fine as granulated sugar. It was bizarre how fine the sand was, and within two throws, Kimber looked like a sugar cookie. After sufficiently wearing her out with the ball, I stopped at a park bench to take in the view. That's when I noticed the Mississippi state flag flying proudly under the Stars and Stripes on a flagpole near the park benches. For those that don't know, the Mississippi State flag has the Confederate flag, also known as the Battle flag in its top left corner. This has caused a lot of stir and emotions to flair, especially since President Trump took office. It also reminded me of a situation last winter.

Prior to leaving Arizona this past winter, I had met some folks from Mississippi camping at Lake Roosevelt. He was a disabled Navy veteran enjoying a week with his cousin and girlfriend by the lake. We quickly became friends and were sitting around the campfire when a couple walked by, out for an evening stroll. Without even a hello, they asked why we were flying "that" flag, and that's a Confederate flag, a loser's flag, and on and on. Obviously not from here and with a very distinct NE accent, they kept at it. That's when my friend politely said he was a Navy vet and that is the Mississippi state flag, where he was from. They didn't care. They kept on as they walked by, finally disappearing down the road. About 30 minutes later, a Sheriff drove up to the campsite, rolled down his window, and said, "What's up with the flag?" After explaining the story of what happened, the Sheriff rolled his eyes, thanked us and drove off. We chuckled at how ignorant folks can be. The next morning, my friend's generator had sugar in its tank and cost a disabled veteran a thousand dollars to replace. Pathetic and sad. In my humble opinion, the flag is historical, no it shouldn't be changed, too bad if it offends you, it's over, let it go.

It was starting to get dark, and I was thirsty for an ice cold beer and some dinner. As luck would have it, I found a BDubs just a few doors down from the Walmart. Perfect. After dinner we settled in for the night, planning to visit Beauvoir, the post war home of the Confederate President Jefferson Davis, and his presidential library.

We were up at the crack of dawn as the big rigs in the parking lot fired up their motors. In a hurry to find some coffee, I jumped out of the trailer to throw some trash away and met another RVer doing the same. The dude had a Coast Guard ballcap on, cup of coffee in one hand, trash bag in the other, flip flops and board shorts, walking from a rig with Cali plates. Of course I had to stop and ask where he was from. Turned out he was out of the Los Angeles area, doing some traveling with his girlfriend, while he worked online out of the RV. Seemed to be a trend. I told him about my travels and how we were headed to Florida to see some spring training. He too was heading to Florida; we exchanged info and got them set up on my book page, hoping to meet up for a game next month. Super cool! I love meeting the coolest folks and becoming "road friends," keeping in touch, exploring new places, and giving advice and tips of places already visited to newbies heading that way. Keep in touch bro!

After breakfast we went back to the beach to visit Beauvoir, the Jefferson Davis Library and home. The tour of the house itself was pretty amazing. The most impressive being that the house was built prior to the Civil War with heart of spruce flooring that was under three feet of water during Katrina, and remained flat with no warping. From a former home builder's standpoint, that was amazing. They also showed how they painted the corners to give a 3D effect, like having an ornate crown molding.

The house was actually built by a friend of Davis who offered her guest house for him to write his memoirs after his release from prison. He later bought the home from her friend, after completing his book "The Rise and Fall of the Confederate Government." Today, Beauvoir is not only the family home, but his Presidential Library and a Confederate Cemetery. An interesting beginning to my Civil War expedition. I honestly hadn't even given it consideration that there would be a Confederate White House, Confederate Presidential Library, and other such iconic institutions that we have today. Interesting.

This stop was the perfect starting place, as it gave me the much needed groundwork into history that wasn't taught in school, or at least not to this depth, such as the different flags the Confederates used, uniforms, and a timeline of events prior and leading to the war. It also went into depth about the Davis family, how Jefferson Davis served as Mississippi U.S. Senator, Secretary of War, and was an engineer who graduated from West Point. He was also in charge of building the dome on Congress that we see today. I highly recommend this tour to all history enthusiasts, it's eye opening.

The night before at Walmart, I was charting my route through Mississippi by marking all the Anytime Fitness locations, mountain bike parks, national forests, and of course battlefields, when my cousin called me. She had been through Mississippi and said I needed to take what's called the Natchez Trace, some sort of road that goes through the parks system. So with all that spinning in my head, I found Natchez on the map, with a couple bike parks and a gym on the way. Off we went, after giving Kimber the chance to imitate a sugar cookie again, of course. This dog!

The first bike park was just outside of town, with a small bathroom and even picnic tables and remnants of a fire pit. According to the map, we were in the DeSoto National Forest, something I had no idea Mississippi even had. I assumed Mississippi looked about the same as Louisiana with mainly swamp and farmland. Instead, we found lush pine and fern covered foothills that had some banks and climbs rivalling any mountain, but the floor was a combo of pine needles and fine sand. Add some pretty steep ravines down to rivers and creeks and it made for some awesome single-track riding. Kimber had a blast keeping up with me, which wasn't hard as I was trying to catch my wind in this foreign entity called humidity. I decided to camp right there and grill some dinner that evening, which was awesome, as we met so many folks out to enjoy the forest. With Kimber being the welcoming party to anyone passing by, we met plenty of new friends and page followers.

Next stop was the Wiggins Anytime Fitness for a quick workout and much needed shower, then NW toward the town of Natchez and the start of the Natchez Trace. We found an interesting bike park just north of the town of Brookhaven on the edge of the Homochitto National Forest, called Mt. Zion. It looked to be private property but set up just for mountain bikers. It had a sitting area with fire pit, several bench swings, a place to hose down and wash your bike, and even a refrigerator with popsicles. They asked for a donation for upkeep, but didn't require it.

The trails had all types of obstacles and levels of experience. What a great place; wish I could've met the owners.

At this point I was ready to settle into a campsite for a few days and relax. I love to be on the go, but boondocking and surfing Walmart parking lots can take a toll, plus we had two weeks to kill. The Clear Springs Campground in the Homochitto National Forest was just the ticket with full hook ups and showers! Half price was $12.50 a night, a bit of a splurge but so incredibly worth it.

It was a great campground with lake, fishing, swimming, and hiking/biking trails. Most importantly, they had nice facilities with hot showers, flush toilets, and sinks with mirrors. Things we take for granted, right? It only lacked one thing, cell reception. Normally it wouldn't have been an issue, but we didn't even have radio reception. We were in a bit of a valley, especially down by the lake, with no reception whatsoever. I didn't even notice or miss it honestly, until Kimber and I left for a hike.

The campgrounds were basically empty save a few campers and the volunteer camp host. It was still early in the season and weather was supposed to be coming in. Overcast but cool, Kimber and I set off to hike a trail to the hilltop, scouting out mountain bike possibilities for later, when I caught a raindrop on my cheek. A big one. That's when I realized the sky had gotten a lot darker and clouds were looking ominous. We had just broke the crest of the hill and could see weather was definitely heading our way. That's when my phone startled me with a message tone. We had service. The message was from a family friend asking if I had been blown away by a storm. Not sure what he was talking about, I called him. Turned out New Orleans just got pounded by a hurricane level storm, literally days after we had left! And now it was turning inland... toward us.

Needless to say, Kimber and I picked up the pace going downhill and back to camp. As we got closer to our site, I noticed all the other campers were gone, with fires still smoldering and fresh firewood left behind. They left fast. I walked past the camp host's spot to see what the news was. She said she would honk her truck horn to let me know if I had to take shelter. The showers were made of block and doubled as a storm shelter. Oh lovely. Flashbacks of South Dakota started flooding my mind, here we go again. Luckily only some very hard rain, and plenty of leaks in the camper, was all we had to suffer through. I still can't believe we were just in New Orleans. Thank you, Jesus!

Still dreary but not pouring rain, we broke camp and headed into the town of Natchez to find a Walmart for supplies and some breakfast. Just outside of town was the beginning point for the Natchez Trace. This was a road that cut through the center of Mississippi, from Natchez all the way to Nashville. Natives first used this road, followed by settlers, traders, and even immigrants until as late as the 19th century. Today it's operated by the National Park Service, with certain portions deemed as historical sites. So basically, it's a very long country road, gorgeous scenery, a couple small campgrounds, a lot of stops with historical information and bathrooms. One strange stop was an ancient Indian burial mound or something to that effect. It was like somebody made the first level of a soccer field sized pyramid and called it good. Seemed more like a raised landing platform to me. Either way, it was an interesting visit.

The Trace does have one leg of the road that splits off towards Vicksburg, which is where we visited our first National Military Park. The first thing I came across was the Mississippi Visitor Center, just south of town, overlooking the Vicksburg Bridge and the Mississippi River. Good place to get some info, stretch our legs, and set up a game plan; not to mention the "free coffee" sign didn't hurt.

Inside, I found the coffee, some free maps of the state and local area, and some recommendations for supper. Outside, there was a walkway to an overlook that actually was a small part of the Vicksburg Battlefield. It was a gun embankment, with a couple of cannons and some placards explaining the position, and the town's importance to both sides. This was basically the main shipping hub for the South, a major victory for the North, and a pivotal turning point for the war. I took a picture of the huge cannon, with a modern hotel and street signs behind it. So strange to see this in an urban setting. Something I would soon learn was the norm for the South.

One old, metal, historical placard that I had found interesting was right outside the Visitor Center's front door. It read, "Beginning on May 16, 1863, Gen. U.S. Grant held this city under siege, cutting off all supplies & driving citizens to caves to escape shells. C.S.A. Gen. John C. Pemberton finally surrendered July 4." Pemberton? Wait a minute. Back in Texas at the Battle of Palo Alto, we saw the sword that Pemberton earned for gallantry, which he now surrendered to U.S. General Grant. WHOA! They served together in the U.S. Army as lieutenants against Mexico, and now facing off as enemies. That's right, now I remember! Ok, now that's pretty cool. You got my attention, Vicksburg.

From there we drove around the town and port of Vicksburg. I'm not gonna lie, the place was rough. Really rough. With only a small area that had some tourist restaurants and shops, this town was falling apart, maybe due to the historical aspect, maybe lack of jobs, whatever; Vicksburg was pretty bad. I wasn't even comfortable at the Walmart for the night, opting for a truck stop further up the road.

The next day we went to the Vicksburg National Military Park just north of town. The park map shows that it actually surrounds the city of Vicksburg, which makes sense as Vicksburg is located on a bluff, high above the Mississippi River. I see why it's called a Military "Park." It's like driving into a huge county park, with a visitor center, trails and roads filled with bicyclists, hikers, and joggers. The only difference is the huge stone markers, giant marble memorials adorned with unbelievably ornate bronze statues… and cannons, lots of cannons.

First thing I did was go inside the Visitor Center where there was usually a short video and a museum of artifacts unearthed from that area. This was the way you got a solid idea as to what happened here, who was fighting who, and all the other parameters of the situation. Then you walk out and see the weapons, clothes, artifacts, etc. on display in the museum. Finally, you're armed with the knowledge and general understanding to go hike or drive the actual battlefield. This is how we learned to roll.

This place was so big that I could have hiked for 3 days and not seen everything. The concrete roads were lined with ornate stone markers, donated from the states that the troops were from, and life-like busts of the commanding officers who lead the troops into battle like giant chess pieces facing the direction they were fighting in the battle. Red placards with Confederate troop information facing one-way, blue placards with Union troop information facing the opposite way, sometimes just mere yards apart. It was an absolutely incredible feeling to stand on the actual ground where the fighting happened. Imagining the scene, following the troop movements, hiking the actual trails and tunnels the soldiers did, not to mention the USS Cairo exhibit. This was one of the famous ironclad ships that was torpedoed and sunk by the South, on display with its huge hole in the hull. Yup, chills were abundant that day.

What struck me the most was the sheer brutality of the time. Vicksburg was a crucial victory for the North, but some pretty brutal tactics were used against the populace. Women and children hid in caves starving, while the North cut off supply lines, continuously shelling the city. None of which I heard about in history class. Added to the sheer number of casualties, it was mind

132

boggling to try to wrap my head around. Almost 20,000 total casualties with 3,000 total dead. That's like 9/11... in one battle! And that's just the combatants. Wow. The worst part is that these weren't North or South deaths, these were AMERICAN deaths. Men who served with each other, now fighting each other. This was just inconceivable to me. I left Vicksburg with a whole new interest in the American Civil War.

We jumped back on the Natchez Trace, which was the most direct route to the Tupelo National Battlefield. Like I said, it's a beautiful country drive, at 35 mph most of the way, with some rest stops, like a very slow expressway patrolled by Park Rangers in Chargers. Great for bicycles, but not for sightseeing Mississippi. Since we were on a bit of tight time schedule I didn't mind, as this was the shortest mileage, cutting diagonally through Mississippi. Gas was cheap, but I still had a long trip ahead.

At one gas stop, near a Piggly Wiggly grocery store, in a very small town, I had an interesting talk with a local lady. I had just walked out of the grocery and was putting groceries away in back of the camper. The door was open as I climbed in and out of the truck to load the bags. Two black ladies, probably in their early twenties, one a few years older than the other, walked past the truck chatting away, until one noticed my "house." She stopped and asked if that was my house in the back of a truck, as if she had never in her life seen a cab-over camper before. "Yes, ma'am. I'm traveling the country, writing a book. Come on up and look!" Her eyes got big as she looked to her older friend for courage, who gave her an approving push. They both just stuck their heads in and looked around in amazement. "This is how you do?" the younger sibling asked, then turned to her sister and said "I wanna house like this!" They thanked me for the tour and commented how they had never met anybody from Arizona before. After just experiencing the brutality of Vicksburg's past, my heart was warmed by this seemingly simple encounter.

My "sister" back in Arizona absolutely loves natural foods, especially honey. She was sure to inform me that Tupelo Honey was supposed to be the best, and I had better send a jar back if I found any. Well, here I was in Tupelo, so off to the honey store I went, at a farmers market no less. I asked for the Tupelo honey and why it was so good here. The old guy looked at me like I should probably have a helmet and limited unsupervised conversations. "Tupelo honey comes from the Tupelo tree... in Florida," he said, leaning forward to add some noticeable emphasis to the word Florida. When I mentioned I was from Arizona, his wife let loose with the "bless your heart." After living in Texas, I knew what that meant; it's the polite way to say "you're an idiot." I just smiled, lowered my head and walked to the next booth chuckling. Yup, I'm THAT tourist.

To my surprise, the Tupelo National Battlefield was just a few blocks down the road and literally across the street from a Walmart. Expecting another massive park like Vicksburg, this was the exact opposite. This was literally a corner on a downtown city block. Two good sized cannons and a tall cement memorial, topped with an eagle, dominated the center of the lot. There were a couple placards, showing the troop movements and giving a general explanation to what on here, all behind the backdrop of a busy street intersection, across the street from Papa Murphy's Pizza and a carwash. So weird.

Apparently in the summer of 1864, CSA General Forrest was harassing Union supply lines, meant for US General Sherman's Atlanta campaign. So much so, that the Union sent 14,000 troops from Memphis to northern Mississippi, to march against Forrest. The Confederate force of 10,000 could not penetrate the Union defense after several attempts, and withdrew. The Union troops returned to Memphis, with the pressure on Sherman's flank substantially reduced. There was no mention of the casualty count from this battle. Then I noticed just to the side of the memorial was a smaller memorial and some gravestones, adorned with small CSA flags and Confederate Battle flags. This was also a Confederate graveyard; maybe that's why this small piece of land is considered a "National Battlefield." So bizarre to know there's dead Confederate soldiers yards away from a downtown city street. Then to think of 14,000 men encamped here, for a 2 day war. Again the numbers are just staggering.

We stayed another day in Tupelo to get some laundry done, hit the gym, and check out the sights. A pretty cool little town, decent size, and of course it's the childhood home of Elvis Presley. We checked out his birthplace and museum, walked around downtown, and stopped into the Blue Canoe for a burger that evening, a cool little tap-house, with some incredible food. I ordered a massive burger with added "crack sauce," white queso cheese, andouille sausage, crawfish and cream cheese. It was unbelievable! So good I took a pint of the sauce home and dipped fresh sourdough bread in it for breakfast the next day. Heaven!

Just outside of town was another small National Battlefield called Brice's Cross Roads. Now, this battle was June 10th, 1864; a full month before the Battle of Tupelo. The memorial was the exact same as the memorial in Tupelo, a concrete pillar with eagle on top. The inscription this time telling of a Confederate Victory. General Bedford Forrest led just under

5,000 troops against a force of 7,900 Union troops, with blinding quickness and veracity Forrest was known for, turning the federal troops back to Memphis. So apparently, this battle was what caused the Union to send the 14,000 troops to Tupelo a month later. I love following the timelines and the progression of these notable players and their battles, once again bringing a whole new perspective to this war.

It was early Sunday morning when I visited Brice's Cross Roads; the small country church across the street was starting to fill with cars. I just happened to be walking back from the adjacent Confederate Graveyard when a car of church goers parked next to the Rig. The little girl was ecstatic to see Kimber poke her head out of the truck window and a conversation with the father ensued. Before I knew it, I was invited to church and introduced to the small congregation, several of whom started following my book page, somewhat shocked I think that someone was giving so much interest to their community's little piece of American history next door.

After the sermon, the pastor came over and started explaining some of the history of the church itself. I had no idea the memorial across the street was where the original church was built in 1852 with a congregation of 25, including 4 slaves. Incredibly, it was used as a hospital after the battle of Brice's Cross Roads. This explained the Bethany Confederate Graveyard across the street, separate from the National Battlefield. How freaking cool is that? I thanked him and the congregation and we said our goodbyes. What an amazing piece of history, in the most unassuming location. Incredible. From here we were just a stone's throw away from the Alabama/Mississippi state line, so on to the next state. Mississippi, state #16... COMPLETE!

Author's note: I almost forgot. Back at the campground where we dodged the New Orleans hurricane, we were visited by a huge red Cardinal. The bird, not the clergy. It stuck in my mind as once again a sign that my AZ Cardinals might finally see a Super Bowl in my lifetime. Little did I know, this was a sign alright, but nothing to do with football.

Alabama

February 12th, 2017. Just like Mississippi, Alabama was all new territory for me. We were right on schedule, with two weeks to explore the state before baseball started. I was excited to visit another National Military Park after seeing Vicksburg, so a place called Horseshoe Bend was the main attraction for this state, other than that we were free to roam.

The first town I recognized from the classic Lynyrd Skynyrd song, "Sweet Home Alabama," was Muscle Shoals. The town itself was pretty cool, with a nice river area and some cool bridges. Somebody said they had a good music scene here. We stayed at the local Walmart that night after a shower and workout. The next day we started out to see an old friend.

Years ago, before I started this journey, I worked as a bouncer at the local bars in AZ. One of the out of town electricians that came to work at the power plant was a dude from Decatur, AL named Donny, but everybody called him 'Bama. He was a huge Alabama football fan, with the mouth and muscle to back it, not to mention having a heart of gold. Donny and I became fast friends and he had invited me to Alabama if I was ever out that way. I told him to count on it.

I hadn't spoken to Donny other than through Facebook for several years at least, so all I had to contact him was Messenger. I sent a message and looked back at some of his posts. Looked like he worked at a place called Herb's Auto Sales or something. Decatur wasn't that big, so I googled it and went to see if he was there. Well, just when it seemed that the whole town knew Donny, but didn't know where he was and wasn't about to give me his number, one guy finally called him about "some dude from Arizona looking for him." He called me right away. "Maaaatty!"... in that familiar, deep southern drawl. He came over and picked me up in his truck, while he ran around all his businesses in town. Now married with children, he owns a couple car lots, has these coin fed ice machines, and who knows what else. It was good to see my brother doing so well. We had a good visit, went to his bowling league, drank some beers and caught up. That's the second-best part of traveling, seeing old friends. Number one of course is meeting the new ones.

After taking the Natchez Trace through Mississippi, I knew I wanted to see the backroads and small towns of Alabama. The second most notable name I recognized was Talladega, which was also a National Forest where I could find some cheap camping. From Decatur, we went through several small towns, some with only a post office and a cafe, stopping at Gadsden to stock up for a couple days of forest camping.

The Talladega National Forest was a surprise to me. I had no idea that there were mountains in Alabama; I assumed it was mainly farming and swamp land. We drove along what seemed to be the crest line of the mountain, passing by resort cabins and private campgrounds near the peak of the Cheaha Mountains. When we made the peak and started down the backside, we ran head on into a wall of thick brown smoke. They had a pretty good fire raging near the road, halfway into the forest. I ended up taking some pretty rough forestry roads to get out of the forest, re-emerging in the small town of Linwood, just north of Horseshoe Bend.

We pulled into the Military Park about 30 minutes after closing, just to know exactly where it was before looking for a place to sleep. There weren't any Walmarts popping up on my map, and the only boondocking site was an old gas station a few miles south. It was about 1730 and I was tired. That turned out to be quite a drive from Decatur. I was tired for sure, but what happened next woke me up.

I was driving down this paved country road, with houses on large lots, set back from the traffic. I was doing the speed limit, lumbering along peacefully, when I noticed a small truck stopped in the middle of his lane. I slowed way down, not sure what this guy was doing. I didn't see a turn signal, but it looked like he was waiting on me to pass, so he could turn into his driveway. It was a kid, pulling a trailer with a single giant roll of hay on board. As I approached, still slowing down, the hay roll suddenly shot up into the air and off to the opposite side of the road, the little trailer lifting up like a spatula flipping a pancake. This made the kid's truck lunge into my lane, just a few yards in front of me. If I would've been doing the speed limit, he would've hit my driver side door, guaranteed. I started to shake, realizing what just happened. Turned out a full-size truck slammed into the back of the kid's trailer. The driver looked like he was moving inside the vehicle, thankfully opening his door. The kid in the truck was also outside his vehicle and fine. Thank God everybody was ok. I was shocked and shaking. I still can picture the boy's mother dropping everything in her hands and running toward the street, screaming her son's name. While mom tended to her son, I checked on the other driver. Dazed but not hurt, he told me he didn't see any turn signal or brake lights on the trailer. Wow.

Now I was exhausted AND freaked out. Kimber could tell, as she was shaking and scared too, sensing it from me. I looked for the first place I could possibly park for the night, which was a truck stop a few minutes away. It didn't really look like a place to boondock; it almost looked abandoned, save for the lights inside. I pulled in next to some big rig trailers, about the same time another truck did. Even the trucker rolled down his window and asked if we could park here. After stepping inside to check, the clerk said no problem. So we were home for the night. Or at least I thought I was. A few minutes later another big rig pulled in right next to my rig, a gas tanker that smelled like it had a leak. The fumes were so bad it was hard to breathe in the camper and I was getting a headache. Thank God I wasn't asleep yet. Where to now? By this time it was dark and there was absolutely nowhere to go. We ended up just moving down to the far end of the parking lot where I couldn't smell gas, and the blast perimeter was much farther away. Jesus, what a day.

The next morning, we headed back to the battlefield along the same road where we saw the accident. Skid marks on the road, a broken mailbox, and some tire marks into the shoulder was all that was left. Still in disbelief that I didn't get T-boned, I just gave a little prayer of thanks, it was starting to become obvious that I was being watched over. Thank you, Jesus!

I was super excited to see the Horseshoe Bend National Military Park. Knowing absolutely nothing about this battle or what it was about, I headed for the video first, then the museum, before exploring the grounds. My excitement quickly diminished when I realized that this was another Indian War. After Vicksburg, I was pretty stoked to explore another massive Civil War park, but this paled in comparison. This was where Andrew Jackson assembled U.S. forces, along with some friendly Native forces, and crushed the Creek Confederacy, thus ending the Creek Indian Wars. Five months later, the Creeks ceded nearly 23 million acres to the U.S., which are now the states of Alabama and Georgia. Now we see why it's a National Military Park.

My biggest take away from this was learning that different Indian tribes sided with the English during the War of 1812, thus making them enemy combatants. That's a little bit of a different story from the U.S. just rounding them up and moving them to Oklahoma, just to "steal" their land. I was starting to see that my standard public school education in American history didn't quite explain the whole picture.

It was still early in the day, and there was another great piece of American military history just down the road. The Tuskegee Airmen National Historic Site was our next stop, a place I'd heard about and a great story. This is where they trained the very first black fighter pilots. A truly inspiring story of how these military men helped pave the way for the U.S. military to desegregate, ultimately adding to the civil rights movement of the 50s and 60s. Amazing to look down at the runways and realize this is where that all began.

After a quick lunch in the back of the camper, I decided I had better start looking for a camping spot. We still had two weeks before March and a little bit of time to kill. At this point, we were just east of the state capital, Montgomery, Alabama. When I looked at the detailed map of the city, I saw several historical places including the "First White House of the Confederacy."

With all the civil rights movement history here, I guess it caught me off guard that Jefferson Davis' house would be here, and they would actually call it that; once again flying in the face of what I thought was a bunch of rag tag southern boys taking up arms. This was a parallel government with all the same institutions and traditions as our own. That's when you realize, it's because they are all Americans. They were us, we were them.

The house itself was in a very odd location. It stood on the corner of a city block, sandwiched between a huge parking garage and a hospital that towered above it. The structure just looked like an old house that the owner must've held out and refused to sell to developers. A very small sign acknowledged its history and offered tours, but sadly was closed while we were there. We chose to move on to find a campsite, I needed to settle in for a bit.

We ended up staying at an Army Engineers campsite, between Montgomery and Selma for a few nights, trying to save some money and burn some time. We explored the town of Selma and ventured back into Montgomery to look around before we headed south to Mobile, Alabama. I wanted to make a stop at the USS Alabama, a virtual floating battlefield.

Within just a few minutes of setting up the camper for an extended visit, another Cardinal dropped in. Sitting in a tree just overhead, I took a picture that I posted to the Facebook page, once again pronouncing the future Super Bowl champs, when a friend sent me a link to an article online. The article spoke of a Native American folklore that described a visit from a Cardinal as a visit from a male family member who has passed, showing you that you are loved, protected, and on your path. I was shocked. I had seen Cardinals in every state since I left AZ on this leg of the trip. I instantly thought of my paternal Grandfather who had raised me most of my life. A Navy veteran, who joined just after Pearl Harbor, too young to join at the start of the war and an avid Giants fan. It had to be my Grandpa Neville; suddenly my eyes sprung a leak.

After our stay there, I was eager to move, so bright and early, off to Mobile we went. It was a pretty muggy day, but clear and beautiful. The USS Alabama is a massive WW2 battleship on display along with a WW2 submarine and several static displayed aircraft. There were also several memorials to different aspects of military service; a service dog memorial, a 9/11 memorial, and each branch had its own display featuring the wars and battles that were the most noteworthy to each branch. I quickly found the large piece of brown granite with the USMC eagle, globe, and anchor engraved in gold on top, with all the famous battles engraved below, from the Revolutionary War to the War on Terror, even some battles I hadn't heard of, but one stood out more than the rest. I swelled with pride when I saw "Somalia" engraved in the granite; a sad rarity. Then I noticed a section labeled "War between the States," followed by a list of the major battles such as First Manassas, Fort Sumter, and Mobile Bay. Then below that was something that took me by surprise. The inscription read, "Lest We Forget -CSA Marines." It suddenly dawned on me that our military split and there would be Confederate Marines. The idea of a Marine killing a fellow Marine was unfathomable to me. I would have to research more on this.

The battleship itself was your typical museum type atmosphere, with several school field trips going on. I opted to leave Kimber in the truck, as it was pretty busy with lots of people. So much so that I found myself walking pretty quickly, trying to see everything, but yet get out of the crowds as quickly as possible. Ya, some things never change, welcome to my world.

After the battleship, I walked over to the small WW2 era submarine, a very small boat as compared to what we think of today. I'm not one for confined areas and claustrophobia has always been kind of an issue for me, but I was here and paid for the ticket. Can't be that bad, right? As I stepped in through the small hatch, there were about a dozen boy scouts listening to the beginning of a tour guide's speech. I stepped toward the rear to see if I could listen in, when another pack of scouts showed up at the door, these a few years older. Quarters got tight, but I was interested in what the guide had to say, so I stood strong. It wasn't 5 minutes before boys started to be boys, sport farting, giggling, and carrying on. All that and then add the humidity, I decided to move along and make some distance between me and this sweaty nightmare. I moved along looking at the sleeping quarters, engine room, and finally to the torpedo room, telling myself, "see that wasn't bad." Before my brain could form the word "bad" in my mind, things suddenly became immeasurably worse. There was no exit. Whoa, what? This was a one way in, one way out display. Why I assumed there would be a way out down there at the nose of a sub, I'll never know, but right then all I could think about was going back through that mob of smelly little bastards. Then I heard it, like squirrels fighting, they were getting closer. Suddenly the air in that giant, metal, death tube was like inhaling air from a room humidifier, with a sweaty sock as a filter. The walls were closing in fast, I made my move, parting the armpit high, sea of stench, like the Red Sea. When I finally broke through the crowd and found daylight, it was like I had never smelled fresh air before in my entire life.

Just north of us was Fort Blakeley, a Civil War Battlefield, that also had a campground with showers. Perfect. When we pulled into what was best described as a city park with an office at the main gate, the sign said the campgrounds were full. I went inside anyway to get some information on the battlefield. The gentleman inside handed me some flyers and information about the fort and the battle that took place here, along with a trail and campsite guide. He must've heard my lack of southern drawl and asked where I was from. I told him Arizona, and about my travels. He became very interested then, asking about my military service and what not. After our chat he then asked if I had reservations. I told him no, and that I had forgotten it was the weekend, and asked how much to just see the battlefield. The gentleman then looked down at his desk calendar and said, "Go check out the battlefield, and come back here at 5pm." Ok cool, so off we went.

The campground was pretty good sized, with lots of secluded RV spots, group campsites, a graveyard, and several acres of entrenchments, or what's called "redoubts." Basically a man made dirt embankment used as a shooting position, something like a giant foxhole. It was so strange to see campfire rings and a shower house less than a hundred yards from tombstones.

The Battle of Fort Blakeley was known as "the last grand charge of the Civil War," the climax of a campaign ending with the Union forces capturing Mobile. I was astonished once again by the sheer numbers. 16,000 Union troops attacked a dug-in force of 3,500 Confederate defenders, along a three mile battle front. Then to read that even while surrounded, the men fought until the bitter end, even resorting to hand to hand combat. Most of the men were captured, but over 100 lives were lost and thousands injured in just under 30 minutes. Unreal. To think that these guys continued to fight to the death, against overwhelming odds, showed me a perseverance by common people that left me in awe. Once again an ALL American trait.

At 1700 we rolled back up to the office to see what the clerk had me come back for. I assumed he was hoping somebody would leave early and a spot would be open. It was a Saturday to make things worse, nobody leaves on a Saturday. The gentleman was outside, smoking a cigarette with another clerk when I pulled up. He saw me and motioned for his buddy to follow him as he walked my way. "This is him," I heard him say as he handed me another campsite map, this time with a spot marked. "I had to wait 'til my night guy showed up," pointing at his co-worker. "Just go right here by the showers, you can park there tonight." "Wow, really? That's awesome! Thank you. How much do I owe you?" I replied. He waved his hand

and frowned. "Have a great trip and be safe," he said as he started to walk away. I was shocked. Before I could say another word, he turned and said, "Hey Marine... Oohrah!" with a sheepish smile. He was a Marine this entire time. "Errr," I replied with a grin, and spun the Rig around for a hot shower and a relaxing evening. Tomorrow we cross into Florida, let the baseball begin! Alabama, state #17... COMPLETE.

Florida

March 1st, 2017. Florida, the Sunshine State, another state I'd never once set foot in, but would be the most ambitious "mission" yet. I wanted to see a game in every one of the 13 Grapefruit League Parks, Florida's version of MLB spring training. This would take us up to opening day of regular season, when we would visit Miami and Tampa as our first MLB ballparks of the year. There were at least two battlefields to visit, and if possible, a little break down in Key West at a Navy Fam Camp for a few days, schedules and cash permitting. So that was the plan. As always, money would be the deciding factor, but we were going to do this as cheaply and quickly as possible. Florida, here we come.

Eager to get to the Tampa area to start the Florida Grapefruit League Spring Training Parks "circuit," while still following the coastline as closely as possible, we crossed into Florida on Highway 98. If you didn't see the "Welcome to Florida" sign tucked away on the side of the road, half covered with bushes and trees, you'd never realize you crossed into Florida... until you stopped for fuel. Gas prices jumped about 15 cents per gallon between the two southern states, giving me an ominous feeling of what's to come. I was pretty concerned how I would be able to afford the tickets for all 13 spring training parks, 2 MLB parks, pay for gas all the way around the state, and still be able to eat and enjoy myself. The most logical idea was to hop Walmarts the entire trip, saving on campsites. There's usually a Walmart in a city large enough for a spring training park, at least that's what I was betting on. I mean, come on... it's the South.

The Florida coastline was completely different compared to the West Coast or even the shoreline around the Texas coast. The most noticeable and interesting change was the color of the water, when you could actually catch a glimpse of it. Turning from an almost muddy brownish, to an emerald green, it was quite a beautiful surprise. But as I said... when you can actually see the water. Driving the coastal highway of Florida you rarely see the water, let alone a beach. The coast was congested with huge houses, monster resorts and hotels, or very high foliage that was waiting to be built on. All the beach access points seemed to be privately owned, with no trespassing signs prominently marked. The only way to the beach was at the public entrances that of course had huge "No Dogs" signs. You had to search high and low for a dog beach in the area, usually on an inlet into the bay. Kimber was not pleased to say the least. Also, you didn't dare throw a ball into an inland lake for fear of alligators! Poor girl was gonna be in for a long month, seeing as the temperature were starting to rise, along with the humidity.

We passed some incredibly beautiful places along the way. First, Pensacola, which was a fairly high dollar area, boat filled marinas at every turn, and a very upscale retirement area. We drove through the Pensacola Naval Air Station; wow, what a great place to be stationed! Then on to Destin for our first overnight Walmart stop. The town of Destin was like a miniature Las Vegas, minus the casinos. Huge LED screens acting as billboards, fancy restaurants, and monstrous resorts and hotels, lined the beaches. The resorts had massive water parks and Vegas style shows, but all seemingly family friendly. They call that stretch of coastline, from Pensacola to Panama City, the Emerald Coast, which is the perfect description for the color of the ocean here. Panama City Walmart was stop #2.

Spring break was upon us and it was beginning to show. Panama City is a huge spring break town and the kids were slowly starting to show up. Even the Walmarts had huge beach displays with everything from boogie boards to Mardi Gras beads in all the local college colors. Oh to be 20 years younger! I was more interested in sampling the local seafood and finding cheap beer.

Our first Florida battlefield was just outside of Tallahassee, a place called the Natural Bridge Battlefield State Park. Nestled back into the Apalachicola National Forest, it was a small, well manicured picnic area with a monument to the fallen, and a few restored earthworks that were interesting. Strange to see an earthen embankment for a cannon in what looked like a jungle. Kimber was eager to play some ball, but being that far into the bush, and near a small pond, I was too worried about her becoming gator bait and chose to move on. Not to mention the flurry of mosquitoes and gnats that Kimber stirred up just walking through the grass, helped with that decision. As for the battle itself, the plaques were so old and faded, we couldn't make much of them. Not a national site, no time to waste.

The next several miles of coast highway was more inland, away from the coast as it became marshlands. The highway was straight as an arrow, lined with dense pines, ground ferns and magnolia trees. This was the view for miles, with an occasional town, gas station, or roadside fruit stand popping up to break the monotony. One such fruit stand was in Chiefland, FL. I was always on the lookout for a farmers market or fruit stand to sample the local harvest, and this one didn't disappoint. Much like the fruit stands in NorCal, this had about everything imaginable under the sun, and some things I'd never heard of. This being Florida, there were several different hybrids of citrus, eggplant the size of footballs, and Honeycrisp apples the size of softballs. Honey also seemed to be a commodity here, with the revered Tupelo honey being the caviar of the beeswax world. It's apparently a rare honey, and this year just happened to be the first crop in a couple years. How they know the bees only go to Tupelo trees, I don't know, but I bought a jar for my sister back home anyway, as the lady from Tupelo's voice whispered in my ear, "Well bless your heart." I still cringe when I think about it. They also had wildflower, orange blossom (my favorite, tastes like oranges) and several other blends. Nope, I'll just take the damn Tupelo.

As I walked around the fruit stand, I happened to meet the owner, a younger guy named Jeff, who had one hell of a fruit stand business going. Extremely knowledgeable about all the produce in his shop, we started talking about my trip and the book. He asked what kind of dog I had, and when I said English Staffy, kinda like a mini pit-bull, his eyes lit up. He went behind the counter and brought out his own dog. An American Pocket Bully, which Jeff bred on the side. This thing was a beast, but only knee high. Such a neat dog. Best way to compare an English Staffy to a Pocket Bully is by comparing a UFC fighter to a bodybuilder. I went and got Kimber out of the truck for Jeff to see. We both fell in love with each other's dogs. Jumanji was a sweetheart, Kimber not so much. Snarling as usual when around a bigger dog, Jumanji took it all in stride. Jeff and I still keep in touch, great guy and when in Chiefland, check out his fruit stand. See ya soon, bro.

Out of Chiefland, we continued south to our second Florida battlefield: the Dade Historical Battlefield State Park. This was actually another Indian Wars battlefield involving Seminole Indians and Andrew Jackson's effort to relocate them to Oklahoma. It was a much larger battlefield with a visitor center and some re-constructed earthworks, more of a nice place to have a picnic than a battlefield. Unfortunately, the museum was closed and only a few plaques explained what took place here. It was interesting to see that the Seminoles actually won this skirmish which gave rise to the Florida State Seminoles name. With it only being a state park, I decided to move on. The next town over had an Anytime Fitness adjacent to a Walmart, where I showered and relaxed for the evening. From there we returned to the coastal highway and ventured into the North Tampa Bay area, eager to see some baseball.

The Florida Grapefruit League is quite a bit different from the Arizona Cactus League in that the parks are spread throughout the state, not concentrated in one area like the Phoenix metro area. So tickets are a bit harder to come by, drastically more expensive at times, and you always run the threat of being sold out with the more popular teams playing at a smaller town with only one venue. All of which I learned along the way. It's best to catch the games early in the month, when Spring Training and Spring break just begins, rather than later in the month when the bigger name players come out to prepare for the regular season and it gets crowded. But even during the last week of the month, there are usually season ticket holders or scalpers, eager to sell you a ticket... for a price. The parks are situated in a ring around the central and southern part of the state, with a few on each coast and a couple inland in between, making a round "circuit" that would put me back in Tampa for the Rays' regular season opener. Then I hoped to go back to Miami to catch the Marlin opener with an old Marine Corps buddy of mine. I hated to backtrack, but to see my buddy Jeff after 25 years, I'd gladly make the trip.

I found an online map of the Grapefruit League parks and chose Florida Auto Exchange Stadium in Dunedin, FL, home of the Toronto Bluejays, as our first stop. Dunedin is a small suburb town, west of Tampa along the coast, fairly close to the second park in Clearwater. Luckily, we found a Walmart in between the two parks that became our home base. The plan was to meet up with the couple that I met in Biloxi for a Blue Jay game the following day before they left for their next destination, then catch the Rays the following day in Clearwater. Awesome! Kimber and I settled in for the night, stoked that baseball was about to begin!

When I drove into the tiny town of Dunedin bright and early to scout out the parking situation, it didn't look good. Dunedin is a very small, older community, just northwest of Tampa. It's a part of a giant suburb of little towns that makes up the bay peninsula. The park was nestled in a residential neighborhood, with a school on one side and a library on the other, neither of which you were allowed to park at. The only parking close by was the VFW across the street that wanted twenty bucks. This was no bueno. I decided to start slowly trolling the outside neighborhoods for a spot that the homeowner wasn't trying to get more than ten dollars for. Apparently pimping out your lawn as a parking spot is a money maker in Florida. Some even had signs, with children waving flags and shouting to help make the sale. Finally, I noticed a smaller lot on school property, not chained up like the larger school lots, with what looked like game ushers parking their private vehicles and walking into the park. I decided why not, pulled into a shady spot near the back and camped out, waiting for game time. While I was in the camper, I heard a couple of old retirees greeting each other on their way into the ballpark. One gentlemen asked the other guy just exiting his car, "Whose rig is that? With the San Francisco license plate on his bicycle?" in a strong New Yorker accent. "Oh, I bet it's that Larry guy from Oregon last year, he was a Giants guy," answered his work partner with the classic Canadian accent. Then they changed the subject to the weather and who was going to be back this year, as they walked toward the park. I stayed quiet until it was game time. Thanks, Larry from Oregon!

The game itself was rather disappointing and even discouraging. The park had no grass seats so the cheapest ticket was nineteen dollars, with no veteran discounts at all. Then again, this IS a different country's baseball team. Duh. The look on the cashier's puzzled face when I asked if they had a military discount was worth the rejection. The park was no bigger than the Babe Ruth field I played on as a child. Snack bar prices were typical of the major league parks and then of course, the whole traffic debacle. It was really making me second guess attempting to see all the parks with the cash flow that I had. I was downright discouraged, and then they played the Canadian National Anthem first when everybody sang, and the American National Anthem with pretty much me and a couple others practically shouting the words to make up for the lack of singers. It was appalling. Thankfully, I still had a good time with the friends, hitting up a local pub for beers before parting ways. Happy travels, my friends.

In the same area just south of Dunedin was Clearwater, where the next game was. Our Walmart spot gratefully had complete, all-day shade, making the camper comfortable for Kimber even in the midday heat. I didn't want to lose this choice spot by driving to the game, when I suddenly remembered a trick me and a buddy used to do. We were only two miles away from the Clearwater park, and today was perfect to take the beach cruiser to the game. Why didn't I think of this before?! Like a charm, I rode right past all the backed up traffic, chained the bike to a power pole, along with a grip of other bikes. Nice! Now to the ticket counter to see what this was gonna cost.

While I was waiting in line to buy my ticket, the guy in front was trying to get two seats next to the seat on a ticket someone had given him. Apparently he had no luck and bought three that were together in the shade; then he turned around and asked me how many tickets I needed. "Just one," I replied as he handed me a front row, box seat ticket in the shade! Wow! Super cool.

Spectrum Field, the Spring Training home of the Philadelphia Phillies, was more of the type of park I was used too. Plenty of grass seats, Cabana Bar in left field above the bleachers, palm trees galore, nice cool ocean breeze. Now this was what I expected Florida Spring Training to be like. I fully expected to see Jimmy Buffet walk by any minute.

With this shaping up to be a great day and looking forward to enjoying this amazing box seat, I walked around the park taking pictures. As I worked my way back around to my section, I reached into my pocket for the ticket to show the usher... and it was gone! I must've dropped it somewhere. Unbelievable! I told the usher my story about the free ticket, luckily, he believed me and said, "Go ahead and catch a seat, if ya gotta move then move," then let me into the box seats. I was amazed he believed me. It was awesome, tragedy averted, for a couple innings at least, then I had to move because ticket holders showed up. Twice. After that, it just got embarrassing, so I decided to get a beer. I found a standing room only table in the shade with only one guy at it, so asked if I could join him. He was a Tampa fan, dressed in Rays gear from head to foot. Phillies were playing the hometown Rays, so lots of Tampa fans were here sporting their gear. Cool guy, we were having fun, talking baseball, when a few more folks joined the table. More huge Rays fans that worked at a nearby bar, one guy was a Navy veteran. We all had a blast drinking beers and watching the game. They gave me some great tips on places to see in the Keys and where I needed to eat or have a drink. Awesome new friends! Once again, everything happens for a reason!

The very next day, the New York Yankees were playing at their home park in Tampa Bay, just a few miles inland. I know it gets confusing with who plays where. Tampa Bay Rays play their regular season here but have spring training in a different city. Anyway, the scheduling gods were shining upon us, so off we went to Tampa for a Yanks' game.

Almost instantly we lost the cool ocean water breeze and the humidity and temperature both went up about fifteen degrees. It was in the low 80s and not even noon. This wasn't good, for Kimber's sake. I drove by the field, that happened to be across the street from the NFL stadium, and saw that parking was plentiful, but no shade and expensive. Just a few blocks back, I noticed a huge mall with a few restaurants in the parking lot that had some large trees. I decided to park the Rig under some broad leaf Magnolias near the road; the camper would be completely shaded for a few hours at least. With the camper windows open and the fans on, it was nice and cool. I loaded Kimber up with water, put ice in her bowl, some food, and even turned on the radio. I hate leaving her in a busy place, even though I know she'll be fine. I wasn't going to stay long, I never do with her being alone... or maybe it's me being alone. I also refused to run the generator while I was gone. Fire and fumes were worrisome, I couldn't stand being gone for a minute, let alone a couple hours. Once I had thoroughly convinced myself that Kimber was safe, I grabbed the beach cruiser and headed for the game. I was pedaling like a fat Forrest Gump in a wife beater, Dickey shorts and sandals, stoked to see the game, but in a hurry to get back to Kimber.

George M. Steinbrenner Field was as big and impressive as any major league park I've ever seen. When I said there was a New York presence in Florida, I wasn't even close, this place was Southern New York. There were plaques with the numbers and information of all the Yankee greats, from Mantle to the Babe, there were a grip of them. There was also an incredible tribute to 9/11 with a piece of burnt steel in front of a tall chrome statue of the towers. Inside the park was just as impressive. There was a huge grandstand, giving it that nostalgic look, yet, pretty much brand new. Check out the right field cabana bar with lounge area if you happen to visit. Literally, I sat on a leather couch with misters, watching the game. Lots of bar top spots were available to eat your meal, and not a word from the ushers. Best park so far.

At this point, my gray wife beater was obviously a poor choice in attire as my man-boobs had left sweat marks that, well, let's just say weren't exactly flattering. The humidity was climbing and Kimber was in the truck. Time to get back. When I did get to the truck, it still had plenty of shade, and I could see Kimber, sound asleep on the bed, safe and sound. My worries gone, all was well. I bowed my head and gave a little thanks; that little dog is my world. Back to the coast and the cool air!

I was pretty ecstatic about our progress so far, three parks complete and it was just now the first of March. Payday eased the cash crunch a little, but we still had a long ways to go. The next park was just south of the Tampa metro area, but still seemed like a suburb; all the coastal towns were pretty much running together at this point.

The next stop was going to be in Bradenton, to see the Pittsburgh Pirates who had an early game the following day. I found the local Walmart, hoping to settle in for the evening before the game. It was about 1900 when we pulled in and realized that wasn't gonna happen. First thing were the two police cruisers parked side by side, just chatting through their windows. Then the cameras on this "Lot Cop" camera tower, complete with red and blue lights came into view. After that, who needs to post the no overnight parking signs? Just at that moment, my buddy in Miami called me, asking where I was at. I told him, "Bradenton Walmart. Dude, it's like a war zone," to which he replied, "Get out of there! That's like the heroin capital of Florida." Lovely. Sarasota had the next closest Walmart, which was like the Hilton compared to the last one. Sarasota is also the home of the Baltimore Orioles camp, and just happened to have a game the following day, followed by a Pirates game in Bradenton the day after that. Perfect, I'd make the commute back... in broad daylight.

My buddy Jeff had also called to tell me that he was going to see a World Baseball League game with his son at Marlin Park, and asked if I wanted to go. What?! Well hell ya, I wanna go! The World Baseball League is like a worldwide tournament that's held every four years, I think. USA was playing Canada, so I'd get to see five of my favorite Giant players in the Miami Marlin's MLB Park with my old Marine buddy I hadn't seen in 25 years? Hell yes, I'm in! This gave me until the 12th to be in Miami. It'd be close, but we got this.

We had a day to kill before the Orioles game so we scouted out the local Anytime Fitness and headed for a workout and a shower. Kimber needed a place to run so after the gym we headed for the beach. Luckily, after walking around the boat docks, looking for a patch of sand, we came across a dog friendly cabana bar that had its own little beach. Other dogs were chasing balls into the water, making Kimber even more excited to get off the hot concrete and join in. As I reached for an ice cold beer, in this sweltering humidity, I paused to take in the scene. Now this I could get used to.

The drive back to Walmart that evening was what made that day interesting. I turned down one street that apparently had a very large population of vacationing Amish. Suddenly, my mind jumped to a scene from one of my favorite shows... *The Amish Mafia* series on History Channel... the episode about the Amish girls going wild on their Florida vacation. Suddenly, the streets were filled with nothing but Amish in their traditional dress, beards and hats, bonnets and long dresses. Buggies and bicycles everywhere, some two wheeled, some three, some were even tandem. I was surprised to see some of the bicycles were motorized, but hey, it is their vacation, let them live a little! Yup, apparently, Sarasota is where they go to party... Amish style. I had to laugh and text my buddy in Arizona about driving through a girls gone wild video, but with my luck, of course, it would be Amish girls.

Ed Smith Stadium, the Home of the Baltimore Orioles, was just a few miles from the Walmart we were staying at, a little too far for the beach cruiser but with plenty of parking in a huge, grass, overflow lot across the street. It was much cooler here, and Kimber could get some ball time in before the game. Always good to wear her out, letting her sleep while I was gone. I had lunch in the camper and ventured across the street a few minutes before game time. Ya, that's worth the ten bucks for parking, when you can tailgate and make a day of it.

The park itself was a little bit older but incredibly clean and well maintained. It had an open veranda, lots of upper deck shade, and plenty of covered benches around the field itself, a nice park, pretty much standard for the league. There seemed to be a lot of elderly, maybe it was more of a retirement town, although it was a weekday day game.

The next day, we ventured back to Bradenton for a Pirates game, still not in the best part of town, but we were in broad daylight. Parking was scarce. We ended up paying twenty bucks to park across the street and down a couple blocks from the ballpark, but at least it had a couple of cashiers at the entrance, making it easier to leave Kimber in the camper while I watched the game. Lecom Park was all in all a pretty cool park. It had huge grandstands that reminded me of the black and white pictures of Babe Ruth in his heyday. A real old timey look, with plenty of mid-day shade. The location was just rough, on the corner of a used car dealers strip. As I write this, I see that they have moved to Sarasota. Looks like another road trip!

The next park was down the coast a ways, finally breaking away from the Tampa/St. Pete sprawl. It was good to do some backcountry sightseeing, the city was weighing on me. Actually, as I looked at what I'd been doing and where I'd been so far with this Florida run, I was doing surprisingly well with the crowds, traffic, humidity, and obviously meeting and talking with folks. This too was a good change. Correction, this was a great change. Thank God.

Port Charlotte is home to the Tampa Bay Rays spring training facilities, and wow is it nice. Much like the Diamondbacks Salt River Park, this place was huge. Lots of different fields with Rays players working out, fielding drills, and batting practice. It was surprising to see how many kids were actually there trying to make the team, or even play in a game. Hundreds I bet, not just the squad you happen to see play that day. Hard not to dream about being one of those kids, that's for sure.

We had gotten there pretty early for a day game. So early that the guy thought I was a player and was waving me into the inner lot. After saying that we were just going to tailgate and throw the ball for the dog, he had me park in a back corner under a tree with lots of soft grass. Kimber was ecstatic and so was I! We had lunch, played ball until she was completely worn out, and I went in and enjoyed the game. Well worth the ten bucks to park.

The park was called the Charlotte Sport Park, and both the Tampa Rays and a minor league team called the Stone Crabs both shared this facility. It was pretty standard with the cabana bar in the outfield, grandstand style, decent shade, and clean! Get there early, with it being in a small town and the MLB home team favorite, they sell out early and often.

That night we stayed at the local Walmart that was near my gym; a much needed scrub down, and an early night to bed was on the agenda. I just realized how fast we'd been moving by how tired I was. Thanks to being unbelievably blessed with the game schedules lining up perfectly, we were crushing the time crunch to meet Jeff for the WBL game. The next day's game was no different. The next park down the coast had the Red Sox at 1300. See what I mean? Unreal! Off to Fort Meyers, first thing in the morning.

Fort Meyers was another small little coastal town, lots of retirees everywhere, reminding me a lot of Sun City, Arizona, the blue hair, golf cart capital of AZ. When there's more golf cart parking spaces than normal car parking spaces, you know you're in Sun City.

Fort Meyers was also the home of the Boston Red Sox's Jet Blue Park, my favorite of the leagues so far. What makes this park amazing is that it is an exact replica of Fenway, complete with the green monster, deep center pocket and rounded right field fence line. Makes sense that they would train on a replica of their unique and difficult home field. Left fielder has to practically play handball with that short field and crazy tall wall. I couldn't wait to see Fenway in person next year.

With it being a Sunday game, the park was pretty much packed. Standing room only ticket was my cheapest way in. Ya, it was actually that busy. As luck would have it, my knee started to act up. It had been taking a beating lately, so I asked the guy if he had a spot for an old vet with a bad knee, just for a few minutes. He replied with, "A few minutes my ass, you sit right here as long as you want," pulled back a plastic chain to a bar top counter and let me in. What a relief and one of the best seats in the house. Thank you, sir! Great park, great people. A must see if you're a Sox fan!

Unbelievably, even with the next day being a Monday, our next game was just down the road in Naples, the very next day, a day game at Century Link Sports Complex, home of the

Minnesota Twins. Almost the exact routine as the day before. We got there early, played ball with Kimber, then watched the game. Maybe I should've been a baseball scout, I was getting used to this job.

Century Link Sports Complex was another large and very nice facility. For some reason the park looked like the Kentucky Derby could've been running instead of baseball. Very southern plantation looking with arched lattice and half circle, red, white, and blue flags that they hang from railings during parades. Inside the park was hot. There was very little to no shade, and it was muggy. The skies were overcast enough that shade didn't really matter, I ended up having a hot dog and getting back to Kimber.

It was too hot, I was physically exhausted, and I was finally reaching my boiling point with people, crowds, and traffic. It was now the evening of the 6th, and the game with Jeff in Miami was our next planned ballpark. We had five days with only the Florida Keys standing between us and Miami. Key West here we come.

I noticed on my campsites app that there was a Naval Getaways Fam Camp on what is called Dredgers Key. When they dredged the ocean floor, to make it deeper for the supersized cruise ships to visit, they stacked the dirt and rocks up and made Dredgers Key, exclusively for military and veterans. At least that's what the website said. I plugged it into the GPS and off we went.

It was a long trip through the Everglades, which is basically a huge swamp with things that want to eat you. Needless to say, there were no potty breaks for Kimber until we got on an island far away. The first "key," basically mini islands that are all lined up, was Key Largo and instantly, The Beach Boys were singing in my head. Flashbacks to washing my dad's truck every Sunday, with only two cassettes to listen to: Beach Boys and Jim Groce. I know every damn word.

The water was breathtaking, like a neon aqua marine color, maybe teal is closer. Either way, it was like there was a giant backlight under the green glowing water, against a dark blue sky, with pure white puffs of clouds. It was spectacular. I had never seen a body of water this color before in my life. I thought the emerald coast was impressive, this was just amazing. Waist high, warm as bath water, for miles.

The Keys themselves are little rock and brush islands that hold small communities. A lot of tourist stuff mainly, but some very cool residential spots that would be a great place for an RV pad. After about an hour and a half of very slow traffic, we made it to Key West and found the

Fam Camp. I was worried they wouldn't have a spot for us, but not only did they have a spot, it was literally 15 yards from the water. No hook ups, but it had a shower and laundry facility, a gym, tennis courts, and a small commissary. All for around 16 bucks a night. I couldn't have asked for a better setup, and I was ready to take full advantage of that ocean being on our doorstep.

With a quick stop at the commissary for some real groceries: a nice fat ribeye, pork loin for the smoker, 12 pack of Stellas, lots of fresh fruits and vegetables, enough for a solid and well-fed three or four days. I didn't plan on moving that truck but maybe to go sightseeing, and even that could be done on a bicycle. With our chores complete, Kimber was more than excited to see the ball splash down in the crystal-clear water, like a gift from God falling from the heavens. With beer in hand, knee deep in the calm warm water, I couldn't agree more.

With full bellies, worn out from driving and playing ball, Kimber and I retired that evening expecting to sleep like a baby. As we did... until about 0600. That's when a bull elk, apparently in rut, and about 5 ft from my sleeping head, let loose with a call that must've made it to Cuba. I sat straight up out of a food coma, smacking my head on the camper roof. What in the literal F was that? I jumped down and swung open the door, exactly as the old buck turned and looked me dead in the eye and said, "Morning neighbor!" The buck was an elderly gentleman, former Korean War veteran wearing a Navy tank top, some sort of Pooka shell necklace, board shorts and barefoot, holding a conch the size of a football. This was the instrument that brought the chariots of hell this morning. All I could say was, "Why?" The reply was "Island life, baby!" then blowing into the damn thing again, as he had for the last 16 years. Enter my buddy Victor. Facing the sunrise, as the sun crests the water, blowing into the conch as a welcoming of the new day... or something to that effect. Right on man, I feel the vibe... right after coffee.

After I was fully caffeinated, I caught Victor just before his morning kayak trip. I introduced myself, and a conversation ensued. Turned out Victor was an 81 year old, Navy Commander, who served as a Russian spy during the Korean War. Yes... 81. He had a Signals Intelligence background and went to Russian linguist school. Yup, you guessed it, in Monterrey. This man was the exact person I had joined the Corps to be. Anyway, it was amazing to hear his stories; this guy actually did what I dreamed of doing. It was bizarre in a way, like looking into the face of an old me in a way. We bonded instantly and became friends. He introduced me to his wife who was about the same age, but was suffering from terminal cancer. A very sweet and amazing

153

love story, that unfortunately would soon come to an end. Victor was healthy as a horse, and brought his wife here to the beach for her last days. None of which brought either of their spirits down. They carried on like teenagers, hugging and kissing playfully, then she'd need her rest and Victor would go play.

That evening, Victor was knocking on the camper door, "Hey Marine, let's go get a slushee." Slushee? Ok, I was game for an ice cream and more of Victor's spy stories. Then another old guy came around the corner. "Is this the Marine with the dog?" he asked. Victor had brought his running buddy with him, a spry 72 year old who was the pacifist of the group. A much more timid, hippy kinda guy. "Meet my buddy Tom." Victor leaned over and whispered, "He's Air Force, go easy on him," and chuckled. "I heard that, asshole!" came Tom's voice from around the corner, as we all piled into his little Subaru.

Slushee bound, we drove down to what is basically known as the Strip, like a small Bourbon Street with bars and restaurants galore. Very tropical, very Jimmy Buffet, and starting to get very crowded; spring break was upon us. Parking was scarce, and there would be no way for me to get the Rig parked down here. Tom pulled into somebody's driveway just off the Strip. He honked his horn, which made an elderly lady, possibly in her 80s, peek out from behind the curtain, get visibly excited as she waved her hands in a very happy hello. "She hasn't had her fix in a few days," Tom said. Victor smiled. Oh God, I thought as I cringed for what was coming next. I mentioned that I was afraid to ask what that was all about, which gladly came the response of nothing sexual. Whew! The old lady lets them park in her spot if Tom brings her a slushee. These must be pretty damn good slushees. We walked to the side ally and up just one restaurant, before we turned into Fat Tuesday's, a Mardi Gras themed Daiquiri bar. Now it all made sense. These were slushees like I had back in Louisiana. High octane. And these guys were bringing in their own sippy straw, refill cups. What? The bartenders greeted these two guys like they were rock stars; even the bouncers and DJs all waved or stopped by our table. Unbelievable! Vick walked up and whispered something in this gorgeous 24 year old waitress' ear, who brought me an empty sippy cup. Victor winked. Then he grabbed all three of the cups and walked to the bar, for our first "refill." And so it began. Drinking slushees, dancing with girls who could be their great-granddaughters, and generally loving life. It was classic. They literally stopped their enjoyment to drive my drunken self home. I wasn't drunk but I was getting there. These old

154

dudes drank me... yes, a Marine... under the table, to which they took great pleasure, almost as much as the old lady who finally got her slushee. I still think there was more to that story.

On the way home, Victor wanted to get a sandwich for his wife, stopping at a Cuban sandwich shop. I hopped out of the truck, curious what a Cuban sandwich was. I walked up to the counter just in time to hear Victor put in our order in perfect Russian, then was obviously flirting with the young girls in their home country language, as they giggled insistently. Spanish was obviously their native language, but many were versed in Russian, which made sense if you think about it. Sandwiches in hand, we headed back to a nice evening of laughs and joking around the fire with Tom, Victor, and his wife. What a great set of people. Oh and Kimber, of course, who Victor couldn't put down. I felt so blessed to have been a part of this special time for them. Not sad in any way, but a celebration of an incredible life together. I had witnessed true and perfect love.

After the fastest five days of my life, I wasn't exactly eager to pack up the Rig and get back into the hustle bustle of Spring Training, especially heading into the Miami area. I was eager to see Jeff, though, and eager to get another MLB park checked off the list. Even though the Marlins weren't playing, I could still say I'd seen the park. Best part was, what a great and unexpected way to see it, with a Marine buddy from what seemed like another lifetime ago.

Kimber and I left the Keys the morning of the game, northbound for the foreseeable future, but just to Jeff's place. He lived in an area just north of Fort Lauderdale called Pompano Beach. I chose not to take the coastal route through Miami, instead, opting for the most direct route. That was apparently going to cost me. Seemed like every inland road was a toll road, and usually required exact change. Well, I guess I'll be getting a radar ticket back home then, because I didn't have exact change the fifth damn time I had to toss money in a basket. Who carries that much change? Anyway, I finally got to Jeff's apartment a few hours before the game. He shares a nice place with his new fiancé, making my Rig an obvious eye sore.

Man, was it great to see my old Marine buddy again. We had met during electronics school in Twentynine Palms, CA. Spend a year in the high desert of California, out in the middle of nowhere, with no car, you got to know your barracks buddies real well. Lots of beer, pizza, playing cards, and fights. Oh ya, there was some training and Marine stuff to do too – pretty much our attitude about it, for an entire year. From the "Stumps," as we affectionately called it, Jeff and I were stationed together at Camp Pendleton, CA, sometimes roommates but always nearby, where we once again tested our livers while we served our country proudly. Both of us even met our wives in Oceanside and had our first-borns around the same time. Now bald like me, but slimmed up, he was looking good in his old age. We both laughed about the old times over some beers, waiting on his son to show up and head to the park.

Marlin Field, the obvious home of the Florida Marlins. Tucked away in a rather older part of town, it was this huge, extremely modern building, surrounded by small run-down duplexes, with little old Hispanic ladies selling their front yards as parking spots. Jeff was a regular at the ballpark and knew right where a spot was, the lady recognizing him as he paid.

We were only a block or two from the park, and wow was it crowded. Like a sea of Hispanic people, all somewhat shorter than me, literally filled the streets. The Puerto Rico v. Dominican Republic game was just letting out. Yes, a literal sea of people. Here's the crazy part about this tournament. They actually run everybody out of the park between games, so all these folks were leaving, as an entire new crowd was just showing up. It was pure chaos, then of course, it started to rain. We stood with five hundred other people under the awning, waiting for the park to open their gates again. Finally they opened up and we all filed in.

Marlin Park was huge. Not only huge, but a mechanical marvel. I had no idea that it had a retractable dome roof. I assumed the weather was pretty mild, but didn't realize how much it rained here... and rained hard! The park also had giant windows looking toward the ocean, that open like massive sliding glass doors when the weather permits. Unfortunately, that night wasn't one of those nights. The inside had this enormous catwalk around the outfield, with some pretty amazing food to be had. It was a great park and a great reunion with my old buddy Jeff; next time I see him, he will be the blushing groom. Best of luck to ya, brother. With more time spent with my bro than running around the park, I'm gonna call it here. Marlins Park, MLB park #9... COMPLETE!

The next day, Kimber and I ran around town, looking to pick up some replacement clothes while we waited for Jeff and his girl to get off work. When you travel, you carry only what you need, and I needed shorts desperately. A quick search of the local Goodwills and we were off and running. Goodwill had been a life saver on this trip. Why buy new stuff when you camp for a living? I buy what I need, use it until I can't, then throw it away. I save a lot of space and money that way. So after finding a couple good pairs of cargo shorts, Kimber and I stopped by a dog park for the afternoon, grabbed a shower at the local Anytime Fitness, and had a great meal with Jeff and some more amazing people that evening. Perfect way to kick-off the second half of Florida, but with no time to waste, we headed up to Palm Beach for our next game the following morning.

That evening in the camper, I sat down and made a route and schedule of the last few parks, trying to get a time frame patched together. Looked like we would be able to see the last 4 or 5 parks with almost a week to spare before the Tampa Bay home opener. We were going to make it, but I wasn't going celebrate until I was sitting in the Tropicana Field with beer in hand. Knowing good old Murphy as well as I do, I'm not counting on anything just yet.

The Ballpark of the Palm Beaches, is home to both the Houston Astros and the Washington Nationals. That day, the Astros were playing the New York Mets. I was stoked to see that deGrom was pitching, and it was rumored that Tim Tebow would be playing. I quickly found the Met's bullpen and sure enough, there was deGrom warming up, long hair and all. About that time, a whole crowd of people turned and started clapping and taking pictures. Tim Tebow walked onto the field, towering over what looked like the head coaches. He wore a number 97 jersey without a name. This usually meant he's brand new, and not expected to make the squad. Funny, he was escorted by all the big coaches and cameras though. First time up, he crushed a deep fly out; first time in the field, probably explains his 97 number. It was a routine fly to left, and there was no way in hell old Tim was going to have the wheels to get to that ball. Oh well, maybe a DH is in his future.

The park itself was very plain, I guess you could say. A lot of just blocky grey concrete made up the majority of the building, with only one level, and a sunken style field. It honestly reminded me of something you'd see on a military base. Very governmental, I guess you could call it. Lots of grass seats, with little to zero shade, I was grateful for the overcast. After seeing Tebow's debut and deGrom throw a few innings, I went back to Kimber. It was starting to get hot, and we needed to find some shade for the afternoon.

The next day we finally had some downtime. A one day break in the baseball action, perfect for a much needed beach visit. Just down the A1A, which is the coastal highway, we found a public access dog beach. Kimber was so excited to be off leash and chase her ball. Beautiful blue water this time, not as bright and clear, and somewhat darker, rolling up on a granite grey beach. I got some good pictures of Kimber chasing her ball, once coming out of a wave looking exactly like a seal. Needless to say, that was Kimber's last deep swim in the Atlantic, especially during

Shark Week. The rest of the day was spent at a city park across the street from the beach, certified shark and gator free. Afterwards it was a shower at the gym and back to the same Walmart for night number three. They were going to think I was homeless for sure.

Our next game was in Jupiter, FL at the Roger Dean Stadium, home to the Florida Marlins and the St. Louis Cardinals. Jupiter was far enough away from all the major beaches down South that it had a bit of a small-town feel. Once again, being outnumbered by senior citizens, I figured it was a retirement community. A nice park, but strangely small, I was surprised that it was shared with the home state Marlins. The other home state teams, Tampa and Arizona, both have massive parks; this was about the size of my Babe Ruth field, just with a bigger grandstand and announcer's booth. I was surprised to see the bullpens out in the field, mound and all, in the foul ball territory. What if a starting infielder tripped and tore an ACL on the practice mound rubber, chasing down a foul? Didn't make sense to me, bad liability, but great for crowd exposure. When they warmed somebody up, it was up close and personal for the front row seats. Once again, crowded and hot was the name of the day, as I hit the exit around the fifth inning. Easy in, easy out. Perfect. Next up, New York Mets... on St Paddy's Day. This should be good.

March 17th, we pulled into the First Data Field, in the town of Port St. Lucie, bright and early the next morning. This town gave the vibe of being just a regular coastal town: strip malls, subdivisions, no overwhelming senior citizen occupation, no crazy drunken college kids; just us working class folks. It was actually a nice break.

Much like its New York rivals, the Yankees, this field was no slouch. Much older but just as massive, this park was as good as any MLB park. Huge stadium style seats with a massive concrete overhang for shade, it had some grass seats in left, with a ton of picnic benches and covered bar areas up and down the baselines. A spacious right field area with a small island bar was pretty neat, and a great view of the game.

I had scouted out a Buffalo Wild Wings, located in a local strip mall for my St. Paddy's day meal, mainly because it was going to be free, but also because I love their wings. I hadn't seen one since Texas, so it almost felt like a homecoming of sorts. Then, with a Walmart within walking distance, it was an evening meant to be. Sadly enough, my old leprechaun self was in bed before the sun was down; we had a bit of a road trip to make before our next game.

We had two days to make it up the coast to Cape Canaveral, then turn inland to Kissimmee, home of Disney World and the Atlanta Braves. Driving up this part of the eastern Florida Coast was basically all the same, lots of coastal homes with sporadic small towns breaking up the line of beach properties. The more north you went, the older the buildings were. Skyscraper style apartments that looked like something out of a 70's movie overlooked the ocean. Some were rest homes, some assisted living, some just apartments. It was definitely an older part of Florida.

Kissimmee, Florida, pronounced "keh semee" not "kissa me," in the local dialect that my buddy Jeff quickly corrected me on. "Don't say it like that. They'll know you're not from here," he warned. "Well, I'm from Arizona, soooo..." I replied. "True," he chuckled back. I've actually found that playing the naive tourist card, and asking questions of the locals, finds you in most people's good graces quickly. They're proud of their hometown and will want to show it off. I always listen to the locals for advice on food, sights to see, places to avoid. Most will direct you the right way, with a kind "bless your heart" to follow. I'm on to ya, Tupelo Lady.

We arrived in Kissimmee a day early, with enough time to stop and let Kimber play in the water on the way in from the coast. In a shallow tidal pool, well north, I was pretty sure she would be safe, as I saw other folks with kids swimming nearby. I found the closest Walmart to Disney World, and was settling in with a Walmart roasted chicken, a bag of Caesar salad, and some tortillas, when my whole camper lit up with lights. I jumped up and opened the camper door to a local police officer, who saw me, turned off the light and asked if I had any beer. "Beer?" I asked. "No… kids. Do you have any kids in there?" he asked in a louder voice. "Kids? God no! I got a dog," I replied. He smiled and said, "Ok, thanks. Somebody said they heard someone shouting." Someone must've heard me get after Kimber for not laying down, which would sound something like this: "Go lay down. Hey! What the hell did I just tell you, GO. LAY. DOWN. You better start listening. (Growl, low mumble talk back) Don't you talk back to me. LAY DOWN. Before I whoop your butt." Yup, that got the local po-po called on me. Lovely. "Do I have to move? I'm going to the ballgame tomorrow," I asked, to which he shook his head and said, "Nope, have a good night." Well, at least he was cool about it, it could've went way worse. After that, I turned off the iPad and went to sleep, for about an hour. Then there was a loud knock at the door. This time, a security guard saying I had to move to a different part of the lot. Well, there went sleeping for the rest of the night now. Just a nod off here and there, like being on watch, sleeping with one eye open the rest of the early morning.

The next day came bright and early. The busy shopping center, in a super humid town, filled up quickly with the cool morning shoppers. After making a stout cup of coffee, we drove over to

Disney World, where the next ballpark was. You could tell that this was the grand mecca of all things Disney, when the electrical poles on the side of the freeway were in the shape of mouse ears, a large circle with two smaller ones on top that the high voltage lines attached to. Crazy. As we got closer to the park, I started to realize the enormity of the place, along with the summer crowds. Thankfully, the ballpark was one of the first features as we drove into the park. ESPN Wide World of Sports Field, or something close to that, another crazy long name. Lots of different sports are played here, from tennis, to what looked like an indoor hockey rink, and of course the baseball ballpark.

We parked under a nice big shade tree, near some other large vans and buses, toward the back of the lot. There was a nice lawn area we backed up to, so Kimber had her fill of chasing the ball before I ventured inside. Inside of course, was still all things Disney with the Atlanta Braves logo. Every character dressed up in team garb adorned the walls of the pro shop, which you conveniently had to walk through to get to the field. Genius. From there was a large veranda overlooking a good size field, seats leading down to ground level, and a large upper deck area. Here's the kicker, NO SHADE. The top veranda covers the last few rows of the lower deck, but there's only lattice on the upper deck for shade. I found a small patch of shade in the grass, but had to move every few minutes to stay in it. Pretty standard park except for the massive Jumbotron in the outfield, which of course advertised all things Disney, but was a monster for just the Spring League. Super cool for instant re-plays though. It was an unusually hot day and it was getting crowded; a situation that I was not going to be in, so I scooted on back to Kimber and the Rig. One more park to go, and I was eager to get there, and get 'er done!

This time we had a four day wait, which meant a lot of downtime in Walmarts and other places that I could run the generator/AC. I scouted out the local Anytime Fitness in the area, along with all the local boondocking sites available, and pretty much just bounced around and saw the local sights. One stop was at the Lakeland Brewery, located downtown, near a freeway overpass. I parked near the rear of the parking lot, backing into a shaded corner with the driver's side of my truck facing the overpass and the passenger side facing the brewery. Kimber stayed in the camper, with the windows open and door locked, after I let her out to pee. After my lunch, I came back out to get Kimber and walk her around the city lake, just across the street. When I came back to the truck after our walk, I unlocked the door, put Kimber in the back, and sat down in the front, reaching for my phone that was on the charger. Key word: was. I had laid it right where my tablet was too. What's the key word... yup gone too. That's when I realized Kimber's back window was down a few inches and had big greasy handprints where they had pulled down the window I had left cracked. They grabbed the phone, tablet, and chargers, but left the cordless DeWalt drill, and tool bag. Idiots. The phones would lock anyway, and I made sure to keep the cloud updated. So hopefully, I'll get my book and pictures back.

After filing a police report to hopefully get my insurance to cover it, I walked behind my truck to the overpass and saw a homeless guy down there. I said, "Man, somebody busted into my truck and stole my phone and tablet. I got my work stuff on there. I'll give ya 100 bucks to get them back." He looked at me and point blank said, "Shit, for a hundred, I wish I had them." He wasn't lying, but he wasn't going to tell me where my stuff was either. So much for leaving my windows cracked. The law came and took a report, my insurance kicked in only $250, so it looked like I was off to Verizon to buy a new phone. And no, it was a used phone that had been given to me after the North Dakota nightmare, so no insurance. I opted for the best of the best. The brand new Apple I-7plus 256 G, with payments at 30 bucks a month no interest, why wouldn't I, and the camera on this thing was amazing!

Friday, May 24th, we pulled into Publix Field at Joker Marchant Stadium, the 13th and final Florida Grapefruit League Park. Wonder if they could squeeze another sponsor into that name? The park was also in Lakeland, springtime home of the Detroit Tigers. With ticket in hand, I officially declared victory, we did it. Mission complete and it was only the 24th of the month. We saw a game in every spring training park, one in a MLB Park, and 5 days in the Keys, and still made it with a week to spare.

After posting my victory lap on the book page, I got a message from a vet who started following my page in 2016. He told me Detroit was his team and to take a ton of pictures. He had always wanted to see them in Spring Training, so I was teasing him with photos of a bucket list item of his. How cool is that!? Absolutely I would and did, and now have a standing invite to Detroit when I get that way next summer. That's what I'm talking about! How freaking cool. That made me wonder how many other people were living vicariously through me because of that Facebook page. How many vets were saying, "Shit, I could do that." Many, I hope. Little did I know that this would soon become my soul source of inspiration.

Publix Field has to be the most kid friendly, family-oriented park in the Florida system. Huge grass areas in the rear and to the sides of the outfield. Kids were playing catch, there were several huge blow-up bouncy things, corn-hole tables, and a radar gun on a pitching mound to see how fast you can throw. This made me curious. I was in the park early, so there weren't many people around to embarrass myself. I paid for three balls, stepped up to the mound, reared back and threw as hard as I could. 53 mph. Wow, that's it? Reared back and threw again. 54 mph this time. That's it, I got this. I took three good hops and threw the last one like an outfielder, as hard as I could. 52 mph. This thing is broken. A respectable toss for a quadragenarian I guess, but not worth waking the 35 year old elbow pain. Wow, that brought back memories.

'Bout the time I was feeling pretty good about myself, this kid stepped up and bought three balls. He was maybe ten or twelve years old, 65 lbs soaking wet. He glanced at the radar with my 52 still displayed, then glanced at me and smirked. What the... I just got called out by this little shit. He walked up to the mound, gave his shirt sleeve a tug, reared back and threw. First of all, the sound of the ball hitting the back stop was like a bullwhip snap. 63 mph. What the hell? Another smirk. Next pitch, 65. Shut the hell up, how old was this kid? Then his Dad showed up. "Come on, Trav, that's all you got?" his Dad shouted. Third pitch, 66 mph. I just walked away.

The next morning, we stocked up with a week's worth of food and found a cheap campsite where we waited for the Tampa Bay Rays' opening week to start. After almost a full month of Walmarts, I was wanting to settle in and fire up the smoker. The Rays were on the road for the league's opening day, so I'd actually catch their home opener on a Tuesday evening. Sweet. Shouldn't be a problem getting tickets on a weekday, night game. Funds were low, but payday was just around the corner.

Alexander Springs Recreation Area in the Ocala National Forest was what the sign read, as we pulled up to the campground's guard shack. This was run by a private company, a bit pricey but still not bad for half price, plus you had access to the cold water spring. In this heat, that was definitely a selling point. The campsites were pretty secluded with heavy ground palms, moss, and vines hanging from the trees. It was as close to a tropical rainforest as I have ever seen. They say that this is where they made all the old Tarzan movies from the 30s or whenever. Legend has it, they released all the animals into the forest when they were done filming. So there's supposedly monkeys, massive boas, and other fun critters, besides just the lovable alligators. I swear, EVERYTHING, in Florida, wants you dead. Gators, snakes, spiders, sharks; now add spider monkeys in for some fun. This should be interesting.

The cold springs was pretty cool, pun absolutely intended. The water was like 40f, absolutely freezing, but fantastic in the sweltering midday heat. Sadly, Kimber couldn't go in the spring, so I had to find a way to get her wet and cooled off. Luckily, we were one of the only people camping, so we had the run of the place. I turned on the campground's water spigot that was outside the bathrooms and let Kimber roll around under the water. I've never seen a bully-breed dog take to the water like Kimber does. She enjoyed her bath, and we headed back to the camper.

When I got back to the camper, I bent down to pick up Kimber and just about freaked out. There must've been at least a dozen teeny tiny little ticks all over my feet and ankles. They were just hatched and must've been over by the water. I'd never seen so many at once and especially on me! When I was a kid, I had an itch on the inside of my belly button. When I scratched I felt something, looking down into my belly button hole, I saw a tick. My dad grabbed some tweezers and by the time the thing let go, my belly button was pulled out like 3 inches, and snapped back. That's it, that's all it took. Traumatized for life. I fucking hate ticks. Pardon my French.

After completely going over Kimber and myself, I went inside and grabbed some fly spray, painting the ground all around my camper, hoping that this would kill, or at least keep the ticks away. I had just finished dinner and settled in for bed when Kimber started growling. Oh boy, here we go. I grabbed this monster flashlight I have, 2900 lumens, I've run bears off with this thing. I opened the door, hit the go button on the flashlight and came face to face with a street gang of raccoons. I'm not exaggerating, these things were as big as dogs, stopped what they were doing, turned and looked at me like they were gonna whoop my ass. I fully expected one to say "What?" while spreading his arms in an exasperated, Joe Pesci, *Goodfellas*, like motion. They were going after the garbage that was on one of those poles with a big hook to hang garbage up high. You know, the ones so raccoons don't get in your trash. One was literally on top of the pole, swinging at the garbage bag like it's a piñata, half of it already emptied on the ground. That was the noise I heard. None of them ran, none of them. They just stood there looking at me, a couple even starting to slowly turn my way. Nope. I just slowly closed the door; I'll pick the trash up in the morning. I hit the truck alarm this time, which seemed to do the trick as they all scampered back into the woods. No more peeing outside at night for this guy and pup... Jesus.

The next day, after cleaning the garbage up, Kimber and I went for a hike. No mountains at all to climb, but a really cool plank walkway that went on for at least a mile into a swampy area

163

nearby. Needless to say, Kimber was glued to my hip with the leash tight. Neither of which she was happy about; better than being gator bait, little girl. It was so hot and humid that only a mile out and we were done. Back to the camper for some AC. I broke down and fired up the generator, trying to conserve fuel until payday. I left Kimber in the camper, after wiping her down with a wet cloth and turning the AC on high, while I went to swim in the cold spring again. It wasn't going to be long and the generator was far from the camper, so I felt safe to leave her.

That evening I got some writing done, cooked dinner and settled into the bed. Kimber was already up there, passed out from the day's heat. We slept good that night until the generator quit, after running out of gas. Shit! I had fallen asleep with the air on and ran out of gas. Great, just great.

Well, it was already morning by now, so I decided to get up and get moving. I felt an itch, or more like a bite, in a place where a man NEVER wants to feel an itch or a bite; quickly, I reached down and scratched my sack. My nail hitting something hard attached to my skin. What the hell. I jump up and put on my glasses and grabbed the flashlight. As hard as I tried, my fat ass couldn't see anything down there. I needed a mirror. I threw on some shorts and practically sprinted to the bathroom. Not caring if anybody walked in, I dropped trough, lifted up my scrotum and peered into the mirror. Sweet Jesus, help me. It was a tick, buried in my sack. A plethora of options flooded through my head. Vaseline is supposed to make them back out. Let me tell ya, when you got a tick, knee-deep in your scrotum, you're not going to stand around smearing petroleum jelly on your junk, hoping the thing isn't going to give you the plague, or worse yet, Lyme disease. Thankfully, I brought my shaving kit, just in case my worse fear was legit. Out with the tweezers and all my childhood nightmares. I grabbed that little bastard and started pulling. At this point in your life, remembering whether it's clockwise or counter clockwise, just wasn't that important. They say you have to worry about leaving some of the tick inside of you... not this time. The monster had a piece of me in his jaws, bigger than daylight. I took a close-up picture, and sure enough… O. M. G. THAT HURT. Did I mention I hate ticks?

By this point I was done, but was still two days away from payday and five days until the game. I had to see if they would give me a refund, or something. I told the desk lady all the drama we had with the ticks and the raccoons, and asked if there was any way I could get a refund. I told her I was a disabled vet traveling the country and could use the money, but either way, I couldn't stay here anymore. I know, pathetic sob story. Did I mention the tick on my junk? She asked where I was heading next, which I replied with most of the southern states. She told me she could give me credit and if I found a campground run by their company, I could use my days there. Ok good enough, either way, I was out of that tick infested jungle.

A few days later, with my direct deposit firmly in my account, the next few days would be much easier to navigate. It was kinda cool going back to the Tampa area because I already knew my way around somewhat. Whenever I go to these amazing places and don't have the money to eat someplace, I always say "next time." Well, now it was next time and I got paid. I had passed on this place last time, but now I was crushing a monster pastrami sandwich, at a place called The Lucky Dill, that was to die for. We stayed at our favorite Walmart with all the shade, hit the gym that was right around the corner, got some laundry done, and even some beach time for Kimber. We were all set for the kick-off of the MLB season, and I was ready to get out of Florida.

April 4th, we kicked off the 2017 MLB regular season with opening day at Tropicana Field, home of the Tampa Bay Rays. As usual, I got there bright and early, scouting out the parking possibilities for the Rig. The park is located in downtown Tampa, with plenty of uncovered parking, so that wasn't an issue. I found a shaded spot in a back lot that apparently was for employee parking. After I had parked the camper, a couple cars pulled in close enough for me to hear the people who got out of them talking. They were concession workers, first day on the job, introducing themselves to each other. Déjà vu, for sure. I stayed in the camper with Kimber for most of the afternoon, until the sun went down and I could slide out of the camper and walk to the game. I'll take free parking any day, especially if it means my dog is even safer where we parked. By this time, they had a lot attendant at the driveway, checking IDs.

Tropicana Field looked like a giant circus tent that had fallen down on one side. A round building with a dome roof leaning strangely to one side. At night it looked like a giant UFO landing in some 50s sci-fi movie; you could almost make out the strings holding it up. Inside was more like walking around a shopping mall. It had three levels with open walkways, lined with storefronts, offices, and eateries. There was no sign of the field; I actually had to look for where my gate was to see the grass because the field wasn't open to view like most parks. There was no mezzanine to walk around while you watched the game from different areas. You found your tunnel that went to your seating area. You could move around in the park, but it was limited. They also had this crazy dome ceiling that looked like a spoked rim of a low rider with three rings and about a hundred or so "spokes" coming off the center, all white in color except for the metallic beams holding the spokes. All I could think of was that poor outfielder, trying to see a white ball, against a white roof. All in all, it was just a weird park. Either way, Tropicana Field, MLB park #10… COMPLETE.

Now get me out of this state, back to the Atlantic coast, and the cool ocean air. That's exactly what we did. After a good night's sleep, we hit the road bright and early, this time taking the Interstate back to the coast where we had left off. Starting with Daytona Beach, we worked our way north through dozens and dozens of small coastal beach towns, until Jacksonville, where we were forced to take I95 to the Georgia border. Florida, state #18, and Grapefruit League Spring Training... COMPLETE!

Georgia

April 4th, 2017. Happy to be leaving Florida, not due to the visit, I was just eager to explore another state that I'd never seen. The plan for Georgia was to continue up the coastline to Savannah, see an Atlanta Braves game, and visit the state's two National Battlefields; other than that, we were wide open for exploration.

We hit the Georgia border just in time to catch the tail end of a pretty bad storm. It was starting to get dark, with storm clouds churning above. I've lived in the South long enough to know when it's getting ready to pour and I needed to get somewhere quick. The next major town was Brunswick, GA, that thankfully had a Super Walmart just off the main interstate. As I made the corner into the store parking lot, I saw the familiar armada of various RVs and travel trailers, which was always a welcome sign. I found an open spot toward the end of the row and turned off the motor. In my rear view mirror I saw an older gentleman, mid 70s I'd say, walking up to my driver's side window, like a cop on a traffic stop. I rolled down my window and waited to see what he had to say. "Could you please pull up over there," he said while pointing at a spot on the edge of the parking lot. I looked at his shirt and hat, expecting to see a Walmart logo or a security officer badge, but there was nothing. His clothes were actually somewhat dingy, stained and dirty. "Why?" I asked. He began to ramble on about the weather, the weekend, and how many RVs he's going to have to fit into the parking lot. At this point, I was pretty sure he wasn't all there. The spot where he wanted me to park was on the corner of the lot next to the main road and a fast food joint. Traffic everywhere, and way too close for Kimber's safety or my sleep, I cut him off and said, "I'll move," while starting the truck. Just wanting to get away from this dude, I drove to the far side of the Walmart and parked near the back. Before I could even finish checking the weather on my phone, this guy was at my window again. "What now?" I snapped at him as I cracked the window. Now he says they will tow me if I'm not in the RV section. It was starting to rain. He wasn't being rude, he was actually apologetic. That's when he told me that they let him park over there, if he keeps the RVers in the specified area and keeps it clean. So he was homeless, that explained a lot. "Ok man, no sweat. Thanks." I backed into the originally requested spot; clinging to Kimber, we crawled into the camper before he could walk back across the lot. I will forever remember this dude as the Sheriff of the Brunswick Walmart.

Later that evening, I decided to eat a nice meal out; it was time for dinner and I was starving. Next to my truck was an older model pick-up with a camper shell on the back. I did notice that it had a Navy Veteran sticker on the back window. Not thinking much about it, I let Kimber out to do her thing, then set her up with food and water so I could go find my own supper. When I stepped out of the camper, the shell door on the truck next to me was up, with a tarp over the end as the rain was starting to pick up. I saw someone in the back, heating up some coffee on a burner. Thinking it was another traveling vet, I said hello. It was the old, homeless, sheriff guy. He's a homeless vet!? My heart sank. He crawled out of his makeshift bunk. "You're a vet?" I asked, pointing at the sticker. His face sunk slightly, a look of embarrassment came over his face. "Yup. Vietnam." I held out my hand, "Marine Corps, 89-95, Desert Storm and Somalia. Welcome home, brother." He hesitated for a split second before reaching for my hand, slightly nodding at what I had just said. We chatted briefly but never about his status or how he got here. I motioned at the fast food joint across the street, "Hungry?" He immediately said no and that he was fine, obviously embarrassed to take a handout. I could see why he was directing traffic, he didn't want to park for free. I came back from the fast food place with two extra cheeseburgers and some fries. "Man, I'm stuffed. Here, take these. No way I'm going to finish them. They screwed up and gave me an extra order of fries too," I said while I sat the bag on his lowered tailgate. "Ya sure?" he asked. "Throw it in the trash if you don't want it," I said as I opened the door to the camper. "Have a good one man," I said, crawled in and shut the door. The bag was gone before I could get in the camper and look out the window. I knew that would be the only way his pride would allow him to take that meal. How do I know? I've been there. God bless that man.

The rain was brutal, it pounded the camper for hours, giving way to an entire new crop of leaks. I pulled the mattress back to mop up the water, when I saw the camper's wood interior was completely rotted and moldy. This wasn't good. I just needed this thing to get us home, then I I'd have enough cash saved to buy a travel trailer or a newer cab-over. I sprayed bleach and water on the mold, dried it the best I could, and marched on.

The next day was sunny and beautiful. Not wanting to take the interstate, but unable to drive the sporadic coastline, we followed Hwy 17 north, which basically mirrored the interstate all the way to Savannah. With tall pines lining the road, we passed through numerous small towns, reminding me a lot of east Texas. The weather was perfect as we pulled into the visitor center in downtown Savannah.

My friends from Minnesota, Nate and Laurel, had mentioned this place to me when they stopped here on their journey north. The visitor center was right in downtown Savannah, walking distance to all the hot tourist spots, the marketplace and the riverwalk included. Amazingly, they offer a two-day stay at 8 bucks a night for RV camping. This had to be the best kept secret in Georgia. The history and beauty of this city was unparalleled thus far. Lots of Irish pubs and history here too, along with an actual battlefield just a block away in the heart of the city!

That evening I explored the marketplace, had some amazing pizza, and enjoyed the nightlife of Savannah, while Kimber comfortably slept a couple blocks away. The next day, we explored the riverwalk, old town Savannah, a couple of Irish pubs and the Battle of Savannah battleground, a Revolutionary War Battle where the Patriots overtook an English redoubt. Notably, General Pulaski was killed there, which led to the naming of Fort Pulaski, located just off the Savannah Coast.

With new knowledge that there was a military fort just a few miles away that was used not only in the Revolutionary War but also the Civil War, we had our plans for the day. We left the Savannah visitor center heading for Fort Pulaski, bright and early the next morning. When we arrived, I was surprised to find out this was designated as a National Monument, but was also a battlefield, another sub-category of the National Park designators to keep an eye out for. The Park Service offered a self-guided tour, which I opted for, that gave access to the entire fort; and they also planned to shoot off a 30lb cannon later that day. Even far away in the truck, I knew Kimber would not be amused; but I sure was! That thing was loud. Also, the entire shape of the fort resembled a baseball field, which I found out the Civil War troops had played on, even displaying a hand-carved bat at one of the exhibits. Well worth a visit if in the area.

While exploring the grounds, I met a woman in her late thirties I assumed was also enjoying the displays. Enter my friend Honey, a Space-X employee from Florida, on a road trip of her own, checking out our nation's forts. She was the daughter of an Air Force veteran and loved our country's military and its history. Hmm, sounds familiar. I told her about my travels and exchanged information. As of this writing, Honey had moved to Colorado, fallen in love with the state, and is now a homeowner near Colorado Springs. This is what's so awesome about traveling and exploring, you will find your own little slice of heaven eventually. Soon, I too, would find my happy place... very, very soon.

From Fort Pulaski, we turned northwest toward Atlanta, once again opting for the country highway rather than the interstate. I had found some mountain bike trails near a campground that looked promising, just outside Milledgeville. It was also the closest National Forest I could find for a much needed break from the public. Once we found a spot and settled in, I jumped on the bike and went for a few good runs. Lots of good trails, pretty sandy, but shaded, helped with the sweltering humidity... and it was only April. When I hopped off my bike after a couple hours of riding, I noticed my hips were aching. Weird. I'd never had my hips ache before. I pretty much just chalked it up to old age and forgot about it.

After a couple days of solitude, I wanted to see where the Braves ballpark was; also to stop by the Kennesaw National Battlefield, both located on the northeast side of town. First stop was the gym, as a shower was definitely in order, and I really needed to get my joints moving with a workout or something. That morning I had woken up pretty sore, all my joints this time. In the back of my mind I was starting to think something more was wrong, but quickly discounted any reason to have to see a doctor. So once again, getting old sucks. Ya that works, let's go.

Next stop was SunTrust Park, the brand-new home to the Atlanta Braves. This was the inaugural season for the Braves' new ballpark, and I wanted to catch the very first day game, that just happened to be on Easter Sunday! We found the box office, hidden by all the delivery trucks and construction equipment. They were literally just finishing the build, and stocking the food and beverages; it was a crazy scene with the first game of the first home series being just two days away. We scored a good centerfield seat, with a military discount it was just 15 bucks. Ticket in hand, it was nearing supper time, and I was done for the day. Instead of Walmart in the big city, I went back to the Anytime Fitness from the morning's shower and parked without a problem.

Since we were here and had some time to kill, I decided to go to the nearest VA hospital to get my cortisone shots. I'd been getting them in my elbows and shoulders for about a year now, although I had a suspicion that I really needed surgery. Just weight-lifting injuries, nothing substantial, but tendinitis sure is annoying and painful. When I finally found the Atlanta VA, I couldn't believe what I saw. It was like they tried to cram a big old building into a little tiny lot. Construction going on made it even worse, with no parking other than in a parking garage; obviously it was not going to fit the Rig. I found a spot to park, after moving a orange construction pylon out of the way, and was immediately run off by a VA cop. Ok, well so much for my shots, I'd have to try again somewhere else. North Carolina would be the next closest VA hospital according to my primary care nurse back in Phoenix, who had to coordinate my care with whatever VA I go to. I learned my lesson from Idaho surgery.

It was only noon, and the Kennesaw National Battlefield was just a few miles away, located in one of the outer suburbs of Atlanta. It was a very popular place for locals to exercise and for school field trips, as the parking lot was almost full. Luckily when I pulled in, a Park Ranger moved a small yellow cone, allowing me to park in the designated "bus" area. "No way you'd fit in any of these spots," he said as I pulled into the long bus lane. Super cool! Kimber and I jumped in the back and had some lunch before we headed up the mountain. Apparently, this battle was fought on the side of a steep hill, because some of the hikers coming down looked beat up… bad. This would be interesting.

The Battle of Kennesaw Mountain took place just NE of Atlanta in the town of Marietta, with only the Kennesaw Mountain and 65,000 of the Confederate General Johnston's troops separating the Union's General Sherman and company from Atlanta. We all have heard of Sherman burning Atlanta to the ground in history class, so this was the battle just before Atlanta burned. So much for a spoiler alert, Union wins and absolutely brutalizes Atlanta and its population. I found it interesting that at one point in the battle, a cannon had set fire to the dry grass on the hill and was basically burning the wounded alive. The Confederate Commander jumped up on a cannon and yelled, "This is butchery! Stop firing and come collect your men." Which both sides did, pulling the dead and wounded to their respective sides, stomping out the fire, then resumed fighting! But not before the Union Officer gave a fine set of pistols to the

Confederate Commander for appreciation of his action before hostilities resumed. Cool right? But then came the absolute savagery of the Union Army upon the civilians, as Sherman ordered all things aiding the southern war machine burned to the ground, to include railroads, hospitals, stores, and farms. Even to the point of forcing the remaining locals to leave the city, they were pushed further south or north, in order to make Atlanta a "military city" for the Union. An interesting addition to the lack of accuracy from my high school history education. Once again, always keeping in mind that these were ALL Americans, committing these atrocities on fellow Americans; it all seems so surreal.

The visitor center to the Kennesaw National Battlefield Park was beautiful. A very modern looking, apparently fairly new or remodeled building held the video and small museum with artifacts from the battle. The outside grounds was basically a wide, well maintained hiking trail that led up to the top of the mountain and along its crest. It was a humid and hot day, but the trail was busy with locals hiking or jogging and tourists interested in the history. Along the trail were information placards, describing the different areas of the battlefield, and a few small cannons placed around earthworks, representing the dug in Confederate positions. At the top of the mountain, you were rewarded with a great view of Atlanta and of the local town, Marietta.

After the hike, I was ready to find a campsite to hide out until the game. The closest National Forest to the ballpark was quite a drive north, but was the only thing I could find that was even close to affordable. I didn't want to hop around Walmarts for another three days waiting on the game. If we were going be here for a week or so, might as well set up a home-base. It was also nice to take the basket and the bikes off the truck while in the big city for obvious reasons, but mainly for the parking. I found a campsite in the Chattahoochee National Forest, about an hour from Atlanta; hopefully there won't be a gang of raccoons and an army of ticks there to greet us.

The drive was longer than I had expected, due to an incredible grade that we had to climb. The campground was situated at the bottom of the OTHER side of the mountain from Atlanta. They failed to mention that in the description. At least the beauty of the drive made up for time and mileage. Beautiful farm country, then up a tall mountain, and down the backside into a small valley, with the Pocket NF campground, yup that's its name, nestled in the foothills near a large creek.

I found a nice spot in the back, away from the weekend campers and all the kids screaming in the nearby creek. I suddenly wasn't feeling well. I had one helluva headache, and these achy joints weren't getting any better. That's when I noticed my skin felt funny; ugh, I really was getting sick. Sure enough, for the rest of the day and on into the night, I suffered through some brutal fevers, sweats, and chills. It was like a really bad flu, minus the vomit. Luckily, I was able to set up camp before it got really bad; I had plenty of food and water, and nothing to do until Sunday. I had packed some NyQuil just in case, took a good swig, and drifted off to sleep. Saturday wasn't much better, I stayed in and just did the NyQuil boogie all day and the next night. Finally feeling halfway decent Sunday morning, thank God, I headed to the gym for a shower before heading to the ballpark. That had to be the worst 48 hour bug I've ever had.

Easter Sunday, 2017. The first day game of the Braves' new SunTrust Park, how freaking cool is that. I had no idea they had a new park, nor did I plan to be here for this specific game. The timing, once again, was uncanny. Without any covered parking tall enough for the Rig, I had to take a spot about a mile away at an office building, selling parking spots with lot attendants. It was well shaded, gate security, and offered a free shuttle, so the twenty buck price was worth it. After Kimber was secured with all her amenities safely in the camper, I climbed on the shuttle bus and headed for the park.

I was there nice and early, with the players still doing warm-up drills. The park was basically empty which gave me ample time to explore and take pictures. The park featured an incredible museum walk, right in the main concourse, showing off a lot of the great Hank Aaron's gear, and more of the Atlanta Braves' history. They had a display that caught my attention, team jerseys dating back to the inception of the team. I knew they were the Milwaukee Braves before Atlanta, but had no idea they were originally from Boston!

The game didn't start until 1305 and right now it was just barely noon. I finished walking this amazing park, with all of its modern amenities. The kids area made me wish I was 9 again. They had everything from a virtual reality batting cage to a rock wall and zip line! I was able to get all my pictures, grab a burger, and get a beer once it was officially the afternoon. I walked up to a beer cart, that had like three guys standing there, with no help in sight. I asked if they were waiting on beer to which one replied, "No beer until 12:30. It's Sunday." I had to smile. Oh ya, we're back in the South now. I had lived in a dry county back in Texas, I should've known. By

1230 the beer lines were halfway around the park, but the clear plastic mug with crystal looking tomahawk for a handle was well worth the wait.

After the Braves had some batting practice, the center fielder, Encinarte, tossed a ball right at me, which I caught with one hand, not spilling my beer, much to the enjoyment of the folks around me. Then about three rows down, where the ball may have been supposed to go, a guy turned around with his little baby girl strapped across his chest in a sling contraption. I instantly handed the ball down to him. He had his hands up too, but was the only one with a baby. Once again the crowd loved the gesture, just like Oakland. Not gonna lie, back at the campsite that night, I contemplated what I had done. I caught a hand tossed ball from Ender Inciarte, on the first day game of the new SunTrust Park, on Easter Sunday, while on my trip. That kid better be a baseball fan. The best part was that little girl would always have that ball, and I will always have that memory. Suntrust Park, MLB park #11… COMPLETE!

It was about 1500 by the time I got back to a peacefully sleeping Kimber. In no hurry to rush to camp, and wanting to soak up as much truck AC as possible, I set the GPS to "no highways" and hit the back roads home. Unbelievably enough, I came across a small Georgia State Civil War Battlefield, commemorating the "Battle of Resaca."

Located about halfway between Chattanooga and Atlanta, near the town of Resaca, is where Confederate General Johnston withstood two days of repeated Union assaults, before withdrawing to Kennesaw Mountain. This small battlefield was the first battle of Sherman's Atlanta Campaign. Reality check, I thought it was just a grass field where I could throw the ball for Kimber. What an amazing find! So apparently, we're following Sherman backwards, from Savannah (his ultimate goal), to Atlanta, now Resaca; ALL BY CHANCE. How freaking cool is that!! Unreal!

Back at the "Pocket" that night, it was quiet, way too quiet. All the weekend campers, who were mainly locals, had left. We were literally the only ones there. With zero cell service, no town within miles, my mind started to wander. Northern Georgia, isn't that where that movie *Deliverance* was made? I was a sitting duck for any hillbilly that wants to add a truck and dog to his possessions. May sound a little paranoid, but you really have to think about your surroundings, but with a realistic mindset. Not everybody is there on vacation, and lots of bad folks prey on the good-hearted. It's just life, deal with it. After checking the map, and realizing I was a good two hundred miles from the Appalachia, I slept slightly better.

We slept in that next morning, before heading north to the Chickamauga National Battlefield. After Resaca, I was super curious to see what started Sherman on this brutal campaign through Georgia. Now it was turning into something like a history geo-cache game. I was digging this! Just outside the park was a small town with another Buffalo Wild Wings across the street from a Walmart. Perfect timing for happy hour, my favorite wings, watching some baseball, and then get a good night's rest before Chickamauga.

Just as I paid for my meal, it started to rain. Not just normal rain, but a don't be the third monkey on Noah's ramp kinda rain. Buckets upon buckets came down, completely soaking me by the time I ran to the camper. Of course some windows were down so everything inside was wet, including Kimber, who was now drying herself nicely on my pillow. Lovely. About that time, I got a text from my Dad, asking where I was. After catching up on my travels, I sent him a picture of this weird bruise on my thigh, which I assumed was another tick bite. It looked like a dot, with a ring, and maybe even a bigger ring around that one, but very faint. It was also raised quite a bit and had been there for awhile. Nothing on my sack though, but a hard bump. I told him about the aches and fever I had a couple weeks after the tick nightmare. My Dad is no doctor, but he's taught high school level advanced biology for decades, so he was the closest thing I had to a doctor consult at the moment. He said it sounded like Lyme and I had better get to a hospital. This prompted me to pose the question to the Facebook page community, to get their input. Also an overwhelming GO! With the weather calling for rain the next two days, I guess I might as well make the three-hour trek to Asheville, NC.

No way was I going to Atlanta again, so first thing the next morning, when the rain slowed down slightly, I hit the interstate for Asheville. I figured I'd just take the freeway there, see the doc, get some shots or whatever, and come straight back, picking up right where we left off. Even though I'd be going into Tennessee and North Carolina, I wasn't going to count this as an official visit.

After a very long and rainy drive, Kimber and I arrived in Asheville around mid-afternoon. Not in the mood to sit at the VA emergency room after a 4-hour drive, I decided to visit the local Anytime Fitness, grab some food, and park at the local Walmart for the evening. All was fine until we got to the Walmart, where they didn't allow overnight parking, and there weren't any other RVs or semis there. It was attached to another strip mall, so I parked right between the two parking lots and hoped for the best.

Early the next morning, I headed for the VA hospital, which was enormous! It took me awhile to find the emergency room entrance, and to my surprise, I was the only one in the room. After explaining to the nurse what happened, they saw me within 5 minutes, took about 3 gallons of blood, set me up on a week's worth of antibiotics, and said the tests would be back in about 5 days. They asked if I could stick around the area until the tests came back. Ugh, that was a long time to wait, especially without a friendly Walmart to stay at. When I asked if I could get my cortisone shots, they said I'd have to be seen by their orthopedics department, and made an appointment for a couple weeks out. I was shocked at their efficiency! Where was I again? I'd just have to time my travels right to be back in NC by my appointment date. Sweet! My elbows were screaming by now, and Motrin wasn't cutting it.

With it still raining, there really wasn't much we could do but drive to the next town where they had another, more traveler friendly Walmart... and wait. Since we had all the time in the world and another week until payday, I set the GPS to backroads again, following Hwy 23 toward the Waynesville, NC Walmart. Along the way, I noticed a small country market that was advertising fresh local veggies, called the Owl Produce Market, in an old, run down building, alongside a creek that separated the roadside market from the steep, densely forested mountainside. I walked inside to be greeted by the most friendly elderly lady working the counter. She had seen my Marine tattoo and asked if I was a Marine. "Yes Ma'am, I am. Once a Marine..." I began to say, when she finished my sentence, "Always a Marine," with a glimmer in her eye. "My late second husband was a Marine!" she said with a sly smile. "Lord, I loved that man!" From that point on, Kimber and I were like long lost family. After loving on Kimber, she showed me around the store, explaining to me what everything was. Things like Amish Hard Candy and FROG jelly, which is an acronym for Fig, Raspberry, Orange and Ginger. Super tasty and a local favorite. She also showed me these small green onion looking plants that she kept in an airtight chest cooler. She called them "Ramps" or "Spring Tonic," a very small and extremely strong leek/garlic plant that only grew in that area. Mixed in a moonshine concoction of some kind, it's supposed to cure you of everything. After she told me this, I had to ask her, "Do you sell moonshine for the tonic too?" as innocently as possible. She looked up at me and said, "You mean white lightning? We haven't had any of that around here since he passed." She was pointing at an 8x12 framed picture hanging on the wall, high above the register. No freaking way! I had to get closer to make sure I was seeing it correctly.

There were two men, just their faces, smiling into the camera. One had a long grey beard, a worn Appalachian felt hat, and eyes that I couldn't have missed anywhere. "Is that..." I stuttered. It was Popcorn Sutton, the famous moonshiner who was caught, convicted, and sentenced to 20 years at the age of like 75. "Popcorn" obviously wasn't going to live out that sentence, and killed himself before he was to be incarcerated, but not before making an amazing autobiography of his life making moonshine. A must see. The other gentleman was the owner of the store, apparently a close family friend. I was literally in Popcorn Sutton's hometown! How freakin' cool is that!? This was my first real dose of Appalachia… and a weird sense of belonging.

After only a couple of nights in and around the town of Waynesville, I received a call from the doc giving me the all clear. No Lyme, oh thank God! Turned out it was a type of tick that didn't carry Lyme, but mimicked it for a few days of pure hell. After learning what Lyme can do to you, and how you carry it forever, I hit my knees and just gave thanks. Another serious bullet averted, I felt truly blessed. Now back to Georgia and Sherman's Atlanta Campaign.

Keeping the setting on backroads, I reset the destination to Fort Oglethorpe, GA, and followed the map. This time Google decided to take me through the Great Smoky Mountains National Park that actually straddled the state line between Georgia and Tennessee. Absolutely gorgeous land, with wild turkeys and blooming Dogwood trees, plenty of trails and picnic spots, with the Appalachian Trail across the summit. A view that was worth the fairly steep hike to the peak. One day I'll attempt the Appalachian Trail, soon as I can figure out how to get dropped off in Maine and picked up in Georgia.

We exited the park on the Georgia side, into the vacationland of Gatlinburg, TN. This was quite a shock, driving through the amazing wild beauty of the Appalachian Mountains into what seemed to be another mini Las Vegas, minus the casinos. Famous chain restaurants had bigger and fancier signs than normal stores. Shows and amusement parks were advertised on billboards and digital screens everywhere. It was a very busy scene, literally just a mile or two from the Park's gate. From there, we followed the winding backroads through Tennessee just south of Knoxville, eventually finding our way back to the Walmart at Fort Oglethorpe, this time not submerged in a lake of rainwater.

Not only was I clueless about what happened at the Battle of Chickamauga, I'd never even heard of it. When we rolled through the park gates bright and early the next day, I realized that this place was even bigger than Vicksburg. Just south of the town of Fort Oglethorpe, and literally three times the size, sat the Chickamauga Battlefield. Turns out that this is actually only one battlefield within the entire Chickamauga and Chattanooga National Military Park. Yup, this battle covered two states, and about five separate battlefields. Just the Chickamauga Park itself, was 5,300 acres, with hiking, bicycle and horse trails. There was a large reception center that had a video about the entire campaign, a large artifact museum, and the Fuller Gun Collection; the most impressive display of period firearms I'd seen since Cody, Wyoming.

Ok, so quite a bit went on here historically; I'm gonna try to keep this short. We're literally stepping into the middle of the fight, so stick with me here. The two major players were US Major General Rosecrans and his Army of the Cumberland, versus CSA General Bragg and his Army of Tennessee. Rosecrans, fresh off his victorious Tullahoma Campaign, now positioning his forces to run the Confederates out of Chattanooga, thus opening an attack on the largest southern supply hub... the City of Atlanta. CSA General Bragg, being pushed from middle Tennessee to Chattanooga by Rosecrans, tried to hold the city, but failed. In short, Bragg was forced out of Chattanooga, only to regroup and bolster his numbers with Confederate Lt. Gen. Longstreet and the Army of Northern Virginia. The counter-attack pushed the Union Army back to Chattanooga, while the Confederates held the surrounding hilltops. So Chickamauga was a win for the South, and a crucial Union defeat; maybe that's why I'd never heard of it.

Now this began what is known as the Battle for Chattanooga. US Generals Grant, Sherman, and Hooker all show up to bolster what's left of Rosecrans command. Grant is given command of Union forces in the west, replaces Rosecrans with Maj. Gen. Thomas, and begins to push Bragg's Confederates back into Georgia. Bragg is weakened by Longstreet being dispatched to assist Gen Burnside in Knoxville, thus retreating back into Georgia, hoping to protect Atlanta from attack, bringing us full circle to Sherman's Atlanta Campaign. Whew, that was a lot.

Newly armed with all this info, I wanted to get some hiking in before it started to rain again. Kimber and I hit the trail for what would turn out to be a 7 mile walk through some amazing history and crazy goosebumps. I also learned that this park was the model for Vicksburg, which explained the similarities. The same amazing bronze statues, intricate carvings into granite as unit position markers, all donated as tributes from their home states, thus seeming to try and out do other states in a contest of patriotism and pride.

I stood in the center of what's called "Battle Line Road," a street lined with dozens of massive statues representing the troop unit placement and total numbers. Thousands of Union men lined one side of the street, while only one lone statue faced them as an enemy on the opposite side of the street... The State of Texas. I had to chuckle, after living in Texas, imagining how many Texans would LOVE that monument, and make sure everybody within earshot knew they were Texan. Don't mess with Texas, for real.

About that time, an elderly gentleman was jogging by. He had a white V-neck t-shirt, blue jeans, and windbreaker tied around his waist. He saw Kimber and stopped to say hello. I was apparently still smiling from amusing myself, when he asked what was so funny. I explained the Texas against the world thing, and we both had a laugh. Enter my buddy Keith. After explaining the whole book thing, like a sales pitch I'd memorized by then, he told me that he too was a veteran. He was a WWII truck driver, kept stateside because he knew how to drive a manual shift 18-wheeler. His dad teaching him to drive as part of the family business actually kept him out of the war. Here he was, a mere 90-year-old, not on any prescription medications other than glasses, jogging in blue jeans, in the crazy hot Georgian humidity. Wow. I want whatever he's having! Got a couple pics of Keith and Kimber, what an inspiration.

That's when I noticed that there were all types of people out enjoying the park, from elderly tour buses, to Cub Scouts earning a badge of some sort. There were bicyclists and hikers, a few dogs on leashes here and there, trailers with horses, and even some re-enactments of the battle; but mainly, just the community enjoying these beautiful grounds. Neat to see a place that held such a tragic event bring the future generations together to enjoy. Actually, that's exactly how this park came into being.

In 1889, the surviving Union veterans from the battles of Chickamauga and Chattanooga, decided to invite their southern counter parts to a large BBQ feast and reunion that they planned to have in Chattanooga. That olive branch offered was what began this amazing place. Later, as those veterans became senators and congressman, legislation was passed to memorialize this place and that BBQ. Now that's pretty cool.

That night, we went back to the Fort Oglethorpe Walmart for a much deserved, good night's sleep. Tomorrow, we venture over the border into Tennessee. Georgia, state #19... COMPLETE.

Tennessee

April 24th, 2017. We crossed into Tennessee bright and early that next morning. The storm was still upon us, but the worst had passed. With a weird combination of warm, humid air and a light but steady cool rain, this combination spelled doom for the camper, which was about to disintegrate already. Every corner was wet, every window leaked, including two spots just above my pillow. Lovely, now I get can water boarded while I'm trying to sleep. I found a Walmart that was attached to a huge mall, with miles of parking. I got on the other side of a big tractor trailer, shielding me from noise and visibility from the store, and just hung out for the day. A much needed break to chart out the route and plan our Tennessee visit.

First things first, we had to see the Battle of Lookout Mountain, and finish the Chattanooga side of the Military Park. One of the Park Rangers back at the Chickamauga Museum was a Marine who told me not to miss that one. There were a couple National Battlefields north toward Nashville that were also a must, not to mention, a couple high school friends who were following the Facebook page I needed to drop in on. Lastly, I really wanted to see Johnson City for some strange reason, like I was compelled to go. Maybe I liked that song, "Wagon Wheel," too much, maybe I was just batshit crazy, either way, we were going to see Johnson City. Besides, from there I could cross into North Carolina and only be twenty minutes from Asheville for my VA appointment. So ya, JC, we see you last. Funds were definitely low, I'd be Walmart hopping, but we would be fine. Yup, that was the plan. Now we'd see what God said about it.

After only a few hours, the rain stopped abruptly, clouds gave way to spots of sunshine. It was the South; if you don't like the weather, give it ten minutes. It'll change. I'd heard that in just about every southern state thus far, and stood true every time. Rain or shine, we headed up the hill to what's called Lookout Mountain, to see what I wasn't supposed to miss. A very narrow, winding road through what looked to be a very affluent neighborhood. Beautiful old custom homes loomed on huge manicured lots, with an eagle's eye view over the city of Chattanooga and the Tennessee River. At least I could see glimpses through the gates and walkways as we kept climbing to the very peak of the mountain. Wow! Just wow! My brother Marine, you were so right.

As you crested the top of the hill, you're immediately greeted by a huge stone entrance, like a castle, complete with two towers that look like giant rook chess pieces. Above the gateway entrance is a creepy, solid black eagle, standing on a globe. Old I guess, but definitely different. The ticket booth is inside the castle, past a steel gate. Not sure if security is needed here, or it's just really old. 1940s is what the plaque said inside, it looked even older.

From this point, you have a complete panoramic view of the entire City of Chattanooga, and miles of the Tennessee River, all within cannon range. How the hell the Union took this position by coming up that hill, literally just blows me away, no pun intended. There were several static cannon displays, all pointing toward the city. I got a great shot of what it looks like to peer down the cannon sights, with the exact center of Chattanooga in the crosshairs. The pictures from here were amazing; this place is a definite must see for history buffs and photographers.

While I was snapping pictures of all the park signage with battle information on them, standing just a few yards away was a gentleman about my age looking out across the valley. We started talking about the view and the battle. Turned out this guy was a pilot, big planes if I remember right, and also a huge history buff. After telling him the book spiel, he asked if I had been to Shiloh. There's another huge National Battlefield literally just a few miles above Bryce's Crossroads in Mississippi. I didn't even see it on my map, must've had baseball on the mind. Wow... thanks, man. He's followed my page and chimed in quite a bit about different Battlefields, steering me in the right direction more than once.

This time my memory completely fails me, as well as my notes, apparently, but I believe he also asked if I had seen a Lookouts game, the local AA team. I looked them up and they just happened to be having a doubleheader for five bucks that very evening. Well, I am now, sir! Thanks again.

I decided I had seen enough battlefield for a minute and wanted to get a beer downtown before the game. This part is Gold. Remember New Orleans had that parking lot downtown, 24 hours for 8 bucks or something. Same thing in Chattanooga, right below the Lookouts Park! There were signs saying no camping, but it was a weekday evening and pretty much empty. I set up Kimber as usual, and headed for a brewery that I found online just down the street.

While I was in the brewery having a sampler tray, a black dude with thick black Stevie Wonder glasses, a black felt cowboy hat, and a bright red Members Only jacket, walked in the door. Yes, you read that correctly. Members Only in bright red. He was carrying some flowers, trying to sell them to guests. I thought the bartender was going to throw him out when he said loudly, "Hey Sandy! Regular?" With a big grin the guy answered, "Yes sir!" then walked into the dining room. I looked at the bartender, who I had been talking to earlier and knew my story. "He was a Marine," the bartender said, nodding toward the dining room while making Sandy's drink. "Vietnam. Recon I think. All the restaurants kinda take care of him." Then Sandy walked up to the bar where his Gin and tonic was waiting. "You hungry?" the bartender asked him. Sandy nodded in the affirmative and asked for a burger. "Fries?" the bartender asked. "You're too good to me," was Sandy's reply. Then the bartender introduced me, mentioning I was a Marine, to which I received a hearty "OOHRAH Marine!" followed by a huge hug and a rose shoved in my face. "I don't have anybody to give it to, Sandy," I said. "Give it to yourself, brother! You're beautiful!" For that he got my 5 bucks and I told him to give it to the prettiest girl in the dining room. On my way out the door, through the bar mirror, I saw him give it to a very elderly white lady, sitting in a wheelchair with her family. Kneeling down to say something, he then kissed her cheek. I had to wipe the tears from my eye sockets before I could see my way out the damn bar. Brutal. Well played, Sandy sir. Semper Fi.

The park was starting to fill up, even with the sky starting to turn grey with storm clouds. The park was good sized, and the locals love their hometown team, the Lookouts. Hot dogs were a couple bucks, craft beers for 5, as it should be. They were playing the Tennessee Smokeys, a huge rival and Chicago Cubs farm team. I stayed for the first game but wanted to check on Kimber before the second game. It was dark now, and starting to get a little cold. When I got to the trailer, Kimber was spooked and shaking uncontrollably. Then I realized they shot a cannon or something after each Lookout home run, which there were a few. Well, that settles that, our night was done. I put on some headphones, curled up with Kimber, and watched a movie on the phone. That was one heck of a day. Baseballs and Battlefields indeed!

A thick fog covered the road as we made our way west toward the Shiloh National Battlefield. It was so thick that truckers were pulling over and sitting this one out. If truckers are doing it, I'm gonna pay attention. So I too pulled over in the long line of both trucks and passenger vehicles. The fog was super thick, but within an hour I thought I'd be good, plus I wanted out in front of these semis starting to rumble back to life. Within a couple hours the fog was starting to clear again, and I was able to make out the next road sign. Lynchburg 120 miles. Wait, Lynchburg? We're in Tennessee, right!? It must've been a message from the divine, shining through the lifting fog, Jack Daniels Distillery here we come.

Even if you're not a whiskey fan, the Jack Daniels Distillery is still a must see. Truly an iconic American brand that dates back to our country's prohibition days. The Old No.7 is the first distillery to gain a federal license post prohibition. Interestingly enough, the distillery is located in a "dry county" but only the distillery itself can sell alcohol. Our tour guy, the big grey bearded guy in overalls on the tv commercial, had mentioned that two truckloads of whiskey just happened to make it to the capital building the day before the vote to allow Jack Daniels to sell liquor from his own distillery within county lines! The "Angel Taste" tour is highly recommended and be sure to get your military/veteran discount. Pure Americana right there.

From Lynchburg we continued west toward the Shiloh Battlefield. I was astonished at how much Tennessee looked like my childhood home of Northern California. Rolling hills and farmland cleared from oak and pine forests that continued on for miles; the terrain was almost identical, except for the mountains surrounding the Sonoma Valley. My favorite tree was the Sugar Maple they used for the charcoal that filters Jack Daniels whiskey. It's a dark bark, with almost neon green leaves, that seemed translucent in the sun. Along with the maple shaped leaves, the contrast of the dark and bright green was hard to miss. Absolutely beautiful.

That night, we stayed at a Walmart in Fayetteville and ventured into the Shiloh National Military Park early the next morning. The day started off cool, but I knew the heat and humidity would show up fast. I walked into the visitor center just as soon as the Ranger flipped the open sign. I was beginning to be an old pro at this. Straight to the movie, walk the museum taking pictures, grab Kimber and hit the trails to see the monuments and skirmish sights. I also enjoyed NOT researching the battle first, but letting the park tell the story. I seem to learn a lot more this way, as compared to what school had ever taught me. It's also starting to become apparent that the southern state battlefields tend to be more forgiving of the South, as compared to what we've been taught in school. An interesting paradigm that I assume will shift as we venture further north.

The Battle of Shiloh took place in the Spring of 1862, between CSA Generals Johnston and Beauregard, and US Generals Grant and Buell. What was initially a win for the South, turned into a devastating loss due to the Confederate Army being short on rations. While the South initially pushed the Union troops back, the CSA officers were unable to stop the Confederate troops from pillaging the Union camps for food and supplies. This pause gave Grant the opportunity to bolster his line with fresh troops and riverboat cannon support. The Union now 40k strong, launched a counterattack against the fractured 20k CSA troops. Johnston was killed, making him the highest ranking CSA officer killed to date. Total casualties 24,000, making Shiloh the bloodiest battle in American history to date. From Shiloh, Grant would move on

Vicksburg the following year, eventually taking Chattanooga. Again, we seem to be working backwards, giving an interesting aspect to the timeline of the war.

After the video, I explored the museum as quickly as possible, knowing the heat outside was climbing by the minute. I was surprised when I read the very first placard explaining the commanders of this battle. The plaque read "Northern Commanders" with pictures of US General Grant and US General Buell. The caption under Grant's picture read as follows: "Grant's military career began inauspiciously, graduating in the middle of his class at West Point. He served gallantly in the Mexican war, but the tedium of peacetime led to drinking problems. He resigned to avoid a court-martial. He volunteered for service when the Civil War broke out and gained attention with his victory at Fort Donelson." Wow, this is a US President they're speaking of, and in such a derogatory and slightly disrespectful tone. Even the picture showed Grant somewhat disheveled. This confirmed my observation of "view point." I'm in the South and this battle was essentially a Confederate victory… at first. It seems like whenever a battle is won by the Union, it's a well-known piece of history; whereas a battlefield with a Confederate victory seems smaller, older, and less notable. Something to keep in the back of your mind while we continue exploring our country's battlefields. He who wins the war, writes the history.

Outside now, Kimber and I enjoyed some beautiful scenery as we hiked the different areas of the park. One site of great interest was the Hornet's Nest, where the Confederacy had the Union surrounded with the sound of mini balls flying through the air, mimicking a hornet's nest. This was where the highest concentration of casualties occurred. You could just tell this was sacred and somber ground, with a heaviness in the air and goosebumps galore.

Suddenly I was attacked, brutally and continuously, by something unseen yet blatantly apparent. Chemical warfare the likes I hadn't experienced since the beloved gas chamber in the Marine Corps boot camp. My allergies just took a dive off the deep end. It started with a sneezing fit and an accompaniment of an uncontrollable, yet remarkably steady, flow of clear liquid evacuating my face, followed by my eyes starting to slowly swell and close. Yup, Spring in Tennessee was in full bloom, beautiful but brutal.

I made a beeline for the nearest Walmart to find the magic elixir called Xyzal or something. I just grabbed the most expensive, top shelf stuff I could find and gratefully, within an hour, I was back to normal. At this point, I didn't even know what town I was in, but knew I needed both an ice cold shower and a beer to match. Luckily, there was an Anytime Fitness just down the road where I could clean up, cool off, and get some bearing.

After a well deserved shower, I found myself pulling up to a very old and run-down beer joint on the outskirts of Lexington, TN, one of two places that sold beer near town, according to Google. There was a pretty good storm about to hit, so I didn't plan on venturing far from the local Walmart. I pulled the Rig into the back parking lot, hopped out of the truck, making my way toward the back patio door. There were two guys on the deck, sitting down at a picnic bench, with several empty beer bottles between them. They looked like local businessmen enjoying a happy hour beverage, when one turned to me and asked where I was coming from. "Arizona," I replied. "Traveling the country, writing a book. Baseballs and Battlefields. Just coming up from Shiloh." After living in the South, I knew to throw in a little reverence for the local history when around the natives. Southern pride is alive and well, and always a good way to break the ice. Immediately they offered me a seat and a beer. After talking about my travels over a few cocktails, I noticed more folks from inside had come out to hear my stories. Turned out one of the guys I had been chatting with had gone inside and said, "There's a Marine out here, traveling the country writing a book. Man you gotta meet this guy." He even got on the phone and called the local American Legion Post Commander, who was a Devil Doc in Vietnam (Navy Corpsman serving in a Marine unit), to come and meet me. After several rounds of beers, and plenty of good stories and laughs, I was invited to speak at the Legion Hall the following night. What a complete shock and an absolute honor.

As the evening rolled on, another local veteran asked me if I wanted to park the Rig at his place, just down the road. "You're welcome to the place. Will have some breakfast for ya in the morning." Enter my buddy Kaya, an Air Force veteran who served sometime after Vietnam. A bit down on his luck, living in a single-wide trailer near the bar, the man couldn't afford another beer but was eager to open his home and give me what he had as a fellow veteran helping out another. The storm was bearing down, so I accepted his offer and drove him home.

Kaya absolutely loved Kimber who wasn't shy about showing the old vet some love. He giggled like a kid as Kimber jumped into his lap, licking his face and ears at every opportunity. In the morning, Kaya made a breakfast fit for a king, with everything from eggs, sausage, bacon, pancakes, coffee and milk. All of which I knew he didn't have much of, being on social security and near the end of the month.

The next night, I ventured down to the American Legion Hall to meet the guys. The commander graciously introduced me to every member of the post, including the Ladies Auxiliary who prepared the dinner. I was nervous yet excited to share my travels with these elderly patriots, who seemed to appreciate the reason for my travels, and enjoyed some of my stories regarding veterans I'd met along the way. It was definitely a motivating moment for me.

That evening, I returned to Kaya's with a cheap 12 pack of beer. He was ecstatic about the gift as we sat and told military stories for the rest of the evening. The next day, once again, Kaya prepared a breakfast feast. After breakfast, I told him I had to go to the gym and stretch my back. It was a small white lie to buy me some time while I grocery shopped for Kaya. My check had hit direct deposit, and I wasn't about to let this man be out the food he had given me. When I returned, he wasn't sure how to accept the groceries I had bought. With a noticeable watering of his eyes, he reached for an old Air Force Unit patch that he promptly held out for me to take. This was pretty much his prized possession, an old A-10 Warthog patch, given to him by a dear friend. Thank you, Kaya. Honor and Respect, my friend.

I decided to give my high school friend Heather a call, since I was starting to head in her direction. Heather had gotten in touch with me at the beginning of my journey, telling me to be sure to drop by if I'm in the area of Big Sandy, TN. Heather graduated high school with me in NorCal back in 1987. We weren't super close, but I knew her and her sister well enough from my senior year to stop in and at least say hello. Unfortunately, Heather was somewhere near Chattanooga, taking her daughter to tour different colleges, as she was to graduate high school this year. Heather said they would be back in a few days, and would love to see me and meet Kimber. So, looks like we had some time to kill, which wouldn't be a problem with all the battlefields nearby.

From Lexington I headed north on Hwy 22, taking in the beauty of Tennessee in the spring, with copious amounts of antihistamines at the ready. The rain had passed, the air was cool, and the grass was wet, all of which made for perfect driving weather. It was early still, so I thought I had better get Kimber some ball time in before it got crazy humid and hot.

I noticed a small ballpark just a few miles north, near the small town of Parker Crossroads. What I didn't realize was just under the tree line, a few feet from the right field fence, was a 12lb Howitzer cannon. At this point, seeing heavy artillery near a city ballpark wasn't anything unusual, but the picture of a cannon with the baseball field in the background was iconic, maybe even a possible book cover. Most of all, it meant I was near a battlefield, and sure enough, directly across the street was a placard that read, "The Battle of Parker's Crossroads."

Turns out that this was where the Union made an attempt to catch the elusive CSA General Nathan Bedford Forrest on his first raid into Western Tennessee. Forrest was sent by CSA General Pemberton, the guy we read about in Texas, who had served with Grant during the Mexican Wars, and later surrendered his sword to Grant at Vicksburg. Ya, that dude. Pemberton sends Forrest and 1800 Calvary to disrupt Grant's rail communications, hoping to stop the eventual attack on Vicksburg. After a very successful raiding campaign, Forrest and the Confederates were camped near a store for two days, where Union sprung a surprise attack. This is where Forrest's famous command of "Charge them both ways!" was given. The swift counterattack of the Calvary units, while being caught between two Union brigades, enabled Forrest's escape. Due to Forrest's raids, Vicksburg stayed in Confederate hands for another 6 months.

Next stop was in Paris, TN, just a short drive from Big Sandy, where Heather lived. I wanted to scout out the local Walmart and get some bearing on where I was, so as not to wander too far off from the area. Turned out that the closest Walmart was in Clarksville TN, a bit of a drive, but it also had an Anytime Fitness and a Buffalo Wild Wings, not to mention that another National Battlefield was along the way. Perfect, let's do this.

Fort Donelson National Battlefield was almost exactly between Paris and Clarksville. The actual visitor center and movie was in the town hall due to renovations, with the actual battlefield grounds across the street. A little-known battle, at least to me, turned out to be one of the most important victories for the Union Army and US General Grant. It was here that General Grant earned the nickname of "Unconditional Surrender Grant" and propelled his career to eventually the Presidency.

The battle was in two parts, the naval attack upon Fort Henry, followed by the ground and riverboat attack of Fort Donelson. Grant was effectively able to take both Confederate forts, thus securing the Cumberland and Tennessee Rivers, both being major Confederate supply routes. This also gave Abraham Lincoln a much needed major victory in the west. An interesting side note: CSA General Buckner sent Grant a note requesting a truce and terms of surrender. Buckner, a fellow Army Officer and friend of Grant's, expected generous terms, as he had loaned Grant money to get home after he was forced to resign his commission due to suspected alcoholism. Grant's reply was, "No terms except unconditional and immediate surrender can be accepted." This came as a shock to Buckner, who had to accept. Although some Confederates were able to escape to Nashville, Grant's victory opened up Tennessee to the Union Army, thus leading to the Battle of Shiloh. My head is spinning at this point with all the names and battles, seriously contemplating a separate book of just American Battlefields. Wow.

The grounds were well maintained, with several exhibits describing the battles. Lots of very cool earthworks, cannons, hiking trails, and interpretive placards. Unfortunately, another storm had settled in on us, and started to pour rain while making our way along the driving tour. After jumping out to take a few pictures, while completely soaking myself, both Kimber and I had seen enough. Next stop, Anytime Fitness in Clarksville. A shower, a meal, and catching some baseball on TV were top priority at this point.

The next couple days we spent exploring the city of Clarksville, home of the Army's 101st Airborne Division. Note to self: NO ARMY JOKES IN THE BAR! A good-sized town with all my favorite places. A military base, Buffalo Wild Wings, Anytime Fitness, and a hospitable Walmart, all within about an hour from Big Sandy. We visited Fort Sevier, another small battlefield in the heart of town, but once again, ran off due to hard rain. We finally retreated to Walmart for our second night before back tracking to Big Sandy to see Heather and family.

Heather looked great after all these years, doing extremely well after taking over her dad's orthopedics practice. She even diagnosed my elbow with needing surgery, and NOT more cortisone shots. Something the VA had failed to find all these years. She was married to a great guy named Sonny, who was an ER nurse at the hospital Heather worked at. Still on their first-year honeymoon, they were absolutely loving life and each other. They had recently come back from a Metallica concert in Texas, where Sonny had worn his favorite Eric Church t-shirt. Once a country boy, always a country boy. They opened their home to me. Sonny even took me over the Kentucky State line to one of his favorite BBQ joints for lunch. Kimber played with the other dogs, one being a big brindle pup, who she wrestled with non-stop. All in all, a great visit with an old friend, and now some new ones.

Kind of a funny story is when Sonny took me to lunch at the BBQ place. The place was set up like a regular diner, a couple of booths, a couple of tables, and a counter with several stools. We sat at the bar-top where we were waited on by the owner, an older lady with a no BS attitude, but in a funny way. I ordered the pulled pork sandwich. "Hot or mild?" she asked. Thinking to myself, I'm from AZ and had Texas BBQ before... "I'll take the hot," I proclaimed. She narrowed her eyes and said, "Ya wanna taste it first?" This time vocalizing my being from Arizona and liking hot food... as she walked away mid-sentence to get my sample of her sauce. "Ok, sure," I said as she sat the plastic cup in front of me, staring at me like the gauntlet had been thrown. I took a healthy sip of what could only have been the devil's own recipe for BBQ sauce. I instantly coughed and broke out in a sweat, which brought a smile to the woman's face, and a hearty laugh from everybody within ear shot. Then she hollered to the guy making my sandwich, "Mild!" Which brought even more laughter... and gladly, a huge glass of sweet tea. Touché lady, touché.

According to the map, our next battlefield was in Nashville, that would lead us through the small town of Dickson, TN, where an old high school football buddy had moved to. Scott and I played high school football together in Sonoma, before I moved to Sebastopol for my last two years of school. Scott also served in the military, and was still serving, this time as a police officer. With two young sons and a great career, it was awesome to see another classmate doing well. Two different friends, from different parts of the same county in NorCal, both moved to Tennessee. I'm starting to see why. We decided to stay in Dickson that night, as once again another storm was rolling in, and I wasn't sure what the parking possibilities in Nashville would be.

On the road, bright and early, I dialed in the GPS for the Battle of Nashville and off we went. Strangely, the Battle of Nashville marker was in a small park, nestled within a quiet residential neighborhood, with only one marker and a few inscriptions. One inscription was a poem about the civil war, but the other strangely mentioned WW1. Other than that, there were no other markers or information on the battle. It wasn't a National Battlefield per say, but still curious as to what happened here. Staying true to the travel portion and only reporting what I see, I was off to the city for some sightseeing.

Two things I wanted to see and do in Nashville were the famous "Music Row" and tasting some world famous Hattie B's hot chicken. First things first, we scouted out where Hattie B's was for lunch later, and then began the hunt for a parking spot big enough for the Rig, while we explored the town. We got lucky with a great spot behind a car dealer that had a semi-truck and a huge motor-coach bus. I asked the guy washing cars in the dealership if I could park here overnight, pointing at the RV. He said, "That bus has been there all week. Go ahead." Gold! We were literally two blocks from the main strip.

Downtown Nashville was super cool! Really cool, rustic brick buildings that housed everything country you could imagine. Every other door seemed to be another bar with live music as early as 0930. Like a country music Bourbon Street is the best way to explain it. One wall on a corner building had a giant banner selling Ole Smokey Mountain from Tennessee that had a startling familiar face. Popcorn Sutton's beard and felt hat are hard to miss. Instantly, I heard the lady's voice from the market back in North Carolina, "Not since he's been gone." I wonder if these folks know he was from NC? Interesting.

After walking around downtown most of the morning, the concrete was getting a little warm for Kimber's feet, and I was hungry. Hattie B's time! Heather raved about how I just had to have Nashville hot chicken, and Hattie B's was the best. So Kimber went to the camper, and I set out for some of this amazing food.

When I turned the corner, there was a line forming literally halfway around the block, and it was only 1100! Striking up a conversation with a guy in line, who was also there for the first time, we ended up sharing a picnic bench inside. We both ordered the "Damn Hot" and a couple beers. I know, I know; you'd think I learned my lesson back with Sonny at the BBQ place, but in my defense, I did go with a lesser heat level than the hottest "Shut the cluck up" with a "burn notice" attached.

When the chicken got to our table, you could literally feel the pepper invade your face, like a swirling cloud of vinegar and fire. They should've used this for the gas chamber back in boot camp. Wow. The fried chicken quarter was a deep, dark red, laying on a piece of white bread, now saturated with dark red grease, and a couple of dill pickle slices on top. It came with a small bowl of potato salad, and a matching bowl of collard greens. The first bite of chicken was good. Lots of spice, good flavor, not really that bad heat wise. Second bite, whew, it got a bit warm in here. Third bite, I think I need a respirator. Good God, what was I thinking, or better yet, what were THEY thinking when they made this?! Three bites and I was done, my buddy in line didn't make it to the second bite, and the dude across from me slid his plate over and asked if I wanted his. Ya, it was that hot.

For the next two hours, I thought I was having a sustained heart attack. I would've killed for even a teaspoon of milk. Why I took a to go box with all that chicken dressed in molten lava, I'll never know. The cab was literally filling up with pepper fumes, like a slow-moving gas chamber. I stopped at the first gas station I saw to dump this toxic waste, and get some antacid. When I was leaving, I saw a homeless guy digging into the trash can, then came up with the bag of Satan chicken. Well, at least it didn't go to waste. Good luck bruh, you're gonna need it.

From Nashville we headed south to Murfreesboro, to yet another National Battlefield; that's four in Tennessee alone. Wet and dreary outside, with a congested and busy Friday morning commute, this was starting to feel like work, and I was really missing me some baseball. Little did I know that this next battlefield would be the biggest eye opener of this history lesson thus far. Welcome to Stones River National Battlefield.

Ok, so let's take a quick 30k foot view of what was going on December 31st, 1862. Up to this point, we've been following the western campaign and Grant's Army of the Tennessee who had taken Fort Donelson, took a beating at Shiloh yet won, and was now moving toward Vicksburg. CSA General Lee and his Army of Northern Virginia, has the Army of the Potomac, the now largest Union force, beat down in Richmond. Which leaves the Army of the Cumberland and the new Union General Rosecrans to deliver a much needed victory to Lincoln, bolstering the morale in the north after Antietam, and hopefully "turn the tides of war"; all this according to a museum placard. Lincoln also needs a huge win to gain political support for his new decree: the Emancipation Proclamation. This is where it gets good!

After the video, I started to tour the museum as I always did, taking pictures of the historical placards and artifacts from the battle, when I read this. The poster heading was "The Stage Is Set" with the word "Emancipation" below an old drawing of a freed slave family. It looked like a type of political poster. Then it read, "The war's moral tone changed in September 1862. President Abraham Lincoln announced that he would declare slaves free in rebellious states. Ironically, this Emancipation Proclamation would not apply to Union states. The Battle of Stones River would provide a victory to support the new order." Whoa whoa whoa... wait a minute. What do you mean "changed" the "moral tone"? We were taught in school that the Civil War was all about slavery and freeing the slaves. What do you mean Lincoln didn't roll this out until halfway through the war? AND ONLY FREED THE SLAVES IN THE SOUTH, NOT THE NORTH. WHAT!?! I almost walked outside to see where I was. This is a NATIONAL Battlefield right? I honestly couldn't believe what I had just read. Ok, now I'm hooked. What the hell is going on here?!

Here's some interesting facts about this battle. 81,000 men lined up for three miles in preparation for the morning's battle. Within two days, each side had lost almost a 1/3 of its men. 23,525 total killed, wounded, and captured. Even though the Confederates had once again pushed the Union back the first day, they suffered horrendous losses the second day. 1,800 Confederates were killed in less than an hour by artillery. The numbers are astonishing. This would also be the exact ground where CSA General Nathan Bedford Forrest would be captured two years later. So much history right here, that it's hard to wrap your head around. Super cool!

The weather stayed somewhat wet and dreary the rest of the day. After the battlefield, we called it a day and settled into a Walmart for a little break. Pizza and a DVD was on the rainy day agenda. The next day, I set the GPS to backroads once again, plugged in Johnson City, and off we went. I had nothing but time at this point, and with a week or so before my doc appointment in Asheville, we meandered our way through the "middle" Tennessee countryside until finally reaching Johnson City, Tennessee.

One thing I've learned during my travels, is how to judge the economy and price of goods in the area by the gas and milk prices. I was astonished to see gas as low as $1.80 a gallon and milk even cheaper! Cost of living in Tennessee was right up this DAV's alley. Land was incredibly cheap too. A small farmhouse, with 10 acres of land was selling for under $35k here! This was effectively the first place I'd seen that a DAV could afford a house and land on VA disability; that's something I thought I'd never be able to afford again. Add the incredibly nice people, Tennessee was starting to look a lot like "home."

We pulled into Johnson City fairly early on a Sunday morning. I found a nice downtown park with dog poop bag dispensers; dog friendly is always a major plus. It was a beautiful day to just relax and take in the scenery… after I made some coffee. Kimber and I jumped in the back of the camper, and as I opened the curtains, a bright red Cardinal swooped down and landed on the park bench right next to the Rig. He was a big bright male, and in the sun he almost glowed. What a beautiful bird. Good morning, Grampa, well, I'm here, now what?

After coffee, Kimber was stoked to step out of the camper and play ball. The Cardinal was gone, but the sentiment of the visit remained. We threw the ball for several minutes until the park started to fill up with people; it was a gorgeous Sunday morning and folks were starting to come out of church. Downtown consisted of about 4 main streets. It was a two Walmart town, even had two Buffalo Wild Wings, and an Anytime Fitness. It's a college town, with a good baseball team, a VA hospital, and you're nestled right at the foothills of the Smokey mountains. Well, there's my mountains. Maybe that's why I needed to see Johnson City. Tennessee was exactly like home, except for the mountains; now we had mountains.

I walked Kimber into a downtown brewery, the Yee-Haw Brewing Company, that was actually a remodeled train station. It had an adjoining gourmet taco shop, which pretty much made this place impossible to turn away from. Great beer and amazing tacos, the owner even gave me a Yee-Haw trucker hat in thanks for my service. Thanks, guys!

After lunch, Kimber and I walked a few more blocks around town and stopped in some shade to let Kimber cool off, and I could check my phone. Just then, a Johnson City police car abruptly pulled up to the curb in front of us, and a young female officer got out. What the hell? My mind raced with what I might have done. I know I picked up the poop, uh-oh maybe because she was off leash chasing the ball... "I just wanted to say hi to your dog!" she said from the curb. "Of course!" I replied, as I tried to calm my pulse down and catch my breath. Thank God. She was a pretty lady, but that wasn't why my heart was racing! As usual, Kimber did the ear cleaning and kissing thing as the officer giggled. Next thing I know, Kimber jumps in the squad car and sits in the driver's seat! Jesus. The officer answered with more laughs and by taking pictures with her cell phone. This dog is the best. I had noticed the officer didn't have a southern accent at all. Turned out she went to college in New York, but wanted to move away, so she threw a dart at a map and here she was. She said she loves it here, I can definitely see why. Great town, great people. So far, Johnson City, you have my heart.

That night, we stayed at a Walmart on the outskirts of town. The next morning, we would sadly leave Tennessee, heading south into North Carolina. Never in my life would I have ever thought that Tennessee, of all places, would make me want to put down roots. The land, the people, the history; what a great state. Tennessee, state #20... COMPLETE.

South Carolina

May 10th, 2017. I know the header says South Carolina, but first we have to make a quick stop in Asheville, North Carolina; it's finally time to get my cortisone shots at the VA. My shoulder and elbows are on fire; I don't think all this driving is helping much either. I will definitely be asking this orthopedic surgeon about what my friend Heather had said regarding possible surgery. It was kind of like getting a second and third opinion, which is unheard of at the VA!

Another side benefit of traveling; if you don't like what a VA doctor says, drive to another state and see another VA doc. Works for me.

Asheville VA has got to be one of the very best VA hospitals I've ever been to. The orthopedic nurse took x-rays of my shoulder and elbows, and told me she would give me my shoulder shot, but not the elbows. Well, this obviously wasn't going to work for me; I've got a lot of miles yet to cover before I started back home. Pleading with the nurse, I promised I'd get it fixed as soon as I reached Arizona. She still refused and had the actual surgeon come in. After explaining what I had going on, he very reluctantly gave me the injections. He also agreed with Heather that surgery is what I more than likely would need, and not to do anymore shots. The nurse was visibly pissed that he had given me the cortisone shot, which was a good thing, as she wrote a detailed and scathing account of my care up until this point in my record. That should get some wheels moving a little faster with the VA back home. We shall see, but for now, I was pain free for another 3 months.

Not wanting to explore North Carolina quite yet, we continued south on I26 to the South Carolina border. The plan was to visit two National Battlefields just over the border, then make our way back to the coast. Starting with a visit to Fort Sumter, then working our way north, continuing our coastal exploration through Myrtle Beach and then into North Carolina.

First stop was at the Cowpens National Battlefield, near the small town of Chesnee, just over the South Carolina state line. Excited to see what this battle was all about, I was taken by complete surprise to find out this would be our first, national level, American Revolutionary War battlefield! I was pumped! This is where my real interest lay, in the war that gave birth to America. And once again, we were stepping right into the middle of it.

The Battle of Cowpens took place in January, 1781, toward the end of British General Cornwallis' "Southern Campaign." Commander and chief of the British forces General George Clinton sent Cornwallis south, to secure the southern colonies, while the northern armies were at a virtual stalemate with George Washington's Continental Army. At one point, English strategists even considered New England a hot bed of sedition and a loss, not worth the effort and cost; but they felt the more important crops and textiles of the South were worth bolstering the southern loyalists.

The Southern Campaign began with the brutal defeat of Charleston, where Cornwallis turned loose his most destructive and blood thirsty Calvary Officer, Banastre Tarleton. Tarleton

193

and his men were known for the butchering of hundreds of surrendering Continental troops asking for "quarters," making the phrase "give them Tarleton quarters" a rallying cry for the Americans. Side note... remember the Mel Gibson movie, *The Patriot*? Remember the really bad guy who was after Gibson and his sons? That was Banastre Tarleton.

Tarleton and his troops, now faces off against Daniel Morgan and a tough unit of Continentals, backed by the local militia. General Nathaniel Greene had dispatched Morgan and Washington (George's second cousin) to stop the British advancement. With a famous, yet almost accidental, tactical maneuver called a "double envelopment," the Americans were able to lure Tarleton into a trap, where he was effectively pushed back and forced to retreat, narrowly escaping from Morgan's men. Even though the Battle of Cowpens was a small skirmish, it was the first real American victory against battle-hardened English regulars in the South, and considered to be a turning point for the entire American Revolution.

After the museum, Kimber and I took the short walking tour of the battlefield. Beautiful green fields littered with oak trees that were used as cattle pastures back then, gave the area its name. The pastures were divided by a dirt road that meandered through the trees and grass. Only a few cannons and placards told of the troop positions and actions, which was fine by Kimber, as the temperature and humidity was starting to rise dramatically. We took our pictures, and headed back to the Rig. I wanted to make the other nearby battlefield before the heat became unbearable.

Kings Mountain wasn't only a battlefield, it was another National Military Park. Normally this would be a plus and I'd be super excited, but after the early drive this morning, already seeing one National Battlefield, and the heat starting to bear down, walking around a massive park wasn't gonna cut it. So off to the local Walmart, hopefully to get some writing done.

The closest decent sized city was Gaffney, SC, where I happily found a Walmart full of semis. Knowing that this evening's boondock spot was secured and RV friendly, I decided to hunt down an ice-cold adult beverage and get some food. Much like Tennessee, the first place I saw that sold beer was a small gas station/hotel that had a bar and grill. When I pulled in, I realized there wasn't any shade, and it was really starting to heat up. So I went inside and asked if they minded a support dog coming in. I usually ask first because she isn't a true service animal and I know from being a bartender, it's just polite; and I get a feel for if they're dog people or not. I don't just take her in anywhere, the place has to be good enough for my dog.

The lady bartender, which is always a plus for welcoming Kimber, said of course she could come in, and asked if she needed water. Perfect! Yup, my kind of place, and Kimber stole the show as usual. The four or five older folks, sitting at the bar, all had to have their turn meeting Kimber. About that time, an older guy in his mid 60s came over and sat down next to me. Enter my friend Thomas. He was originally from Connecticut, with a thick New England accent, bald head and goatee. He thanked me for my service and asked what kind of dog Kimber was. He too had a small pup, and was apparently another dog lover. He saw my tattoos and asked if I rode a bike. If it's not veterans, then it's usually bikers who come up to talk, tattoos and dogs being a commonality amongst both. We sat and talked bikes, baseball, and dogs over a couple beers, while we watched the Braves on TV; after which, I said it was time to grab a bite and head back to Walmart for the night. Thomas then said, "Walmart? I work at Walmart, that's a dump. Nah, you can park at my place just down the road. We'll go over to the Legion for supper." It was like déjà vu of being back in Tennessee… gotta love the South.

After dinner and meeting half the town, we headed back to Thomas' place where he had me park on his front lawn, and I had access to the house bathroom. He apparently had to work early and just asked me to lock the place up when I left. Yup, this was definitely the South. Thanks again, my friend, see ya soon.

Just a few miles east of Gaffney was the Kings Mountain National Military Park. I knew to be there bright and early; it was already muggy and the forecast was hell, or close to it. The visitor center was surprisingly modern, and really interesting. The entire inside was like walking through the forest, more like an interactive Disney studio than a National Park Museum. It made the amazing and very important story of the battle come to life.

The best way to summarize the Battle of Kings Mountain is to pair it with the Battle of Cowpens. Basically, where Cowpens was a victory over English troops, Kings Mountain was the first battle won between Tories (sympathizers to the crown) and Whigs (American Patriots). This was in all actuality our FIRST American Civil War, this was Americans fighting Americans. These two victories were what helped propel the morale of Washington's armies in the north and win the sentiment of a new nation.

Outside the visitor center was a huge area with several horse and hiking routes. The parking lot was starting to fill in with school buses, and their normal crowd of completely uninterested adolescents. I grabbed Kimber from the Rig and hit the trails, hoping to get a head start on the field trip crowd. This park was gorgeous; we walked through dense forested areas while_taking an interpretive history tour of the main battlefield. The path itself was made of that spongy, rubberized pad mixed with rock, obviously modernized from the park's inception in the early 1900s. Unfortunately, our visit was cut short again due to the unforeseen cannon firing exhibition at the top of the mountain. As you can imagine, after the first volley, the hike back to the Rig was more of a power sled pull for Kimber, as she literally pulled me down the mountain by her leash. Poor little girl, sometimes I think she's the combat vet and I'm just along for her support.

It was still late morning when we left Kings Mountain, but the weather was starting to change drastically. The sky was turning an ominous dark, with clouds beginning to roll in. My old camper can barely stand rain coming straight down, let alone wind driven from the front, so I decided to look for cover. The next town up was York, SC; please God please, let them have a Walmart.

Not only did York have a Walmart, but they had an Anytime Fitness in the same parking lot! Thank you, Jesus! Just as soon as we pulled into the gym parking lot, the sky opened up like something fierce. Kimber was not having a good day at this point. I couldn't leave her. To the side of the shopping center I noticed a do-it-yourself car wash, with one extra tall bay. Perfect. I parked inside the big truck washing bay, grabbed Kimber and jumped in the camper. She instantly stopped shaking as the rain wasn't pounding down on our roof. Looked like I found home for the night. Kimber and I rode the storm out for the next two days right there in that car wash bay. Nothing like free covered parking to keep dry.

By Sunday we had a break in the weather; it looked like a clear and sunny day from York all the way to Charleston. So bright and early, we hit the road. Working our way down to Charleston via Hwy 321, but then we opted to take I26 outside of Columbia, to make up some time. By the looks of the weather radar, we were traveling in the "eye" of this big, slow--moving storm. I wanted to take the Fort Sumter boat tour before the second part of the storm hit. Plus, it was Mother's Day, and I was hoping Ft. Sumter wasn't exactly high on a Mom's list of things to do, so maybe crowds would be at a minimum.

Ft. Sumter National Monument is another perfect example of a "non-listed" National Battlefield. With all the designators used by the National Park Service for historical sites, you really need to do some research to find out if that National Monument or National Historical Site was actually a battle site, which Fort Sumter obviously was. There was plenty of parking at the

Ft. Sumter dock, a visitor center and a small snack bar. A nominal fee of under 20 bucks was well worth the hour-long bay cruise to the island, where you were greeted by Park Rangers for a free tour, or you could do your own thing. The view of Charleston was amazing, and the weather was absolutely perfect.

As we all learned in history books, this is where the first shot of the American Civil War began. Fort Sumter was almost completed by the time South Carolina decided to secede from the Union due to the election of Abraham Lincoln. What we didn't hear in school was that the US Army built Ft. Sumter as a premier port security base for the bustling city of Charleston, on a small island that was within South Carolina's state boundaries. When South Carolina left the Union, they told the US government to vacate their land which included Ft. Sumter. They were basically repossessing state land. The first actual shots fired were by cadets attending the Citadel, who fired upon a ship trying to resupply the fort. Three months later, Lincoln sends troops into Northern Virginia. Ok, wait a minute. So a war that we were told was all about slavery, actually started over a state's rights/property dispute with the federal government. The secession from said government, was due to the election of a President, and the threat of an Emancipation Proclamation that wouldn't be rolled out for another three years? That doesn't sound right. So in all actuality, Lincoln attacked after South Carolina reclaimed their property. I'm starting to see why the South calls this the War of Northern Aggression.

After the boat ride back to the dock, I was eager to get Kimber out of the truck. There was plenty of grass around the parking area, so we found a quiet, shaded area in the back to get some ball time in. It was lunch time, and I was starving. My friends from Minnesota had been through this way a few weeks ago and told me I had to try the duck club sandwich, with duck fat fries at a place called The Tattooed Moose. Yup, I'm all over all of that! Another added benefit of "road friends," the recommendations are priceless! And so was the sandwich. Wow!

The rest of the afternoon was spent driving up the South Carolina coast to Myrtle Beach where we found a Walmart to spend the evening. The second half of the storm wasn't nearly as bad up here, enabling a relaxing evening before we ventured over the North Carolina state line the next morning. South Carolina, state #21... COMPLETE!

North Carolina

May 15th, 2017. First things first, coffee for me, and this little dog needed some beach time. What an absolutely gorgeous day! The storm had passed with very little rain last night, giving way to a beautiful sunny day, without a cloud in the sky. We found a sparsely populated area just outside Myrtle Beach where Kimber could sneak in a little ball time. "No dog" signs were everywhere, but no people; defiantly, Kimber sprinted past the sign and down the beach after her favorite tennis ball. Happy dog, happy day. Next stop, North Carolina.

I had a buddy in the Marine Corps from North Carolina, and I'd seen that fishing show about the "Outer Banks" a few times; other than that, North Carolina was brand new to me. The night before, I mapped out a tentative route between the coast and the two nationally designated battlefields, then back to the coast, of course swinging by Camp Lejeune if at all possible. Weather was good on the coast, but I knew as soon as I turned inland, it was going to be brutal. Funds are good, Rig is stocked. Show me what you got, NC!

First stop was Moores Creek National Battlefield, but first we had some coastline to cover. Just as soon as you cross the North Carolina State line, the highway jags inland, well away from the coast. Taking the first road I could to keep us within sight of the beach put us into the small town of Southport... and a dead end. There was a bar across the lane, like a railroad crossing, with a stop sign attached. Past the barricade, the road looked like it used to go over a small bridge or something. I was about to turn around when another car came up behind me. Then I noticed the signs to my right, covered by an overgrown tree branch. Looked like we were first in line for a ferry ride.

I was concerned if the Rig was going to fit under the bridge, let alone on a tiny ferry. I had no clue to the size of this thing. Gladly, about that time the ferry showed up, plenty big for all of the vehicles that had now lined up behind me. Second concern I had was if they only took cash like a toll bridge; if so, I was possibly screwed again. Nope, not this time, all the ferries are free! So nothing to do now but enjoy the short boat ride up the coast.

The ferry dropped us just outside of Fort Fisher, a North Carolina State Historic site. A battlefield in itself, Fort Fisher flew under my radar due to it being a state park. Another lucky find. A beautiful park, right on the beach, with a tremendous amount of history. This fort stood in defense of the last open port in the Confederacy. The site of two of the largest land-sea battles in history took place here toward the end of the war.

Fort Fisher also had the first mention of the United States Marine Corps role in the American Civil War that I'd seen. This really made me curious; was there a Confederate Marine Corps? When I asked the tour guide, the answer was rather interesting. Turns out the South did not like the Marine Corps, even thought of them as traitors. Whereas all the other branches had defectors from the Union Army and Navy, the Marines stayed loyal to the Corps and to their country. I almost sensed a bit of animosity in the old guy's voice, after he told me that. Pride runs deep in the South, very deep. Another reminder of this pride was an unknown soldier's grave outside the visitor center, whose tombstone read: "Our unknown Confederate soldier," keyword "Our."

From Fort Fisher, we took the 421 north through Wilmington to the Moores Creek National Battlefield. It was still fairly early, but the day was heating up fast and we were still on the coast! The battlefield visitor center was pretty much empty, with plenty of shaded parking. That's when I realized the museum was closed. The open hours in the window said it should be open, but it wasn't. Oh well, it was getting really hot, and I wasn't in the mood for a hike anyway. I'd just have to research this battle later. About then, a bright red Cardinal landed on the trailhead sign. I heard that passage from my friend's message run through my head, "...you're on your path." I was thinking this time it was stick to your path. Ok, Grandpa, got it. Let's do this.

It's hard to explore a battlefield that you know nothing about without seeing the intro video, but we pushed on and read every sign, trying to piece it together. Turns out Moores Creek was another Revolutionary War battlefield, and a tremendously significant one at that. This is where the first major victory for the Patriots occurred that ended English control over the colonies in February of 1776. This battle spurred North Carolina to be the first American colony to vote for independence. Three months later, the United States ratifies the Declaration of Independence. Wow! And to think I almost skipped this. I was pretty bummed the visitor center wasn't open, but I did get the park pamphlet and another info card about the battle. This would be enough for the book at least. All because of a red bird. Thanks, Grampa, good lookin' out!

It was only two in the afternoon, and already a very humid 93f. Well, from this point forward, we tried to hug the coast or stay as high up in elevation as we could, neither of which was even close to being feasible for the next few stops. I was done with hiking for the day, and the next battlefield was an hour away. So we decided to call the Clinton Walmart home for the evening. Clinton, named after General Sir Henry Clinton, Commander and Chief of the British

Forces. We found a quiet spot with a run of grass and some trees in the back lot and called it a day, after some ball time for Queen Kimber of course.

The next morning, we continued north to the Bentonville Battlefield, part of the North Carolina Civil War Trails. While I waited for the visitor center to open, I found a brochure about the Civil War Trails with a detailed map of literally hundreds of Civil War battles and historical places. I could spend an entire summer right here in North Carolina. I was shocked at how much there was to see statewide.

The brochure said that this site happened to be a farming family's home that was commandeered to be a field hospital. The entire downstairs was the hospital with surgical tools and beds, while the family was forced to live upstairs. Can you imagine the sounds those kids must've heard, or the horrors they had to have witnessed? Wow, Just wow.

About then, a couple of gentlemen walked up, also waiting for the visitor center. They were having a conversation about some of the issues the country was having, everything from politics to weather, and preparing for an electrical issue due to weather or civil strife. One of them happened to notice the Marine tattoo on my neck. "You a Marine?" the younger of the two asked while pointing at his neck. I thought they were father and son at this point, with dad being Vietnam Era, son about my age. "Yes sir," I replied as a typical Jarhead would. Thanks for service was given in all directions. Then to join the conversation, I mentioned how I'd be in a hurt locker if suddenly I didn't have access to my bank account because of an electrical interruption of some sort. That and I can only carry so much in way of supplies. That's when the older gentlemen spoke up, "Son, you're a Marine. You're in the South now, you'll be ok," with an assuring smile and a firm hand on my arm. That was pretty cool, the South does love its military, even us Marines... after all.

By this point, I'd discovered if I show up at opening time for the visitor center, get our outside hiking done by mid-morning and then spend the afternoon traveling in the AC; I not only beat the heat, but I beat the crowds and the traffic. Bonus! Next stop was Guilford Courthouse National Military Park, just outside of Greensboro, a few hours away. This set up the town of Sanford, NC, with its Walmart and Anytime Fitness, as the perfect place to stop for the night. The park looked to be close to downtown of a fairly good-sized city, so first thing in the morning we were back at it.

I realize the monotony of bouncing from Walmarts to battlefields, is probably putting you to sleep right about now. Trust me, I was getting battlefielded out myself. I was really looking forward to a baseball game or even just posting up at a nice campsite for a week, but I had to press on. We still had a lot of land to cover and still make it back to Texas to catch the Ranger and Astro games by September. Forgot about those, didn't ya? So back to it, hang in there. Ok, where was I?

Guilford Court National Military Park goes down as one of my favorites so far. Absolutely gorgeous walking path in a bustling downtown area depicting the epic stand-off of the Patriot Nathaniel Greene versus his mortal enemy England's General Charles Cornwallis. Absolutely amazing statues memorialize the events of this battle, but the enormous bronze statue of Greene mounted on his horse, was something to behold. It was stunning and massive all at once. It made the very humid 4.8 mile walk well worth the sweat.

As for the battle itself, you could call this Cowpens/King Mountain Part three. So after Morgan basically chopped up Tarleton's troops back at Cowpens, General Greene decides it's time to take on the English General Cornwallis. Much too weak to take on the British military machine head on, he sets out on a rabbit chase, enticing Cornwallis to blindly follow. Trying to gain momentum, Cornwallis dumps gear and rations hoping to gain on Greene's Patriots. Finally, Greene and Morgan meet at Guilford Courthouse, where they are able to make a "last stand" before retreating into Virginia for reinforcements. Surprisingly, Greene's few hundred Federal troops and a grip of mountain militia locals, damaged Cornwallis' troops significantly enough to weaken them drastically, as they gave chase into Virginia. This English victory was at an extremely high cost. Cornwallis' fixation on capturing General Nathaniel Greene would ultimately lead to his demise and the birth of a new nation.

It was about three in the afternoon when we left the Military Park; we were beat up from the hike, and soaking wet with sweat. Kimber was just as hot and exhausted as I was. Gratefully, we were as far inland as we needed to go for North Carolina; now we headed back to the coast and some much cooler weather. Once again into a local Walmart for the night before we ventured west.

Like I had mentioned earlier, I was jonesing for some baseball, big time. That's when I realized, while looking at a map later that night, that we were going through Durham, NC the next day. Wait, Durham, like Bull Durham? Sure enough, this was the home of the Durham Bulls minor league baseball team, immortalized by the greatest baseball movie ever made, *Bull Durham*. Greatest ever, fight me. Better yet, they had a home game the next night! Hell ya, I'm in! How cool is that gonna be!? That night, my dreams were full of baseballs and beers, while I slept like a child on Christmas Eve.

We headed into downtown Durham bright and early the next morning. I wanted to scout out the parking situation before we figured out how to stay occupied until game time. The Durham Bulls Athletics Park is in what's called the American Tobacco District, part of the Duke University Campus. Super cool brick buildings that were the original Lucky Strike Tobacco Company were now a conglomeration of classrooms, businesses, and restaurants. There was also plenty of uncovered street parking for the game later.

Outside the old brick cigarette factory were several large office buildings surrounding a small park with a fountain. Kimber needed some water, which quickly turned into a bath, much to the delight of some college girls nearby. Good girl. Then I noticed some placards off to the side. They were Civil War Trails placards, titled "Durham's Station; Prelude to peace." Then went on to describe Sherman meeting Johnston to open negotiations for the Confederate surrender in a small house just blocks from here. Here's the kicker, Sherman has a messenger's note in his pocket saying Lincoln was assassinated. He had to keep a secret in fear that his men would take it out on the city of Raleigh. Whoa what? Well ya, I gotta see this place. A perfect find to keep us preoccupied until first pitch later that evening.

We arrived at the Bennet Place, a North Carolina Historic Site, according to the welcome sign, around 0930. Another banner hanging from the welcome sign read, "Site of the Largest Surrender of the Civil War. April 26th, 1865." The grounds had a visitor center and two replica homes of the ones the treaty was signed in. Only the chimney from the original house is still intact. With the signing of this treaty, in a tiny country farmhouse, 36,827 North Carolina Confederates and 52,453 in Georgia and Florida, laid down their arms. Lee had already surrendered to Grant at Appomattox. The war was over. Yup, I got chills. Wow, what a great find just by taking Kimber for a walk.

Later that night, a storm began to roll in, gladly dropping the temperature down to tolerable levels, also giving me some piece of mind for Kimber. I set her up in the camper with her usual array of snacks, also known as bribes, to keep her occupied until I was gone at least. I'm pretty sure it was more helpful to me than it was to Kimber. She's just fine, I'm the big baby that can't stand to be away from her for more than an hour. I know some of these big venues scared her pretty bad, and I think it's therapeutic for me to venture into crowds on my own now and then. It helps tremendously knowing she's safe and content, thus the treat array. Now fully content, she's good, I can relax somewhat while inside.

The first thing you see as you walk into the Bulls park is a huge billboard of the Bulls' jersey that resembles the Tampa Rays logo, obviously a farm team. The park looks a lot like a brick mall that I went to as a teenager, but once inside, it becomes a really nice ballpark, fairly new by its appearance, with giant video screens making up the outfield wall. The best part of the entire park was they had brought the original Steakhouse bull sign from the original park, now standing proud above left field. Yes, the one from the movie where it says, "Hit the bull win a steak" and every time someone hits it with a home run shot, the eyes turn red, steam shoots out its nose, and the tail moves up and down. Which I was able to witness for myself in person after back to back shots at the bull. Super freakin' cool! It was brought here when they moved from the old "AA" park to the new "AAA" because they had to add 10k seats when they made the league jump. The old park, from the movie, is now a community park for softball and Little League.

The coolest part about this park is how the community packs this place on a weekday evening, and everybody seems to know everybody. Little League teams in their jerseys, different schools wearing their school colors, high school teams in uniform, all backing their local baseball team. I met two local guys who gave me the scoop on the park history over some local craft brews and tacos; I had an absolute blast. This is what Southern AAA baseball is all about.

The next morning, the storm had passed and the day was heating up dramatically. One last stop was at Camp Lejeune, then back up the coast to Virginia. I stopped at a local breakfast place, just outside of base. I love eating breakfast at these little "greasy spoon" restaurants, especially around military bases. They're usually full of old vets talking politics or local gossip. It's a good way to get a quick intel dump as to the local population's viewpoints. That and a quick walk through the local Walmart is pretty telling too. Anyway, this restaurant didn't disappoint, all the way down to the crusty old vets playfully giving crap to the old Philippino lady who was waiting tables and also apparently owned the place. She in turn would fire back, putting them in their place, all to the amusement of the other vets who chuckled at her unfiltered replies. There were also a couple of active duty Marines sitting at a booth, apparently recovering from last night's libations. Yup, typical military base town.

I had just ordered my meal when a couple in what looked like their late 20s early 30s, with two small children in tow, walked in and was greeted by everybody. It reminded me of back when I was still in the Corps, having breakfast with my wife and kids. Seemed like an eternity ago. Then the father of the family stopped at the table with the two active duty Marines. Obviously knowing each other, but somewhat reserved in their conversation, I was curious as to how they knew each other. That's when the two Marines stood up to leave, turned, and over their shoulder said, "See ya later, Gunny." Whoa what? Gunny? That kid looked like he was... That's when I saw what an eternity actually looked like and realized, I too, was one of the "old" vets having breakfast.

Well, after that slap in the face with the reality bat, I decided it was beach time for me and the Princess. It was an absolute gorgeous day, and Kimber was wound up like a cat on caffeine. We stopped at North Top Sail Beach for a round of ball, then continued our trek up the Atlantic Coast until we ran out of road at the Cedar Island Ferry Terminal. From there we took the ferry over to Ocracoke Island and the beginning of what's called North Carolina's "Outer Banks."

I took a cool aerial picture of the Rig parked on the ferry, from an upper level forward facing deck, then posted it on the book page. Instantly, I got a double dog dare from a veteran following my travels. He dared me to do the "Titanic" scene where Rose puts her arms out from her sides in front of the ship as if flying. Gauntlet thrown, and replied with vigor. Instantly, I asked the two older guys that happened to be a few feet away if they could take a picture. I assumed the pose, leaning over the second level bannister, chest out, arms wide and hands back. I think the beard, ballcap on backwards, and on my tippy toes with board shorts and flip-flops completed the shot nicely. The group of college aged kids on the top deck must've agreed as they knocked on the glass all clapping and laughing. Double dog dare... pffft. You forget, I'm a Marine. The two old guys just looked confused.

From Ocracoke Island, we took another very short ferry to Hatteras Island, putting us back on the road near the southern part of the Cape Hatteras National Seashore around 1700. The skies were clouding up, becoming dark and somewhat menacing. Yup, we were about to get slammed. The further we drove, the darker it got with both clouds and retreating daylight; we needed to find a place to hunker down before this thing hit.

It wasn't but a few more miles into the drive when the rain started coming down, and I mean in buckets. Now it was dark, the wind-driven rain slammed into the windshield hard. The streets were starting to flood, giving me a mini-heart attack every time we hit a deep puddle, flooding the windshield and temporarily blinding what little vision I had. It was nerve wracking, but there were very few places to park, all with no overnight signs in most beach parking lots, which really didn't matter at this point. The storm was bad enough that I decided to press on until we got to a populated area. Kimber would be a wreck anyway, having South Dakota flashbacks; might as well take it slow and drive through it.

After what seemed like an eternity, the storm finally let up just as we passed over the Virginia State line. Not realizing how far we had driven, we completely drove past the North Carolina Outer Banks. I was bummed in a way, but grateful we were out of that storm and finally parked. I'd be back to check out the beaches there when I had more time and dry clothes. North Carolina, state #22... COMPLETE!

Virginia

May 23rd, 2017. We woke up at a Walmart just south of Chesapeake, VA, with more rain. Not a wind driven storm, but a slow, steady soaker. Not much fun to go sightseeing at Virginia Beach in the rain, so we hunkered down for the day and got some writing done. Not only is there very little fun in exploring in the rain, but why take the chance of an accident and jeopardize Kimber, the Rig, and my traveling. Plus, we've been putting in some serious miles! A well needed "zero sum" day worked for me. That's what I call a day where we put out zero expenditures. Didn't use gas, ate food we already had, zero money spent. That's always a good rainy day.

The next day was cloudy and overcast, but no rain, temperatures still low from the past day's storms, so all in all, a good day to drive. Last night, I had researched the route I planned on taking through Virginia, or at least a rough idea. Wow, Virginia was like one giant battlefield. This would definitely be the highlight of the Civil War portion, not to mention Yorktown and the surrendering of Cornwallis!

So first stop was Yorktown, right on the coast with Virginia Beach on the way. Then I had hoped to stop in on another old Marine buddy near Richmond before venturing inland to all the Civil War sites. From Richmond to Washington DC's border, I hoped to follow the battles up the east side of the state, then finally turn west and come back down the Shenandoah Valley to

Lexington, before crossing over into West Virginia. Buckle up my friend, there's a whole lot of history heading our way.

Driving through Virginia Beach was just like driving through any other beach town tourist destination, with all the same assortment of tourist traps, t-shirt vendors, and chain restaurants. We didn't stop at this point, nothing new to see here. Over the bridge into Newport News was super cool though, looking down on aircraft carriers in various stages of construction. Traffic was thick so we headed straight for Yorktown, a few more miles up the coast.

As we followed Cornwallis and Greene through the Southern Campaign of the American Revolution, we knew that the final battle was in Yorktown where the English surrendered; otherwise, I wouldn't have realized that the Colonial National Historic Park was even a battleground. The park encompasses not only the battleground itself, but also most of the historic "downtown" of Yorktown during that period. Complete with a very modern visitor center, movie and museum, redoubts and cannons along the battlefield trail, and a whole lot of American history. We spent the entire day here, as every American should. To actually walk the field where the English laid down their arms, ending all hostilities; to stand where the actual American Experiment began, was something truly amazing to behold. I quickly found myself swelling with the pride of patriotism once again. I did realize there was a huge difference between Revolutionary War sites and Civil War sites… the lack of politics. We were ALL Patriots in the revolution, no sides to choose, no blame to place.

Yorktown is where our exploration of the eastern coast came to an end for the year. We would have had to turn north from Virginia Beach, across the Chesapeake Bay toward Maryland, in order to continue up the coast. From Yorktown we turned the Rig west for the first time, which also meant we were halfway done, and heading home. Looking back at what we had accomplished thus far was impressive, but we still had a long ways to go. Next stop Richmond.

I called my buddy Jay who I had served with at Camp Pendleton to let him know I was in the area, but as luck would have it, he too was out of town with the family for another few days. With this extra time, I plotted out a small loop where we would venture inland to Appomattox Courthouse, then return to the Richmond area battlefields, just in time for Jay and the family to return.

I decided on taking the fastest route to Appomattox which was almost exactly 100 miles from Richmond. Hoping for an interstate to hop on, we ended up taking Hwy 60, which was just a two-lane country road, but as close to a direct route as I was going to get. It really didn't matter once we left the urban sprawl of Richmond, the absolute beauty of the Virginia back country made the drive seem momentary.

We didn't get our usual early start, putting us at the Appomattox Courthouse National Historical Park shortly after noon. The parking lot was completely full, with school buses everywhere. Definitely not my scene. I decided to stake out the local Walmart and maybe find Kimber some grass to play ball. That's when we passed by the "Museum of the Confederacy" and decided to stop and have a look.

All I can say is, man am I glad I stopped to see this place. When I set off on this southern state trip, I wanted to see the Civil War from the southern perspective; and wow, did I find it here. A private museum, it was dedicated to the Confederacy during Lee's surrender at Appomattox Courthouse. The artifacts in this place is what makes it absolutely incredible. Families of the men who fought for the South have donated everything from articles of clothing and firearms, to pictures and documents that are literally priceless. Included were the General's frock that Lee wore, the gloves he laid on the table before Grant, even Lee's incredibly ornate sword that he offered to Grant, which Grant famously refused. There were also flags galore, hand sewn and ragged, some with blood and bullet holes. But the most impressive and somewhat creepy, was General Lee's actual death mask. It really showed how much the South revered this man, and how much this man loved his state. When asked to command the US Army prior to the Civil War, Lee replied, "Save in defense of my native state, I never desire again to draw my sword." - Robert E. Lee, April 1861. That statement speaks volumes to me. He chose to fight for his state, being that back then, we were truly states of a republic, rather than a republic of states.

I was so glad that I stopped and took in the information from that museum, giving me a head start on what I would find at the battlefield the next day. Much like the Colonial Park in Yorktown, Appomattox Courthouse was set up as an entire town, with surrounding battlefields and a National Cemetery. It was incredible to walk down the same road General Grant took to meet Lee on the morning of the Confederate surrender. This was the same road where Lee had planned his escape after being chased from Richmond but was eventually surrounded by Grant's forces. I could just picture the 70,000 cheering Union troops lining the road as General Grant rode his horse past. I could see the house where General Lee would be waiting, the unassuming structure that would witness the end of the American Civil War. What an amazing scene that must've been.

So basically what happened was, when Lee was pushed from Petersburg, he was hoping to escape to the west to later meet up with General Johnston in North Carolina. His plans to re-supply and feed his starving troops were thwarted by none other than the boy general himself, Major General George Custer, who intercepted the shipment. At this point, Lee was surrounded and had no option but to surrender. Johnston followed suit a few days later in Durham, surrendering to Sherman. I had to chuckle at once again, by no grand scheme whatsoever, we were following the war in reverse. Why change now right? So off to Petersburg we went, to see how Lee was driven from the Capital of the Confederacy.

Petersburg National Battlefield is a few miles southwest of Richmond, that pretty much now encompasses Petersburg proper. We got there bright and early as usual, on a cloudy and wet morning that apparently kept the tourists away, happily giving us the run of the place. This was definitely an older battlefield, by the looks of the signage and visitor center. It was designated as a "battlefield," and a massive artillery battle at that, so the park was geared mainly toward a driving tour with an unbelievable amount of cannon and mortars on static display. It was warm enough for shorts, but the mist was heavy and rain was sporadic. As long as you stayed in the non-wooded portion of the walking tour, you got wet; but, when you ventured into the woods you were instantly breakfast for every winged insect in the immediate area. Kimber wasn't liking the rain much, so after the visitor center, we stayed in the truck most of the time, grabbing some pictures here and there along the way. One of which was of a big, red, male Cardinal, keeping watch from above.

The Battle of Petersburg is the last battle of what's known as the "Overland Campaign." Basically, it's a series of battles where Lee tried to block Grant's southern push in a series of battles from Fredericksburg to Petersburg. Almost a full month of fighting, with casualty numbers that you just can't wrap your head around. So it looked like I had my work cut out for me. Next stop Richmond.

Rain sucks for sightseeing and we had a lot of both coming up, so I decided to look around for a Buffalo Wild Wings and catch up on some baseball. Low and behold, there was a BWW literally next door to an Anytime Fitness in a strip mall, just across the street from a Walmart.

Bingo, I'm in! Mix in a little laundry and grocery shopping, and I had a full rainy day afternoon. Perfect actually, as Jay said he would be back in town the next evening, and to plan on a BBQ.

The next day was beautiful, bright and sunny, without a single cloud in the sky. The last night's rain was keeping the temperature down nicely as we pulled into downtown Richmond and the first stop of the Richmond National Battlefield Park. The visitor center explained that the park is made up of several historic civil war era sites, to include the Tredegar Iron Works factory, the second White House of the Confederacy, a hospital, a prison, and several major battle sites, all around the city of Richmond and the surrounding area. Wanting to focus on the battlefields themselves, I took some pictures of the Iron Works factory, where they made the cannons and mortars for the Confederacy, before heading out to Cold Harbor, the next battle of the Overland Campaign.

Cold Harbor is an area west of Richmond, in the surrounding farmland that was becoming "suburbanized" with housing developments creeping in. The battlefield itself was a wooded area with hiking trails, giving you a view of the earthworks and entrenchments, while interpretive plaques described the horrific scene. This was two weeks of trench warfare with estimates of casualties reaching 2,000 a day, 18,000 at Cold Harbor alone. It's literally unfathomable to think of trench warfare in America, but yet, here it was. Un-freaking-real.

We completed the entire Cold Harbor hiking trail by 1030, just as the heat and humidity was starting to become a factor. From there I scouted out a gym for a quick shower before heading into Mechanicsville where my Marine buddy Jay and family lived. Like Jeff, my Marine buddy in Florida, I had served with Jay back in San Diego at Elmaco or Electronic Maintenance Company. After I had married and became an NCO (non commissioned officer), I always invited the junior enlisted guys who couldn't make it home for Thanksgiving over to our place for football, beer, and turkey. Jay was one of those troops. To this day, he tells me how that was one of best memories he has of the Corps. I'd have to say, ditto for me.

Jay was a Lance Corporal (E3) back then, who later got his degree and got out of the Marines as a Major. Now doing well in the business world, he's married with two boys. We sat in the backyard catching up, telling old Corps stories, while Kimber and Jay's big yellow lab chased the ball around the yard. Some of the best, and completely unexpected, parts about this traveling thing is the reconnecting with old friends. Great to see ya, brother, hope to see you again real soon.

Thankfully, it was payday, funds were starting to get pretty tight, but I was still sticking to my budget, and was even stashing a little bit away in savings every month. Once you get the hang of this boondocking thing, you can actually save quite a bit of money living the RV life. Of course, that depends on your lifestyle, and right now mine's about as minimalist as you can get. Granted, I'd probably never have been able to pull this off if I was married with children. Luckily, Kimber is pretty low maintenance. Either way, we had a full tank of gas and a full bank account, for at least the next 30 days.

When I was at the visitor center in Richmond, I had grabbed a brochure for the Fredericksburg and Spotsylvania National Military Park, knowing I'd be heading up there next. According to the brochure's map, this park was also made up of several different exhibits located in and around the local towns. First stop being the Stonewall Jackson Shrine. Shrine? And a Jackson at that, this should be interesting.

It was only a 45 minute drive from Jay's to the small farming community named Guinea, where the Confederates had established a major supply depot at Guinea Station in 1862. Confederate camps blanketed the local farmland, one such farm belonging to the Chandler family. At one point, Stonewall Jackson himself, General Lee's right hand man, had camped there, refusing to take a bed from the family but instead pitching a tent nearby. In 1863, the Chandler family had planned to sell the farm, but before they could, General Jackson returned. This time he had been wounded, lost an arm, and was awaiting a train to take him to a hospital, but it was too late. Stonewall Jackson had succumbed to his wounds, and passed away. This was an absolute major blow to General Lee and the Confederacy.

So the "Shrine" is actually a small, one bedroom, white farmhouse situated in the center of a couple acres of farmland. There was a double set of train tracks on the edge of the property, that had serviced the Guinea Station back in the day. The farmhouse was furnished as it was then, with the original bed and bloodstained linen that marked where General Jackson had died. Everything was exactly as it was, according to the Park Ranger giving the tours.

Ok, so I've obviously become very interested in Stonewall Jackson, as he shares my maternal Great Grandfather's last name. Benjamin Franklin Jackson Jr. was my Great Grampa Jackson. I had reached out to my second cousin in Oregon about Stonewall Jackson and asked if we had any relation, to which she promptly sent back a family tree with all the known relatives. Not seeing any direct ties to Stonewall, I was astonished to learn that we had Jacksons going all the way back to 1814! Francis Jackson, my Great X4 Grandfather, had married in 1814 and moved to Rock Creek Oregon. We don't know where he moved from. His son was George Washington Jackson, who had a son named Benjamin Franklin Jackson Sr., and then my Great Grampa, Ben Franklin Jackson Jr. So yes, I am indeed a Jackson. Now I was super curious about who Stonewall Jackson was and if we were related.

When I got to the visitor center at Fredericksburg National Battlefield, I realized I was actually in the middle of two separate Civil War campaigns. The first being a Confederate victory at Fredericksburg and Chancellorsville, with CSA General Lee pushing the Union Army back North, only to have US Generals Grant and Meade return a year later on their march to Richmond, known as the Overland Campaign. I guess I should've left the Jackson Shrine for last, even though his death was actually right in the middle of the timeline, with his passing just 10 days after being wounded in Chancellorsville. Confusing, I know. Ok well, let's just take this one battle at a time.

After checking out the visitor center at Fredericksburg, I let Kimber out of the truck and explored the battlefield. Once again, the stories of the individuals who fought here, and the sheer amount of casualties that were sustained by both sides really made an impact on me. It was just mind numbing to realize that almost 200k men engaged in battle here, with close to 20k in casualties and losses. Names like Burnside, Hooker, Grant, Lee, Jackson and Longstreet, just to name a few of the heavy hitters that fought here and in the surrounding area. What an amazing piece of American history.

Fredericksburg National Cemetery was also here with its countless headstones lining the grassy hillside. Kimber and I walked among the graves, with a very ominous and heavy feeling. I was really uncomfortable being there for some reason. I felt like I wasn't supposed to be there, like I was not welcome. It was so bizarre. Then I thought, wait a minute, this is a Union cemetery, where they never buried Confederate soldiers. I'm a Jackson, my relative probably put some of these guys in here. I was somewhat amused by the thought that these fallen soldiers didn't appreciate me among them, and were letting me know it. Now that's some creepy shit, and the goosebumps on my arms verified it.

While we explored the cemetery, another gentleman was there taking pictures. He was a black guy, about my age, wearing a Marine Corps ball cap. Of course, I walked up and said hello with the customary, "Semper Fi Devil dog," to which he quickly responded with a hearty

211

"OOHRAH!" Turned out he was a former Marine Chaplain, taking pictures with some crazy camera, trying to capture the supernatural on film. I was rather taken aback, hearing this coming from a man of God, but at the same time I was very interested. I told him about my being a Jackson and feeling like I wasn't supposed to be there. He laughed and said, "You too, huh? I feel the same at all the cemeteries." He then commented on how the Confederates obviously weren't happy with his presence, but the Union wasn't sent here to free slaves, but to secure the Union. Wow, amusing and creepy, all at once. We chatted for a few minutes and parted ways after a selfie with Kimber of course, with thankfully no supernatural visitors doing a photo bomb.

We stayed in Fredericksburg that night and started out for Chancellorsville bright and early the following morning. It was only about a twenty-minute drive west from Fredericksburg, and was really nothing but the foundation of a large brick inn, owned by the Chancellor family, situated at a key crossroad. There was a wooded area near the home that had a hiking trail with information placards and the battlefield's visitor center.

Once inside the Chancellorsville Battlefield Visitor Center, you suddenly realize the importance of this battle. This was the place where Stonewall Jackson was mortally wounded, and surprisingly enough, by his own troops. Coming back from a night reconnaissance that Jackson personally undertook with a few other men, they were mistakenly fired upon, hitting General Jackson in the left arm. He would later succumb to his wounds at the farmhouse in Guinea Station.

It was incredible to see the outpouring of emotion the public had upon Jackson's death. Soldiers and civilians alike scavenged for souvenirs to remember their hero. There was a framed photo of Jackson in the museum that had a lock of his hair, and a piece of his uniform, along with his profile. The place where he was shot has a massive boulder marking the spot, with a later addition of a granite obelisk memorializing the location. The South loved their Stonewall, that's for sure. General Lee was devastated by the news, and even likened Stonewall's death to the loss of his own right arm. Even the Union officers, elated by the news of his death, respected the warrior that he was. Not gonna lie, at this point, I was hoping I was related to this guy, and even found myself swelling with pride over his military achievements. Don't get that twisted; it has nothing to do with slavery or racism, it's all about the person and his military accomplishments. Remember, this is from a veteran's perspective, and now a possible family perspective.

Next stop was the Wilderness Battlefield, just a few miles up the road. Apparently, this part of the military park was a driving tour, as we passed one exhibition that had a locked metal gate across the entrance, with the name "Ellwood" welded into the frame. It was a national park site, but apparently closed. Across the street was another brown National Parks sign, pointing to an area that was Grant's Headquarters with the number 1 in a yellow circle. There was just a small parking lot with another trailhead leading to a bivouac site.

Lacking an actual visitor center for the Wilderness Battlefield, the first significant stop was called the "Wilderness Battlefield Exhibit Shelter." Basically, it looked like a bus stop with several information placards, a large area map labeled May 5th and 6th 1864, a few benches, and what looked like a trailhead, with a path leading into the nearby woods. Ok, so now we are at the beginning of the Overland Campaign, and the multiple engagements between Grant's Army of the Potomac, and Lee's Army of Northern Virginian, while moving south toward Richmond. All taking place almost exactly a year after Fredericksburg and Chancellorsville.

Kimber was happy to get out of the truck and get some hiking in, although the heat wasn't going to make it a very long one. The interpretive signs along the way described "Gordon's Flank Attack," a Union victory that saved the entire right wing of Grant's Army. I was taken aback by how dense the forest was in this part of the landscape, trying to imagine thousands of men fighting through this. Add the ground fires ignited by muzzle flash, it literally must have been the landscape of hell itself, with another 17,500 Union and 11,000 Confederates losing their lives here.

After our short hike, we retreated back to the shelter for some solid shade while I waited for the Rig's AC to cool the cab. That's when I noticed two small pamphlets, just copied pieces of paper folded in thirds for visitors to take. One with a map of the area and the hiking trail that we just walked, describing what happened at different places along the way. The second was about a homestead called Ellwood, describing a family farm that was used as a Confederate hospital around the time Chancellorsville was going off. Wait, that's the place we passed but was closed. It described how the house changed hands during the war, from Lee staying there on his way to Gettysburg, to Ambrose Burnside taking over the farm and using it as a Union headquarters a year later. The kicker was a small excerpt on the back page, the header read, "The Cemetery." It went on to describe a family burial plot on the edge of this farm, where several soldiers were buried after passing in the hospital. The most famous of which was Stonewall Jackson's left arm. I about dropped the piece of paper. Say what!? They buried Stonewall's arm!? Sure enough, after he was shot, surgeons amputated the arm in a nearby tavern. The following day, Jackson's chaplain carried the arm across the field and buried it in the family cemetery, where it remains today. No freakin' way! I gotta see this. We jumped in the now chilly Rig, made a U-turn, and drove back to the Ellwood gate. There was no way in hell that I had come this far, and wasn't going to see a tombstone marking the burial place of Stonewall Jackson's arm!

Now with a recon mission of my own underway, I parked the Rig across the street near the Grant HQ trailhead, got Kimber out of the truck once again, and made our way to the locked gate. There were no cars or people to be seen anywhere. I took a ball with me to explain that Kimber had run off with it, and I was merely giving chase, if anyone was to stop us. I know, I know, but it was the best contingency plan I could come up with on short notice. I'd just play the dumb Yankee tourist who got lost. Who's gonna be mad at her when she looks up and performs her magic, anyway?

With a quick flick of the "chucker stick," Kimber was off, down the tree lined dirt road chasing her ball, me dutifully following behind. The place was empty, no cars, no people, nothing; we had the run of the place. Once back near the house, there was no way we could be seen from the road, which made me relax just a little. Kimber was ecstatic to play ball, regardless of temperature at this point. Following the drive, eventually stopping at the farmhouse, we followed the interpretive signs around the property and down to the family cemetery.

The cemetery was basically a grassy area with what looked like several depressions, presumably the unmarked family graves, with only one weathered granite tombstone near the center. The area was lined with an old wooden fence, under a few oak trees, other than that, there were no other markings or signage. When I walked around to face the canted, granite marker, I was able to read the inscription. Just 4 words and a date: "Arm of Stonewall Jackson May 3, 1963" was carved into the stone. First thing that went through my mind was how much of an actual bad ass did you have to be, that the public would mark and bury your body parts! Wow, what an amazing find. I quickly took some pics, one with Kimber posing nicely next to the marker. Now with my mission complete, I needed to regress from the objective undetected.

Another toss of the ball down the drive, putting our cover into motion, we found our way back to the Rig. Now that was freakin' cool!

It was the hottest part of the day now, and my brain was on information overload. We scouted out the nearest Walmart, just a few miles north of an area called Lake of the Woods, fired up the generator for AC, and called it a day. I needed to get some of this knowledge on paper, and figure out the next day's adventure. We still had one more stop within the Fredericksburg and Spotsylvania National Military Park ahead, but first, a small diversion to another incredibly historic place, James Madison's Montpellier estate was just up the road.

The next morning, we waited long enough for the Montpellier grounds to open, before leaving Walmart and venturing somewhat off our path, to the home of President James Madison, known as "the Father of the Constitution." First stop was at the Montpellier Train Depot, a small, newly remodeled train station building, just outside the main entrance to the mansion grounds. There were two entrance doors, one marked "white" and the other marked "colored" on the wood trim above. The sign out front explained that William DuPont built the depot to increase passenger and freight flow to Montpellier, which he had purchased in 1901. It went on to say that the Montpelier Foundation later restored the depot to document this time of legalized segregation in American history. When I tried the entrance doors, they were locked, and the building was basically empty. I was somewhat confused as to why they would talk about what this place was remodeled to represent, rather than stating the actual history of the building. I should have seen this as a sign of what I'd encounter next.

I wasn't going to put this into my book as it really had nothing to do with battle, but I thought it significant to explain after what I had found completely enraged me. I made my way through the expansive estate, complete with horse racing track built by DuPont after acquiring the land, to the very modern and ornate gift shop, snack bar, and ticket counter. The actual house where Madison penned the Federalist Papers was a guided tour exhibit that required a purchase ticket of almost 20 bucks, and no pictures were allowed to be taken. When I asked if there was a veteran or military discount, the rude lady behind the counter said, "This is a private museum, not the Park Service," and pointed at the prices. I paid for my ticket, while biting a hole through my tongue, and wandered around the gift shop until the tour began, somewhat surprised by all the literature concerning slavery alongside our fourth president and founding father's books of accomplishments. Why are they so concerned about the slavery of the early 1700s? This was a way of life that, although detestable by today's standards, was the norm during Madison's. I just don't get this.

I still had about 30 minutes before the tour started so I ventured outside to look around the adjoining grounds. I noticed there was a huge tent being erected with several folding chairs nearby, setting up for some sort of a celebration, maybe a wedding or something. Then I found another building, where the Madison's slaves were quartered. Several brand-new plaques described in detail the horrors of slavery, the slave families that lived here, their daily lives and struggles, etc. The interesting part is all this was completely free and open to the public without a guided tour. The next building was under the final stages of construction, but also dedicated to slave life of the time period. That's when I asked a construction guy what the outside tent was for. "They're opening this part of the museum tomorrow," he replied. "Oh, so they will start charging to get in then?" I asked. He shook his head, "no sir, it's free." So they charge for the tour of the home of a founding father, author of the Constitution and Federalist paper, not to mention our 4th President, but overwhelmingly include the lives and struggles of the slaves he owned, completely free to the public. This along with no picture taking allowed inside of the home, but take all you wish of the newly remodeled slave quarters. This was my first experience of the rewriting, or maybe the "re-emphasizing" of a certain narrative, or what I call the reshaping of our national history, is a better description. Either way, I was pissed. Once again, don't get it twisted, this should be about the man who helped form our country, not about the perceived evils of the time by today's activist "historians." Sure, a mention of slavery is noteworthy, but shouldn't be the focus of this man's life or legacy. Ok, off my soapbox. Let's get back at it.

After wasting 20 bucks and a half day's time on this so-called historic tour, Spotsylvania Court House Battlefield was our next stop, which was also the next major battle of Grant's Overland Campaign. The largest battlefield and hiking trail yet, it mainly described how combat had changed from the beginning of the war where forces would fight, retreat, and rest, giving way to Grant's relentless maneuvering and attacks. Coupled with the dug in and deeply entrenched Confederates, protected by earthworks and artillery, this led to the worst combat and fatalities in American history. The losing of the race to Spotsylvania and its critical crossroads would pretty much seal the fate of the Confederacy. From here our next stop would've been the Stonewall Jackson Shrine that we had already visited, so instead, we headed back to

Fredericksburg for a shower, a meal, and to call it a night at the local Walmart. Next stop, the town of Manassas and the Battle of Bull Run.

The following morning, we woke up to a little bit of weather coming in. The heavy mist and light sprinkling of rain was a happy reprieve from the heat and humidity we had the last few days. Up bright and early, trying to avoid traffic, we ventured north toward the Manassas National Military Park. Not realizing that we were basically in a suburb of DC, the morning traffic was brutal. I had thought to visit Arlington National Cemetery on my visit to Virginia, but after seeing this traffic, it could wait until next year's adventure into the North East. I wanted to be at the visitor center right when they opened so I could get on the closest freeway and head back to the country quickly, once we were finished with the Battle of Bull Run. The park didn't open for another hour or so, giving me time to locate an Anytime Fitness and grab a quick workout and shower.

First thing I learned at the Manassas National Military Park was that the Battle of Manassas and the Battle of Bull Run is actually the same conflict. The Southern troops, being generally from rural areas and farmlands, named their battles after the nearest structures such as train stations, courthouses, churches or small towns, due to not many buildings or man-made structures being nearby. In contrast, the northern troops being from major North Eastern cities were impressed with the South's geographical features such as rivers, streams, mountains, and valleys. While fighting in unfamiliar territory, these natural formations were easily remembered and recognizable. Bull Run was a small creek, known as a "run," that troops were firing across as the Union pushed toward the Henry Farm, located in Manassas. So the North retreated from the defeat at "Bull Run," while the South celebrated its victory at the Battle of "Manassas." Same battle, get it? Keep that in mind with other battles near the border states between North and South.

It also turns out that this battle was fought more than once on this land. The first battle of Manassas/Bull Run was the actual first battle of the Civil War. Fort Sumter was the first bullet fired, but was mainly an artillery bombardment of the island that didn't include ground troops. Both sides assumed Manassas/Bull Run 1 would be a very quick battle to end hostilities directly. Man, were they wrong. The onslaught was something neither side expected. Civilians bringing picnics and chairs to watch this "grand battle" were overrun as gunfire and artillery erupted. With mainly inexperienced troops to include cadets from West Point, confusion and mayhem reigned. Lincoln pushed hard for Union troops to get this battle over with, and moved troops into Northern Virginia first, thus the South naming this the War of Northern Aggression. Incredibly, the South was able to push the Union troops back over the border into Maryland and DC. The reality that this was not going to be a one-off battle, but a long and bloody war, now became apparent to both sides.

The most interesting to me personally about this battle was the introduction of General Thomas J Jackson to the war. This battle is where Jackson earned his nickname "Stonewall." Learning that he was a geometry and artillery instructor at the Virginia Military Institute prior, not to mention a West Point graduate and veteran of the Mexican American wars, explained how he knew to roll his cannons slightly down the backside of a rolling hill, exposing only the wicks of his cannons as they bombarded the Union positions. Remember that these officers commanding the raw ground troops were seasoned veterans who served with each other prior to the rift between states.

CSA General Bee was the man who gave Stonewall his name. Wounded but not yet dead, Bee was attempting to round up his scattering ground troops. The granite marker, memorializing the spot where he died read, "Form! Form! There stands Jackson like a stone wall! Rally behind the Virginians!" At that moment a star, a legend, and even considered by some, a savior of the South, was born.

The Manassas National Battlefield Park had an amazing Visitor Center and expansive grass covered grounds. The main attraction was the Henry family farmhouse that was burnt and reconstructed after the war. My favorite thing being, of course, the static display of cannons peeking over a berm line, backed against a wooded area, representing Jackson's "stone wall." All the guns were facing the Henry farmhouse, being led into battle by a massive stone and bronze statue of Jackson atop his horse, also facing the farm. Jackson's body literally looks like something out of a superman movie, with horse just as muscular and ripped. The pedestal that the statue sat on was taller than me at 5'7", with statue towering well above that. It was as impressive as the Nathaniel Greene statue back at Guilford Courthouse in NC. Only three simple inscriptions were chiseled onto three separate sides of the base. Facing the front was "Thomas Jonathan Jackson 1824-1863," then on the sides were "First Battle of Manassas July 21st,1861" on one side, and "There stands Jackson like a stone wall" on the other. What was peculiarly different about this monument was the color. The base was of shiny black granite, while the bronze bust of horse and rider were also a dark black rather than a bronze or even greenish color. Interesting.

Surprisingly, there was no mention of the second battle of Manassas/Bull Run in the visitor center, but only as I passed a couple of old steel historic markers a few hundred yards away from the Manassas Battlefield Park entrance, did I hear of the second fight. A much larger battle than the first, and just a month later. Here, Stonewall Jackson performed a wide flanking march and captured the Union supply depot near Manassas. Only after Confederate reinforcements arrived was the Union once again pushed back to Bull Run. I only mention this as being significant because this was the battle that emboldened Lee enough to begin his Maryland Campaign and his first invasion into the North.

One last notable entry for the First Battle of Manassas was the entry of the United States Marines Corps into the war. A small detachment of Marines were sent in support of Army ground troops, 350 total with only three weeks of training at the Barracks in D.C. After Union troops had fallen into disarray after a brutal fire fight, the Marines made two more final attempts at taking the farmhouse on Henry Hill. Both attempts obviously thwarted by the Confederacy, the Marines' conduct and reputation as warriors received praise from both sides. OOHRAH!

By this time, the light rain had picked up significantly; a serious storm was heading our way. It was still fairly early as we jumped on Interstate 66 west toward Strasburg, VA, officially marking our halfway point, and began the long trek home. It was recommended to me by a retired USMC Sgt Maj buddy of mine, who had taught at the Virginia Military Institute, to travel the Shenandoah Valley and make a visit to the VMI museum. So the plan was to make it to Strasburg and wait out this rain, then head south along the Shenandoah Valley to Lexington, VA, ultimately over the border into West Virginia near White Sulphur Springs.

The rain intensified brutally. I knew I had leaks over my bed already, and doing 65 mph into a torrential downpour would pretty much guarantee me a wet mattress, let alone the water damage to the old camper. I dove off the interstate, stopping under an overpass, waiting for the worst to pass. I wasn't the only one. A motorcycle state trooper and another RV were there too, all waiting for the rain to lighten up enough to drive. Man, I felt sorry for that motors officer. He just sat there stoically watching traffic, not minding that we were parked several yards behind him. About 10 minutes later he must have had a call as he fired up his bike and took off. Rain still coming down, I chose to take some backroads at a much slower pace to the Strasburg

Walmart. Home for the next few hours, bed not too wet, I counted my blessings and holed up there for the rest of the day and evening, waiting for the storm to pass. Thank God for Walmart!

First thing in the morning, we rolled out to explore the Shenandoah Valley. Instead of taking the major Interstate 81, I opted for the scenic route, Hwy 11 that basically mirrored the interstate. The storm had finally broke, giving way to perfect temperatures and beautiful cloud streaked blue skies. We passed several small but historic towns, one being Mt. Jackson, VA, where I stopped to refuel. The elderly lady behind the counter was friendly as most southern folks seem to be, commenting on the beautiful weather outside. I told her how I needed to get my little dog out for a hike since she'd been cooped up in the truck for awhile. Instantly, she asked where I was from, my lack of southern accent giving me away. I explained my travels and aspirations of writing this book. I then told her that my Grandfather was a Jackson and ran down the lineage that my cousin had sent me. The look on her face was of almost shock. "That mountain right there," she said as she came out from around the counter, pointing across the street toward the east side of the valley, "That's named after your family, son. That there's Mt. Jackson, named after Stonewall." Suddenly, I felt like royalty. She reached out and grabbed my hand introducing herself and asking my name. She quickly wrote it down on a pad, and shook my hand like she had just met the President. That was amazing. She then told me of a battlefield just down the road a few more miles, and not to miss the museum. With a chest filled with pride, I thanked her and said goodbye. Next stop New Market, VA.

Just as the lady had described, the New Market Battlefield signs started popping up a few clicks down the highway. Not the brown National Parks sign, this was a Virginia State battlefield marker. Like the 2nd Manassas sign, it was white painted metal with raised black letters and black outlining. It gave a brief description of what took place here. Basically stating that the Union Army was thwarted by the cadets of the local Virginia Military Institute after they captured a Union battery. Then came a brown Virginia State Parks sign pointing toward the exit.

As I was following the signs to the New Market Battlefield, the first building we came to was in a manicured grass field with headstones and a parking lot. The building was tan with huge white Roman columns at the entry. The sign read "New Market Battlefield Military Museum." I must be in the right place. When I entered, I realized that this was a private museum and not the county park visitor center a few miles further up the road. Well, since I was here, I might as well pay the 6 bucks and check it out. Man, am I glad I did. This would be the most amazing collection of war history that I'd ever seen. Not just civil war, but ALL wars!

I could have spent all day in this museum. Every war from the Revolutionary War, to modern day, but mainly about the American Civil War, was covered with several different exhibits. There were an amazing amount of small personal pictures and trinkets next to typed captions pinned underneath. All were donated by families who not only lived in the area, but from all over Virginia and other states in the South. Several pictures of Stonewall Jackson adorned the walls, from when he was a lieutenant during the Mexican Wars, to his teaching days at VMI, and ultimately his death after Chancellorsville.

The most shocking display in the museum was of the late Abraham Lincoln. Amongst other pictures was a real photograph of the President laying in state, his face fully visible from only a few feet away. It was a chilling black and white photograph that you instantly knew was genuine. Along with several photographs were captions, typed on paper, glued to cardboard, and hung with pins like paragraphs in a book. A few read as follows: "During the election of 1860, Northern voters cast a quarter of a million more votes against Lincoln than did the entire South." Let that sink in a minute. Thinking in terms of the electoral college, how did this happen? Or was it purely a loss of the popular vote? "June 7th 1864. Federal employees learn that they are expected to contribute 5% of a year's pay to the Lincoln Campaign." Whoa what? The next card read, "Lincoln signed the Emancipation Proclamation, freeing slaves in the Southern States ONLY. Further, he invited free blacks to join the U.S. Army." Ok, that's twice we've heard this, both at a Federal level and now at a private level. Confirmation I'd say, to something that would NEVER be taught in public schools. "Not once during the war was Abraham Lincoln heard to use the term 'the enemy,'" because we were all Americans and he had to convince his troops it was to save the Union, not free the slaves. That's my take at least. And finally, "President Lincoln and Confederate President Davis were both born in Kentucky, barely 100 miles apart and within 8 months of each other." Ok, wait a minute. What happened to Honest Abe from Illinois? Nope, born further south than Davis himself; no wonder the South considered him a traitor. I'll check into this more when we go to Kentucky.

See what I mean about the information that you receive from local and private owned museums as compared to the National Parks Service? It really makes you question what we were taught growing up in the 1980s. Isn't there a saying that goes, "He who wins the war, writes the history books," or something like that. It's very interesting to see this war from the eyes of the South, a perspective that you won't get through public education. So it's up to these little private museums to pass on the true history of country. I'll be on the lookout for more non-governmental museums going forward.

Like I said, I could've spent the entire day in this building, an absolute priceless personal collection of American History I believe I've ever seen. Local history, with stories and captions from the folks who lived through and served in these wars. When I asked the gentleman behind the counter, who happened to be the owner, how much insurance was to protect this amazing place, he told me that the cost of one month of insurance was more than he collects in entrance fees a year. His insurance policy: "I live upstairs with a shotgun." God bless ya, sir, and thank you for sharing your amazing home. If you love history, you have got to see this place. Unreal!

Another few hundred yards up the road was the actual Commonwealth of Virginia, New Market Battlefield and Virginia Museum of The Civil War. I'm glad I didn't see this sign until after visiting the other museum as I would have skipped the private, pay to play museum for a government one. The state-run Visitor Center was also a pay to play museum, that mainly covered just the Battle of New Market, summarizing once again about the cadets from VMI securing an artillery battery, forcing the retreat of the Union Army. The most significant fact about this battlefield, beside the VMI cadets' bravery and a few that were entombed here, was that this would be the final battle to take place in the Shenandoah Valley.

It was only midmorning by the time we left New Market, Kimber was visibly anxious and needed some exercise; my waistline concurred. So off we went to the Shenandoah National Park, a portion of the George Washington National Forest. I was hoping for a little down time so I could get all this information in some kind of order. My head was swimming with all the battlefields we had visited, I didn't want to confuse them later. Hopefully, I'd find a nice boondock spot or even a cheap National Forest campground to spend a couple of down days and get some hiking in. The weather was good and we just had a payday, so I stocked up on groceries and headed for the hills.

We took Hwy 211 up to the crest of the Shenandoah Valley mountaintops, looking as far as the eye could see east toward Washington D.C. The trees were overgrown with dense vines, covering the forest with what looked like a giant green blanket. The only camping places we found were private "resort" like campgrounds that were way too pricey for just a couple of nights. We ended up finding a very popular hiking trail that led down to some waterfalls below. As Kimber and I traversed the fairly steep trail, I kept thinking, what goes down must come up, remembering New Mexico and the cavern elevator disaster. I was mindful of the distance, but yet enthralled by the absolute beauty of what seemed like a completely untouched forest. We kept seeing these crazy looking growths on the side of the trees that I assumed were some sort or mushroom. They literally looked like brown pancakes with lighter edges, glued to the side of the massive oak trees. Later I was told that this had to be an "ancient forest" for those type of mushrooms to be prevalent. I started to think, this was probably one of the first "National" forests, being so close to DC and being named after George Washington, and therefore protected from way back then. Only a speculation but it made sense. After the 5 mile total hike, with climbing the equivalent of 45 flights of stairs, both Kimber and I were done for the day and I needed a much deserved shower... bad!

We followed what was called Skyline road across the ridge of the mountain, not realizing that it mirrored the Appalachian Trail just a few yards into the forest on the east side of us. Someday I gotta do the Appalachian, what a cool book that would be. I found an Anytime Fitness between the cities of Waynesboro and Staunton, near a fast food, fried fish place and a coin operated laundromat. Workout, shower, laundry and lunch; now that's what I call one stop shopping. Perfect.

As the laundry was drying, I stepped over to the fish place that was advertising a piece of fish, small fries, and a small drink for $2.99. Kimber and I had already had a sandwich at the trailhead, but a little snack for that price sounded tasty. I stepped in and made my order, paying with the spare change I had from the laundromat coin machine, the lady patiently waiting while I counted out the quarters and gave her exact change. When I picked up my food, there was three pieces of fish, a couple of shrimp, and a huge portion of fries. She then held out a large cup for me to take. That's when I said that this order wasn't mine, and that I had ordered the special. "That's the Marine special." I was shocked and bewildered. Then she explained that she had seen me pull the Rig into the parking lot, adorned with a USMC license plate that I had screwed to the back. Her brother was serving in the Corps, and she knew I could eat more than just the special, she told me. Amazing. I thanked her profusely for the meal before heading back to Hwy 22 and the Staunton Super Walmart for the evening, just before the rain started again. I planned on a good night's sleep before exploring the Virginia Military Institute first thing in the morning.

The Virginia Military Institute is in the small town of Lexington, VA, with a very long history of accomplished military graduates such as General Patton and instructors such as Stonewall Jackson. What I didn't realize was that they had an incredible museum and several memorials around the campus. The campus was amazing; pristine grass and manicured grounds with static cannon displays and other war monuments, all with the graduates' names who served in them. I was completely impressed and actually jealous, wishing I would've been told about colleges like this when I was in high school. Welcome to growing up in California.

I found a parking spot only after circling the grounds a few times which drew the attention of a passing security guard. I explained to him I was there to see the museum. He nodded, stepped back to look at the Rig, and told me to wait right there. He actually found me a spot next to a construction lift and told the construction crew I would be there about an hour, then came back and guided me to the spot. I thanked him for hooking me up with oversized parking place, to which he replied with a hearty "OOHRAH!" followed by a sheepish grin. Once a Marine, always a Marine, isn't just a buzz line, it's for real.

The VMI museum is truly something to behold. The museum could've been named the Stonewall Shrine, as it housed and explained all that pertained to their famous, former instructor. Everything from the India rubber raincoat that he wore on that fateful night he was shot, complete with bullet hole in upper left arm, to his original desk and some papers from his classroom instructor days. Even his horse that he had ridden the night he was wounded was stuffed and on display. I was surprised to find the museum had an amazing firearms collection, to include many air guns from early France. Why, I'm not sure, but still cool to see. It also had displays of some of its most famous students, to include General George S. Patton, and seven Medal of Honor winners from different campaigns. I learned from the cadet running the gift shop, that Stonewall's home was open for tours downtown, and that he's buried in the town cemetery. Another bonus, General Lee and his horse are buried at the college next door. Guess my day is planned, as long as the weather holds out.

Storm clouds were moving in fast at this point. The temperature had dropped to an outstanding 71f, with it forecasted to soar back into the 90s in four days. Just enough time to wrap up Lexington, and head over the border into West Virginia. Looking back at the trip so far, I'd have to say that we'd caught the weather almost perfect, following the rain had kept the temperatures relatively livable. The AC had been unusually quiet so far, which was a good thing.

That and when you start the humid season actually being in the South, it's much gentler and easier to become climatized, compared to just stepping off a plane into pea soup air. Huge difference for sure. The downside is a lot of hurrying through places I would have liked to spend more time, added with quite a bit more time in the camper than I expected; still, I'll take the rain over just hot and humid anytime.

From the college we drove into the super cool, historic little town of Lexington, VA. I found a parking place just outside of the only home Stonewall Jackson had ever owned. Out of the three visitors that were in the downstairs gift shop, I was the only one interested in taking the tour of the house. With Kimber by my side, a tour guide took us through every room, describing Stonewall Jackson's family and what everyday life looked like, pre-civil war. There were letters and artifacts on display throughout the home, also giving insight into Jackson himself. He was an avid gardener, health enthusiast, and methodical as a computer in everything he did. A West Point graduate and hero in the Mexican Wars, he studied the Bible as if it were a textbook with the Roman Catholic priests in Mexico City. This led him to becoming an extremely pious man, praying before even drinking a glass of water. He even went as far as to teach the slave children Sunday school, an illegal act at the time, yet he felt that they too had a soul worthy of saving. He loved to travel, and traveled abroad extensively before taking up his residence in Lexington to teach and help found the Virginia Military Institute. I could go on an on about the man Thomas Jackson, the similarities between our families becoming strikingly apparent.

The tour ended with Stonewall's death mask, similar to General Lee's back in Appomattox. Creepy as hell, but very interesting. A fantastic and simple timeline of wars Stonewall participated in explained exactly why the Jackson name was so prevalent in the Shenandoah Valley. Seven months after the first Manassas battle, Jackson commenced his "Valley Campaign," known as one of the most remarkable campaigns in modern warfare history. In 6 battles he faced vastly superior numbers, defeating three armies, and disrupting the Union effort to reinforce US General McClellan. Two short months after the Valley Campaign, the second Manassas kicked off. It was Stonewall's second victory at Manassas, that drove US General Pope back to Washington, enabling Lee to drive north for the first time. At this point, Lee splits his Army, sending Stonewall to take Harper's Ferry before he ultimately joins Lee at the Battle of Antietam. The incredible loss at Antietam drove the Confederacy back into Virginia, where the Battles of Fredericksburg and ultimately Chancellorsville were fought, ending Thomas

"Stonewall" Jackson's career and finally his life. Amazing. Once again, something you won't read in standard history books.

After the tour I had told the lady running the bookstore about my family name and heritage. She instantly reached under the counter and brought out a book titled "The Genealogies of the Jackson, Junkin, and Morrison Families" where we found a Benjamin F. Jackson in 1856. There was unfortunately, still no obvious direct ties to Stonewall and my side of the Jackson Clan. How many Jacksons were there in the 1700-1800s? Guess I'm gonna have to find out. Turned out, the lady who ran the gift shop actually lived in the Jackson house back when it was a hospital. After his death the building became a hospital for almost 50 years before being reverted back to a home and ultimately a museum. We had a great talk, exchanged my book information, and now she's also following our travels. Another Kimber fan is born.

From the Jackson home I decide to walk the exact same route Stonewall Jackson took everyday on his way to class, from downtown Lexington back toward the VMI campus, passing the Washington and Lee University. Here we stopped to enter the church and visit the Lee family crypt buried underneath. Through a metal gate you could see the tomb of General Lee amongst other family members. Also, you could see the office he worked in as President of the college after the war. Just outside the metal gate leading into the mausoleum was a small bricked area with a marker that read, "Traveller, Horse of Robert E. Lee." Yup, his horse is buried here too.

The clouds were getting pretty dense at this point, I had one more site to visit before we retreated back to the local Walmart for the evening. Stonewall's grave was on the other side of town, buried in the city cemetery. I found this odd as Lee was buried on campus, and with all the statues and dedications to Stonewall at VMI, I wondered why he wasn't buried there. When I got to what was the city cemetery, the sign actually read "Stonewall Jackson Memorial Cemetery, Jackson's Tomb." An absolutely ancient graveyard, with tombstones so close to each other they almost touched, except for the large granite marker in the center of the cemetery grounds. Atop a tall granite pedestal stood General Thomas Stonewall Jackson in full uniform, binoculars in one hand while leaning against his sword with the other. Only one inscription underneath: "Jackson 1824-1863." Around the base was the headstone marker of his infant daughter, between Jackson and his wife's markers. Other family members, some high-ranking military, were buried around the base as well. Outside the family plot were statesmen such as John Letcher, Virginia War Governor, and other tombs with CSA markers here and there. What I found remarkable was that there was no specific boundary separating the Confederate graves from all the others. This looked to be a city cemetery, with local family plots, regardless of wars... as it should be. We're ALL Americans, something that we can never forget.

I could've stayed in Lexington for a solid week, taking in all there was to see, both historically and modern. I loved the way the town continued on as a regular small town, managing day to day activities amongst such incredible history. A norm on the east coast, yet so foreign to those of us from the West. That night, we had pizza at a local high school favorite spot, watching sports teams come in like I did as a child back in California. This was the town meeting place where all the teams came together as friends and family. Super cool. That night, we slept soundly, with a light rain tapping on the metal camper roof. Tomorrow we venture into West Virginia, saying goodbye to the state with the most amazing history yet. Virginia, state #23... COMPLETE.

West Virginia

June 9th, 2017. The storm had passed by sunrise the next day, once again keeping the temperatures down to something this AZ boy could gratefully handle. With very few backroads crossing the Appalachian Mountains, we opted for Interstate 64 west, to a town called White Sulphur Springs. I had charted where the next battlefield would be, hoping to find a quiet campsite for a few days. I had run pretty hard the last few weeks, putting a pinch on the already tight funds situation. I needed a place for a "zero sum" week. I was exhausted, had about my fill of people and traffic; I needed some forest time to get my head straight and relax. Kimber was done driving too, becoming more and more stubborn when it was time to get back in the truck. We needed a break and as always, the good Lord put us right where He wanted us.

The Blue Bend National Recreation Area was just a few miles up the road from White Sulphur Springs on the way to a state battlefield. It was a national campground, so only 8 bucks a night with my access pass, perfect for a few days of decompression. I found a quiet spot, explored the grounds, and threw the ball for Kimber into the ice-cold river, something she enjoyed immensely. That night, I passed on the writing and settled in for a very sound sleep. Something about sleeping in the forest is just incredibly relaxing, like your soul reaching out to where it belongs. For a once proudly pronounced "city boy," I find myself much more at home in the mountains. I think aging has something to do with that.

227

The next morning, Kimber and I crossed the river and found a trailhead leading further upstream. It was a beautiful hike surrounded by vine covered trees, ultra-clear water in the river below, and beautiful broad leaf plants that stood about knee high, overgrowing into the trail. I had my regular shorts on, with hiking boots, when something bit or stung my calf. It felt like a fire ant bite, dammit that hurt. Guess I better be on the watch for, OWW, another bite, opposite calf this time. I stopped to inspect my leg but found no insects. Just a rash of some sort. Must be some type of No-See-Um or flying insect, yet nothing was there. Shrugging it off, I took a few more steps forward, brushing some of the saw-tooth edged leaves with my calf as I walked. Again, these needle-like pokes hit my skin. This time, figuring out it had to be the plants, I took a picture and posted it to my Facebook page with the caption, "What is this green plant from hell!?" I promptly received a bunch of laughing emojis saying that I was walking through a giant patch of STINGING NETTLE. Lovely, I'd heard of this plant before but never experienced one up close. Yup, just like fire ants, but in plant form. I slowly backed out of the crop of Satan's ferns and tiptoed carefully back to the campsite. "Welcome to WVA" one of my followers wrote; "Live and learn" I replied.

My campsite neighbor was a younger kid, probably in his early 20s, but already down on his luck. He was staying in a tent that his girlfriend had bought for him after he had been kicked out of her parents' home. Jobless, homeless, yet trying to stay in his children's lives, I couldn't help but feel sorry for this one. He reminded me of myself, a young single father, trying to find his way. We sat and talked by the fire for a couple hours while he unloaded all his grief on me. Working in the bar scene for years, I guess I'm just one of those people folks feel they can talk to. It must be the bartender lineage I come from. Either way, I recommended the military to this kid, something he hadn't thought about. Then something happened. I reached over and took his hand, and asked him if I could pray for him. This is something that is completely out of the norm for me, but something compelled me to just do this. He nodded as he took my hand and I started talking to Jesus. Not like a pastor, but like another lost soul who after years of bad decisions, was starting to find his way. The kid started to cry, which made me cry. He really was a good kid, trying his hardest to stay afloat. He only had a day left on his campsite, and now broke, was moving to a boondock spot on the outside of the rec area. He actually asked if he could travel with me, to which I replied with an apologetic no. I encouraged him to stay and fight for his kids, for his girlfriend, and most of all for himself. He hugged me and said "thanks." Hope he's found his way, for the children's sake.

It wasn't long after the kid had packed up his tent and left that a new neighbor was eyeballing the spot. It was a single lady about my age, trying to back up a vintage camper into the tree-lined spot. She was having a hard time navigating the trailer backwards, so I walked over to help her out. After guiding her into the spot, she exited her truck and said thank you, while introducing herself. Enter my friend Tina, an aunt with no kids of her own, setting up camp, waiting for her sister, nieces and nephews to show up. "I hope you don't mind kids" she chuckled, as all of them would be under 12 years old or so. I politely lied, and said, "No problem," which I followed up with the truth that Kimber would be excited. This was a very true statement, and the kids actually kept Kimber busy in the river, while I got some words on "paper."

That afternoon, the camp host drove by in his golf cart, stopped at the edge of my campsite, and walked up to tell me something. Kimber, being her customary friendly self, ran up to greet the host, receiving a stern welcome. "You need to keep that damn dog on a leash," he yelled as he walked further into my camp. I called Kimber to me, and being scared, she came immediately. While putting on her jacket, I replied back to the guy, "She was fine until you pulled up. Just relax, she's my support dog," to which he continued on about not caring and rules were rules. Not much I could say as I didn't want to be told to leave, so I put Kimber in the camper and then turned to the elderly host. "Anything else?" I asked, with a pretty pissed off look and tone, after which I followed Kimber into the camper and slammed the door. The camp host took the clue and left. Afterwards, I took Kimber out of the camper and put her on a long lead I had just for such an occasion. Tethered to a tree now, Kimber wasn't pleased at all. Then I went inside to start making dinner, and to get a much needed beer. Suddenly, I heard Kimber growl and some commotion outside. I caught a glimpse of another dog, a short-haired spaniel looking dog, extremely lean and muscular, with a thick orange collar and some sort of a transmitter attached to it, chasing Kimber around the tree! Like a momma bear, I was outside instantly, ready to do battle, when the dog saw me, stopped, and came to me, wagging his tail, friendly as could be. Kimber, tied to the tree, wasn't having any of it. She was scared shitless. I grabbed the male dog by that huge collar and walked him all the way down to the camp host site, asking an elderly lady who came out of the tent where he was. In a very harsh tone I said, "Your husband came down yelling at me about my dog being off leash, and this thing shows up chasing her around the damn tree." The lady explained that the spaniel was a bear dog, and they had no control over it being off leash. The hunters turn them loose, following them by GPS until they tree a bear. "A bear dog!? And it was going after my dog?! She didn't have a chance, tied to the stupid tree!" I exclaimed. She could tell I was livid. I left the dog at their campsite and went back to Kimber in the Rig. She wasn't going to be on leash anymore. The next time the camp host drove by, he didn't even look at our camp or Kimber. Warning shot sent, and apparently received.

The next morning, I was at the end of my time there. Tina was up early making breakfast over the open fire with a metal pot of some sort. She asked if I was hungry for some biscuits and gravy. "Well absolutely!" I said, while she took some bacon out of what she called a "Dutch oven" hanging over the fire. "Here, watch, this is how West Virginians make biscuits." She popped the can of biscuits, hey, this is modern West Virginia, took one of the raw ones and sopped up the bacon grease on one side of it, then flipped it over into the grease to "bake." She did the same with all of the biscuits, replaced the lid, and then poured me a cup of coffee. "Give it a minute," she said. The kids were still asleep, when we started talking about my travels. "Seneca Rocks is a place you should see. It's a WVA favorite." Then she said, "wait a second," and looked at her phone. "I've got a cabin I rent out during the summer, over by Summersville. It's open the next two days, you're welcome to it if you wish. Free of charge." Turned out my new friend also was a real estate agent who then handed me her card with the directions on the back. How freaking cool was that!? She said it had satellite tv and a hot tub; oh hell ya, I'm in! Then she realized the biscuits were done. I was amazed that the Dutch oven actually baked something over a campfire, a city boy, remember. Now it was my turn to say thank you, as I packed up the Rig and got ready to pull out. I waved at her and the family, about the time the camp host drove by. I waved at him too, but I guess he didn't see me. Too funny.

The first thing you notice that's different between Virginia and West Virginia is the terrain. Virginia's mainly flat, rolling pastures, and farmland with dense forest in between, changed to West Virginia's mainly mountains with some farmland in between. What didn't change was the growth and density of the forests, just steeper terrain. We were definitely in the heart of the Appalachian Mountains, a place I felt strangely at home.

Droop Mountain Battlefield State Park was perfectly situated between me and the cabin. Not gonna lie, my mind was filled with hot tubs, take-out pizza, and baseball games on a huge TV, not so much with war. This was going to be a quick stop. Strangely enough, there was nobody to be seen, anywhere. The visitor center was open, lights on, but no park staff anywhere, which just made this an even faster visit. I parked in front of what looked to be a Confederate cemetery, only some very uneven, moss covered earth mounds with large flat-faced rocks used as headstones. Some plastic lilacs were laid next to the cemetery sign. The area was surrounded by wood post fences and a small trail leading to a log cabin. "Museum" was carved into a small wooden sign with an arrow pointing to the cabin. The inside of the rustic cabin only had a few maps and paintings on the wall, and several newspaper clippings and articles. It was interesting reading the New York Times description of the South. Remember, we learned that Lincoln never once called the South an "enemy," yet the headlines of the Times read, "The Rebels justify their barbarities" and "Interesting misc. intelligence" sounded like an anonymous source to me. I guess some things never change. There were also several artifacts in two glass cases, mainly rusted muskets, mini balls, and some uniform items.

The information plaques explained that Droop Mountain was an important ridgeline road that ran north to south, connecting two major east/west crossings of the Alleghenies. It was the only way to move artillery and supply wagons to support either side's army. When West Virginia was admitted into the Union in 1862, Droop Mountain was a must-have for both sides. Eventually, the Confederates had to retreat from West Virginia to protect Richmond in 1864. Droop Mountain would be the last significant battle in West Virginia and would stay under Union control from this point forward.

Since nobody was around and they had a nice grassy area with picnic benches near the entrance, Kimber was elated to dive at her ball in thick, soft, West Virginia grass. Nothing decreases my angst more than to watch this little dog just be a dog. It was almost noon, and I didn't want to miss out on a second of "cabin time." Back in the truck and off to Summersville. Yes!!!

The cabin was actually just down the freeway from Summersville, which was the largest town in the area, nestled in the community of Mount Lookout. The address was not on GPS, so I had to rely on the handwritten directions on the back of my friend's business card, who is a West Virginia native and local. You know where I'm going with this. After a couple U-turns in driveways of folks that must've thought I was crazy, I finally asked for directions to Old Government Road, and where the two trash cans were that was supposed to mark my friend's driveway. The guy I asked, standing in his yard, staring at me, said, "Ya, that's Tina's place just around the corner, keep going... past the cans." I was glad that they must be used to strange cars driving up their somewhat private road, I mean this is West Virginia. Finally, I pulled the Rig into what was the perfect little slice of heaven.

Tina had said her uncle left her this place after he passed; she now rents it for short term visitors. A very rustic looking, single-level wood cabin came complete with wraparound deck, and a beautiful green lawn surrounded by manicured hedges. The back faced a cliff overlooking a forest, with a hot tub, gas grill, and lawn chairs. The inside was modern and perfect, having the exact amount of WVA wild charm, mixed with just enough modern to make it relaxing. It came complete with kitchen, bed linens, and coffee maker, everything but the food, which the Summerville Pizza Hut took care of perfectly. What an absolute treat after the innumerable Walmart parking lots we had called home. I was set to just relax and watch baseball for two days, heaven indeed!

That evening, just before dusk, Kimber alerted me to her needing to go outside. Since the driveway sloped down to the house, and the property was completely surrounded by trees and dense brush, I felt confident stepping outside onto the lush grass with just my boxers on. I know, probably a little TMI, but it adds to my carefreeness of the moment. Kimber was happily sniffing around the yard looking for that perfect spot to do her thing while I stood by just taking in the scenery. Then I saw something. In the bushes, about 10 yards in front of me, I saw what looked like a small yellow light turn on, then off, almost like the glint of an animal's eye, and about the same size. Like when you take a picture of your dog and the red eye is present, it was the same thing but orangish/yellow. There for a second, then gone. Maybe it was an LED to a security camera, it wasn't red or green, so laser optics were out; either way, I was hoping for electronics, rather than the animal hypothesis. Yup, at this point, I had no clue, but my mind was running wild with conspiracy theories, while reminding myself I had no shoes on. Then the light appeared again but about 5 yards to the right of the original spot. Whoa what? That thing moved that far, that fast, and SILENT, not to mention right in front of me. I quickly looked for Kimber, who was on the far side of the yard, still sniffing. Good. Not sure what this thing could be, but she's far... Then a light went off about a foot from my right shoulder, just catching a glimpse of it with my peripheral vision. With a shriek like a little girl, I ran one way, Kimber ran the other, both of us meeting at the cabin door in mid-flight. I slammed the door and peeked out the window, with Kimber peeking around my leg. By now it was practically dark, and the lights multiplied by a 100. I slowly opened the door, still half naked, and walked out into something I had never seen and only heard about. Fireflies filled the night sky like Christmas lights twinkling in the trees. I haven't laughed that hard, out loud, in a very long time. Kimber then went outside and had the time of her life chasing the infinite amount of "laser pointers" from God, dancing just above her head. Too freaking awesome and too funny!

After two very short but blissful days, I hated to leave Tina's amazing cabin. Time was closing in on the halfway mark of the baseball season, and I still had quite a bit of land to cover, not to mention in the hottest part of the year, in the hottest part of the South. Remember, I still had the two Texas ballparks to see by September. Seneca Rocks was quite a bit out of our way, but I was told over and over that I just gotta see this place. So off we went, north toward Stonewall Jackson State Park, then east to Elkins, WV, where I found a Walmart plus an Anytime Fitness, which equals home for the evening.

I even found a cool little brewery where Kimber and I could cool off with a cold one. The staff more than welcomed her into their establishment, with everybody stopping by to pet her and say hello. About that time, a couple with their high school age son walked in and asked if they could sit next to us. "Absolutely!" I responded, scooting down a stool so they had some more room. Quickly, conversation ensued. Several beers and stories later, Laura was sitting on the floor with Kimber while James and I talked civil war battles. They were enthralled with the stories of my travels to this point and offered for us to park at their place on my way back through from Seneca Rocks. They said they had a farm in Philippi, WV, plenty of room for Kimber to chase balls, and would be honored if I stopped by. I promised we would, taking their number and address. Super nice folks and another chance to experience local life in West Virginia, yup, I'm in!

The drive from Elkins to Seneca Rocks was gorgeous, climbing back into the Appalachian mountains, crossing the Eastern Continental Divide through Monongahela National Forest. I loved how even in the steep mountains you found small farms with cows and horses grazing grass in whatever pasture land they could find amongst the rocks and forest. Seneca Rocks was an area with a huge, jagged rock formation jutting out from the forest canopy. Across the street was a National Forest campground that I was hoping wasn't going to be full. Other than that, Seneca Rocks was a rock climber's destination, a very small town with its own climb shop, coffee house, and a small grocery store. This too was the only place to get cell service, as the picnic benches were crowded with coffee sipping, screen addicts getting both their morning fixes, myself included.

I was stoked to find out the campgrounds not only had plenty of spots, but it also was run by the same company from the tick infested Ocala National Forest we escaped from in Florida. Remember the place that gave me a week credit after I bailed out of Florida early? They sent me a credit in the mail, that my brother Chongo took a picture of and sent me. I couldn't believe that I actually found another place they managed, how lucky is that! On my path indeed. I told the camp host the situation, showed him the credit letter from the other campsite, and boom, I had a free spot for the next 5 days. Well, pre-paid, not quite free, but with funds tight, it might as well have been free. The park employee that I had talked to asked if it was a full hookups spot or dry camp. I replied that I wasn't gonna lie, and no it wasn't full hookups, but I could sure use some in this heat. "Otherwise I'd have to run my generator a lot in this heat, I got my dog." The clerk looked at my truck with Kimber hanging out the window. "Can't have that now, can we. Thank you for your service," handing me a receipt for 5 days of full hookups, right next to the bathrooms. Man, I love these people! So for the next 5 days, Kimber and I explored the area, completed some crazy hikes up to the Seneca Rocks, and took in the incredible scenery from this beautiful place. Now with batteries fully charged, but with funds on low, we decided to head back and take up the folks from the brewery on their offer of a parking spot for the next few days.

Philippi, WV is just a few miles north of Elkins, a small community where James and Laura have an amazing piece of property, around 500 acres total, with a beautiful landscaped yard and barn. I asked James if it was a lot of work for him and his son to tend to a place this size. He just grinned and told me he lets people hunt his land in exchange for yard work and help around the farm. I can see how that would work out nicely!

I ended up going to town with Laura and James, attended their church, and they even took me to a nearby battlefield that claimed to be the first ground battle of the Civil War. At first, I thought it was a small town being proud, but after some research I discovered the Battle of Laurel Hill was indeed the first land battle of the Civil War. It's also known as the Battle of Philippi or the "Philippi Races," a description of how fast the Confederacy ran from this battle. Laurel Hill is where the Confederates regrouped briefly before being pushed into Virginia. Lee had instructed commanders to rally the troops in West Virginia to protect railroads, prior to the vote for Virginia to secede from the Union. Lee underestimated the animosity of the western region toward Richmond, and ended up losing West Virginia to the North. This all took place with zero fatalities and less than a month before the Union invaded Virginia. A super cool find that you'd never hear about without looking for it.

I was impressed with how the community here pitches in for everything. You always hear about West Virginia being so poor, yet there was always some kind of free food going on somewhere most nights or weekend mornings. From fire departments to churches, pancake feeds to fish fries, there was a meal somewhere to be had. James told me when somebody's roof blows off, the entire town is there to help. That's the mystique of Appalachia that I love, true neighbors... when you're accepted as one. With the Scotch-Irish settling here, the clannish lifestyle isn't far lost. Church and community here is everything. As it should be.

Our last night at James and Laura's, we were sitting inside having dinner when I heard Kimber let out a rare bark. Not a playful, or get my attention bark, this was a rapid fire, one breath, rahrahrahrah, which translates into DAAAAAAD!!!! Like a shot, I was up from the table and at the front screen door. The bottom was wood so Kimber didn't know I was standing there. I heard her growl and then let loose again with a rapid fire set of high pitch barks. There were three deer in the yard, a buck with two does, and the buck had his head down, walking toward the porch. Poor Kimber was backed up against the door. I opened the door, stepping over the now rolling backward, scared shitless, little dog and out onto the porch, scaring off the deer. Turns out that I had run off "Apple," the deer she feeds most nights. Poor Kimber was in shock; I'll never forget her screaming for dad, sad but funny.

With a freshly filled bank account due to direct deposit hitting on an early Friday (Military folks understand the joy of that), Kimber and I headed south toward one last place that bullets flew in the name of liberty here in WVA. Ok well, maybe not liberty this time, but it sure did make a mark on American history and legend. Our next stop was going to be our last for West Virginia, but perfect for the transition into Kentucky. I was super excited to see this place, as the three part series was amazing. Yup, next stop was going to be the Hatfield cemetery, on the WVA side, followed by the McCoy's cemetery on the Kentucky side. Weather was cloudy and with a bit of a late start, we said our goodbyes and headed west.

A full day's drive from Philippi, with the sun starting to set, we stopped at Charleston for some Buffalo Wild Wings and to post up for the night at the neighboring Walmart. While I had some dinner I met a couple in town on business who just happened to be from the neighboring city to Johnson City, Kingston, TN. I guess I didn't realize we were only a few hundred miles from that corner of Tennessee, and even closer to Lexington, VA, a new favorite spot. Ya, I'm really liking this part of the country, a lot.

The follow morning, we were up with the truckers, filling my big bubba coffee mug at the corner store and continuing on toward the southwestern WVA/Kentucky state line. The storm was gone, streets were wet and extremely foggy, which made the ride into a not so wealthy part of West Virginia just a little more creepier than I had planned.

I kept reminding myself that "Deliverance" was filmed in Georgia, not here. But as the locals peered out their windows and half cracked doors, watching me get out of a camper with AZ plates and start walking up the side of the local mountain to a grave yard, it was just a little unnerving. Kimber was curled up asleep, locked up tight in the cab of the truck. I just smiled and nodded as I locked my door and started up the trail. The metal arch over a small bridge read "Hatfield Cemetery," thankfully with "visitors welcome" painted on a wooden sign just below it. There was also a roadside, historic place marker, explaining the history of the Hatfield and McCoys. If you haven't heard of them look it up. It's a famous family rivalry between one family who fought for the South and the other for the North. A bitter feud that is alive to this very day, but mainly on a reality show. The second plaque was marking this as a place on the national register of historical places. There, see, I told you this was important.

I was pretty winded by the time I got up to the actually grave site, but you knew it when you did. A fenced off plot had a 10 ft tall statue in the exact likeness of CSA Capt. Anderson "Devil Anse" Hatfield, the obvious patriarch of this family. His likeness carved out of granite, reportedly done in Italy, marks his grave with a Confederate Battle Flag waving nearby. Looking around the graveyard, I learned that the Hatfields had served in just about every war America has fought. From WW1, WW2, and Korea to Vietnam, the Hatfields have had a relative who served. Impressive to say the least. I took some pictures and got out of dodge. A cool place to check out, but I wasn't trying to spend time there. My mind was on Kimber, as I skidded back down the trail to the Rig. From there we crossed over to Kentucky to visit the McCoy cemetery. West Virginia, state #24... COMPLETE!

Kentucky

June 27th, 2017. We crossed over the Kentucky state line around 0600, right after leaving the Hatfield cemetery. Now that I check the time of these pictures, I didn't realize how early it was. No wonder the locals were wondering what the hell I was doing. That's kinda funny. Anyway, we crossed the state line, which is actually the Tug Fork River, coming from Logan WVA, entering Kentucky at the town of Williamson.

There was no real plan for Kentucky other than to check out the McCoy cemetery, follow the "Bourbon Trail" up to the Louisville Slugger factory and museum, while catching a couple of battlefields along the way. With no major battles here, and quite honestly after Virginia, I was about done with history, I was really looking forward to some baseball. With those waypoints circled on the road map, I set the GPS to the McCoy cemetery and hit go. Ok Kentucky, show us what you got. Except the hot sauce, I got that already. I remember you, lady, I can never forget that sauce.

I stopped for breakfast in the town of Williamson, WVA first, introducing myself to the neighborhood by turning the wrong way down the only one-way street in town. Some folks were outside the restaurant, waving me down, as I was rolling down my window and asking "what?!" "Wong way!" they yelled over my motor while pointing up at the one-way arrow. Oh ya, great first impression. They were nice enough about it, telling me it happens all the time, once I walked into the diner. Then one asked where I was from. Oh, here we go. "Arizona ma'am," as I cringed for what was coming next. Like slow motion in that *Christmas Story* movie, I could see the words starting to form on her lips... "Bless... your... heart." I just smiled and put my head down as I followed the waitress to my booth.

After breakfast, we headed further down the Tug fork where the GPS claimed the McCoy cemetery was. The road was getting narrower the further we followed it until finally, I saw a historical marker in front of an old, white, federal style building, with five tall pillars in the front. The plaque told us this was Sally McCoy's birthplace and childhood home. Sally was the love child of Rosanna McCoy and Johnse Hatfield, a huge part of the clan wars. Super cool!

Just past the house was a sign pointing down the dirt road that read "McCoy Cemetery." Another narrow road, winding deep into the woods, didn't exactly give a welcoming feeling, as the imaginary banjos picked away in my head. Unlike the extravagant headstone for "Devil

Anse" Hatfield, the McCoy family was scattered across a hillside with flat and knee-high headstone markers, but plenty of flowers and American flags. Here too were many veterans from many different wars. Another cool piece of "Americana" where bullets flew in the shaping of what we know as America.

Outside the McCoy cemetery, I decided I had better cover some ground, as we were entering July, giving me about three more months before the end of baseball's regular season. I also had to remember the 4th of July was near and I had better find a secluded campsite for Kimber. With all that in mind, I set the GPS for the Louisville Slugger museum, clear across the state, this time opting for the shortest route possible.

About 30 minutes up the road I saw a large concrete obelisk, with two information placards and a small parking lot/rest area. Kimber was due for a bathroom break, and this had to be some type of war monument, so we stopped to investigate. Sure enough, this was another Civil War skirmish known as the Battle of Ivy Mountain, a precursor to the larger Battle of Middle Creek. An interesting player here was the Union forces commander, Colonel James A. Garfield, who would later be elected as the 20th President of the United States in 1881.

The plaque mentioned Middle Creek; a quick search on Maps marked a destination named "Middle Creek National Battlefield." Whoa what? A "National" Park? There was no mention of this in any of the literature that I had from the NPS, and nothing with a google search of National Battlefields. Interesting. There was also a Walmart in the nearby town of Prestonsburg that sounded pretty inviting after such an early start and with already two hours of driving in.

Right before Prestonsburg was a Y in the road, one route going to town, the other going to the Middle Creek Battlefield, another 10 miles away. I was tired, and in need of a little down time. Staying with folks we meet along the way is great, but I never really get rest as I'm too busy experiencing, learning, or writing about what's going on. That and it's just rude to hide in the camper when you're a guest, even though sometimes meeting strangers is enough to rattle the nerves and seclusion is much needed. Just another aspect of how therapeutic this trip is, even when it forces me to move past the grip of anxiety. At least that's what I keep telling myself; seems to be working. I also didn't realize I was battling the time change, not realizing you could get "jet lag" while driving cross country. Anyway, I chose to hang out around Prestonsburg and catch up on some much needed sleep. Surprisingly, Kimber agreed and slept quietly curled up next to me.

The weather held the heat back nicely that evening, so no need for the generator and AC to be running, thus not drowning out a noise that made me sit straight up in the camper, smacking my head on the roof above. This low guttural vibrating sound that increased in pitch and volume, abruptly stopped and then repeated, shortly followed by what sounded like an army of whatever this thing was, just outside the camper window. Bull frogs, huge ones, all letting loose at once it seemed. Loud enough to wake me up, and annoying enough to make me leave the parking lot at 0400. I did not realize I had parked next to a small pond that was blocked by a neighboring semi who had left in the night. So much for a not so early start this morning.

I pulled into the Middle Creek National Battlefield at 0412, pissed and tired. Sun still not up, I grabbed Kimber and crawled into the camper, drawing the curtains and hoping for a good hour or two nap, before having to get up due to other visitors pulling in. About 20 minutes into my attempted nap, the sound of a vehicle with tires rolling over the dirt parking lot made Kimber growl, and I once again sat straight up, smacking my head on the camper roof. Groundhog day had commenced. What made it even more special was explaining to the State Trooper, why I was trying to grab a nap before exploring the battlefield at 0430 in the morning.

After convincing the Trooper of what I was doing there, the sun came up a few minutes later. So much for the nap. Now that I could see the surrounding area, I was somewhat confused as to what this was. Here was another dirt parking lot with a few plaques around a hiking trail and a large wooden sign reading "Middle Creek National Battlefield." The weird part was, these weren't the customary brown NPS signs, they were state level. A metal one describing what occurred here had the Kentucky Department of Highways name under the text, while the information placards along the trail didn't have any source. They explained how Kentucky was a border state, unsure of what government was going to control the region. Basically, the Confederates never regained a strategic advantage in Kentucky as a result of this battle, thus securing it for the Union. After some further research on why this was named a "National Battlefield," it turned out this was made an "Historical Place" at the federal level, therefore assuming the local government added the "National" to the battlefield title.

Exhausted with war at this point, I was much more interested in seeing the sights of Kentucky than chasing another small civil war conflict. I pulled up some top destinations nearby, with the first being Red River Gorge in the Daniel Boone National Forest. It sounded interesting and hoping for a good hiking trail for Kimber, I turned off the highway and drove into a very dense forest. The road was basically a lane and a half wide, with no markings whatsoever. With zero shoulder on either side of the road, oncoming traffic proved interesting with the size of the Rig.

I should've filled up back in Prestonsburg but forgot with the early morning exit, so now we were running on fumes. Lovely. At least the gas buddy app said we were only 12 miles away from the next station. No biggie, a quick drive to the freeway, then back to the Red River Gorge. About 2 more miles ahead, the road disappeared into a mouse hole drilled through a mountain sized rock. There was a small yield sign leaning next to the hole that grew to life size as I got closer. Through this tiny, one lane... wait, one very small, slightly larger than a go-cart lane... so-called tunnel, was the only way I wasn't going to run out of gas. It was 32 miles if I had to backtrack out of the forest. It looked like a tiny dark hole in this massive ivy-covered stone cliff. The small sign said it was 12.5 tall, a full foot and a half above the Rig height. Ya ok, I'll take your word for it. The width is what bothered me. Dead centered on the road, my driver side mirror was about 6 inches from the tunnel wall, ditto on the passenger side. Knowing that my entire rig is a couple inches narrower than my mirrors, I clenched my teeth, amongst other body parts, and eased the truck into the tunnel. My biggest fear was getting stuck in the tunnel halfway through, and looking at the deep scrapes along the tunnel wall wasn't exactly comforting. After the longest, darkest 100 yards of my life, we emerged on the other side. Luckily nothing happened, not even a scrape. I accelerated past the parked, oncoming traffic, staring at me while I was laughing and filming the whole thing. Wow, that was close. I think at this point, I blessed my own heart.

Another 25 miles up the road in Winchester, KY, we came across a Walmart where I decided to stop for the rest of the day. Still needing to catch up on some sleep, we pulled in early, fired up the generator/AC and relaxed the rest of the day. There was also a nice green area that had shade, perfect for Kimber to get her ball on, and finally crash out with me watching baseball. A nice lazy "park and bbq" day was perfect.

After a fantastic night's sleep, and hearty egg breakfast, we were back on the road. We took what's called the "Bourbon Trail," basically the country highway that is home to several large whiskey distilleries. I stopped to take pictures at the Jim Beam distillery, but it was way too early for the taste tour. We must've passed half a dozen distilleries and some of the most amazing horse farms I've ever seen. Bourbon and horse racing, yup, we're in Kentucky alright. Next stop was Louisville.

Parking the Rig was tough in Louisville, especially on a weekday morning. Luckily, I found an uncovered parking lot about a block away, that would accommodate the Rig. It was already getting pretty warm, and with very little shade, I knew I had to move fast to get back to Kimber in the camper. I set her up with cold water with ice cubes and opened all the windows. After I was convinced she was good for a couple hours, I literally jogged a block and a half to the Louisville Slugger plant, making sure I had time to take it all in.

A monstrous giant replica of a wooden baseball bat leaning against the factory building is what meets you at the front door of the Louisville Slugger Baseball Bat plant. An incredible museum of all the great MLB players who used a Louisville Slugger as their tool of choice, was an awesome surprise, along with lots of information and history about the bat itself. Super cool and free to the public. The behind the scenes tour is well worth the ticket price, and a must see for all. You see how they're made to individual player specification, including weight and color. They show the making of college level bats, but the pro bats are top secret. Each player gets about 30 bats a year. At the end of the tour they give you a mini wooden bat, and an end off an original blank of a bat, cut off after the lathe process. A unique experience that won't break the bank if you take the family. A must-see, bucket-list item, for baseball fans of all ages. I even picked up a full size, natural bat with burnt end, with "Baseballs and Battlefields, Matty and Kimber, 2017" laser engraved on the barrel for around 60 bucks. A very cool memory, and a must-have splurge.

It was closing in on two o'clock and the heat was substantial at this point. We were almost starting July, and continuing inland, far away from the cool coastal winds and mountain elevations. By the sheer grace of God we'd been blessed by nightly rain that kept the temps lower than usual, but now that we were almost down to sea level, closing in on the Mississippi River, the heat and humidity multiplied almost instantly. This created a drastic change to our lifestyle. I couldn't leave Kimber in the truck at all after high noon, only early mornings with windows down. I used the support dog vest to get her inside some restaurants or small bars to cool off when it became crazy hot. So not a lot of sightseeing in the afternoons, mainly finding a spot to run the generator and AC through the night was the early afternoon chore. This time we found a truck stop just outside Lincoln's birthplace to call home for the night. Yup, we're still in Kentucky, and that plaque was correct; Lincoln was indeed born in the South.

The next morning we visited the Lincoln Birthplace, just south of Hodgenville, KY, just as the private museum in Virginia had described, only about a 100 miles away from Confederate President Jefferson Davis' birthplace and monument. So much for honest Abe from Illinois, he really was a Southerner. There stood a huge, white, federal style building, complete with massive staircase climbing up to the towering Greek columns. The first thing you see as you enter, is an old log cabin. Presumably the same cabin that President Lincoln was born and raised in. You could only walk around it and look inside through the door or window. There were some other small statues of Lincoln in the corners of the massive stone building housing the cabin. All in all, a pretty simple self-guided tour. That was about it, ok, back to Kimber. We had another battlefield to see before it got too hot.

About 50 miles due east was the Perryville Battlefield State Historical Park. I really wasn't going to cover this state level battlefield, because I didn't want to drive that far back east; but after seeing that the New Market private museum's claim about Lincoln's birthplace proved true, I was curious as to what else we'd find. Plus the Battle of Perryville had a significant number of casualties, enough to rank it as something I needed to check out.

The first thing that sticks in my mind when I think about the drive to Perryville was the rolling fields of wildflowers, as far as the eye could see. Like a living rainbow, swaying to the music of the wind. It was truly a magical sight, leading to a place of tremendous sorrow. Makes you wonder if this was by some divine plan.

The battlefield itself had a small building housing the museum, with gifts and memorabilia for sale. Outside was manicured green grass, cut back from the wall of wildflowers, surrounding the grounds. There was a massive monument with a Confederate soldier perched on top, marking a mass grave of over 200 unknown Confederate soldiers. The plaque read that the Union dead were removed and buried, while the Confederate bodies were rooted by hogs and eaten by crows. Local farmers and slaves buried the bodies in a mass grave under this marker. An absolute brutal scene described the aftermath of the fight. After walking around the grounds, waiting for the visitor center to open, I had felt the heavy, solemnity of this place. Then for it to be surrounded by such immeasurable beauty, was something near impossible to wrap my head around.

Basically, what happened here was CSA General Braxton Bragg's failed push to rally troops and political favor amongst the Kentucky people, lost the state to the Union as early as 1862. Although this was a tactical win for Bragg on sheer casualty numbers alone, he was outnumbered and hastily left Kentucky in the middle of the night, leaving the dead and wounded to be taken care of by the locals and the Union. It was this battle that pushed the Confederates out of Kentucky at the same time Antietam pushed them from Maryland, giving President Lincoln the victory he needed to roll out the Emancipation Proclamation. Yet another reference to the eradication of slavery being used as a war measure, and only against the South. One plaque read, "With Confederate armies pressing into Maryland and Kentucky, Lincoln realized that he could not issue the proclamation until the Union secured a major military victory." Even more interesting was the last sentence, "In addition, Lincoln feared how Unionists in Kentucky, Missouri, and Maryland would react, although the Proclamation did not free border-state slaves." That's twice we'd read this, notably now in a "Union" state.

I was intrigued to see so much about the Emancipation Proclamation here in Kentucky, but after realizing we were in a border state, and now taking in a more Northern perspective, it made sense. This battle was pivotal for its release. The most interesting plaque on the property was one that described how soldiers from both sides reacted to the release of the Emancipation Proclamation. Quotes were reprinted here under the subtitles Southern View and Northern View. The southern quotes were from a military general and a politician, which were basically a call to arms. To be expected. The Northern quote from two enlisted men, was what astonished me, but it echoed the same response as the Union soldier character actor back at Appomattox Courthouse. "Sister, you may I think the above a singular confession for a federal soldier but it is true. I enlisted to fight for the Union and the constitution but Lincoln puts a different construction on things and now has us Union men fighting for his abolition platform, and this making us a horde of subjugators, house bumpers, negro thieves, and devastators of private property. - John T Harris, 22nd Kentucky Union Inf. Reg. Jan 9th, 1863." Two more quotes from enlisted men echoed the same sentiment; they were here to fight for the Union and the Constitution, not to abolish slavery. I also found it interesting that a Northern politician made the comment about how the troops have a "noble" purpose. Typical politician, apparently the troops didn't see it that way.

Still early in the day, and now turning head-on into a thunderstorm, made for a nice cool drive to the Jefferson Davis Monument and birthplace. This thing was absolutely massive. You could see it from miles away, a giant white obelisk, much in the fashion of the Washington Monument in DC. With the dark clouds rolling in behind it, the picture was amazing. It towers above a visitor center and museum, tucked away in a small residential community just east of Hopkinsville, KY. The price of admission to the museum and the fact that this wasn't a battlefield, I decided to pass on this one. I learned all I needed about Jefferson Davis back in Mississippi at his Beauvoir home and library. Besides, it was absolutely dumping rain outside, and I was sure Kimber wasn't pleased.

I needed to find shelter, and while passing a car wash, I remembered my South Carolina trick. We pulled in and spent the next few hours hiding from the torrential downpour. I broke out the map book, looking to see what was next, when I realized I was just north of Clarksville, TN, and only a couple hours from Heather and Sonny's house. Sitting in the trailer, at a car wash, in a thunderstorm, wasn't exactly uplifting. The 4th of July was coming up, and for some strange reason I just didn't want to be alone this time. I gave Heather a call, asked if they had any "lake life" for a lonely traveler this 4th of July. The answer was, "Come on." With that being said, Kentucky, state #25... COMPLETE!

The next three days we spent with brand new friends and family, soaking up some of what they call "lake life." We loaded up Heather and Sonny's boat with beer and snacks and headed for their designated anchor spot on Kentucky Lake. Much like AZ, all the boats meet at a certain area, moored side by side to each other, fire up the country music, grab a "diaper" and hit the water.

Ok, so remember those lifesaving devices that were made of that squishy plastic-coated stuff, like your grandpa's boat key, floating keychain. Imagine a kickboard made of that stuff, with two half circles cut out about 1/3 of the way up the board. Like a floatable "diaper." You put the small part in front, legs in the holes, and larger part in back. Holding on with both hands, one front and one back, you just jump in. The diaper keeps you afloat about chest high. Add floating koozies, a floating snack table, dogs in floating life jackets, and about 15 adults just bouncing up and down in the water, beer in hand, music blaring... you got Tennessee lake life. An absolute blast!

From Heather's house, they shot fireworks off over the lake. I knew that Kimber was about to lose her mind, so I retired early to the camper to hold my shaking little puppy. As I laid there, holding my canine vibrator, I couldn't help but smile. Something about Tennessee, I just felt at home here, and now with new friends. I was truly excited about starting fresh here after my travels.

I told Heather about what the VA doc in North Carolina had said, confirming her diagnosis. I even asked if she could do the surgery; luckily her hospital did take VA veterans, so it shouldn't be an issue. How cool is that! My high school friend will be the one cutting on me, and in Tennessee of all places.

On the way out of town, I noticed a campsite near Heather's house that would be perfect for when that time came for surgery. I still had a couple years of traveling, but stopped to check on monthly rates anyway. After talking to the lady inside the office about my travels and possible stay, it turned out she was a Gold Star mother who lost her Marine son in Afghanistan. She worked at this campsite, but was in the process of building a place with her husband for vets to rehab and recreate, the Blackhorse Lodge, named after their son's unit. She said they hoped to have fishing, wood working, archery, etc. for PTSD and handicapped veterans. What a great cause, and a great memorial to their boy. Semper Fi, ma'am.

Missouri

July 5th, 2017. From Big Sandy, Tennessee we set out for Missouri, and most importantly a baseball game... finally! We were completely rested, stocked up, and prepared for the next couple months, knowing they were going to be grueling. We were going to be hitting the flattest, hottest, and most humid terrain yet; I prayed that my generator/AC holds out, I was not up for lake hopping, like Nebraska last year.

The plan for Missouri was to first head north for a Cardinals game in St Louis. I was about done with battlefields, they were pretty much all running together at this point, and baseball was the perfect break. That's what I loved about mashing these two together, Baseballs and Battlefields, when the solemnness of war became too much, baseball was the happy alternative. Anyway, from St. Louis we would head west for a Kansas City Royals game, then south to Wilson's Creek National Battlefield, before dropping into Northern Arkansas. With the weather being this hot and humid, we would be covering some serious land in a very short amount of time. The biggest question would be how to keep Kimber cool while I attended the games.

St. Louis wasn't exactly known as an RV destination, so finding a Walmart that was safe enough to leave Kimber and the Rig while I ventured my way to the game, wasn't gonna happen. Instead, I found a casino on the Illinois side of town that had an RV Park and included a shuttle to the game. Although 60 bucks a night was way out of my league, it was sensible this time to come out of pocket for the night. We were buying piece of mind, and that stuff gets pricey, but worth every dime. I was able to park in a secure location, with full electric hookups to keep Kimber cool, and even had transportation to the game and back. Not to mention showers/bathrooms, cheap buffet for breakfast and entertainment that night if needed. I made reservations for the following day and headed into the city to buy our tickets at the park, and do a little downtown St. Louis sightseeing.

Parking downtown was insane, the Rig making it doubly so. I wanted to see the St. Louis Arch, and take the ride to the top for some pictures, then walk a few blocks to Busch Stadium to buy tickets and get some daytime pictures. We finally found some parking down by the river front, amongst some other RVs and buses. As soon as I opened the truck door, my plans instantly changed. Not thinking about the heat while driving at 9am with the AC on, it was already way too hot to leave Kimber here. Oh well, guess it's time to make the donuts, girl. I packed a couple bottles of water in a backpack, strapped on Kimber's jacket, and headed toward the Arch.

Things didn't start off so great right from the beginning. As soon as we climbed enough stairs to finally see the base of the Arch, is when I saw the "under construction" signs and all the orange plastic fencing blocking the entrance. Ok, so scratch that, let's get the tickets and get out of here. Off we went toward Busch Stadium.

By this time the heat was unbearable; we ran from shaded area to shaded area, still on the regular concrete sidewalks. When we got closer to the park, the walkways turned to brick as well as the surrounding buildings. There was a day game that had already started, so the crowds were thick. Kimber kept pulling really hard, either to get out of crowds or to get to the shade. Mainly the shade I'm thinking, it was crazy hot. We had stopped several times for water, but ran out, pouring it on her back, trying to wet her jacket down.

After buying the tickets, I had to get her back to the truck. She just wasn't listening to anything I was telling her. Then I reached down and touched the brick walkway, it was like a damn frying pan. I swooped her up to see her feet; red but not burnt, but tender to the touch. No wonder she was pulling so hard. Now I was pissed.

I carried her most of the way back, stopping across the street from the ballpark, near some park benches. I was checking her feet again, looking around for a water faucet, when I saw a homeless guy asking the nearby vendor for a glass of ice water. I didn't pay attention, picked up Kimber and started to walk off when he said "Hey, this is for the dog!" I turned around to see him walking toward, me holding out the cup of cold water. I thanked him profusely, and let Kimber drink the entire cup. He just watched Kimber intently, then she instantly jumped up on him an gave him plenty of kisses. I could tell he had some special needs to an extent, speaking at about an 8 yr old's level. I reached in my pocket and handed him the few dollars cash that I had. He said thank you and goodbye to Kimber. That was both heartwarming and heartbreaking all at once. I did notice I wasn't pissed anymore, how could I bitch about ANYTHING in my life after seeing that.

Just as Kimber and I got past the brickyard area and was crossing the multi-lane road in front of the clock tower building, two loud explosions of some sort went off. They were loud and close enough to feel the concussion. With Kimber tucked under my arm like a football, I broke into a sprint, sidestepping the bumper of a car like Barry Sanders in his heyday, before finally getting to the other side, and hearing the roar of the crowd. Somebody hit a damn home run. Sweet Jesus, I thought it was a bomb. After controlling my breathing and adrenaline, I started laughing, then crying, then laughing again. Don't ask me why, it just happened. With no real thoughts behind it, other than what the people around me must've thought, I noticed I was clenching Kimber, almost as much as she was clenching me.

We pulled into the Casino Queen RV Resort about 1400 the following day, after a restless night's sleep in a St. Louis suburb Walmart. Enough said about that. My weather app said it was 100f but with humidity, it felt like 112f. In reality, it was at least 150f, easy... this is coming from an AZ guy though, it's a dry heat, remember? This was freaking brutal, no wonder this was the murder capital of America. Thankfully, we got a nice spot with some tree shade, and a full 30 amp plug that made the AC sing like a heavenly mechanical choir, while condensation formed on the windows from the ice-cold air. We napped for a few hours, until it was time to get ready for the game; then Kimber continued to nap. She could care less if I was leaving; she was fed, cool and comfortable. See ya, fat boy, I'm good.

The shuttle picked me up in front of the casino and dropped me across the street at a place called the Ballpark Village. A massive bar and restaurant, with huge screens all with the Cardinal game on. This place was awesome. If I didn't have a ticket to go inside the park, or it was a sellout, I'd be here for the game! With a short walk across the street, I was at the centerfield entrance. The streets around the ballpark were blocked off and flooded with people, like a massive block party. Super freaking cool!

Busch Stadium has to have one of the best backdrops in all of baseball. With the Courthouse dome, iconic St. Louis Arch, amongst all the other skyscrapers, the view from behind home plate is spectacular. Add the Arch that is cut into the grass, mirroring the one towering above, makes this park one of my favorites so far.

The ticket was a little pricey at $28, but included a military souvenir Cardinals ballcap, complete with desert camouflage bill and branch insignia embroidered on the side. Pretty cool, with my eagle, globe and anchor proudly represented. The funny part is that most vets here would probably be Vietnam era vets, with the tag inside the free hat reading, "Made in Vietnam." I chuckled to myself, thinking somebody didn't quite think this one through. Still a cool memory from the trip. Oh and I definitely saw plenty of Cardinals for my Missouri red-bird sighting. Busch Stadium, MLB park #12... COMPLETE!

That night, I realized that we were back to scheduling our travel around home game schedules, giving us about 5 days to kill before the Royals' next home stand. One of the veterans that started following my page was a fellow Somalia veteran that invited me to his hometown to check out the General Omar Bradley War memorial and have a beer. It worked out perfectly that Moberly, MO was just a few miles north of highway Interstate 70, the most direct route to Kansas City.

I met my friend Ken, an Army Motor-T veteran, at a local sports bar in Moberly, Missouri, a small farming/railroad town from what I could tell. It was the largest town among several small communities, one being Omar Bradley's hometown of Clark just a few miles down the road. Always a little unsure about where to meet folks, I pulled into the first restaurant that had a Bud Lite baseball banner on the patio railing. When Ken walked in, he said jokingly, "Oh ya, had to pick the high dollar place in town," putting me instantly at ease. Hey, like I said, all veterans are brethren in arms, but Marines and any Somalia vets are truly brothers. We instantly became friends and ended up sitting for hours at an even smaller, more bikerish bar downtown, a place that suited both of our likings. It wasn't long before Ken's wife came in the place looking for him. Not realizing we had been talking for hours, she was worried. He just disappears with some strange dude in a camper for hours on end. She was understandably alarmed, I couldn't blame her.

After he calmed her down and introduced her to me, everything was good again. He told her we were going to head over to the war memorial, and he would be home shortly afterwards. I told him it was good to have family, to which he smiled lovingly without saying a word. Later at the memorial, after walking around some of the statues commemorating all our military branches, Ken and I said goodbye, with big hugs and promises to meet up again at a Wall ride in DC one day. It's a rare thing to meet other Somalia vets, regardless of branch, who served with boots on the ground in the Moag. A different kind of family, but strong ties nonetheless. Looking forward to it, brother.

Now I needed a cheap campground, preferably by a lake, where I could hole up for about 5 days, until the Royals come home. Ken told me of several spots, but the closest one turned out to be absolutely perfect, an almost empty campground with rolling green grass and shade trees, along side the Thomas Hill Reservoir. Looked like we were back to lake hopping after all, but this time with AC and a full freezer. Kimber was in heaven, chasing the ball over land and/or into the cool water, returning only to lounge in the thick, soft grass. Happily, this allowed me to get some decent writing done, and chart out the next few stops on our Missouri visit.

About two days into our short hiatus, we were attacked in the night by a numerically superior and relentless force. Not realizing that we were surrounded on all sides, with the enemy laying in wait amongst the blades of dense grass, unlike the dreaded kamikaze mosquito attacks, this was more of a harassing barrage meant to confuse and dismay. As I stepped outside to get a better perspective of enemy numbers, I realized we were completely outnumbered and the onslaught had begun. With every footstep, a dozen of these winged demons took flight, landing on my arms, legs, face, glasses, under my glasses, between my toes, and every other conceivable crack, to include my truck windows that I left down over night. What crack were you thinking!?! Yup, the entire park broke out with a Mayfly hatch. Once I realized what they were, I went down to the shore; as I suspected, the fish were jumping like popcorn. Shortly, an armada of fisherman came rolling up to the boat dock, and me without a pole. A few hours later, a small storm was approaching, and just like that, they were gone. One of the weirdest things that I've ever experienced.

The Royals first home game was on a Friday night, the weather was amazingly cool, with rainstorms popping up intermittently. First stop was going to be at Kauffman Stadium, home of the Kansas City Royals, to buy a ticket and scout out parking before the night game. It was still too early for the box office to open, so we ventured into town, near the Kansas City Zoo, where I found another Civil War battlefield.

The Battle of Westport visitor center and museum was situated on the east side of the Kansas City Zoo property, in a not so great part of town, apparently. I got there somewhat early of course, with about 30 minutes to wait before the museum opened. I decided to get Kimber out for a little ball time while we waited. This actually was a good thing, because the few homeless folks that I hadn't seen, didn't care for Kimber running around, and had come out from the bushes near the visitor center, and walked away. Yup, this was definitely not a good part of town. When the museum opened, which was a privately funded one by the way, the curator was surprised I was there to see the place. They don't get many visitors, which was also obviously apparent.

The Battle of Westport was part of a Confederate raid conducted by CSA General Price late in the war. Trying to draw Union support away from Richmond and Atlanta in October 1864, Price engaged in almost daily skirmishes, wreaking havoc on the Missouri Countryside. It mentioned something about the Battle of Wilson Creek being a part of this whole raid, so I decided to dig into this more at the National Battlefield. My mind just wasn't on wrapping my head around who did what and when; Kimber was outside in the truck. Did I mention it was a bad neighborhood? Off toward the game, I wanted out of there.

I noticed when we drove by Kauffman Stadium, that it was an arena type park, with an ocean of parking spots and grass areas, perfect for tailgating and spending the day. So us getting there at 1300 was perfect for seeing the 7pm game. Tickets were plentiful and fairly priced. With the vet discount, I was on the third deck, behind the plate, my favorite, for under 20 bucks.

After buying the ticket, we pulled up to the parking section, where the lot attendant said we had to park in the RV and bus area, up the hill, in the back. Then he pulled back for us to pass without taking my money. Ok, guess they will charge me up there. At the top of the hill was a large tent being set up, with catering vans and rental equipment being off-loaded from some trucks. There were a couple vans and a truck by the back corner, where I slid in amongst the other cars, with the back of the camper facing a grass field. I wasn't trying to hide from paying the parking fee, but these were the only vehicles on top of the hill, so I parked. Either way, nobody came to collect, saving me an oversize vehicle $30 parking bill. I'll take what I can get.

After a few hours of ball play, a good couple hour nap, and some dinner in the camper, I set out to see Kauffman Stadium, home of the Kansas City Royals. The parking lot was full of tailgate parties before this first home game on a Friday night. Glad I got tickets early, I never expected a crowd like this. I was pretty excited to see this park, with all the tributes to my childhood hero, Royals iconic third baseman, George Brett. I had every baseball card, wore the #5 or increments of, played third base, and read his book "The Art of Hitting .300" cover to cover; now I would finally get to see his "corner" in person.

There was so much fun going on outside the park, I almost didn't want to go in. They had live music and people dancing with beers in hand. The weather was perfect as the storm from the morning passed through, leaving a nice cool evening. Still pretty humid, but at least it was not hot. Inside the park was really nice, with the last bit of sun now setting behind home plate; whoever situated this park, nailed it. No direct sun heat, and zero glare.

The stadium itself was huge. With an upper deck that looked like a curved blue football field. My seat was pretty much the very last row, but directly behind home plate. Once you got past the vertigo, it was a great seat, no net to obstruct and the entire field in view. Then again, the space station had the same view, but hey, they don't have beer. There was a giant concrete walkway around both sides, leading to a kids' amusement park behind the massive crown shaped Jumbotron towering over center field. All in all, a pretty cool park, and one of the biggest open-air stadiums I'd seen yet.

While I was sitting in my assigned seat eating a hot dog, a family of three sat next to me. The father was early 30s I'd say, a black guy and judging by his accent, from Jamaica or Haiti. His wife appeared to be white, spoke American English, carrying an infant about a year old. They all sat down, and he said hello. "Hey, thanks for your service, brother!" he said with a heavy accent, while looking at my Marine tattoo on my neck. With a mouth full of hot dog, and somewhat surprised, I nodded and waved back in thanks. Turned out that he was active duty Army Reserve, an E-4, who as a child was rescued from Haiti, became a citizen, and absolutely loves his new country, choosing to serve as a guardsman, like the ones who saved his family.

Now that my friends, is super cool. He then met his wife, who is also an Army veteran who recently had their first child, and man does this guy love his Royals! We had a great time, watching the game, talking about service, country, and family, and yes, God too. He told me he thanked Jesus for his new home, every single day. Amen brother, so do I. That right there is what becoming an American is all about. Embracing OUR culture, not bending it to make it more like the place you left or even fled from. Thank you for YOUR service to OUR country, brother. Kauffman Stadium, MLB park #13... COMPLETE!

After the game, Kimber and I spent that night at a Walmart just south of town, back at it bright and early the next day. I wanted to put some miles in, as we had only two weeks before August hit us with the worst part of the summer. The upside, we had plenty of time to see both Texas teams before regular season play ended. First things first, we had two more states to finish before we hit Texas.

I noticed the Carthage State Battlefield was on our way toward the Wilson's Creek National Battlefield, giving us a straight shot down Interstate 49 to Carthage, just outside of Joplin, MO, then east on Hwy 96 to Wilson Creek, just outside of Springfield, MO. The Carthage site was a small park, just off the main highway. A few picnic tables with a nice grassy area, were surrounded by woods and a small stream in the back. Information placards were within an enclosure, describing the politics of Missouri at the time, and where the state stood on slavery versus secession.

I knew the name Carthage sounded familiar. When I did the research on a timeline of battles, mainly to see when the Battle of Philippi went down, it mentioned Carthage as actually being the very first ground battle, followed by Philippi and then Manassas/Bull Run.

Most Missourians believed in what they called "Conditional Unionism"; they desired to remain in the Union, but would remain neutral, not entering into war with their sister southern states. The battle known as the "Steeple Chases" was between the State Governor and militia, who refused to be dictated to by a federal government, and a Unionist state senator who had the backing of a popular Missouri born Union General. Ironically, the state governor's name was Jackson, who was ultimately ran out of Missouri, making it a staunch Union state thereafter. Ok, so we have this battle in the very beginning of the war, and the other raid, at the very end of the war. Just trying to keep this straight. Off to Wilson Creek.

A straight shot east on Hwy 96, which is actually a portion of the historic Route 66, put us just southwest of Springfield, Missouri, at the Wilson Creek National Battlefield. It was only 0845, so weather was still somewhat cool; this was a good thing as I would be at this battlefield for awhile. I had no idea what made this battle so significant as to deem a "National" recognition, but I was sure about to learn.

Ok, so back at Carthage we heard the state was torn over slavery, but just not to what extent. We also learned that the state's governor sided with secession, thus making the state guard Confederate troops. What we didn't know was after the Governor and troops went to southern Missouri, while the Union General Lyon went north to Illinois; he soon returned to attack the state militia troops, thus driving the "Confederates" out of Missouri early in the war. Doesn't sound like anything special, right? Then I noticed the dates. Battle of Wilson Creek started in June of 1861, a month after Carthage and the original state political split, but also an entire month BEFORE Manassas. Even more astonishing, it didn't end until a month AFTER Manassas, the battle we were told started everything. Missouri was so war-torn by the end of the Civil War, that it ranks as the third highest in number of battles behind Virginia and Tennessee. This specific battle marks when Missouri became a solid Union State.

The park itself has the standard visitor center, short film, and artifact museum; the only thing new here was an incredible library. If you had a relative that fought in the Civil War, they were probably documented somewhere in this room. A very extensive collection of military and federal records, lineages, and even ancestry websites, were free to use. I had a Ranger gracious enough to print off Jackson lineage clear back to North Carolina and Pennsylvania in the early 1700s. No ties to Stonewall so far, except by name, just an interesting family split shortly after the Civil War to the Oregon Trail. Looked like more research for another time. Super cool resource and a must see for Civil War buffs.

One very interesting thing did come up while researching the family tree. My Great Grandma Jackson's maiden name was Coe. The Ranger at the museum was kind enough to also look up the Coe lineage, also listing names and dates as far back as the early 1730. It turns out I have great x4 grandparents buried in unmarked graves somewhere on Baker's Ridge in North Carolina. A quick google search of Baker's Ridge about made me drop my phone. Baker's Ridge is directly over the mountain from… Johnson City, Tennessee. Ya, I got goose bumps too. So not only do I have a pre-Revolutionary war heritage on the Jackson side, but now on the Coe side as well. Talk about being the original OG! Can we change that to old patriot instead? No wonder I felt so at home in Appalachia.

The rest of the park was mainly a driving tour of a young family's ranch and farmhouse, where the battle broke out in their cornfield. The house had a tour guide who explained the situation and some facts about everyday life, especially to include slavery. Funny how that's always a prominent aspect of the Union States' perspective of the war. The biggest takeaway here was the price of the family farm as compared to the price of just one slave. Ok, this is hard, but try to remove yourself from the whole "slavery" thing and see this in the eyes of a young family, starting a farm with some inheritance. According to the park historian/tour guide, the value of the 300-acre farm was around $30k while the price of the slave was around $80k. This blew me away. Many times a slave was willed or given as wedding presents from the parents. Trying to wrap my head around this, I equated it to a truck driver. A trucker spends 100g on a truck, or a farmer spends the same on a tractor, both needed to make a living and support the family. Now the government comes along and says the means by which you make your living and feed your kids, is now illegal. Ya, I can see some folks willing to fight for that.

Second massive takeaway form this: 85% of the men who fought for the Confederacy were between the ages of 16 and 30, and never owned a slave. As a matter of fact, if you owned slaves, you were exempt from war because they needed you to supply the war effort with whatever your farm produced. Once again giving way to the southern precept that this was a battle for one's way of life, as compared to the battle over the newly perceived evils of slavery. An interesting argument about the destruction of Confederate monuments must ensue. Why are these young men and families, fighting for their homeland against a perceived tyrannical government, not afforded a tribute to their service and gallantry? Historical fact outweighs personal emotion, in my opinion. Get over it, learn from it, and move on.

It was now 1230 and unbearably hot. The weather app said it was currently 93f, but with the humidity, it felt like 107f! That's what the app said. No exaggeration. With nothing left to do, we worked our way down to Pea Ridge National Battlefield, just over the Arkansas border. We ended up stopping in Branson West, MO for some dinner and another night at Walmart with the generator running full blast. Even with the soothing mechanical rhythm and the wonderful cold air pulsing out of the vents, Kimber sat straight up in bed and started shaking instantly. That's when I woke to the sound of pop, pop, pop, something loud in the distance. Suddenly, a rainbow-colored flash came through the tint of the camper window. Fireworks. "It's freaking July 15th, are you shitting me!? Ugh!" were my exact thoughts out loud... very loud. Now Kimber was really shaking, ok, so much for a restful night's sleep. Happily though, Missouri, state #26... COMPLETE!

Arkansas

July 16th, 2017. Well, the good news is, we were in Arkansas; the bad news is, we were in Arkansas in mid-July. I've lived here before and knew pretty much what to expect. Lots of green, lots of heat, and lots of bugs. All I kept thinking was "Good Lord please, just don't let the generator die." The plan was nothing more than to visit the one and only National level battlefield, then straight to Texarkana, where my buddy had a motorcycle/AC business. From there the plan was to haul ass to Houston for a game, then up to Dallas for a game, before entering Oklahoma, Kansas, and finally back to AZ for the winter. Ok, so those were my plans, let's see if God is laughing yet.

Crack of dawn, we were up with the truckers. Best reveille in the world is a couple semis firing up their rigs at 0500. That worked, I knew the weather was going to be brutal, so time we hit the road too. We pulled into the Pea Ridge National Military Park really early, about 0730, well before the visitor center opened. It was a semi-cloudy day, with air thick enough to chew before you could inhale it. The grass was wet with morning dew, which made the best morning ever for Kimber, who used it as the world's largest slip and slide after diving for her ball. Perfect! Every chance I can get to wear her out early before I go research a battlefield, is absolute gold. Now completely soaked, but with an unmistakable canine grin, I dried my little stunt dog off, and headed for the door the Ranger had just unlocked.

The park grounds were well kept, lots of parking, and a good-sized building. Inside was a very small museum and gift store, with mainly just maps and information placards, very little in way of actual artifacts. After browsing the gift shop, I started to read the plaques and instantly realized I was now in a southern state. The emphasis here was more on the actual soldiers who fought here, their original motives, both north and south, and much less about the Abolitionist movement. There's also the military achievement of course, solidifying Missouri for the Union after the Battle of Wilson's Creek.

My first major takeaway about the Confederate Army of the West was who made up its ranks, specifically the Native Americans regiments. It described the 2nd Cherokee Mounted Rifle, second meaning it's the second unit raised from this area. So basically, there were at least two of these units. Here's the crazy part. The plaques went on to read, "Loyalty in the Five Nations were sharply divided between North and South. Slavery was legal and widespread in Indian territory." Whoa wait, what? "Hundreds of Cherokees volunteered to fight for the Confederacy as early as July, 1861. The Cherokee Rifles served as a home guard unit inside Indian Territory for most of the year." It went on to say, "When Van Dorn gave the order to march north into Missouri in 1862, he asked General Albert Pike to mobilize as many Indian troops as possible and meet him in Bentonville. Because Van Dorn's army moved so fast, only two Cherokee regiments had joined him before battle broke out. Choctaw, Chickasaw, and Creek troops were still on the way." This fascinated me, my head reeling with questions. What do you mean slavery was widespread in the Indian territory? You mean the Native Americans owned slaves... and actually took up arms to protect them? This made me wonder about all we've been told regarding the "slaughter" of the "innocent" Native Americans. I mean at this point, why wouldn't Union soldiers now view the Natives as enemy combatants, not just being torn from their tribal lands as we have been taught. More to come on this thought.

After the museum, I jumped in the Rig and began the driving portion of the tour. This being a Military Park, it had quite an expansive road system. The Park basically encompasses the Elkhorn Tavern and surrounding valley, with several parking areas facilitating small trailheads and walking paths, including one to a veranda overlooking the entire valley and battlefield. Last stop was Elkhorn Tavern; that's when my Cardinal showed up.

Little did I know that the accumulation of my entire Civil War History revelation was about to be unveiled. The questions that I had regarding so many strange and obscure facts that I'd discovered on this trip, were about to be answered. Such as, what was the political divide that led to Lincoln's running on an abolitionist platform; why was slavery only outlawed in the South; what was the inspiration of the northern soldiers to pick up arms if not to end slavery? On and on, my mind seeing all these facts like a pile of bricks, but with no mortar to hold it all together. A gentleman at Elkhorn Tavern was going to be that mortar.

While Kimber and I were driving through some of the more forested area of the park, a bright red male Cardinal swooped down in front of the Rig. Traveling the exact speed as the Rig, it flapped its wings to rise and fall exactly three times, covering a good 100 yards, before veering away from the road, and directly into the parking lot of the Elkhorn Tavern. Almost as if escorting me to the grand finale of this year's trip. The Tavern was a remodeled National Park Service exhibit, showing the makeshift hospital and the Inn itself. Much like Wilson's Creek, it had a couple of Park Rangers dressed in the period as Union soldiers, discussing the scene.

I had an interesting conversation regarding the true beginnings of the war, searching for some of the questions I wanted answered, with one of the Park Rangers and tour guide. A very well read, younger gentleman, extremely knowledgeable about the situation and era he portrayed, told me to wait for the show, I'd get some answers I was seeking then. About that time, he stood up, and while stretching said there was enough folks waiting and to "Get this show on the road." To which I agreed as the heat and humidity were climbing quickly.

The Ranger then grabbed a replica musket leaning against the wall, stepped out in front of the crowd of visitors and proceeded to give his speech on exactly what I had been curious about. Turned out this gentleman had a master's degree in history, was a 12-year Army Combat veteran, and now serves with the Army in some type of historian function; so basically, this guy knows what he's talking about. He went on to describe the two economic systems colliding, the industrialization of the north embracing "free labor," and the aggregate slave-driven economy of the South. Most astonishing to me was that Lincoln did not run on an abolitionist platform, he ran on the Republican platform of not allowing the expansion of slavery into the western territories. The Unionists saw slavery much like how we see illegal immigration today, wages would drop in the western territories if slavery was allowed to produce "free labor." The northern working class saw this as unfair for their pioneer expansion and especially during the gold rush. The South on the other hand, believed that states' rights and the Constitution allowed them to take their legally owned property (slaves) with them as they also looked to pioneer the west and cash in on the gold rush. Ok, now this finally made some sense. Then when South Carolina votes to secede, the north viewed this also as unconstitutional and had the added patriotic view of preserving the Union; neither of which was a reason to enter combat due to the humanity of slaves. Ok, so this explains why the Emancipation Proclamation was described as a "war measure" deployed against the South, much later into the conflict. Once again, I had to take mental note that I'm in a Southern state. I wonder what next year's travels into the Northeast will show me, obviously from the Northern prospective.

After the gentleman's 30-minute discussion that I recorded and posted to Facebook, I had my first "viral" video. Well, viral for me anyway, with a few thousand views and hundreds of shares. Super exciting to watch, but now it was 1100 and the heat was unbearable. I knew Kimber would have to spend the majority of our time in the camper with generator and AC running, from this point on. Like I previously explained, I had lived in Texarkana for a few years after the Marines and pretty much seen all there is to see there. We stopped at a couple of local battlefields and graveyards on the way to Texarkana, TX, choosing to stay at a Walmart once, before pulling into my buddy's motorcycle shop for the evening. Now happily plugged into some real electricity, AC running at full throttle, we had made it back to Texas. Two more states, two more parks, were almost there. Arkansas, state #27... COMPLETE.

Texas (again)

July 17th, 2017. It had been a good twenty years since I had been back to Texas, let alone Texarkana. I was a prison guard here shortly after being discharged from the Marines, and always had considered this area as a possible landing spot after my travels. It was good to see my buddy Kevin after all these years, it wasn't good to see and hear what had happened to my friends who stayed in this area. Apparently, meth had taken a toll here, like it did in so many small towns over the past couple of decades. Prominent business owners were losing everything, upstanding folks either in prison or dead. It was shocking and sad, to see how far this place had fallen, I didn't even recognize the place well enough to navigate the streets without GPS. It was truly shocking.

The next day, I said goodbye to Kevin, and started south into Texas, to see a Houston Astros game. The weather was brutally hot, and funds were going to be tight, but it had to be done. I had scouted out an RV park in downtown Houston that advertised a safe, fenced area, with security, full hookups and laundry for 60 bucks. It was expensive, but what else was I going to do. I had to have a secure place to park the Rig, and had to have electricity to keep Kimber cool. If the generator kicked off while I was gone this time, Kimber would be dead. A chance that just wasn't gonna be taken. No way.

Once tucked away into our spot, electricity hooked up, and Kimber happy, I met the Uber driver just outside the "Compound." The park was protected by a tall fence with barbed wire across the top and an electronic cipher lock to enter, thus resembling a military compound. As we drove out to the ballpark, the area around us came into full view. Definitely saw why the security was so tight and so glad I chose to handle the Kimber situation the way I did; no way in hell I was going to relax with Kimber alone in the camper, unsecured, in this part of town.

I quickly learned that this was going to be the most expensive game I'd attended so far. 60 bucks for the parking spot, another 46 bucks for the round-trip Uber ride, and now no veteran discount at the window. This was the first park that only offered the military discount online and not at the ticket window, which made zero sense to me. So add another 28 bucks for a ticket. By this point, all I wanted to do was get a bite to eat and a much needed beer. Add another 23 bucks for a hamburger patty with a slice of cheese, on a stale bun, with a 16oz beer, then being pointed to the condiments station for mustard or ketchup. The absolute worst, not to mention expensive, food of any park thus far. Wow, this wasn't a great start for Minute Maid park and the Houston Astros.

After I found my seat and finished my "meal," I started out to take some pictures of the park. For some reason I still thought Houston had the old Astrodome, so I was pleased to see that the park was still enclosed and most importantly, had AC. The park itself was nice, reminiscent of the Miami park with its dome and large glass window beyond the center field fence. Strangely, a train carrying oranges would drive across the front of the windows when the Astros would hit a homer. I don't remember Houston having oranges. The absolute best part about this park was the fans. Obviously from a strong Hispanic area of the country, the enthusiasm was like something you'd see at a soccer game, although having a first-place team this year probably helped. Massive sombreros and ponchos in bright orange and blue lined the terrace above the right and center fields, with the majority of partying fans hanging around the Torchy's Taco stand in center field. If you go see the Astros at home, just buy a "get in" ticket for as cheap as possible and go early, head to the center field area and grab a spot at the first come, first serve standing room only area. Torchy's Tacos is where the party's at, and made the cost of the visit all worth it. I just wish I had eaten there instead! Minute Maid Park, MLB park #14... COMPLETE!

Later that evening, with Kimber snoring contently by my leg, I started to map out our route for the next game in Arlington, TX. It was then I realized that we had four very hot and humid days to wait before the Rangers next home game. That posed a serious problem. I didn't want to sit around and sweat for almost a week at a campsite, stuck in the camper with the generator running, coupled with the fact that we were halfway through the month and funds were already running tight. That's when I remembered my buddy Nick was in Austin, and had said to stop by if I was in the area. I've known Nick since junior high school, back in Sonoma; we played sports together growing up and were good friends. It had been 33 years since I had seen Nick, so I was looking forward to the visit. Unfortunately, when I called he told me he had moved to Dallas, which would've been great, but he was out of town on business also. Well, dammit. He was bummed too, but we made plans to see each other after the Rangers game.

Back to looking for a campsite somewhere along the freeway from Houston to Dallas that has a lake or some water. I even thought to stay along the coast and just make the drive up to Dallas in a day; ya, I was getting that desperate. Worst case, I'd just keep Walmart hopping and looking for shade, or a pond to throw the ball for Kimber. Anything to keep cool at this point. I had gone as far as to post my woes on the book page, and surprisingly, another old friend from high school sent me a message that I could stay at his place, and we'd catch the game together. Once again, thank you, Jesus. We had a place to relax, I didn't have worry about parking or dealing with Kimber while I went to the game, and I got to see another old friend and former Marine.

Wes and I knew each other in school, played football together once, I think with his brother Craig too. He had also joined the Marines, served about the same time I did, and became an airline mechanic now working in Dallas. Like Nick, I hadn't seen or heard from Wes since my sophomore year, so it was quite a surprise to hear from him, let alone see him after all these years, and in Dallas of all places. Gotta love the marvels of social media.

For the next few days before the Rangers game, Kimber and I had the run of Wes' place, as he worked mainly nights. Lots of time spent relaxing in front of the TV with baseball on, soaking up the precious AC. Never in my life would I have known, what a little humidity would do to a man after living in the desert for 20 years. Like kryptonite to Superman, I was unapologetically content to lay there like a bum for three days until game day.

Globe Life Park, Home of the Texas Rangers, is actually in the town of Arlington, the "taint" between Dallas and Fort Worth. I've always liked the Rangers, mainly because their spring training park was in Surprise, AZ, where I was a home builder. Lots of good times were had with family and friends. Maybe that's why the first thing I noticed was the lattice trim on what looked like office buildings in the center field outfield, giving that "old timey" 1920s feel.

Liken it to watching Babe Ruth warm up in front of the TV camera, in black and white, that kind of look. It was similar to the AZ park.

I had heard on the radio and from my buddy Wes that they wanted to build a new park, being as this one was open aired, with no dome or AC. Even at the night game it was unbearably hot and super humid. Such a beautiful park, great location, lots of parking, and the best food of any park so far; it would be a shame to see it go. We sat in the upper deck, behind home plate, which gave us a little breeze, but was still very uncomfortable. Either way, it was still a ballgame with a high school buddy and former Marine, which makes it all so worth the sweat. Globe Life Park, ballpark #15... COMPLETE!

After saying goodbye to Wes, we drove an entire 45 minutes over to Nick's place in Fort Worth. It was great seeing my buddy Nick after all these years. We played football, basketball, and ran track together, not to mention junior high and high school. Now Nick is a successful businessman, logging in more frequent flyer miles than anyone I know. This dude is always on the move, so it was cool to spend over a week at his place while he was in town. He had a beautiful home with a pool that Kimber and I took full advantage of as we waited for payday to roll back around.

Since we had some time to kill, I decided to head into downtown Dallas to see a place where bullets flew in the shaping of our country, Dealey Plaza, where President Kennedy was assassinated. At least in my thoughts, it is a place that can arguably be referred to as a "battlefield." Even with the crowds of tourists, and regular businesses operating as usual, there was a heavy solemnness that was unmistakable.

I walked Kimber along the same path as Kennedy's motorcade took, noticing an "X" painted in the center lane of the three-lane, one-way road. This is the exact spot where JFK was shot. Chills went up and down my arms and spine like electricity. I was shocked by the tourists, running into the middle of the road, dodging traffic, to get a picture standing near the "X." I thought how morbid could you get, but then again, I was there to see the same thing. I must've said it out loud as a gentlemen standing next to me with a very expensive camera said, "The city keeps removing it, but people keep putting it back," referring to the "X." That made me think. Who is "putting it back"? By the looks of the neighborhood, I don't think historically passionate locals are repainting the marker, nor would the tourists all flocking to take pictures next to it. Obviously, the culprits are the street vendors selling old copies of the Dallas newspaper proclaiming the death of an American President. Others were selling picture books, discussing different "conspiracy theories" regarding that day. Even this place has been commercialized.

As we walked further down the street, I took notice of the famous book repository window, where Oswald was claimed to have made three shots and three hits on the President. This is going to get a little graphic, you've been warned. From where I was standing on the sidewalk, directly across from the "X" in the road, it had to be at least a 300yd shot. They say he used a bolt-action rifle (must be cocked between shots), shooting at a moving object, hitting the President in the head three times from behind, throwing his brain-matter backward on the trunk. Sorry folks, but there is just no way. I'm a Marine, qualified expert with the rifle, and could never have made those three shots with that weapon, let alone make the aftermath fly backward.

Behind me was the famous "grassy knoll" where the "conspiracy theorists" believe at least one of the shots was fired from. I walked Kimber up the grass slope to the tree line. There I found a wooden picket fence with years of graffiti written in layers, most saying RIP to JFK. I followed the fence to the parking lot that it separated, and around to the back side. There was one plank that had the top missing, as if broken off years ago. I lowered my head down to peek through the missing slate, and as suspected... it lined up perfectly with the "X." Chills instantly ran up my spine. I'm not saying that this was a gunman's possible location, but it sure made you wonder.

It was just after noon at this point, and Kimber was getting noticeably tired, time to get back to Nick's amazing pool. On the way back to the truck, we walked past the book repository, where I saw a brass plaque mounted to the wall explaining the events of that day. What I found interesting was that the word "allegedly" had circles scratched around it, and the word had been touched so many times that it was noticeably shinier than the rest of the plaque. I see I'm not the only one with doubts.

Back at Nick's I was planning out the last month of our travels. With no more baseball parks to see for the year, my attention turned to where to go until Arizona cooled down enough to be inhabitable. That gave me at least two months before I even thought about heading back, plenty of time to knock Oklahoma and Kansas off the list, before I head up in elevation to wait out the heat. The next day, we said our goodbyes to Nick, and headed north to Oklahoma. Although it's been counted already, Texas is now officially complete.

Oklahoma

August 7, 2017. I had only been to Oklahoma once, for a biker rally in Broken Bow, several years ago. Other than that, all I knew was Oklahoma was flat and windy. After doing some research into the state, I found there were two National exhibits worth making a visit to. The first was the Oklahoma City National Memorial Museum, site of the Oklahoma City bombing, and the second being Washita National Battlefield, where General Custer is involved prior to Little Big Horn. Also along the way was the hometown of a very close family friend back in AZ who set me up at his favorite local eatery and bar for the evening. Turned out it's the first and oldest bar in Oklahoma, with a ton of history and the best fried chicken around. Yup, I'm in! After mapping the waypoints on the road atlas, filling up the bubba mug with coffee, we turned north for OKC.

Absolutely incredible that after almost two weeks of scorching hot weather, a storm rolled in the night before we left Nick's place, keeping the temperatures nice and cool for our OKC visit. A much smaller city than I had expected, we easily found some street-side parking for the Rig, about a block away from the bombing site. Vaguely remembering what happened here, I never realized the size of the tragedy that occurred. Scars from the blast are still apparent on surrounding buildings, especially on the church that used to stand across the street. With one of the most powerful memorial statues I've ever seen of a weeping Christ as he faces where the oldest church in OKC once stood, face in hand, crying; I too was brought to tears.

There were two giant black archways that were the entrances to a very large reflection pond. To one side of the water was a grassy area with several metal chairs, representing the fallen on the different floors of the building where they died. The other side had a large tree, that withstood the blast and had been surrounded by burning vehicles, yet was unscathed. There was also a museum and a children's area behind a chain-link fence strewn with stuffed animals, pictures, and prayers. Even with kids coloring with concrete chalk and climbing on the jungle gyms, there was once again a heavy solemnity in the air. A much more powerful place than I had ever imagined. Another "battlefield" of sorts, where liberty and lives were lost in the shaping of our America.

Okarche, OK was just a few minutes outside of OKC, a rural farming town where my buddy Lee grew up. He's always talking about this local bar called Eischen's where all the locals go to eat fried chicken. He was going to have his brother meet me there, but unfortunately work schedules prevailed and I sat at the bar solo that evening. Once I said I was Lee's friend and was just passing through, they treated me like family. Showing me around the bar, making sure I had plenty of food, they even gave me a gift bag with some plastic Eischen's tumblers, cozies, and books of matches to take on the road. What a great place to be from, and thanks to Eischen's for making me feel at home.

That night, we boondocked at the local Walmart just up the road in Kingfisher, OK, before driving west to the Washita National Battlefield. Here we find once again another "slaughter" as described by the National Park Service. The "Boy General" and former hero of the North, General Custer, who now is in service of the US Army, just three years after the Civil War, descends on a sleeping tribe of mainly women and children, killing everyone. Continuously they're describing how the battle was due to "clashes of cultures" while villainizing the former Union General. After learning that slavery flourished among the native tribes back at Pea Ridge, and that some tribes took up arms against the Union during the Civil War, made it hard for me to accept the description that the park service was portraying.

I left the video before the other visitors did, hoping to get some pictures of the exhibits before it got crowded. That's when a Park Ranger happened to walk up and ask if I had any questions. I told him of my travels, and what we had learned about at Pea Ridge regarding the Natives role in the Civil War. That's when his eyes lit up and he said, "Well, you will appreciate the 'rest of the story', making air quotes with his fingers as he spoke. He went on to tell me some interesting information strangely omitted from the video. He told me that Custer had killed his first and only two Indians here at this battlefield prior to his death at Little Big Horn; but he had killed hundreds of white southerners throughout the course of the war, yet his "legacy" has made him an Indian killer. He also said that the Cheyenne and Choctaw, amongst other tribes, had a flourishing slave trade, stealing women and children from settlers and merchants who were crossing the plain states on the way to the west. Ok, well that confirms what we learned in Arkansas. Stories of the natives taking white women to Mexico, raping and beating them visibly so that Mexicans felt bad enough to buy the slaves. Custer freed a white female slave and child along with a Mexican merchant during this battle, but only the slaughter of horses is mentioned. Those same horses were captured from settlers and used on future raids, making up the bulk of the reason for the horses to be killed. Keep in mind that this battlefield was in Oklahoma, where the Indian Tribes were all sent during the Trail of Tears, canting the view of this somewhat; but also remember that this happened only three years after the end of the Civil War. Why wouldn't Custer view these as enemy Confederate sympathizers or even combatants? Clash of culture? Sounds like one of my favorite sayings, "one man's freedom fighter is another man's terrorist." I thanked the Ranger for this interesting addition to the Indian Wars narrative.

The grounds of the battlefield didn't have much to offer. The actual battle took place a few miles down the road, that offered a viewpoint overlooking the valley where the fighting occurred. There was a hiking trail which was pretty muddy from last night's rain. Not gonna lie, I really had zero interest in seeing anything to do with war and battles at this point, regardless of which war. I was sorry to see our last ballgame for the year go by, and was ready to just find a nice cool campground on top of a mountain somewhere. The less people the better, I was done with this trip. With that in mind, I crawled into the camper with Kimber for some lunch, and looked for the next destination.

So back in Missouri I was taken off guard by the Kansas City Royals actually being a Missouri team. I had planned to see them when I visited Kansas. And here I am a huge George Brett fan and never knew they played in Missouri. Anyway, I was pretty much in the middle of nowhere, but pretty close to the Kansas border. The famous western town of Dodge City was just a couple hours away, and bullets definitely flew there; plus, I'm pretty sure my grandpa would enjoy the visit. Well, I guess we're heading to Kansas. Oklahoma, state #28... COMPLETE!

Kansas

August 9th, 2017. We pulled into the Dodge City Walmart around dinner time, just in time to find a secluded spot between a couple tractor trailers and finish the massive to-go box full of Eischen's chicken, fried okra, and white bread. I broke out the road atlas, tracing our last miles with a drumstick, contemplating where to go after Dodge City. Kansas, huh? Well, like I had said before, this was just going to be a quick visit to Dodge City, check off Kansas as being touched, and then off to higher, and much cooler, ground for the rest of the summer. After throwing the ball on the lush grassy patch next to the parking lot for Kimber, we crashed out for the night.

Up with the truckers, bright and early the following morning, I laid in bed thinking of the day's adventure. I sure wished my grandfather could have seen this town, some of my fondest memories were watching westerns on the wood encased TV set, with Grampa sitting in his chair by the window. Lord knows how many times he's watched that episode of Bonanza or Gunsmoke; my only wish is being able to sit and watch it with him one more time... just once more. This one's for you, Grampa.

Short on pocket cash, I pulled the Rig across the street to a bank with a walk-up ATM. There was a huge sign in front of the building, with a digital screen displaying the time and date as I approached it. After my transaction, while walking back to the truck, just as I was directly in front of the digital screen, the time and date changed to a huge red Cardinal. I almost dropped my keys. Nothing like a 4 ft tall, bright red LED Cardinal at sunrise to get your attention. Ya, I think Grampa is excited for today. I just sat in the truck, looking at the giant Cardinal on the screen... while tears gently rolled down my cheeks.

Dodge City was originally a Military Fort, that later became the location for bringing Texas Longhorn cattle to market. We of course know it as the original western town, home to names like Doc Holiday, Big Nose Kate, and of course Wyatt Earp. Famous shootouts in the original Long Branch Saloon, gave way to a car dealership and a public sidewalk. Now the entire scene is enclosed in a small amusement park type setting, with museum and gift shop. I was glad to be able to attain my goal of having a cold beer in the Long Branch Saloon, while listening to a piano player and watching can-can girls, even if it was just a replication of the original bar.

After walking all the streets of downtown Dodge City enough to wear Kimber down, and to take in all the possible sights this historic town had to offer, it was time to head north. Not in latitude, but more in elevation. After our brief Red River, NM visit from last year, I knew where I was going. That's the joy of travel, scouting out all the places I want to come back to visit, Red River being one of them. After a visit to the grocery store for a couple weeks' worth of supplies, we were off to cooler climates. Kansas; state #29, and the final state of our "Southern Perspective Tour"... COMPLETE!

Normally, this would be the end of the story for 2017, but sadly and unexpectedly, it wasn't. After coming down from of the crisp Red River, NM air to resupply in Taos, after finally getting some cell reception, I caught word of the Las Vegas shooting. First thing that went through my head was Heather and Sonny. Not sure if I had explained earlier, but they were huge country music fans, Sonny's favorite being Eric Church, who just happened to be playing at the Vegas Harvest Festival. Heather and Sonny had just returned from a Metallica show in Texas a few weeks before I had seen them. So this prompted my call to Heather. I don't really remember if we spoke or just texted, but this is what was said: "Hey girl, you guys weren't in Vegas, right?" I typed into the text message on my phone. The answer was almost immediate. "You didn't hear? Sonny's dead," was Heather's reply. This time I did drop my phone. What!? I couldn't believe what I had just read. She went on to tell me how they were in front of the stage when the shooting started, and how she felt Sonny get hit twice as he gripped her shoulders, pushing her down. He saved Heather. This was the nurse who saved his surgeon wife that was all over the news. Eric Church was in tears on stage at the Grand Ole Opry weeks later, describing how Sonny had come to see him specifically, which prompted Eric's song "Why you and why not me?" The Tennessee Titans wore a green rubber wrist band in his honor the rest of the season, while they are still naming bridges and landmarks in Tennessee after Sonny.

I was overcome with all kinds of emotions after the news. First shock, then I was pissed. This isn't supposed to happen here, this is why we fight over there. All I could think of was the story she told of trying to revive Sonny, while bullets kicked dirt up around her. Finally, two guys came and grabbed Sonny, laid him in a truck bed and sped him to the hospital while Heather performed CPR, before turning back to get more victims. I was so mad that this happened, that Heather had to experience "combat," let alone lose her husband. I was mad that I didn't have my buddy back in Tennessee anymore, and saddened that a family and town had lost a son. It took me a good while to wrap my head around what happened, the whole time seeing Heather go through a whirlwind of drama online. It was hard to take. Strangely, it made me feel like I did as I watched the downed pilots being drug through the streets of Mogadishu, watching this while sitting in separations with tears in my eyes. Send me back, I wanted to fight. Yet there was no war to return to. It was all so confusing and brutal to accept. My heart goes out to Heather and Sonny's family for their incredibly senseless loss.

Looking back at the past 8 months of travels, I was shocked at what I had accomplished. We covered 16 states, 19 baseball parks, including all 13 Florida Spring Training camps, and countless American Battlefields and historic places. No wonder I was exhausted. Now it's back to Arizona to get all this on paper, and get some well deserved rest. Year 3 of Baseballs and Battlefields is now… COMPLETE!

The Northeast and Lake States Run

2018

It's hard to believe that I'm on year four of this trek. Time has flown by so fast that it's inconceivable. It seems like yesterday that I left on this adventure, yet when I go back to AZ, I realize that life marches on without me. I asked a friend if he wanted to go to the bar and watch some football, his reply surprised me. "I'm married with a two-year-old now, bro, you've been gone for 3 years." Wow, that's a wake-up call. I guess when they say, if you find something you love to do, you'll never work another day in your life, it's so very true. Time has literally passed at lightning speed; but with what I've experienced thus far, there are definitely no regrets. Memories are gold, while all else fades away.

So this year brings big changes to the Rig. During last year's trip I was able to save almost $500 a month while traveling; boondocking for free, rather than spending money on camping and RV spots, proved very beneficial. With that cash I purchased a 2003, 26ft Ultra-Lite, bumper-pull, travel trailer, fully self-contained, with shower, toilet, full kitchen, couch and queen-size bed. The timing couldn't have been more perfect, as the aluminum siding under the cabover portion of the old camper came loose with a bang, ironically just after putting the cash down on the new trailer. It held in there just long enough, until I was able to purchase the new trailer, then let loose. It was done. With a glance at the heavens, I just said, "Thank you." That right there, was nothing less than heaven sent!

My plan for this upcoming year was to park the camper in a centralized location, and use the truck with a newly added camper shell, as a "3-day bug-out" vehicle, complete with sleeping cot, beach chair, Walmart "Yeti" cooler, and a portable propane heater. I was hoping that this would give easier access to parking while venturing into the major cities, seeing as I'd be visiting 15

MLB ballparks in the last 18 states of the lower 48. That's 15 MAJOR cities to navigate and find parking in. Can you say stress? Hopefully this works out. Quite honestly, it has to, there's no other way. Along with the baseball parks, we planned on wrapping up the Civil War from the Northern perspective, dive into the War of 1812, and finish the Revolutionary War; all the while, trying to complete the coastal drive of the entire U.S. Definitely the most ambitious leg of our adventure so far. And you thought last year was busy.

We left Phoenix on March 28th, 2018, heading for our first "home base" at Camp Atterbury, ID, a joint services training base run by the National Guard. No safer place for my Rig than a military base, while we ventured out in the truck. The route I chose was going be about a 4-day trip, stopping at a casino near Albuquerque our first night, then a family friend's place, Lee and family moved back to Okarche, OK, setting up our second stop. Next was a truck stop in Effingham, IL, finally arriving at Camp Atterbury, ID.

This was my first time pulling such a long trailer for any amount of distance, let alone the cross-country trek we were embarking on. I was so nervous about towing my "house" that the drive out of AZ was definitely a white-knuckle affair, to say the least. Thankfully, it wasn't long before I got my "sea legs" and was easily cruising eastbound on Interstate 40, also known as the new Route 66.

The trip was proceeding as planned, when good old Murphy raised his ugly head. As luck would have it, 98 miles from Okarche, my truck transmission started downshifting kind of hard. Then I realized it wasn't shifting at all, with a big number "4" on the dash, it wasn't shifting out of 4th gear. Well there it goes, my transmission is toast. Traveling with the heavy load of the cabover camper and pulling the old bike trailer for the last 100k miles, my quarter ton transmission finally gave out. My biggest fear just came to fruition, my trip was over. Frantically, I called my friend Jim in Phoenix, whose knowledge of cars far exceeds mine. After venting my frustrations and explaining the situation, he told me to find a dealer ASAP. I grabbed my phone and searched the nearest Ram dealer location. To my absolute astonishment, it told me to take the next exit and make a U-turn. I looked off to the side of the highway, low and behold, there was a Chrysler/ Dodge/ Ram dealer! I couldn't believe my eyes! Oh Jesus, thank you! I must've looked desperately worried as I explained the situation to the lady behind the service counter. She told me to go ahead and unhook the trailer next to the other one in the lot, and bring the truck around so they can run a code on it. I was shaking with anxiety, my mind racing a mile a minute, this was bad, really bad. Without hesitation, the service manager went out and coded my truck and came back with a diagnosis. The manager and the service lady both looked at the screen, and then each other. The look on their face was like a doctor getting ready to break the news to a terminally ill patient. "Ya... you might wanna have our tech look at this," she said. Turns out the shift solenoid was bad, a $1200 job, if that's all that was wrong. I told her I had purchased an extended warranty, and if they didn't cover this, I was screwed. She took my warranty information, told me the tech was at lunch, and she would let me know what the warranty folks say.

While I'm sitting in my camper, anxiously awaiting a call from the dealer, I received an email from Carshield, the warranty company. It read, "Thank you for choosing Carshield, it was a pleasure speaking with you today. Please rate your experience below..." Without a word from the dealer, my heart sank, assuming that it didn't get covered. When I went in the office to ask what the verdict was, the service lady said, "They're buttoning it up now. All you owe is $100 deductible and a filter." WHAT!? I could've jumped over the counter and kissed her! So in less than 4 hours, the solenoid was installed, along with a tranny flush, new oil, gasket, and filter. I went back to the camper and hit my knees with tears in my eyes... thank you, Jesus! Even my friend Jim was astonished. "Somebody is looking out for you," he said. I couldn't have agreed more.

The weather at Camp Atterbury was an experience in itself. It snowed the night we arrived, then warmed up to 70f the next day. The camp host stopped by to inform us that there was a tornado watch in effect. Pointing at a huge siren on a pole and then pointing at the cinder block shower house she said, "If that goes off, get in there. You can walk behind that last row of trailers and still see metal in the trees from 2 years ago." Whoa what?! That was not something I needed to hear. So there we sat for the next few days, scanning the weather apps on the phone, watching the news, and listening for the siren. This gave me the chance to research some sites in Illinois, reserve a hotel room in Chicago for the city's two baseball parks, and get some writing done. Hopefully, the weather holds out for the two games I chose see.

Illinois

March 28th, 2018. Ten days of sitting around Camp Atterbury, waiting for the weather to let up so we could begin our Illinois tour, was brutal. Snow, wind, tornado alerts, and the surrounding gun ranges made it rough on Kimber too. Finally, we saw a two-day break in the weather around the Chicago area, reserved a hotel room in Evanston, IL, packed up the truck and headed out for the Windy City. First stop was the Guaranteed Rate Field, Home of the Chicago White Sox, formally known as the historical Comisky Park. Not remembering that there was a time change between Indiana and Chicago actually worked to our benefit and put us at the South Side of Chicago an hour early, just as the gates and box office opened. The weather was still extremely chilly, and I was concerned about Kimber staying in the truck. Looked like she was going to see her second MLB park today. Hope it's warmer inside.

Guaranteed Rate Field, Chicago, IL

I was a little concerned about our safety at this park too, especially leaving Kimber in the truck during the game. Soon as we hit the city limits, the song, "Bad Bad Leroy Brown" kept playing in my head. "The South Side of Chicago, is the baddest part of town, and if ya go down there, ya better just beware, of a man named Leroy Brown." All that was quickly put to rest when I met a group of guys tailgating next to where I parked the truck. They invited Kimber and me to join them for brats and beers before the game. Turned out they were a group of CPDs finest, and explained to me the layout of Chicago. They said that the far South Side is rough, but the majority were mainly just working-class folks, blue-collar people, and not to believe the hype of the news media. I'd have to agree at this point. From the parking attendants and employees at the park, to the group of off duty police officers and others tailgating in the parking lot nearby, I was taken aback by the generosity and kindness. Amazing people. The group of CPD guys even had an extra ticket and wanted me and Kimber to join them. They had much better tickets than my regular "get in" ticket, and they weren't going to accept anything but hell yes for an answer. With the beer flowing and the weather warming up nicely, a great time was had by all. Kimber settled in nicely under my chair, after being passed around by the fellas for pictures. The dog has a nationwide fan club to be jealous of. Then a 3-run homer was hit to win the game, followed by a volley of fireworks, bringing the crowd to their feet. So much for Kimber settling in. She was in my lap for the rest of the game, which wasn't bad since it started to cool down with the cloud cover. One great story my local friends told me about old Comisky; some seven decades ago, Yankees immortal Babe Ruth used to sneak across the street from Comisky Park to the late, great McCuddy`s Tavern to chow down on a few hot dogs and beers, between innings of Sox v.

271

Yankees games. The Babe said they had the best dogs in town. How cool is that? Gotta love baseball history!

After exchanging information and saying goodbye to my new South Side Chicago friends, we headed north into the heart of Chicago, right at rush hour. My second biggest worry was driving in a huge and very dense city such as Chicago. West coast cities like L.A. and Phoenix seemed to be more spread out with fewer tall buildings to hinder your navigation. I have driven in San Francisco plenty of times, this was pretty much the same, minus the hills, and a lot bigger. But this was rush hour in Chicago. I was not just a little concerned, I was petrified with a full-size 4x4. Once we were on the freeway and heading toward the city, and not away to the suburbs, traffic was actually easy to navigate. We took in the sights of the famous Lake Shore Drive, driving between the city face and Lake Michigan. We passed Soldier Field, Navy Pier, and more public parks than S.F. ever had. Once we turned onto the surface streets, the full-size truck was a little cramped, but if a fire truck could do it, so could we. Traffic wasn't a problem at all. We found our hotel room and got settled before I went on the hunt for a true Chicago-style, deep-dish pizza.

After asking friends and putting the question of where to find the best pizza in Chicago to my Facebook page, the overwhelming answer was Lou Malnati's. (Except from the CPD crew, but they knew I wouldn't be venturing deep into the South Side for their favorite ma and pa pizza joint, next time my friends.) Incredibly enough, I chose a motel that just happened to be exactly one mile down the road from the original Lou Malnati's store in Lincolnwood. After getting Kimber situated with food and water, I headed out for a brisk walk to the restaurant.

As consensus would have it, the pizza was incredible, and for a surprisingly reasonable price. Picture a medium pizza with a single giant sausage patty that covers the entire pie, along with plenty of cheese and a crisp butter crust they are famous for. I chose to add pepperoni and a salad to the feast. The great part about finding the original store was the incredible sports memorabilia from local teams adorning the walls. The bar had a baseball theme going, complete with pictures of many Cubs greats and the owner, a glass case holding signature bats, and even a glove and pair of cleats from the early 1900s. The main dining room had football memorabilia, where apparently Mike Ditka was a regular guest. There were even some hockey memorabilia here and there situated around the restaurant. What a great bonus! Once again, this trip just takes on its own path. Amazing!

Wrigley Field, Chicago, IL

April 12th, 20108. Just before I left for Chicago, my USMC buddy Jeff from Miami asked when I was planning to see Wrigley Field. Turns out his brother lives here in town, and knew a group of former Marines who are Cubbie fanatics, putting me in touch with a close family friend of the group. Within minutes I had a text from Mike, telling me when and where to be for a meet and greet before the game. Confirming our meeting place at a popular Cub's bar directly across the street from the centerfield bleacher entry gates called Murphy's Bleachers, I called for an Uber and said goodbye to a less than pleased Kimber. Knowing she's safe and sound in the hotel room was well worth the price. Wrigleyville, here I come!

When I arrived at the bar, Mike and his friend Kyle already had a table, beers in hand. Welcome to Wrigleyville. The streets were already blocked off and full of people, the bar was already pretty busy for an early start to a day game. The memorabilia on the walls would make any baseball fan drool. Pictures of Cubs players, autographed everything from jackets to baseballs, and even an exact miniature replica of Wrigley Field itself. It was amazing to see pictures of the iconic bleacher entrance in black and white photos from the past, and then step outside and see the same entrance just across the street, completely unchanged. I love that, history intact.

Closer to game time I had to go to will call to get the ticket I had purchased by phone, while Mike and Kyle had bleacher tickets. Mike checked to see what the bleacher tickets would cost, and as luck would have it, they tripled in price as game time approached. No big deal, I like walking around and taking pictures by myself. We decided to meet up after the game for more bar tours and beers around Wrigleyville.

Walking around the outside of this iconic and historical park was incredible. The front side of the stadium had a large grassy area, surrounded by restaurants and bars, with a huge tv screen showing pregame activity inside. Families were enjoying the first sunny and warm day pretty much all week. The streets were packed with pedestrians, the Cubbies mascot posing for pictures with kids, frisbees flying; it was truly an unexpected sight for a weekday day game. I couldn't wait to get inside and experience this iconic piece of baseball history firsthand.

After walking the concourse, and then around the lower deck, taking all the pictures I could possibly want, I found my way to the nosebleed section. Opening day this ticket was $85, three days later, 10 bucks. I slipped my way down to a seat directly behind home plate, right on the rail for some great shots of the field from above. About that time I received a text from Mike. It was a picture of a bleacher ticket and a message saying to meet him at the left field entrance. I thought he had bought me a ticket, but actually Mike is such a regular here that he knew the ushers and beer stand personnel by name. He handed me the ticket and told me to have her scan me in. There were ushers at both bleacher entrances scanning tickets in and out. I don't know what he did, but I wasn't going to ask any questions. Next thing I know, I'm sitting with Mike and Kyle in the famed Wrigley Field Bleachers! This is where the true definition of a Cubs baseball fan was born. Watching the video of the late great Harry Caray singing "Take me out to the ball game" on the Jumbotron, while the entire park stood and sang along, gave me chills and tears all at once. Truly an incredible sight! What a great experience, thanks to Mike and Kyle. Semper Fi, my brothers!

After the game we started walking, looking for a place to eat and have some more beers, of course. Just as the bars emptied into the ballpark bleachers at game time, the ballpark empties back into the bars for postgame libations. We found an Italian Beef joint just down the road, another staple of the Chicago food scene. From there, we all piled into an Uber and headed downtown. My tour guides took me on quite a hike and tour of the Riverwalk area, pointing out landmarks, iconic Chicago buildings, and of course some great hideaway bars along the way. I truly couldn't have asked for a better taste of what Chicago had to offer. Absolutely amazing! Chi-Town has my heart, and I will definitely be back to Wrigley and Guaranteed Rate very soon! With that I can proudly announce that Wrigley and Guaranteed Rate fields, MLB parks #16 and #17... COMPLETE!

While in Chicago it was highly recommended that I check out Starved Rock State Park, best hiking in Illinois I was told. Enough said, I'm on it. We headed out of town on the I55 with an amazing view of the Chicago cityscape as a farewell. Just outside of town I remembered my vow to avoid interstates, so after a quick fuel stop I jumped off the I55 and onto Hwy 52, then to Hwy 71 toward Norway, IL. Along the side of the highway I came across a small memorial, complete with a sign framed in wooden dragons from the head of a Viking ship and a few headstones with plaques. Of course, I made an immediate U-turn and then saw the road sign, "Norwegian Settlers

State Memorial." Unbelievably enough, there were several graves with headstones from several Norwegian families, including one with Erickson inscribed on it. My half Norwegian, half Swedish, paternal grandmother's maiden name was Erickson. Even though her name came from the Swedish side, it was still an incredible coincidence that I just happened to take this small rural highway, found a town named Norway, and then found a headstone with Erickson on it. I was floored. I was literally in the middle of nowhere, back on my path I see.

Unfortunately, the crazy spring weather this year was not cooperating. Forecast said heavy rain today or tonight, the sky definitely confirmed it. Between weather and my incredibly brutal hangover courtesy of Wrigleyville, I chose to save Starved Rock for next time. Even though hiking was out of the picture, we did come across a small town named Ottawa, IL. First thing I noticed was the incredible murals around town. When I got closer, I recognized it was of Abe Lincoln giving a speech. Then I noticed a store on my right that had another mural of Union Calvary soldiers adorned in American flags. That was enough for me. We found a parking spot, put Kimber on the leash and headed out to explore. Turns out Ottawa was the site of the very first Lincoln/Douglas presidential debate on August 21st, 1858. Another amazing find, I was definitely on my path.

I stopped for some lunch at a local brewery, hoping to get a quick break when one of my Marine buddies from Wrigley called and said he knew the second in charge at Gruntstyle T-shirts, and he'd like to talk to you about what you're doing. Whoa what?! Ya, I had mentioned to him at the game how cool it would be to get a sponsor; I had no idea he'd do this! My mind filled with all kinds of grandiose ideas, picturing Baseballs and Battlefields t-shirts and promo codes, all to be dashed by the CFO of Gruntstyle who had more realistic ideas. Either way, it was still an honor to be addressed as "Devil" by the former Marine, CFO of Gruntstyle T-shirts, and be able to tell him my story. Not going to lie, I was a little bummed, but it was this moment that set a light bulb off in my skull. Don't take a dime from anybody in way of sponsorship. The VA is your sponsor. Show veterans there's life outside the VA, and they too can do this on the "VA dime." It was then that my adventure took on a whole new meaning.

With the skies getting darker every mile we drove, I decided to jump back on to I80 west and get to Rock Island where I read there was a National Cemetery that used to be a Confederate POW camp during the Civil War. Also not having a truck camper and just the bug-out set-up, kept me active until bedtime, a big change from having my own "house" to relax in. When we arrived at Rock Island, I realized that this was an active duty military base; thankfully, the trip wasn't wasted due to my military ID and base access. Even though this wasn't a battlefield, it was an interesting find. Not only is it an active base, but it has a National Cemetery. The only remnants of the POW camp was a separate Confederate Cemetery that had 2,000 Confederate graves. Turns out in 1863 just after the Union won the battle of Gettysburg, Union and Confederate forces stopped exchanging prisoners and some 10,080 Confederate POWs were held here, with no hospital. Smallpox broke out and 993 men died in the first 3 months. The plaque on the memorial reads, "In memory of the Confederate prisoners who died at Rock Island prison camp. May they never be forgotten. Let no man asperse the memory of our sacred dead. They were men who died for a cause they believed worth fighting for and made the ultimate sacrifice." As it should be! I think that only veterans truly understand that statement. Take away politics, they are still men who fought for their country and their way of life, just as the thousands of other veterans in our country's wars since then. This is why their memory too shall not be forgotten.

We stopped in the city of Rock Island, thinking to call it a night. With daylight savings time here, there was still enough daylight after I ate to make it down to Springfield, IL, where I wanted to tour Abraham Lincoln's home. Clouds were darkening, wind was picking up, but no rain yet. I fired up the truck and headed south. From Rock Island, we took the I74 south through Galesburg on to Peoria where I headed further south on the 155 to Springfield. Now the rain made its first appearance. I found a Walmart right off the interstate and hunkered down for the storm. It was a pretty sleepless night as thunder cracked, rain poured, and Kimber and I tried to contort into some reasonable sleeping position on the one man, and now add one dog, cot.

A few hours later, and only a few hours of sleep, I was happy to see the sun come up while heading to the Anytime Fitness across the street for a shower. The Lincoln Home tour didn't start for another couple hours, so I went to Circle K for a coffee and looked for a Denny's. All you could eat pancakes was on top of my to-do list, unfortunately no Denny's in Springfield. The convenience store clerk was a mountain of a man, in his 60s I'm assuming, so while paying for my coffee, I asked, "You look like a man that can point me to a good breakfast." He smiled and replied, "Best ma and pa breakfast is just down the street." I knew he would steer me right. Shortly, I was feasting on the breakfast version of a dish that is the local pride, called a "Horseshoe." Invented here in Springfield, the original Horseshoe is two pieces of white bread, with two hamburger patties on top, covered with French fries and cheese sauce or gravy. The bread was supposed to represent the horse's foot, the meat part was the shoe, and the fries were the nails. They didn't offer an explanation for the gravy or cheese sauce, and I wasn't about to ask. The breakfast version was biscuits with sausage patties, eggs, country fries and gravy. Now we're talking! Filling up enough that I surely wouldn't need lunch today, I had plenty left over in case I did. Thank you, Circle K giant, good call.

It was pretty ironic that last year I visited the Confederate President Jefferson Davis' home Beauvoir in Mississippi, prior to any of my Southern state battlefields, and now I was starting this year with Lincoln's home. Again, I was on my path. The Lincoln Home was interesting, as a young self-taught lawyer, the Lincolns were considered very wealthy in their time. Much like the Davis Home, the house was larger than most and decorated with full-length curtains, extremely loud colored carpet instead of a bare wood floor, and fine furniture from Europe. Old Abe came a long way from the one-room log cabin with dirt floor that we visited last year in Kentucky. Although the story and history were impressive, it wasn't a battlefield. After the tour, I did notice that the Lincoln Tomb was nearby so headed in that direction to check it out.

One thing to note, within the museum was another information placard that read, "Lincoln issued the Emancipation Proclamation as a military measure, at the same time that he understood its awesome symbolic value." I had to do a double take of what state I was in. This was a National Park Service exhibit, in Lincoln's own home… in Illinois! I guess that will put the naysayers to rest about the real intentions of the Emancipation Proclamation. Ya, good luck with that.

When I pulled into the Springfield Cemetery there was some type of re-enactment taking place at the foot of this massive memorial. Everyone was dressed in mid-1800's attire, complete with Union Army color guard, Union Army band, civilian men, women and children all dressed in period correct costumes. I had just happened upon Lincoln's Tomb at the exact time and remembrance ceremony of his death. I was once again amazed at another unplanned coincidence! While speaking to one of the period actors, he explained to me that they are all relatives of those who actually attended Lincoln's internment on April 16th, 1865, and that every year since then they gather to lay a wreath in honor of the slain President. This is a sight that everyone needs to see once in their lifetime.

After some more exploring of the cemetery grounds, I decided my Illinois portion of this incredible adventure was complete. The forecast called for snow in the area, and another night on the cot wasn't sounding too appealing, so we turned the truck toward the Indiana border and headed back to Camp Atterbury. Illinois, state #31... COMPLETE!

Indiana

April 14th, 2018. After a much needed rest from an amazing four-day Illinois adventure, it was time to explore our home base state of Indiana. Without a MLB park or any obvious National Battlefields in the state, it took some digging to find anything relevant to my book. Once I did my research, I was excited to learn that there were actually three battlefields that would pertain to not only the War of 1812, but also my first Revolutionary War battle of this leg of the trip, and a famous Civil War Confederate raid! So I packed up the truck for another 3-day bug-out and hit the road. Unfortunately, the Tippecanoe Battlefield was closed, so I turned south toward Vincennes, IN and the Battle of Ft. Sackville.

The weather wasn't exactly helping out with our Indiana adventure, but with time running out on the month long stay at Camp Atterbury, we needed to keep moving. We were burning days, not just daylight. So come rain or shine, Kimber and I hit the road. It was extremely cold, but the little bit of snow that welcomed us back to Indiana had stopped and didn't stick, which was good news. I had the Buddy propane heater, so wasn't too concerned. It kept us extremely warm in Springfield during the rainstorm, so confidence was high, which was good since later that evening, I realized I forgot the blankets. There's always something.

Spring was trying hard to break through the extended winter. The pastures were blooming with some type of purple, flowering land cover. Dogwood trees, that may have been ornamental wild Cherry trees, were in full white bloom. Lush green grass divided the four-lane highway, but Oaks and other trees were still barren of any color. Mud was the big issue and the reason why my mountain bike was starting to acquire spider webs and rust once again. You had to be careful on these narrow farm roads to not get into the shoulder where your tire would sink into mud, while at the same time just barely squeezing by oncoming farm equipment and school buses. The Indiana road system is in serious lack of attention.

While I'm on the topic of roads, I've learned something that will more than likely be a prominent issue with the rest of my northeastern trip. Potholes. Not just small, sporadic potholes,

I'm talking holes so deep you can see the rebar holding the concrete together, and large enough for a small child to swim in. Ok, I may be exaggerating just a bit, but not much. These things will tear apart a vehicle, and run unsuspecting, non-snow state drivers off the road. It has to do with the salt applied to the roads to melt the ice, then add a continuous flow of big rigs, cars with snow tires, and very little money put towards repairs. It's pretty bad, to the point of dangerous. That coupled with all the major interstates in Indiana which seem to run north to south, pretty much all roads leading to Indianapolis in route to Chicago, with only little more than farm roads running east to west. Therefore, giving a detailed route of my travels is pretty time consuming, so I will just list cities and towns going forward.

The town of Vincennes, IN was the first stop on our trip, a small college town on the western border of the state, with an incredible amount of history. I was surprised to find not only the location of a Revolutionary War battle in the state of Indiana, but also an incredible monument to the American Revolutionary, George Rodgers Clark. The George Rodgers Clark National Park was the home of the largest battlefield monument in the nation, falling just a few feet shorter than the Lincoln monument in D.C. Also on site was an incredible Catholic Church with a small graveyard that held the remains of several American and French Patriots from 1750 to the mid-1800s. To the rear of the church was the National Parks visitor center, complete with video and museum, all enclosed in what was called Patrick Henry Square. Like I said, lots of history.

I love going to these National monuments on weekdays when it's relatively quiet and few visitors; today was a perfect example. After watching the video of the Battle of Fort Sackville, I was lucky enough to get basically a private tour of the George Rodgers Clark Monument by one of the Park Rangers. It was like what I could only imagine stepping into the Vatican must have felt like. It was enormous, with a prominent bronze statue of Clark in the center of the grand rotunda. A glass ceiling with the Federal Seal in the center was surrounded by giant paintings depicting different scenes from the Battle of Fort Sackville. To my amazement, the paintings were done by Ezra Winter in his studio on linen, and then later hung on the monument walls in 1934. Known for his paintings in the Radio City Music Hall and the Library of Congress, it took Winter 2 1/2 years with 6 assistants to paint and hang these incredible works of art. The entire floor and benches of the monument are carved from what looks like solid marble, with a detailed carving of Patrick Henry giving George Rodgers Clark the commission for the raid on

Kaskaskia, and eventually the Battle of Fort Sackville, mounted above the entrance. The statue of Clark himself sat upon a decorative piece of either marble or polished granite, with a large brass inscription laid into the floor circling the pedestal that read, "If a country is not worth protecting, it is not worth claiming." No truer words spoken today.

Our next stop was Evansville, IN where I had a standing invitation from another fellow veteran following the Facebook page. This time we'd see an old .45 ACP bullet factory from WW2 and a tour of Bosse Field, the third oldest active baseball park in the nation. Enter my buddy Scott, who has been following my travels since 2016. Scott, who served in Afghanistan with the Army, and friend Adam, who I call the town historian, met me at what is now a distribution center for a sporting goods company. They had arranged a walk-through of the older part of the building that was once a Chrysler automobile plant turned Sherman tank and .45 ACP round manufacturer for the war. The floor and the ceiling were all that were left intact from those days, but it told an interesting story. The floor looked like it was laid with brick, but if you looked closely you could see that the brick was actually the end of a 4x6 stud, with the circular core in every 3-foot post pounded vertically into the bedrock of the Ohio River coastline below. I was amazed. Every single post was the heart of the tree, which obviously gave it the most strength. I guess if you're making tanks, concrete just would not do.

The ceiling above still had the steel girders that ran the hoists and cables used to lift such heavy equipment. The roof had windows that were mechanically driven to open for fresh air ventilation. It was entertaining to look up old pictures of the plant and compare them to the photos that I had taken of the warehouse today, all these features readily recognizable. It was especially interesting to see rounds being made on such a huge scale, due to my hobby of reloading my own .45 rounds at home. Maybe this helps explain to the reader why my dog's name is Kimber, after my favorite 1911 style .45 ACP pistol, of course. I've always got a Kimber by my side! Pictures of brass shells back then had the letters E P stamped into the ring denoting the Evansville Plant, and I even found a picture of FDR touring the Chrysler plant back in the day. I absolutely love seeing modern day reach back and touch recognizable history.

From there my two tour guides took me to Bosse Field, home of the Evansville Otters. Built in 1915, and named after Evansville Mayor Benjamin Bosse, Bosse Field was the first municipally owned ballpark, and generally thought of as the third oldest of the still active ballparks, right behind Fenway and Wrigley. Although it is currently the home to a minor league team, tonight it was hosting a local high school game. What an incredible experience for these youngsters to be playing on the same field as the great Don Mattingly, Warren Spahn, and Bob Uecker, just to name a few. Not to mention, this is one of the many parks that the Tom Hanks movie, *A League of Their Own,* was filmed, portraying the Racine Bells home field. Adam knew one of the groundskeepers of the park and was able to give me a look inside some of the training rooms and groundskeeper areas. We then walked around the entire ballpark where Adam clued me in on some of the more historical areas of the park, such as the "negro" section from the days of segregation, to the old block building about 100 ft behind the centerfield fence that Don Mattingly hit with a homer while still in high school. Did I mention that the centerfield fence had a 400ft marker?! Unbelievable!

From Bosse Field, my friends wanted to take me out to dinner and a couple beers; but not without a stop by the riverbank to see an old WW2 LST ship, docked a couple miles up the bank from us. Turns out this city also made ships for the war along with P47 fighter planes. The Ohio River was used as a conveyor belt of sorts at the different levels of the ships' build.

From there, we went to a popular German restaurant downtown that used to be the local hardware store. It was interesting to learn that this town was populated predominantly by German immigrants, who in turn built some of the major tools used to defeat their former countrymen and homeland during WW2. Proof again that we are ALL Americans. A special thank you to Scott and Adam for an amazing private tour of your city's rich American history. Until next time my brothers, never goodbye. Kimber and I retired for the night at the local Anytime Fitness parking lot, preparing for the next day's adventure.

While researching the state's battle history, I came across a series of skirmishes known as Morgan's Raid. In July of 1863, CSA General John Hunt Morgan ferried 2,000 men across the Ohio River from Brandenburg, KY to just outside the town of Mauckport, IN, while under fire. With the intention of drawing Union troops away from Gettysburg and Vicksburg, Morgan began the furthest northern intrusion by the Confederacy during the Civil War. Within just 26 hours of Morgan's crossing, US General Hobson crosses the Ohio with 4,000 Union troops in hot pursuit. The race was on. With that being said, we were off to Mauckport, IN, bright and early on an overcast and rainy day.

Just before the bridge crossing over the Ohio River, we found a familiar cluster of signs that appeared to be information placards. The large signs were labeled "John Hunt Morgan Heritage

281

Trail" with a large numeral one in the upper left-hand corner. The title read, "Six Days of Terror" and showed 24 different locations on a map of Indiana. Beneath the map, pictures of commanding officers, and information of the site, was directions to the next location. "Next sign: SR11 and Morgan's Landing Road." How cool is that!? Like a historical scavenger hunt, we were off to the next stop.

No need to set the GPS to back roads for this portion of the trip, as I couldn't have asked for a better "back-country" tour. Morgan's Trail took us through the SE Indiana countryside, finding state information placards literally at the gate of a family ranch house, across rivers that I had to put the Rig in 4WD for, and several small towns where the most significant incidents of the raid occurred. From the southern border of Kentucky, to the eastern side of Indiana, we followed little black and white signs, shaped as arrows, that read, "Morgan Tour."

The first portion of the raid took us past a ranch where the Confederacy stopped to bed down for the night. The locals had been warned about Morgan's arrival, fleeing in such haste that they left hot food on the table, readily consumed by the hungry troops. When the family refused Confederate money as payment, they burned the farm, leaving only the mill. Whoa, what? They tried to pay? From here, the Confederates marched on to Corydon where the first major battle of the raid occurred. The rest of the stops described different places where Morgan and his men created chaos, such as cutting phone lines in the town of Palmyra, the absolute devastation of the town of Salem, and the plundering of Canton. Yet what took me by surprise was the hospitality and respect shown by both the raiders and the locals, as if it wasn't personal, but had to happen. One story summed it up perfectly.

With early notification that Morgan and his crew were coming, one farm owner was ready. Morgan himself approached a farm that he intended on commandeering for the night, while inside, a mother quietly loaded a revolver. She opened the door, invited him in, and fed the Confederate officer. He then retired for the evening. In the morning, she fed him again, gave him her warmest quilts and fresh bread, while he thanked her and bid farewell. Why would she have done that; why didn't she kill him and end this? Her answer, "Because my son is fighting somewhere in the South, and I hope that a southern mother would show my boy the same kindness." That makes my eyes leak just writing it. We are all Americans, remember?

It took us the rest of the morning and all afternoon to find all 24 stops, before the raid crossed into Ohio just outside Cincinnati; setting us up perfectly to resume the raid and catch our next ball game to kick off the Ohio visit. It was now about 1545, the clouds once again beginning to roll in, and I had a decision to make. Either find a Walmart here and call it a day, or head back to the comfort of my bed, that was a whopping two-hour drive away. Even though I was exhausted from driving, my back chose the later, instead of another night on the cot. Ya, that cot stuff all looked good on paper, my back begs to differ. Anyway, off we went back toward our home base of Camp Atterbury, hoping to navigate the crazy farm roads before it got too dark.

Kimber was a little wound up being in the truck all day, while I was feeling the exact opposite as usual; so a coffee and ball stop was in order. I found a truck stop with a nice, long, green grassy area, perfect to launch a couple for Kimber, while I got some caffeine in my brain. Just as soon as I threw the bright red ball, that bounced once near a row of hedges, a bright red Cardinal swooped down at the ball as if it was another male in his territory. The Cardinal then landed in the tree just above my truck, watching Kimber as she retrieved her prey. With the second throw, the angry male must've realized he was duped, flying back into the thick brush. With a smile and nod toward the sky, we turned the Rig west, toward my bed. Yup, that was a good day, Grampa, I agree.

Back at the camper, we were stuck again for another couple days due to snow and rain. It was now the 21st of April, the Cincinnati Reds were back in town starting on Thursday the 26th, giving me only 4 or 5 days to see all of Ohio, and catch the Cleveland Indians game too, before our month at Camp Atterbury was up. Here's the crazy part, the Cleveland Indians just happened to be in town that weekend also, giving me a chance to see them on either Saturday or Sunday. The pressure was definitely on, the timing was going to be close, and the weather wasn't helping whatsoever. Perfect, wouldn't have it any other way. In the meantime, I still had to go north to see the Tippacanoe Battlefield. Not a National Battlefield, but still a notable one. Plus, if Kimber didn't get out of the trailer for at least a truck ride, we would both go insane.

"Tippacanoe and Tyler too" was President Harrison's famous campaign slogan that I remembered from some distant history class. I guess that's what made me curious to check out this county level park and museum. Turns out that the future president, General Harrison, who was also governor of the area, led a small army of 1,000 men to destroy Tecumseh's "Prophet Town" while he was away recruiting natives to join his Indian Confederacy. Upon entering the village, Harrison agreed to withhold hostilities until a meeting with Tecumseh the following day. That night, Harrison's camp was raided while they slept. Fortunately the "prophet" was known for not keeping his word and his aggression toward white settlers, so his men were somewhat prepared. Harrison repelled the attack and destroyed the town, while Tecumseh joined forces with the British. It was this battle that kicked off the War of 1812 and secured Harrison's future presidency.

The very first paragraph of a typed explanation describing what occurred here, that I found inside a newly erected bulletin board, read as follows. "These grounds surrounded by the stately iron fence, was the site of a deadly battle on a cold, rainy morning the seventh day of November in 1811. It was on this site that the American Indian lost his grip on the fertile midwestern lands he had roamed for thousands of years." This was the first thing that you would read while walking toward the building. So if you didn't go inside to learn the truth, and only read this, your view would be completely different from someone who actually went inside and read the information placards. Lost his grip on fertile grounds? Well then, don't attack U.S. troops that agree to peace talks, and don't side with the English, after the Americans kick your ass for doing it. Here's the best part, when I drove down the road to see the "Prophet Town" exhibit, an info placard said that English weapons were found, proving that Tecumseh was being supplied by England, thus kicking off the War of 1812. Once again, the bleeding heart, poor Native narrative crushed by actual history. Brutal but true.

Rain once again was the word of the day as we made our way back to the camper. Would it ever let up? I was desperately hoping the Cincinnati game wouldn't be rained out, or I would have to come up with a whole new plan for Ohio. Dragging this trailer was proving to be very, very expensive; and sitting around burning our month's worth of rent wasn't helping. Please, Jesus, please, just let up on the rain for a few days is all I ask. With that being said, save a few standby and travel days, Indiana, state #31... COMPLETE!

Ohio

April 26th, 2018. By the grace of God we actually had a break in the rain, just in time for the ball game in Cincinnati. I thought it would never let up, the campsite was starting to look more like a boat launch, with the common area under a foot of water. I had packed up the cooler with cold cuts, loaded all the blankets on the cot, hoping to save my back this time, and left just before dawn to catch the one weekday ball game Cincinnati had at home this week. From there, the plan was to pick up Morgan's Trail where we had left off and follow it all the way up to Cleveland for an Indians game on Sunday. That gave us two days to wander the countryside and explore Ohio. Ambitious for sure; I just hope my lower back is up for the challenge.

First stop was Cincinnati to pick up a ticket and find some parking. We got to the park around 1000 for a 1235 game. I love these "Businessman Special" day games. It's the best way to see a game, with the least amount of crowd. Parking typically isn't too bad, there's usually a deal to be had on tickets, and there's very few kids because the folks are at work. It's just one of the many perks of being "retired."

Great American Ball Park, Cincinnati, OH

April 26th, 2018. Parking at Great American Ball Park, that's the actual name of the park, was easy enough, with a huge underground garage that seemed to cover an entire city block. Parking was cheap enough, and the stairway from the garage emerged right in the center of the "bar district," with all the businesses just opening their sliding doors and turning on their giant TVs. From there, it was literally just a half block to the ticket office and the stadium. I felt confident leaving Kimber in the cab of the truck, secure with blanket and water. It was a little noisy, but cool enough not to worry about her.

When I found my way to the ticket booth window, I asked if they had any military or veteran ticket deals. The kid behind the counter said, "yup" and turned to the keyboard, fingers typing faster than I could ever attempt. Without asking me where or saying how much, he tore a ticket off the printer and handed it to me. "There ya go." I was shocked by the lack of questions, until I looked at the ticket. Row 0, seat 3, lower box. I about dropped the ticket. I just said thanks as I stared at the front row, box seat numbers. What!? I've never sat this close to behind home plate! This was amazing! Turns out that most weekday day games have season ticket holders who give up their tickets for veterans or military when they can't make the game. Whoa, that's cool! I've got to pay attention to that moving forward. That's huge!

There were still a couple hours to kill before first pitch, so I checked out the Reds Museum, found just across the courtyard from the ticket booth. Downstairs was the gift shop, but for ten bucks, you could walk the incredible two floors full of Reds history. I had no idea the Cincinnati Red Legs were the very first team to enter MLB. The baseball history enshrined in this museum was the most amazing display yet. Regardless of who your team is, this place is well worth the price of admission. And if you're a Pete Rose fan, and what real baseball fan isn't, this place should be ordained a holy place. Everything Rose was found here. The most impressive was the view above the rose garden that was once part of the original field, where one white rose bush in a field of red, marks where his 4,192nd hit landed, breaking Ty Cobb's all-time major league record. If they won't let Pete in the Hall of Fame, he definitely has his Hall in Cincinnati. They love their Charlie Hustle here.

Inside the park, I was astounded at how clean the place was. The polished concrete floors made me shudder, thinking of the wheel-buffed hallways of the USMC. It was that clean! The park overlooked the Ohio River, with a giant replica steamboat as its centerpiece. The stacks would light up and blow a loud horn for every home run. Thankfully, Kimber was far out of earshot, as the game was a slug-fest. They had a huge bleacher area under the massive Jumbotron, with the Cincinnati skyline behind home plate this time, making for some great shots of the park from centerfield.

Every time I go to a ball game now, I ask the 700 or so followers I have on the Facebook page about what's the best food, or what I need to see or try. This has turned out to be the very best part of the trip. Now I have locals telling me where to eat! Some even ask when I'll be in their city, and would like to meet up for a game. Now how cool is that! Anyway, the consensus this time was a "Skyline Chili" dog and craft beer from one of the local breweries; it was the Skyline Chili that was the target. A typical bun with a beef dog, covered in chili, and then packed with shredded cheddar cheese. Craft beer with just a little hops was the perfect closer. Good call! Great American Ball Park, MLB park #18... COMPLETE!

By the fifth inning, the score was like 8 to 2, I had my taste of Cincinnati, and now it was time to get out of the city. This was actually the perfect formula for me. Just enough time in the city to see what I need to, before the crowds and anxiety start to get the best of me. Then back to Kimber and the countryside as we search out more battlefields. Then when the somberness of war becomes too much, back to the fun and excitement of the ball game. It was the perfect cycle. Which made me think. Was this by design the entire time? Look back in history, even as war waged, Americans turned to sports and Hollywood for relief. It's like war and sports go hand in hand. This is why I call Baseballs and Battlefields a story of America's two favorite pastimes, Baseball... and war. Ya, I keep repeating that, also by design.

Not wasting anytime, knowing that we would be pressed to make all the markers by first pitch in Cleveland, only two and half days away, we got right to work. Just outside of Cincinnati, back toward the Indiana border, we found the last information signs of the Indiana side of the raid, where we had left off the previous week. From there, it was just across the bridge (state line), and down the street into the town of Harrison, where we found our first "Morgan's Ohio Raid" signs. These signs were noticeably newer and better kept, but laid out the exact same way as the last signs, with directions in the bottom corner and each numbered on the top. Placard #1 starts out interestingly describing the entry of Morgan into Ohio. 10,000 Union soldiers laying in wait, and a decoy move to attack Cincinnati, resulting in the "longest non-stop march of a calvary division in US History." The sign had a map showing the 56 stops on the tour, from Harrison to East Liverpool. FIFTY-SIX! Don't threaten me with good time. If Morgan could do it, so could Kimber. Gauntlet thrown, we're off!

From the raids of Harrison, past the Confederate rendezvous point at Bevis, to a train station in Glendale, we followed the little black and white Morgan's Raid signs through the Ohio countryside. Some were a challenge to find, hidden in a downtown construction zone, in the center of a turn-about circle, and some in the drainage ditch on the side of a two-lane highway. You took your life into your own hands in some traffic congested areas, but what a great time was had, chasing down American history.

We passed through several more small towns along the way, before it was finally getting too dark to see the road signs and placards from the truck. In July of 1863, the town of Williamsburg was the first campsite in Ohio that Morgan and his 2,000 cavalrymen bed down for the night. His troops were so tired that they were falling off their horses asleep; even some horses were seen staggering as if drunk from weariness. Kimber was close, but not that bad, as we pulled into the closest Walmart. Williamsburg, Ohio would be our first bivouac spot also. Just think that this was sign number eleven, and we're in a vehicle reading about what these guys did on horseback. Good, bad, or indifferent, that's quite a task for horse and man. Wow. We slept like a rock that night, with a huge day ahead of us in the morning.

The next morning we were back at it before dawn. Not quite so bright-eyed, and definitely not so bushy-tailed, we set out for coffee, a bathroom, and about a 20 mile drive to Georgetown, our first stop. Turns out that Georgetown, Ohio is US General and former President Ulysses S. Grant's boyhood home. Morgan had made a quick stop here looking for food. The information placards downtown once again described a sight that you wouldn't expect in time of war. The sign read a letter from a local town's lady to General Grant just after Morgan's departure, describing what had occurred and what the damage was. It read, "Some raiders went to each house asking for food. They were all very polite and bowing and lifting their hats when leaving. The Colonel (Morgan) asked Mrs. John Stuart for a piece of bread and butter with a glass of buttermilk, but was interrupted by an orderly half finished. The bugle sounded and in less than five minutes they mounted and left town." Once again, the civility and respect of the time toward fellow Americans was astonishing, yet heartwarming in a way. The people, the American people, saw this not as a personal attack against each other, but more of a business task to be completed. A solemn one at that, yet still the calm indifference and lack of rage toward the person is what intrigued me. If it was a foreign invader and not a fellow American, would the public have been so cordial to "enemy" soldiers? Definitely an interesting thought. Some would see this as false, when you hear about the hate between soldiers; but even in battle, the respect between warriors, and the reverence for those slain, is unheard of in modern warfare.

While in Georgetown, I decided to search out the actual Grant home, hoping for a museum and a walk through. As I approached the home, there were a couple cars in the driveway unloading white tents, chairs, and tables. The two older men doing the work were dressed as Union soldiers, setting up for some type of school presentation. Unbelievably enough, I happened upon President Grant's boyhood home… on his birthday. Are you kidding me!? Once again, the timing was uncanny.

It was great speaking to the guys setting up for the junior high school exhibition. Several more period actors showed up, one being General Grant himself. Unfortunately, I forget the guy's name, but he works for the National Parks Service, has a PhD in US War History and travels the country portraying General Grant. After telling him about my travels, he was super interested and took me around the house and grounds on a private tour, telling me stories about Grant. It was absolutely surreal, like having General Grant, in uniform, show you his home. The guy was a dead ringer for the General and an absolute wealth of knowledge. We had an interesting conversation about the political atmosphere of the country in the years leading up to the Civil War. He made some startling similarities to where we are today as a nation. Basically saying, the fringes on both sides of the political spectrum make 90% of the "noise," while the rest of the country is caught somewhere in the middle. An interesting thought in the era of

President Trump, and an ominous insight into the future of our country in modern times. Super freaking cool!

The cannon crew was kind enough to let me know that they were about to test fire the cannon, just in case Kimber wasn't a fan of the boom. Gratefully, I said thank you, and bid our farewell to the General and Kimber's new artillery crew brethren, hustling our way back to the truck. Just as I was hoisting my princess puppy into her backseat throne, I heard a bird whistle from above. Yup, a huge red Cardinal sat on a blooming Cherry or Dogwood tree branch, literally right above the truck. Ya, that was pretty special, Grampa, pretty special indeed.

The rest of that morning we chased the little black and white signs through the now eastern side of the beautiful Ohio countryside, basically following the Ohio River through what I was surprised to find was actually the Ohio Appalachians. When I think Appalachia, southern states come to mind: WV, TN, GA, not Ohio. Rolling hills started to appear, much like those from last year's descent into Kentucky from the West Virginia Mountains. Something else I hadn't realized; we were entering Amish Country. Driving down the dirt roads, we saw huge farms with bright white fencing and massive matching barns. Some were very modern, made of metal, with several women dressed in long skirts, with small white bonnets, tending to the flowers and vegetables for sale. There were kids on these ancient looking scooters and bicycles, boys in pants and suspenders with wide brimmed straw hats, and girls in long dresses and bonnets, waving as they pushed or pedaled by. The dead giveaway that a farm was Amish, was the 25 yard long clothesline that ran up to the peak of the barn from the farm house. Long drawers, white granny panties, and slips flying in the wind like a battleship flag line, proudly professed their lack of electricity.

The countryside was gorgeous with rolling hills, bright green pastures, clear bubbling creeks at every turn. It was beautiful to drive through, but a pain in the backside for finding road signs. At one point, I so completely frustrated that I was about to just use my GPS, move on to the next town, and skip the missing road marker altogether. I whipped off the road, into a small parking lot in front of a market, trying to regain some composure. I was getting tired, it had been a long day already, and I was pretty much done. I threw my hands up and said out loud, "I quit!"; then, I looked up just in time to get tower buzzed by a huge red Cardinal. Just as I looked up, a Cardinal flew past the truck, from the front corner of the truck hood, wings tucked, dropping in flight as he spread his wings and flapped once again, raising his body to the top corner of my windshield, before disappearing in my rearview mirror, flying down the road in the exact opposite direction. Like slow motion, I could see his black mask and bright yellow beak; if it was only for a split second, it seemed like a still photo. I was shocked it flew that close to the truck. I too thought I must be crazy, as I said, "Ok Grampa, if you say so," while turning the truck in the direction the Cardinal flew. I know you're gonna say oh come on, now he's just embellishing. No, my friend, if I'm lying, I'm dying. The damn sign I was looking for was back about a mile, covered in overgrown grass, on the OPPOSITE side of the road. Ya, I couldn't believe it either. On my path indeed.

We continued following Morgan's Raid, up the coast of the Ohio River, deeper and deeper into the Ohio Appalachians. Through several more small towns and numerous backcountry roads, we ended at Old Portland where we found Morgan trying to escape across the river to West Virginia. In what was obviously to be his capture, turned out to be another daring escape by Morgan. Back on the road again, we followed more of Morgan's antics up the coast of the Ohio River, until a massive road construction block had us pretty much stranded in deep Appalachia... with no GPS service.

It looked like a rockslide, maybe a road widening, either way, we weren't getting past it. It was starting to get dark and I needed to find my way back via a different road, just to make it past this construction zone. About a quarter mile back was a house with what looked like a pretty substantial dirt road. I decided I had better ask for directions. There was a family of two small girls, and a couple about my age, in the yard with some dogs. I pulled up, without getting out of the truck and kindly asked if there was a way around the construction zone. The father approached the truck waving, "Yessir, just follow this road down to the T and make a right. Then make your distant left into Johnson's Holler, highway is up a mile." And then the inevitable, "Where ya'll from?" "Arizona, just passing through." He just nodded while backing up to look at the truck. "Ya, you'll make it through the holler." "Great, thank you," I said as his words echoed in my ear. "Make it through the holler"... lovely.

Even more frightening than experiencing the joys of the "holler" was what I saw in the road, about a mile from the couple's house. A group of about eight cats were huddled in the middle of the road, all but one scattering as the truck approached. It was dead. Obviously hit by a car, just outside a small house on the side of the road. Instantly I tried to remember the last car I had seen. None... for hours. Rapidly my mind puts this scenario together. Crazy Ohio Cat Lady comes home to find one of her litter dead from a vehicle. Family down the road says they told a Yankee from AZ in a silver truck to go that way. Ya, I'm pretty much guaranteed to take the rap for this one. I hit the accelerator to make some distance. Just then a set of headlights popped up over the next hill, heading my way. I was about a half mile from the dead cat. I pressed harder on the accelerator. Still no GPS. Sun just falling below the tree line. I blew by the car in a blur, hung a hard right onto the next road, gratefully paved this time. Suddenly, the GPS roared to life, the highway was two miles away. Holler, where's the damn holler he spoke of? Then a quick glimpse of a sign to another side road, showed me where he was talking about. I trusted the GPS, continuing straight and got on the highway with a huge sigh of relief. Dead cat bounce indeed. We crossed into Parkersburg, WV where I had staked out a Buffalo Wild Wings, Anytime Fitness and a Walmart. Day two of Morgan's Ohio Raid complete.

The next morning, we crossed the Ohio River and continued where we left off with marker #31, just outside of Reedsville, Ohio. Through Vinton Station, Creola, and into Nelsonville, we followed the Morgan's Raid road signs until another dead end and traffic change. This one was much more enjoyable, as the blockage was for the town's incredible classic car show. Antique hot rods, flawless classics, and even a few rat-rods, were parked in front of 100 yr old stone storefronts. The picture possibilities here were endless, yet the mission at hand had a strict schedule.

We continued on through so many small towns they had finally become a blur. One interesting aspect of the history here, was seeing this half American Flag/ and half Confederate Battle flag, flying in front of many homes. I mean a single flag was made with half of it being the Stars and Stripes, while the other half was Stars and Bars. Very interesting, obviously depicting the divide, or maybe more so the unification, amongst families along the Ohio. Some small towns flew banners on every streetlight, with photos of soldiers from the area who served. From Revolutionary War veterans, to Afghanistan veterans, their award and service proudly displayed by their hometown. I've never seen so many American flags flying on overpasses and highway fencing. Ohio is truly a patriotic state.

Finally, with miraculous timing right at dusk, we found the final stop and complete surrender of Morgan and his band of raiders. Just outside the town of West Point, Ohio, along a small country road, in front of a storage company was the final placard, #56. Even though this wasn't a National Battlefield, it was the most incredible journey through Indiana and Ohio I could have asked for, and an absolute recommendation to all history enthusiasts. A truly incredible and memorable experience. That night, we parked at the East Liverpool Super Walmart, relaxing and preparing for the game in Cleveland the following morning.

Another one of the social media sights I like to follow is the "Drinkin' Bros Baseball" page on Facebook. It was here that I posted some pics of the parks I've visited and explained my journey. This page was one of many started by a former Army Ranger and has a huge veteran base following. When I had mentioned that I was on my way into Ohio for the Cincinnati and Cleveland games, and asked if any vets would be there, I received a reply from a veteran, telling me that she had season tickets, and a spare one for this Sunday's day game... the exact game I was hoping to catch. Hell ya, I was all in! This was truly beginning to be the best part about this journey, meeting new veterans and hearing their stories. So after some coffee and quick ball throwing session for Kimber, we were off to meet our new friend Kerri, for a Cleveland Indians game.

Unbelievably enough, Kerri even set up parking for me with a reservation on an app called SpotHero. This turned into an invaluable tool moving forward. But, as luck would have it, being aware of one's vehicle height is crucial in older city parking garages. The Rig wasn't going to make it. I was about two inches too high at the camper. It would take three people to stop traffic enough for me to back up into the busy downtown street to get out of there. Plus, Kerri already paid for the spot; I had to make this work. Then it dawned on me. I reached down and released some air from the airbags, dropping the truck just enough to scrape the top of the camper, but still make it in. Thank God for a used Camper and rattle can paint job. I'm pretty sure the parking attendant lady thought I was crazy, especially when I said I had a dog in the cab and asked where she could go pee. By the time I found a spot of grass for Kimber to do her business, and walked back in the garage, the attendant lady was Kimber's new best friend, having me park closer to her kiosk in a reserved spot, promising to keep an eye on the truck. God, I love this dog!

Progressive Field, Cleveland, OH

April 29th, 2019. Progressive Field, Home of the Cleveland Indians, situated in downtown Cleveland, was a newer park by the looks of it. At street level, I approached the right field gate that gave way to an open air pavilion, looking down onto the field. A huge grandstand on the right, and a massive screen over the outfield bleachers, allowed only a glimpse of the Cleveland cityscape to peek through. I met Kerri just outside the park; she had a ticket and a bag of five nice cigars in one hand and held out her other, inviting a handshake. "Welcome to Cleveland," she said as she handed me the cigar bag. How freaking cool is that! Second question was, "Where's your pup?" A question that has become the norm.

Kerri showed me all around the field, from the lower display of bronze plaques, sporting the bust of all the great Indian players, all the way to the top, overlooking the basketball arena next door. Turns out it was the NBA playoffs, and they had a basketball game going on at the same time as the Indians game. Security was definitely increased, as they had an "NBA Experience" going on in the adjoining concrete pavilion between the venues. That's when Kerri started jumping up and down, waving at something. I looked over to see what I hoped were two of Cleveland's finest glassing the crowd with huge binoculars. They were obviously police snipers who noticed Kerri, and actually stopped to smile and wave back. I had to laugh. Ticket to get into the Cleveland game... free, beers with new veteran friend... 18 bucks, said new friend getting the Cleveland police snipers to wave at you... PRICELESS! Yup, she's a vet.

The rest of the game was spent enjoying craft brews, yelling for the home team, and watching the pitching duel; not on the field, but on the pitching challenge machine behind our seats. College kids had moved in, and the challenge was on. I think they had more spectators than the game itself. Afterwards, Kerri and I headed for the parking garage to get Kimber, and then Kerri showed us around her town. A super cool old town, it had lots of brick work that I love, and some incredible old buildings that you just don't see in the fairly new cities of the Southwest. After venturing only a few streets, Kimber had had enough. Lots of people from both sporting events were filling the streets, as the sun going down gave way to a city-wide party. Both teams had won, Sunday evening be damned, it was party time, which meant exit stage left for Kimber and I. We said goodbye to Kerri and jumped on the freeway back to Indiana. What a great experience, and another great new friend. Now I had one day to get back, break camp, and head for Pennsylvania. Ohio, state #32, and Progressive Field, MLB park #19... COMPLETE!

Pennsylvania

May 1st, 2018. That night, we enjoyed one last night around the campfire with some new neighbors, before hooking up the trailer and making the big move to the next predestined camp spot, this time with another old friend from my Marine Corps days. Susan was formerly married to a classmate of mine while in Marine Corps Electronics school out in 29 Palms, CA. We were a pretty tight knit group of friends back then, and had now become Facebook friends since I began my travels. Susan invited us to park at her farm in Muncy, PA, which was perfectly situated almost dead center of the state, giving me equal access to both the Pittsburgh and Philly ballparks, and still fairly close to Gettysburg and other PA sights I wanted to check out. So two National Battlefields and two MLB ballparks, not to mention experiencing life on a "vegan" farm and exploring the PA countryside; this was the plan for the next couple weeks.

The drive into PA was still a terrifying experience, dragging that trailer with a half-ton pickup. The wind threw us all over the road, with intermittent showers to keep things interesting. Thankfully, the roads improved dramatically once we hit the PA state line, the potholes through Ohio and Indiana now just a bad memory.

Interstate 80, our most direct route via the freeway, which was recently resurfaced and smooth as glass; was an absolute gift from above, after traveling other freeways in the Midwest. We stopped at a truck stop somewhere on the PA side of the border the first night, putting us into Muncy that following afternoon. Muncy's a cool little farming town, with several small family farms and ranches nestled away in the rolling hills just west of the emerging Appalachian Mountains. You can tell when you enter older portions of the country by the spiderweb of roads, made more for horse and carriage than for full-size trucks and 26' travel trailers.

Susan's house was picturesque for what I believe was a turn of the century farmhouse, a typical Shaker style square home with additions to the family room and kitchen. A very cool blend of natural and modern. She lived here with her husband and two boys, growing organic veggies for some of the local markets, while her husband worked on his family's much larger production farm closer to town. It was an interesting experience to live in a vegan home for a few days; trying to immerse myself in their "culture" wasn't as easy as I had thought. My carnivorous diet stubbornly refused to go out without a fight, as I opted for Buffalo Wild Wings in town for lunch the next few days. To each his own, and more power to Susan and her family. It just wasn't for me. The farm was incredible though, with ducks, cows next door, chickens, dogs, and plenty of grass for Kimber to get her ball on.

Rain, rain and more rain seemed to be the outlook for the next few days. My back was absolutely on fire due to the lack of exercise. Just sitting in the trailer, trying to write, watching baseball, was both aggravating and depressing. I had a lot of land to cover and not a lot of time to do it. Monday would be Mother's Day, which would be perfect for a road trip to Gettysburg. It would give Susan and family some alone time, and would get me out of this stir-crazy rut. Rain or shine, we hit the road in two days.

In the meantime, I went to church with Susan and her family in Williamsport, PA. Susan taught Sunday school, so had to be there early, giving her husband and me some time to check out the Little League Hall of Fame where they play the Little League World Series. A place of my childhood dreams, sadly we were too early for the museum, but were able to take some pictures of statutes and memorials to folks who started the whole Little League institution. One engraved piece of marble had the familiar Little League hatpin above an inscription that read, "At this site on June 6, 1939 was played the first Little League baseball game." Turns out that this is the birthplace of the largest organized youth sports program in the world! A super cool part of baseball history for sure.

Monday morning was wet and overcast, but only a heavy mist; no rain so far. It would have to do, the down time at this point was killing me. Not just in wasting time, but not being active was putting a toll on my back. Driving was now just as painful as sitting at the dinette, trying to write. I had to hike or find a gym. I guess I'm finally to the age of "move or die," my joints wholeheartedly in agreement. Either way, we were heading south to Gettysburg today, and I was ecstatic.

I wasn't really a fan of Civil War history, the Revolutionary War being more my thing. I guess because there's no picking sides, we were all Americans then, it was all about liberty. But now, with what I had learned from last year's travels, I was stoked to learn the "rest of the story," and especially now from the Union perspective. Gettysburg was the crown jewel of all Civil War battlefields, and with the Park Services restoration, it truly did live up to its name. The visitor center was massive and brand new, housing a cafe, book/gift store, several information kiosks, and different tour tickets to include other local sites not associated with the war. There was also a very modern museum, large modern theater, and something called the Cyclorama, which was this circular painting and light show thing that was interesting, other than the 23 middle school students that could care less. I did mention it was Monday, right? I forgot about school field trip days.

Gettysburg National Military Park was definitely a two-day minimum visit, just to take it all in. Like Vicksburg, I could've stayed there a week. After finding a spot to park amongst all the school buses, we made our way to the ticket booth. Unlike the older parks, this one had a price for just about everything. I opted for just the video, museum, and cyclo thing, $7.50 with the access pass. Not bad for what you get, and hey, they had to pay for this beautiful building somehow, right?

It was pretty amazing, looking like a resort lobby when you first walk up. Stone floor, timber frame construction, they spared nothing on this place. I had watched some YouTube videos about the park while we waited for the rain to break back at the farm. I had to laugh when I saw the same tour guide from the video at one of the info kiosks. He was about 5 years older than me with a beard. I walked up and said, "Hey, you're famous." He laughed and said, "You must've been really bored." He was surprised I recognized him from the video, it had been awhile. About then a big security guard walked up. "Ya, that's our resident movie star, don't let him fool ya." We had a good chuckle, then he asked where I was from. After explaining the book thing, he was pretty interested. He grabbed a local map of town, telling me different places to check out, including the brewery locations and best food! Always good to buddy up with the Rangers!

The museum was incredible; it had plank hardwood flooring, huge wall-size murals, a fantastic firearm collection, and some of the cleanest and intact artifacts from the actual battlefield that I'd seen yet. They definitely went all out here. The most impressive was the art gallery with oil paintings depicting everything from a life-size Lincoln portrait, to realistic battle scenes coming to life under the direct light. The detail and texture of the paintings were beyond reason. Absolutely incredible American treasure here, a must see.

After seeing the exhibits, it was pretty close to lunch time. I rescued Kimber from the truck, grabbed a sandwich and an apple from the Walmart Yeti, and headed for the walking trail. Little did I realize that the "walking trail" was actually a leg of the driving tour. Also like Vicksburg, the battlefield included a good portion of Gettysburg proper and the surrounding countryside. No biggie, Kimber needed a good walk, and so did I. It was actually partly cloudy, with the sun finally shining through, cool enough… for now.

We walked past several small farmhouses used as makeshift hospitals, before getting to what could be called "monument row." It was pretty much ground zero for the entire Battle of

Gettysburg. As usual, it had all the Northern Units facing one way, with a large statue of US Maj General Meade in the rear of cannons and granite unit markers. Toward the end of the road was a massive memorial that looked like something from Greece. Four white granite pillars adorned with life-size bronze statues of the commanding officers involved, holding a massive ornate bronze dome, were all on top of a granite platform large enough to be a small parking lot, with numerous bronze plaques around the outside walls, memorializing the names of the soldiers who fought here. After you climbed the steps of the platform, there was an old, metal, spiral staircase in one of the columns that let you walk on the roof, around the dome. The most memorable thing here was the bronze disks embedded in the granite that had arrows pointing to where the major battles took place. You had a 360 degree view of the battlefield from up top. To imagine 72,000 Confederate soldiers and another 100k+ of Union men, all battling in the farmland and rolling hills around you, was emotional and humbling all at once.

This was a new emotion, like a mixture of awe, sadness, pride, and gratefulness flooding my soul all at once. Was it me feeling this, or was I feeling what was surrounding me? Then a strangely comforting feeling of understanding washed over me. At first, we all recoil at the thought of death, then immediately judge it. We quickly jump to "oh those poor boys," placing blame on the aggressor, siding with the victim, all depending on where you fall politically, of course. But that's not what is needed in such a place as this. What's needed is to place yourself in the soldiers' shoes. That's what I was feeling. As if they were saying, don't place blame, just understand what took place here, and remember those who lived it. All for a cause they felt strong enough about to die over. Maybe this only make sense to vets, I don't know. That's the best I can explain it.

So let's get an overview of what we've learned so far. Going back to Chancellorsville, Jackson is now dead, but Lee needing to ride the wave of momentum, turned his army toward the North once again, but this time without his chief strategist and right-hand man. Lee also needed to push as far north toward Washington as possible, to pull the Union away from Vicksburg, and also to take advantage of the peace movement making its way through the North. Due to the movement's popularity, we now see General McClelland (US General fired by Lincoln for his inaction), now running against Lincoln under a Republicans for Peace platform. Gettysburg would be the last big push by the Confederacy, its last gasp, if you will. The stories and legacy of this battle not only shaped America, it defined her. The final accumulation of four years of absolute death and carnage, came to its final climatic phase, beginning with Gettysburg. From here, we saw Lee escape Gettysburg, to be chased through the Wilderness Battlefield, back to Petersburg and finally Richmond. This was the beginning of the end.

Gettysburg has got to be one of my favorite towns on this trip so far. I didn't realize it was a college town, with the Gettysburg College being one of the most expensive and prestigious private colleges in the area. Interesting. It had a bustling nightlife, due to the college and tourism, with this amazing 1800s small-town feel. We ventured into one of the breweries recommended by the movie star Ranger, nice but all tourists. I wanted to see what was really going on, and the college kid bartender was happy to help. "Ya gotta go to the Blue and Grey Bar. Make it for the happy hour food." That's all I needed to hear; I was starving, but it was still fairly early. I still had time to explore the town.

Just down the road, and right outside the back entrance to the Military Park, I passed a building that made me turn around and look again. The sign in front of this very English Pub looking building was in the shape of a baseball diamond, with a black and white picture of a really old baseball player. Old like 1800s tobacco card old. The kind you only dreamed about finding as a kid. This is why it caught my eye. The name of the place was Gettysburg Eddie's, a bar and grill named after a local baseball legend. Are you kidding me? Of course I gotta see this place.

The front half of the restaurant was empty, with only a few sitting around the bar in the back. The walls were adorned with pictures of this Gettysburg Eddie guy with greats like Babe Ruth and Ty Cobb. A banner above the bar showed his Hall of Fame induction date of 1946. There were even pictures of him with boxer Jack Dempsey, and Presidents Wilson and Taft seen at his games. Who the hell is Gettysburg Eddie? Well, I was about to find out.

The bartender was a young college-age girl, tending to a couple old guys and a wife, to which one, I wasn't sure, but definitely locals. They were arguing over the baseball game on the TV. My kinda place. When I asked the bartender about who Eddie was, it was like time stopped. The place was silent, all looking at me. "Ya, I'm a tourist. Sorry," then explained why I was in Gettysburg. Suddenly, the shy little bartender turned into a tour guide at the Gettysburg Baseball Hall of Fame. "That's Eddie Plank, one of the greatest pitchers to ever play the sport," and she went on to tell me how he went to Gettysburg College, played ball locally, and is the town mascot basically for anything baseball. She took me around the bar, explaining the pictures and

298

even gave me roof access to more pics of the local minor league team. What an amazing find. The guys downstairs were pretty impressed about my travels, for about two minutes, then went on to argue about 1850s politics. The bartender just rolled her eyes and smiled. Some things never change, apparently.

Ok, now I was hungry. Blue and Grey bar was the choice for dinner that night. What could be more appropriate for Gettysburg right? The place was packed and I quickly learned why. Shrimp boil happy hour, New England shrimp boil for like 5 bucks a pound. Add local craft beers, TVs in every direction, and nothing but standing room... it was a blast! Great place, super cool people. A must visit!

After dinner I walked across the street to the Union Cigar shop. Another super cool find. Lots of military memorabilia, free beverages, and of course, a smoking lounge where once again, the discussion of politics both past and present were the focal points. I felt very nostalgic, puffing on a General Grant Torpedo, discussing the hypothetical implications of the South winning Gettysburg, while sipping on a cup of coffee with "Irish additives." And while I'm here, let me answer that question. Lee himself said, when asked what he would do if he took Washington, that he would have humbly laid a letter of truce on the President's desk; of course, what would occur after was the true speculation. An interesting thought indeed. Another must see place with some fantastic people. Thanks, boys!

That night was spent at the local Chateau St. Walmart, with a bright and early start at the driving tour of Gettysburg Military Park. This was like Morgan's Raid, once again searching for red arrows on small, white road signs, usually with a star. The trail took you through parts of downtown Gettysburg, out to the local farmlands and pastures, to the rolling hillsides and local forests. Unbelievable stories such as the Battle of Little Round Top, and the snipers in the Devil's Den, brought waves of emotion, but nothing like walking the same dirt as Pickett's Charge. Imagine 12,000 men, on a line a mile long, marching over a mile, up hill, under deadly cannon and musket fire. This was the final push of Lee's Army of Northern Virginia. After losing over 6,000 men in just one day, Lee was heard saying, "It has been all my fault." From here, the retreat back to Virginia begins. Amazing history.

It was about 1000 when we left Gettysburg. We touched all the important spots, but passed over several exhibits due to school tours; some things just aren't worth the aggravation. The plan was to head back toward Muncy, making a stop in Hershey and Lebanon. Chocolate and *Amish*

Mafia were on my mind. Yes, I love that stupid show, both of which we ended up just driving through. No Levi to be found, maybe they're still down in Florida from last year; and the tourist trap that is the Hershey compound was too expensive for this guy. Gotta stick to the mission. The drive was nice, through some amazing countryside, but the clouds were closing in.

Back at Susan's the rain came again, this time so bad that I had zero reception for any of my devices. If I was going to be cooped up inside, I'd better get some work done; without maps and google, this would be impossible. Fortunately, Susan's husband, Keith, made arrangements for me to move down to his parents' farm, close to the freeway and 4G reception. This was another cool farm, much bigger, producing flowers and "u-pick them strawberries" at the moment. It was another cool experience to see how a large farm works, helping Keith and his dad lay out water lines for strawberries, while his mom was selling floral arrangements at the roadside store. All this in between torrential downpours every couple hours.

Across the street from the farm was a bar and grill that had a pretty popular wing night, that had my name all over it. I was starving and didn't feel like cooking. While I was sitting at the bar watching the baseball game, I inadvertently pulled out a roll of cash that was mainly singles, and counted what I had left from Gettysburg. After putting the cash in my pocket, the young lady who was sitting with a male friend, who I only said hello to when I sat down, asked if I was a "Gashole." "A what? Nah, I'm just a vet, passing through. What's a gashole?" That's when she laughed and went on to tell me about the gas company people, kind of like the oil workers that travel, they have the same in natural gas. Apparently, they throw a lot of cash around this place. They told me the ranches that I saw driving through PA, that looked like they were just abandoned, were farms the gas company bought out, just for what's under the ground. The family sells the land, farm goes dormant, town suffers. Sad but true. Some abandoned houses still with property in them isn't out of the norm around there, she explained. About then, the bartender showed up with their to-go order, we said our goodbyes; now a new friend is following the book page. Awesome.

Right after that, another single guy, younger than me, sat on the previous girl's stool. We struck up some conversation about baseball and the military; he too was a veteran. I told him about what I was doing in PA, which caught his attention, and quickly he joined the book page. Later, I got a message from him saying how motivational it was to hear what I was doing, and one day he'd like to travel. That's the most amazing inspiration to me; to hear from a fellow veteran that I could possibly have even nudged him toward his dreams, no matter what they are, is incredible. But mainly it's humbling, and even as small as it may be, it's a way of giving back for me. I'm so incredibly blessed to be able to do this, it's the least I can do but share and hopefully motivate. There really is life outside of the VA.

I had already decided on catching the SF Giants v. Pittsburgh Pirates matchup back in Indiana; I never miss a chance to see the old home team. It was the first game of a home stand for the Pirates, and a night game, giving me time to check out the Fort Necessity National Battlefield on the way in. So the next couple days we spent on the farm, before heading out for a pretty lengthy road trip. Luckily, the rain was predicted to be spotty, but supposedly clear over Pittsburgh that evening. Fingers crossed!

We left bright and early for the three and a half hour drive to Fort Necessity. Choosing freeways this time, trying to lessen the drive, the GPS took us on Hwy 99 south, clear into Cumberland, MD, then back up Hwy 40 to Fort Necessity National Battlefield. A long but beautiful drive, briefly passing through the mountainous "Cumberland Gap," historical and beautiful; I hope to see this area again when we explore Maryland.

We pulled into the Fort Necessity Battlefield about 0830, not sure what to expect, but eager to get it done and on to the ball game. I knew it was a Revolutionary War Battlefield, at least that was my presumption, but it's actually PRE-Revolutionary War, where we find George Washington as an English Red Coat. The entry sign explained the main gist of the museum. "Welcome to Fort Necessity National Battlefield. Here in 1754, George Washington suffered his first defeat of his military career." Then it changed subjects, "During the 1800s, the United States first federally funded highway passed by only a few hundred yards from here. The new route linked the Atlantic coast with the Ohio River Valley and helped to make the country's westward expansion possible." So half War, and half First Interstate; ok, got it.

Past the welcome sign was the information desk and gift shop, the typical National Park museum layout. What wasn't typical was the Ranger sporting a mohawk, huge hoop earrings, not the normal dangling kind, but the ones that are like tire rims in your earlobe. He also had tribal tattoos of some sort up his neck and a few other tats on his arms; all that dressed in a Park Service uniform. It was almost startling when he said "Semper Fi Dog" in a fairly loud baritone voice. What? No way! The dude was a former Marine turned Park Ranger who had Iroquois blood, and was allowed to sport his heritage while in uniform. Of course it helps that the Iroquois tribe sided with Washington in this battle, making this Marine brother the perfect park guide. Well played, dog! Err.

Ok, so Fort Necessity was basically where the French/English war began. Sound crazy, huh? Hang on for more. So Washington was a captain out on patrol when they ran across some French soldiers. The countries were not at war at the moment, but through a series of blunders and bad luck, Washington's men ended up in a battle with the French, killing them. Then in a missed translation from French to English, Washington is depicted as assassinating the Frenchmen. This leads to a French retaliation at Fort Necessity, escalating into the battle between France and England. Interesting to think, could this have been done by some higher design? The same man who commanded the American Revolution and becomes our nation's first President, starts an incredibly expensive and painful war for the country he is currently serving, only later to revolt against her; or is that just by incredibly lucky happenstance? A cool thought to ponder.

After the museum, I went back to the truck to grab Kimber for my new Marine buddy to meet, and to explore the hiking trail. It was still pretty wet out, but Kimber didn't waste any time when she saw the green grass. There was nobody around, so I dropped the leash and let her stretch her legs. She ran around the small wooden picket structure, that was the actual Fort Necessity, doing a sort of flip onto her back just below the English flag, rolling on her back, trying to catch her tail. I had to laugh. My English Staffy is on English soil, and apparently loves it. Well, she is a Brit, appropriate yet embarrassing, I chucked to myself.

Further up the pathway from the museum we found another unexpected site. It was a large building at the top of a fairly steep walk; it was George Washington's Inn, yup, our first President was a bar owner. A smart one at that, as a land surveyor, he helped chart the very first highway, talked about in the museum. What better place to put a roadside inn and bar than at the crossroads of the east and west? The door was open as Kimber and I walked in. The foyer had a few pamphlets and a bench, with the entrances into other rooms blocked by plexiglass. Inside the rooms were scenes depicting the times. Bedrooms were set up with multiple beds for travelers, the bar had card tables and spittoons, with others dining at tables. It was super cool to think that I was walking on the same wooden floors as George Washington! And to think he could look out a window and see the same battleground he fought on so many years previously.

Back through the museum, Kimber made her rounds, saying hello to all the guests and employees alike. We said goodbye to my Iroquois Ranger friend and got a recommendation for some good food just up the road, which was a sound call, the steak and blue cheese salad with french fries actually in the salad was amazing! Apparently, that's a thing in PA.

Traffic started getting thicker the closer we got to Pittsburgh, it was Friday night and we were catching rush hour head on. It was easy to find the park, just follow the procession of cars adorned with Pirate flags, stickers, or occupants wearing the famous yellow and black. There was plenty of parking at the stadium, unfortunately most of the close lots were private and/or full. Still, parking for 10 bucks about three blocks from the park was easy and affordable. Kimber was safe, secure, and satisfied after a long day in the truck, running the grass field at the battlefield, and a full belly of dog food sprinkled with steak. Bribing the dog when I leave had become standard operating procedure lately. Either way, she was good, truck was fairly safe with parking attendants nearby, and I was off to the game.

PNC Park, Pittsburgh, PA

May 11th, 2018. Right off the bat, pun intended, I was learning baseball history on the walk into PNC Park. A large, blue metal street sign with yellow lettering from the Pennsylvania Historical Commission read, "In October, 1903, National League Champion Pittsburgh played the American League Champion Boston in Major League Baseball's first modern World Series. Boston won the 9 game series, 5 to 3; prominent players included Pittsburgh's Honus Wagner and Boston's Cy Young. Games 4 through 7 were played near this site at Exposition Park, Pittsburgh's home from 1891 to 1903." WOW! How freaking cool is that!

The park itself takes up an entire city block, with the Allegheny River as its rear border. First things first, I jumped into the ticket line, which was unusually long for a Friday night this early in the season; so much so, I was worried about getting a ticket. When I asked one of the other obvious Pirate fans in line why the crowd, he explained that this was Andrew McCutchen's homecoming, first game back in Pittsburgh since his trade to San Francisco. Ok, that makes sense, but how crazy is it for a huge baseball town like Pittsburgh to show up for the other team's player?! They definitely love their Cutch in Pittsburgh.

The nosebleed seat I ended up getting was in the deep left field, upper deck, and already filled elbow to elbow. Ya, that's not gonna work. I decided to just walk the park as I usually do when I'm attending solo. What a great park! There's an incredible backdrop over center and right field of the Pittsburgh skyline, highlighted by this giant, Pirate gold, expansion bridge across the river. The park had great bar venues looking over the river, and still seeing into the park. Then there's the Rotunda.

The Rotunda, as it's called, is this giant metal and concrete spiral walkway that climbs the height of the park. Located in the home run alley of left field, this is where the Renegades of the Rotunda gather on the top deck. A group of hardcore Pirates fans are dressed like the supporting cast of *Pirates of the Caribbean*, waving massive "Jolly Roger" flags, and snarling at anybody in Giants' gear. Enter me, with a Giants hat, sipping a beer a few feet away from this group, when suddenly one spots me. Next thing ya know, I'm being Shanghai'd by this group of scallywags! Had a great group shot, with me in the middle, of about 7 of these guys and one fair lass. Best part was watching the kids come up for pictures with the Pirates. They weren't paid mascots, just loyal Pirates baseball fans. Super cool, now that's America.

After getting all my pictures I needed from around the park, it was dinner time. Once again, a fan from the book page told me I had to eat a Primanti Brothers Sandwich, a Pittsburgh classic. It took me awhile to find the sandwich shop as the park was starting to really fill up. When I got to the register, I told the guy it was my first time in Pittsburgh and to give me what the locals eat. When I finally found a place to eat my food, I wasn't exactly enthused by what was inside the bag. Some type of mystery meat patty, maybe sausage, I couldn't tell, with French fries, lettuce and tomato, on white bread. I guess some tastes are acquired, this one just wasn't mine. Maybe he gave me the wrong thing. Anyway, belly was full, game was in the 5th, and I missed my dog. PNC Park, MLB park #20... COMPLETE. We're in the final countdown folks. 10 more parks to go!

Back at the truck, Kimber was sleeping contently when I popped the locks on the doors. I could tell because her face was all smooshed on one side, with her tongue half hanging out, looking completely confused and startled by the door opening. I was glad to see she was calm and able to sleep; I'm always so concerned about her when I'm gone. Well, now we had a decision to make. It was now 2000, dark with wet roads, and a 3.5 hour drive back to Muncy. It was either find a truck stop or rest area outside of town to bed down for the night, or make the drive in the rain that had just begun. My lower back spoke up right about then, "The cot? Ya, right! Get some coffee fat-boy, we got a drive in front of us." There was no way I was going to sleep on that cot. I set the GPS to "Interstate," set the cruise control to 75mph and started the trek

304

home. It was rough, but we made it back to the farm around midnight, exhausted, highly caffeinated and unscathed.

The plan was to check out Philadelphia from Muncy, but after checking the schedule, that wasn't going to happen. They had a fairly long road game stint just starting. Next game was like a week away. That was just too much downtime, so I called a friend who had offered us a spot in Delaware, asking if we could drop by a little earlier. With confirmation and a weather report from Delaware as all clear, we just waited for a break in the weather locally. Two days later, we were off for the coast... and the DC metro nightmare I'd been dreading. At this point, we enter Delaware, but still have to visit Philadelphia, so PA... to be continued.

After saying our goodbyes, we hit the Interstate for Delaware, a 4-hour nightmare of a drive. The closer we got to Philly, the worse the traffic and roads became. I was really missing my Cabover camper right about now, and cursing this trailer I'd been dragging behind me. We took I80 east to the 246, south to I95 and into Wilmington and finally Felton, DE. White knuckling it most of the way, especially when lanes got tight, potholes got much larger, and then they made you pay a toll for all that enjoyment. Needless to say, we survived the excursion, arriving safely at some dude's house I'd never met, later that afternoon.

So last winter, when I was back in Arizona making the swap into the larger camper, I had made a post on the Facebook page about the new pad. I think I must've voiced my concern about pulling it into the NE metro areas, like DC and NYC; because shortly after, I got a call from one of the vets who'd been following the page since 2016. Glen and I talked quite a bit over Facebook as he had lived in my hometown area of Northern California, but was a huge Dodger fan. So we had some familiar hometown ties, talked a lot of Dodger/Giant baseball trash, and most important of all, both served in the Moag. He too was a Restore Hope Veteran, serving as a C-5 Flight Engineer with the Air Force. Glen served in the military to full retirement and now works for the post office near Felton. Anyway, he calls me up and tells me he has a 1/2 acre in Delaware where I was welcome to park the trailer and use as a "home-base" for the DC metro area. So here I am now, pulling into his driveway, meeting a "Facebook" friend for the very first time. Ya, if stepping out of my PTSD comfort zone is what I'm supposed to be doing... this is definitely it!

The address took us to a small house on a long country road, in what I was frankly surprised to find as farmland. When we pulled up, a massive white Sheppard instantly jumped up on the fence and let us know exactly whose house this was, and I wasn't him. Then a small Jeep pulled up right behind us; Glen had told me they were on the way back from the store. If there was any nervousness, it didn't last too long as Glen and Nancy instantly put me at ease, especially with Glen's comment after thanking him so much for opening his backyard to a stranger. "Well, we've been following your page for awhile, and nobody's said you're an asshole," Glen chuckled while shaking my hand. I laughed. Yup, he's a vet, and now a brother.

The house was on a half acre lot, with a shop and huge class 3 motorhome. They too were RVers; ok, this is making more sense by the minute. When one is bitten by the wanderlust bug, to help a fellow traveling friend is almost a given, and you know what they need from your own experience. So Glen had me park the trailer next to his bus, under a shade tree, in thick beautiful green grass. He even sent me a picture of a Cardinal a few days prior, perched in the tree above my spot. Need I say more? Now I just hope I don't wear out my welcome, something I'm always so cautious and worried about when meeting and staying with new friends.

Arris was Glen's giant white Lab/Sheppard mix that met us at the gate. A 7 yr old lumbering male, super friendly other than his bark, that tried his best to play with Kimber, but due to his size and age, for whatever reason, Kimber would have none of it. Delilah was Nancy's female Dalmatian, about the same age as Arris, who was having none of Kimber near her mom, toys or food; and she could care less about me too. Typical first day dog drama, they'd be alright in a few days. Even though she was in a new place, and out of sorts for a minute, Kimber was definitely happy about the grass being right out our doorstep, equating to her belief that dad should do NOTHING but throw the ball all day. Happy dog indeed.

Ok, so here's the plan for the next few weeks, using Glen's house as a home base. We now are at the whim of the weather, baseball schedules, and cash flow, so scheduling is going to get a little dicey. As you probably noticed, I didn't check Pennsylvania as complete, we still have battlefields on the eastern side of the state and of course, another ball game in Philly; so hold that thought as we jump around the area for a bit. I'm hoping to explore Washington DC and see the Nationals; explore Maryland with Antietam and the Orioles; check off Delaware and New Jersey; finish PA; and try to get into NYC for one of the Mets or Yankee games; all from Glen's backyard. Ambitious is an understatement. Ok, well, strap in, here we go.

The next couple days were spent just getting to know our new hosts and exploring the local area. Glen took me on a brewery tour, excited to show me the local craft beer scene. From the famous Dogfish Head Brewery to his local favorite right around the corner, we saw them all. I was still surprised by how much farmland there was in Delaware, and then add to that miles of beaches, all in a place the size of an Arizona county. I guess I was just expecting endless suburban sprawl this close to DC. I found the local Anytime Fitness, the corner bar and grill, and a new favorite grocery store called Aldi. It was a nice 3-day break, before it was game time in DC.

Glen and I caught the Sunday afternoon Nationals game, while Nancy graciously watched over Kimber for me. The ride into the nearest DC metro subway station from Delaware was around an hour and half, then another 45 minutes or so on the train into downtown. I was super glad Glen said we would take the subway and could show me how to get around, as I would be venturing back into DC to see the Capital by myself in a few days.

Not gonna lie, I don't think I've ever been on a subway in my life, especially not a massive train system as DC's. It was a daunting obstacle and something I had been dreading and trying to avoid, but now had to conquer. So Glen's help here was enormous. He showed me the ticket machines, and how to read the routes on the map, explaining the route colors and waypoints of where the routes intersect and how to tell which direction the trains were going. It was all very confusing at first glance, but became pretty apparent as we traveled into the city.

The stations themselves looked like something out of the movie *Batman*. Massive grey concrete tunnels formed from these huge rectangular blocks, making a honeycomb pattern on the roof and walls. Floor lighting shining up toward the roof, with multi-colored digital signs atop dark metal poles, separated the concrete benches facing the train tracks on both sides, one traveling the opposite direction than the other. It was a strange mix of industrial and modern, yet with a gothic flair. Just picture the "Capital" in the movie *Hunger Games* to get my drift. Then of course, the crowds, people facing toward their designated train, earbuds or headphones on, staring at their phones, saying very little to each other. Typical cattle car mentality if you will, just like what you see on TV.

Nationals Park, Washington DC

May 20th, 2018. The train dropped us within a block of Nationals Park, home to the Washington Nationals. The Nationals were formally known as the Montreal Expos, prior to their move back into the U.S. from Canada just a few years ago. So the park was pretty much brand new, being built in 2013, but was rather lackluster for a modern ballpark. The entire place was once again constructed of mainly plain grey concrete, the outfield backdrop was of hotels under construction, with huge crane booms filling the blue sky. That's when I realized the lack of skyscrapers and just architecture in general, all around the park, or even the city itself. Fun fact, no building in the DC area can be taller than the capital building, therefore no massive skyscrapers fill the sky. It was a strange setup for sure. Actually mimicking their spring training compound in Florida, the park had the same non-descript concrete and very little in the way of outside signage.

The most distinctive part about the outside of the park were these very strange bronze statues of some of the Senators greatest players. Instead of just having the bust of a player, they portrayed them in this weird, modern, action type of pose. For instance, Walter Johnson had his body in a throwing stance, left arm and glove by his side, but his throwing arm or "arms" were three individual arms in different positions of his "throw" with more bronze "shadows" in between them, looking more like the MLB's version of the Hindu God Sheba. Another was of a player, Frank Howard, but this time swinging a bat, catching multiple "still frames" of the bat in motion, is the best way I can describe it. It was just creepy in a way. Again, think *Hunger Games* Capital kind of creepy.

Glen and I made our way around the concourse, snapping all the pics I needed, taking in the sights, and of course enjoying some local craft beers. I enjoyed seeing the pictures of the old Washington Senators, who were the original franchise's mascots from 1901 to 1960. Even the food vendors got in on the DC vibe with names like "Steak of the Union" for a sandwich shop.

It was a great day weather-wise for the game. Rain had subsided, keeping the weather fairly cool, even with the humidity that was pretty much constant at this point, yup, summer had begun. The saving grace here was an almost constant breeze, I was assuming because the ocean was so close. It was only mid-May, so ya, it was going to get nothing but warmer from here on in. This is when I'd be happier to drag the trailer around, with its shower, cold AC, and refrigerator full of frosty beers. The real test would be Michigan in August; hey, it can't be worse than Houston in August, right? Quit laughing, I'm trying to comfort myself here. Anyway, it was a great game in DC and a great time had with a fellow Somalia veteran. Awesome! Nationals Park, MLB park #21... COMPLETE!

That very next night, Philadelphia had a home game, and the skies were starting to clear for the most part. Glen had to work and Nancy graciously watched Kimber for me once again, as I jumped at the opportunity to catch this game. I'm glad Kimber wasn't with me as traffic into Philly wasn't great, and my Irish temper got the best of me a few times. It was also a blessing to be able to park in a regular garage, and explore downtown Philadelphia on foot, without worrying about what to do with my dog. She would be too hot in the truck, and lose her mind walking in a huge city with all the loud noises and crowds. It won't be a cake walk for me either, trust me; maybe that's why it's so hard on her.

I first found the National Park's headquarters and ticket sales building to get a map of the area. It was like a visitor center for the entire downtown historical district of Philadelphia. A map was crucial as there was a whole lot to see. Independence Hall, Ben Franklin's tomb and printing press, and of course Tun Tavern, birthplace of my Marine Corps. First stop was the closest, the Liberty Bell exhibit, and surprisingly would be the most eye opening of them all.

The Liberty Bell exhibit was housed in another National Parks building, that looked as if it was built in the 70s, while the walkway, meandering its way to the front doors, looked brand new. There were brick walls that guided you along a path to the front doors, adorned with information placards and paintings depicting different historical scenes. The line to get in was substantial, so I had plenty of time to read the information and look at the artwork. That's when I realized there was something different going on here.

The first painting showed the scene of a funeral procession, men in colonial white wigs, carrying a coffin down the center of a street lined with mourners. The title on the picture read, "Promoting the Abolition of Slavery" and had a caption below stating, "on April 21, 1790 nearly 20,000 African and white Philadelphians lined the streets to view the funeral procession of Benjamin Franklin. Once a slave owner, Franklin was president of the Pennsylvania Abolition Society at the end of his life and sent a biting parity attacking slavery to the press as his last word on the subject."

Whoa, what? This is the Liberty Bell exhibit, as in our liberty from England to start our great nation, and the first thing you read is about the abolition of slavery? There was so much wrong with this painting that I laughed angrily out loud. First of all, the mourners in the painting had about a 1 to 4 ratio of black versus white amongst the crowd. You're telling me, out of the 200,000 people reportedly there, a quarter of them were black... in 1790!? Secondly, they distinguish the black Philadelphians from the whites, by calling them specifically Africans, requiring a capitalization, while generalizing the white mourners with just the word "white"... uncapitalized. And then the worst part of all, they went on to discuss Ben Franklin owning slaves and being an abolitionist, before describing him as one of the architects of our country, our government, and our way of life as a whole. Like Madison's house, I was disgusted by the redirection of attention away from the true history of the founding fathers, due to this ridiculous and demeaning account of non-modern political correctness of the period. No wonder these kids today have no respect or love for this country; they're not being told the whole story, just a politically driven version. This set the tone for the rest of my visit, and this was just the beginning.

The next placard was an informational placard, talking about the formation of a new government. It began with the signing of the Constitution and where to locate the capital, then it suddenly jumped to the Naturalization Act of 1790 and quickly the topic changed to immigration with this strange caption, "Race was fundamental in determining citizenship in the new nation. In 1790, Congress debated a bill about the requirements to become a naturalized American citizen. While disagreement arose about religious and political affiliation, moral character, and length of residency, all agreed on the most fundamental point: future citizens must be 'free white persons of good moral character.'" I had a feeling where this was going and the next paragraph confirmed it. "In the 1790s, indigenous peoples occupied much of the land of this continent. The Chiefs of the Iroquois and other Indian nations received peace metals from President Washington, beneath this façade of friendship simmered a struggle to define the relationship of the land, autonomy, and citizenship on the North American continent. While many European immigrants were becoming American citizens, citizenship did not apply to most native Americans because they belong to their own sovereign nations." I almost threw my phone at the wall. You have got to be kidding me! Remember this is at the LIBERTY BELL EXHIBIT, why is this even here? Oh but wait, kind sir or ma'am, there's even more.

The next placard continued on with this "history" lesson. Four more sections, the first talks of the First Bank in the U.S., then something about the Whiskey Rebellion. The third was titled "Driving the Indian nations out of the northwest territory" and the final caption titled "Closing the doors against 'Dangerous Aliens.'" So let's review; we covered Ben Franklin was a slave owner, our immigration laws are racist, Bill of Rights only were for white people, and we drove the Indians from their land. So far nothing about the Liberty Bell, or about the Constitution, let alone anything else about Ben Franklin besides him owning slaves. Wow, just wow. We haven't got to the front door yet!

My mind raced with who would have approved this politically slanted historical account to even be published on a National Parks exhibit. Who even wrote this factually inaccurate dribble? The biases here was so pathetically obvious to those attentive to even the basics of government and history, who would be appalled. Then came the final coup de grace, it showed a picture of a historical pamphlet dated May 30th, 1793, titled "Principle Articles and Regulations agreed upon by the members of the Democratic Society." Beneath was the caption, "ABOVE/RIGHT: Democratic societies with revolutionary ideas spring up in the capital. President Washington and his administration objected to their passionate political criticisms and tried to suppress them." What? Why would this be here? What are they trying to say with this statement?

Then all my questions were answered and put into proper perspective. Underneath this section, but still emblazoned on the National Park Service placard was a picture of President Obama and family with the following caption, "ABOVE: when Barack Hussein Obama was sworn in as a 44th president of United States in January 20, 2009 he became the first person of African dissent to hold this office. Pictured here with the first lady Mrs. Michelle Robinson Obama and daughters Sasha and Malia." From Ben Franklin, straight to Obama. Interesting. Remember when I said he who wins, writes the history; apparently that serves for elections as well. All of these exhibits were installed under the last administration. Reshaping history, anyone? Regardless of your politics, this should be alarming to all Americans. Sadly though, we're still not done.

The final "exhibit" you're forced to walk by on your way into the Liberty Bell Museum was a human-sized wooden crate, made of wooden slats, each with a different AFRICAN country's name, such as Senegal, Guinea, and Sierra Leone; representing the countries where AFRICAN slaves were from. I highlight the word African, as there was zero mention of any Irish slaves or European indentured servants whatsoever. Let that sink in.

At this point, I couldn't help but think what a 15 yr old child on a school trip to the Liberty Bell would be thinking about his/her country as a whole at this point. I mean after that, I'd be depressed that I was American. Thankfully, inside the museum things were as one would expect. At least for the first couple of exhibits.

The exhibits went into the history of the bell, the forging of it, the crack, etc. There was one display describing how it rang when the Constitution was signed, announcing our independence from England, and the birth of a new country. Then the very next exhibit, straight back into the abolitionist movement.

I understand the idea of liberty for all and the Bell symbolizing that Liberty, and the exhibits inside the building discussing the correlation to slavery and other movements are perfectly acceptable... as supplemental information. I just think the spotlight needs to be on the ACTUAL history of the Bell and the powerful message it represents to our country and the world. But hey, I'm just an old Jarhead, what do I know.

Constitution Hall was next on my to-do list; unfortunately, only a certain number of tickets are sold per day, and I was about two hours too late. It was enough to just walk the same grounds as our founding fathers did in 1776, to give me goosebumps thinking of what occurred here. The same place where Ben Franklin was asked what they had given the country, "A Republic, if you can keep it." was his reply. No truer words spoken… ever.

Just a few blocks away was Ben Franklin's home and print shop. It was amazing to walk the same brick-lined tunnel that Franklin passed through every day on his way to work. The Park Service had set up an authentic printing press from the time period, and were printing actual copies of the Constitution, on the same parchment style paper that was commonly used back then. For just 5 bucks, I now own a copy of the US Constitution, printed from an authentic press on period paper, from Ben Franklin's actual shop. How freaking cool is that!

Down the street from his shop was Franklin's Tomb. Strangely, his grave was placed right at the street corner, just behind a brick wall with bars to see through. The cemetery was gated off, and his marker covered with coins. I can only imagine how many people have visited this grave site, and the amount of spare change collected.

At this point I was starving, and an authentic Philly Cheese Steak was on my heads-up display. I was told by so many people that you can't leave Philly without going to Tony Luke's. There was quite an argument on the Drinkin' Bros Baseball Page when I posed the question as to who had the best steak. Tony Luke's won out, besides it wasn't far from the ballpark.

Not in the best part of town for sure, I found the place under a freeway, with just street parking, and fairly empty. I was a little concerned I picked the wrong place. I walked up and said the same thing I did in Pittsburgh, "Give me what the locals eat." The lady behind the counter then asked, "Wid or widout?" "Huh?" I wasn't sure if that was even English. "Wiiiid or wiiiid oouut," she said again, obviously slower, staring at me intently. I glanced at the dude behind me, puzzled. "With cheese whiz or without," he explained amusingly. "Cheez whiz? On a sandwich?" He just shrugged. I chose without and grabbed a seat. Within about 3 minutes I devoured that amazing culinary masterpiece. Sliced ribeye, with peppers and onions, and especially the bread. Baked on site, it's definitely all about the bread. A must eat bucket list item for sure.

Citizens Bank Park, Philadelphia, PA

May 21st, 2018. Citizens Bank Park was just a few blocks away from the restaurant, with nice easy access to the park and plenty of parking. I noticed a long line of cars parked on the curb, even under the no parking signs, with an open spot, fairly close. I asked the folks a few cars ahead of me, who were tailgating on the curb with lounge chairs and bbq, if parking here was ok, just in case. "You gotta go down and ask that cop" pointing at the cruiser parked in the middle of the street a few hundred yards away. Ok, no problem. After taking a tongue lashing about paying for a spot like everybody else, and how he's going to lose his job, he finally gave me the ok. It was almost like asking your dad to borrow the car on a Friday night. I thanked him for his service and walked back to the truck chuckling. That was worth the twenty buck parking savings.

Inside the park was pretty standard. Stadium style park, built mainly of red brick, with its light poles and metal girders painted to match. The backdrop was pretty sparse, as the park was located in the industrial part of town, far from the downtown skyscrapers. There was a standard size Jumbotron in left field, a much smaller "liberty bell" tower that lit the bell and made the neon sign look like it was ringing when homers were hit. Right field had the only bleacher section, with the food court directly behind it all.

The centerfield food court has only local Philadelphia food establishments, with low and behold, Tony Luke's proudly in the center. I was surprised to see the prices were the same in the park as at the restaurant. Friends from the Facebook page said I had to try the crab fries too. Basically, they're French fries with Old Bay seasoning and a white cheese dip on the side. Not bad, but nothing like that steak sandwich.

Around the promenade there was a lot going on. They had an amazing place for kids to play ball, basically a small stadium including its own mini Jumbotron, where your kids could see themselves at bat on the big screen, just like the pros. It was pretty cool how they set it up. They also had Greg Luzinski there signing autographs, not at the kids park but in front of his own BBQ shop. Unfortunately, the all-star Philly didn't get off his cell phone or even look up as he signed my "First Philly Game" certificate.

It had been a long day and I still had a couple hour drive back to Delaware that night. Not to mention, I missed my dog horribly. By the fifth inning I had taken all the pics I needed, and had my fill of crowds. Glad to have two of the four ballparks I hoped to visit from Glen's place completed, with just Baltimore and maybe a New York team left. Slowly but surely, we're getting her done. Citizens Bank Park, MLB park #22... COMPLETE.

Back at the trailer, we were bogged down by rain again. A welcome change from the intense humidity, but still not much fun to explore in. I really wanted to cover Brandywine Battlefield and visit Valley Forge, before wrapping up our PA visit for good. There was a break in the weather after about three days, so I packed up the truck to include Kimber this time, and once again headed back to PA. See what I mean about dragging the trailer for a home base, the trip doesn't "flow" the same as when I had my cab-over camper. I hate backtracking.

Brandywine Battlefield wasn't a National Battlefield, so I almost skipped it. Luckily, my desire to learn as much about the American Revolution as I have about the Civil War got the best of me and off we went. About 70 miles straight north, out of Delaware, back into PA, is the Brandywine Battlefield Park. A small but beautifully manicured public park, run by a private organization that included a few small buildings and a large rolling hill. The flowers and trees here were in full bloom, the grass was as lush as I've ever seen a lawn. Thank God for allergy medication. They also had a museum, a short video, and a small walking path between structures. The locals were eating their lunch at the scattered picnic benches as it was just about high noon.

With not really much to see outside, the stone house that was used by George Washington as a headquarters was about the most interesting. The doors were locked, but you could peer in from the windows at the period decorations such as jarred food on the shelves, and an American blue military smock hanging from the back of a chair, as if it was Washington's, flung over a chair after returning home from a long day of commanding a revolution. Am I the only one who is scared that when you press your face to the glass of an old building, cupping your eyes from the glare to see what's inside, that somebody is going to be on the other side peering back? I chose to just push my phone up against the glass and take a couple shots. That way, if old George is looking back at me, I can freak out in the car, instead of running through the park, dragging Kimber, screaming like a child. Just keeping it real.

Ok, so let's talk about what happened at Brandywine. Relax it's quick. Here's what the sign read, "September 11th, 1777 (I know, creepy right!?), Washington and about 11,000 men attempted to hold a British advance into Pennsylvania. The Americans were defeated near Chadds Ford on Brandywine Creek by approximately 18,000 British and Hessian troops under Howe." So basically, this is after the Declaration of Independence and Washington has already driven the English out of Boston, and has his Army sitting in New Jersey. It's fall, winter is coming, and so are the English. British General Howe shows up in Maryland and is heading north for the American capital of Philadelphia. Washington meets Howe here at Brandywine, loses to the English and the German Hessians, and heads north to Valley Forge for the winter. That about sums it up. Still amazing to walk the field that George Washington fought on, goosebumps were pretty much constant. Great piece of history right here. Kimber loved it too, as ball play was inevitable with all that green grass.

While inside the museum, I had read something regarding the Battle of Paoli, where some type of controversial attack happened, going as far as to label it the "Massacre of Paoli." Now plugging the Paoli Battlefield into the GPS, gave us a pin drop just a few miles away. Sweet! I love this part, when one place leads you unexpectedly to the next.

When we approached the battlefield, we began seeing road signs, directing our way. A small white road sign, that read "Paoli Battlefield." It was a combination of city park, combined with an open hayfield, a wooded hiking path, and a monument area, next to a very tall flagpole. There was a wooden information stand with a description placard that looked like it was handwritten in some type of calligraphy. The first paragraph of the lengthy story read, "These memorial grounds commemorate the engagement in the Revolutionary War known as the Paoli massacre, an attack by the British Army on American troops, that took place near this spot toward midnight of September 20, 1777. About 150 American soldiers were killed or wounded in this action in which the British used only bayonets. 53 of the Americans were buried here in a common grave, now surrounded by stonewalls and capped with a monument erected in 1877." Basically, the English killed these guys in their sleep with knives, as to not alert the local townspeople. The rallying cry "Remember Paoli!" stemmed from this incident.

After reading this, I walked over to the monument area. Just as reported, there was a block fenced area with a massive marble marker. The marker was so worn that someone had made a plexiglass enclosure for it. This was the mass grave described in the information placard. Around this monument were several others commemorating our military branches and wars that they fought. My heart swelled with pride when I saw Somalia listed on the Marine monument. That's something you don't see everyday.

The bizarre thing about this place was the small cardboard signs, like campaign lawn signs, that read "Paranormal Tour," with a date of "June 7-11th." After looking up the "tour" online, it appears that this is a hot spot for ghost hunters; apparently there are some pretty pissed off American soldiers who still want to tell you about it. That was enough for me to head back to the truck. I got a thing about ghosts. I leave them alone, hopefully they reciprocate. If you've seen what I've seen... well, that's a whole different book.

It was pushing up on 1400, and I still wanted to see Valley Forge, just another 45 minutes north. No problem. Well, 45 minutes in traffic at 1400, turned into 2 hours. By the time we got to Valley Forge, we were pressed for time, and this place was gigantic. It had a long driving tour, amazing museum and visitor center, including a great video. I was able to catch the museum and film before they closed. For some reason, I thought a battle was fought here, but it was actually just where Washington bivouacked for the winter, before making the famous Delaware River crossing on Christmas Eve.

So now, I'd put myself in a helluva spot. Venturing north to Valley Forge had led me almost 3 hours away from Glen's place. In rush hour traffic. Just outside of Philadelphia. Ya, this was gonna suck. I didn't bother with the driving portion of Valley Forge, and opted to jump into traffic, headfirst, and get this drive over with. Thankfully, we made it home, once again unscathed. Finally, I can say: Pennsylvania, state #33... COMPLETE!

Maryland

May 28th, 2019; Memorial Day. It was partly cloudy, possible showers that afternoon, but sunny as we drove into Baltimore to catch the Orioles game. The day after I had returned from wrapping up our PA visit, Glen had knocked on the trailer door. "I got tickets for the Memorial Day at the O's.," he said. "Dude, that's awesome!" I responded. "Ya, and then you're gonna drop us off at the airport and we're going to Alaska for ten days, will ya watch the dogs?" And with that Glen, Nancy, and I were off to Baltimore two days later.

Glen and Nancy had decided that I was worthy to watch over their fur babies while they took a long planned trip to Alaska. They had a dog sitter set up, but now that I was here, and passed the sniff test, we both decided it was a great trade for me, barging in on them for a month. I was flattered and somewhat shocked when he asked; a total stranger entrusted me with his home, motorcycle, RV, and most of all... his pups. On top of that, he wanted me to drive his truck into Baltimore and back, then take the electronic toll pass from his truck and use it in my own, while I finished my exploring! That was huge, as highway and bridge tolls add up fast in this part of the country. Hell, it's 6 bucks just to drive to Walmart and back! That and the thought of having a house, with Netflix, a bath tub, and a recliner, was more than enticing.

Camden Yards, Baltimore, MD

I arrived at Camden Yards on Memorial Day, with a new veteran buddy and his wife, exactly 4 years to the day since I pulled out of AZ on this journey. It was a special day indeed. Glen had purchased some awesome box seats, that included food, on the second deck in left field. This gave me access to the box suites for pictures, a place usually denied by my "get in" ticket. After an inning or two, I excused myself to go take my pictures and explore the park.

I'm gonna go ahead and let it out of the bag early. Camden Yards is easily my number 3 favorite park in the MLB system. I know I'm jumping the gun here, but I can't emphasize enough how cool this place is. It's not just a ballpark, it's a Baltimore experience. From the outside, the place looks like a giant brick compound, taking up an entire downtown city block and then some. Along the right field fence is a giant brick warehouse, renovated into retail stores, restaurants, team offices, etc. Then there's a wide brick walkway separating the field from the restaurants, with several small brass markers laid into the brick, each one engraved with a name and a date, marking where home runs were hit by famous players. The highest marker was on the wall of the brick office building, just above a restaurant door, a shot by Ken Griffey Jr.

The park itself resembled the Orioles Training camp back in Florida. Giant archways opening to the outside street, with only bars blocking the entrance, made the whole park feel really open. The backdrop at Camden Yards wasn't much to talk about, with only a few hotels and an old clock to look at. It's Eutaw St. with its massive "brickyard" behind left field that is the main feature of this park.

After walking the concourse several times, taking as many pictures as I could, I returned to watch the rest of the game with my friends. Lots of military pride and salutes went on that day, even handing out ball caps to the veterans in attendance. Shortly after the seventh inning stretch, I dropped Glen and Nancy off at their hotel, and started back to Delaware to check on Arris and Delilah, and begin my dog sitting duties. Camden Yards, MLB park #23... COMPLETE!

Back at Glen's, Arris and Delilah weren't exactly tickled that I pulled up in Dad's truck... with no mom and dad. Arris, the big male Sheppard, stayed outside laying by the fence, as Delilah went to her kennel, keeping a watchful eye on Kimber and the guy in her Dad's chair. It didn't take long before Arris and Kimber were chasing each other around the yard, and Delilah was content to lay on the couch, keeping a watchful eye over everything. For the next two days we just sat around and got used to each other. Binge watched a show recommended by Glen called *Peaky Blinders* and just relaxed. It was a wonderful break, but we still had work to do.

Payday finally hit, and I was ready to get out of the house. It had rained the majority of the time, keeping us inside and at home for the past three days, giving me time to research and plan my Maryland excursion. This was going to be an ambitious run, to say the least. I decided I wanted to venture all the way to Harper's Ferry, a place I had wanted to see last year, but decided against the drive from Seneca Rocks. I wanted to follow Stonewall Jackson's movements from Harper's Ferry to Antietam, and then catch the Monocacy Battlefield before nightfall, putting us back into Delaware for a late dinner with the dogs. This was going to be a long day, but it had to be done. I wasn't going to leave Glen's dogs outside overnight, even though he said a night or two would be ok. Nope, not on my watch.

Kimber and I left Felton, Delaware around 0400, breezing through the Baltimore morning traffic with little delay. The rain was still sporadic and it was heavily overcast. I opted for the freeway on this trip to make up time, plus it wasn't the weather to be sightseeing. We basically split the DC/Baltimore Metro area, eventually catching Interstate 70, and arriving in Harper's Ferry around 0600.

The reason why I chose to go back to Harper's Ferry is due to it being the prelude to the Battle of Antietam, and another incredible feat of Stonewall Jackson. It's now 1862 and Lee has made his first push into Maryland. His right-hand man, Stonewall Jackson is still alive at this point of the war, and is set to make history. Lee and his Army of Northern Virginia has now pushed north to just outside Antietam, making Harper's Ferry and its Union garrison now behind enemy lines. With Harper's Ferry being a major supply route, situated on the point between the Shenandoah and Potomac Rivers, the Union was still able to wreak havoc on Lee's supply routes. In a daring and historic move, Lee separates his forces, sending Stonewall Jackson to Harper's Ferry to take the Union garrison. The result was the largest surrender of American troops until WW2; 12,500 Union soldiers were captured, including artillery, carts, and small munitions. One Union soldier was heard shouting to his comrades as Stonewall rode by reviewing the troops, "Boys, he's not much for looks. But if we'd had him, we wouldn't have been caught in this trap!" Once again, the respect and reverence for one's enemy is what takes me by surprise every time, swelling my heart with American pride. Never forget, these were ALL Americans.

The parking situation at Harper's Ferry was something to be desired. The entire town was built on a hillside with very narrow roads. The rains had made the rivers rise quite a bit, turning the Potomac into a mud colored rushing monster, flooding out the Park Service parking lots. So basically Kimber and I didn't stop for long. I jumped out at a few choice places for pics of information placards, we hiked back to where John Brown's House was, then called it a day and headed for Antietam. We still had a lot to do, and the clouds were getting darker.

Antietam National Battlefield was just a short, twenty-minute drive from downtown Harper's Ferry. Even with the sporadic showers and darkening sky, the drive through the rolling farmlands of Northern Maryland was beautiful. Lush green grass, giant Oaks, and gentle rolling hills was the lay of the land. I tried to put myself in the mindset of a soldier in 1862. A city boy from NYC, seeing the strange beauty of the Maryland countryside for the first time, or the country boy from Tennessee, on somebody else's farm, but with a rifle instead of a plow. The confusion of what they must be thinking, all lead to the same conclusion of thought that formed the words in my own head, "Why am I here, why me?" No matter how hard I tried to mentally "place" myself here, nothing could have prepared me for what I was about to "see."

It was now around 0900, the sky was actually showing some clearing while I sat in the semi-round glass room, overlooking several miles of farmland, waiting for the Park Ranger's presentation. Wow, much better than a movie! This park actually assigns you a Ranger who gives a guided tour throughout the park, to include 6 major driving spots. You can of course just take a map and roll the driving portion yourself. The noticeably older visitor center also had a fantastic museum with artifacts and uniforms from this actual battlefield. I listened to the Ranger's presentation, took my pictures in the museum, then grabbed a map and headed back to the truck, hoping to beat the crowds to the first stop on the driving portion.

You can tell that Antietam National Battlefield was one of the oldest and original parks. The visitor center was made of stone slabs, looked like 1960s architecture, with a large wood sign that matched the age of the building. I assumed this is what Gettysburg looked like prior to its incredible renovation. You could see giant marble or granite memorials along the side of the county road, along with some very old farm buildings and a church. The map showed 11 major stops on the driving tour, starting with "Dunker Church." Well, it must be that way, target acquired, let's do this.

First, let's get some background about what's going on here. First, Manassas kicks off the war, Shilo breaks out in Tennessee, then the Second Battle of Manassas is won by the Confederacy. General Lee, not wanting to lose momentum, invades Maryland, igniting the Maryland Campaign. Lee wanted to move the battle out of his already war-torn state of Virginia, and into Pennsylvania, liberating Maryland, a Union State, but also a slave-holding border state with Southern sympathies. Upon arrival in Maryland, Lee separates his forces, sending Stonewall Jackson to Harper's Ferry. What's left of Lee's forces now tries unsuccessfully to block Union advancements, and is forced to retreat from South Mountain. Lee was ready to return to Virginia when news of Stonewall's success at Harper's Ferry made him reconsider. It was Lee's decision to stay that lead to the bloodiest, one-day battle in American History; and one of the strategical wins Lincoln needed to roll out the initial Emancipation Proclamation.

Like Gettysburg, the most gripping information placards are the ones with a picture of the subject on the day of the battle, in front of the same subject, now standing in front of you. Maybe it's just me, but it just leaves me in awe to see a physical structure or a particular land formation, and imagine what actually took place there. To see it in black and white on the day it happened, really sends that home. Usually goose bumps were the telltale sign of this revelation, and there were plenty this day.

Dunker Church marking the first battle, named for its version of the Baptist church that participated in whole body immersion baptisms (true story!), was dead center of the Confederates 40,000 man line; Lee's men to the left, Stonewall's artillery to the right. US

General McClellan moves 15,000 men to assault Stonewall's position the night prior. At dawn the 4 hours of intense fighting and unbelievable carnage began. Folks, this is only a portion of the battlefield, and merely the first skirmish of the day!

We followed the driving portion, sign by sign, reading about the unbelievable numbers of combatants at each spot. Imagine looking out your farmhouse window, looking across your farms rolling pastures, and seeing nothing but a sea of men, smoke, and the atrocities of war. Unfathomable to think the population of a major city is battling it out in your corn pasture, and your living room is now a hospital. But that's exactly what happened to Clara Barton, founder of the Red Cross. She was appalled by the lack of supplies to the front lines, packed up supplies and delivered them herself. She and her helpers prepared meals and took them to the wounded, comforting them where they lay. This was one of many battles she worked. Later she established the American Red Cross in 1881. Wow.

There were so many incredible stories, and so many worthy notables, that I could write an entire book on just this park alone. One though, brought me to tears. After driving through the South, and hearing these incredible stories of heroism and grief, this particular portion of the Battle of Antietam hit me hard. A place called the "Sunken Road," later to be known as the "Bloody Lane."

Imagine a country road, worn down from wagon and horse travel, making about a four foot berm of dirt on each side. Atop the fairly steep rise to the pasture is a wooden picket fence, stretching for miles on both sides. This is the sunken road. Now add 7,200 Confederates approaching the Sunken Road from one side, while 5,000 Union approach from the opposite side. At 1030 in the morning, the bullets began to fly. One Union survivor described being able to see the enemies' face light up with his musket fire. They were at point blank range, firing between the picket fences across that sunken farm road. When it was over, 5,000 men laid dead in and around that sunken road, now forever renamed the Bloody Lane.

At the end of the Bloody Lane was a giant stone watchtower, built as a memorial to the men who died there. It had an observation deck, looking down on the Bloody Lane, but also gave a view of the entire battlefield. That's when I lost it. I don't know if it was just the battle in general, or this specific skirmish that got to me; all I know is I broke down crying. To walk down that sunken road, literally feeling what went on there. No, not like physical pain, but like a heaviness from the inside. I truly had a heavy heart. By the time I got to the tower, I had had enough. Tears welled in my eyes, and I just wept. For whatever reason, I still am not sure, I just wept.

Back at the truck, I just wanted to hug Kimber and leave, but I forced myself to finish the entire park. What an amazing place this is. Don't get me wrong, it's brutal, sad, and heartbreaking; but it's a must see for everyone who claims to be a true American. To think, 87,000 Union and 38,000 Confederate troops "engaged," 28,000 total casualties and losses... in a single day. These are American lives, every single one of them. Absolutely brutal. It was now 1300, I was mentally and physically exhausted, and we still had another battlefield to see.

Heading back toward Baltimore, our last stop was at the Monocacy National Battlefield, just outside the city of Fredrick, MD. This would be our last Civil War Battlefield, and surprisingly one of the most interesting. I'd never heard of this battlefield in school, which is usually a good sign that there's something not so popular being discussed, but important enough to memorialize it. That's exactly the case at Monocacy.

The battlefield itself was a visitor center, located in a small field on the outskirts of a good-sized city. Not quite the suburbs, but the farmland was disappearing fast, giving way to houses and traffic. The rest of the battlefield was a driving tour, with only a few stops within a couple miles of here. Traffic was starting to pick up, with Monday evening rush hour closing in quickly; so I needed to make this quick. I wasn't but three information placards in when I knew I'd be there for more than a minute.

First placard read, "A Border State: Maryland, Delaware, Kentucky, and Missouri were 'border states' — slave states that remained in the union. Because Maryland surrounded Washington DC on three sides, it assumed special importance. Early in 1861, secessionists tried to sway Maryland, but President Lincoln took strong action to foil them. In September, union authorities arrested pro-secession members of the Maryland state legislature, preventing a vote that might've taken Maryland out of the union. As the war progressed Lincoln took care not to alienate Maryland and the other border states. When he issued the Emancipation Proclamation on January 1, 1863 the president excluded the border states. Maryland would abolish slavery on its own in 1864." WHOA WHAT!? Lincoln arrested state senators who were going to vote to secede, and now here's proof that he indeed only freed the slaves in the southern states. That's insane! Talk about going against everything we've ever heard about Lincoln. Apparently, that private museum back in Shenandoah was spot on. But wait, there's more.

The next few placards got into the political climate of the time. Lincoln is looking at his re-election campaign coming up, he couldn't have any more losses on the battlefield, to sway public opinion; and he needed the votes of the 1000s of men fighting across the country. Lincoln decided to open voting for soldiers outside of their home state. And just like that, the absentee ballot was invented. "In 1864, 19 states would allow soldiers to vote from the front. These men would vote overwhelmingly for Abraham Lincoln and total victory over the Confederacy. If Lincoln lost the election, it was assumed that a peace agreement would be made with the new administration and the war would be lost."

Finally the last few placards described the actual battle, I'm summarizing here. With the main Union Army positioned in Virginia, pinning down Lee at Petersburg, Lee knew the capital of Washington DC would be lightly defended. In a last-ditch effort, he sent CSA General Early and half of Lee's men to travel up the Shenandoah and attack Washington DC, while Grant continued his push on Petersburg. Grant suddenly gets a letter from US General Meade that two deserters informed him of Early's troops moving up the Shenandoah Valley. In a rush, he sends troops by sea back to Washington, stopping CSA General Early at the northern edge of Washington itself. The Confederacy's victory at Monocacy left DC within 1 hour of falling, all due to the luck of two scouts seeing troop movement. It was said that Abraham Lincoln himself could see the smoke plumes and hear the cannons from the White House. Luckily, the Union was able to get there in time to thwart the attack, saving the capital and the war. Wow, after all 5 years of incredibly atrocious battle, the war was almost lost within just a few minutes. No wonder you don't hear about this place in the high school history books.

Well, it was now 1700. Traffic was at its worst, and I had about a 2 1/2 hour drive back to Glen's place. I had two very hungry dogs waiting for me, and a very tired little one passed out on the back seat. It was time to get home. After stopping for some wings, we hit the road, putting us back at the house around 1830. Wow, was that one helluva day!

The next day, weather permitting, we planned on checking out the Maryland beaches and Ocean City for lunch, wrapping up our Maryland visit. So at this point, I'm happy to proclaim Maryland, state #34... COMPLETE!

Delaware

June 6th, 2018. So now with Glenn and Nancy still in Alaska, I decided a little downtime with pups was in order. The weather was still pretty wet outside, giving me some time to plan out the rest of our "DC Metro" visit. There was a NY Mets game coming up on the 6th; a rare, Thursday "businessman's special" day game, that even offered free tickets to veterans at the window. When I called the Citi Field box office to confirm this, they said to get there early because they never know how many tickets they will have. Apparently on weekdays, season ticket holders donate unused tickets to veterans like in Cincinnati. How sweet is that!

The plan was to catch one of the NYC teams while I'm here at Glen's, then drive down to the other game, which will be the Yankees, from our Massachusetts destination. There was zero in the way of RV parks around NYC, so the challenge to get into the city for baseball was one of the situations I was dreading most. Knowing that Kimber was in a safe place would make the Mets game so much easier and enjoyable. We also had to explore the states of Delaware and New Jersey, both of which could be done in an afternoon. There were a couple smaller battlefields between the two states worthy of a visit, and I wanted to see where Washington crossed the Delaware into New Jersey. Finally, a visit to downtown DC when Glen and Nancy get back, will wrap up our visit. No rest for the wicked. Let's do this.

After setting up the big dogs outside with a bowl of food and fresh water, I did the same for Kimber inside the house. She was going to sit this one out. I wasn't convinced that Delilah and Kimber were kosher yet, and I also didn't trust the English Staffy's uncanny ability to escape yards. My male, Deuce, was a damn Houdini, I swear! So with a very unhappy look, Kimber watched through the window as I backed the truck out of Glen's driveway around 0600, and began the 3 1/2 hour trek into Queens, NY.

Thanks to Glen's "Easy Pass" I was able to fly right through the toll gates, jumping onto the famous New Jersey Turnpike, heading into NYC. A friend of mine said that whenever you meet somebody from New Jersey, you ask "what exit ah ya?" Apparently, the Jersey turnpike is the main artery through the state; everything has an exit number. Traffic wasn't too bad, until the NY/Jersey state line. Then it was bumper to bumper all the way to the park. The most notable part of the drive was the George Washington Bridge. The toll for my truck was $15.00, if I would have pulled my trailer, it would have been $80.00! Note to self, go around NYC on the way to MA. Second note to self, thank Glen profusely for the use of his traffic pass thingy.

Citi Field, NYC, NY

June 6th, 2018. I arrived at Citi Field around 1030, plenty of time to find a cheap parking spot and get some pictures outside the stadium. One of the things I like to do is walk the entire outside of the park, seeing everything being set up is like a behind the scenes tour before the game. This park was older, with a surprisingly large parking lot for downtown NYC, that wrapped around half the park. The other side was the subway with a designated stop right at the park's ticket office, and a back street with tire and rim shop signs saying something in Spanish. There were flags of all the great players from years past, and some brass plaques embedded in the concrete walkway describing great moments in Mets history.

After I received my ticket, I headed inside, just as they opened the doors. Formerly Shea Stadium, now Citi Field, wow this park is huge! I was able to walk right down behind home plate and get some great pictures, free of ushers giving me the stink eye. Another perk of showing up early. That and the players were just getting on the field for warm-ups and batting practice. Always cool to see a lot of players stopping to sign autographs for the gaggle of kids waiting by the dugouts. It was "Schools Day" with about a million rug rats going to be in attendance. So getting my pictures now, and finding my seat way above the sea of snotty noses and cold bugs, was top priority. Getting sick on this trip is not an option! First things first, pictures, beer, food. In that precise order.

The backdrop for the Citi Field is a massive bleacher complex in left, a massive Jumbotron in center with a giant apple adorned with a Mets logo beneath it. I'm assuming something happens with the apple when a home run is hit. Right field is more bleachers and another, smaller digital screen. There was also a three-deck bar area between right and center that had a replica of a bridge above it. That was it, no cityscape or even a skyscraper in sight.

After walking the entire park and seeing all the food options, I chose the most New York thing I could find, a hot pastrami sandwich. This thing was amazing. Thick cuts of pastrami piled literally 3 inches high, with kraut and mustard on rye bread. Wow. Add the beer while looking over the ballpark... I love my job.

I knew that I could only stay a few innings before having to make that 4-hour drive back to Delaware. It was around 1400 when I jumped in the truck, hoping to beat some traffic heading out of town. I wish I could've spent more time, but I had dogs waiting. Mets were one of my all-time favorite teams, and where my hometown SF Giants originated. Fun fact... the blue and orange on the Mets uniform is SF Giants orange, and Dodger blue, memorializing where both teams originated. With that, I can now say, Citi Field, MLB park #24... COMPLETE!

Back at the farm, the dogs went nuts when I pulled up. Big Arris standing up, paws on the fence, was announcing my arrival, with a much smaller, muffled bark coming from inside. Even Delilah was excited, grabbing her toy in her mouth and throwing it up for herself to chase. I need to teach Kimber that trick! Kimber bolted out the door to join in the fray as soon as I slid it back enough for her to wriggle out last. All three dogs, excited and playing, made me grin. It's funny how dogs change when the owners are gone. Now they all get along and are having a blast. Nice. We all settled in for an evening of *Peaky Blinders* on Glen's big screen TV and recliner couch, glad and relieved that one of the NYC parks was done.

We had a couple days of downtime, with the rain letting up enough to mow the lawn. I had asked if there was anything I could do while Glen and Nancy were gone, Glen said, "Sure! Mow the lawn." I'll let my Facebook post explain the situation...

Joys of Living on the Road... #432

When dog sitting at a friend's house, and said friend asks you to run the riding lawn mower over his 1/2 acre of green grass once while he's gone… SAY NO. This is a two parter...

"It only takes me about 40 minutes with trimming," he says. "Sure, it will be fun." Dog sitter says. 4 1/2 hours later...

Dog sitter...

1. Never assume that you know how to mow a damn lawn on a riding mower, let alone a 1/2 acre. You're from ARIZONA FOR CHRIST'S SAKE!

2. Don't wait a week in Delaware for grass to dry out after 3 days of rain. Grass NEVER dries in Delaware. And grows approximately 1/2 inch every single damn day.

3. Have said friend explain that you should mow in such a fashion that the cut grass ejects OUTWARD. Instead of having a 1/2 acre long row of mowed grass as high as the Appalachian Trail.

4. Rabbit mode is far more efficient and exhilarating than turtle mode. Thank you John Deere, for not explaining that part with ACTUAL WORDS.

5. Going back over said Appalachia in center of the yard on a higher mower setting, DOES NOT spray grass nicely as possible mulch. Instead, you have what resembles kiddie bumper rails at the bowling alley... for a 1/2 acre.

6. After spending hours raking said bumpers into piles, you realize that the lawn now looks like a bad barracks cut on a Monday inspection morning, with Beaver mounds every 8 ft.

7. When back muscle pulls, throw the rake, grab a beer at 10:30am and go in to the AC. You're a damn dog sitter from Arizona... idiot.

Friend...

1. Don't ask your former Marine dog sitter from ARIZONA, who lives in a trailer (with no lawn) to mow your half acre jungle on a damn midget tractor with hieroglyphics for instructions.

2. MOW YOUR OWN DAMN LAWN.

PS. Sorry Glenn Nutter, I tried. Dogs are good!! □□□.

PPS. Pretty sure you have some explaining to do to the neighbors.

With giant grass "beaver mounds" left in Glen's yard, of course it would start to rain again... for three more days. Once again, hoping for a break in the weather to dispose of the lawn massacre evidence, I also had to get some more book work done. This time, packing up Kimber for the ride, and leaving the other two pups in the house, we headed out in the rain to wrap up Delaware and New Jersey.

First stop was the Battle of Cooch's Bridge, the only real battlefield I was able to find in Delaware. Located up toward the PA border, it's a Revolutionary War skirmish that occurred right before Brandywine. Basically, it was a harassing force meant to slow the progress of Howe's British forces from its march on Philadelphia. With 40 lives lost on both sides, the tactic was successful, delaying Howe and allowing Washington to position the Continental Army at Brandywine.

The battlefield itself was an old colonial style, white pillar farm home with what looked like a barn fashioned into a visitor center, surrounded by lush green grass and some information placards. The bridge was on the corner of the property and is an actual working bridge today, with stoplight and plenty of traffic. I took some pics, let Kimber have a ball break, and set out for New Jersey.

New Jersey

June 10th, 2018. The main thing I wanted to see in New Jersey was where George Washington famously crossed the Delaware River, from PA into NJ, to make his attack on Trenton. Just north of Trenton, south of Titusville, was the Washington Crossing Historic Park. There was a small hiking trail park with a very small house and an information placard describing what took place here. There was also an old bronze plaque on the house's wall that designated it as a National Historical Place.

To stand on the exact spot that Washington disembarked from his famous Christmas Eve maneuver, was truly awe inspiring. We've all seen the iconic paintings of Washington crossing the frozen river, with a lantern held above. Ya, I had chills. Amazing. What I didn't know was that he was on his way to the Battle of Trenton. So back to the truck, plug in Battle of Trenton into the GPS and off we went.

Ok, so this next stop really chaffed my backside once again. GPS took me into the heart of Trenton, NJ, to a giant concrete pillar with a bronze George Washington perched on top. The column was large enough for a small visitor center underneath. The visitor center, which was more like just a room under the monument, was barred and chained. The concrete around the monument was broken and unkept. There were beer bottles and an empty syringe laying near one of the park benches. The worn plaque on the side of the monument, covered in overgrown ivy read, "This monument erected by the Trenton Battle Monument Association to commemorate the victory gained by the American army over the forces of Great Britain in this town on the 26th day of December." Sad to see this in such horrible condition, infuriating actually.

At the opposite end of the small courtyard was a much more recent fountain, also adorned with a brass plaque. This one read, "dedicated to the memory of the black soldiers and patriots both free and enslaved who served in the American Revolution 1776-1783." Besides the horrible decay of this historical monument, now they have to interject race, separating the black patriots from the white ones. The original plaque read "American Army," why people feel the need to separate due to race is unreal to me. In the USMC you were either a light green Marine or a dark green Marine, because we all bled red. Another example once again of what I see as the

328

reshaping of U.S. history, due to a political opinion, under the premise of inclusion. Well folks, sorry to break it to ya, not everybody is included in every aspect of American history. Get over it. Once again, the victors of war get to write the history books, but the winners of elections get to rewrite them. Can't they see that this inclusivity that they seek, is actually segregating and even more so, just plain racist? It's a term completely overused today and something they claim to hate the most. I just don't get it, but I digress.

While looking up the location of the Battle of Trenton, a couple of other locations popped up on the GPS that were also nearby, the Princeton Battlefield and the Princeton Battle Monument. The battlefield itself was basically four large white pillars that was once a house, at the edge of a large grassy field. Behind the columns was a brass marker designating a mass grave of both English and American soldiers who had died here. No plaques numbering how many by race, in case you were wondering. Excuse my sarcasm.

The Princeton Battle Monument was actually a very interesting site. Located near Princeton University, if not on the grounds itself, it's hard to tell as the town and University seem to intermingle quite a bit. It was basically a courtyard with a massive carved granite monument depicting Washington at the Battle of Princeton. Words can't describe what this thing looks like, ya gotta just google this and check it out. Absolutely gorgeous, majestic, and a bit creepy all at once.

There was also a separate, much smaller, brass plaque mounted atop a stone platform dedicated to the "Marines in the Revolution." It had an amazing brass plaque with a picture of a Marine dressed in the period, while standing in the wind. Modern and beautifully done, the inscription below read, "Dedicated to the continental Marines who fought with General Washington's troops during the battle of Princeton January 3, 1777." To think, my glorious Corps was only three years old. Amazing.

Traffic and rain were really starting to wear on my last nerve; it was time to get back to the farm. We meandered our way across the small state, back to the turnpike, and eventually home to Delaware. This won't be our last time in Jersey, as we will once again back up the turnpike when we head to Massachusetts for our next trailer location. With only a trip to DC being left on the "DC Metro" itinerary, I'm going to go ahead and declare both Delaware and New Jersey, states #35 and #36... COMPLETE!

Washington DC

June 14th, 2018. By this time Glen and Nancy had returned from Alaska to two very happy fur babies, and the two interlopers in their back yard. Glen keeps telling me that when I go to Alaska, I won't come back. Can't wait to experience that myself, but until then, I got a huge challenge in front of me. Today I venture into downtown DC, on the train, without Kimber. Not going to lie, since it wasn't a real state, I was good with skipping DC; the congestion, traffic and crowds was enough of a deterrent to make me want to pass. But since they have a baseball team now, and there are all kinds of stuff I really wanted to see, I pushed the anxiety beast as far down into my soul as I could and mustered the courage to do this. Not to mention, who knows if I will ever be here again, I gotta do this.

First stop was back at the same train station as Glen had showed me the day of the Nationals game. I had a decent understanding of the color coded map, and Glen had shown me where I would get off for Arlington, where I wanted to start this adventure. Plan was to get off the train at Arlington National Cemetery and work my way to the Capital Building. I didn't have the money to really explore all the museums and really cool things, so a long hike down the "Mall" and pictures of all the famous monuments and buildings would have to suffice, at least for this visit.

The subway dropped me off to what I believe was just north of Arlington National Cemetery, within a couple blocks of the US Marine Corps War Memorial, an obvious must see. A massive bronze statue of the iconic raising of the flag at Iwo Jima, stood atop a black granite base, with the countries and years that the Marine Corps served there inscribed with gold lettering. I found the "Somalia 1992-1994" ominously next to "Afghanistan 2001- ," with the end date obviously empty. I noticed other people taking pictures with big smiles in front of the memorial, something I just couldn't do. I had a younger kid take a picture of me standing in front of the Somalia inscription, I looked more somber than happy.

First thing that I did not know about Arlington National Cemetery was that this is an active military base. I entered from the north and not the main entrance, quickly flashed my military ID to a gate sentry, and I was in the cemetery, map in hand, and alone. No crowds, nobody else nearby, it was just me... and what seemed an eternity of graves. Standing in an absolute ocean of white marble tombstones, my heart started to race. I began to notice that most of the graves around me were fallen Marines. One after the next, I read the names, dates, and ages. As far as you could see, the markers went on and on. When my eyes finally filled with enough tears that I couldn't see, I suddenly burst out in song. Why, I have no clue. And if anybody else would have been there, there's no way I would've done this. Suddenly, I just started singing the Marine Corps Hymn. Maybe it was in my head, maybe it was out loud, all I know is I sang. With tears rolling down my face, I sang. All I could think was this, this right here, is why we stand for our flag, our anthem, and our country. By the time I had finished the hymn, I felt relieved. Like a release of sorts had just happened. I can't explain it, I just felt... lighter.

As I made my way to the Tomb of the Unknown Soldier, I happened to look to my right, and there was Omar Bradley's grave, reminding me of my Somalia vet buddy Ken back in Missouri, showing me Bradley's monument. Then I passed the tomb of Robert Todd Lincoln, thinking back to Lincoln's tomb, where he and his wife are buried, describing that the son was buried here. It's crazy how everything from this trip is intertwined, and how cool it is to have been at these other places, giving even more relevance to today.

I passed the John F. Kennedy Memorial with the never extinguished flame, Jackie Kennedy by his side. Robert "Bobby" Kennedy's grave nearby, along with Senator Edward Kennedy's. A sign posted asked for silence and respect, which of course the foreign tourists couldn't read. I took some quick pictures and moved along, not before shushing an obnoxious Italian dude, who quickly got checked by his wife.

I walked along a path named "Lee Avenue" that lead to the Lee house, which was unfortunately closed for renovation at the moment. The information placard told an amazing story that is one of my favorites of the entire trip. Prior to the Civil War, General Lee was an up and coming Army Officer and knew he would be traveling to DC often. He decided to purchase a ranch near Washington DC, but on the Virginia side of the Potomac River. After the Civil War began, it came time for Lee to pay his property taxes. Back then you couldn't just mail in a payment, they were made in person. Lee knew he would be arrested if he crossed the Virginia state line, and he couldn't send his wife to do it, women couldn't even vote at that time. So the Union Army seizes his land, and out of spite began to bury their dead on Lee's ranch. That piece of land today is called Arlington National Cemetery. Yup, I got chills too. Incredible!

Finally, I found the Tomb of the Unknown Soldier, hoping to see the changing of the guard. As I made my way up the hill, I noticed there was already a large group of people, and a lot of Army personnel in full dress uniforms, standing around, waiting for something. I walked up and asked a couple of the soldiers what was going on. Turns out I was there on the Army's birthday, and the top brass was about to arrive for the ceremony. Wow! Perfect timing!

There was a large crowd of mainly school kids on a field trip, and several old veterans, myself to be included, apparently. I gently worked my way through the crowd to get to a place where I could record a video. The ceremony was full of the typical military formalities. The Secretary of the Army and a couple of 4-star generals laid a giant rose wreath at the tomb, then stood for a moment of silence before the band broke out with the Army Hymn. What's pretty cool as I write this in 2020 and look back at the pictures is, the Secretary of the Army was Mark Esper, now Secretary of Defense, and one of the 4-star generals was General Milley, now Joint Chief of Staff. This explains what happened after the bigwigs departed the scene, and I quickly made my way to the shade, looking for some relief from the hot sun. As I fanned myself with the map I was holding, I glanced to the roof of the building to see two security guys watching me make my hasty move to the shade. Ya, a bearded guy with tattoos, amongst a bunch of school kids, suddenly wants to leave right after the Secretary and generals do; I'd be watching me too. I nodded to them, waving my fan a little faster in front of me. They slowly backed away from the building parapet, speaking into their wrist mics. Just trying to cool off, Officer, good looking out though! I decided to go ahead and make my way to the main gate, trying to stay ahead of the crowd, and any other issues.

From Arlington, I walked across the bridge above the Potomac River to the Lincoln Monument. It was a bright sunny day, and humid as hell. The crowds were manageable this early in the day, mainly school groups, foreign tourists, and locals jogging or exercising in some form or fashion. Even had a dude in spandex doing yoga while people filmed him. Hey, whatever floats your boat. It's America.

I climbed the steps of the Lincoln Memorial, reading the massive inscriptions of his famous speeches carved into the white granite walls. The enormity of the thing was what was amazing, Lincoln looking almost life-like. It really was impressive. From there, I walked down the cherry tree lined pathway, along the reflection pool. I passed through the World War II monument, the Washington Monument, took a few pictures of the White House, and made my way to the Capital Building. 9.1 miles total that day, before finally sitting down at a pub, with a cold beer near the train station. I did it, lots more to see, but not this time. I saw enough, I want my dog. Washington DC... COMPLETE!

Massachusetts

June 17th, 2018. Father's Day came on a Sunday this year, which in my mind made it even better to drag this trailer up to Boston at 0300 in the morning. I was hoping that traffic would be at its best, if I left as early as possible on a Sunday morning... especially one with a holiday. So that's what we did, saying our goodbyes to Glen and Nancy, we began the 400 mile trek to Hanscom AFB, our next predetermined "home base."

It was a good move, making our run early; the freeways were pretty much empty save a few delivery trucks and big rigs. I took the New Jersey Turnpike to the Garden State Parkway, rolling through downtown Newark around 0600. Perfect, traffic was still very manageable, as we finally hit the New York State Thruway. You can pretty much tell from the names like turnpike and thruway, that these were pay to play roadways, to the tune of about 80 bucks in tolls by the time we pulled into the Hanscom AFB FamCamp. There were so many toll booths in Massachusetts that I decided to roll the dice and see what the "pay by plate" option did. Like putting your toll tax on layaway. When my buddy called this place "Taxxachusetts," he wasn't lying.

Once outside NJ, the drive became amazing. A new interstate carved into beautiful rolling hills of green grass, tall trees lining both sides of the road. The sun was out and absolutely gorgeous, especially when you passed the peak of a good-sized hill and could see across the green treetops, against the blue sky backdrop. Even the rest stops were like small city parks, much to Kimber's appreciation, as she got to play ball with every one of my coffee induced bathroom stops.

Author's note: Even though we saw the Mets play in NYC and still had a Yankee game to catch here, we only passed through the state of New York to get to Massachusetts. I'll cover New York as a state, when we come back across the northern border. So basically, we're going to count NYC as its own little world. So many smart-ass remarks could go here, but I'll refrain. You're welcome.

I had looked into Hanscom AFB back in AZ when we were in the planning phase of this trip. A popular FamCamp that allows you to stay as long as you wish, took reservations but also had a good-sized first come first serve section, and a huge field that could take overflow if needed. The lady said they have never turned anybody away. That was music to my ears! I chose to play it by ear and take the overflow if necessary, not having any clue really what exact day we would be pulling in. Luckily, they had plenty of spots, with us choosing a secluded area in the back, a forest for our backyard. It had water and electric, a bathroom and shower close by. A community fire pit was the evening attraction, and a lush green grass field that made Kimber the happiest of campers. Coffee in the morning with the fellas, nice quiet evenings, save for the AFB runway a few hundred yards away. Then of course, you have a modern military base with a gym the likes of Club Med, and a commissary like a high-end grocery store, fast-food and PX. AND being only twenty minutes from downtown Boston, sandwiched between both Battles of Concord and Lexington... this place was an absolute gold mine of a find!

So the plan for our "New England" adventure was another ambitious one. We had two iconic ball games to attend, a trip down to the Bronx for a Yankees game, and then my first visit to the oldest park in the nation: Fenway. When it comes to the battlefields, we had landed at ground zero for the Revolutionary War. We would be visiting Concord and Lexington, followed by the Liberty walk in Boston, ending at the Battle of Bunker Hill. Then with time permitting, there's all of downtown Boston to explore. I also planned to make a run into Connecticut and Rhode Island from our Hanscom home base, before packing up the trailer once again for our Maine visit. Did I mention we had about two weeks to do this in?

Ok, so now it's a scheduling issue. I had to figure out what games to see, in the time frame I'd permitted, and according to weather; so here's the itinerary. I found another Thursday afternoon businessman's special for the Yankees game, and a pre-planned Red Sox game for that following Sunday, leaving us the next three days wide open. The weather was perfect minus the humidity, so we took advantage of both time and weather, and set out for a couple of small battlefields in Connecticut and Rhode Island, but only after a solid day of rest and relaxation.

Connecticut and Rhode Island

June 19th, 2018. We left camp bright and early, not knowing what to expect traffic wise. We took the freeway to get out of town, and then set the GPS to backroads once we got into Connecticut. I was taken aback by how dense the forest was lining the freeway, almost tropical as we got closer to the coastline. Our first stop was going to be at Fort Griswold Battlefield State Park, a place I had looked up prior to leaving. Situated on the mouth of Thames River between the towns of Groton and New London.

It was a beautifully landscaped park with a well maintained Revolutionary War era fort, several static cannon displays, and a small visitor center that of course was closed on Tuesdays. The view over the water to New London was phenomenal; an incredibly beautiful backdrop to the tragedy that happened here.

I was in awe when I heard the story of the Battle of Groton Heights, a horrible massacre led by none other than the American traitor, Benedict Arnold. Arnold, now defected from the U.S. and in charge of the British Fleet was tasked with destroying American privateers in New London, capturing any military supplies stored there. On September 6th, 1781, Arnold landed, easily taking several forts while looting and burning the towns. It is still under speculation whether the troops at Fort Griswold surrendered or not, still mercilessly slaughtered by Arnold's men. Here's the kicker... Benedict Arnold was born and raised in Norwich, Connecticut. The bastard did this to his own home state. Wow. Just wow.

I still wanted to cover as much of the coastline as possible, even though I skipped most of New Jersey and all of Long Island. From Groton we took Hwy 1 toward Rhode Island, passing through some of the most beautiful country I'd seen since PA. I was surprised that there was this much heavy vegetation so close to the beaches, let alone between NYC and Boston! I guess I assumed it would be all urban sprawl.

Just before crossing into Rhode Island, we came to a town called West Mystic. Mystic? Why does that sound so familiar? I started humming Van Morrison's "Into the Mystic," a personal favorite due to some great memories, trying to remember why Mystic, Connecticut was so familiar. I was starting to get hungry too, especially when the smell of pizza hit me while stopped at a traffic light. Low and behold, on the corner across the street was the memory I had been searching for. *Mystic Pizza*, one of my favorite movies that had me head over heels for a new actress named Julia Roberts. That's what it was! I knew that sounded familiar, and absolutely, I stopped for lunch and a beer. Great food, great people, and a cool gift shop now added to the original pizza place.

After lunch I walked around downtown Mystic, an absolutely gorgeous little seaside town. I was definitely getting a California vibe here, especially when I stopped in at an old record shop. I started picking up old LPs that I had owned another lifetime ago. The Rolling Stones iconic red "Tattoo You" album cover caught my eye, along with about three decades of memories all at once. Then The Clash's "London Calling" smashing guitar cover instantly appeared in my hand, with my wallet in the other, before I had to remind myself I don't own a record player anymore. Wow, I felt like I was 14 years old again, standing in my favorite underground record shop called the Record Vault, back in San Francisco. Suddenly it was 1985 all over again. I had a great talk with the shop owner who was excited about my book and travel stories, taking my information and demanding a copy when I print. What a great shop! Thanks again for the care package, brother!

We crossed the Rhode Island state line around 1300 near the town of Westerly; the weather was amazing and the drive fantastic. I wanted to see the beaches and Misquamicut Beach State Park was just up the road. Absolutely gorgeous homes hugged the coastline, with large stones and incredibly bright flowers along the beach. Definitely not what I expected for Rhode Island. I stopped for some pictures and let Kimber get in the water. She hadn't been in the ocean for awhile, and immediately began where the last "Battle of the Waves" left off. Eagerly chasing the tide out, but this time not scared of its return, she lunged into the oncoming frothy white crested waves. I'm still floored by how much this little dog loves the water.

From the beach we started back toward camp, hoping to stop at another battlefield called Prescott Farm, but sadly not being able to locate it. We continued winding our way through the back roads of RI, still taken aback by how dense the vegetation was and only a few miles from the beach. I stopped once to look at my GPS, making sure I was still on the right track home. When I looked up from my phone, the first thing I saw was a mailbox on the roadside, in front of the house where I had stopped...with a bright red Cardinal painted on the side of it. It's almost uncanny how as soon as I begin to question myself, this reminder always appears. Yup, I'm good, almost home. Even though it was short and sweet, I'm glad to say both Connecticut and Rhode Island, states #37 and #38... COMPLETE!

Ok, now back to Mass... kinda. Before I had left for this trip, my buddy Alex from Arizona, remember he's the Vietnam vet/ Massachusetts State Troopa that watched Kimber for my very first ballpark in San Diego. Anyway, he was going to be just a few minutes away from Hanscom AFB, visiting his son in New Hampshire, and said he would take Kimber again while I went to the Yankee game. This was a huge relief when we made the plans back in AZ, and gratefully, I made it to Massachusetts on schedule to take him up on the offer. So after a full day of rest, I dropped Kimber off with Alex and Dawn, just over the state line in New Hampshire, and once again made the 4-hour drive into NYC.

Yankee Stadium, NYC, NY

June 21st, 2018. Using my new found trick of reserving a parking space online, I found an uncovered spot within a block of the park for around $25; pretty sure that was a good deal. The parking attendant was even good enough to make sure I could get out after only a few innings visit. It was just on the other side of the subway drop-off from the new Yankee Stadium. From here, I just followed the crowd of blue and white clad Yankee fans to what looked like a modern version of the Roman Colosseum. It reminded me of walking up to Caesar's Palace in Las Vegas. It's made of massive concrete blocks, with tall white pillars surrounding the entire complex, save the side next to the above ground subway tracks. The typical flags of all the great players adorned the streetlights, with a few vendors about; but mainly massive concrete barriers directing the crowds. Police officers in full riot gear with M4 rifles was definitely the most eye-catching aspect of the whole scene. That and a sea of elderly folks my grandparents age. Senior citizen day, oh great. Hope I get a ticket.

As luck would have it, all that was left was a standing room only ticket, which was the cheapest anyway. I'm just glad I didn't have to pay a NYC scalper's price. Inside the park looked like a giant mall with a ball field in the middle. Built in 2009, I was sad to realize that I missed the original Yankee Stadium. All that was left was black and white posters of great players and moments along the roofline of the main promenade. Below the giant pictures were glass entry doors to retail shops and bars on clean shiny concrete. Literally like walking in a shopping mall. All that history... gone. Ya, I was very disappointed. I guess I just didn't realize they had a new park. That lasted for about a minute, then I remembered we were still in NYC at a freakin' Yankee game! Yup, life was good then. One of the most dreaded parks to visit due to logistics, timing, traffic and parking; but now all that was left to do was take some pictures and enjoy the game.

Don't get me wrong, this park was amazing. Absolutely massive ballpark, with four full levels, and multiple box seats and suites in between. The backdrop was mainly just the massive Jumbotron in centerfield, with two smaller screens flanking it. There were ample bleacher areas on each side of a standing room only bar, with the bullpens on each side, just below the bleachers. It was quite the party scene in centerfield, no doubt. I opted for a standing room only spot on the 4th deck behind home plate; great view, cool park, nice people. I was lucky enough to see Aaron Judge play at home, and got a pack of the 2018 team baseball cards, with Judge's rookie card on top to prove it. All in all, a huge victory for me and my PTSD. By the fourth inning, though, I needed my dog, something fierce. And I had one helluva commute home in front of me. Yankee Stadium, MLB park #25... COMPLETE!

Kimber was ecstatic to see me of course and took a minute to calm down. That's when Alex told me he had Red Sox tickets for that Sunday. He had mentioned that he knew a retired veteran that was somehow connected to the Red Sox organization, and was getting us some really good tickets. He said Kimber could stay with his wife Dawn, who didn't care to go, and we'd take the train into Boston. So I get to see Fenway with a great friend and veteran, that grew up seeing games in Boston, and worked here as a state trooper?! Hell yes, I'm in! I couldn't wait to hear the old stories and of course see Fenway Park, the oldest park in the MLB system. Sunday couldn't get here fast enough, but in the meantime, Kimber and I took a couple of well deserved days off to enjoy the AFB amenities.

With the trailer's fridge now nicely stocked, thanks to the base commissary, and a couple of much needed visits to the incredible, on base, fitness facility, it was time to head back to Alex and Dawn's place. Sunday was finally here, and it was time for baseball. First, Alex and I jumped on a commuter train at Lunenburg, MA, then caught the archaic Boston subway somewhere downtown I assumed, since we were underground the entire time. From there, it was a quick trip over to Fenway Park, dropping us about a block away. The subway seems like it was built by Washington himself, compared to the DC Metro, just saying. It was actually kind of cool, like stepping back in time about a hundred years. All I know is we took the "green-line" to the game, and if I had to find my way out of here, I was screwed.

One of the best stories I heard from Alex was when we hustled across the freeway overpass toward the park. "See that roof right there?" Alex asked, while pointing at a rooftop across the street from the left field wall, affectionately known as the Green Monster. "There used to be a sign on that roof that we would climb up when I was kid to see the game." It was then and there, I knew I was in for a once in a lifetime experience.

Much like Wrigleyville, the streets were flooded with a sea of Sox fans, sporting all things red and white. We walked down Lansdowne St., the street that separated Alex's sign from the actual park, and stopped at a bar and grill that's actually built into the Green Monster. A place called the Bleacher Bar, had a large roll-up door where people could sit and eat while watching the players warm up right in front of them. The funny part is when I was inside the park, I noticed they shut the roll-up door before game time. Sorry folks. "No tickey, no laundry," to paraphrase Jack Nicholson in one of my favorite Boston movies ever, *The Departed*.

Fenway, Boston, MA

June 24th, 2018. After lunch, we met up with one of Alex's good buddies from the Massachusetts State Troopers, Charlie, a monster of a man, in great shape for being somewhere in his 60s. We stood and talked while watching all the excitement as the crowd starting filing into the park. That's when Sgt Major Davidson (retired) showed up with the tickets Alex had spoken of. After introductions and handshakes, I was handed a ticket from the Sgt Maj. with a quick "see you guys up there," before he bolted off to find some other ticket recipients. When I glanced at the ticket, I almost tripped over the curb we were walking past. The ticket price was $195.00, followed by "Private Suite." I was in shock when I showed Alex the ticket with a WTF look on my face. That's when he explained who Sgt Maj Davidson was and the ticket.

Back when Alex and I made plans to meet up in the NE last winter, he had mentioned that he knew somebody that could get us tickets, and maybe even get us on the field. I was stoked, dreaming of a picture with me leaning against the Green Monster in left field. As time passed, I didn't really think about that, as it wasn't a for sure thing. All I knew was that I'd be seeing the Red Sox at Fenway with my brother Alex. So now Alex looks at the ticket and smiles, and tells me how this came about.

One of Alex's junior officers and subordinates was a Captain named Jack Hammond. Jack later became Brigadier General Hammond retried, and in charge of the Red Sox grounds crew. Alex calls his old General buddy and says, "Hey, Jack. I got this veteran, served in Somalia, diagnosed with PTSD, traveling the country, writing a book about baseball parks. What's the chance at a line on some tickets?" Jack responds with a "I'll call you right back." That's how we learned to meet Sgt Major Davidson, who works with an organization called "Home Base," working with veterans suffering from PTSD and TBI, for our ticket. Wow, just wow!

Just when I thought it could not get any better than this, it turns out the Red Sox ace, and starting pitcher, Chris Sale, reserved the box and sprung for all the food and beer us veterans could consume. I'll never forget when we walked into the suite, where two full boxes of Chris Sale autographed baseballs were sitting on the table. "Welcome! Grab a beer, grab a ball!

Enjoy!" was the greeting from the Sgt Major. Whoa what!? This was way too good to be true. Then around the 5th inning, they called us all into the suite to take pictures with... get this... the Red Sox World Series Championship Trophy from 2013. It was carried around from suite to suite by its white felt glove wearing staff. An absolutely incredible experience, and one I was so humbled to be a part of. Thank you, Alex, Sgt Major Davidson, General Hammond, Chris Sale, and the Home Base organization. Author's note: Later that year, Chris Sale would lead the Red Sox to the 2018 World Series win. Not gonna lie, I love me some Boston, and this just put the icing on the cake.

I know I didn't cover much of the Fenway with this visit, only because I knew I would be coming back to the park for a second game in just a couple of days. One of my friends back in AZ wanted to fulfill a bucket list item of his by catching a Red Sox game at Fenway while I was there. This was perfect as I didn't want to be rude to Alex and leave that amazing suite to take pictures and roam around the park. This would also give me a chance to explore downtown Boston and do the tourist thing. Not to mention my friend's mother sprung for a hotel room downtown, making it much easier to deal with Kimber while we explored the town. Until then, I had some battlefields to see.

Monday is always a good day to explore a National Park or any other tourist destination during the summer. Most parents are working, and kids aren't going to go learn about history by themselves, which leaves the parks happily vacant or close to it. Perfect time to catch the Battle of Lexington, which was literally just a few miles from camp. After some breakfast and a little bit of ball time for Kimber, we were off to two of the most important battles in American history.

I pulled into the town of Lexington about 1030, completely disoriented as to what direction we were facing or really where I was in general. The road system in Massachusetts is literally a spiderweb of interconnecting two-lane roads, meandering through amazingly dense trees, broken up by farmland and pastures. Town signs pop up out of the blue and suddenly there is a small town square or plaza with businesses and shops. Like Alex told me, they made a road out of every goat trail since the 1600s. It definitely shows. If it wasn't for GPS here, I'd be pulling over every three miles to consult the map.

We couldn't have asked for a more beautiful day. The sun was out with a cool gentle breeze, allowing Kimber to stay in the truck comfortably as I explored the Lexington Common Historic Site. This is where the GPS gods brought me after typing in Battle of Lexington. A large triangular shaped grass field surrounded by giant Oaks lining its edges. A beautiful city park, with a massive flagpole, had several informational placards embedded in large boulders and a massive marble monument. At the point of the "triangle" facing town, which was the direction the English advanced from, stood a bronze statue of a lone patriot holding a musket atop a mound of boulders, now completely covered in a light green patina, yet still standing in defiance. I'm not sure if this is Paul Revere or just a depiction of a "Minute Man," either way, it was this spot that began the American Experiment.

As I walked around the Lexington Commons, I came across a young lady in period dress, a long dress and bonnet, standing next to a granite monument marking where one of the first "meeting houses" stood. She was employed by the Chamber of Commerce and was an absolute wealth of knowledge. She pointed out where all the most important episodes took place, and directed me toward a visitor center downtown with maps and what not. This was not a Park Service visitor center, so I opted to just walk the park and then follow Paul Revere's ride to Concord.

The next display was a giant boulder with a very old bronze plaque mounted to it. The plaque read, "The site of the old Belfrey from which the alarm was wrung April 19, 1775 this tablet was directed by the Lexington chapter Daughter's of the American Revolution. 1910." The alarm was wrung? So this is where the local townspeople heard Revere and rung the bell, warning of the English advancement? I'm kind of confused at this point. Maybe I should've went to the visitor center after all. Let's just keep exploring.

Across the street was a large yellow house with a Lexington Historical Society sign saying "Buckman Tavern c.1709. Gathering place of the Lexington Militia. April 19th 1775." An interesting exhibit that had a pay to play entry fee, but also had a Park Service pamphlet for a "Minute Man National Historical Park." After a quick scan of the map and timeline inside the brochure, I had some bearing as to what was going on here. So Buckman Tavern is where the militia waited for the English troops to arrive. But let me back up and give you an overview first.

Ok, so in a nutshell, here we go, timeline first. The excerpts from the pamphlet read, "1765-1770, Taxation and Rebellion. To pay for the French and Indian war, Britain begins taxing its American colonies. Colonials protest; they do not believe Britain has the right to tax them. Tensions mount and British soldiers arrive in Boston to restore order. Soldiers fire into a mob, killing five colonists in what rebels call the Boston massacre.

"1773-1774, Tea Party and Trouble. Britain repeals most taxes except on tea. The rebels respond with the Boston Tea Party, dumping tea into the harbor. Britain closes the ports and strips Massachusetts of self-government. The Massachusetts provincial congress recommends towns raise companies of 'Minutemen' from the militias who can respond 'at the shortest notice.'

"1775, Preparations. The British army begins patrolling beyond Boston. Militia companies and Minutemen continue to drill; colonies continue to stockpile gunpowder and supplies, enough to supply an army of 15,000. Rebels in Boston keep a close watch on British movements. In turn, subjects loyal to Britain spy on the rebels."

Ok, now we're up to nightfall, April 19th, 1775. "One if by Land, Two if by Sea. Paul Revere learns the British Army is preparing to cross the Charles River and march to Concord to capture weapons. A man hangs two lanterns in North Church to alert colonials, using Revere's code: one if by land, two if by sea. Revere crosses the river, mounts a strong horse, and races west to spread the alarm. William Dawes gallops out along the southern route." So far so good. But who's this Dawes character? Never heard there was more than one rider, I always thought it was just Paul Revere.

The pamphlet now breaks down April 19th, 1775 into an hourly description. The next one surprised me. It read, "1am Captured! In Lexington, Revere and Dawes encountered Samuel Prescott, who joins in spreading the alarm. The British patrol surprises them and captures Revere." Whoa Whoa Whoa! Revere got caught?

I read on, "5am First Blood. 77 militiamen await the British Army on Lexington Green. A shot rings out and the British soldiers fire a volley. Eight colonials die." Ok, now I have chills. You mean, I was walking on the same grassy field where Patriot blood was first spilled in the creation of America? Wow, just wow. So was this the famous "Shot heard around the World" as described in our school history books? And who fired that shot? Interestingly, this was not that famous shot. The truth is, historians actually have no idea who fired the round that propelled the English to open fire. Then where and when was that famous shot made that echoed around the world? Follow me grasshopper, you have much to learn.

The next pamphlet entry read "7am Concord's Early Light. Several hundred militiamen watch from nearby hills as the British start searching Concord." Ok, so at this point, the English are moving on Concord. I stopped reading and decided to move along what's called "Battle

Road"; looks like we're on another historical scavenger hunt. I still want to know what the hell happened to Paul Revere!

So according to the map in the Park Service pamphlet, the towns of Lexington and Concord are both part of the Minute Man National Historic Park, to include the path in between. It was that path, Battle Road, that we were taking now toward Concord. It also said there was an award-winning visitor center somewhere in between. So after letting Kimber chase the ball on the lush green grass of the historical Lexington Common, we were off to Concord.

The drive toward the first stop looked extremely familiar; it should, being as I'd driven by it several times on my way back to camp. We were literally about 2 miles from the trailer. The information placards next to the small parking area described the retreat of the British back toward Lexington. Shit. This was the LAST stop of what looked like would be a very long day. I was exhausted from the week's activities already, and we had to meet my buddy at the hotel room tomorrow evening. Not to mention, the heat and humidity were kicking in. Ya, I'm calling it, back to the trailer to soak up some AC and relax before a busy couple of days in Boston. Kimber concurred, knowing full well there was plenty of grass next to the Rig for some ball time.

Not quite fully rested but 100% better than yesterday, we left bright and early to wrap up the Minuteman Park, before heading into Boston that evening to meet Rick. This time, I decided to go straight to the visitor center, which I should've done in Lexington the first time. Of course, since the Park name didn't have the tag word "battlefield" in the title, I had no idea this was even here. See what I mean about National Park designators? The visitor center itself was absolutely state of the art. Of course the building replicated an old, stick built barn, its content was the most modernized I'd seen yet. Maps had red and blue LED lights describing troop movements, the theater was as if you were in someone's home, watching the fight through the window. It was a well-done display for sure.

The very first placard I read answered my question about the capture of Paul Revere. As Revere and Dawes left Boston on separate routes, they both arrived in Lexington around midnight. Now check this out, this gets good. Sam Adams and John Hancock were hiding out at Rev. Jonas Clarke's house after leading the Massachusetts Rebellion. Within an hour of Revere and Dawes alerting Lexington, the town Belfry bells began to ring.

Now both Revere and Dawes are riding to Concord, when they come across Dr. Samuel Prescott returning home from a night of "courting." He quickly learns of the mission and offers his assistance. As they pass through the town of Lincoln (interesting name for a man not born yet), all three are stopped by a British ambush. Instantly the three chose to run; Prescott jumping a stone wall, Dawes making for the road, and Revere across a pasture. Only Revere was recaptured but quickly released, when the English heard the sound of gunfire and bells from Lexington. If they only knew who they had! Meanwhile, it was Prescott who finally made it to Concord and sounded the alarm. Ok, so that's answered, now where was "the shot heard around the world" fired if it wasn't in Lexington?

Back to the Park Service pamphlet. We left off where the colonials were on a hillside watching the English sack Concord. "9am Homes on fire? British soldiers burn weapons and military supplies, but militia men think homes are burning. They advance to North Bridge." Next entry reads, "9:30am North Bridge. The militia men confront British soldiers, who fire and kill two colonials. The militia officer orders his men to return fire, an act of treason against the British government that would become known as the shot heard round the world." Apparently we're off for North Bridge.

A quick glance at my watch proved that I was going to have to hustle if I wanted to see everything before heading into rush hour traffic toward downtown Boston. This was the most important battlefield of them all, as far as I'm concerned; I definitely don't want to rush this. We still had Thursday and Friday this week to explore this properly, so once again, I headed back to the trailer to prep for our Boston excursion. Besides, I could drive into the city early and skip a lot of the traffic... I hoped.

Later that evening we met Rick at the hotel, set Kimber up in the lap of luxury, and headed out for some dinner. The drive into town was bad but could have been worse; we got to the hotel early, giving me some time to look up restaurants. First place that came to mind was the original "Cheers" bar from one of my favorite '80s television series. This wasn't the stage set bar, this was the ORIGINAL underground bar that the show was based off of. A very small bar with a few dining tables and unbelievable Boston memorabilia decorated the walls. Definitely a popular place, luckily we were able grab a seat to sample their famous Boston Clam "Chowda," a must have if visiting the Bostonian. From there, we just rolled back to the hotel, had some beers, and got some rest for the very busy next day.

We were up first thing, set Kimber up in the hotel room, had some breakfast at the hotel, and were standing in the Boston Commons by 0800. This was the starting point for what's known as the "Freedom Trail." The night before, I had downloaded an interactive app that takes you on a 2.2 mile guided tour of downtown Boston, from the Commons to the Battle of Bunker Hill. It was going to be a bit of a push before we caught the game tonight, but the history would be amazing.

I was stunned by the architecture of the old buildings surrounding this massive grass park with giant Oak trees, that I learned were actually Great Elms lining the walkways and sprouting up intermittently in the field. Ornate stone cut into buildings, some with cornerstones dating back to the 1600s. In 1634, only 4 years after the Puritans settled the Shawmut Peninsula and created the town of Boston, the Commons were set aside as an English-style "commonage," or common area for Boston's townsfolk. Everything from recreation, religious congregations, a place to air grievances and a cemetery; the English even used it for camp and drilling prior to the Revolutionary War. I can't believe I walked on this incredibly ancient, and in some ways sacred, piece of land. This truly is the birthplace of America.

First stop on the map was just across the Commons from where the Uber dropped us off. The Massachusetts State House and the Boston Massacre Memorial. The memorial was in the Commons, a massive white granite obelisk, with a very old bronze statue of a woman and an eagle breaking chains, perched above a bronze plaque directing the horrific scene of the shooting. The inscription on the backside read, "Erected in 1888 by the commonwealth of Massachusetts in honor of those who fell at the Boston Massacre." There were no information placards describing the event, so I'm still unclear as to what happened. Hopefully, it will be explained later, there's a lot of stops to see.

Just a few steps up to the street from the memorial, you have an amazing view of the gold covered dome on the Massachusetts State House, again reminding me of the film *The Departed*.

There was a fence barring access to the actual building, but the view from across the street was awesome. A giant brick building, with white colonial pillars, reminiscent of the Capital Building in DC, but on a much smaller scale. The obvious difference is the brick and massive gold dome. One of the signs explained how the dome was temporarily painted black during World War 2 as to not attract enemy aircraft. That's kinda cool.

The path you follow is actually bricks inlaid into the sidewalk, or sometimes just a painted curb, all with brass markers pointing directions as you wind your way through Boston's side streets. We passed the church where the song "America" also known as "My Country 'Tis of Thee" was written and sung for the first time. We stopped at the absolutely ancient Granary Burial Ground with such famous occupants as Paul Revere, John Hancock, Samuel Adams, and the slain from the Boston Massacre, only to name a few.

Ok, we finally found out what the Boston Massacre was and I recognized it immediately. This is when the townspeople surrounded the house and shop of a "Tory" sympathizer and customs agent named Ebenezer Richardson, throwing rocks and snowballs at his windows. Richardson opens his window and fires into the crowd, killing a small boy. 11 days later on March 5, 1770, British troops shot and killed five demonstrators in what was called the Boston massacre. Now I remember, I think we saw a film about this in school.

We walked past the Irish immigrant memorial, a refreshing change to see that white Europeans also suffered from slavery. I saw the Old State House, where the Declaration of Independence was first read to Boston, the Revere House, and of course the North Church where the famous lights were hung, giving the message as to whether the Red Coats were attacking by land or by sea. Finally, we ended at Bunker Hill, where the famous order "don't fire until you see the whites of their eyes" was said to be given. This is a very broad recap, as an entire book could be written about this 2.2 mile walk. So much to see and learn. This tour was an absolute must do if you're in Boston. Absolutely incredible! It was a little warm and humid, but hey, it's Boston; there's a cold beer on every block.

We got back to a very anxious little Kimber dog in the hotel room. After a quick walk outside, a good 30 minutes of ball time on a chunk of grass near the hotel, and a belly full of dad's sandwich, all was forgiven. At least until we left for the game about 3 hours later.

Back at Fenway later that evening, the scene was even more chaotic than the Sunday afternoon game, shockingly busy for a Wednesday night game. It was nice having an Uber drop us off right at the park, instead of hunting for parking. Luckily, we didn't have too far to walk as Rick was having some trouble with calf cramps. A few years older than me, I think he pushed it a little too hard on the Freedom walk yesterday. We pushed through the crowds, found our seats in the lower deck on the right field side, and got Rick in his chair to rest for a minute. This gave me a chance to weave through the crowd to check out the park and get the pictures I needed.

First place I went was back down to Lansdowne St., where Alex and I had first approached Fenway Park a few days earlier. I was amazed at how original the park still was. I imagined perfectly what a game in the 20s and 30s may have been like by just imagining the scene in front of me through my mind's black and white filter. I'm pretty sure only the cars and the clothes styles would be different. It was just amazing.

Where Wrigleyville had a somewhat finished look to the outside, Fenway was all industrial. Red brick lower structures with massive steel girders painted in Kelly green were visible from all sides. The narrow side streets, with small shops and bars facing the stadium, reminded me somewhat of the French Quarter in New Orleans. There were Boston's finest on every corner, smiling and friendly; jersey barriers and metal detectors guiding you into the free for all happening within the cordoned off streets. Like Wrigleyville, a massive block party was in full swing. Apparently this is what EVERY Red Sox game looks like.

Inside, it too was much like Wrigley, a low ceiling on the bottom deck, with piping and wiring running just above your heads. I happened to enter the park right at the home plate entrance, so first things first, I had to see the Green Monster from the batter's point of view. Just as soon as you get a glimpse of the field, the massive left field fence is the first thing your eye catches. Wow, is that thing tall, with people seated on top, these were the seats to have if you could afford them. The ushers were kind enough to let me walk down to directly behind home plate for a picture. One of my childhood dreams was to hit one over that massive Green Monster. I had chills and fought back tears of joy. This was just amazing.

I then climbed the stairs to the top deck to get a shot of the entire park from above the backstop netting, walking past the old bleacher style seats that still had the wooden slats for your backrest and red steel armrests. These things had to be 100 years old at least. Climbing the stairway to the top deck, you get a great view of the city, and I was surprised to find a huge vegetable garden, growing most of the greens served at the restaurants in the park. Walking up to the edge of the upper deck, facing centerfield, was a sight to behold. Downtown Boston's skyline is to your right, just beyond the Samuel Adams Brewery sign perched above right field. Centerfield had a giant John Hancock insurance sign, replicating the founding fathers' signature. I had to wonder how many people realized that the two single most stringent patriots of the Revolution were prominently represented for this evening's game. Interesting.

I could see the one and only seat in the right field bleachers that was painted red, marking Ted Williams' longest home run in Fenway history; a 502 ft shot that hit the occupant of the seat in the head. In dead center, adjacent to the Green Monster, is a blacked out section of seats called "Conig's Corner" where the hometown star Tony Conigliaro had them covered because he said his eye couldn't pick up the ball flying toward the plate with all the brightly colored fans in that section. And then of course, the massive green wall in right, loved by the fans in Boston, and famous throughout the league... The Green Monster.

The history was so thick, you could cut it with a knife. I was so humbled and amazed to walk the truly hallowed grounds of MLB's oldest ball park, built in 1912. It wasn't until after I had left Boston that I learned of a $50 tour that takes you inside the belly of the Green Monster, where it's rumored... get this... to have the signatures of every player who has ever played at Fenway. Let that sink in for a minute. They say it's like graffiti for miles, as far as you can see. This I will most definitely be back to see.

After taking all my pictures, I met back up with Rick just as the National Anthem had ended, and settled in for the rest of the game. What a mad house for a Thursday night game, and apparently the norm for a typical Red Sox crowd. What a great experience to see this from the box suite with my veteran brothers, and again with a buddy checking off a bucket list item. I couldn't have asked for a better Fenway experience! Fenway Park, MLB park #26... and my all time favorite park so far... COMPLETE!

The next morning after breakfast, Kimber and I said our goodbyes to Rick, and headed back to camp. The plan was to take the rest of the day off and catch up on some rest. Kimber's plan wasn't even close to that. The compromise was lawn chair on the edge of the grass in the shade, with a beer cooler within reach. No rest for the wicked, but we can at least be comfortable. It wasn't long before Kimber was sufficiently worn out that we retired to the trailer for AC and a bed. We had one more day to cover Concord before we had to checkout of our trailer spot and start making our way north to Maine.

We finally come to the last day of our Massachusetts excursion, what a crazy busy couple of weeks this has been. Now with a solid day of rest under our belts, Kimber and I were back at it bright and early, pulling into the town of Concord around 0600. I wanted to first and foremost beat the mid-day heat, cover the final portion of the Minute Man National Historical Park in the morning, and get back to camp to pack up the trailer and prep for the drive to Maine.

The first thing you see as you pull into this small town is the "Entering Concord Inc. 1635" sign at the edge of town. A super lush area, green leaves of all types of trees and ground cover, were dripping wet from the morning's dew. I found the famous North Bridge with a small parking lot across the street. In the parking lot were some construction workers, sipping coffee and waiting for their crew to show up. I pulled to the far corner of the lot, next to what looked like a newly built, replica farmhouse from the 1700s with a National Park Service information placard near the front. Once again, I felt my blood pressure start to raise as I read the NPS sign.

The Parks display was titled the "Robbins House," with a brand-new placard in the same design as we saw back at the Liberty Bell in Philly. One sign was a large billboard that had a picture of a very old black man with the caption reading, "Journey with us as we explore the African-American history of Concord and its regional and national importance." Standing to the billboards right was a sign that had two separate timelines, but both within the same time period. The title of the placard read, "What does Independence look like? The Robbins House - Concord's African American History. This c.1823 farmhouse was home to the first free generation of the Robbins family and relatives who farmed, worked, went to school, supported anti-slavery efforts and follow their own paths to independence. Here's how those paths are connected to local, state and national milestones in American history." Whoa wait, what does independence look like? It looks like that bridge across the damn street, that's what Independence looks like... but I digress. The words Local and State were color coded to the top timeline, where National was separated below. I'm not going to list the entire timeline here, but I will give the first few and last few entries.

The first entry on the local and state timeline reads, "1641 Massachusetts is the first American colony to legalize slavery." Ok, I've already got an issue. We had just learned that the Boston Commons were created in 1634, just four years after the pilgrims landed. So we're already hyperbolic about the dates of slavery, and the next entry proves it. The National timeline entry below says, "1400s-1800s Atlantic slave trade: 12 million Africans in slaved; 2 million more die in transport. Slave resistance coincides with slavery." So apparently, the Native Americans had a thriving slave trade 200 years before the Pilgrims landed? This is unbelievably inaccurate. It gets worse. Next entry, state and local timeline: "1725 A Concord tax roll lists "six slaves" the earliest record of slavery in Concord." And the National timeline below: "1775-1783 American revolution; many African men seek freedom by fighting with either BRITISH or

American armies." So let's see, in the first two entries, coming up to the Revolutionary War and the shot heard around the world, this sign talks only of slavery.

On and on this went, with dozens of entries such as The Underground Railroad, the Third Fugitive Slave Act, the Emancipation Proclamation, the 13th Amendment, Brown versus Board of Education, Rosa Parks, the 1964 Civil Rights Act, the Voting Rights Act of 1965; until it reached the final three entries. Where I completely lost my shit. The last three, in this order, keep in mind this is a NATIONAL PARKS SERVICE placard, "2008 Barack Obama is elected for the first of two terms as the first black US president." With a picture of the 44th President's face, right next to Rosa Parks sitting on her infamous bus seat. Finally, came the kicker, the next entry read, "2012 Black Lives Matter movement begins after the killing of Trayvon Martin." What in the living hell does Black Lives Matter have to do with the North Bridge and the single most important action taken in the creation of this great country we ALL love?! I was absolutely livid and disgusted. Once again, the "reshaping" of history for the sole purpose of inclusivity, based on nothing more than a politically driven ideology... and one hell of a massive ego. Ok, I'll get off my soap box, now to the real history.

As I made my way across the street, I saw that the entrance to the bridge was fenced off and under construction. That's what those guys must be here to work on. I walked over to them to find out what the deal was. I told them I was from AZ and came all this way to take a picture for my book. They said it was being renovated, but I could squeeze past the edge of the fence and get some pics if I wanted. Absolutely I wanted to, like Stonewall's buried right arm, there was no way I was leaving Massachusetts without seeing the North Bridge in person.

After squeezing past the fence, I approached the North Bridge on the same path as the English troops would've taken. A dirt road, lined with massive trees had a slight rise before dropping down to the creek bed covered by the old wooden bridge. The first thing visible was the top of a granite obelisk, the original 1837 monument placed on the British side of the attack. Facing the obelisk at the west entry to the bridge stands the bronze statue of a Minute Man, representing a farmer who leaves his plow and picks up his musket to defend his land and liberty. This is it. This is where it all began. The shot heard around the world, giving rise to the single greatest nation in history. I just stood there and took it all in. No words to describe the feelings giving rise to chills up and down my body. Absolutely incredible. THIS is what Independence looks like.

After leaving the North Bridge, we followed the path laid out on the Park Service pamphlet, knowing it would lead us straight back to the RV. First stop was in downtown Concord, where I had another rise in blood pressure. A quaint town, with of course unbelievable history. The buildings were well kept from the period, with an ornately decorated church and its customary graveyard attached, some old inns and tavern, and a most interesting white "church" that looked more like an old town hall with clock tower, and tall white pillars at the entrance. There was an old bronze plaque inlaid in a granite memorial that told of the building's amazing history. "The first provincial congress of delegates from the towns of Massachusetts was called by conventions of the people to meet at Concord on the 11th day of October 1774. The delegates assembled here in the meeting house on that day and organized with John Hancock as president and Benjamin Lincoln as secretary, called together to maintain the rights of the people, this Congress assumes the government of the province and by its measures prepared the way for the war of the revolution." Wow, that's super cool, but sadly, politics once again came into play.

Next to the granite block was the street sign for the Church, that now resides in this historic building. "Gathered in 1636 the First Parish in Concord Unitarian Universalist." Ok, not sure what all that is, but the curious thing is, there was a rainbow sticker on the Church's sign. Not put there defiantly by a passerby, but as a part of the actual sign. The rainbow of course standing for the LGBTQ rights, instead of the true meaning of God promising not to flood the earth, but that's a whole different tirade. Then I noticed a large black sign with white letters, tied between two of the pillars. "BLACK LIVES MATTER" in bold white lettering. Ok, what in the hell is going on here? A building that John Hancock presided over the provincial congress, is now some sort of gay church with a racially motivated group's message hanging from its pillars. Hey, just keeping it real. John Hancock would have rolled over in his grave at the sight of this. Once again, someone choosing to divide, rather than unite.

It's amazing how when you travel the country, you pass through this landscape I describe as being full of these massive "media bubbles." It only takes a few minutes of listening to the morning's talk radio shows to know exactly what type of political climate you've just entered. For instance, if you drive through Nashville, the sun is out, the birds are singing, Trump is our president and all is good. Then you pass through somewhere like Boston, suddenly the world is ending, Trump is a Russian plant, and we're all doomed. It's so starkly obvious to the traveler, but completely oblivious to those caught inside the bubble with little means of escape. You're stuck working there, raising a family there, you have family history there. It's rare you leave that area, and when you do it's on vacation, with politics being hopefully far from your mindset. I'm not picking one side of the aisle or the other, both sides of the media tell their own version of the story. It's just the constant bombardment of one side of the story that's killing our country. Whether you love him or hate him, when President Trump said the media is the enemy of the people, he sure as hell wasn't lying. Both sides are finally discovering this fact.

From Concord, we followed the path of the English retreat toward Boston, stopping at just a few historical information signs along the way. The most notable being the spot where Revere, Dawes, and Prescott were captured. We finally returned to the RV, just before the heat of mid-day came into full swing. That's it, we're done with the Bostonian and the beginning of the Revolutionary War. Wow, was that a jam-packed couple of weeks. Now it's north to Maine, where I had previously reserved another RV spot, this time at a Navy FamCamp resort. A very much needed decompression in the woods, far away from all the crowds and excitement. I was exhausted, but man was it worth it! We had just completed the most stressful portion of this entire adventure. I was relieved and proud all at once. Massachusetts, state #39... COMPLETE!

Maine

July 1st, 2018. Happy to see a payday and absolutely amazed that it's July already, we were happily cruising up the I95, bright and early that Sunday morning. Great Pond Naval Getaways was the destination on the GPS, and life was good. I was absolutely ecstatic and relieved that I made it through the worst of the Northeastern big cities unscathed. The proverbial ton of bricks lifted from my shoulders, now it was time to relax.

My next predetermined destination for the camper was going to be a short drive east of Bangor, Maine; a place called Great Pond Outdoor Adventure. It was a Navy FamCamp that I had seen on the brochure from our visit in the Florida Keys last year. It was the most economical and centrally located campground I could find, besides, with it being July already, we weren't going to be staying too long. So with a quick stop at the Bangor Walmart for about a week's worth of supplies, we pulled into the Great Pond Rec Area around noon.

A cool clubhouse with fireplace, sofas, chairs, restrooms, a store, and kayak rentals next to an absolutely gorgeous lake surrounded by dense forest, greeted us as we pulled in. One look at the lake and Kimber could hardly control herself. As soon as I opened the door, she bolted out, did a hard U-turn, then sat up, tongue out, looking at me like, "ball please!" With a quick toss of a tennis ball, Kimber notified all the other swimmers that she had arrived. Quickly, before I had any adults take notice, I threw on her "support" vest, and went inside to check in.

As usual, Kimber could do no wrong inside the clubhouse, kids asking to pet her while the staff clamored over her. It still amazes me what effect she has on people, it's uncanny. Either way, her antics got us a much better spot than the one they had originally fit me into on such short notice. Now instead of the only pull-thru spot next to the toilet, I had a nice back-in spot, a ball throws away from the water.

They had water and electric as way of hook-ups, with a bathroom/shower nearby. There were only about 15-20 spots and a few cabins here, so I then realized how lucky I was to have gotten it. I had just reserved the last space while at Glen's house, completely guessing at when I hoped to be here, and nailed it perfectly. Later, when walking out of a much needed shower, I noticed the yard flag that was hanging from the shower house post... a giant red Cardinal. A huge smile and a knowing nod was sent the flag's way. On my path indeed.

All day Monday, we just sat by the gorgeous water, beer in hand, throwing the ball for Kimber. From what I can remember of the movie *On Golden Pond*, this had to be the place it was filmed. No mountains in sight, just calm clear water with an unusual golden-brown tinge. Almost like swimming in iced tea, it was perfectly clear and surprisingly clean. From what I was told, the color is due to the iron ore in the lake bed. It was an incredibly beautiful place, dense forest giving way to sandy beaches. It was fun to watch Kimber navigate the reeds with her ball like a Labrador with a duck. An absolute perfect place to decompress from the biggest cities, and the most people that I've ever seen.

That evening, I sat down to figure out what the plan was for the next week. I kind of gave up on following the coast when it got to New Jersey, so I'd like to at least see the Maine coast. Also there was one battlefield of interest near a place called Bar Harbor, which just happened to be on the coast. Ok, so there's one road trip to do. What else? That's when I remembered to give my friend Amy a call.

Remember the young lady I had met at the Snake River Brewery in Jackson, Wyoming? She was there river rafting that crazy-ass river, just traveling by herself. Ya, so she had been following the book page since then and got in touch with me to hit her up when I got to Maine. After speaking to her, we set up a bit of a pub crawl for the following evening where she wanted to show me the sights of her hometown, partake in some local brews, and have some lobster for dinner. How freaking cool is that!? Man, I love traveling and meeting these amazing people who are truly lifelong friends. I'm humbled and blessed to be able to do this.

The next day was clear but crazy humid. I found that out when I woke up soaking wet from sweat because the power had gone out sometime during the night. Try waking up like that and then not having the coffee maker work. It wasn't a great start to the first half of my two-week vacation from "work." The office said they were having some electrical upgrades done, and it just tripped the breaker. No harm no foul, forget the coffee, I was ready for a beer and the lake. Don't judge, it was a very long past couple of weeks. The entire rest of the day was spent in the water with Kimber, ending with a fantastic bbq, and a night's rest equivalent to a mini-coma. Let's just hope the AC stays on.

The power stayed on, just long enough for everybody to start their coffee makers and microwaves, then off it went. Over and over, the resetting of the circuit breaker looked like a zombie parade of "dads" to the circuit box up by the shower house. The guy who worked on it last had decided to split for the 4th of July weekend, so this was the new norm for a few days. It was hot and I wasn't happy. Positive thinking, breathe, ok, let's go for a hike since we're already sweaty.

I changed into a long sleeve t-shirt and pants, ball cap, and grabbed the dog. Bug Spray? Nah, it's just going to be a short one. Bruh, big mistake. ALWAYS wear bug spray in Maine. I was absolutely molested by every kind of insect indigenous to Mother Earth, and I'm pretty sure some from Mars too. They were insane! I wasn't a quarter mile into the woods, following a river bank along a rough hiking path, before the mosquitos, flies, and whatever else decided to take a bite of the back of my neck, as I ran from the forest like the *Blair Witch Project.* Nope, back to the lake, where we stayed until the drive into Bangor that evening.

Not trusting the camper AC to stay on, I decided it was best for Kimber to go with, rather than leave all the windows open and worry about her the entire time. So off to Bangor we went, quite a bit early with a couple hours to kill.

This would actually be my 2nd visit to Bangor, Maine. Pronounced Bang-Or, and the locals will let you know it with the favorite Maine joke I must've heard 5 times from Boston to Bangor. If you pronounce it "bang-er" the standard local reply in the pub would be, "Bang ha? I don't even know ha! Spoken in the Maine dialect, followed by a hearty chuckle from all in the know. Anyway, ya, this would be my 2nd time in Bangor, the first being about 27 years ago.

Coming home from Desert Storm, our very first stop in CONUS was at the Bangor International Airport to refuel, before heading to March AFB in California. We were allowed to debark, with the pilot announcing over the intercom, "Welcome home, we're all so proud of you. There's a few people outside who'd like to tell you about it." To our complete amazement there had to be at least 2,000 people forming a winding walkway from the bird to the building. At 0200 local time, they were playing the song, "Eye of the Tiger" from the iconic *Rocky* movie, over a loud speaker, people cheering and waving flags, some even asking for autographs. At the end of the long walkway of cheering townspeople was a line of veterans from the Legion Hall and VFW, that would take two Marines and walk them into the bar and buy them a beer. How freaking amazing is that! Funny thing is that was the first beer we had had in over 5 months; the lines for the bathroom ran up and down the aisles of the plane all the way to Cali. Memories a 19yr old Marine will never ever forget. So ya, I had a soft spot for Bangor, Maine. When I told my friend Amy that story, she said, "Oh, you saw the Bangor Troop Greeters." Apparently this was a thing back then and became well known, enough to still be remembered to this day... as it should be.

It was so cool to see Amy again, it had been over two years now, but we kept in touch thanks to the marvels of social media. It was still fairly early and I had reached our meeting spot about 45 minutes before Amy said she'd be there. It was a small English style pub, that offered some pretty good food and a great selection of local craft beers. When I pulled up in front of the place, I noticed they had a huge rainbow flag hanging in the window. Normally, if I wasn't alone, I'd walk into a gay bar no problem, but this time I hesitated. I thought to myself... here I am, a fairly large guy, with a fresh beard trim and haircut from Boston, walking a mini pit bull with a pink leash, into a gay bar. Umm. I text Amy back, "Hey girl! I'm in front of your bar (she said it was her favorite) how far out are you? She replied saying that she was about 20 minutes away and to go have a beer. "Well, I have Kimber with me. Are they good with that?" She confirmed that Kimber was fine. Dammit. Deep breath. "Ok. Girl, no offense, but I'll wait for you. Feel kinda weird walking into a gay bar by myself," then explaining the flag in the window. Amy sent a HAHAHAHA back. "It's not a gay bar, silly. It was Pride Week last week, they haven't taken the flag down from the parade yet." Ok, so I had to laugh out loud at that, as

Kimber and I walked into an awesome little pub with fantastic tacos. There ya go over thinking again, dumbass. Hey, I grew up near San Francisco in the 80s, gimme a break.

After beers and taco appetizers, we stopped at an Irish pub with authentic Celtic beers and another appetizer of some sort, before finally stopping at Sea Dog Brewing Company. The place was run buy a former Marine First Sgt who, after seeing the eagle, globe and anchor tattoo on my neck, greeted me with a hearty OOHRAH MARINE! Kimber of course was welcomed with open arms here, with the 1st Sgt showering her with Sea Dog Brewery swag, to include a collar and leash, and a "Marine Only" beach hat not offered for sale to the general public. We drank from the ten beer sampler, and dined on my first authentic Maine Lobster Roll. What a super cool brewery with the best people. But we still weren't finished yet! Amy then took me to a wine and dessert bar where we completely overindulged on artisan cupcakes and flourless chocolate cake. What a great night, with a great friend! Thank you, Amy, I'm sure our paths will cross again, or maybe our rivers.

4th of July, happy "scare the crap out of your dog" day. Luckily for Kimber, no fireworks allowed at the Great Pond, Kimber gets a reprieve. Actually, it's me that gets the break, from a shaking little dog that won't be comforted unless she can possibly crawl inside of you. So it was a happy 4th this year, with a hot dog burn at the clubhouse, sitting with my lawn chair halfway in the lake, tossing the ball into the warm, copper colored water for Kimber to give chase. We had a couple more days here, before stormy weather returned to the forecast. Tomorrow we'd head to the coast, another day or two by the lake, and we'd pack it up for New Hampshire. We'd be heading west for the first time this summer, and the last time for this book.

Due south from Bangor, along the Penobscot Bay shoreline, we found Fort George, originally known as Fort Penobscot. This was an English Fort that had some notable figures involved worth mentioning. The most important military action relating to Fort George was the Penobscot expedition of 1779, the largest American naval expedition of the Revolutionary War. Due to some treasonous actions by American Commodore Saltonstall, by not attacking the British ships docked nearby and allowing English reinforcements to arrive, turned the Penobscot expedition into the worst defeat in US Naval history until the attack on Pearl Harbor in 1941. Paul Revere was in charge of artillery for the expedition, although acquitted from a court martial, his reputation was permanently damaged. Wow, bummer battlefield here for sure.

The Fort itself was made of tall earthen redoubt walls, shaped in a square. The mounds and field were all covered with lush green grass, save the dirt baseball diamond in the far corner. Whoa what? Baseball? Yup, the city actually turned this place into a softball field, and a group of folks were getting ready to play. Now that is freaking awesome! A battlefield turned into a baseball park; who would've thought that the dreary depiction on the sign would give way to the joy of baseball? Well played, fine people, well played.

We were pretty close to the Arcadia National Park, which was on the way to Bar Harbor, the place I was told I had to see. A massive island park with tall mountains had a view that went on for miles and miles. It gave a great shot overlooking the town of Bar Harbor, with this huge, pirate ship looking day cruise, just entering the docks. With lots of people and it being still fairly warm and humid, we just made this a driving tour. Bar Harbor was definitely a popular place, with zero parking and the sidewalks spilling over with pedestrians. Maybe another time, I was done with crowds for a minute.

I wanted to stop for another lobster roll or some kind of seafood while I was here. You always hear of the famous New England crab boils, and I was dying to eat some shellfish. I found a place that had these huge baskets with something boiling outside the building, with a line of people waiting to get inside. I think I found my spot. Luckily, I walked up to check the prices first. You can buy a whole, live main lobster for only 4.99 per pound, but a damn lobster sandwich was 18 bucks. What? Ok, well, looks like my lunch will be an early supper back at the trailer. Concluding our day trip to the Maine coast, at this point, driving was the last thing I felt like doing; we will have to finish the NE coast another time.

As the forecast predicted, the next day was solid rain. Kimber completely undeterred by this, chose to spend our morning in the lake, which was as warm as bath water. Later that afternoon, we packed up the Rig and searched online for a National Forest in New Hampshire that looked promising. I had another couple of weeks before I'd have to start paying attention to the Toronto Blue Jays home schedule. In the meantime, funds were already very tight, so a cheap campground, and a nice hikeable forest, was on my heads-up display. With a break in the weather early that next morning, we made a run for the New Hampshire state line, heading for a place that had a familiar ring, the White Mountains of New Hampshire and a town named Conway. That's it for Maine, state #40... COMPLETE.

New Hampshire

July 8th, 2018. The drive through Maine to New Hampshire started wet and damp, but gave way to sunshine gleaming down on some absolutely beautiful country. We followed the I95 south until just past Lewiston, before veering west again, putting us into the White Ledge National campsite near Albany, NH around 1500. An absolutely gorgeous campsite was going to run us 9 bucks per night with my discount. I sure have missed being in the National Forests this trip; cheap spots, solitude, and the greatest backyard you could ever ask for. Great Pond was nice, but this was heaven.

Our campsite hosts came out to greet us almost immediately. An elderly couple, he being in his early 80s, she a few years younger, were both an absolute joy to talk to. The gentleman came to my campsite later and asked if I would check in with his wife whenever we came back from a hike. "She gets worried like a mother hen. Save me the grief." I had to laugh. They were the cutest and sweetest pair of hippy campers you'll ever meet.

The next day, I was sitting at the picnic table enjoying an amazing day, double checking our itinerary and baseball schedules, when the host gentleman came by again while making his rounds. He told me how he had just done this 4-mile loop that took him about 4 hours, and how his wife cussed him for attempting it. Kimber was ready for a hike by that time, and it was still fairly cool out from the earlier rains, so I asked where the trailhead was and we started out. I could see his wife peering out her camper window, as we took to the trail. I'll have to remember to tell her we made it back. Obviously it won't be 4 hours.

Three hours and 52 minutes later, Kimber and I emerged from the trail of death. She literally bolted to the nearest ground water as soon as we hit somewhat level dirt, with me right behind, dipping my hat in the water and then over my head. How old is that dude!? So the first half mile got me to the base of the mountain. Nothing drastic, a good climb though... for the next 3 miles. I didn't think we would ever make it to the top. The humidity was brutal, but the bugs were only bad when you were in the shade and where it was flat enough for water to pool. So all the cool, shady, flat places to rest was where you walked the fastest. Then, for some unknown reason, the steepest part of the climb was always covered with rock and in the full sun.

By the time we got to the top, I was toast. Our water was gone, Kimber and I shared the last granola bar, and my phone said we were 3.1 miles into the 4-mile hike. Ok, so the math isn't working out on this. You're saying that I've got a mile to go... then it's got to be... Yup, you guessed it, straight f'ing down. You got to be kidding me. With my legs shaking like jello, flailing at every tree branch along the way trying to slow down, I was actively seeking an upcoming landing place that would produce the least amount of damage. Ya, it was that steep. This time, with Kimber following behind me, it was basically a mile long, controlled fall, from the top of this freaking mountain. 82 years old, my dying ass. Yup, almost exactly 4 hours later, I see the lady in the window. I wave, she waves, the old man laughs. Well played, good sir, well played. Needless to say, I wasn't heading out for beers that night. Neither was Kimber.

Back to our schedule I was in the middle of figuring out, when that wild-eyed banshee told me about the death march. I had planned to give the three non-baseball, non-National Battlefield states (ME, NH, VT) up to a week visit in each, before heading into upstate NY. I listed all the home games of the last 4 teams we HAD to catch this trip, putting us into Minnesota by September and the end of the regular season. I made reservations in Niagara for our venture into Canada, set up a stop with a cousin I'd never met in Michigan, picked out a fairground in Milwaukee for a tentative spot, and a surprise for you in Minnesota. What an incredible relief to at least see the end of this year's baseball quest on paper; now we just have to stick the landing.

The next day, Kimber and I ventured into town. Yup, Alex was right, this place was amazing. Gotta love a state whose motto, "Live Free or Die," is emblazoned just under the "Welcome to New Hampshire" road signs on every state line crossing. Conway is a resort town, with ski lifts in the winter and awesome mountain bike trails in the summer. The touristy part of town is North Conway, much like Pinetop where I started this journey from. Then Conway itself is just down the road, a much larger town, like Show Low back in AZ. It was almost identical, not to mention that these are the White Mountains of New Hampshire, Pinetop/Show Low are in the White Mountains of Arizona. The similarities were uncanny, but the accents brought you back to reality. Not quite a Boston accent, not quite Canadian, but they were definitely prominent.

We walked around both the downtown areas of each town, found a mountain bike path and got in a few miles, while Kimber jogged happily behind, then decided to hunt down a Taco Tuesday somewhere. I was dying for my Taco Tuesday standard, something not so celebrated in the Northeast. I now see why. You just don't go to Taco Tuesday in New Hampshire, stick to crab and lobster. When in Rome, don't act like you're in Phoenix.

While having my mushy tortilla filled with stew meat and unmelted cheddar cheese "taco," the guy next to me asked if they were good. I just kind of looked at him and said, "I'm from Arizona." After a good laugh, I met my friend Jaime. A tall guy who lived and worked here locally, was sitting with his buddy from Germany. Both men were a few years younger than me, and both travelled abroad together in Bangkok, amongst other places. We spoke of traveling the U.S., about why I was here from Arizona, and generally just had a good time. Several beers later, Jaime's girlfriend showed up with a few other friends, and the next thing you know, I'm invited to an authentic New England Crab boil! I was stoked. Finally, I get to stuff my face with never-ending shellfish. An Irish Viking's dream date.

The heat was brutal the next few days, leaving the camper unbearable until the sun passed enough for the trees to give it cover again. For some very odd reason, I thought I had run the AC with this generator before. Either way, it would power the microwave or the toaster, and charge the batteries just enough to run the fans. Forget about the AC, and now suddenly realizing this is our first camping spot without power, I found the generator too weak. Actually, this wasn't as catastrophic as most Arizonans would consider it, we had the amazing Sack River to cool off in. An extremely slow current, with the max depth of about 5 ft and ice cold, it was perfect to lounge in the sand, throwing the ball for Kimber. So that's exactly what we did for the next three days, so peaceful and refreshing. I was really liking this place.

Saturday night finally rolled around and all I could think about was lobster and crab. I absolutely love shellfish and I was stoked to finally experience a boil, especially with my new local friends. Jaime and the crew did not disappoint; I couldn't believe what was being laid out before me. One of Jaime's friends put in an order to a local seafood store and came back with an absolute shellfish feast. There had to be at least two dozen lobster in a giant styrofoam box, steaming hot and ready for butter. As if that wasn't enough, then came a bucket of steamed clams, like half a Home Depot bucketful. Jaime grabbed a plate, slapped two whole lobsters down, then poured a handful of clams over them and handed it to me. I was in shock. It might as well have been a proposal, I think I was in love. He then pointed to the table where a giant community bowl of melted butter awaited our arrival. I wasn't sure how to actually go about this monstrosity of shellfish delightfulness in front of me. Was there a method to this madness, some type of Northeastern protocol for this sacred event, maybe just a quiet prayer to the creator of all living... a loud crack came from across the table. There was Jaime's girl, the full body of a lobster in one hand, claws dangling to her wrists, the tail of the beast in her other hand, missing a large crescent-shaped bite that she wrestled trying to keep in her mouth as she redunked the wounded tail in for more butter. Valhalla indeed! My kinda people. We had an absolute blast eating this feast, followed by some type of Romanian liquor and more laughs. A great time was had by all; I couldn't have asked for a better "boil!" Thanks so much to Jaime and the crew!

Monday finally came and so did the rain. Buckets of it. The upcoming drive to Vermont was basically all backroads, so bad weather was definitely an issue right now. We chose to wait it out. Tuesday came, rain still here, Wednesday... same same. Ok, now I'd chewed up a couple of my "wiggle" days, I had to get moving. Rain or shine, we pulled out Thursday morning, this time heading for the Green Mountains of Vermont. New Hampshire, my live free or die state, #41... COMPLETE!

Vermont

July 19th, 2018. Vermont, the Green Mountain State, is what the Welcome sign reads as you enter the much softer, green rolling hills of Vermont. Compared to its wild and woolly neighbor, New Hampshire, the mountains gave way to green pastures and ample forest covering a much more forgiving terrain. Looking at the artisan cheese farms, passing vineyards and fruit orchards, even the small dairy farms, gave me a very odd sense of déjà vu. That's when I realized this place was exactly like Sonoma County, CA. Take the wine country back home, add a couple ski resorts here and there, mix in a funny accent and voila, you have the Northeastern Sonoma County. It matches its age of residents, its heavy sense of community, and yes its politics. This is the land of Bernie mixed in with Ben and Jerry, right? "Hey, when in Rome, bro!" my inner hippy exclaimed.

The drive started out rough but the skies became blue and everything took on a beautiful summer shine. Unbelievably dense vegetation when there wasn't a farm or small shopping center breaking up the forest. The Hapgood Pond Recreation Area, deep in the Green Mountain National Forest, was just a few minutes from the town of Londonderry. It was one of the most beautiful campgrounds that I'd found yet, including a few heavily shaded spots with towering Pines and Oaks, a few spots in the tall grass near a stream that had ample sunlight. There was a perfect little swimming/kayak/fishing pond, with a one-mile loop that circled the pond and the campsite, making for a great morning walk, or a decent lap on the mountain bike. Did I mention they had hot showers and flush toilets? Ya, this place was a gem of a spot; at ten bucks a night, I was ecstatic to call this place home for the next week or so.

We ended up in one of the full sun spots, but even then, when the shade was down, surprisingly, the heat nor the insects were much of an issue. Of course with a pond nearby, the hot hours were spent throwing the ball into the cool pond for Kimber to give chase, something I could do all day. That afternoon, we started out for a walk to the closest little town nearby called Peru, where they had a gourmet coffee shop serving the famous Green Mountain coffee, something I'd heard of but didn't realize was in Vermont. That's when we stumbled upon a tall granite obelisk war monument a few miles outside of camp.

It was off the street and perched on top of what looked like someone's side yard. Maybe it was some state land between homes, either way, here was this 15 ft tall granite obelisk with the following inscription: "Encampment of General John Stark August 6, 1777, while on his march, with one thousand men from Charlestown, N.H., through the woods, to the Battlefield at Bennington. Erected August 7, 1899 by the sons and daughters of Vermont." Wow, this monument itself was 119 years old, and described somebody and something I'd never heard of. This was awesome! Now to research the Bennington Battlefield, and whoever John Stark is.

Well, I had plenty of time to research our next move, but instead chose to move my camper out of the mud pit that our spot had become. The deluge of rain that hit us for the next three days turned that little creek behind the camper into the Mississippi Delta. The ground around me turned into a giant, muddy sponge, barely allowing me to pull the trailer up to a newly opened shady spot on high land. After moving camp, cleaning the mud off of pretty much everything, I managed to find out where the Bennington War Monument was, and planned a road trip for the following day. Rain or shine, after three days of solid rain, I was stir-crazy as hell and had to get out.

Finally, a break in the weather. The next morning, I got Kimber in the truck, armed myself with a big mug of the famous Green Mountain coffee, and headed off to learn some history. The Bennington Battle Monument was about an hour away, near the much larger town of Bennington, VT, right at the corner of NY, MA, and Vermont. A massive obelisk towering above a small mountain, it overlooked the town. This thing was visible for miles, and looked taller than the Jefferson Davis Monument from the freeway.

The structure was built in 1891 to commemorate a battle that took place in 1777, and was actually fought across the NY border in the town of Walloomsac, NY. This was due to John Stark, a veteran of the Battle of Trenton, Battle of Princeton, and who even fought at Bunker Hill, now the Brigadier General in command of the New Hampshire Militia, deciding to cut off the English attack of the Bennington supply depot in New York, rather than defend it at point-blank range. Thus, the monument marks where the English's goal once stood.

Ok, so this battle was actually in New York; well that's cool, but doesn't help my Vermont experience. Guess I know where I'm going when we move on to NY. I read, "The Northern Campaign Begins. Burgoyne's plan in the summer of 1777 was to divide New England from the rest of the United States, down along Lake Champlain and the Hudson River to New York. On July 5th and 6th, American forces withdrew from Fort Ticonderoga in New York, and Mount Independence in Vermont, leaving these fortifications to the British. The British followed the Americans southward, until they were delayed by a rear-guard action at Hubbardton. The only Revolutionary War battle fought entirely on Vermont soil, the Battle of Hubbardton gave American forces a chance to regroup for what became the first successful resistance to Burgoyne's plan."

Ok, as in true Baseballs and Battlefields form, we entered this Northern Campaign, somewhere right in the middle of the action. Burgoyne is the English commander who now owns Fort Ticonderoga, and is heading for Saratoga looking for more property. Ol' boy runs out of chow for his troops, tries to raid our pantry with his tired, cold and hungry army, who were extended way too far from base, thus losing this battle. History in a nutshell my friends. Next stop apparently is Hubbardton, but that's for another day. First things first, groceries and laundry, since we're in a decent sized "town." Afterwards, it was back to camp, this little dog needed to be in the lake.

Once again, the rain returned. This time a steady soaker that just wouldn't let up. Three days later I was completely stir-crazy and had to make a move. I decided since I would be headed north to Hubbardton Battlefield, that I might as well extend my journey to what appeared to be the beginning of Burgoyne's Northern Campaign, Fort Ticonderoga in New York. With the plans set for the following day, we were back in the lake for the rest of the afternoon.

The following morning I received a knock at the camper door. One of the young Park Service Rangers who had been collecting the camp fees the last couple days, asked whether I wanted to ride out the summer as the camp host. The lady who was currently running the place had a sick child and decided to go home early. Oh man, I wish I had the time to stay here for another couple months, but I was so close to finishing this book, I could taste it. With much regret, I turned down the offer, although flattered to be asked. He said to keep them in mind, and that they were always looking. Nice, something to think about for another time.

After chatting it up with the Rangers for a minute, Kimber and I set out for Fort Ticonderoga, New York. It was a 71-mile drive, with the Hubbardton Battlefield directly in route. The weather was overcast, but at least it wasn't raining. It was actually the perfect weather to do this in, as it stayed cool enough to not worry about Kimber in the truck while I explored the Fort. Everything happens for a reason, right?

The town of Hubbardton is nothing more than a traffic intersection, dividing a couple of small farms. Just up the road was the Hubbardton Battlefield State Historic Site, the one and only battlefield on Vermont soil. It was basically just a granite obelisk monument in front of a visitor center that of course was closed. There was a large grass field with a walking path around the exterior explaining what happened in different areas. The view over the top of the green rolling hills was incredibly beautiful, even in the dreary overcast.

I took Kimber out and tossed the ball a few times for her, while I took in the view. The hills changed color as they stood farther away. The first green, the second a subdued green, the farthest a slate blue, finally disappearing into the grey sky, like a giant watercolor landscape. I noticed an old metal road sign, erected by the Historic Society of Vermont that read, "Battle of Hubbardton. The only battlefield on Vermont soil. Here on July 7, 1777 successful rear-guard action by Colonel Seth Warner's Vermont Massachusetts and New Hampshire troops ended British pursuit under General Fraser. The American army, retreating from Fort Ticonderoga and Mount Independence, was saved to fight again near Bennington and Saratoga. Burgoyne's 1777 drive to divide the colonies, first resisted at Hubbardton, ended in defeat at Saratoga."

Ok, so as the Americans gave up Fort Ticonderoga, for what reason we still don't know, Seth Warner and what has come to be known as the Green Mountain Boys, successfully harassed the English, allowing the Americans to escape. This is the "rear-guard" maneuver they spoke of. That's simple, ok, got it. Now off to Ticonderoga to figure out why we ran.

We didn't have to venture too far into New York to visit Fort Ticonderoga as Lake Champlain, which looks more like a river, doubled as the state line. Just a few miles north of the bridge, on the New York side was Fort Ticonderoga, a massive stone structure built on a large jetty, patrolling the riverway into Lake Champlain.

The Fort was a huge tourist attraction, beginning with a row of information placards giving a timeline of the Fort and who occupied it at various times. It was interesting to see signs printed in both English and French, rather than English and Spanish. The first sign had the date of 1609-1754, describing the French and Native Indian conflicts. The next sign was dated 1755, discussing both English and French troops being deployed during the French/English War. 1757, the Natives side with the French against the English, but the alliance is short lived. 1758 gives way to the bloodiest battle on the continent until the American Civil War. Nearly 2,000 English and American casualties as the French surprisingly take the Fort. 1759, when Quebec is threatened by British attack, the French leave the garrison lightly guarded, the English regaining control of Ticonderoga. Keep with me, we're almost there.

1760-1775, Canada surrenders to Britain, effectively ending the French and Indian War. From 1760 up to the American Revolution, the Fort was lightly manned by the English. Now it gets good. 1775, less than a month after the hostilities between Britain and the American colonist began, a small force of colonists under the joint command of Ethan Allen and Benedict Arnold delivers America a major morale and material victory. Yup, there's our buddy, Mr. Arnold again, but this time a hero. And Ethan Allen? I always just thought that was a furniture store. Ok, so Americans owned the place. So why did we run?

December 1775, Washington orders nearly 60 tons of artillery, 59 cannons, to be taken from surrounding forts and sent to relieve the siege of Boston, a whopping 300 miles away. It's December, imagine the snow in upstate New York, and you're dragging cannons over mountains... in 1776... with horses! Now the battered, withered army returns to the Fort, only to be overrun by Burgoyne's Northern Campaign. Now the Fort belongs to the English and surprisingly the Germans, at least until news of Burgoyne's surrender at Saratoga. Wow, that was one helluva intro when waiting to buy a ticket to see the Fort.

The Fort itself was definitely impressive. Built with stone walls in a strange star like formation, giving a 360 degree field of fire for its numerous cannons and mortars. The amount of hardware laid out on various levels made this the most heavily fortified and armed Fort I'd visited yet. Inside it was more like a 17th century hamlet, housing many people, not just soldiers but their families too. I couldn't help but be reminded of *Monty Python and the Holy Grail*, the part with the body cart helmsman shouting, "Bring out your dead!" I know that was medieval times, but the sanitation situation here had to be close.

There were many displays of weapons, clothing and tools, all artifacts from the Fort's historical grounds. There was an interactive, "dress-up" area for the kids, with period actors walking about the grounds, interacting with guests. They had a tool area, also for kids to try their hand at 17th century trades work. Afterwards there was a cantina, cafe, and refreshments area, along with a large gift shop. All in all, a very well done historical site, important to many counties. Well worth the somewhat expensive ticket, especially for kids.

On the drive back to camp, I found my mind wandering to the places that we'd seen prior to Ticonderoga that led up to the battle between France and England. Remember, we saw Washington as a British officer, a Red Coat, back at Fort Necessity in PA, as he was mistakenly instrumental for basically starting the French Indian Wars. But now I see that we were actually part of England then, fighting the French. So now we see the French and Indian Wars over with, England needs to pay for this expensive worldwide war, and begins to tax the American colonists to help foot the bill. Well, that wasn't happening. Now we see Boston rise up, and surround the old boys house, setting off the Boston Massacre. Well, the English weren't having any of this dumping tea, and other basic tomfoolery, so they send in troops to disarm the colonists and quash this insurrection. Big mistake. Lexington goes down, then Concord, the fight is on. All that artillery gets sent to Boston from upstate New York, weakening our already tired defenses, and boom, here comes Burgoyne, trying to be the hero and split Boston from New York. And that's where we are today. See, boys and girls, history can actually be fun. Next and final stop, Saratoga, clear at the other end of Vermont.

On the way back to camp, I stopped at a great little bar and grill in downtown Londonderry. It was happy hour on a weekday, with only one stool open at the small neighborhood eatery. The folks in the bar were everything from blue-collar road workers, just getting off work, to wealthy retirees, discussing the crazy politics of the day. That's when an older gentleman next to me asked where I stood, being from across the world in Arizona. I mentioned that I was happy with our President, which surprisingly received a hearty reception. Wait, this is Vermont, right? That's when I got the low-down on what's really going on here.

Turns out that Vermont is the ski resort state for New York, like New Hampshire was for Boston. So the folks who ski the winters in Vermont, end up retiring out there. They want it to be everything NYC isn't, as they pass laws to keep this country environment pristine, something I have a hard time arguing with. Such as, there aren't any billboards in Vermont; nor can you build on top of a mountain, another similarity between Sonoma County and its laws.

The older gentleman who explained all this to me had owned his own company and was apparently retired and wealthy, his wife wearing a New York Yankees ball cap, actually voted for Trump. He told me a great story about arguing with his friends over politics. He told me how he and his two buddies walked a mile every morning. Halfway into their walk is a mile marker. He told me the rule is that they talk politics up to that marker, then they talk about sports, which they agree about, on the way back. This way, they're still friends by the time they return. I had to laugh. If only the entire country could have that rule. See what I mean about just letting people be people? You'll be surprised what you find most times.

It was now July 31st, our last day at camp, and also the payday that I needed desperately at this point. It was going to be a real tight couple of months while I dragged the trailer home to Arizona. I wanted desperately to wrap up the Northern Campaign with a visit to Saratoga, and contemplated seeing it now, or backtracking quite a distance after we find a spot for the camper in New York. First things first, let's figure out where we're going to land in Upstate New York, then decide on how to see Saratoga.

Ok, this part even left me surprised. The plan for our upcoming visit to New York was to make a stop at the MLB Hall of Fame in famous Cooperstown, New York. An obvious must see for the book, and another major bucket list item to check off. From there, it would be a week or so in Niagara Falls where we would venture into Canada to see the Toronto Blue Jays, and then on to Michigan. Without any National Battlefields to see, I was satisfied with Fort Ticonderoga and soon to be Saratoga, filling the battlefield gap.

I checked all of my regular camping apps, hoping to find something even close to reasonable around Cooperstown for just a couple of days. As luck would have it, the inauguration ceremony was the week prior, and most places were booked solid or way out of my price range. 60 bucks seemed to be the average per night in an RV park, for the area, and all the nearby forests were state and not local, and also expensive. Once again frustrated and about to give up, I checked the FreeCampsites app, and low and behold, there was one spot just outside of Cooperstown, on the opposite side of a nearby lake. The ad gave a phone number for "Ed and Sue's house" that I called just to see if this could possibly be true. Surprisingly, an answering machine picked up,

"You've reached Ed and Sue's house, please leave a message." So I explained to this machine that I had seen their ad, was traveling the country writing a book about ballparks, and was hoping to stay there as I visit the Hall of Fame. Within a few hours I got a call back from Sue, a super friendly lady, asking about when I planned to be there. I was shocked. A free spot, close to Cooperstown, and being held just for me. I was ecstatic. Absolutely amazing. I couldn't thank her enough as I decided then and there to visit Saratoga from our spot here in Vermont, that very next day. So for all intent and purposes, we were officially done with our visit to Vermont, state #42... COMPLETE.

New York

July 31st, 2018. The drive from Londonderry to Saratoga was nothing less that gorgeous. Every small town we passed was like stepping back into colonial days. Absolutely dense forests of Beech and Oak, some indigenous hardwoods completely foreign to me, but all were stunningly beautiful. We crossed the New York state line about 0830 that morning, to a welcoming committee of some pretty nefarious road signs to someone from Arizona.

The first was your standard Welcome to New York sign, proclaiming the title Empire State. The next sign, literally 20 yards past the welcome sign read, "New York State, HANDGUN LAW, violation mandatory one-year JAIL SENTENCE." So welcome to New York, but leave your constitutional rights at the border. And by the way, here's a threat of imprisonment if you don't obey. Well, alrighty then. This is the perfect case of a major metropolis like NYC, dictating law to the rest of the state. Apparently, the term "Empire" State is exactly that. This is why we need to make the electoral college a state thing. Either way, I had a Kimber by my side, and not afraid to use her.

My buddy Alex told me that New York State is three separate states in reality, one completely different from the next. There's NYC, Long Island, and Upstate, and so far I couldn't agree more. Upstate New York was nothing like I'd ever expect New York to be. We all hear about NYC being the "Big Apple," passing all the apple orchards finally explained why. It was crazy to think that the terrain of New York was very similar to Sebastopol, CA, my childhood home in the middle of Gravenstein Apple country. Rolling hills, apple orchards for days, and roadside fruit stands selling cider definitely brought back some fond memories.

The closest town to the Saratoga National Historic Park, which houses the Saratoga Battlefield was a place called Schuylerville. A small town just west of the Hudson River had a nice grassy park with plenty of open grass for Kimber to play ball. There were a set of softball and little league fields in the back, with giant Oaks giving shade to the public park portion near the road. I grabbed Kimber's ball and gave it a good chuck. Off went the brindle and white express, chasing her red bouncing ball, like a mini bear chasing down its prey. That's when I looked up to notice another metal historical sign, just a few feet from where I parked the truck.

I couldn't believe my eyes; the thought that I'd just happen to stop right there next to this sign. "Fort Hardy. British supply post 1755-63. Here, General John Burgoyne defeated British troops in the ruins of the fort, lay down their arms, 1777." Then just a few yards further up the road, another much older metal road sign said, "On these fields the British Army grounded arms at the surrender." So you're telling me that this is the field that the defeated General Burgoyne's stacked arms and surrendered... AND NOW IT'S A BALLPARK! I'm blown away by how this journey just takes on a life of its own. On my path indeed.

In the center of town was a large cemetery, with once again a massive concrete obelisk. When you get closer, you realize that it's actually made of bricks; life-size individual bronze statues depicting soldiers who served here stood on a precipice above the entrance door. On the structure's corners were eagles carved from granite, glaring down like gargoyles perched on the eaves of an ancient church. This was the Saratoga Monument, a place I had found by catching a glimpse of a road sign out of the corner of my eye while driving by.

There was a walking trail, named the Victory Wood Trail, that cut through the center of the ancient graveyard, leading to a wooded area called Victory Woods. The National Park Service sign explained, "These grounds witnessed a monumental event. In October 1777, over 2500 defeated and weary British soldiers, their wives, and children retreated here following the battles of Saratoga (fought 8 miles south). Surrounded by the American army, they were forced to surrender a pivotal Revolutionary War victory which led to American independence and freedom." Apparently, this is a brand-new edition to the larger Saratoga National Historical Park.

As Kimber and I walked out of the cemetery and into the wooded area, there was a lady Park Ranger looking at some trees. A middle-aged lady, wearing a standard National Park Service uniform, turned toward us as we approached. "Are you marking them to be cut down?" I asked, making small talk while I quickly corralled Kimber and got her on a leash. The Ranger explained she was a botanist and was checking something to do with the trees, as she bent down to greet Kimber with open arms. As usual, Kimber seemed like she had known this woman forever. I told her about our travels, the book, and that we were headed to Saratoga. She quickly offered to show me some of the redoubts and earthworks not pointed out by the signage. Heck ya, I'm in!

As we walked, she explained the different areas of the woods and the scene that happened here. She explained that the Americans who finally corralled the English here, prior to surrender, were pretty brutal to their prisoners. Starvation, disease, bitter cold was the norm; folks were forced to eat their horses. It was war, and the gruesomeness of it was horribly bad here. She continued to show me a swampy area that was the size of a small lake. Then things got a little crazy.

She started to explain how some modern day "ghost hunters" for lack of a better term (she called it something much more scientific), actually brought out all this high-tech equipment that quit working as soon as they put it in the water. She said that one of the people doing this test asked why he was eating horse meat and his chest hurt like pneumonia. Ok, so I'm a pretty spiritual guy, but that right there was freaking creepy. And the place definitely had that "heavy" feeling about it. But wait, it gets creepier.

After her story, I said, "Oh, you believe in that kind of stuff? I've got a story for you," and began telling her about my Cardinals. Just as I was getting ready to tell her about my grandfather, she literally cut me off by asking, "Who's Carl?" The only Carl I know is my Great Grandfather Erickson, the Swedish immigrant turned Court Clerk/Justice in North Dakota. I also had a buddy from high school that spelled his name Karl. So I asked, "Spelled with a C or a K?" Almost instantly she replied "C." I told her the only Carl I knew was my great grandfather, and before I could say another word, she said, "Ya, he's helping you write your book," while nodding her head, her eyes looking away as if confirming a memory. My jaw hit the floor. Wow, just, wait, what? I was confused and stunned all at once. First, because I've only met my Grampa Carl once as a very small child, and second because I automatically assumed it was my Navy grandpa who raised me. "Oh, I bet there's a few grandpas up there watching over me," I replied with an uneasy smile.

After that, we walked back toward the entrance of the wooded area, where another dirt road disappeared into the forest. I began to walk that way, when the Ranger stopped me and said, "Oh, that's not the park down there, it was so good to meet you," shook my hand and started walking down that dirt road, looking up at the trees as she passed. I had this strange feeling when we parted ways, and for some reason, I knew she'd be gone when I backed up and looked down the road she had left by. She was nowhere to be seen. There was no car parked anywhere near here either. Kimber and I literally flew back to the car. What in the hell? Then, I scrambled to get out my phone, thankful that there was a normal picture of her with Kimber, and not Kimber hugging an invisible vampire lady. How in the hell did she know my grandfather's name? And he's helping me write my book?! It all just hit very close to home. One of my friends on the Facebook page said she was probably one of the English who passed there... an interesting thought to process.

Just a few miles up the road was the Saratoga National Historic Park. This could've been named a military park, just because it's based upon this last battle that was strewn all over the countryside, making this mainly a driving tour. There was a very good visitor center that went into detail about who fought here, including the infamous Benedict Arnold. The day I was there, they happened to have a local grade school there, with kids learning to wash laundry by hand, darn socks, and other household duties of the time, all while dressed in period clothing. I found it interesting that the girls were mainly interested in the domestic stuff, while the boys were chasing each other around the grass yard with makeshift swords like idiots. Except for one young lady, who donned a sword and shield, beating on the boys like a young Joan of Arc. Well played, my lady, well played.

So back to Benedict Arnold. I've always wondered why Benedict Arnold was considered a traitor; we all know the name from school, and that he committed treason. But I don't remember why, well, here ya go. It was because of pride, pure stupid egotistical pride. Maybe that's what makes this so bad. Turns out Benedict Arnold literally kicked the English's butt here, playing a huge role in a pivotal battle, even losing a leg to prove it. His commanding officer, when giving his after-action report, left Arnold's name out... apparently they weren't friends. So now Arnold is pissed, starts "wining and dining" the English, and gets a deal to turn West Point, and possibly Washington himself, over to the British. As if that's not bad enough, he acts upon it by requesting a command at West Point where he funneled real time intelligence to the English, all for 20k pounds and a British military commission. His plans went to crap when his courier got nabbed with notes condemning Arnold to treason. Arnold then escapes to England where he demands to be paid for his failed mission, and is still considered a traitor even by the English. Once a traitor, always a traitor.

It was well into the afternoon heat by the time we finished up the entire driving tour. Completely exhausted, but not tired enough to catch the cot in the back of the truck for a night, we made the long trek back to the Hapgood Pond campsite. That's when I looked over and saw that original war monument that directed us to the Battle of Bennington. To think... if I never would've seen this, I probably never would have made the trek to Ticonderoga, or even stopped at the Saratoga Monument and had that talk with the Ranger lady. So in the past 5 days we covered the entire Northern Campaign and learned about my ghost writer grandfather (literally); all because I happened to choose this campground on a whim. On my path indeed.

Pulling the trailer through New York wasn't too bad at all. We retraced our route south to Bennington, then taking Hwy 7 into Troy. The drive was absolutely gorgeous, until the city traffic started to be a factor. Still not too bad at all, as we made our way down to Hwy 20. I chose 20 instead of winding north on the interstate, and even though there were several small towns to negotiate the camper through, I don't think I could've picked a prettier drive. Highway 20 runs parallel with Interstate 90, from Albany to Buffalo. If for some reason you find yourself traveling New York State... TAKE THIS ROUTE! Upstate New York is much like Vermont terrain wise, but with diminishing hilltop peaks, into more slightly rolling farmland. With lots of fruit stands and apple orchards everywhere, it really felt like the Sebastopol area of Sonoma County.

Ed and Sue's house was a couple of miles off the highway, near the town of Springfield Center. I drove past their road twice, seeing only Amish farms. I called Sue, who told me I was correct, and to follow the road up to the left. She and Ed would come down to meet me. The first thing that went through my head was, are they Amish? This ought to be good.

Standing by a grass clearing in some high bushy vegetation, stood a middle-aged couple, somewhere between me and my dad's age, smiling and waving. Behind them was their own 5th wheel, and a lush grassy spot perfect for one or two more trailers.

We parked the truck and jumped out to meet my new friends. Two of the absolute nicest folks you'd ever meet, Ed is a large animal veterinarian, basically a cow doctor. I believe Sue was retired or stayed at the house with their two huge Dobermans. They lived on top of one of the few peaks in the area, with the RV parked below. We clicked right away, as I had been speaking to Sue on the phone, giving updates on our trip. There had been some rainstorms we came through that she was concerned about. Kimber came out of the truck like a flash and was also instantly friends with Ed and Sue.

After our meet and greet, Sue held out an envelope while she said, "I've got a friend that works for the city (maybe it was the museum), that I told about your journey. These are for you." I'm paraphrasing completely, but something to that effect. Inside the envelope were tickets to the MLB Hall of Fame, plus two more tickets to a Farm Museum and one other exhibit, plus a map of downtown. There was a sticky note that read "For Matt" stuck to the package. Wow, how freaking amazing is that?! I asked how the weather has been, besides the intermittent showers, and mentioned how I was concerned about the heat for Kimber in the truck or the trailer. Almost instantly Sue said not to worry, Kimber could stay with her. Wow, just wow. I couldn't thank them enough; absolutely amazing people.

I decided to head into Cooperstown on Saturday, then check out the area on Sunday, setting us up for our reservations in Niagara Falls on Monday. So that Friday, Kimber and I were just setting up the camper and enjoying the cool morning air when Ed came down to go out on a call. He was on his way to deliver a baby calf. Looking back, I probably should have taken him up on the experience, but the thought of blood and guts, let alone the sight of it, is something I'm still not great with. I must've made a funny look when I politely declined the invite, Ed just chuckled with an understanding smile. Hell, I hadn't even had my coffee yet.

Saturday, I took Kimber up to the house for the first time. What a cute little wooden house, carved into the side of the hill, with a nice deck looking over the valley. It was perfect. When I knocked on the door, I noticed several firearm manufacturers stickers placed on the windowpane in very obvious view. Ok, so now I'm gonna go ahead and stereotype this situation, then laugh at myself.

When I met Ed and Sue, him being a veterinarian, obvious travelers using the freecampsite boondocking app, opening their home to strangers, and both somewhere near the "hippy" age, I just assumed they were of the liberal variety to one degree or another. Now I'm looking at their front door, with the same gun stickers that I have had on my own truck window, at one point or another, completely and utterly confused. I mean this is New York, right?! Didn't they read the road sign? Turns out that not only are they hunters, but Ed's a big game hunter with several full-size standing and head mounts on his walls. They've been to Africa on safari, and Ed proudly proclaims he's eaten everything he's killed. As it should be. When I told Sue I was confused for

373

a minute she laughed, "Ya, we were worried you weren't a Trump fan too." We both laughed. As I said all along, let people be people and you'd be amazed at how much you have in common.

With Kimber safely stowed away with Sue, I was off to check the box on a HUGE bucket list item, a visit to the Major League Baseball Hall of Fame. Where history meets sports, where politics and war go out the window, where America has united itself, time and time again. My only wish is that my Grampa could've made this trip, although I'm sure there's a bright red Cardinal around Cooperstown somewhere, keeping a close eye on my every step.

The small town of Cooperstown itself is everything baseball. From the street names to the local businesses, everything has a baseball theme. Toward the end of the Main Street was the actual museum, with only a few city blocks making up the entire downtown. In the middle of the main drag was a very old ballpark flanked by gift stores, restaurants, and all the typical tourist trap businesses. I was glad I chose to park on the outskirts of town and take the shuttle into town, as the surface streets were filling up quickly, even as early as 0900.

The museum was built in 1939, housing over 250k photographs, 14k hours of moving images and recordings, 40k artifacts, and 260k yearly visitors. Now those are some serious numbers. The building is three stories tall, each floor housing an amazing array of priceless artifacts from over 100 years of baseball. Skipping the ticket line and heading straight to the entry, beating most of the crowds still waiting to purchase a ticket, made me feel like Grampa Charlie with the golden ticket to the Chocolate Factory. Thanks, Sue!

The tour oddly begins on the second floor with an exhibit called the "Locker-Room." The exhibit had a locker-room "stall" for each team, holding famous players' gear from exceptional moments. For instance, the Red Sox locker had David Ortiz's shoes, Xander Bogart's batting gloves, and the score card from the 2013 World Series win. Also, in each locker was a card giving each team's statistics; year founded, retired jersey numbers, world championships, etc. This went on for all 30 teams, and that's just the first exhibit!

Other second floor exhibits included Grandstand Theater, Taking the Field in the 19th Century, Babe Ruth: Life and Legend, Diamond Dreams: Women in Baseball, Pride and Passion: The African-American Baseball Experience, and Vive Baseball.

Third floor had the Sacred Ground exhibit, Hank Aaron gallery and records, Who's on First, the New Face of Baseball, and Autumn Glory, Postseason Celebrations, just to name a few. This was definitely an all day, maybe a couple day event. The Sacred Ground exhibit, displaying all the ballparks throughout the history of the game, explaining their beginnings and builds, was the most fascinating to me, absolutely incredible American history.

Finally, the tour brings you back to the first floor, and now I see for good reason. This was the actual "Hall" that folks talk about. It's a magnificent room, 20 ft tall ceiling with black granite pillars, hundreds of bronze plaques, all with the players' faces and information/stats, hanging from the marble walls. From the first class in 1936: Ty Cobb, Babe Ruth, Walter Johnson, Honus Wagner, and Christy Mathewson, to the newly enshrined class of 2018: Jeff Bagwell, Pudge Rodriguez, and Tim Raines, to name a few. One man who deserves to be here, but was sadly excluded, the great Pete Rose.

I felt it to be pretty hypocritical of the MLB to use all of Pete Rose's uniforms, artifacts, and an entire display dedicated to his hitting title, but will not admit him after all these years. Players since then have been in trouble for far worse, and it's the man's achievements that should be recognized and remembered rather than punished for life for a one-off mistake. "Charlie Hustle" will forever be in my greatest player Hall of Fame. Just my two cents.

I spent the rest of the afternoon walking the downtown streets of Cooperstown, enjoying the scenery, and breathing in all things baseball. There was fantastic craft beers, a cigar shop worth stopping in, and the oldest little league park in the nation with some type of tournament going on as we speak. What an amazing experience for a young kid, to play ball in Cooperstown NY. Super cool, and a once in a lifetime experience for any baseball fan. Major League Baseball Hall of Fame... COMPLETE!

Back at the camper, Kimber was ecstatic to see me finally return. You'd think 5 hours was an entire lifetime, but in fact, it probably felt that way for me more than her. We ended up visiting the rest of the evening with Ed and Sue before packing up the trailer and heading to Niagara Falls. I couldn't thank Ed and Sue enough for their hospitality and kindness. More lifelong friends that I truly hope our paths will cross again. Thanks, guys!

Our final stop in New York was Niagara Falls, at the only decent priced campground in the area, about two hours away from Toronto, on the U.S. side. Sadly, you get what you pay for, a pretty rough looking motel, with several campgrounds around a green grass field in the rear. It wasn't bad, but at over 30 bucks a night, it wasn't great. What was worse was the entire town of Niagara, on the American side, was an absolute dump. It was like driving into a 1950s summer resort town, that nobody stopped to paint, repair, or upgrade since. Antiquated roller coasters and mini golf places, trash and abandoned buildings, and tweekers. Ya, this wasn't a great place, but I had no option.

The Toronto Blue Jays played a six-game home stand, starting Tuesday and ending on Sunday. I decided that I wasn't going to unload the camper entirely for a full week, because if I could make tomorrow's Tuesday night game, I could checkout on Wednesday and save some cash. I called the desk to explain that I may be leaving early, and asked if I'd be able to get a refund, which the lady at the desk confirmed as not being a problem. Well, I hope I made the right call, we shall see. About that time, I looked up from my phone, due to a scratch of a branch on the back window. Low and behold, a big bright Cardinal was literally in the bushes just outside my window. The sound that got my attention and then the bird sitting right there, bigger than life, made me about drop my phone. Every time I wonder about a decision, choose an unsure route, or anyway else second guess myself... a Cardinal appears. Got it, Grampa, I'm right where I'm supposed to be.

So now that we're catching tomorrow night's game, then breaking camp, I had better go across the bridge to see the Niagara Falls light show. Jaime's German buddy back in New Hampshire said it was a must see, but the view from the Canadian side at night was the best. I left Kimber in the trailer and ventured into downtown Niagara Falls. The scenery didn't get much better downtown, with somewhat of a bustling nightlife, but still that lingering feeling of watching your back was on the forefront of your mind. I paid the parking fee at about 2100, then started for the pedestrian bridge, following the signs toward the Canadian border. I was shocked at the amount of fencing and concertina wire there was for Americans to pass into Canada. For what I thought was such a friendly country, it had the equivalent of check point charlie to even get over the bridge.

I followed the fairly constant stream of people walking back and forth across the expansion bridge, with the country border directly in the center. First stop was at the Canadian border crossing office. I moved to the counter when I was called by the Mountie, sliding my passport under the bulletproof glass. First time to Canada, what's your trip to Canada for, how long will you be staying, and do you have any weapons... like three times. All of which I shook my head no, he handed me my passport without a stamp. "Don't I get a stamp?" Now it was his turn to just shake his head. Well played, sir. I took my passport and followed the crowds to the view area across from the falls, just a few hundred yards down the road.

It was completely dark now, but the streets were packed. I looked around at what looked like a booming resort town, with casinos nearby, streets filled with pedestrians, lots of signs and lights. I was taken aback by how I was in Canada, but all the restaurants and hotels were American brands. Guess you have to venture further east to see the French stuff. Maybe Toronto will be more like a different country; this place felt more like Laughlin, Nevada. As for the light show, picture two deep bathtubs with overflowing faucets on high, while holding a three-color flashlight, switching colors every 5 seconds. Congrats, you just imagined Niagara Falls.

I guess after all the waterfalls I've seen, like Bridal Veil Falls, or anywhere in Colorado, you will understand my comparison. It just wasn't very impressive. Upon re-entering the glorious United States, you have to actually pay a dollar toll to walk back across to the U.S.; best part is, the turnstile only takes quarters. So now, picture a crowd of newbies, all frantically digging in their pockets and purses, some even asking their children for pocket change. There were two change machines, one empty and one with a line longer than the one to get into Canada. Thankfully, I had the correct amount of quarters to pay the ogre under the bridge and quickly bypassed the crowds.

I stopped for a few pictures of the "light show," before crossing the bridge and being directed inside by a couple of border patrol officers to show my passport. I was literally the only one in the building, standing behind the red line, with only one border patrol agent at the desk. I stood at the line as instructed by the sign, before he raised his head and yelled, "Next!" I looked around amused, then stepped to the desk. The agent looked up at me, while reaching for my passport. "What was your purpose for visiting Canada this evening?" he asked with the typical monotone, midnight shift, government employee excitement. "To see the waterfall lights," I replied in the same unexcited tone. "Was it absolutely breathtaking?" he asked, this time detecting some sarcasm. "I think my swimming pool has more colors. Apparently nobody's ever seen Vegas here," I replied in the same tone. To which he replied, "Indeed. Exit left, please. NEXT!" while handing back my passport. I smiled and looked back to the red line; the place was empty. Classic.

Back at the camper, Kimber was sleeping intently, not even getting off the bed to greet me. I didn't blame her, this had been a long run. Tomorrow I'd drive the truck into Canada for the very first time, then back on the road to Michigan. Hard to believe that I had only four more major league parks to see, before completing all thirty. I was amazed as I looked back at what we'd done so far this year, with two more months of baseball to go. We were almost done, and I'm not going to lie, I was glad it was almost over. I was damn tired too.

The next morning we slept in later than I had in years. The exhaustion finally caught up to me, but we can't stop yet. After a hearty breakfast, and a good session of ball throwing for Kimber, I spent the rest of the morning unloading the truck. I wasn't going to have anything in my truck that would turn me around at the border. I emptied the entire bed of all tools and camping gear, scoured every crack and crevasse for spent shells from target shooting over the years, made sure all my truck registration/insurance paperwork was all organized and at easy reach. I felt like I was preparing my vehicle for a base inspection. All I know is what happens to you if Mexico finds a shell or a bullet in your car, I sure as hell don't want to go to prison in Canada either. Although a Canadian prison sounds much more appealing than a Mexican one. Just saying.

The drive to Toronto was fairly uneventful. This time driving through the border, I waited my turn behind the dozens of camera lenses and red stoplight, until it was my turn to approach the window. I rolled down all my windows and handed the Canadian Mountie my passport. He mumbled something that I couldn't hear. When I asked him to repeat, he yelled, "Turn your motor off," which I did immediately. Oh boy, does that mean they're going to search the truck? Ok well, at least I prepared for that. He shuffled through my paperwork, scanning my passport into the computer. "What's your purpose for your visit today?" he asked. "Going to the Blue Jays game," I replied. "Where are you coming from?" was his next question. "Arizona," I replied. "Awfully long way for a baseball game," he replied, this time watching my response. "Yup, seeing all 30 parks" was my answer. He looked at me somewhat exasperated and asked, "Where are you staying?" "Oooooh," I replied once I knew what he was getting at. "The Princess Motel in Niagara." At which point, he handed back my paperwork and told me to have a nice day. Well that was relatively painless. Then we approached another toll gate about a mile ahead.

This time they were collecting the actual toll for the highway or the bridge. When I pulled up to the window, I realized I had no Canadian money, and I had passed the exchange office a few hundred yards back. Assuming that a U-turn right about now would draw some undue excitement my way, I asked the young man working the booth if they took American currency, which of course they did. Then I asked if I should get Canadian money before going to the game. The 20 something year old said, "It's easier if you do, plus you'll get the right exchange rate.

Just park in front of the booth here and walk back to the office. I'll cover for ya." Ok, a little weird leaving my truck here, but if he says so. Not sure if I should not run as he specifically said walk; don't want to draw any sniper attention either. So I walked briskly to the office, received my Canadian Monopoly money, and walked quickly back to the truck. With a nod and a wave from the kid, I was on my way to Toronto.

So the very first thing you have to figure out when driving in Canada, is how to read your speedometer in kilometers. 100 kph was the speed limit, with massive signs in English, reminding Americans to convert from miles to kilometers. The next thing was how flat it was here; mainly farmland and what looked like wineries, slowly giving way to the suburbs and ultimately downtown Toronto. Thirdly, the amount of very large mosques between our border and Toronto was surprising.

There were at least four massive complexes, with the crescent moon above its rounded domes; something not so prevalent in Arizona, and definitely not as numerous. I had noticed on the Canadian side of Niagara Falls, about 30% of the women were dressed in full Muslim garb, some with just the hajib headscarf. Now in Toronto, that number increased dramatically. Blame me if you want, but from a Marine's point of view, who's served in the Middle East, I believe we need to be just as weary of our northern border, or even more so, than our southern. It was a real eye opener to see this within a couple hours of our country, with a wide-open northern border. Before you hit me with the Islamaphobe garbage, I understand that there are peaceful practicing Muslims, but until they get ahold of this extremist ideology, we have to be prudent for national security; political correctness be damned.

I had reserved a parking place a few blocks from the Rogers Centre, home of the Toronto Blue Jays. When I emerged at street level, I was immediately taken aback by the beauty of this city. The skyscrapers looked as if they were all made by the same builder. Different in size and architecture, but all constructed in what looked like brushed aluminum, the windows all had the same type of bluish-green reflective tint, giving this ultra-modern downtown the look of the Emerald City. I made my way along the hustle of the busy streets and sidewalks, walking past several, very nice, outdoor cafes. There was definitely every type of nationality you could think of here. I heard French, Arabic, East Indian, and English, in both Canadian and English varieties. It was an interesting mix of the familiar and the foreign.

Rogers Centre, Toronto, Canada

August 7th 2018. The ticket office for Rogers Centre was outside at street level, with massive concrete steps leading up to different gate entrances, circling the park. Right next door was the massive space needle like structure, looking over the city and the coast of Lake Ontario. Across the street was a warehouse district turned into shops and a brewery, and across the courtyard was an aquarium of sorts. Definitely a busy recreational area, especially when the Jays are in town.

One benefit of seeing a game in Canada was the exchange rate. My get in ticket was only 13 bucks. Even then, I asked the lady if they gave a veteran discount, just to see her reaction. She just looked at me with a blank stare and slowly shook her head no. Either she didn't know what to say, or she must've thought I was an idiot. Either way, 13 bucks for a behind home plate, nosebleed seat, was good enough for me. Inside, the savings continued with beers and food being extremely reasonably priced. I had to laugh at myself when I just had to give a handful of change to the girl, to take what she needed, as I was not well versed in the land of loonies and toonies at this point. I'll explain that later.

I found my way to my seat first, then headed out to explore the park. First and foremost, you're probably wondering why I'm watching American baseball in Canada. Trust me, I'm not a fan of there being teams outside of CONUS. This is a purely American sport, with its founding in the United States. I didn't like the fact I needed to get a passport, and travel to another country, just to see one of the 30 parks. Of course, all the blowback of them naming the championship series the "World" Series confuses a lot of people. That was because of the American and National League coming together for the first time, to compete in a grand championship. Back then this WAS all the teams in the world. An interesting fact: the San Francisco Giants were originally slated to move and become an expansion team. Wow. I think I just felt my grandfather roll over in his grave. Imagine if that actually went through back in 1977, when the Blue Jays were founded.

The stadium has a retractable dome that was wide open for tonight's game. The centerfield backdrop was a massive Jumbotron, flanked by what looked liked windows with curtains, either open or closed. Turns out that there's a hotel built into the backside of the stadium. You can literally get a room, and peer down on the centerfielder's head. Some Boston folks were hanging Red Sox flags in the windows, giving away the Jays' opponent this evening. Gotta love Bostonians!

As you walk the concourse, you get an idea of how large this place really is, which makes its cleanliness astonishing. It's a gorgeous park with some slight differences from stateside venues. First of all, a Budweiser is considered a domestic beer, served to you with a sippy lid installed. Much like a coffee cup lid, this thing was ingenious. I mean, how often are you bumped and lose a couple sips of your adult libation? This person deserves the Nobel prize for inventing this. Well done!

Then there's the food. Remember the burger condiment stand in Houston; wilted lettuce, limp sliced tomatoes, mustard, ketchup and relish? The Canadian condiment bar looked like an all you can eat salad bar with every kind of fresh vegetable, several different sauces, and several pickled garnishes to boot. My foot-long, all beef (everything was all beef and healthy here) looked like a Chicago dog with veganistic tendencies. Man was it good! Seemed like everything served here was far more healthy than what you see in the States.

If I had to do this park all over again, I'd just buy a get in ticket and head to the second deck, outfield area. Basically, there's a line of different themed bars, all facing out to the park from centerfield. From a whiskey bar to brewery tap room, this is where the party was at. Even as I left the building somewhere around the seventh inning stretch, there were young ladies entering the second deck, looking like they were dressed for a night at the club. Oh to be twentysomething again.

With that being said, I found my way back to the truck and started for the border. The American border agent asked me the same questions, where were you and where are you coming from, to which I replied the same as before. "That's a long ways for a baseball game," he said sarcastically. Some things just never get old. Now safely back on American soil, with a wiggling and whining, happy little puppy dog in my arms, I'm glad to pronounce, Rogers Centre, MLB park #27... COMPLETE! And while we're at it, let's call New York, our 43rd State... also COMPLETE! Michigan, here we come.

Michigan

August 8th, 2018. With a payday under our belt, and finally some clear skies above, we were on the road to Michigan. This time we're staying with a distant cousin that I had never met. I grew up with my great aunt's daughter, from the Jackson side, my cousin Judy. So this would be her cousin, from her dad's side. Ya following me so far? Anyway, my cousin Judy in Oregon, had called Audra and asked if I could stay at her place while visiting Michigan, unbeknownst to me. Next thing I know, Judy sends me a phone number and says, "This is Audra's number, my cousin. She's expecting you." Well alrighty then, I'm all in on meeting new family. With a quick text to Audra saying hello, and some status updates along the way, we arrived in Grand Junction, Michigan two days later.

The quickest, most direct route was going to be Interstate 90 west, through Buffalo and Cleveland. This made the anxiety level rise to newfound levels, trying to navigate about 40ft of truck and trailer through the downtown traffic of two major cities. I just kept reminding myself, if semi-trucks can do it, so can you. We ended up stopping for the night about two hours away from Grand Junction. I was starving, tired, and needed a shower before presenting myself to new kin. Thankfully, the Coldwater Walmart with a Buffalo Wild Wings and Anytime Fitness nearby, fit the bill perfectly.

After my workout and shower, I stowed Kimber away in the camper with her supper and some water, and headed into B-Dubs for the same. While sitting at the bar, waiting for my food, a local couple came in and sat on the stools next to me. We struck up a conversation, and of course, ended up talking about my travels and what brings me here. They warned me not to take a certain road this weekend, as it was "yard sale" weekend. Apparently, it's lined with people selling things for literally miles. It's the largest yard sale in the world they said. "The road is packed for miles, and there's a lot of wrecks. Trust me, I own a tow truck company." Well, that's good to know, as the roads heading to the tiny, four corners town of Grand Junction are all pretty much backroads from here.

We continued on with our meals and conversation, lasting well into the evening. When it came time for me to get back to Kimber and catch some sleep, I was confused by how quickly this couple agreed, stood up, said goodbye, and left. Not thinking much if it, I finished my beer, and asked for my bill. The bartender smiled, "Nope you're good. They covered it." Wow! How freaking cool is that. So I mention this to give a shout out and a thank you to those folks for welcoming us to Michigan with a great meal and some great conversation!

We pulled into Audra's around 1100 the following morning. It was a quaint little white wooden house, with a good-sized backyard, large enough for their own camper that was now at their gun club. Bob, Audra's husband, greeted us at the street and helped guide the camper back into the trailer spot. Audra came down shortly with big hugs and welcomes, like she had known us forever.

Turns out Audra is a proud veteran also, serving on an Army helicopter air crew in 1975. After her Army stint, she became some sort of an instructor for the Department of Defense. Apparently that wasn't enough for Audra, as she climbed behind the wheel of an 18-wheeler, driving the open roads, to include the ice roads of Alaska. This is where she met her husband Bob, a former lineman for the electric companies, who decided to jump in the cab with her, and become a team. Now with Bob retired, Audra is working from home as a call service rep for an appliance company. Did I mention she's 69 and he's 79?! Amazing people right here, opening their home to complete strangers. I'm always amazed by that.

So the plan for Michigan was to make our way into Detroit for a Tigers game, visit the River Raisin National Battlefield Park, and make a trip up to the "U.P.," the Upper Peninsula of Michigan. We also had a planned visit with a veteran who had been following the FB page since 2017, and wanted to show me the Ford Museum. A busy itinerary, but at this point, we had plenty of time before the Milwaukee game to enjoy the visit.

We spent a solid five days just relaxing and visiting with Audra and Bob, before hitting the road to Detroit. The River Raisin National Battlefield Park was only a few miles south of Detroit, making it a perfect day trip, before catching the Tigers game that afternoon. Now that Kimber was being absolutely spoiled at Audra's house, and my new cousin telling me to take her small, much more city friendly and fuel-efficient car, I was on the road at zero dark thirty. About a two-hour drive across the state would put me at the River Raisin Battlefield Park about 0800, right at opening.

First thing you notice about the park is that it is under some serious construction. The original, small and antiquated visitor center sat near the front of what looked like a typical city park with some farmland in the rear. Across the street, in front of the park, were several small dilapidated houses, marked for demolition. These too were soon to be part of the newer expanded park, that will show an old English Fort with small houses for soldiers' families inside. At this point I was still confused about what this battle was, or what it was about.

Inside the visitor center you learn that this battle was fought during the War of 1812, with the familiar names of Governor William Henry Harrison and Shawnee leader Tecumseh, taking center stage once again. Remember our visit to the Tippacanoe Battlefield and Prophet Town in

Indiana, where Tecumseh and his brother tried to ambush American troops, and later found that they were backed by the British, thus kicking off the war of 1812. Surprisingly, here we hear about what a great warrior and leader Tecumseh was and how the Indian tribes, due to constant persecution and attacks from white settlers, fought valiantly against American intrusion. Blah blah blah. See the difference between National and local museums, not to mention the politics of the state that we're currently in. So what really happened here? Why was "Remember the Raisin" an American battle cry? This is what I learned.

One thing that I always find interesting with these older battlefields, the outside signage that usually has been there since the park's inception, always tells the story in a pragmatic and straightforward depiction, free of the moment's political clime. Like the first one I read while waiting for the visitor center to open. I'll let it describe the scene, the information placard read, "The opening months of the War of 1812 were disastrous for the isolated American outpost in the west. Fort Mackinac, on Mackinac Island, had fallen in the first action of the war. The inhabitants and Garrison of Fort Dearborn, at what is now in Chicago, have been massacred. Detroit had surrendered August 15, 1812, and the Frenchtown settlement on the River Raisin was controlled by the British."

So now with Michigan basically a complete disaster, Harrison sends troops from Kentucky to take back Detroit. A small, poorly supplied army, moves north, assuming that this would be a simple rout of a sparsely manned British outpost.

This is when the story gets a little mucky. Some say the Kentuckians attacked every Indian settlement they came across while moving north toward Detroit, while other accounts say they were harassed and attacked repeatedly by several tribes along the march. Either way, they were exhausted and depleted by the time they reached the English Fort known as Frenchtown, built along the River Raisin. Ok, so that's what they're tearing down those houses across the street for. After successfully running off the English, the American troops took over the Fort. It was then that the native forces, siding with the English attacked in the night, dragging out the Americans and slaughtering them. They went as far as to post the heads of the deceased on pickets around the encampment. Now the controversy kicks in. Some say the Indians were justified in their attack, as it was a boiling over point for all the attacks they'd suffered. Others say the Americans used this to show the brutality of the Natives, and how they were backed and supplied by King George and Britain. Either way, "Remember the Raisin," became an American battle cry to remember the massacre that occurred here. A rough synopsis, but you get the idea. Ok cool, I'm ready for some baseball.

Comerica Park, Detroit, MI

August 15th, 2018. Comerica Park, home of the Detroit Tigers, built in 2000, took the place of the 88-year-old Tiger Stadium, several blocks away. Across from the famous Fox Theatre, the outside of the park resembled a circus more than a baseball park. The exterior brick walls were adorned with massive tiger heads perched like gargoyles with baseballs in their mouths. Prowling the roof line above were absolutely massive, full body, concrete colored tigers, snarling and growling at the fans below. Wasn't there some big scary looking dogs in the movie *Ghostbusters*? Something like that, except an obvious tiger. Pretty cool actually, like something you'd see on the strip in Vegas.

Although this new park lost all the history from the old Tiger Stadium, much like the New Yankee Stadium, its history is encapsulated in glass displays along the main concourse. Most of the pictures and artifacts showed the great Ty Cobb, along with other Tiger immortals. A car theme of course took precedent, with either a Ford vehicle or the Ford emblem in plain sight, everywhere. The centerfield backdrop showcases what was at the time of the build, the largest Jumbotron in the league, with grandstands behind left field, and a large ivy-covered wall in right. A nice view of the Detroit cityscape was visible from my nosebleed seats behind the plate. Also visible from above were the two distinct differences separating this field from other MLB parks. First, the dirt walkway connecting the pitcher's mound to home plate, sometimes called the "keyhole," then the shape of the dirt surrounding the plate and batter boxes is the same pentagram shape as home plate, instead of a circle.

By the 7th inning, I was ready to go. Traffic would be picking up soon, and I still had two hours of driving ahead of me; that and I missed my little dog horribly. I polished off a quick hot dog, finished taking all the necessary pictures, and started back to where I had parked the car. Detroit Motor City's Comerica Park, MLB park #28... COMPLETE! Only two left, people, wow, I can't believe we're almost done.

Back at Audra's, Kimber could care less that I was gone, as the showering of snacks and attention kept her at Audra's feet most of the day. This became the routine for the next few days, as I ventured out to the gym and finally rode my neglected mountain bike, waiting for the weekend to meet up with my veteran buddy and explore the Ford Theatre. I was going to take full advantage of Kimber being happily distracted.

When I pulled up to Eric's house, I was greeted by a friend I've only known through my book page. All I knew was Eric was an Army veteran, post 9/11 Iraqi vet, and a huge Tigers fan. We started talking when he had asked me to take a lot of pictures of the Tigers spring training camp down in Florida, which of course I was happy to do. I thought that was super cool, to be able to do that for a veteran friend, living vicariously through my travels. If I could only make that a career somehow. Anyway, after meeting him and his family, Eric and I were off for the museum.

To explain the Ford museum in a paragraph, would be like trying to explain the Smithsonian Institute in 50 words or less. There just is no describing this place, it literally is a book of its own. The building itself had to be measured in acres, housing everything from airplanes suspended in air, to arctic snow trains with massive plows towering above. It had the actual bus where Rosa Parks defiantly refused to give up her seat, and President Lincoln's actual bloodstained chair from the Ford Theatre (not the same family as Henry Ford). They had Reagan and Kennedy's presidential limousines, describing the assignation attempts, and also Teddy Roosevelt's presidential horse carriage. Not to mention the original Mustang prototype and several other iconic Ford models. All under the same roof! And that's just the museum; outside was an entire town, with some pretty significant residents.

Behind the museum was an actual town, rebuilt by Ford with some iconic historical buildings imported from all around the country. First was the Wright brothers' home and bicycle shop with period actors explaining how they decided to make an airplane. Harvey Firestone's working farm was on the outskirts, with period actors growing and cooking authentic food from the time. Ford built replicas of his birthplace, with his mother's house furnished exactly the way it was during his childhood. The most amazing display was Edison's Menlo Park laboratory, where Ford imported several tons of dirt with the original building, so that it could be placed on Jersey soil back in Michigan. I had no idea Ford was such an eccentric.

We ended the visit with my favorite exhibit, the baseball diamond outside. There were two teams dressed in authentic, 1800s style uniforms, using these clubs for bats, and crazy old gloves, warming up for a game. One of the players was walking around talking to folks, answering questions. He explained that this is an actual league that has several teams from around the country. They use all original equipment, and play by all the old rules. How freaking cool! What an absolutely incredible place; I could've spent weeks here, absorbing all the incredible history Ford had accumulated with his vast wealth. I was kind of surprised that artifacts like Lincoln's chair wasn't in DC, enshrined in the Smithsonian. I thanked Eric for showing me this amazing place and started back for Grand Junction.

So at this point, we were just waiting for the Milwaukee Brewers to return from the road, kicking off a 5-day home stand. Also, the RV spot at the fairgrounds I had reserved, located perfectly downtown, was in the middle of the Harley Davidson anniversary celebration and the spots were ridiculously expensive. So with a few days to kill, and wanting to give Audra and Bob a break from our extended stay, we packed up the truck and headed for the UP of Michigan on a sightseeing tour. Following the coast up what's called the Michigan Lake Circle, we followed the coastline all the way around to Traverse City for our first night's stop.

I had been to Traverse City once before, visiting my step-mother's parents, who owned a cherry farm here. I remembered all the candy sweet fruit, my favorite being cherries, so was looking forward to passing through this super cool town. We stopped for dinner at a brewery that had at least 6 or 7 food trucks, all different types, surrounding a large picnic area with a live band. You could sample small servings from each truck, grab a craft beer from the brewery's indoor bar, and sit outside with strings of lights and live music. It was an awesome experience. That night, Kimber and I parked at the local Walmart, remembering why we hadn't slept on the cot in awhile.

The next day, we continued following the coast to the Mackinac Bridge, the entry into Michigan's Upper Peninsula. I stopped for gas and to get exact change for the bridge at a convenience store a few miles ahead of the toll booths. Inside, they had an assortment of meat sticks made from pheasant, deer, and other game meats, stuffed with cheese that I just had to have. On the glass case was a sign that read "Fresh Pasties 2 for 3 dollars." I turned to the older gentleman working the register and asked, "What's a paisty?" "They're PAAASTYs, paisties go on titties," the perfect answer from a guy that resembled one of the *Grumpy Old Men* cast. Anyway, they're some sort of Finnish Piroshki, which I passed on.

The Upper Peninsula of Michigan is like driving into another country. Sparsely inhabited, it has dense wooded forests much like Maine, and the water of Lake Michigan is a dark beautiful blue. Even the beaches seemed empty as we followed the coast Hwy 2 west. I was hoping to follow the border of the Upper Peninsula all the way around, ending back at the Mackinac Bridge, until I realized how big the U.P. actually was. It was over 300 miles just to drive to the furthest western border; it could've been its own state. So I chose the one place I wanted to see, Picture Rocks National Lake Shore, where there appeared to be a few National Campgrounds.

From Hwy 2 west, we took the 77 north to the coast of Lake Superior, following the water west to Picture Rocks. I was stunned as I looked down on this incredibly clear, emerald green water, slowly fading to a deep dark blue as the water deepened, ending at the horizon with the dark blue instantly becoming the baby blue sky. The coastline was lined with small gold colored beaches, before rising to the granite rock formations and finally the deep green forest above. The lake went as far as you could see, both left, right, and center. Like the calmest ocean, with 3 to 5 foot waves lapping at the rock clad, sandy beaches. It was absolutely breathtaking.

I found the nearest Ranger station, hoping to find a campsite while it was still early in the day. Sadly, even on a Thursday, the place was booked solid. Well shoot, now what? We could look for a boondocking spot, maybe a Walmart or a sympathetic VFW. No such luck, plus my back wasn't exactly looking forward to another night on the cot. I decided on a day hike down to the water, have a little prepackaged lunch, while Kimber adds to her already impressive body of water list. I figured we would just enjoy the scenery for a bit, before heading back toward the Mackinac Bridge; worse case, I go back to the Traverse City Walmart for the evening.

It was about 1800 when we crossed the Mackinac Bridge, putting me in the quandary of whether to subject my back to the cot, thus taking the side road to Traverse City, or stay on the Interstate and make it back to Audra's, and my bed, by 2100. Eight hours of driving after the day hike, wasn't exactly what I had in mind, but my back had the louder voice, and we made the drive back to Grand Junction. Now happily in my own bed, thinking about what was next, it was almost time to make the move to Wisconsin. Only two more ballparks and three more states left for this run… we're so close.

The next couple days were spent hanging out with Audra, before heading further west. Money was very tight, and payday on the horizon; Audra must have sensed I was somewhat concerned about having the cash to make it back. Pulling this trailer, added a serious gasoline cost burden that I halfway expected, but not to this extent. The day we were packing up to leave, she handed me a credit card. "Take this for gas. Throw it away when it quits working" were the instructions given by a woman who wasn't about to take no for an answer. What an amazing lady. I thanked Audra and Bob for their hospitality, said our goodbyes, and pointed the Rig due west for Milwaukee. Michigan, state #44... COMPLETE!

Wisconsin

August 31st, 2018. We still had a few days before my RV spot at the Milwaukee Fairgrounds would be available. With Labor Day weekend in full swing, I was concerned about finding a campsite on some water, let alone one that had electric for the AC. It was August, and the humidity was as bad as Houston at this time last year. One of the camping apps found a place right on the Wisconsin/Illinois state line, Illinois Beach State Campground, a huge campground, next to a fairly busy beach, right on Lake Michigan. The price was fair, so we jumped at one of the open spots that they had left. This was my first mistake.

The plan for Wisconsin was to dock the Rig at the Fairgrounds for three days, catch the Brewers game with another veteran following the FB page, drop in on an old friend from Arizona, and with time and cash permitting, visit the Harley Davidson Museum and the Pabst Brewery. The camping spots for this week, bike week, were about 150 bucks more per night than usual. So a few days at Illinois State Beach was the cheapest way out, until we actually hit Milwaukee. Apparently, you get what you pay for. Gunshots, screeching tires, people speaking every language BUT English, it was the very first time I've felt unsafe to sleep in the entire country.

The next morning, I took Kimber for a walk to the beach. She was excited, ball in mouth, pulling me all the way to the water. When we got to the beach, the first thing I noticed was the no trespassing signs to the north. There were two large circular towers, like old dilapidated water storage or something, with one tower obviously leaning to the side. Wait a minute... why is there a nuclear hazard symbol on the no trespassing sign? A quick question posed to Senor Google showed that those water towers were actually shuttered NUCLEAR REACTORS! What!? And one's leaning... a lot! Ok that's it, I'm outta here. Wow, was this a shocker. With that being said, it was back to pack up the Rig, and get the hell out of Dodge. I'd find a Walmart for the night somewhere. With a quick call to the Fairgrounds RV Park, they said I could check in a day early for the standard price, a huge relief. We're outta here!

Finally, we reached Milwaukee, the camper parked, AC plugged in... and we slept. Catching up on last night's rest, and fueled by pure exhaustion, Kimber and I both slept like babies to the hypnotic hum and cool breeze of the AC. It was late in the afternoon when Kimber decided it was time to eat. What she didn't know was that she was going to see one of her long-lost fan club members.

Way back in 2015, when we came back from our very first summer of travel, Buffalo Wild Wings was my favorite happy hour place to watch baseball and get some food. This was when I met my friend Kristin, who had kept my reward card nicely stocked for me all this time and several waitresses who literally sat on the floor behind my stool and visited with Kimber. This was Kimber's "fan club." So in 2017, one of her fan club members had moved back to Milwaukee, and told us to drop in on her when we finally made it to her hometown. So off to a local sports bar to see our friend Emily, and get the low-down on Milwaukee.

As expected, Kimber was excited to see one of her old friends, and of course to meet all the soon to be new ones. Everywhere this dog goes, she's a rock star. It's insane. Anyway, after the meet and greet and a cold beer for Kimber's human, we were eagerly awaited the arrival of a pub pizza and some cheese curds. The rest of the evening was filled with baseball, pull-tabs, great stories, lots of laughs and of course, beer. I love this "do as the Romans do" part about traveling.

I made plans with Emily for lunch and some day drinking tomorrow on her day off. It's a bartender thing, relax. Besides, did I mention we're in Milwaukee, the only place in the country with apparently more bars than Boston. Outside of downtown had an interesting vibe. The buildings and houses all looked old, with relatively few high-rises. For some reason, it reminded me of the TV show *All in the Family*, or at least in that time frame. Or maybe it was *Laverne and Shirley* with the brewery. You get the point. The city was old, but with a strangely new reprisal from old brands that are now the fad and fashion. Pabst Blue Ribbon, Harley Davidson, even the Brewers are having some good years as of late. A historical hipster vibe if you will; I was digging it.

The unbelievable humidity was put on hold the next day or two, this time happy to see thunder clouds and rain coming in. By lunch time it was pouring. Undeterred, we ventured out to see Emily and experience what Milwaukee had to offer. We met up at Jackson's Blue Ribbon Pub, an all Pabst Blue Ribbon themed bar/restaurant, for more cheese curds and PBR. Then over to meet some of her friends, one of which was the bartender at a place the shape of a triangle. If there's enough room for a keg and a stool, they'll make a bar out of it in Milwaukee.

Soon it was time to head back to the camper with only a couple of hours until game time. We were meeting up with yet another veteran following the page since 2016. Enter my buddy Chris, prior Navy, who had followed my page after seeing a post I made on one of the many military/veteran FB pages. We had stayed in contact and chatted often about baseball and all things related, as I finally made my way to Wisconsin. It's always a cool experience, meeting someone for the first time, but feeling like you already "know" them. Ahh, the wonders of social media.

Miller Park, Milwaukee, WI

September 5th, 2018. Chris picked me up at the camper, leaving Kimber to her food and assortment of chew treats, while we made the short drive to Miller Park in the never-ending rain. Not realizing the park had a retractable roof, I was excited to get this opportunity to hang out with a veteran about my own age, and not worry too much about getting all my pictures in. It was dark anyway, and Chris had picked up some amazing seats just off the first base side. We made our way around the park, getting the shots I needed, before settling in for the game. All was well until a very large gentleman, putting it nicely, who apparently had season tickets, made his way down the aisle to sit next to me. A massive soda in one hand, a hot dog and God knows what else in the other, he positioned himself in front of the seat and basically did a controlled demolition fall into the under compensated seat below. He was like a giant human wedge, simultaneously pushing me and the lady on the other side of him to the wayside, without a care in the world. I'm not one to judge, but when it's just your arm and maybe a knee that may periodically come in contact with mine, that's one thing, but if I can feel your pulse from the roll of fat that can't be contained in your own seat, I got a tad bit of a problem. There was no attainable position in my seat that made it so I WASN'T in contact with this man in some form or fashion. This is exactly my luck, every single time. A few innings into the game, Chris could see I was in obvious turmoil, offering to relocate to a standing room only bar. I felt bad since Chris bought the seats, but undauntedly we enjoyed the rest of the game, while learning some cool facts about the park from my buddy Chris. For instance, the old Brewers ballpark is still in the parking lot, transformed into a little league park; and there's a bronze plaque somewhere in the parking lot, that marks where Hank Aaron's last home run landed, outside the old County Stadium.

First of all, Miller Park is absolutely massive. Even with the equally massive Bank One Ballpark (now Chase Field) being built in my own home city at the time, this place seemed even bigger. Built in 2001, it replaced the old Milwaukee County Stadium, where the great Hank Aaron once played. The Brewers were Milwaukee's original team from 1902-1952, at which time the Boston Braves took up residence in the newly built County Stadium, moving the Brewers to Toledo. The Milwaukee Braves then moved to Atlanta, making room for the Seattle Pilots to become the new Milwaukee Brewers in the spring of 1970. Aaron then came back to Milwaukee as a manager from 1975-76. Ok, so this explains why I had Hank Aaron baseball cards in a Milwaukee uniform. It's crazy I didn't realize this until now, especially after seeing all of his memorabilia under glass in Atlanta. Then again, I was 8 years old, but can still picture that card distinctly to this day.

The roof of Miller Park was a mechanical marvel. The entire roof opened up like a fan, with home plate being the pivot point. The centerfield backdrop was the typical Jumbotron, surrounded by what looks like windowpanes making up the stadium's exterior wall. There's a small waterslide or something, that the mascot slides down when there's a home run in left field, and a large bar area in right. It was all pretty nondescript, with the sheer magnitude of the building being the wow factor. Tomorrow, when it's daylight, I'd come back to see County Stadium and search for that home run plaque. Until then, it was just beers, baseball, and good times with a newfound friend. Miller Park, MLB park #29... COMPLETE!

The weather was cloudy and cool the next day, but this time no rain. Today was going to be a full day, backtracking to Miller Park to see where the old County Stadium had stood was first on the list. As Chris had described, it was now a brand new, miniature version of a MLB field, little league sized, complete with green wall, grandstand, concession area, and ground crew. Around it was some granite memorials to the history of the park, including a life-size bronze depiction of Aaron himself.

I followed the left field line, straight out into the now empty parking lot, the logical place for a Hank Aaron home run to land. I found the plaque about 50 yards from the little league field fence, inlayed into stained red concrete meant to look like bricks. The plaque read, "This marks the landing location of the final home run of Hank Aaron's career, #755, hit at County Stadium on July 20, 1976." Just below that was Aaron's signature. I put one hand on the plaque and took an awkward photo. I just wanted to remember that I touched the spot where the final, all-time record holding home run landed, hit by the one and only Hank Aaron. I was almost as excited about this as I was standing on the spot where Washington crossed the Delaware. Almost. Editor's note... it's understood that Barry Bonds Jr. now holds the title, sadly an obviously dubious honor.

After Miller Park, my last must-see in Milwaukee was of course the Harley Davidson Museum. I had purchased my first Harley shortly after getting out of the service, and was immediately bitten by the lifestyle bug. It probably helped in the ending of my marriage, as my mother once said, "No wonder she left, her officer and a gentleman turned into a biker." The same lifestyle that almost killed me a decade ago, but that's for yet another book. Now being without a bike for the first time since my kids were born, it was a bittersweet visit to a place that I had always considered sacred ground. Milwaukee Harley Davidson, where it all began.

The grounds of the museum had a bar and grill, gift store, several office buildings and of course the museum. I don't think this was the actual manufacturing plant, but more of its showcase location. There were large white tents and hundreds of folding chairs being taken down and moved to trucks, all from the last week's anniversary festivities. I wasn't sure how long the cool weather was going to last, the sun was starting to break through, and the humidity was already becoming a factor. With Kimber in the car, I was going to have to be mindful of the time, so I went straight to the museum. There was no way I was gonna have money for anything else here.

Inside the museum was motorcycle nirvana. Every model of every year was on display somewhere in this huge two-story building. The history here was incredible, with a display of Harleys being used throughout our nation's history. From military messengers to post office couriers, police bikes to ice cream vendors, the Harley Davidson brand has been an iconic symbol of Americana for over a hundred years. There were hands-on displays about the inner workings of the Harley motor, an entire wall of gas tanks all painted to different year's paint schemes, and a view into a working restoration shop, that looked more like a scene from *American Pickers*, with antique Harley parts hanging from the walls. I could go on for days about all there was to see; the history here is worth the visit, Harley fan or not. As for this Harley enthusiast... that's a huge bucket list item checked off the list!

The rest of the day was spent downtown, walking the old Pabst Brewing complex, checking out the Welcome Center that looked like a castle, then having some lunch in one of the original brewery tap rooms from back in the day. I wish I had more time to visit this history packed town, but the last ballpark of the book awaits. Two more states and we're finally done with this run. I was eager to get moving, so back to the camper to pack up for the road, it's off to Minnesota in the morning. Short and sweet, Wisconsin, state #45... COMPLETE!

Minnesota

September 7th, 2018. With a payday having already arrived, a gas card from my amazing cousin, and basically the entire month of September to find a single home game on the Twins' schedule, I was all smiles as the Rig lumbered across the Minnesota state line. Remember, I had mentioned there was a bit of a surprise coming up? Remember our friends Nate and Laurel, the couple from Minnesota that we had met on the Texas coastline and followed into Louisiana? Yup, we're ending this year's run with a visit to my "old" friends. Nate, now a manager at the Little Thistle Brewery in Rochester, and Laurel now a stay at home mom, with their beautiful little one-year-old daughter. See what I mean about time just disappearing before your eyes? Amazing.

Nate and Laurel had purchased a very nice, newly remodeled farmhouse on several acres of land, about twenty minutes outside of town. Gorgeous property, with lots of grass, fruit trees, and pines lining the backyard. Kimber would be in heaven with three solid days of ball throwing, literally right outside our door. Which meant no rest for dad; that's ok, this little pup deserves a doggie vacation too. The plan here was to catch the Minnesota Twins game in about three days, other than that, just relax and tell travel stories with my old roadie buddies. Nate was crazy busy with work, and of course a first-time mom having a one-year-old wasn't exactly easy street for Laurel, so Kimber and I stayed occupied until Nate came home and we all could relax and visit.

Just up the road, in a small country town was an Anytime Fitness. With a lot going on the last few days, and plenty of white knuckled, tense driving, I definitely needed to work the kinks out of the old Dad bod. This gym was a nice one, with large weight and machine areas, and some pretty big dudes. This was more of a real weightlifting gym than the regular silver sneaker crowd. I had struck up a conversation with another vet in the gym, when one of the staff walked by, overheard us and asked, "Were you in the Corps?" while pointing at his neck in the same place my Marine Emblem tattoo is. "Ya, 89-95" I replied." "Me too. Were you in the Moag?" he asked, now stopped whipping the equipment and walking toward me. "Lido Pier, and the Golf

Course. Yup, I was there." Before I could get the sentence out, the manager of the club gave me a big hug; "Ooh-rah" was all he said. "Welcome home, bro" came next.

At this point, I've sadly forgotten this Marine's name, but not only was he the manager at their kick-ass Anytime Fitness, but he was also the road manager for the heavy metal band Lamb of God, who just got done touring with my favorite band Clutch recently. Whoa what!? How freaking cool is that. We joked around a bit as two long lost brothers would do, telling a couple lighthearted war stories, intermingled with shit-talking to any other poor non-Marine veteran within ear shot… What can I say, it's a Marine thing.

Then the conversation turned to PTSD. We talked about some dark things, also as two Marines would do, looking for that bit of understanding from a place you'd rather forget. Then my Marine brother got very serious. "Bro, DO NOT go about 3 miles down the road to the east. It's like driving in the fucking Moag." I looked at him perplexed. "Obama dumped 70k of them here, it's ridiculous." The look on his face confirmed his consternation. Why here? Why in the coldest, most non-Somali like place in America? My buddy explained it's because of the benefits. Lots of bad weather, lots of down days, lots of welfare.

Wow, I was shocked by this. Then I remembered the soccer field in Louisiana, where me and my Minnesota friends felt uncomfortable enough to leave, and the old man outside of Joplin Missouri, describing how the town was taken over by migrants. These folks aren't coming here to embrace our American institutions, to raise their right hand and swear to uphold our laws and constitution. They're not coming here to leave their culture behind and adopt the ones of their new home country. Instead they come here at the hands of politicians, placed into specific areas where they need the votes. Agree or not agree, the facts are the facts. These folks are not assimilating or conforming to our ideals and values, instead they demand we bend to theirs. This my friends, will come back to bite us, regardless what side of the aisle you fall. Mark my words.

We had planned to stay with Nate and Laurel for the entire week, opting for a Wednesday night ball game where they could join me. Plans changed after just a few days of relaxing, as my back was starting to act up again, and I was just plain exhausted. This trip was definitely taking its toll. So instead of waiting, I made the command decision to head into Minneapolis for the Monday evening game, expediting the dreaded drive back to Arizona. I just wanted this done.

It was nice having the grass field right outside the camper door, giving Kimber ample time to wear herself out before I left her behind. She always seems less concerned about me leaving without her when she's collapsed on the floor, in a puddle of cool water that splashed out of her drinking bowl. With her happily down for the count, I slipped away for the two-hour drive north into Minneapolis. A bittersweet moment, thinking of all the parks I had seen, and now with the last park in front of me, I could only think of my grandfather. God, I wish he could've seen this in person. Then a tear rolled down my cheek as I thought of all my red Cardinals. I swear I heard a voice say, "He did."

Target Field, Minneapolis, MI

September 10th, 2018. With the magic of my new best friend, the SpotHero parking reservation app, I found an open-air lot, without any pesky height limitations, within a block of Target Field. When walking up to the ball park, I was confused as to how old it might be. The park looked as if it could be brand new and almost space age like, or 50 years old and also almost space age like. Something about the park's architecture reminded me of the Jetsons cartoon. Old space age. The main grandstand having a smaller base than the top made the tall stone walls made of tan granite tiles lean outward to support the larger roof. The park's lights were enclosed in some type of metal enclosure rather than being exposed on top of a pole, giving the appearance of a wing of sorts. It was all very Star Trek meets the Jetsons, space age, yet Art Deco.

Once you step inside the park, which is incredibly similar to Cleveland's park, you realize that this place is brand new. Well, brand new as far as MLB parks go; built in 2010, Target Field will be one of the great parks in about 50 years. Built with an open-air design with no expectation of ever adding a roof, it was very similar to Cleveland's setup. Sunken field, open-air concourse in right field, wrapped around the entire park. Unlike other open-air setups, this one had grandstands wrapping around the entire park, save for a small space in center that housed a two-level bar below the Target Field sign. The park's Jumbotron was on top of the grandstand in left center, with another smaller Jumbotron above left field. There were some interesting lights that seemed to be video screens, but up-close turn out to be long strips of small LED clusters. It definitely had the best audio-visual experience of all the parks, adding to the modern feel.

This park was definitely one to buy only the cheapest get in ticket, and experience the gambit of bars and restaurants throughout this place. From taco bars, to a Vegas like sports bar, this place had it all. Funny story at the taco bar. I look up from ordering my beer, and there's a dude dressed in a full-blown white wedding dress, Twins ball cap for a tiara, pounding shots with his buddies. I had to walk up and ask, "Getting married or lost a bet? "BOTH!" all three of the bachelorettes exclaimed. "Lucky lady," I replied with a thumbs up, to which they all laughed and offered me a shot of tequila, which I politely refused. Too funny. Best part was I saw the same dude on Sports Center later that evening. Now that's awesome! With that being said, and several pictures later, I climbed back in the truck and went home to my surely snoring little princess. Unbelievably, with tears rolling down my face, I'm so humbled, yet chest poundingly proud to proclaim, Target Field, the 30th and final Major League Ballpark... COMPLETE. We did it Grandpa, we freakin did it!

The following day we celebrated with Nate and Laurel, the baby, and their parents, over a some great bbq'd burgers and some cold craft beers. Laurel had put together a Minnesota care package for me, a gift bag with bacon spam, some local chocolate, caribou coffee, salted nut rolls, a can of Hormel tamales, with a sticker and t-shirt from Nate's brewery. Attached was a hand drawn Minnesota state shaped note, tied to the bag with a bow. The note read, "Matt and Kimber, what a journey! We're so glad to have been a part of your story and that you are a part of ours. Thank you for stopping by our home state, you're welcome back anytime! Safe travels and all the best as you sit down to write the book! Cheers! Nate and Laurel." I couldn't have thought of a better place or with better people, to end this amazing journey. Thanks guys, see you soon. Minnesota, my visit was way too short but definitely sweet, state #46... COMPLETE!

Iowa

September 11th, 2018. An ominous date to begin our journey back home. With only Iowa to visit on our way back to Arizona, I began to feel something I hadn't felt in a very long time; I was depressed. Not full blown, PTSD, crawl in my cave depression, but definitely the downturn of excitement for the future. There were no more ballparks to visit, and now only one National Battlefield to visit, Pearl Harbor. Which brought up an entire new set of challenges that I was dreading to face. Basically the trip was over. Now what do I do?

These bummer feelings persisted with an occasional tear rolling down my cheek now and again. Maybe I was just exhausted, still not sure. Iowa, not having a ballpark, and nothing really in the way of battlefields, became just a pass-through state. Flat and uninteresting, mainly due to my attitude, I really couldn't get through Iowa fast enough. Sorry to disappoint any readers from the Great State of Iowa, but I'm gonna call this one "touched." Iowa, state #47... Complete.

Thus ended the final state of our Northeastern Run. But wait, you're probably thinking, that's only 47. You missed one, or miscounted. Ahh, my fine friend, you would be correct, one state was skipped. Yet strangely enough, Nevada, taking a more prominent place in the book by inadvertently saving it for later. Stay tuned for next year.

From Iowa, I once again cut through Colorado, stopping at a friend's for a few days until Arizona cooled off enough to go home. This time I was so ready for home, so mentally and physically exhausted, I needed to find a spot in the woods for the next month or two just to decompress from the people, traffic, road, and chatter. Add that strangely familiar feeling of impending dread, mixed with the triumphant return of an explorer who attained his goal and now returns, it was an emotional, yet fulfilling time in my life. One more year, one more battlefield, then what? That's what's been bothering me. Then what? I finish my travels next year, I finish the book. Then what? I find a place I like and start new. Cool, then what? We all know how I get when I'm sitting still, spinning my wheels; not good. Then what? My 5 year plan, the 5 years of travel, the five year mission, is over. NOW what. What was THEN, becomes NOW. I'm thinking this is supposed to be a happy time, but quite honestly, I was scared to death.

The Final Chapter:

Nevada, Alaska, and Hawaii

Baseballs and Battlefields 5.0, the grand finale. I can't believe that it's been 4 years since I left on this expedition. Amazing. It's very apparent when I come back to Arizona and old friends are now married with children, a phenomenon I'll never get used to. Proof of just exactly how fast our time here literally flies by us. Yet at the same time, it's a good sign, showing me that I've now found a lifestyle that suits me perfectly. Yet, I still wasn't exactly excited about making this final leg of the trip.

So after six months of downtime, to include elbow and shoulder surgery, not to mention a tooth implant and three root canals, I was ready to pop. Unfortunately, the folks around me could sense that too. The good thing was, I had a place to stay and get the Rig put together while I recuperated and got some writing done. An added benefit of surgery was I lost a total of 34 lbs, and am back down to the weight I was when I started this trip. This would definitely help crawling in and out of the trailer shell. I just hope everything heals well so I can get back to the gym. In the meantime, it's fishing, hiking, and healing.

There was no way I was going to drag that travel trailer all the way to Alaska, with as much as it cost me last time to drag it around the Northeast. So this time I decided to go as light as possible. Thanks to the 2x4s we used to mount the older model camper shell to the new style truck bed, I had a perfect wooden "beam" to build off. I was able to fit a regular $99 dollar firm twin mattress on a wooden platform that I had built in the truck bed, then added the 3" topper that failed miserably from last year, cut down to twin size. It actually feels pretty good, so I'm hopeful my back will comply. Actually, since I've lost that weight, my back has been much better. Fingers crossed.

Also inside the shell, I installed a long drawer that slides under the bed platform to store canned veggies, fruit, rice, beans, fish smoking seasoning, bacon spam, corned beef hash, and bbq utensils. Pretty much everything you need for two weeks, except the fish.

I added a metal cargo basket to the top of the shell, which sits on a wooden platform I had built to help with shade, hoping to keep as much sun off the shell as possible. I fastened rolled up tarps to the side and rear of the roof platform, that could be rolled out and secured to the ground or to nearby trees for more shade. I also put a reversible window fan in the open slider window for exhaust and cooling, powered by one of the huge batteries from the original cabover camper. I wired the battery in parallel with the truck's battery so the alternator charges both. Other than lights, the fan, and charging the phone/tablet, there was little draw on the batteries.

I also installed lights to the basket with a "panic button" next to my head, that will light up the entire area around my truck. I can also set off the car alarm from inside the shell, to scare anyone or thing if need be. After that, it's bear spray, a huge Bowie knife and me jumping out the back like a fat trunk monkey. Pretty sure I'll be picking up a shotgun in Alaska. Security check complete.

Secured to the roof basket, I had two large plastic tubs with lockable, watertight lids, one for fishing and sporting gear, another for tools, campsite gear, axe, saw, etc. Behind those was a brand-new propane smoker/grill and a milk crate that holds the 20lb propane tank. We were also bringing the rear basket from two years ago with 15 gallons of gas and 14 gallons of water. Finally, two Home Depot buckets, one full of dog food, and one with cedar chips, toilet paper and plastic bags. You can figure out what that one's for.

It took about five months, but the camper shell build turned out perfectly. I also installed a small wooden counter inside the shell, with a burner for coffee and/or soup if raining outside. We have the little buddy propane heater for heat, and also an electric space heater if we find power along the way. Add some floor carpet and pillowcases for curtains, courtesy of Goodwill, and we're ready to rock. This set-up really is ideal for this run, or at least it looks damn good on paper.

Mechanically, the truck is doing well for the mileage and the load that's been put on it. I'm definitely sold on Ram trucks. We did go ahead and replace all the brake rotors and pads, new lifted struts in the front, new taller off-road tires, and got an oil change package for the trip. The rear differential is starting to hum, let's hope it doesn't turn into a howl. Other than that, I'm feeling positive about the Rig. She'll make it.

The Plan

The plan is to finish up the lower 48 with a visit to Nevada. If you remember back to the second year, when I had surgery in Idaho, there was a schedule change back home. I didn't have to return to AZ, so I turned back toward Montana instead of going into Nevada. Also, I had been to Nevada many times, there weren't any real battlefields, and of course no MLB team, so thought I'd save it for a Vegas celebration, after finishing the lower 48. Well, everything happens for a reason, but maybe not as we immediately perceive it. Now fast forward to present. I'm going to Nevada to see the place where my new friend Sonny had lost his life. The Vegas Shooting will be my Nevada Battlefield, in honor of Sonny and Heather. From there we're off to Alaska, hoping to stop in on friends in Idaho and Kelowna, BC on the way up. Other than that, the trip to Alaska is wide open.

Then after coming back home along the west coast, I plan to fly to Hawaii for a week, hoping to rent a minivan to camp, fish, and explore the island for 5 days. Then capping it all off with Pearl Harbor as the final battlefield, my 50th and final state, on my 50th birthday. Can't make the finale any better than that, can we? We shall see my friend, we shall see.

Ok, so back to why I wasn't looking forward to this trip so much, and what was really freaking me out. What was so different about this trip was the lack of direction. I mean, of course I know where I'm going, but there's no definitive route or agenda. No waypoints to navigate through, no schedule to adjust to, just wide-open exploration. You would think that this would be the ultimate leg of the trip, and if it goes anything like the rest of the trip, it undoubtedly will be. It's just that there was no specific mission other than drive to Alaska and eat fish. It was actually hard for me to even get excited at first about this trip; even my friends thought I was nuts for not being beside myself with excitement. It's so hard to put into words. I guess it just reiterates what I've said all along: Vets need a well-defined mission... move or die. More on that later. Right now, I just need to get back at it, back on the road.

Once winter had subsided, my joints healed up to serviceable levels, and I began building the Rig, my mood elevated greatly. Now I was getting excited. I purchased all my gear, researched the routes, memorized town names and highways to look for. All systems were go, I was now in full-on exploration mode. Deep down, there was still that nagging anticipation of what are we going to do when we're done, but for now, I was ready to go to Alaska.

Nevada

April 30th, 2019. After a quick checkup and a green light from my orthopedic surgeon, we were off to Pahrump, NV, home to Frontsite, a tactical shooting training facility that I had attended once before. I had purchased a life-time membership at the gun show a couple years back while home in AZ, but still haven't made it back out for a class. I was hoping to scout out a trailer park for next winter; might as well get some training in while I'm waiting for winter to pass by.

The town was about an hour and a half from Vegas, had an Anytime Fitness, a couple small casinos, Walmart, plenty of restaurants, lots of softball fields, and cheap RV "resorts" you can spend 4 months at a time in during the winter. Don't get me wrong, it's not paradise, but it would be a nice change from Arizona, and close enough to still visit. We stayed one night, threw the ball for Kimber at the softball park, caught a quick workout and shower, and headed into Vegas, unsure of what this next stop was going to bring.

I've read and researched so much about this tragedy; it really makes the whole situation look pretty shady. Then when you actually see the location, it really didn't make sense. We found an oversized vehicle lot directly across the street from the Mandalay Bay. An eerie sight looking up at the golden towers we saw so many times on the news. Of course there was no way to see a difference in the glass, all was exactly as it was before. Nothing to see here. We parked and walked down the street looking for an area that would be the size required for the country music venue. It was actually katty-corner from the Mandalay Bay, surrounded by two fences, white sheeting blocking the view, and cameras everywhere. Looking back at the top of the tower, then looking toward where the stage was, was well over a hundred yards away. As a vet, and a gun enthusiast, I've obviously shot an AR-15 before, even one with a bump stock. Much like Dealey Plaza in Dallas... I wasn't buying it.

It didn't take long after I started snapping pictures and trying to see over the fence, before a security guard suddenly appeared, walking toward us. I quickly assumed the grieving tourist role, explaining I had lost a friend here, and asked where the memorial was for the victims. "The city donated land and moved everything down by old-town" was his reply. He was actually very kind and sympathetic.

As for downtown Vegas, outside of the Mandalay Bay, near where the concert was, it was business as usual... except for the barriers. Concrete barriers surrounded the city block, encircling a white screened chain-link fence that was backed up by yet another, taller, screened chain-link fence. Multiple cameras were posted at the corners, facing every direction. For what looks like an empty lot, they sure didn't want anybody in there. It was a very creepy feeling in general. There was a banner of Carrot Top looking demonic, next to some sort of Devils bar across the street. All very strange. Sin City for sure, I couldn't wait to get out of there; neither could Kimber.

The old-town memorial was completely different, and actually quite moving. There were several different displays of the victims, each having their own tree with pictures hanging from the limbs. I found my way to Sonny's tree, recognizing his smiling face dangling from one of the branches. So sad to see such a young life gone, and my friend Heather's life shattered. Some ask why I used this as a battlefield. Americans lost their lives here, also lost was their liberty. That's a battle in my book, and my friend Sonny is the hero of this story.

The area was just a corner of a small park, but the monuments and all the messages from loved ones was incredibly powerful. Vegas Strong was the theme, with beautiful waterfalls, walking path, "victim trees," and several dedications from surrounding businesses. It was a beautiful sentiment, and much props to the City of Vegas for making this happen. Ok, enough sadness, time to explore.

From Las Vegas we headed up Hwy 93, north past Ellis Air Force Base, stopping for gas in the small town of Ash Springs, when I spotted a road sign that read "Extraterrestrial Highway." It was a government road sign that had stickers all over it like a brewery or skateboard shop. It also had pictures of a stealth fighter and a flying saucer. Could this be the road that leads to Area 51, and do I dare go see? Well, ya! Off we went to see aliens.

Sadly, the only alien we saw was a 30ft tall statue of a "Grey" alien standing outside a gift shop about a mile or so up the road. After that, there was nothing. Miles and miles of nothing. Then I saw a weird government sign that said Aspen Gate or something like that, and a very long road fading away into the desert hills miles away. Then more miles of complete nothing, except for yucca plants and dirt.

Then I noticed something out of my left side window. A wisp of what looked like a plane's vapor trail, making some serious banks and zig-zags, very faint and slowly disappearing as you looked at it. That means something just did that. I worked at Luke AFB long enough to know what a vapor trail looks like. I pulled over and turned off the truck to listen. I could definitely hear a jet, but had no clue to where it was. Then I saw another wisp of white smoke with a very sharp turn to it, slowly disappearing again. Whatever it was, I heard it but never saw it. And only vapors on the banks and turns, maybe he's accelerating then. There was that sign of the stealth fighter on the sign. Who knows, but what I did know is that I probably should keep driving.

A few miles from there I came across a small airfield with a few houses nearby. I always heard that they flew the Area 51 people to work; I wonder if this was that airport. I stopped to take a picture when the first one showed up. A white truck driving pretty fast to the intersection that I was approaching. I had the green light and rolled through, as the other guy came to a pretty hard stop. All I saw of the driver was glasses and a beard. He pulled behind me and kept a few car lengths back, never attempting to pass even though I was doing only the speed limit. Then as I got through the small residential area, another white truck came to a stop sign as I passed by. Not pulling out, just sitting there, watching. Clean cut guy with sunglasses this time, same type of white government pickup. Yep, time to scoot, I'm thinking. When I made the first mountain pass out of town, the guy behind me was gone. There was nothing out there, so he had to have turned around and gone back to that airport. Crazy!

We followed the ET Highway all the way to Tonopah, then north through the only green National Forest patch on the map, hoping for a change of scenery. Green on the map saying it's a National Forest, doesn't mean that it's not more dry desert. We finally came across a campsite just east of Austin, NV, where we stopped for the night. It was closed, apparently under construction, but had some boondock sites near the entrance. Good enough to sleep for the night.

It was a chilly 21f when we woke up in the morning. I didn't bother with the little buddy heater, assuming that it wasn't going to get that cold. Deserts can be very deceiving with their cool temperatures. Just like in Taos, there was ice on the inside of the windows, and Kimber was buried in the sleeping bag, spooning the back of my legs. Next stop, the little buddy gets fired up, that was damn cold.

After a quick breakfast at an overpriced diner in Austin, we headed north to I80, then east to Elko. I found a small lake just north of Elko that looked promising, a place called Wild Horse Reservoir. Just a few hours south of Boise, it was a good spot to stop for a night. For six bucks, we parked right on the water, not a soul in sight. Then the wind came in, blowing off of the very cold lake, right at us. I ended up parking the truck behind a rock to shield us from the cold wind. Then tragedy struck. The little buddy wouldn't fire up. The pilot light wouldn't stay lit... again. I had thought I fixed it when we were testing the Rig. Apparently not. So I put on sweats and a hoodie, pulled out all the blankets, and ran the burner intermittently to knock down the chill. We actually were fine under the covers, Kimber is a great heater. I love this dog!

In the morning, I made coffee and crossed the Idaho line around noon, making Nevada, our 48th and final state of the lower 48, officially COMPLETE! Thank God. I've had enough of dry-ass deserts and cactus to last a lifetime.

May 3rd, we pulled into Boise to stop and see my old high school friend, Gabe, a Coast Guard veteran living in Boise, now married with two kids. We had some steaks that evening, caught up on the last 20+ years, and even got some range time in the following day, before pushing up to Moscow, ID.

I was somewhat surprised by Boise, Idaho. It reminded me exactly of Mesa, AZ, with its grid like streets, flat terrain, surrounded by barren mountains with only a few trees here and there. Just add a few cacti, subtract about 30 degrees of heat, and you've got Boise. I will say though, I didn't stick around to go downtown where they say the trail systems are worth visiting. Next time. I got Canada and Alaska to deal with right now.

I decided to follow the Snake River north to Moscow, Idaho. We passed some cool little towns and amazing campsites that were along the river, free to stay for 10 days at each spot. From what I was told, the fishing here is impressive a little later in the summer. Again, something to keep in mind for next time. Then I came across something that I had completely forgotten about. The White Bird National Battlefield was a place that I had planned to visit our second year of travels, but then opted to head back to Montana instead. Best part, it was a complete toss-up as to which road I was going to take north, choosing the Snake River route at the last minute. On my path indeed.

The White Bird National Battlefield is actually a visitor center of sorts, with an open-air platform overlooking the valley where the battle took place. Several information placards explained the scene on June 17th, 1877. Apparently the Nez Perce Tribe was pissed about being forced to live on a reservation that continued to shrink in size due to the discovery of gold in the area, thus disregarding a treaty they had made over the land. At an apparent meeting to discuss terms, shots rang out from an unknown origin, igniting a firefight. This time the Nez Perce defended themselves, but knew that the soldiers would be back in force. Thus, began the sad trek of the Nez Perce, and the start of the Nez Perce wars. I grabbed a few pictures, took some notes, and climbed back in the Rig. I was excited to see my friends from 3 years ago, in a town that I absolutely adored.

We stopped in Moscow where I had received my elbow surgery back in year two. It was so good to drop in on friends we made from that trip. Like it was yesterday, they welcomed Kimber and myself back with open arms. Well mainly Kimber, but I'm used to it by now. I gotta say, Moscow, Idaho is definitely on the possible landing spot list. Love this little town, not to mention the northern part of this state.

May 5th, Cinco De Mayo, or like my Boise buddy said, "Ya, we call that the 5th of May in Idaho." Shows I've been in Arizona too long. After lunch with my "Idaho family," I decided to move on to Spokane, WA for the evening, stopping at one of the three local Walmarts for the night. I guess I picked the wrong Walmart as I couldn't believe what was going on in the front parking lot. Full-size camper trailers, unhooked from vehicles, some on blocks with a couple cars parked in front were scattered around. One bumper pull camper had four cars parked in front, two guys working on one of the cars, with a pit-bull tied to a chain by the front door. These folks were straight up living in the Walmart parking lot. Wow, this was a first in all 48 states. We ended up parking in the back between two big rigs, and still had people coming up to panhandle and beg. The State of Washington has completely changed in the last 4 years, and obviously not for the better. Sad but true.

We crossed into British Columbia at a small border crossing town called Midway, not far from Spokane. One of my Idaho friends recommended it because his kid used to play hockey there. The one border patrol agent, 9 to 5 crossing, was supposed to be a little more laid back than the main border crossing. When I pulled up to the small building with camera and stop signs, it said that over-sized vehicles stopped on the uncovered left lane, while regular cars went into the covered area closer to the building. With my truck having the baskets and bike rack, I stopped on the uncovered side. That was my first mistake.

The Canadian Border Guard was a good-sized dude, bald head, goatee, and a very unfriendly demeanor. First thing he said was, "I need you to back up and pull into this lane," pointing at the covered lane under his feet. So much for laid back, this wasn't a good sign. So I moved the truck over and rolled down the passenger window. He then had me roll down ALL the windows and asked for my passport. I handed him my passport book that had Kimber's shot record and health certificate folded and tucked inside. He glanced at the passport picture and handed it back to me saying, "Can you take the cash out, please." I didn't realize that I had kept a blue, $5 bill from the Toronto Bluejays game last year as a souvenir... in the passport. Great, now I'm going to jail for bribery. I removed the cash and handed it back with a smile. He took the passport and went inside. He then came back and looked at the bike rack in front of the truck. "Where's your bumper?" he asked. "A pole in AZ needed it worse than me. Been like that for 3 years," I replied jokingly. He wasn't amused. Once he found out that AZ doesn't require a front plate, he handed back my paperwork saying, "Well, you're going to get pulled over in Canada and the ticket will be pricey. Up to you." "I'll roll the dice, I gotta get to Alaska," I replied. He shrugged his shoulders, asked what I had on top in the crates, attempted to look through the truck shell's tinted windows, and then walked inside the building. That was it. Well, at least he didn't find the extra 20lbs of contraband dog food I had onboard and over limit. Either way, I was officially in Canada.

The drive to Kelowna was beautiful but slow, taking the backcountry road that turned into dirt a few different times. Kelowna is a fruit and wine growing region of British Columbia, built around a massive lake. Not once, but twice was I followed by police and sat at a red light next to a police car. No problem with the bumper or the bike rack, not even a glance my way.

I was excited to be able to drop in on my old friend from the Texas Coast. The same time I met my Minnesota friends on Padre Island, I also had met my buddy Rusty. A retired truck driver from Canada, he mentioned the next time you're in BC to give him a shout. Well, here we are. We had a great visit at Rusty's little house that he had built himself, got some advice on what to expect traveling through his neck of British Columbia, and of course caught up on travel stories.

We only spent a couple days at Rusty's as I was eager to explore Canada and get to Alaska. From Kelowna, we decided to follow one of the routes on the "Milepost," a road map book with several driving route options up to, and inside, Alaska. The route would take us along the Canadian Rockies, to the town of Dawson Creek, where the Alaskan/Canadian Highway begins. I was absolutely stunned by the beauty that we were passing. It made the entire state of Colorado look like a gas station town that you had better not blink, or you'd miss. It was that massive, and that absolutely breathtaking. We stopped at a few waterfalls along the way, had some lunch, and finally pulled into the town of Prince George, where we found a Walmart to park for the evening.

It was an absolutely amazing drive with plenty of roadside overnight parking spots from Prince George to Dawson Creek. Basically, if it's not marked "no overnight parking," feel free to stay the night or two. Canada is very forgiving to its travelers this way. Super cool and greatly appreciated as camping and RV spots are pricey without my veteran discount. We drove another couple hours before I found a spot next to an amazing river that I just couldn't pass up. This was absolutely amazing country, that I needed to slow down and enjoy. Kimber and I relaxed with an evening of ball play, while dining on cold cuts and delicious Canadian Peach Cider, courtesy of Rusty. The sound of the rushing river lulled us to sleep like a lullaby. I could get very used to this!

The next stop was Dawson Creek, BC, where the "Mile 0" marker is and the beginning of the Alaska Highway, also known as the AlCan. I found a campground just outside of town that had hot showers, laundry, and 10 bucks Canadian per night dry camping. Can't beat it for 6 dollars and some change. Perfect place to take a couple days off and recoup from the drive. Kimber even had a nice grass field all to herself for ball action. She also needed the break from the road, although it was gorgeous, it was still a long drive for that little dog. You gotta remember BC is the length of our entire Western Coast of America. We were covering some serious miles.

After exploring the town of Dawson Creek, learning that no, this town isn't where the TV show was named after, I stocked up on some supplies and decided to stop in at the local pizza place for a bite, and hopefully watch some baseball. With my truck windows down and radio up, I didn't hear what this lady had said, as she yelled something out of her window from the truck next to me. I turned down my radio and looked at her puzzled. "What?" I mouthed not trying to yell at her. I figured something was wrong with my truck. "Thank you for your service!" she shouted again and sped off. Whoa, what? I was shocked. I didn't expect that in Canada of all places. She must've seen the Marine Corps retiree sticker on the shell. That was cool, definitely made my day, as I pulled into a place called Boston Pizza.

Later after my meal, I asked for my bill. My bartender replied, "Somebody covered your meal sir, and here's the gift card they purchased with a few more dollars on it." Wait, what? Who? The bartender said that some lady must've overheard me telling my travel stories to another guy at the bar. Amazing! Wow, I was completely shocked. Never in my life would I have thought Canadians would be grateful for my military service. That's when another guy sitting at the bar said, "We know who keeps us safe; Canadians are well aware of your service." I was almost in tears when I walked back to the truck. I was truly moved.

The next day, Kimber and I headed out to see the Mile 0 marker and do the tourist picture thing. It's pretty obvious you're an American when you're holding your dog for a picture in front of the marker. Just saying. Next to the marker were some locals who were protesting something about Trudeau and a plastic tax. I asked a lady who was with them if she could take a picture of Kimber and me in front of the AlCan sign. When I handed her my phone, she asked if I had enjoyed my pizza last night? At first I wasn't sure what she was asking, then it dawned on me. Whoa, what!? "Did you pay for my meal, ma'am?" I asked. "No, that was my daughter. She bought your dinner," she replied. I was shocked... again. "Well, please tell her thank you for me." About that time, a truck pulled up with a lady and her kids. "This is my daughter," the lady who took our picture said, pointing at the truck. That's when a lady in her mid-thirties walked up and said she was the one who yelled thank you for my service as she drove by! She saw me turn into the pizza place, went in and bought a gift card, and instructed the staff to pay for my meal. Well played, ladies! After a hug and info exchange, we met up for coffee and a hike the next day. Turns out she was previously married to a Marine and said, "You guys don't get the respect you deserve in the States, let alone up here in Canada." Thanks to Shea for a super cool experience, and an amazing new friend in Dawson Creek, BC.

Back at the campground that night, I had noticed a full-sized red pickup with camper shell. The license plate was from Pennsylvania, with a Marine Corps retiree sticker on the bumper. Of course I had to stop and say hello. It turned out to be an elderly couple, he a retired Marine, her a Marine wife of 50+ years, both traveling to Alaska for the very first time. They too were sleeping in the back of their truck, on top of two small cots he had built in the back, similar to my own build. We talked about the Corps, where we were from, and where we were going. He explained how he had always wanted to see Alaska and was finally making the journey. I'll never forget when the old Marine said, "I don't get around as well as I used to. But I sure as hell can drive. I love to drive." They were opting to take in the sights of this incredible drive, rather than board a cruise ship. Then he looked at me and said, "Once a Marine..." to which we both finished in unison, "...always a Marine!" Ooh-rah sir, you folks are a motivation to us all. We parted with an invite to Pennsylvania the next time we rolled through their home state, to which I warned, "We have a habit of taking folks up on that offer!"

Our next stop was in the small town of Fort Nelson where I saw another Boston Pizza and stopped in for dinner and baseball. I had such good luck at the last place, might as well stop again. We ended up staying the night just a block away, parked on the side of the road with the tractor trailers, before continuing on toward Whitehorse. The interesting thing about this stop was the electrical outlets near the parking spaces, so you can plug in your vehicle's block heater during the winter. Something I've never seen, and only heard of. Either way, we had electric for the space heater that evening, although it was starting to warm up enough not to be needed.

One thing that I was completely unprepared for was the sheer amount of immense beauty that we would pass through, especially on this stretch of road between Fort Nelson and Whitehorse, the capital of the Yukon Territory. It was startling to see areas that would remind me of a scene from Colorado or Wyoming, but on such a grand scale that is hard to even imagine. A couple of hours drive on I80 through the Rockies, compared to hours and hours of something absolutely amazing behind each and every turn. One second you can't believe this majestic snow covered mountain peak, the next turn unveils the crystal clear blue river that cuts through that amazing mountain. Every single twist in the road revealed another glimpse of God's majestic country.

The wildlife were emerging from the forest, looking for Spring's first sprouts of fresh food. Everything from deer to black bear... lots of black bear. They seemed to be digging up the dandelions, that I learned later was a great source of calcium and highly sought after. Even the birds were fighting over a dandelion root. It was crazy to see a good-sized black bear, less than a hundred yards away from a wood bison herd. Wood bison are miniature version of our bison, with calves the size of large dogs. Yet the bear were more interested in the dandelion roots. Add the bald eagles, massive ravens, and the occasional elk/deer, and it was like driving through a wild animal park, but for real!

We could have made our entire summer trip out of just exploring British Columbia; places like Muncho Lake, Laird Hot Springs, and staying a night at Strawberry Flats Campground, made it all so hard to pass up. Fuel was a necessity though, and we were running short. Our last stop in BC before crossing into the Yukon Territory was at a two pump, mom and pop gas station in a place called Contact Creek.

While I was fueling up the truck, I heard a voice from behind me yell, "Arizona?!" A white, lifted 4x4 truck, pulling a pretty old trailer, with a huge off-road, Canam side by side, that looked like it belonged to Batman, had pulled up behind me. Its driver, an active duty Army mechanic, hopped out and introduced himself. Turns out his family is from the Payson area of Arizona, where I had stayed this past winter, and he was moving to Fairbanks for his duty assignment. What a small world, 2,000 miles from Arizona, I run into this guy from Payson. That's just crazy. We chatted a bit, gave him my book page information, and got back on the road. The weather was starting to get ugly, and we still had a few more hours before Whitehorse and a Walmart, time to move.

We drove on for another hour or so, stopping at a place called Sign Post Forest for a bathroom break and to stretch our legs. This was basically a chunk of land where people have been posting road signs and placards from their hometowns. There were signs from every state and many different countries, from Ireland to Australia. License plates, restaurant signs, street signs, all shapes and sizes, some with inscriptions and a date. Thousands of signs. It was really pretty cool to read from where they all came. I took some pictures, Kimber peed, and we were back on the road. Only an hour until Whitehorse. This drive is incredible, but very, very long.

The rain started to make its presence known just a few miles into our last leg of the drive. It was coming up on 1700, when I noticed a vehicle pulled off to the side of the road, with its hazard lights flashing. As I got closer, the white truck that WAS pulling an old trailer, looked kind of familiar. That's when I saw my Army mechanic friend, standing in the rain, waving at me as I pulled up behind him. He had a flat tire, with his only spare already in use, and with no tire iron. After a couple of quick jabs at him being an Army mechanic with no tire iron, on a 2500 mile road trip, I gave him a spare iron and said he could give it back to me in Fairbanks. He had a tandem axle trailer, with one good tire to limp on, as I followed him into the next town to look for a spare.

We found a restaurant and hotel in the small town of Teslin, but no spare. The owner of the restaurant put in a call to a buddy, who might know the number to a guy that may have a tire. Welcome to the Yukon. Now that we're in a holding pattern, we decided to have some dinner. While we sat and talked about our travels over beers, an older couple behind us overheard our discussion. "We're from Mesa," said the lady. "Our son is in Anchorage, we're on our way home." More Arizonans in the Yukon. What an incredibly small world, but we already knew that.

As we exited the restaurant, a trailer pulled up to the gas pumps, with at least 4 spare tires, two for a truck, two for a trailer. I asked the driver if they would possibly sell my friend a trailer tire. I explained he was active duty Army, and needed to check in for duty. Amazingly, the guy said that he was stopping in Whitehorse, and my friend could borrow his spare to get to a place where he could buy one. Now that was freaking cool! Later, I found out the guy said my buddy could keep the tire, and good luck in Alaska. One thing I noticed while traveling the AlCan, everybody is overly friendly and eager to help in any way. This really warmed my heart. I would see my Army friend in Fairbanks later to retrieve my iron, until then, I felt he was in good hands. We parted ways as he followed the guy with the tire into Whitehorse, and I decided to stay the night by the Yukon River, right there in Teslin.

After a good night's sleep, we headed into Whitehorse the following morning, where I was hoping to find a Walmart and a shower. With little to no cell reception or places to stop for coffee, I found a spot at the foot of a bridge crossing the Yukon River. It had bathrooms and was a beautiful place to swing by for a pit stop to make some coffee.

When we pulled in, I noticed two trucks, one towing a drift boat, like the ones I had seen on the Alaska fishing videos I've been obsessed with. When I got closer, I noticed one truck had California plates, the other had Alaskan plates. I just had to ask these guys what they were fishing for. Turns out it was two brothers from Humboldt, CA, that were fish guides both in NorCal and in Alaska. After I told him I was a rookie fly fisherman and wanted to float a drift boat, he instantly handed me his card and told me he was outside of Soldotna, AK. Turns out he was a former Army sniper. "You're gonna love it, bro, it's like every badass in the country said fuck it and moved to Alaska," he said as he climbed into his truck. "Sounds good to me, see ya up there." This is getting better by the minute!

Shortly after the fisherman left, a white Ford truck with an Alaskan Veteran plate pulled in and parked next to the water, near our Rig. An older gentleman got out and came right over. "Arizona?!" he asked. "Yup, Payson," I replied as I noticed his Zane Grey RV Park, Verde Valley, AZ ballcap. He went on to explain how he lives in Alaska but has a trailer in Verde Valley too. Wow more Arizona people! Then he told me he came to spread his wife's ashes in the Yukon River. She had just passed away in AZ and he was on his way back home. He wanted to spread them here in the Yukon River and on the Chilikote Trail, where they had hiked in the 80s. He then asked if I had a paper cup. No cup, but I cut a water bottle down to size and asked if this would help. He took the makeshift cup and went back to his truck, emerging with a bouquet of flowers and that same plastic cup now filled with his wife's ashes. I watched as he approached the water, and one by one, tossed the flowers into the river. Then in an arching sweep, he let her ashes loose in the wind as they swirled in a brief cloud before landing on the emerald green water. He blew a kiss toward the floating flowers as they traveled downstream and came back to the truck. I told him I hope he didn't mind but I had some pictures and a video for him. Yes, I was filming the whole time. He was ecstatic when I sent him the photos and short video. Pretty sure THAT right there, was the most beautiful thing I've seen thus far. What an amazing place to stop and make a cup of coffee.

We made it to Whitehorse around noon that day, found a spot at Walmart to park the truck for the evening and hopped out to get more groceries and supplies, unsure of what was going to be available in the Yukon. Sadly, there was no Anytime Fitness, so a sink bath in Walmart was as close as I got to a shower. We had a meal downtown and settled in for a well-deserved early night. Well, what I thought was early at least, it was now 2100 and still full daylight.

The next morning, I had to make a decision. There were two routes into Alaska from here; continue on the Alcan through Haines Junction and Destruction Bay, or take Hwy 2 through Dawson City and enter at the town of Chicken. Yes, for whatever reason, the town is named Chicken. A reason to go that route all in itself. The second route came highly recommended by a bartender at the Yukon Brewery, telling me I had to see Dawson City. When I returned to the truck to see where this place was on the map, I noticed the road crossing into Alaska was named the Top of the World Highway. That settles it, I gotta go that way now.

The drive was a couple hundred miles out of the way, but at this point we had nothing but time. Both entry points into Alaska converge at the town of Tok, so it wasn't too terribly far off course. Alaska was close, so might as well get in some Yukon sightseeing, besides, I would come out of Alaska on the Alcan. This way I can see it all.

The drive to Dawson City was long and desolate. Now the steep mountains of the Canadian Rockies became more rolling, with forests in different stages of growth, after years of forest fires. The Canadians let their fires burn, thinning the forest, and replenishing the soil. It was fascinating to see the signs telling when the fire had taken place, then seeing the tree growth

413

since that time period. Fire areas from the 1980s had trees the size of saplings, making the sense of time in relation to the tree height seem like a blink. It really makes you think of our own existence as truly being just a blip on the radar screen of life.

Dawson City was exactly as the bartender had described it. It was like walking into one of those western theme parks, with bright and colorful storefronts and wooden plank sidewalks, it reminded me a lot of Silverton, Colorado actually. The roads were all dirt, with cars, horses, and bicycles being the main mode of transportation. That weekend was the first weekend of summer, kicking off what they called "Gold Days," a commercial gold mining trade show of sorts. So the town was packed with people, from what the locals said.

They had a casino named Diamond Tooth Gerty's that was a sight to behold. Imagine a not for profit organization that puts the winnings back into the town, while at the same time paying out the most jackpots I've ever seen in a casino. Everybody was winning, and so was the town. Then the stage erupts with an authentic can-can dancer, vaudeville show, hosted by Diamond Gerty herself.

With all this going on, I was sitting at a blackjack table, having a discussion with a gentleman that was here to open the "ferry." This was the boat that took you across the Yukon River on your way up to Chicken. Apparently, the ferry was just opening, but the road over the pass still had 30ft of snow. There was no making it to Alaska for at least another week. This was not good news. Well, so much for my good time in Gerty's, we drove 300 miles out of the way, and now have to backtrack to Whitehorse. I was not a happy camper.

To make matters worse, it was now almost midnight, and looked like it was 1800. I had to find a place to park for the night, and I wasn't finding anyplace near town. Well, it's daylight and I'm wide awake, I might as well start back toward Whitehorse at this point. We drove for about 60 miles, trying to get up in elevation, away from the water, as that's where the mosquitos are congregated. We happened upon a large rest area, where I happily parked for the night. From the top of the mountain, you could literally see the sun just barely setting behind the horizon in one direction, while directly behind you the moon is at its peak. It was a surreal sight, and so were the mosquitos, apparently water be damned.

The next morning I was up bright and early, with just a couple hours sleep under my belt. I just couldn't sleep with the sun shining though the shell window. While making a cup of coffee, I saw a vehicle pull up to the bathrooms at the other end of the parking lot. It was a guy about my age, wearing a long leather slicker and a crocodile Dundee hat. He had a monster of a dog with him, a Bernese Mountain dog, that came lumbering toward me, tail wagging. I turned to greet this massive pile of muscle and hair, with a hearty petting and a belly pat. He just sat there, staring up at me with these crazy yellow eyes. His owner walked up shortly after. "He must like you, or you'd be dead," the guy said in a monotone voice. Wasn't exactly sure if he was kidding or not. "He keeps my place free of bears," he continued. By the size of this dog, I wouldn't doubt it. I offered the gentleman some coffee, and had an interesting chat with him.

He told me he was originally from Alberta, where as a young boy, his dad and his grandfather handed him a .22 caliber rifle and told him to go hunt something for dinner. When he came back empty-handed, his father said it was to prove a point, there were no animals left. That's when his family directed him to the Yukon, the Canadian Last Frontier, where he lives today. He went on to tell me about a recreational mining claim that is available to anyone, not just Canadian citizens. For just ten dollars, you can stake a claim on an unclaimed creek or river, designating a space of 50ft by 100ft that you can build a structure on as long as it's on skids. You can live on this claim for up to eleven months out of the year, but nobody actually bothers to come check on you, he added. Very interesting, and something I will definitely keep in mind.

We made it back into Whitehorse fairly early in the afternoon, exhausted and just looking to sleep. The light situation was something I had not expected. That and Kimber expecting to play ball or do anything other than try to sleep while in the back of the truck with the sun still shining... also completely unexpected. After flooding my nervous system with Tim Horton coffee (basically the extremely popular Canadian version of Dunkin Donuts), we turned north, I think it was north, toward Destruction Bay and the Alaskan Border.

Alaska

May 19th, 2019. Alaska! We finally made it. This last leg was definitely the longest. Maybe because of the severe driving fatigue, maybe because the Yukon Territory is about as desolate a place as they come, either way, I was ecstatic to see the "Welcome to Alaska" sign. Another thing I was surprised by was how dry it was here. Apparently, the Yukon has been in a bit of a drought lately, with Destruction Bay and the Yukon River obviously incredibly low. This didn't stop the big Grizzly we saw on the side of the highway, also foraging for what I assumed was dandelions. Wow, this thing was massive, and it didn't even blink at the truck as I drove by, less than 40 yards away.

The US Border Patrol and Customs checkpoint was further into the interior of Alaska, strangely not on its exact border; but then again, there's not too many migrants pushing the border here, thanks in part to Mr. Grizzly we passed a few miles back. The officer at this checkpoint was completely different than any of the three other Canadian checkpoints, or even the American ones. He walked up to the window smiling, had a dog treat already in his pocket, and barely glanced at my passport and Kimber's shot history. He asked where we were headed while petting Kimber, who happily lavished him with kisses. "Fishing! Gonna see it all. First time here! Heading to Fairbanks first, then down toward the Kenai," I explained. Still preoccupied with Kimber, he mumbled something about wanting to go with us and then handed back my paperwork. Wow, that was pretty cool. I already love this place. Then I saw the trooper.

Still putting my paperwork away while leaving the border guard, not paying attention to my speed, I happened to glance into the rearview mirror, and there's an Alaskan State Trooper right behind me. It was a no passing lane, and he was close; I decided to find a spot on the shoulder to pull over. If he was going to stop me, let's get it over with. Just as I put on my blinker and started to pull off the road, the trooper passed me. Thank God. Then the unexpected happened as he pulled around me, he turned on his lights, chirped his siren, and waved as he went by. What?! Even though I was perfectly legal, other than going a little fast, my heart gladly came down from the 200 bpm adrenaline shot, and I just laughed. Wow, that was pretty cool, I've never seen a cop do that. Yup, I think I'll definitely be liking this place.

A few miles into the amazing beauty of this country, something came over me, something completely unexpected that made zero sense. I started to cry. This weird emotion came over me, my eyes welled up with tears, I choked back a sob, what was going on here? One word came to mind, just one... home. You're home. You're finally home. I pulled over to the shoulder to wipe my eyes. Everybody I've ever met, who knew me all my life, or just met me for the first time, all have said to me in one way or another, "When you go to Alaska, you won't be coming back." I even had a veteran on the book page comment about my post of finally making it to the border. Just two words, "He gone."

Ok, so I'll let this out of the bag now. When my grandparents passed, the same grandparents who raised me for most of my childhood, I lost any resemblance of "home." Their house is where I grew up, graduated high school, and came "home" to when I returned from overseas. When I wrote letters back "home," when I thought fondly of "home" while on guard duty in Somalia, when I uttered anything that had to do with "home," Sebastopol, California was where I was referring to. Even when I married and followed my ex-wife from Texas to Arizona, just to stay close to the kids, neither Texas nor Arizona were ever "home." During this journey, I always mentioned possible "landing" spots from this trip, places that I could possibly call "home" one day. Astoria, OR; Moscow, ID; Johnson City, TN; Conway, NH; all places that I absolutely fell in love with, but none brought me to tears before I even had the chance to truly experience it. Something in my heart, completely absent of any common sense, just said, "you're home." And I cried.

At this point, the coffee was taking its toll and rest stops were few and far apart. There were plenty of turn-off areas with trash cans, which would have to do at this point. The weather was just starting to cloud up, I was thinking it's surprisingly humid as I exited the truck, heading for the small bank of trees just off the edge of the parking lot. Mid-way through handling my coffee overload, I heard them. Just a faint buzzing sound, then I swear you could hear the individual flaps of their wings. Mosquitos. Big ones. I'm talking, these things were the size of nickels, looking like something out of a prehistoric dinosaur horror movie. Mini-demonic dragons with spikes sticking out of their face, looking to drain your blood so they can lay their eggs. Freaking frightening! They were big enough to see the hairs on their backs and legs when they did land on something. When you swatted at them, the wind from your hand movement just blew them gently out of harm's way, then they were coming right back at you. Unreal. Later, I learned that moose can loose up to a pint of blood a day, just from mosquitos!

I zipped up and literally ran back toward the truck. Yes, you can outrun them, barely. Then, back safely within the cab of the truck, Kimber signaled she needed out. Of course. Looking like a Chinese fire drill, I jumped out once again, ran around the opposite side of the truck, let Kimber out. Where did she go? Straight for the mosquito den, of course. Now it started to sprinkle a little. Good! This will take out the mosquitos. After finally corralling Kimber into a grassy area, away from the dragon's lair, we were attacked again. This time by something smaller and faster than the mini-pterodactyls. Small little gnats or something, in my ears, in my eyes, spitting them out of my mouth, they were swarming us. Jesus! Kimber, truck, now! Run run run! We both bolted for the far side of the pickup, jumping inside, slamming the doors. What

417

in the literal hell were those? They were outside my window now, bumping against the glass, like they were saying, "We know you're in there, come out, coward!" Surprisingly, there were no bites on me, except for a little red dot on my earlobe, not a bite, but a chunk of ear missing. Later, I learned these little bastards are called "Whiteheads" and yes, that pronoun is what Alaskans use to describe them too. Biting gnats… isn't that a biblical plague?

Now with our introduction to Alaskan entomology past us, I was just looking for a place to park and get some rest. Tok, Alaska was the first sign of any type of real civilization, to include a gas station, a couple of restaurants, and a hotel. This was the last main intersection of Alaskan highways, before taking the AlCan out of state, or taking the road into Dawson City. One of the veterans on my page is a trucker that makes this drive a lot, and he told me to park at the motel/bar there in Tok, the fellas inside would take care of us. Which they happily did, and we finally got some rest. I was beyond tired, mosquitos or not, daylight still an issue, we slept good that night.

Bright and early the next morning, we filled up at the gas station across the street that happened to have a sporting goods store attached to it. I wanted to see about purchasing a shotgun for the trip, and I needed my fishing license. Perfect. That's when I overheard the sporting goods manager trying to explain over the phone to an obviously elderly gentleman about shipping firearms into Alaska. Becoming agitated, the manager finally, very politely, ended the phone conversation and just looked at me with a face that clearly read, it was way too early for this shit. "Can I help you?" he asked. "Just need a fishing license." That's when I met my first Alaskan Veteran.

The manager was a former Marine, Force Recon, who also served in Somalia. I could tell he was about my age, had the tats to prove his unit and service, with a no-nonsense attitude. I told him how it was my first time here, that I'd been traveling, and was possibly looking to move here someday. He reached behind the counter and handed me two paper books, the Alaskan Fishing regulations, and something about an Alaskan Land Auction. He went on to tell me that there is no other state that treats their disabled veterans as good as Alaska. As a resident I'd qualify for free hunting and fishing, and 25% off of a land auction. There was also something about a guaranteed sealed bid win that I'd have to research a little more about. Either way, he was a wealth of information. The last thing he said, as I turned to walk out, made me feel incredibly good. "Hey, bro. There's a lot of us out here. You're good, man. Welcome home." On my path indeed.

So remember when I was so worried about there not being any real direction to this leg of the journey? There were no schedules or time frames to adhere to, no checking to see what days a museum was open, or whether I'd find uncovered parking. The hardest thing that I'd had to do so far was remind myself to slow down. I was so used to go go go, now it was time to sit back and truly relax. Something I guess I'd basically forgotten how to do. That's when I saw a road sign pointing at a state campground, "Birch Lake Recreation Site." Perfect, time to set up camp and do some fishing. We made it to Alaska, now slow down and enjoy it!

Birch Lake was a small, crystal clear lake with a few campsites near the boat dock. Big beautiful homes graced the far shores while woods surrounded the rest of the water. There were two other campers, an older couple in an RV with a bunch of big dogs, and another couple doing some trout fishing from kayaks. It was still pretty chilly to actually get in the water, but just fine for paddling out to the center of the lake instead of shore fishing. A kayak is something to consider if we're going to make a go of this state.

The older couple happened to be a Vietnam Vet and his wife who have a home in Tok, but came up to fish before the crowds began. They had four large Huskies that would like nothing better than to get a piece of Kimber. None of them were nice, and the alpha male was downright scary. I did get some great information from this Alaskan Veteran, like they usually don't charge the campground fee until Memorial Day, a full week away. He also told me that any disabled veteran, from any state and with any VA disability percentage, can get free camping by visiting the state Parks and Rec office in Fairbanks. Whoa what!? Free camping for out-of-state DAVs!? That's freaking huge!

I stayed at the lake until my supplies dwindled down to almost nothing before finally packing it in and heading to town. I caught our first couple of trout, and had a pan-fried trout dinner, with my Army buddy Justin. He made it to Fairbanks, checked into his unit, got all settled in, and brought back my tire iron. It was amazing to see the fish hatchery truck pull in, stocking this little lake with 2,000 trout and 2,000 Arctic char, all of which were big enough to be a prize catch in Arizona. Baby bald eagles perched on the trees, the sun only going down for a few hours. It was an amazing place, and only our first stop!

I searched for FamCamps on both the local Air Force base and the Army base; both had camping, but no place you'd want to stay. Eielson AFB was the first disaster we checked into. The campground was in a wooded area, at the end of the flight line, consisting of about a dozen spots, all rough looking and unkept. The bathrooms were literally taken apart, either to remodel or maybe destroy; the place was an absolute dump. I couldn't believe a base commander would let this happen. It was disgusting. Hopefully, Fort Wainwright would be better, but sadly it wasn't.

Fort Wainwright was the major Army post for northern Alaska, home of the "Arctic Warriors." A good-sized base that seemed to have a good-sized campground. When I asked the gate sentry for directions, he wasn't sure where the campgrounds were. Not a good sign. Sure enough, it was just as bad as the AFB campground. 16 bucks a night to camp, the bathrooms hadn't been touched since Vietnam, and there weren't even any trashcans, let alone envelopes to pay your fee. There were only a couple of other campers that appeared to be temporary lodging for active duty soldiers, other than that, it was empty. There were even signs of somebody doing "donuts" in a vehicle, and the remnants of a pallet wood bonfire, with burnt ashes and nails in the middle of the road. How in the world does the base commander let this fly? I was amazed. I guess folks don't really camp or recreate on base, I mean it's Alaska, why would you?

I ended up staying here for a week, waiting for a camp host to come by and collect my money. That never happened. So my weeklong visit was free. I was just shocked by the lack of management here, hopefully this wasn't a trend for all of Alaska. I did get a chance to go to the Parks and Rec office to check on the free camping thing. Sure enough, the old veteran was right. After showing the clerk my VA identification card, I was walking out to put a free camping decal on the truck windshield, good for two years! Wow, now that's a game changer. The rest of the week was spent exploring the base, getting some gym time in, hitting the base PX and commissary, and checking out the sights of Fairbanks. Once you've been to one military town, you've pretty much seen them all. Plus, I heard the mosquitos weren't so bad, the further south you went. I was definitely ready to test that theory. Now with a payday firmly in my account, body fully rested, Rig fully stocked, I was ready to get back on the road.

Oh, I almost forgot. Another reason I stayed so long in Fairbanks was our visit to the repair shop. When I took the truck in for an oil change, the tech noticed I had water and oil covering my motor so bad that they had to power wash it to find the leak. Yup, lost the water pump on the way through Canada somewhere. Once again, that warranty plan we bought in Arkansas saved the day. For 100 bucks I now had a brand-new factory water pump and radiator flush. While I sat in the waiting room, I struck up a conversation with an older lady also waiting for her car. "On a clear day, you can see Denali from here. It's that big," she told me. I thought to myself, that's a four-hour drive away, 225 miles by road, there's no way. I guess I was about to find out.

My plan was to drive a giant circle around Alaska, even though only a small portion of the actual land mass has roads. Remember, Alaska is about 2/3 the size of the entire lower 48! So I decided I wanted to hit the interior first, starting in Fairbanks. I heard the interior could get up into the 90s in the summer. I wanted to avoid that at all costs, so inland first, then follow the coast back when the temps come up. See, there is a method to my madness.

From Fairbanks we took Hwy 3 west, along what seemed like the ridge of a mountain. To my right was this massive majestic valley, a huge river, and multi-shades of green valleys and hills, as far as the eye could see. To my left was mainly more mountains, with an occasional view of a valley, nothing less spectacular though, as every view in Alaska is like looking at a postcard.

We followed Hwy 3, also known as the Parks Hwy, west to the town of Nenana, slowly arching south toward Denali. The valley was starting to fill with a haze, blocking the view of the Denali mountaintop. Not sure if it was moisture from this absolutely enormous snowcapped mountain, or weather coming in. After looking around and seeing basically blue sky, you realize this thing is so big, it has its own weather pattern. Driving down the tall tree-lined road toward the Alaskan Range, all you saw in front of you was the road seemingly disappearing into a jagged rock cliff. The top of the mountain, completely hidden by fog, gave the illusion of nothing but a wall. I could imagine what that would look like in a small plane.

First stop was Denali National Park. I'd been looking forward to this for a long time. Sadly though, I was disappointed by the view, and access to the National Park Service was restricted. There was only one road that took you to a campground further into the interior toward Denali itself. You had to have reservations and take the park shuttle service to get out there, unless you had a pass for your vehicle. So the only view you had of the mountain was from 70 miles away. That sucks. But hey, the gift shop and bookstore were pretty nice. Yippee. Just outside of the park was a touristy area, lots of shops to include a Harley "Boutique," selling T-shirts and clothing. This should give you an idea of the price and clientele. There were some fancy resorts and hotels, and I think I saw a golf course too. All of which I had no interest in while visiting a place like Alaska.

Further down the road, in the Denali State Park, you got a full view of this majestic mountain. Colorado's highest peak is 14,000ft, Denali sits at 20,000ft, making it the highest peak in North America. You thought you knew what a mountain was until you saw Denali. Formerly named Mt. McKinley, now renamed to its Native American name, it literally makes you just stand and stare. Suddenly you realize how tiny and somewhat insignificant you are in this world. It was startlingly humbling.

I noticed a road sign pointing at the parking lot to the Alaska Veteran Memorial. Thinking this is going to be as close to a battlefield as I'm going to get, I pulled into the small parking lot to stretch my legs and let Kimber out to do her business. There was a pathway leading to four concrete pillars, with a large star cut out near the top, like a window, each one representing a branch of our military. Curved in a semi-circle, like a modern Stonehenge, the history of Alaskans' service for each branch was carved into the face of the towering blocks. Around these were several Congressional Medal of Honor winners who were from, or became, Alaskans. One in particular caught my attention.

A non-descript granite plaque, embedded into a large stone, read as follows: "In Memory Of, Joseph P. Martinez, July 27, 1920 - May 26th, 1943. Joseph P. Martinez was awarded the Congressional Medal of Honor posthumously for conspicuous gallantry and intrepidity In action at the risk of his life above and beyond the call of duty on Attu, Alaska on the Holtz Bay – Cichagof Harbor Pass, 26 May 1943. Army Pvt. Martinez resumed an advance stalled by severe hostile fire, pausing only to urge on comrades, inspiring followers and eliminating resistance despite knowledge that passage by rocky ridges and snow trenches was barred by the enemy. Martinez nonetheless led troops up, personally silencing several occupied trenches, reaching the top, he was mortally wounded while firing into the last trench. Joe Martinez is the only Medal recipient to fight and die on American soil outside of Hawaii." Whoa what? Trench warfare in Alaska? Sadly, Attu Island is at the tip of the Aleutian Island chain, only accessible by sea or air; but yes, Alaska actually has a battlefield. Amazing.

Back at the truck, with Kimber safely stowed away in the back seat, I tried to make my way around to the driver's side when I was suddenly confronted by what looked like a black and white chicken, with red on its head, and a fanned out tail like a turkey. It first walked right up to me, then veered for the brush. He wasn't trying to get away, but seemed to want me to follow him back into the woods. Nope, not falling for it Mr. Chicken, as he sashayed his fan while strutting away. About that time I heard a flurry of wings flapping. Suddenly, a much less colorful, assuming it was his lady friend, came up on me from behind. She was coming in hot, but stood there looking at me, once again trying to lead me across the parking lot, seemingly away from her "man." I assumed there had to be a nest of some sort in the area, so started looking around the place where she landed. That didn't bode well with her hubby, as suddenly he came storming out of the woods, marching like a Marine, right at me. About two feet out of the brush, he ruffled all his feathers, scratched the ground, and pecked the dirt in front of him like, "Bring it, fat man, I dare ya." I was pretty sure this was a Grouse, and I was about to get groused. Hey, it's his turf, I'm outta here. That was interesting for sure. Later, I found out it was indeed a Grouse, and most hunters will carry a bird shot round as their first shot in the revolver, in case you run across one of these bad boys, that's dinner!

The first state run campground I stumbled across wasn't great; it pretty much looked abandoned, but maybe it was just early in the season. I was somewhat concerned that maybe the free state campgrounds weren't exactly the best places to stay. Luckily, this seemed to be a one-off, as the next state campground was absolutely amazing. A place called K'esugi Ken at Denali State Park, which appeared to be a brand-new campground, was by far the nicest I'd seen on this trip. The drive in looked like a resort; a brand new, meandering road, lined by manicured grass, led up to the forest. The campground surprisingly had full hook-ups for $30 per night, and some hike-in dry camp spots. There was a large log cabin available to rent for parties, and a paved over-flow lot, but the real attraction was the incredible view of Denali that served as a massive backdrop for most of the camp. I stopped to make sure I was allowed to be in the full hook-up site, assuming that dry camp was probably the only free spaces. I was ecstatic to learn that I was good to go for an entire week here, electric and all! Granted, I didn't have anything to really run but a space heater, but it was still a treat to have, and a great place to remember for next time.

During our stay, we found a hiking trail that climbed to the top of the mountain that we were camped on. It was a good climb, but as always, you were rewarded for your effort with views that I have no words to describe. We were above the tree line, so the terrain was rocky with only sparse, unfamiliar ground vegetation. It was like being on a different planet. To one side was this incredible unobstructed view of Denali, so tall that clouds covered the center, giving the illusion of the top of the mountain floating above the base. On the other side was a valley, with a lake about a 1/4 mile away, and then mountaintops as far as the eye could see. Even with my glasses off, and at least a quarter to a half mile away, I could see a bull moose walking along the lakeshore, then turn up the trail that we were coming down. I had to take a picture with my phone, then zoom in to confirm what I thought I saw. Ya, it was huge, and slowly moving our way. We opted to head back to camp, but wow, just wow. The beauty of this place was awe-inspiring, to say the least.

During our week at "Camp Ken," we ventured into the nearby town of Talkeetna, a small, funky little town that is rumored to be the inspiration for the TV show "Northern Exposure." Today it's a popular destination for the younger crowd, serving as a base camp for mountain climbers and popular with tourists in general. The Denali Brewery is located just outside of town, along with other small specialty shops and restaurants surrounding a small city park.

Kimber and I stopped into the brewery for lunch, dining on a prime rib sandwich and a very good IPA. The bartender, a young lady in her early thirties, took interest in my travels and of course Kimber, and later met me uptown to show me around. She explained that the Alaska state law allows you to have three beers in the brewery, then you have to leave. The reason, from what I understand, is the restaurants complained because people were staying at the local breweries where the beer WAS NOT imported, and therefore cheaper. For instance, a pint in the brewery for a fine craft beer was the same price as a pint of Coors Light in the restaurants. So only three, then off you go. Interesting. Here's the funny part. Denali Brewery also makes cider and mead; yup, you guessed it, only three of each type of liquor, then you better find a cab. If you could pull that off, you're probably a local. Oh ya, pro tip: If there's only one parking spot around that little city park in downtown Talkeetna, make sure it's not in front of the only stop sign in town. Ya, I was THAT tourist. Lessons learned.

We continued south on the Parks Highway, working our way toward Anchorage, stopping at the various state campgrounds along the way. They all were completely different, without a whole lot of pictures or explanation in the Park's brochure as to the condition or age. I tried to judge the site by the number of spaces it's advertised to have. If it was just a few spots, good chance it was nothing more than a roadside rest stop that you could sleep at. If there were lots of spots, it was obviously a larger and probably nicer campground. It's obvious when you pull in most times, it's either very busy or basically abandoned. Mosquitos and water nearby also played a huge role. Something you just had to learn the hard way.

Speaking of the blood sucking Pterodactyls, let me give you an update on the Great Mosquito Wars of 2019. So since we learned that a moose could lose a pint of blood a day, I decided we had better learn the best defense against this wily and persistent enemy. Kimber could be sucked dry in a matter of minutes, for God's sake! Ok, a little dramatic, but you haven't seen these things and the literal swarms they travel in. So back at Fort Wainwright, I had plenty of bugs and plenty of time to work up the best defense thus far. We went through every level of bug spray from natural to scorched earth; the winner was the wipes, the higher the octane the better. These were used on my legs and back of my neck, and once down Kimber's back. She had her own "natural" bug spray that didn't seem to do much. I may have worked for those soy-boy, latte-sipping skeeters in the lower 48; this was Alaska, even the mosquitos act accordingly. Next, we tried the electronic, hot pad thing. It worked if this thing was literally attached to you, and there was zero wind. The winner and grand champion... a smoker. Yup, the propane smoker, on low with a big bowl of wood chips, literally smoked out the flying demons before they even got to the truck. Another reason to carry a meat smoker everywhere you go. The kicker that I just couldn't figure out, was how the hell they were getting into the back of the truck. Nothing worse than to be on the verge of sleep and hear one of these things coming in hot at your forehead. Forget about sleep until you kill the bastard. Like little commandos, they were coming up through every little hole I could find in the truck bed. I literally turned on the lights inside the camper, then crawled underneath the truck, stuffing wet toilet paper into every crack and crevice that I saw light. This seemed to help. Also, it was still pretty cold at night, so heavy blankets protected my body, leaving just my face exposed. That's when I learned that if I turn the exhaust fan on, in the pass-thru window, just above my head, the mosquitos literally get sucked to the screen as they try to land on me. Plus, I didn't hear them over the fan motor hum. Double bonus. Kimber, buried under the covers snoring away, could care less. So the wars waged on, but we were starting to get the upper hand.

As we bounced from campground to campground, looking for our next spot, I noticed something interesting at a place called Big Lake. This was a campground on the shores of a beautiful, good-sized lake, much like our first stop. There were only a few campers, all very well kept, with a camp host near the front entrance. That's when three kids, about middle school age, rode by on an ATV. Not a quad, but one of the old school, and now outlawed, three wheelers. I haven't seen one of those since... then I looked up to the loud sound of a motorcycle coming from the water. Here were two high school kids racing on jet skis. No, not a sit down, personal watercraft, the stand-up ones that I think they outlawed years ago too. What!? It was like stepping back in time 20 years, hell maybe 30 or 40. When I turned to find Kimber, I noticed an old pay phone mounted to the stand, near the life jackets and announcement board. There's no way. I walked up and lifted the receiver. Yup, there was actually a dial tone! I instantly thought of my penny loafers back in high school, with two dimes instead of pennies, in case you had to make a call. That was 1984. I'd have to carry a credit card in them now, what's a call from Alaska, twelve bucks?

June 5th, 2019. From our stay at Big Lake, it was time to head for the town of Palmer, where the trucker veteran on my book page was from. Ben was a truck driver who split his time between Alaska and Minnesota. Even though he was currently out of town, he had set up a camping spot for me at the Palmer American Legion, where he was a member. It was awesome to have folks waiting for me when I got to Palmer. The bartender was expecting us and showed us where we would be staying for the next week or so. A perfect spot, on a small freshly stocked lake, with nobody else around except Legion members in the lodge above. Ben had set this up for me before I had left on the trip, my only pre-planned destination on this adventure. It would be a great location to explore the Wasilla Palmer area. That and they had a baseball team!

Later that evening, I headed down to the fairgrounds where Ben had told me they had a summer semi-pro baseball league. Turns out that Alaska has five teams scattered around the state, with a big tournament up in Fairbanks. During the summer solstice they play at midnight without lights. How crazy is that!? All the players in the Alaska Baseball League are on active NCAA team rosters. There was a team here in Palmer, another down the road in Eagle River, a couple in Anchorage, and the last on the Kenai Peninsula. The biggest name I could find that played here was Aaron Judge, oh and Scott my physical therapist back in Payson. I learned all this from a lady selling hats and t-shirts; she ran the league or was in upper management of some sort. Of course I had to tell her about my travels and how cool it was that Alaska had baseball. To which she immediately replied, "Well, you gotta have one of these!" handing me an official Alaska League baseball. Now that's cool. I settled in for a great burger, a couple Alaskan

Ambers and a baseball game with snow topped mountains as a backdrop... at 2100... without lights. Then I noticed, they didn't have any to turn on anyway. Now that's crazy.

For the next few days, we fished for the stocked trout and sterling that were eager to eat after a long winter. More than once we caught a 12 to 14 inch trout that immediately became a pan-fried lunch, sautéed with mushrooms and onions in a pan of butter. We explored Wasilla, checking out a fishing outfitter that my cousin Audra knew from her time driving truck here. Crazy how small this world is. I worked out at the veteran owned and operated gym, walked around some type of festival that was happening that weekend, and decided to check out this brewery everybody spoke of. That's when I learned just how crazy small this planet really is.

The Arkose Brewery looked like somebody's garage, with an added room on the side. I actually drove past it, twice, before I realized it was a brewery. There was only one car there, but the sign in the window said they were open. Well, I'm here now, and the locals at the festival said it's great beer, so why not. When I walked in, the smell of roasted hops and a lady at register were there to greet me. I ordered a flight to sample what they had, and grabbed a seat. While she was pouring my beer, a couple, and someone I assumed was an owner, had just returned from a tour or something. I overheard that the couple was from California and mentioned the town Fresno. Ok, this is where it gets kinda crazy.

I turned to the guy, a dude about my age, Hispanic, with long hair and a ball cap on backwards, and asked, "Fresno? You wouldn't know the Casos would you?" He turned to me and said "no." That's when I explained that I was originally from Northern California, and I had a very close friend whose daughter married a dude named Caso from there. Fresno wasn't that big, there was a chance. When I mentioned her maiden name, he stopped and said "Ernie?" Ernie is my "big brother," my pastor of the church I attended in Pinetop, and truly one of the closest and dearest friends I have. And this guy knew him.

Danny grew up in San Jose also, knew Ernie growing up, and Danny's nephew is even named after Ernie's little brother. Now living in Los Angeles, he was here fishing with his fiancé and some friends. He and his girlfriend just happened to be in Palmer checking out the sights, before heading down to the Russian River. Our paths crossing in Palmer, Alaska has to be the biggest proof of just how small this world is. Or maybe it's that we really are all connected in this craziness we call life. After sending a selfie of Danny and myself to Ernie's phone, the confirmation of "WHAT! DANNY?!?" made my trip full circle. From the place that I stepped off from, to the last state that I drove to; everything just came full circle. Crazy.

Danny invited me to go fish with his buddies down on the Russian River. They planned on hitting it opening day, before the crowds got there. Salmon fishing with experts, in the place read about the most, the Russian River, affectionately known for its "Combat fishing," we'd be "flipping" for Reds. All of which sounded foreign, yet absolutely the reason why I was here. "Hell, ya! Teach me, bro." I was all in, packed up the camp that night, and headed down the next day, hoping to find a camping spot early. Super special thank you to the folks at the Palmer American Legion, see you soon!

On the way down to Anchorage, I decided to catch another Alaska League game in nearby Eagle River. A fun game, with super nice people, but the star attraction for us was the momma moose and her copper-colored calf, who walked up the sidewalk, right next to us, at a stop sign. If you've ever seen a baby moose, they look like a cross between a cow calf and an elk calf, and as bright as a brand-new copper penny. This was one of the cutest things I've ever seen. Gotta love Alaska.

Next stop was at an Anytime Fitness in Anchorage for a shower, then Walmart for the evening. We learned really quick that Walmart in Anchorage is not where you want to camp. They had the tall, periscope camera thing with red and blue cop lights on top, dead center in the middle of the parking lot. Not a great sign for boondocking. Since we weren't exactly stealth camping, with a basket of gas tanks hanging off the back and boxes of tools and gear on the roof, I didn't sleep well that night at all. Not to mention the police, in and out of the parking lot, walking up on parked cars... ya, needless to say, we were out bright and early that next morning, heading for the Kenai Peninsula.

The drive to the Kenai was nothing less than astonishing. Snowcapped mountains so big they would be named in the lower 48, were just one in a never-ending parade of jagged peaks leading to the Kenai. Now take that scene and add a perfectly calm ocean bay to your right, and a massive bull moose eating moss in the middle of some wetlands at the base of a mountain to your left... that's your drive from Anchorage to Cooper Landing. As if that's not enough, add a couple glaciers to stop and check out, purple and red fire weeds along the edge of the roads, and an occasional bald eagle crossing the scene, topping it off with a good dose of absolute freedom.

Ya, it was that awesome. This is when I found the most amazing campsite of the trip, and the occupant just happened to be leaving the next day.

With a couple of days to burn before Danny and Amber check into the hotel up the road, Kimber and I set up camp at a National Forest campground that was directly on the Kenai River. We paid 9 bucks a night, but the beauty of this spot was well worth the cost. I've never seen water so amazing as when the sun hits the Kenai first thing in the morning. There's a greenish blue color that just irradiates with the rays of sunshine. Even with the glacial silt, it was incredibly beautiful, emerald water, beautiful red and blue wildflowers, blue sky with bright white clouds. I could sit at the riverbank and just look at this water rush by, hour after hour. Second only to a house looking up at Denali, I'd like to have a house overlooking this river. Either one of those scenes is what I want to grow old staring at. Words cannot describe the beauty of this land; even if they could, it would never even be close.

It was beautiful yet somewhat foreign. When Kimber and I went on a hike into the Chugach National Forest, we encountered an almost tropical feeling, yet well within what one would consider a forest, far from the ocean. Growing up in NorCal, I was used to the prehistoric feel of the Redwood forests. This was the same feeling, but maybe in Japan or somewhere. There were broad leaf, tropical looking plants, along with large ferns and moss. At the same time, there were towering Cedar and Pine, dense patches of Alder, and several other species I didn't take the time to look up. There were creeks and branches of creeks everywhere, all with crystal clear rushing water. The forest would subside at times, dropping us at the edge of a tall grass slope, with what looked like dill plants and tall reeds grouped together here and there, finally ending at some form of water, usually rushing quickly and ice cold. The array of color from wildflower patches was surprising. I easily took at least a dozen pictures showcasing the different colors, shapes, and sizes of Alaskan Spring wildflower blooms.

Opening day on the Russian River was the Thursday before Father's Day, and apparently the best time to go before the crowds show up. Danny gave me directions on how to get there; they were heading in early, so I would meet them on the river a bit later. The local outfitter, who happened to own a landscaping business back in AZ, set me up with a med/heavy spinning rod and reel, loaded with a spool of 30wt. monofilament line. He also gave me a few different color "Russian River" flies, that of course, as a tourist, I thought fly color mattered drastically, and some 1oz lead weights. I was all set up to catch my very first salmon.

The line was long to get into the parking lot, but there were plenty of spots once you paid the parking fee. The place was a National Park Service parking area with a ferry that takes you to the far side of the river. I was able to park for free with my access pass, but had to pay half of the ten dollar ferry fee. Fair enough, bring on the salmon. With Kimber stowed away in the truck, I headed for the ferry line. That's when I met "Gunny."

While waiting in line for the boat, a guy about my dad's age struck up a conversation, then asked if I was a Marine. He of course had seen my neck tattoo. Next thing ya know, I'm laughing and joking with Gunny and his two veteran buddies. After I told them this was my first time, they had me follow them to the DAV area of the river, to show me what "flipping for Reds" was all about. The banks of the river were full of fishermen, literally hundreds; there was no way I'd find Danny in the crowds, so I took the old vets up on their offer. I could always meet up with Danny later, these guys were put here for a reason.

So let me give you a little lesson on how to catch an Alaskan Sockeye, also known as a Red Salmon. First interesting thing, the fish doesn't eat when they spawn, they have one intent and only one intent, and eating isn't it. They do, however, swim upstream with their mouths continuously opening and closing. So you're hoping to "floss" the fish by throwing a 30wt line, tied to whatever hook is legal for that area, and just enough weight attached about 30" from the hook, so that you feel the weight bouncing along the bottom of the river. The leader portion of line trailing behind the weight will drag across the running river, hopefully running your line through a salmon's open mouth, and dragging the hook into his outer cheek. Basically snagging him on the outside of the mouth. Any other snag not on the mouth has to be thrown back.

After getting the lowdown from Gunny on what the procedure was, I put on my cousin Audra's old waders, strapped on my hiking boots over the rubber wader feet, tied a bungee cord around my waist and entered the frigid glacier water for the very first time. The water was about thigh depth and fairly clear; as instructed, I faced downstream, cast my weight and hook upstream, letting the hook drag across the river bottom. It wasn't long before I got the hang of it, and landed my first fish. Fish On! is the battle cry that moves all the fishermen politely out of your way as you wrestle in your 8-10 lb prize. It was almost too easy. So you're telling me that I can pull a 50 dollar fish out of a gorgeous river, 6 at a time, everyday here?! That's smoked salmon every single day. Like I joke with my friends, that's like crack candy to an Irish/Norwegian, and I'm pulling it out of the river by the pound! Not to mention that this was

430

my very first salmon, and my personal best size-wise. All because I met some dude from Cali at a brewery in Palmer, Alaska.

I quit after catching just two salmon, only because I'm living out of a chest cooler with no refrigerator; so off to the cleaning table I went. That's when I just happened to run into Danny, standing in line for the table. He was glad to see I caught some fish, we made plans to meet up later for some beers, and parted ways. Super cool guy, met under crazy circumstances, that pointed me in the direction I needed to go. Thanks, brother, see you soon. On my path indeed.

From Cooper Landing we headed south toward the town of Soldotna, the town that the float boat guy had said he was from. It was now only a few days before the 4th of July weekend, but no fireworks were going to be flying, much to Kimber's appreciation. Sadly though, a good-sized wildfire had moved into the area. The roads were covered with thick, yellowish orange haze, the smell was like a campfire blowing smoke directly at you. It made sleeping in the camper shell almost unbearable, definitely bad enough for us to break camp and head further south to Homer. Soldotna was an awesome little town that I was eager to explore, but not right now.

Not only the fires were affecting the Peninsula, but also the heat. This was considered a record high temperature year, reaching 88f. I know that sounds silly to think that 88f would be hot enough to make you hunt for shade, or do anything other than enjoy it. I don't know if the sun is at a different angle here or what, but if you're in direct sun, you might as well be back in Phoenix. It was hot; maybe due to higher humidity compared to Arizona? Who knows, either way, it was unbearable unless we had shade. So add that to the list for a reason to get closer to the ocean. And get this, there was an ice shortage at the local stores, with one store clerk directing me to the coin-operated ice machine in the parking lot of the mall. I had to laugh when I saw this, in Alaska they're literally selling ice to proverbial "Eskimos." Gotta love it.

The trip down the Peninsula seemed to transport you to several different lands along the way. Forests, lakes, and swampy marshland on one side; sheer cliffs, covered in plants and wildflowers, some familiar, most completely foreign on the other. Across the water, through the light blue haze, you could make out a line of massive snowcapped mountains. Like driving into a postcard, we pulled into the town of Homer, a small fishing hub on the tip of the Kenai Peninsula.

Homer was a cool, sleepy little coastal town that brought back memories of Bodega Bay in California, minus the snowcapped mountains rocketing out of the calm bay waters. I decided to drive out toward Kachemak Bay on what's called East End road, one of only two ways you could drive from Homer. I took some pictures of the incredible views and sent them to my buddy Glenn, who had just visited Alaska. He said, "Kachemak Bay, that's where the *Kilcher Homestead* is," referring to one of the many Alaskan reality shows. I had to chuckle when I curiously looked up the show to see what he was talking about. One episode spoke of a family member who was too lazy to hunt for meat that summer, all concerned about what he was going to do for winter sustenance. Well, I'd assume he'd drive 20 minutes to Safeway, they have pork chops on sale for $1.28 per pound. Ya, not everything is what it seems on TV.

On the way back into town, I turned south on Highway 1, toward what's known as the "Spit," basically, a long jetty separating the Kachemak Bay from the Gulf of Alaska. The highway was now a narrow and crowded two-lane road, lined with commercial docks on one side, and tourist traps on the other. They had beach camping, but none of the campgrounds were state run, and somewhat pricey. I didn't feel like battling the sand anyway. So we turned north, back up the Sterling Highway, to some state run parks I saw near a place called Anchor Point. Free camping is free camping.

With it being 4th of July weekend, I had assumed it would be crowded, thankfully I was wrong. Anchor Point is the mouth of the Anchor River, a phenomenal place to fly-fish an amazing lazy river, and also a popular boat launch for halibut fishing. We found a nice spot in the back of a fairly empty campground, where we set up camp and had some supper. Getting here a couple days before the holiday worked out perfectly as I knew the place would probably fill fast. I was just glad to find a spot and settle into a non-firework Fourth of July, to which Kimber wholeheartedly concurred.

We had some neighbors pull in the next day, a couple about my age and their boy. They came down from Soldotna for some halibut fishing, when Kimber decided to introduce herself. Great folks, as every Alaskan I've met so far is. We chatted about fishing and what Kimber and I were doing in Alaska, quickly becoming friends. I was shocked when their son offered me a "slab" of halibut, a filet about a foot long and a couple inches thick. Now that I think about it, pretty sure that was my first taste of the poor man's lobster, which I promptly turned into pan fried tacos with red onion and mushrooms. Viva Alaska!

Kimber and I were also invited to join them on a fishing trip that next morning, which we gladly accepted. Quite the experience to be launched into the bay by a tractor in knee-deep mud. The beaches here are mainly fine silt, volcanic rock I think, leaving Kimber a dirty black mess after I threw her ball. Anyway, the tractor guy backs you into the water with a large wheeled farm tractor, then they park your trailer for you. You just call them when you're ready to come in, they come get you with your trailer. Your feet never touch sand. Sweet! Not to mention, the dozens of seagulls and baby bald eagles hopping around the black beach, making the whole scene seem surreal. Sadly, much like Washington, my sea legs have been long gone for quite sometime. Even in the proverbial flat bath water of the Gulf, I started to get sick. Not even an hour in, I sadly wasn't going to make it much longer. No halibut for me today, but the lesson was invaluable.

After a week in Anchor Point, Kimber and I headed back up to Sterling, to a place called Morgan's Landing Campground. The smoke now dissipated some, but the fire waged on. It kept the sky an orange haze most of the following week. I didn't notice it too much, I was way too busy falling in love with my new hometown. For the next three weeks, I would stay right here in the Soldotna/Sterling area, bouncing between the abundance of free state campgrounds in the area.

Soldotna is a city of around 5k people. Kenai, the city just down the road, sits at about 8k. Sterling is on the opposite side of Soldotna, and has the least amount of folks. All in all, it was just like Pinetop and Show Low back in AZ, just add a massive river and a fish filled ocean within 20 minutes of each other, not to mention you're on a peninsula the size of West Virginia. There were several grocery stores, a Walmart, Home Depot, and of course the state favorite Fred Meyers, along with several auto dealerships, a couple dozen restaurants and bars, movie theatre, and even a small indoor mall. It was definitely the most populated area of the Kenai, the perfect combination of civilization and wilderness. I was absolutely loving this place.

The people in Alaska, whether native or transplant, are some of the absolute nicest folks I've ever met. While I was sitting in one of the local breweries, yes there's even two of those, a guy from back east somewhere came in. He mentioned how nice everybody was here, when another guy, a local, said, "That's because nobody's from here." An interesting statement that made me think about my choices of locales to establish roots. Think about it. If I moved to Tennessee or anywhere in the South, the first thing the locals will know is I'm not from there. My lack of drawl instantly makes me a "yankee" or at best, a visitor. I've lived in Texas, remember, great folks, but also very territorial with folks not from there. Family names run deep in the South, as I've learned from this journey. Fast forward to Alaska. Nobody but the natives can claim this place. Another reason to give Alaska a shot.

One of the highlights of Soldotna is their Wednesday concerts in the park. Seems like the whole town comes out for an incredible craft show, farmers market, and to eat at one of the many food trucks. Local acts filled the stage, while locals filled the Kenai Brewery beer garden. Oh ya, I could get really used to this.

One Wednesday afternoon at the craft fair, I stopped to admire some of the best handmade knives I've ever seen. I already owned plenty of blades, but sure could use a sharpening. After asking if he sharpens and how much, the bearded gentleman, maybe a couple years older than me said, "Sure do. Give me a few minutes and you tell me what it's worth." Enter my buddy Dave. A local special education high school teacher who also owns and operates Great Land Knife Co., his summer side gig. Kimber and I walked around the fair and grabbed a bite, before making our way back to Dave. While he was finishing my blade, I explained to him what my little dog and I were doing in AK. He finished my knife and handed me back a razor blade. Wow, that thing was sharp. "What do I owe ya?" to which he instantly said no vet's money was good with him. Wow, super cool. That's when he asked if I fish, we exchanged numbers, and made plans to hit the river at a "locals" spot. Now that's what I'm talking about!

The next day I got a text from Dave, "Wanna build a knife?" Short of fishing, what's more Alaskan than that! Hell ya, I'm in. A few minutes later, I was standing in Dave's garage, turned knife shop. He had everything from a hot kiln, to every kind of metal grinder you could think of. This man takes a blank piece of steel and a block of wood, and makes a piece of art that sells for 100 to 300 bucks. About twenty hours of work go into a knife, only because of Dave's tenacious attention to detail, this dude should have been a Marine instructor. Barking at the three little dots I had left unpolished on the blade. "Attention to detail, Marine!" he laughed as I was frustrated. If you were in the service and ever had to hand a spotless rifle back to the armor for q-tip inspection… for the fifth time. Ya, that frustrated. But as the master knew, my eyes went straight to those dots every time I look at the blade. I told him when I buy land there, I'm naming the place "Threedotna."

I could go on and on about the Kenai; the fishing, the people, the climate, and what they do for veterans and their military. The best way to explain what was happening to me, was when I woke up one morning, bright and early, stepping outside the camper shell for some coffee… I was smiling. For no reason, person, or animal, I was smiling. It was then and there that I suddenly realized that I was truly happy. I was infatuated with this place, and it showed. Even a message from my friend Honey on FB confirmed this. "Alaska has you beaming!" she commented under the picture of me holding a 6 fish limit of Sockeyes, grinning from ear to ear. I was home, and I knew it. My soul knew it. Finally.

People often say they are "happy" and wholeheartedly believe it, I too am one of those folks. While I was traveling, I was happy, a happiness that I was so glad to finally have. In all actuality, I was only assuming I was happy. I assumed that traveling was the peak of my happiness, because it was the closest thing I knew to freedom. Now I find myself in a PLACE where I feel free, the most freedom possibly attainable in this world we now find ourselves in. This place touched my soul. The craziest part is to actually notice that you're truly happy. I mean come on, who the hell smiles before coffee?! Needless to say, it was a sad day when I packed up the truck and started to move my way back down the Alaskan Coast. Literally, I had tears in my eyes as I rolled out of the campground. I miss it here already, but I will be back, very, very soon.

After leaving Soldotna, we made our way down the Alaskan Coast, stopping in Seward, Valdez, and finally Skagway, before turning the truck south, hoping to meet up with my buddy Chris from Milwaukee, for a Sturgeon charter in Washington State. We stayed a few days in each spot, just absorbing the unbelievable beauty at every turn. But I was tired, and Kimber was exhausted. This was one of the greatest adventures I had personally ever embarked upon. To think I was dreading this leg of the journey. To think from that dread, I found my nirvana. I found home… and the sign in front of the Kenai High School, a giant wooden carving of the school's mascot confirmed it, a bright red "Kenai" Cardinal. I suddenly have a new mission. Remember the fear I had when I came home last year? All those, Ok, now whats? I got my answer, stay tuned, my friend. Alaska, my soon to be home, state #49… COMPLETE!

Hawaii

October 24th, 2019. Well, the time has come, a day that quite honestly, I've been dreading since I began this trip. I haven't flown on a plane in over 15 years, and wasn't looking forward to it now, mainly because my road partner wasn't here. Kimber would have a ten-day quarantine before she could explore the island, like she had the last 49 states. There's no way I could afford ten days in Hawaii, just to wait for her to get out of jail, and there was absolutely no way I was going to leave her alone in some cage for ten days. So, once again a DAV with PTSD is stuck-out because she's not a true "Service" dog; even then, I'm not sure what the quarantine protocol would be, nor did I care. All I knew, I was completing the final leg of this 5-year journey without my best friend. So ya, I was actually dreading my first visit to Hawaii, sad but true. Tears uncontrollably rolling down my face as I type this at the airport bar. Irish coffee is the word of the day at 0600.

So the plan for this 4-day expedition was to find my way to Honolulu, pick up a rental mini-van to drive, explore, and camp in, while we explore Oahu and mainly Pearl Harbor. (Even as I type this, I'm correcting the "we" with "I"... ugh). Anyway, after two days of exploring, I would check into the Hale Koa Military resort, the largest resort on Waikiki Beach is what I've been told, and exclusively for military, retirees, and 100% DAVs. I check in on Saturday, then have a tour to the USS Arizona and USS Missouri on Sunday, which just happens to be my 50th birthday. My 50th state, 50th birthday, and the completion of the greatest five years of my life. Dammit, I miss my girl already... bad.

Kimber will be staying with my friends Alex and Dawn, which is kind of cool in a way. Alex and Dawn are the couple that I had met on my first year of travels, visiting my first state, California. My neighbors at Camp Pendleton RV resort had offered to watch Kimber while I visited my very first ballpark in San Diego. Alex is the retired Army Officer and retired Massachusetts state trooper who I had met up with in Boston, for my first visit to Fenway two years later. So it's somewhat appropriate that they would watch Kimber during my last state too. Knowing she's in good hands, and familiar with Alex and Dawn, made it incredibly easier for me to deal with her being gone. This is the first time that Kimber would be away from me for more than one night. Pretty sure she's going to handle this much better than me. Pre-boarding just began, well, here we go. This will truly be the hardest test of my PTSD to date.

I landed in Honolulu around 1100, all in all, an amazingly smooth flight, save for the rather rotund, elderly gentleman in the seat next to me. Ya, that's my luck. Just about every seat I ever get, whether it's a baseball game or an airplane, is next to someone who probably should've bought two seats. Thankfully, the in-flight movie selection was top notch, with John Wick keeping my mind off the seating arrangement.

After debarking the plane, the first thing you notice is how humid it is here. Wow, like Texas humid. I was surprised by this, thinking it would be more like California weather. I made my way to the car rental desk to pick up my soccer mom mobile. The young kid at the checkout counter started to bring up my reservation when he asked, "How many passengers?" "Just me," I responded. He then asked if I had a lot of luggage, realizing that the reservation called for a van.

Not sure if camping in a rental car is against the rules, I just looked at him blankly like I didn't hear him. "We're having a special on high-end SUVs if you'd like something nicer." "I like vans," I said, not breaking my gaze. "Um, ok. Here ya go, sir," he said, and handed me my paperwork with a perplexed look. Ahh, my chariot awaits, let's do this.

I was missing Kimber even more than I thought. So much so, I was tearing up a couple times per hour, ya this was hard. Harder than I had ever imagined. Now add the absolutely crazy traffic while my nerves were already frazzled. I wanted to drive to the most remote place I could possibly find and just sit there. First things first though, I headed straight for the Pearl Harbor Historic Sites Visitor Center. Our one and only WWII battlefield.

The NPS website had said that it's best to get to the newly remodeled visitor center early, as parking was somewhat limited. Since it was Thursday, I figured that this would be less busy than the weekend. Turns out it doesn't matter what day you go, this place is always packed. There was a concrete walkway along the waterfront describing the scene that was happening across the bay at Ford Island. That's the naval station where the USS Missouri and the USS Arizona, among other ships, were docked when the Japanese attacked. There were also a couple museums with some artifacts from that fateful day, mainly pictures, models of ships, and different gear used in the war. One museum detailed the events in Japan leading up to the attack, while the other showcased the actual battle. There was also a gift store, snack bar, and ticket counter for different tour packages.

I made my way around the crowded exhibits, snapping pictures and taking in what I could, as fast as I could. The crowds were on par with the Grand Canyon back in Arizona. Instead of Chinese and Russian tourists that were predominant at the stateside National Parks, the majority of people here were Japanese. I wondered what my grandfather would have thought about that. See, my grandfather had attempted to join the service with his older brother after the attack on

Pearl Harbor, but my great grandmother refused to sign the papers, being as he was just 17. What the family didn't know was that my great uncle was a Marine and died in Tarawa, the bloodiest of all Marine battles. So it wasn't until the clean-up that my grandfather joined the Navy, but he had always held some hostility toward the Japanese. I remember him calling December 7th, Pearl Harbor day, "slap a jap day." Being politically correct wasn't my grandfather's strong point, but could you blame him? They killed his brother. This explained why he begged me not to join the Marines, and came running outside when I had come home from Desert Storm yelling "He's home! He's home!" tears running down his cheek. And here I thought the old man just didn't think I could make it as a Marine. I'll never forget that day. This is my "Cardinal" grandpa, the one who raised me.

After getting back to the van, I decided to go across the bridge to Ford Island and see if I could get some better pictures. Hopefully the crowds wouldn't be as bad. Well, my wish was granted as Ford Island is still an active Naval Base, with an ID check just over the bridge, definitely no crowds. After flashing my ID to the gate guard, I made my way to the dock where the USS Missouri tours began. Since I had already purchased tour tickets to both the Arizona and the Missouri for Sunday, I decided to hold off and check out some other memorials on base.

One that caught my eye on the map was a "Marine" memorial. Unfortunately, after searching for said memorial, it turns out that the "Marine" wasn't USMC but something to do with NOAA as it was inside the building. The good news is I found another monument for the USS Utah, a sunken ship that was unable to be raised, trapping and killing the crew. I found it along what's called the Ford Island Historic Trail. It was along this trail that I had a visitor.

As I began to explore the island, I had mused how my grandfather was going to show me a Cardinal. I assumed it would be a strangely obvious billboard portraying a Cardinal like so many times before. Quite honestly, I wasn't going to get my hopes up of seeing something like that here, even if my grandfather had served here. I even asked aloud while I was driving, "How ya going to show me a Cardinal this time, Grampa?" Now, as I walked this interpretive history path on Ford Island, I stopped to take some pictures of the famous Hawaiian Minaj birds that were feeding in the grass nearby. That's when I was startled by something, and then couldn't believe my eyes. A small grey and white bird with a bright red head and crest that was identical to my beloved Cardinals. I about dropped the phone. He landed within just a few yards of my feet, and refused to fly away, as I walked within just a few feet of him. I was floored. Later, after posting about my visit from this guy, one of my followers sent me a post portraying a Red Crested Cardinal, also known as a Spanish Cardinal. Another friend said the bird just had his "away" jersey on. Awesome. I love you, Grandpa, and I needed to see this more than anything right now. It's so hard to be here without Kimber. Here come the tears again.

At this point, I was so fed up with traffic and people, I decided to drive up the west side of the island, to a state park at the end of the road. Passing several beaches, I started looking for a place to boondock for the night. There were zero RVs here, no bumper pull trailers and definitely no 5th wheels, so camping spots here were pretty much on the beach and that's it. This wouldn't be so bad, but every beach so far has had homeless encampments. I'm talking tent cities, with stacked pallets as walls around many "tenants," all within yards of a school. I was completely shocked. Later I found out from a waitress that the west shore is the rough part of town; ok, so now what? It's not safe to sleep on the beach like so many people think of Hawaii. Maybe on other islands but not on Oahu.

It was starting to get dark so I looked for a Super Walmart, hopefully to find a quiet area to park and crawl into the back for the night. That's when I realized that I'd had the AC on all day, and as soon as the car stopped, the stifling heat and humidity attacked. I'd have to roll down the windows, which would make it obvious I was sleeping in my car. There were no other boondockers here, just roving security. Ok, so Wal-Mart is a no-go. At this point, I was glad Kimber wasn't here, even though I cried at even the thought of her. God, I miss her so much, this is so hard.

So now I knew that my only chance at getting some sleep would be to go up in elevation, and hopefully cooler temps. Ya, good luck with that too. Nothing was high enough to effect the temperature. I was getting worried now, it was dark, I had no idea where I was neighborhood wise, not knowing if I was safe to park or not. Remember, I can't lock the doors, I need the air. So I found a Costco just off the road heading to North Shore. It was 2200 and nobody in sight but some construction vehicles and parked employee cars. I found a dark spot under a tree, parked and crawled into the back of the car. Now the jet lag and coffee kicked in, so nothing but a couple hours of cat naps before I was wide awake at 0300. Well, this sucks. I guess I'll find a Denny's and drink coffee until daylight.

Finally, after 2 hours of drinking coffee and writing at the local Denny's, the sun finally decided to show itself. I headed north to North Shore, hoping the scenery and the beaches would improve from what I saw on the west shore. It was very early still, with nothing open but a small coffee plantation's shop offering restrooms and a bright neon "open" sign. Thank God. That's the other issue, I left my keys back home with Alex in case he needed to move my truck while I was gone, with my key fob for Anytime Fitness attached. So bathrooms, away from the beaches, were at a premium, especially this early in the morning.

I drove the perimeter road from North Shore all the way around to Honolulu in about 2 hours. The beaches up here were much more like what I expected Hawaii to be, pristine blue water, gorgeous plants and trees along the coast. The news had mentioned that there was a high surf warning today, which explained why parking this early was at a premium, with all the surfers coming out to see. I think surfers are the only people that get up early, standing on rocks and truck tailgates, watching the surf like they're waiting for Jesus to return.

The homeless thing was still there, but not nearly as dense; still there was only a few beaches that didn't have tents and tarps littering the coastline. Every beach had warning signs of "high theft" areas, warning to not keep valuables in your car, and even portraying a hammer on shattered glass. Nope, not sleeping here either. Also not excited about sleeping in the heat and humidity again, even if I found a safe place to park. I think it's time to break down and rent a hotel, at which my back concurred wholeheartedly. Unfortunately, this is when things took a turn for the worse.

I stopped at the MCBH (Marine Corps Base Hawaii), formerly known as Maine Corps Air Station Kaneohe Bay, to see if they had any rooms available. Probably a long shot on such short notice and on a Friday night. Unfortunately, the only room available was $180 per night, with the cheaper cabanas being sold out. Well, now what? There's gotta be a cheap motel somewhere, at this point anything under a 100 bucks would be a bargain. I turned to one of the many online reservation companies to search for something decent. The first one looked nice but was still $130 a night. Oh well, I gotta do what I gotta do. I reserved the night, set the GPS for the hotel, and started to head that way.

Downtown Waikiki Beach is a maze of one-way roads with cross streets in every direction. It was extremely crowded with crosswalks full of people. Looking for the hotel, while keeping one eye on the GPS, and the other on traffic and pedestrians, was incredibly frustrating. When I finally did find the hotel, there was zero street parking and the small garage for hotel customers was almost 40 bucks a night. Jesus, now what. After circling the block and nearby streets half a dozen times, I finally gave up. My nerves were shot, anxiety peaking, on the verge of tears again; I needed to do something. I decided to take the car back to the airport a day early, maybe get a refund for the one day. Then I checked the rental car contract, that was a no-go; it said they could charge for early return. Ugh! I give up, back to the parking garage. Now the bill is up to 170. All I want at this point is to get on the fucking plane and go back to my dog.

After parking and checking into my room, I find out there's another $27.50 a day "resort" fee, which is a beach towel, a pot of coffee, and combination to a room safe. Really!? And then the final kicker, they hold another 50 bucks back for room deposit, refunded a few days after checkout. I almost lost it. Doing everything I could not to go off on the clerk, I took my room card and went to find my bed. It was almost 48 hours since I landed with only a few hours of cat naps. I was done. When I got to the room, I broke down. It was a dump. My view was of a burnt-out motel next door, complete with charred mechanical equipment, broken out windows and graffiti. The shower had peeling paint and mold, the coffee pot had residue, stains on the carpet, and a dinette that looked like something you'd see in a crack house. Tears running down my face, I hit my knees and sobbed like a child. All I could think of was my Kimber. I just wanted to go home and hug my dog.

I slept only a few hours here too, waking up at 0300 as usual, and still pinging with anxiety. More tears. I had to talk to somebody so I called my cousin in Oregon. She answered with a happy "Hello!" and then a gasp as soon as she heard my voice. "I hate this place. I wanna go home, Cuz. I can't do this!" And then it let loose, full-on balling. I haven't cried like that since before this entire five-year expedition began. All the healing that I thought I had accomplished while driving this country, came crashing down. The crowds, the traffic, the cost, and now, for the very first time... the loneliness. The PTSD was back with a vengeance, and all I wanted was my Kimber. Why the hell did I do this, why did I ever leave her?

My minor nervous breakdown was probably the best thing that I could've done. The release of stress from a good cry is something that should be embraced instead of embarrassing. I was now able to focus, and set a game plan. All I needed to do now was wait for the sun to come up, checkout of the roach motel, turn in my car at the airport, and find a shuttle back to the Hale Koa. A lot of stress ahead, but now we were on the backside of this 4-day trip, and I was eager to move it along. Thankfully, all went smoothly at the airport, car return was painless, another 20 bucks for a shuttle, and finally, I was checking into the Hale Koa Military Resort.

Whatever fears of dealing with crowds or people suddenly just flew away with the cool ocean breeze. This place was amazing. Formerly a military installation, now turned into a 5-star luxury resort, the grounds of this place went on forever. Two different pools, a children's with full waterslides and toys, and the zero edge adult pool, just a few feet above. An outside cabana bar served Mai Tais to die for, and ice-cold drafts, among other decently priced libations. The food was incredible, but the one thing you must do, as recommended by my friend from Maine, is eat pineapple every single day. You'll never get pineapple like that in the States. Pure candy, and the Portuguese Sausage is something not to miss. My first night in the hotel, I just sat by the cabana bar, sipping Mai Tais, watching baseball on the bar TV, while the sun set over the water behind me. Ok, this Hawaii, I like.

A startling change happened to me here, enough to catch my own attention and make me think. This place is in a major city, super crowded resort, people literally everywhere. Why am I not bouncing off the walls with anxiety? All shapes, sizes, colors and creeds were present at this international resort. None of which I knew personally, yet had a familiar bond with. The Military. We had that one common thread to unite us, we all have served in one form or another. We were all family; this was my tribe. This made me think about how we're told that tribalism is such a bad thing, usually pointing at race or politics being the initiative. Why would being comfortable around people that you're familiar with be racist or misogynistic? The interesting twist here is this has nothing to do with appearance, but with mindset and life experience. We all had the same mindset, to feel strongly enough about a cause, in this case love of country, that we would lay our lives down for it. This bond is sometimes even stronger than blood. And because of this, I was able to enjoy my birthday and this final end to the book. Again, not sure if that makes sense, but felt it should be acknowledged.

October 27th, 2019. I can't believe I'm 50. I really can't believe I'm 50, in Hawaii celebrating, that this evening will be the conclusion of a five-year journey, that seems like it started yesterday. 50 states, 30 MLB parks, countless battlefields, all culminating to this very day. My 50th birthday. One last battlefield, and the journey ends. Prior to Alaska, this would have scared the living crap out of me, as it did just thinking about this moment for the past 4 years. Now, I just want to get this over with, and enjoy the moment. So after an amazing breakfast buffet, I caught the tour bus in the lobby, and was headed back to the Pearl Harbor Memorial.

So we all know the story of Pearl Harbor, and what took place here. I won't bore you with the synopsis and get straight into the visit. Our first stop on the three-part tour, was back at the main memorial, for the boat ride over to the USS Arizona. The exhibit had just been re-opened after a year or so of renovation, another timing miracle of this trip. It literally just re-opened earlier that year, so everything was freshly painted and cleaned. I was taken aback at the starkness of the memorial, that somehow added to its reverence. Only a giant white wall at the end of the memorial with all the fallen's names, and a few information placards, made up the entire exhibit. The silence required by the posted signs, added to the solemnity that weighed heavy on the visitor, as you peered down into rusted remains of the ship below. Just a metal ladder, leading down into the abyss, was chilling to say the least. The most moving was the placard explaining how every survivor of the USS Arizona has had their remains interned here with their shipmates, upon their later passing.

When returned to the main memorial complex, I had about an hour to kill, while everybody went through the different museum exhibits. I had already done this the day before, so I headed for the snack bar and to get some water. That's when I met this gentlemen in the cashier line. An older guy, a bit older than my dad, was there with his wife for the first time. Make a long story short, I ended up walking with these folks for most of the hour. Turns out he had brought her here to see where her father served. She had early stage dementia and he wanted her to see it while she could appreciate it. He had to explain to her several times, who I was and about the book I was writing. They were the absolute cutest couple on the outside, yet trying to enjoy the day with a hidden sadness. I ended up hanging out with them while we made the next stop at the USS Missouri.

The Missouri is where the Japanese signed the final surrender of WW2. Formerly docked in Washington, they brought the Missouri to Hawaii, marking the exact beginning and end of the war in the Pacific. A brass marker on the upper deck denotes where the document was signed, pictures of the signing hung on the walls behind. Other than that, it was another battleship tour, with all the same exhibits, but with Dole Whips and Hawaiian Ice snow cones at the gift shop. Two more must haves while in Hawaii.

After the third stop on the trip, which was mainly a driving tour through the veteran's cemetery and an amazing view of Diamond Head and Honolulu, the bus dropped us off at our various hotels. When we stopped at the older couple's hotel, I stood up to shake their hands and say goodbye. The gentleman slyly slipped a twenty-dollar bill into my hand and whispered, "Happy Birthday, have a couple of drinks for me," before turning back to help his wife off the bus. Yup, my eyes leaked a little. Too sweet for words, thank you, sir.

Back at the hotel, I was on cloud nine. We did it! I did it! Holy crap. Now I gotta write a book! Then my thoughts went straight to Kimber, dammit why couldn't she had been here? Ok, enough of that, it's your birthday, you accomplished your goal… party time. After an amazing surf and turf victory meal, I headed down to the cabana bar to end the evening sipping on a Mai Tai, puffing on a Cooperstown cigar, and watching the sun set over the Pacific. While I was enjoying my drink, a young lady sat down next to me. She had overheard me ask the fellas next to me if they would take a birthday picture for me, to which she told me Happy Birthday. Take a wild guess where she's from… Tucson, AZ. Full circle indeed. And with that, this five-year plan, haphazard and accidental as it was, has come to a perfect ending. Ya, whatever, get me to my dog! I'm out! Hawaii, my 50th and final state… COMPLETE! Kimber, Daddy's coming home.

Conclusion

As I sit here and reflect on the last 5 years, I turn back to the original subtitle of this journey, "A Veteran's search for God, Country, and Himself." Did I accomplish the most important aspect of this trip? Did I forget the true intention of my travels, giving way to social media, book writing, and every other logistical aspect of the journey? Well, let's take a look.

Did I find God? Those who know me, understand that I knew God before I left on this trip, the relationship was there, but it definitely could be stronger. So the answer is… absolutely! I found God in the fact that I'm blessed enough to have even had the means to embark on this adventure. I found God when my stress levels should have shot my PTSD through the roof, but stayed uncannily calm. I found God when I thought I was physically or sometimes mentally lost, or couldn't find lodging, and suddenly something appeared out of nowhere. I found God in the complete strangers who opened their doors, homes, and lives to me and my little dog. I found God in the immense beauty that this land has to offer. And lastly, I found God in the transformation within myself, that happened to me along the way. The renewed sense of worth thought to be lost from a period of bad decisions. I found God in the healing.

Did I find my Country? One thing that I believe every veteran questions at one point in his service. What the hell did I just do?! I just raised my right hand, and swore on the Bible to lay my life down for this country and its people. People I don't even know. Who are these people and where are these families I vowed to protect? Setting my GPS to backroads and avoiding the highways was the single best thing I could have done, to find the REAL America. So yes, I found America on the backroads and less traveled highways, in her ballparks where race or politics don't matter, on her battlefields learning the stories of her heroes who created her, in her rich history, both good and bad, that formed the greatest country in the history of man. Yes, I found America, and I'd raise my hand even more quickly than before to defend her, now that I've finally met her. America is alive and well, if you know where to look.

Finally, did I find myself? Hell, that's a whole different book all in itself. Those that knew me before, know the answer. To find a person who you thought was gone is amazing, but when it's yourself, it's supernatural. Remember when I kept harping about the need for a mission, and how scared I was for this to end? It was that acknowledgment that was transformational, to know that I still have drive and ambition after years of trying to fit in, brought my confidence and self-esteem roaring back. Let me try to explain this.

When I worked for the builders back in the day, running several different sub-divisions, managing about a dozen guys, I'd walk into the local bar at happy hour and would buy the whole place a round. I was the big boss on the spot, hanging with the boys. After I received my VA pension and was not part of that circle, things went downhill. One second you're talking lot numbers and customers, the next second you're listening to your buddy's talk, while you keep asking, "who?" As hard as you try to fit in, they politely just talk around you. That's the first step removed. Slowly but surely, you start to fade from the work world, into a world of depression and guilt. It's brutal. The loneliness and lack of work or goal leads to drinking, which leads to drugs, which leads to death. The worst thing they could do to a veteran is give him a livable wage, with no reason to get out of bed in the morning. Think about that for a minute, in the politics of the time. Without going further, just look for a possible book on this in the future. So, did I find myself? Oh ya! In a way I never thought possible. I guess there's nothing left to do now but prepare for the start of the next 5-year plan. Time to start… Becoming Alaskan.

The End

Made in the USA
Middletown, DE
11 March 2024

51260264R00252